Luminos is the Open Access monograph publishing program from UC Press. Luminos provides a framework for preserving and reinvigorating monograph publishing for the future and increases the reach and visibility of important scholarly work. Titles published in the UC Press Luminos model are published with the same high standards for selection, peer review, production, and marketing as those in our traditional program. www.luminosoa.org

Witness to Marvels

ISLAMIC HUMANITIES

Shahzad Bashir, Series Editor

Publication of this Luminos Open Access Series is made possible by the Islam and the Humanities Project of the Program in Middle East Studies at Brown University.

1. *Forging the Ideal Educated Girl: The Production of Desirable Subjects in Muslim South Asia*, by Shenila Khoja-Moolji

2. *Witness to Marvels: Sufism and Literary Imagination*, by Tony K. Stewart

Witness to Marvels

Sufism and Literary Imagination

Tony K. Stewart

UNIVERSITY OF CALIFORNIA PRESS

University of California Press, one of the most distinguished university presses in the United States, enriches lives around the world by advancing scholarship in the humanities, social sciences, and natural sciences. Its activities are supported by the UC Press Foundation and by philanthropic contributions from individuals and institutions. For more information, visit www.ucpress.edu.

University of California Press
Oakland, California

Suggested citation: Stewart, T. K. *Witness to Marvels: Sufism and Literary Imagination.* Oakland: University of California Press, 2019. DOI: https://doi.org/10.1525/luminos.76

Library of Congress Cataloging-in-Publication Data

Names: Stewart, Tony K., 1954- author.
Title: Witness to marvels : Sufism and literary imagination / Tony K. Stewart.
Description: Oakland, California : University of California Press, [2019] | Includes bibliographical references and index. | This work is licensed under a Creative Commons CC-BY-NC-ND license. To view a copy of the license, visit: http://creativecommons.org/licenses . |
Identifiers: LCCN 2019005276 (print) | LCCN 2019009927 (ebook) | ISBN 9780520973688 (ebook) | ISBN 9780520306332 (pbk. : alk. paper)
Subjects: LCSH: Bengali literature—Social aspects—India—Bengal. | Romance fiction, Bengali. | Islam and literature—India—Bengal. | Sufism—India—Bengal. | Hinduism—India—Bengal.
Classification: LCC PK1701 (ebook) | LCC PK1701 .S74 2019 (print) | DDC 891.4/409382—dc23
LC record available at https://lccn.loc.gov/2019005276

28 27 26 25 24 23 22 21 20 19
10 9 8 7 6 5 4 3 2 1

Frontispiece: Gāji and Kālu ply their magic boat. © The Trustees of the British Museum. This image and the cover image depicting Satya Pīr shapeshifting into an ogre to frighten Basanta Rājā, are from a *pīr paṭ* scroll painting, Murshidabad ca. 1780-1800 (Asia 1955.10-8.095).

The publisher and the University of California Press Foundation gratefully acknowledge the generous support of the Richard and Harriett Gold Endowment Fund in Arts and Humanities.

for Samira

Fabulation, then, means not a turning away from reality, but an attempt to find more subtle correspondences between the reality which is fiction and the fiction which is reality.

—ROBERT E. SCHOLES, *FABULATION AND METAFICTION*

CONTENTS

Preface xi
Acknowledgments xxi
Conventions Regarding Transliteration and Nomenclature xxv
Conventions Regarding Dates xxxi

1. Heavenly Orchestrations: The World of the Legendary *Pīrs* of Bengal 1
   1.1. The Tale of the Birth of Satya Pīr 2
   1.2. The Marvelous Tales of Sūphī Saints 12
   1.3. A Pregnant Ambiguity 25
2. The Enchanting Lives of the *Pīrs:* Structures of Narrative Romance 33
   2.1. The Myth-History Conundrum 33
   2.2. Narrative Bios as Autotelic Fiction 39
   2.3. Prolegomena to the *Mānikpīrer Jahurānāmā* of Jaidi 46
   2.4. Exploring the Romance of Mānik Pīr's Birth 66
3. Subjunctive Explorations: The Parodic Work of *Pīr Kathā* 71
   3.1. Narrative Strategies in Fictional Hagiography 72
   3.2. Entertaining Encounters that Shape the Religious Ideal 82
   3.3. The *Pīr* in a Subjunctive World 85
   3.4. Irony and Parody in *Pīr Kathā* 91
   3.5. Mimesis and Parody in the Tale of Badar Pīr 96

4. Mapping the *Imaginaire:* The Conditions of Possibility 110
4.1. The Reality of the Bengali *Imaginaire* 110
4.2. The *Bonbibī Jahurā Nāmā* of Mohāmmad Khater 123
4.3. The Semiotic Context of Bonbibī's Tale 133
4.4. The *Rāy Maṅgal* of Kṛṣṇarām, Precursor to the Tale of Bonbibī 137
4.5. The New World Order of the Sunderbans 150

5. Manipulating the Cosmic Hierarchy: A Practical Act of Conceptual Blending 155
5.1. The *Gāji Kālu o Cāmpāvati Kanyār Puthi* of Ābdur Rāhim 155
5.2. Gāji's Love for Cāmpāvatī and the Conflict with Dakṣiṇā Rāy 158
5.3. Gāji's Marriage to Cāmpāvatī and the Ascetic Trek 169
5.4. Revisions to the History of Baḍa Khān Gāji and Dakṣiṇ Rāy 174
5.5. Conceptual Blending to Fashion a New Cosmo-Moral Order 182

6. Pragmatics of *Pīr Kathā:* Emplotment and Extra-Discursive Effects 189
6.1. From Literary Emplotment to Social Discourse 189
6.2. The Vaiṣṇav *Avatār* of the Age 202
6.3. Gendered Witness to Satya Pīr's Powers 221
6.4. The Significance of Satya Pīr in *Musalmāni* Terms 232
6.5. The Never-Ending Mission of Satya Pīr 250

Epilogue 255
Works Cited 261
Primary Texts in Bangla and Sanskrit 261
Primary Texts in Translation 269
Monographs, Dissertations, Field Studies, and Two Novels 272
Secondary Works: Articles and Essays 279
Language and Reference Sources 282
Manuscripts Consulted: Satya Pīr 284
Index 287

PREFACE

It was through the literatures of Satya Pīr that I first encountered the world of the legendary *pīrs* of Bengal. The stories of these *sūphī* saints are rife with miraculous events and mind-boggling escapades, the sheer joy of which prompted me to translate eight tales in *Fabulous Females and Peerless Pīrs*.[1] Long before that volume appeared, I had discovered that Satya Pīr was part of a constellation of fictional *pīrs* whose stories have circulated in the Bangla-speaking regions for as long as five or six centuries. The stories self-identify as fictions, *kathā*—a term with a long history in the subcontinent, but it should be noted that the semantic field of *kathā* in the Bangla language does not map exactly onto the Sanskrit term or as it is used in other north Indian vernaculars. While the worlds these *kathās* construct bear a resemblance to the well-known lands of Bengal, their geography is often creative, their temporalities malleable, and their miracles defy the constraints of the ordinary created world as we know it. As fictions their protagonists are necessarily fictional too, though one or another character may have been inspired by an identifiable historical figure. For instance, the misty memory of Pīr Badar of Chittagong is likely the inspiration for the stories found in the prolegomena to the *Mānikpīrer jahurānāmā* that I have translated in chapter 2—but that possibility does not constitute a causal connection, and one should resist conflating the stories of the historical figures with stories told in these fictions, even if they share events, seemingly historical or miraculous. As the life stories of fictional saints, these tales are both literary and hagiographical, but the religion they promote can

1. Tony K. Stewart, trans., *Fabulous Females and Peerless Pīrs: Tales of Mad Adventure in Old Bengal* (New York: Oxford University Press, 2004).

only be described as a generic form of Islam. The tales depend on a generalized knowledge of Islam to tell their story, just as they assume the readers' or auditors' general knowledge of a traditional Bengali culture with all the gods and goddesses, *brāhmaṇs* and kings, and so forth that make up a world steeped in traditional Sanskritic and Indic culture. Because many of the recognized *pīrs* and *bibīs* are credited with miracles, there is a tendency to lump together those historical figures with these fictional ones. Historians either have dismissed the lot or have sifted through those tales, separating "fact" from "fiction" in an exercise that does great violence to the original life stories, discarding the miraculous as legends, myths, folk tales, wives' tales, and so forth, all of which conveniently excuse these scholars from having to address the texts as a whole with all of the interpretive problems these fabulations engender. If we treat the texts as the fictions they are, then we must use interpretive tools appropriate to the genres, and those tools are primarily literary critical. That is precisely the approach I have adopted.

These tales depict a world of miracle-working saints, *sūphī* (Bangla for Sufi or *ṣūfī*) *pīrs* and *phakīrs* (Bangla for *fakīr* or *faqīr*, mendicant), the terms are used interchangeably. Nearly all of these figures represent the ideals of the warrior-saint or *gāji* (Bangla for *ghāzī*), including the matron of the Sunderban forests, Bonbibī. They do battle in an effort to persuade people to recognize the validity of Muhāmmad and the place of Āllā (Bangla for Allāh) as the sole and supreme God, but, more often, they win over people by providing them with wealth, with protection from the vagaries of existence in the miasmic mangrove swamps, by helping the childless gain sons and daughters, and by brokering peace, usually through the fixing of kinship relations in which all parties have a vested interest. To accomplish their goals, these *pīrs*, *phakīrs*, and *bibīs* will conjure entire cities overnight, fly to the heavens to consult with the Prophet, or venture into the underworld of the god of death, Yam (Sanskrit Yama). They display traditional Indic forms of divinity as easily as they perform the recitation of the names of god in *jikir* (from Arabic *dhikr*, Persian *zikir*). And they engineer the most miraculous forms of conception, creating virgin mothers and even theriomorphic birth. Their stories are easily understood as variants of hero-mythology and fall within the category of Romance, but because they are driven by a concern to inculcate an appreciation of Islamic perspectives, and to aid *musalmāni* populations, these tales of saints are fictional hagiographies. The stories are wonderfully entertaining but elusive with respect to their real cultural work.

Much of what follows is an effort to develop strategies for making sense of the *pīr kathās* on their own terms. Because the tales are little known outside of the Bangla-speaking world and they have virtually no interpretive legacy in any language, I have chosen first to tell the story—usually by direct translation or a combination of summaries punctuated with sometimes lengthy translations of key passages—in order to establish a hermeneutical baseline. Only after their retelling do I move to more contemporary modes of interpretation, and those in only a rudimentary way. To retain a logical progression of tellings and explorations, the first five chapters constitute a general semiotic analysis covering the *semantics*, the *syntactics*, and then the *pragmatics* of these texts, illustrating each category with different tales. The final chapter on the literatures of Satya Pīr illustrates all three of these semiotic interests. Under that larger semiotic umbrella, each successive chapter will introduce a new strategy of interpretation, on which the succeeding chapter will build: chapter 1 provides a first glimpse into the *nature of the tales*; chapters 2 and 3 argue for the genre of *romance* and the stories' propensity to *parody*; chapter 4 introduces the concept of the *imaginaire*, and chapter 5 builds on that to trace historical change through the model of *conceptual blending*. Because of the plethora of materials dedicated to Satya Pīr, chapter 6 will show how *emplotment* and *narrative codes* signal religious positioning and condition expectation and reception. The brevity of analysis will undoubtedly disappoint some readers, but without any prior literary interpretations on which to depend (when noticed at all, literary histories only report the stories), these six chapters should serve as a good starting point to enter this literature and perhaps inspire others to look more closely at these dazzling productions and bring to bear an increasingly sophisticated hermeneutic. Though they are fictions, the tales play with religious issues without participating in the primary discourses of theology, doctrine, ritual, and so on; as stories, they can only point to those discussions, but point they most definitely do. The religious sensibilities that drive the plots do, in fact, routinely refer to the world of everyday reality in which their auditors live. What the texts are trying to accomplish religiously will gradually emerge when we examine them as a set—and even though they have been composed over several centuries, they do constitute a set because several of the authors have identified them as such, and because the tales operate in and through a shared *imaginaire*, as will be explored starting in chapters 4 and 5.

In the early stages of gauging the extent of these *pīr kathās*, and anticipating that other regions of South or Southeast Asia might have analogues, I proposed some years ago to several colleagues that we organize a workshop on what I then casually termed "Islamic mythologies." I was informed rather brusquely that Islam had no mythology, that to characterize any Muslim writing as such would be offensive, and under no circumstance would they support such an effort. While I was sympathetic to the desire not to be offensive, what was glaringly obvious to me—that such a literature existed, no matter what you called it—seemed to be truly invisible to my colleagues. I first thought the term "mythology" was the root of their resistance, but it soon became clear that I had stumbled into a much bigger problem. The tales I was reading and translating—stories of Satya Pīr, Baḍa Khān Gājī, Bonbibī, Mānik Pīr, and others that have proliferated over the last five centuries—I had come to realize were not only invisible to my colleagues, but were effaced in much of Bengali *belles-lettres*, in studies of religion and history, and in virtually every other field of intellectual inquiry. Imagine my surprise when in the early

1990s I first surveyed the literatures of Satya Pīr (who is favored by both Muslims and Hindus even today) to discover more than seven hundred fifty manuscripts and one hundred sixty printed titles composed by more than a hundred authors. Statistically, these tales constitute one of the largest blocks of literary productivity in Bangla, yet at the beginning of that project, I could locate fewer than eighty pages of secondary literature in any language focused on Satya Pīr and only a few pages more addressing the other protagonists. When the manuscripts and printed texts dedicated to the exploits of the other fictional *pīrs* and *bibīs* are added in, the totals of unexamined tales climb even further. Scholars, it seems, were on the whole unaware of these tales. I began to realize that the glaring absence of these stories pointed to something much more systemic, which raised serious questions about the intellectual industry dedicated to the re/construction of the cultures of the Bangla-speaking world; on the theoretical level, these lacunae redirected my inquiries to epistemology, especially regarding the issue of "not knowing."

In Western philosophy, the realm of ignorance is but a very small subset of epistemology, which tends to focus on what philosophers consider to be mistakes and untruths, what it means to be wrong, or simply not knowing what is right. More recently the field has moved in the direction of Bayesian statistics, which shifts the emphasis from not knowing to predicting the probability of knowing (probabilistic epistemology)—neither direction being particularly germane to the issues at hand, not least because of (Western) assumptions about the nature of the un/truths under investigation.[2] But in rummaging that literature, I ran across the more genial concept of *agnotology*, a precise term for a concept with which I was already all too familiar (and which anyone who has considered the underbelly of Foucauldian analyses knows well). In the sociology of epistemology, which examines structures of knowledge and their power relations, agnotology is characterized as the failure to recognize or the failure to know (which is not the same as ignorance with its incisively negative connotation, though scholars do sometimes invoke the term): *it is the study of our intellectual blind spots.* The causes range from simply not knowing enough because the state of knowledge has not yet reached sufficient levels of sophistication to reach what we know must be there (e.g., science), or from systems that institutionalize the hiding of knowledge (e.g., state secrets), to more complicated decisions generated in particular discourses that a priori eliminate areas of inquiry as not useful or as uninteresting (e.g., medical

2. The literature on the epistemology of ignorance is not trivial, but among more recent forays, I found the following useful: John D. Norton, "Ignorance and Indifference," *Philosophy of Science* 75 (January 2008): 45–68; and the collected essays on epistemology by Nicholas Rescher; see Rescher, *Studies in Epistemology: Nicholas Rescher Collected Papers*, vol. 14 (Frankfurt: Ontos Verlag, 2007); immediately germane to our purpose are the last three essays in this collection, "On Learned Ignorance" (131–45), "Coping with Cognitive Limitations" (147–55), and especially "On Ignorance and Limits of Knowledge" (157–79).

knowledge of female orgasm), or ideological and doctrinal decisions that make it impossible to think certain thoughts, or at least to acknowledge them, rendering them invisible (e.g., religious commitment). It is these latter two perspectives that I found most provocatively relevant. Nancy Tuana's essay "Coming to Understand: Orgasm and the Epistemology of Ignorance," in the Proctor and Schiebinger volume titled *Agnotology: The Making and Unmaking of Ignorance*, suggested strategies to uncover the stories' apparent invisibility and how I might proceed.[3] It was not long before I could identify systemic blindness and obstruction among Orientalists, sectarian fundamentalists, historians, literary historians, and even linguists. While it has on occasion been tempting to become self-righteous about the pervasive suppression of any discussion of these tales—tales which I happen to find so intriguing—I am convinced now that the blocking of these tales has been primarily a product of the prevailing structures of knowledge operational in the colonial and immediate postcolonial setting of South Asia—which would, of course, include ethnic, religious, and linguistic biases and which were, not surprisingly, conditioned by political agendas far beyond scholarly control, but an exercise in which scholars have been unwittingly complicit. These tales tell us about the ways people have been subtly persuaded to think about religion in Bengal, to think about Islam in a Bengali context, and we have ignored them even though they have been pervasive for centuries. It is our loss if we do not listen to these voices—and from them we can learn things not possible through the dominant discourses of history, theology, and law that drive so much of our understanding of Islam today.

As I have noted elsewhere, the concept of "invisible religion"—a term coined by Assman, following Luckmann—helped to lay open at least some of the stories' religious and cultural work,[4] and without explicitly invoking Assman and Luckman, I have built on that concept through the early chapters of this volume. What is invisible is what makes these tales in many respects culturally Bengali rather than overtly sectarian Muslim or Hindu or some combination. The authors explore the cosmological and social assumptions of a Bengali heritage, its habits,

3. Nancy Tuana, "Coming to Understand: Orgasm and the Epistemology of Ignorance," in *Agnotology: The Making and Unmaking of Ignorance*, ed. Robert N. Proctor and Londa Schiebinger (Stanford: Stanford University Press, 2008), 108–45. The volume covers a wide range of possible forms of agnotology.

4. Tony K. Stewart, "Religion in the Subjunctive: Vaiṣṇava Narrative, Sufi Counter-Narrative in Early Modern Bengal," *The Journal of Hindu Studies* 6 (2013): 53–73. There I point out that Jan Assmann has argued that the invisible religion formulated by Thomas Luckmann, when traced historically, functions as an archive of cultural memory; Assmann, "Introduction: What Is Cultural Memory" and chap. 1: "Invisible Religion and Cultural Memory," in *Religion and Cultural Memory: Ten Studies*, trans. Rodney Livingstone (Stanford, CA: Stanford University Press, 2006), 1–45. For Luckmann's concept of invisible religion vis-à-vis visible religion, see Luckmann, *The Invisible Religion: The Problem of Religion in Modern Society* (New York: Macmillan, 1967).

its mores. That the tales do not play to any explicitly doctrinal position, but to a more generalized outlook, no doubt accounts for part of their low profile in the highly charged political and sectarian space of colonial Bengal and beyond, where religious identity had become a de facto political identity. I will argue that in the period which runs up to the time when identity politics began to take a definitive shape in the late nineteenth century, these stories were *subjunctive* in the exploratory mode of that concept.[5] They were test-driving ideas that could find no other easy outlet. I was pleased to see that in his recently published, incisive, and somewhat controversial book *What Is Islam?*, Shahab Ahmed argued that these kinds of experimental literary forms were to be expected in the efflorescence of Islamic culture in what he terms the Balkans-to-Bengal complex.[6] He wrote, "Unlike many Muslims of today, the Muslims of the Balkans-to-Bengal complex did not feel the need to articulate or legitimate their Muslim-ness/their Islam by mimesis of a pristine time of the earliest generations of the community (the *salaf*). Rather, they felt able to be Muslim in explorative, creative, and contrary trajectories . . . taking as a point of departure the array and synthesis of the major developments of the preceding centuries . . . and made productive of new meanings in a new vocabulary of Islam."[7] The *explorative authority* he invokes captures the tenor of these fictional *pīr kathās*—though I hasten to add he was primarily interested in personal modalities of experience and insight (especially Sufi) that had potentially profound theological implications. That explorative authority contrasts completely, indeed finds itself contesting, the monologic of the prescriptive authority of the conservative elements of the mainstream. As has become increasingly apparent, stories seem to have little place in the latter's heavily politicized discourse. Ahmed's binary may be too broadly painted to account historically for the improvisations that have marked the mainstream Sunni traditions—and even more so the conservative elements, laboring under the strictures of theology, history, and law—but it is heuristically useful, for in its broad strokes it captures precisely the generic nature of subjunctive religious exploration found in the *pīr kathās*.

Ironically, we might further speculate that these tales have not received any attention from the mainstream religious traditions of greater Bengal (both Muslim and Hindu) because they frequently rely on *parody* to make their point—irony of

5. In a different context, Amitav Ghosh recently made a similar point: "But to reproduce the world as it exists need not be the project of fiction; what fiction—and by this I mean not only the novel but also epic and myth—makes possible is to approach the world through a subjunctive mode, to conceive of it *as if* it were other than it is: in short, the great, irreplaceable potentiality of fiction is that it makes possible the imagining of possibilities." See Ghosh, *The Great Derangement: Climate Change and the Unthinkable* (Chicago: University of Chicago Press, 2016), 128.

6. Shahab Ahmed, *What Is Islam? The Importance of Being Islamic* (Princeton: Princeton University Press, 2016).

7. Ahmed, 81.

course being the critical trope for making parody work (following Hutcheon[8]). Parody and humor do not play well among modern religious reformers, so I suppose we should not be surprised that in their eyes these tales do not pass muster as proper religious texts. But there is no question that parody is fully operational throughout, which should astonish no one familiar with Indic literary and religious expression; Bangla literature has a robust tradition of parody. There are a large number of Bangla terms whose semantic fields fit the full range of the English notions of parody, and these texts deploy them all.[9] In the last century, even explicitly declared parodies of the parodies have been performed on stage and circulated in print. I will argue that it is through parody—from positive mimicry to acerbic criticism and everything in between—that the stories of the *pīrs* reach out from their fictional perch and touch the world of ordinary things, invoking texts and traditions in freewheeling fashion. But why this urge to parody and to the subjunctive? As banal as it might seem, I am increasingly convinced that, like so much else in Bengali culture, it is in part tied to its geography.

Today largely composed of Bangladesh and the Indian state of West Bengal, the Bangla-speaking regions are of course riddled with thousands of distributaries of the Gaṅgā and Brahmāputra rivers, their lands' fertility annually boosted from the silt of the Himalayas carried down by the annual floods. But those floods constantly carve the landscape into new forms; in spate rivers can suddenly become ten or twenty miles wide, their courses changing day by day, and with that volume of water and silt, old lands are submerged and new islands (*caḍā*, *carā*) rise in the middle of waterways or extend the land mass further into the Bay of Bengal. It is not hard to see how the contingency of the land itself, constantly shifting, profoundly affects, even unsettles, the Bengali psyche. So ubiquitous is the water that in the early modern period in which our investigation begins, *pār karā* was the verbal form that signified simply "to go" somewhere, that is, to make one's way (using some form of the verb *karā*, from the root *kṛ*-) to the other shore (*pār*).

When *musalmāns* first entered Bengal, they did not shy away from the frontier wilderness, which was just beginning to yield to the pressure of encroaching development.[10] This riparian landscape was laden with natural perils to a degree seldom encountered in the rest of greater India, and one of the most profound affective

8. Linda Hutcheon, *A Theory of Parody: The Teachings of Twentieth-Century Art Forms* (Urbana and Chicago: University of Illinois Press, 1985, reprint 2000).

9. Terms include: *nakal* as copying, copy, reproduction, imitation, mimicry, mimicking, aping, forgery, counterfeiting, plagiarism, and as an adjective, artificial, sham, spurious; *anukaraṇ*, understood as an act of copying, imitation, following, going after, pursuit; *anukṛta*, meaning imitated, copied, mimicked, followed; and as a noun, *anukṛti* as imitation, copy; *lālikā* as jesting, evasive reply, equivocation (such as puns or ambiguous expression), parody; *bhā̃ḍāmi*, which means jesting, buffoonery, drollery, horseplay; and finally *mithya abhinay* as mockery and explicitly dramatic parody.

10. Richard M. Eaton, *The Rise of Islam and the Bengal Frontier, 1204–1760* (Berkeley: University of California Press, 1993).

responses was to seek some kind of supernatural help in coping. *Hinduyāni* followers sought the aid of the gods and goddesses, resulting in a new and unique genre of literary production, the *maṅgal kāvya*. The genre's name can be translated as the "poetry (*kāvya*) of benefaction or auspiciousness (*maṅgal*)." These tales are generally characterized as semi-epics, sagas documenting the establishment and inculcation of the worship of the goddess, but I would argue the genre is more a literature that sought to chronicle the pacification of the land and all its imminent threats. Those threats were multiple. They included the dreaded world of serpents—kraits, pythons, vipers, keelbacks, and of course the cobra, king of all—so Manasā, daughter of Śiv, was celebrated as their master in her many *Manasā maṅgals*. A range of dread diseases were, and to a certain extent still are, endemic to the region, especially prevalent in the southern reaches, so the goddess Śitalā was eulogized to reign over smallpox and other eruptive ailments, skin diseases such as leprosy, leukoderma, and a host of minor but common annoyances, such as wenns, warts, and sebaceous cysts. Threats were social, too, as *hinduyāni* culture increasingly came into contact with indigenous (i.e., non-*hindu*) populations, the *ādibāsīs* or "original inhabitants" of these forested regions, groups that historically stood outside of a proper Indic world as outlined in the classical Sanskrit texts. The goddess Caṇḍī and the god Dharma were invoked in their respective *maṅgal kāvyas* to help settle these *ādibāsī* peoples, creating new, ideal cities in the middle of the forests and integrating their populations. As depicted in these texts, pacifying the wild was a complex process of social, agricultural, and pastoral domestication and urban construction. When *musalmāns* joined the land, their literatures make clear that they joined in these same efforts as their *hinduyāni* equivalents, and here is where the legends of the *pīrs* began to emerge in the popular imagination.[11] In all of these tales, the *sūphī pīr* and *phakīr*, the *shaykh* and *dārveś*, tended to be solitary figures following a call that was their own, even when they were part of recognized *silsilās* or lineages; they were not urban dwellers, and they gravitated to the wilderness, where few would venture. By the time the *maṅgal kāvya* genre was firmly established in the sixteenth century, the exploits of these *pīrs* in the wilds began to gain their own traction, flourishing in concert and eventually outlasting their *hinduyāni* literary counterparts. Those tales mimicked the *maṅgal kāvya*, initially through positive parodies that eventually led to socially biting satires, parody turned to the service of the political.

In these tales of the *pīrs*, we witness attempts to tame the land and make a space to recognize the legitimacy of *musalmāni* presence and practices, especially in the southern and eastern reaches of the region. Figures such as the forest-dwelling Baḍa Khān Gāji became synonymous with control of the vast tiger population, the

11. Richard M. Eaton argues the process had begun even earlier; see Eaton, "Forest Clearing and Growth of Islam in Bengal" in *Islam in South Asia in Practice*, ed. Barbara D. Metcalf (Princeton: Princeton University Press, 2009), 375–89.

great Bengal tiger, *panthera tigris tigris*, but also with establishing a mobile administration of justice in untamed areas. The *sūphī* matron Bonbibī likewise trafficked in tigers, crocodiles, and sharks. As mother to all the inhabitants of Sunderbans, she and Gāji were both involved in settling the land and in building communities among the local populations of *ādibāsīs*. As a protegée of Śitalā, the youthful Olābibī provided prophylaxis for cholera and other water-borne ailments such as dysentery. Each of these figures carved out a special domain for action. Today they are often collectively worshiped by those living in the Sunderbans, crowning a process that began with the demand for recognition and cultural accommodation of a *musalmāni* perspective on the world, exploratory moves that led to more complex interactions of appropriation and even displacement of the old into a new *musalmāni* cosmology. But each figure was also significant in mobilizing, organizing the local populations to settle the land, to create communities that integrated every social, religious, ethnic, geographic, and trade classification. It was the latter that seemed to be a preoccupation of many of the authors, for settlement meant trade.

The tales found in both the *maṅgal kāvyas* and *pīr kathās* routinely depict the adventures of the trading voyage and the other activities of merchants, a preoccupation which is, I think, partially a function of the strategic geography of Bengal, its place in the long history of maritime trade networks of the subcontinent. This fixation on trade, where textiles and spices particularly come to mind, went hand in hand with the domestication of the land, the exploitation of its vast natural resources: salt, timber, honey, and wax. Trade and basic transportation oriented Bengal to the inland waterways, and externally to the Bay of Bengal. As a hub of economic activity in the early modern trade routes, its role expanded further with the colonial intrusion of the Portuguese, French, and British.[12] Considering seriously this orientation to the water and the connections it brought to a larger world, I would caution that we should not automatically look to developments in the practice of North Indian Islam imported overland as the source of inspiration for Bengali *musalmāni* interests. There were connections that can be especially remarked in some of the higher *musalmāni* literary forms (often bypassing North India to go back to Persian and some Arabic stimulation and vision), but the *pīr kathās* of our study seem to be much more local, indigenous efforts. As has been well documented, religious ideas inevitably follow trade routes, and for Bengal, many of those routes skirted around the coasts of the subcontinent into the regions of the Middle East, and in the other direction into Southeast Asia, a pipeline that

12. For an all-too-brief set of essays on the impact of the littoral regions on the movement of ideas and the impact of trade, see Shatarupa Bhattacharyya, *The Magnificent World of the Littoral: The Northern Bay of Bengal on the Eve of Colonialism* (Saarbrücken: LAP Lambert Academic Publishing, 2012). There are, of course, substantial numbers of studies on Indian Ocean trade too numerous to address here.

inevitably worked in both directions, for the great port of Chittagong anchored the kingdom of Mrauk-U, Arakan, from the fifteenth to the eighteenth centuries. I have noticed over the years that the mapping of the expansion of Islam is nearly always visually represented as land-based, an inexorable tide moving across the continents from west to east, in South Asia extended by marauding bands pushing territorial domains ever eastward to the eventual fixing of stable Sultanate and Mughal rules. But given Bengal's relation and orientation to the water, it is worth noting that the generative locus of the tales of the *pīrs* and *bibīs* is precisely where Bengal touched the rest of the world in the early modern and colonial periods, that is, through the littoral regions along Bengal's intricate coast, the maritime highway of trade. Surely that geographical situation with its many points of contact must have had a hand in spurring the novel responses embodied in the *pīr kathās*; and it points to the possibility that "folk" literatures in other areas of southern and southeastern Asia may have performed similar functions. Michael Murrin has convincingly argued that the burgeoning of heroic romance in European languages from the thirteenth to the seventeenth centuries went hand-in-hand with the expansion of trade into Asia, a fabulous spur to the imagination.[13] So we are left to wonder if the romantic narratives of the *pīrs* and *bibīs* in Bengal were somehow indirect beneficiaries of a similar impulse based not in Europe but in Asia—but that historical inquiry must be left to others to explore lest this essay expand to epic proportions. Regardless of the possible connections, these stories suggest, at least in part, how *musalmāni* practices and perspectives were naturalized in the Indic world of traditional Bengal, helping to create an indigenous form of *musalmāni* religious belief and practice that was Bengali in its outlook and appearance, responding to conditions that seem to be unique to the Bangla-speaking world, but suggestive of the more subtle ways the religious imagination rides the literary, a conjunction that is likely to complicate our notions of what it means to convert. If nothing else comes of this book, the stories alone will invite the reader to explore this imaginative realm, no doubt provoking a sense of wonder and humor as these authors hold up a mirror to their Bangla-speaking audiences, an inevitable effect of the subjunctive at work.

Oxford, July 2017
Nashville, January 2019

13. Michael Murrin, *Trade and Romance* (Chicago and London: University of Chicago Press, 2013).

ACKNOWLEDGMENTS

The incubation period of this text stretched over several decades, so a number of institutions provided opportunities for sustained periods of research and reflection. Seminal was my time as a William J. Fulbright Senior Research Fellow, CIES (1991–92), starting with work in London at the British Library (at the time, the Oriental and India Office Collections were housed in Blackfriars) through formal affiliation with Dhaka University and my additional work at the Bangla Academy and the Asiatic Society of Bangladesh; extending those connections was made possible as a senior research fellow of the American Institute of Bangladesh Studies (1993). The University of Pennsylvania Center for South Asian Studies designated me Jubilee Fellow, a time that coincided with sponsorship from the National Endowment for the Humanities (1996–1997). The Wildacres Writing Retreat sponsored by the Blumenthal Foundation (1999, 2001, 2002) sustained early experiments in writing, while several North Carolina State University short-term research grants (1994, 1996, 2010) enabled much-needed trips to the British Library, British Museum, and Victoria and Albert Museum. A Fulbright-Hays Senior Research Abroad fellowship (U.S. Department of Education) when I was attached to Independent University, Bangladesh (2008–2009) allowed important follow-up research. My participation in projects supported by the Fant Fund, College of Arts and Science, Vanderbilt University (2012–2015) and the further support of the Robert Penn Warren Center for the Humanities as the Rebecca Webb Wilson Fellow, Vanderbilt University (2015–2016), coupled with co-directing the John E. Sawyer Seminar, Andrew W. Mellon Foundation (2015–2016), provided important stimuli for consolidating the project. And finally, my time at the Oxford Centre for Hindu Studies as the J. P. and Beena Khaitan Visiting Fellow (2016–2017), and at St. Antony's College, Oxford University, as Senior Associate Member (2016–17), allowed me to complete the manuscript. To these and the many other institutions around the globe that gave me the opportunity to share this work as it developed, I am deeply grateful.

It is of course the provocative conversations with a host of individuals to whom much credit for the sharpening of the ideas in this book accrues—and it is impossible to name everyone, so I trust inadvertent omissions will be forgiven. A special acknowledgement goes to my friends in Bangladesh, starting with the late M. R. Tarafdar, who was my first sponsor at Dhaka University and mentor until his untimely death in 1997. My dear senior colleague and friend Anisuzzaman, retired from Dhaka University, has for several decades extended his warm and generous support. The late Bazlul Mobin Chowdhury, Vice Chancellor of Independent University, Bangladesh, and Omar Rahman, who succeeded him as Vice Chancellor, encouraged my project and extended their gracious hospitality over many years. Other scholars from Dhaka University from whom I have benefited include Perween Hasan, Momin Chowdhury, and Niaz Zaman. For his insights into the Gājikālu cycle, I am appreciative of the help from the late A. K. M. Zạkariah, archaeologist, historian, and former Education and Cultural Affairs Secretary of Bangladesh. Thanks too to Saymon Zakaria, Bangla Academy, and Syed Jamil Ahmed, Dhaka University, for helping me better to understand Bangladeshi folk drama. Those who, now nearly thirty years ago, opened my eyes to the creative side of the living traditions of the Bangladeshi art world helped me to see (even when they did not) how their work was relevant to my own efforts. Tuli and Jamal Ahmed opened their home to me, even naming one of their rooms for my habitation, extending a family nurture that saw me through the inevitable ups and downs of field research. The late nights with Jamal in his studio were inspirational as we discovered we must have been brothers in some earlier life. I also thank Kuhu and Richard Plamondon and Mustaque Ahmed who were always and continue to be gracious in their hospitality. I would be remiss if I did not mention my frequent conversations with artist Nisir Hossain, who provided insights into the history of Bangladeshi arts that have helped me to fathom connections that would have remained otherwise invisible.

In Kolkata, my colleague Amit Dey, Calcutta University, long-time friend and research associate Hena Basu, and my closest friend, Ajoy Ray, my brother in jazz, have helped me maintain my links with that city and its intellectual life. In the UK, Graham Shaw, then Deputy Director of the Oriental and India Office Collections of the British Library, helped me to plumb the depths of their collections, while William Radice, formerly of the School of Oriental and African Studies, long encouraged this work. T. Richard Blurton of the British Museum challenged me to link the stories to the extraordinary scroll painting in their collection, two of which registers serve as the cover art and frontispiece of this volume (after a decade I have nearly completed the long-sought identifications). Talks and shared work with Francesca Orsini of the School of Oriental and African Studies confirmed the direction I was going. Prashant Kidambi of Leicester University, Rochana Bajpai of the School of Oriental and African Studies, Shalini Sharma of Keele University, and Miles Taylor of York University punctuated my reveries with much-needed cheer and stringent queries about my project. In London, Eleonora Giusta has cheerfully extended vital logistical and moral support over the last decade. In Oxford, Faisal Devji of St. Antony's College, Oxford University, provided support and his usual keen insights into how my work fit into larger intellectual and cultural concerns of the subcontinent and the larger Islamic world. Shaunaka Rishi Das, Executive Director of the Oxford Centre for Hindu Studies, with his infectious Irish brio, ventured to support my project, which was unlike anything the Centre had previously sponsored, and two affiliates of the Centre—Jessica Frazier, Lecturer in Theology and Religion, Trinity College, and advanced Mansfield College graduate student Lucian Wong—prompted long conversations that circled around and through my work and much else, often fueled by our ongoing experiments in the world of martinis, cooking, and jazz.

My colleagues at Vanderbilt University have sharpened my eye, especially to the implications of this work; a special thanks to Laurel Schneider, Rob Campany, Issam Eido, Bryan Lowe, Richard McGregor, Anand Vivek Taneja and former colleague Nancy G. Lin. Long before coming to Vanderbilt, my colleagues in the North Carolina Center for South Asia Studies (North Carolina State University, University of North Carolina–Chapel Hill, Duke University, and North Carolina Central University) patiently listened, but did not always comprehend, the direction of this complex project—but the intellectual ferment of that group proved an uncommon pleasure and spur. The Rockefeller Foundation Residency Program (1993–97), titled "South Asian Islam and the Greater Muslim World," directed by Bruce B. Lawrence and the late John. F. Richards of Duke University, proved a turning point in my thinking. In 1997, Carl W. Ernst of UNC-CH and I directed an NEH Summer Seminar, titled "Hindu and Muslim: Rethinking Religious Boundaries in South Asia," in which we hatched our critique of syncretism, and which laid an important foundation for much of the ensuing appraisal of the scholarship associated with the tales of the *pīrs* and *bibīs*. David Gilmartin of NCSU relentlessly pushed me to connect the tales of the *pīrs* to the larger historical world of South Asia, which ultimately led to the formulations that helped to shape the last chapter of this monograph. Anna Bigelow of NCSU, miriam cooke at Duke, and Chapel Hill potter Judith Ernst have variously encouraged me along the way.

I have had the privilege of engaging a number of others at various points germane to my work, some going back many decades. At the University of Chicago, Edward C. Dimock unfortunately passed away as the project was beginning to achieve clarity, but his imprint on it remains. Others there include Ralph Nicholas, who has encouraged this work for a very long time, and more recently Thibaut d'Hubert and Matthew Rich, the latter of whom helped track down invaluable resources. My *guru-bhāi* at Chicago, Robert "Bibliography Bob" Evans, opened his personal library, sharing texts I could locate nowhere else, a continuation of our book-buying jaunts in then Calcutta in the early 1980s. The provocative and seminal works of Farina Mir, University of Michigan, and Akbar Hyder, University of Texas, prompted me to explore avenues that might have been left untouched, and their comments on the final manuscript were much appreciated. Ahmet T. Karamustafa, University of Maryland, in his usual patient manner answered my obscure queries in the final stages of the writing. Others whose work has directly affected my inquiries include: James L. Fitzgerald of Brown University; Indrani Chatterjee of University of Texas-Austin; Glen A. Hayes of Bloomfield College; Sufia M. Uddin of Connecticut College; Edward Yazijian of Furman University; Ayesha Irani of University of Massachusetts–Boston; Annu Jalais of National University of Singapore; Karen Ruffle of the University of Toronto; and Projit Mukharji of the University of Pennsylvania.

Shahzad Bashir of Brown University and series editor of Islamic Humanities, University of California Press, has been extremely supportive of this project; so too the marvelous subvention provided by the "Islam and the Humanities" project of Middle East Studies at Brown University. Eric Schmidt, my editor at the University of California Press, has guided me skillfully through the process and I thank him for it. Copy editor Ben Alexander deftly massaged the text into its final form, while Alexander Trotter adroitly prepared the index. Paige MacKay of Ubiquity Press artfully managed the transition from typescript to the digital or printed text you are reading, while Francisco Reinking of the University of California Press quietly and efficiently oversaw all phases of production. To all of these individuals I owe a debt of gratitude.

Extended conversations with Nilima and Gulam Mohammed Sheikh enfolded me into a world of the arts of India I had only previously glimpsed, simultaneously opening a door to the family that allowed me entry on my own terms. The relevance of what I was doing crystallized there in unexpected ways. But it is to their daughter, my partner Samira Sheikh, that this book is appropriately dedicated. For well over a decade she has endured my wrestling with the project and provided a healthy skepticism and productive intellectual stimulus that has forced me to tighten my analysis and be bold enough to say what needed saying. She saw, when neither I nor anyone else did, where it might ultimately lead, an act of uncommon prescience which enabled the book's completion when I doubted it possible.

• • •

CONVENTIONS REGARDING TRANSLITERATION AND NOMENCLATURE

THE CHALLENGE OF BANGLA

Perhaps more than any other north Indian vernacular, transliterating Bangla into Roman script is an exercise in frustration because orthography and pronunciation diverge so dramatically. One must choose an approach commensurate to the material. That, together with the tendency of Bangla to resort selectively to apocope, inevitably leads to inconsistencies. Orthography in Bangla has always been fluid.[1] The printing press is assumed to have standardized Bangla orthography, as was often the case in other parts of the world, and this seems to be the case within certain genres, such as the novel, which emerged in the late nineteenth century. But orthography and spellings have never been truly stable, as the texts in this study make clear. Even now, after the advent of digital printing and spell-checking dictionaries, change and inconsistencies abound.[2] These issues of orthography and spelling are doubly exacerbated in the materials used in the present study because

1. For issues of orthography, see Muhammad Śāhjāhān Miyā, *Bāṃlā pāṇḍulipi pāṭhsamīkṣā* (Ḍhākā: Bāṃlā Ekāḍemī, 1390 BS [ca. 1984]); Kalpanā Bhaumik, *Pāṇḍulipi paṭhan sahāyikā* (Ḍhākā: Bāṃlā Ekāḍemī, 1399 BS [ca. 1992]).

2. Around 2008, Microsoft contracted the Center for Research on Bangla Language Processing at BRAC University in Dhaka to check the spelling dictionary it had developed for Bangla in Kolkata. As the team checked the text, the number of errors was extraordinary and far beyond anything anyone had predicted. Ultimately it came to light that, in the half-century since the independence of Pakistan in 1947, then Bangladesh in 1971, and into the twenty-first century, Bangla orthography in India had dramatically transformed, much more affected by Hindi, while in Bangladesh, the orthography had retained nearly all of the features common to the first half of the twentieth century (personal communication, Naira Khan, Center for Research on Bangla Language Processing, BRAC University, November 2009).

there has never been a standardized way for words from Persian and Arabic to be rendered into Bangla—and even when the source of a term seems to be obvious, the semantic field of that original term frequently does not map directly onto the Bangla, for the conceptual world of Bangla adds and subtracts meanings and sometimes proposes associations not present in the original. So when transliterating those terms that have Persian and Arabic antecedents, I have chosen to retain the Bangla spellings, which then undergo a second transliteration into Roman script. Pronouncing the transliteration usually makes clear the relationship of a term to its predecessor—but it would be a mistake to assume that the meanings are automatically the same. There is no easy solution.

In the scholarship generated over the last half-century, the tendency has been for those working with the contemporary language, usually anthropologists, sociologists, and political scientists, to use a phonetic transcription that attempts to approximate the spoken word (if followed scrupulously this renders some otherwise familiar words incomprehensible, and even more so in certain dialectical forms). In this approach the scholar would likely transcribe the name of the god কৃষ্ণ as Krishna, or closer to pronunciation, Krishno; one of his worshipers would be বৈষ্ণব, transliterated as *boishnɔb* or *boishnob* or, in some pronunciations, *boishnobo.* Scholars working in older traditions (historians, historians of religion, Indologists) or on Hindu text-oriented traditions that have a strong connection to Sanskrit, have tended to follow a stricter orthographic representation that often strays far from the spoken word: so the god would be transcribed as Kṛṣṇa and his followers would be called *vaiṣṇav* or *vaiṣṇava.*

The interchangeability of */b/* and */v/* creates a different set of problems because both are written as ব and pronounced */bɔ/*, unless of course one is transliterating a word that has entered Bangla from Persian or Arabic, and the character may signify something akin to the English */w/*, so the singular for *saint* can be written বলী or বলি and transliterated as *vali* or *valī*, but pronounced *wali* (also written as ওলি, *oli*, or ওয়ালি, *oyāli*). The distinction in Sanskrit between */b/* and */v/* is often subject to hypercorrection, turning one into the other in both directions.

Most authors writing in English will generate plurals of nouns by following the English language convention of adding an *s* to the transliterated form, and we will do the same. So, for example, we have *boishnobs/boishnobos* or *vaiṣṇavs/vaiṣṇavas*, each of which technically becomes a neologism that in no way corresponds to the orthography or the pronunciation of the Bangla, but it has the advantage of avoiding confusion between the singular and the plural in the English (some linguists add the *s* unitalicized to the end of the italicized foreign word, but I reject that convention as a visual interruption). Similar constructions abound for the importing of adjectives and adverbs, such as brāhmaṇical and dharmically, which suffer the same charge of what we might humorously term "neologismogony."

The apocope, which has already reared its head in these examples, presents a different set of problems. Sometimes it is observed in common with other North

Indian vernaculars, so for instance the final /*a*/ is not pronounced in the word ব্রাহ্মণ, *brāhmaṇ*, often written in English as *brahmin*, though orthographically that inherent vowel is present and would be transliterated as *brāhmaṇa*, as if routinely done for Sanskrit. But when the word ends in a conjunct consonant, the inherent vowel final is pronounced as an /*o*/ with a gemination of the consonants, so বৈদ্য, *vaidya*, becomes *boiddo* and সত্য, *satya*, becomes *shɔtto*—further complicated by the fact that few people can distinguish শ, /*ś*/, from ষ, /*ṣ*/, or স, /*s*/, each pronounced like the English *sh*, with few exceptions, the most notable being the word শ্রী, /*śrī*/ (pronounced *sree*). On occasion, where one would might reasonably expect apocope, the inherent vowel is reinstated, especially in compounds or when two consonants come together which become difficult to pronounce without the retention of the inherent vowel—but there is no hard-and-fast rule for this, rather it seems to depend on the vagaries of local speech and, perhaps of equal import, the dictates of meter. I have followed the simple guide of pronounceability as my standard, so, for instance, the story of the twin boys Nīl and Nal will be written as the *nalanīler pālā*, though apocope would dictate *nalnīl*.

IMPLICATIONS OF CHOICES, NOT JUST A MATTER OF CONVENTION

I have favored a primarily orthographic transliteration of Bangla terms, regardless of their origin, but I have allowed for the apocope as best I can approximate it. When transliterating Sanskrit or Persian or Arabic I have followed what are generally considered standard rules for those languages. Importantly, I have retained the spellings as they are found in the textual passages, regardless of the variation. When we impose our own fixation with consistency in matters of spelling and form, we interrupt, sometimes irreparably, the tenor of the original texts, for these stories attest to a living language that is in flux, reflecting the same instability and fluidity found in the culture itself during this period. In the same sentence you might see the word for a masterly Sufi (সূফী, *sūphī*, or সুফি, *suphi*) written as পীর, *pīr*, or পির, *pir*, ফকির, *phakir*, or ফকীর, *phakīr*; and for women, পীরানী, *pīrānī*, or পিরানী, *pirānī*, ফকিরানী, *phakirānī*, ফকিরানি, *phakirāni*, ফকীরানী, *phakīrānī*, or ফকীরানি, *phakīrāni*, and the matronly বিবি, *bibi*, বিবী, *bibī*, or বীবী, *bībī*. This may seem trivial, especially since each of these paired words is pronounced identically, but to impose a standardized "proper" form—*pīr*, *phakīrānī*, *bībī*—would be to use a measure that ultimately lies outside of Bangla (in this example, from Persian) and would vainly attempt to make the language of the texts conform to a high literary standard that is at best an ideal, but which fails to represent what is actually written. The implications are, at least *in potentia*, not at all trivial. One of the most glaring cases in point is the word for God.

In Bangla the word for God in these stories is spelled আল্লা and transliterated and pronounced Āllā, and that is the form I have used throughout. The more common form in scholarship is to transliterate the Arabic as Allah or Allāh, but Bangla cannot fully approximate those sounds. Were one to transcribe Allāḥ, অল্লাঃ, a Bangla speaker would be depicted as saying "Ollā" according to the rules of euphonic combination. Āllā is about as close a phonetic reproduction as Bangla can project. Starting with some reformist publications in the nineteenth century and continuing today, an author might attempt to Arabicize the spelling by writing আল্লাঃ, Āllāḥ, which leaves the impression of following the Arabic (but more the transliteration of Arabic), but fails to represent accurately the sounds (for many speakers the distinction of the voiced pharyngeal constricted fricative /ḥ/ would not be discernible or would substitute an ever-so-slighty different sound than that of the original Arabic). Similarly, the word in Bangla for Qur'ān is কোরান, transliterated Korān, which spelling I have adopted throughout unless referring to the Arabic original; Qur'ān or Quran corresponds to nothing in Bangla orthography. But perhaps more importantly, the Korān in Bangla should be understood as a dynamic reference. To some it certainly denotes the source of foundational revelation, but that may not always signal a "book" or a "text" as we tend to think of it, and its nature as revelation is probably better understood as akin to the ancient Sanskrit notion of *śruti*, or "heard truth," and so becomes a verbal icon. In many instances it may signal little more than the cultural analogue to the Veda or the *Bhāgavata purāṇa*, whose symbolic value is often greater than its semantic, and as Max Stille's dissertation makes clear, it can generate a sonic experience for the listener quite apart from its content.[3] The point is to remind the reader that the Bangla terms used may not share the precise semantic field of their Arabic or Persian counterparts, or the English glosses; so for me to impose a non-Bangla spelling on any of these terms would, in fact, be to overdetermine the concept, to make a theological as well as historical judgment I am unwilling to make. As I have argued, regional variation and improvisation were central to the spread and practice of Islam, and the use of Bangla inevitably demanded such adjustments.

By resisting the grand scheme of homogenization that plagues so much of the study of Islam (and the attempts to make its theology and practice uniform, especially among those who wish to propose that there is a transnational Islam that is simply one), we do well to remind ourselves that regionalisms are potentially significant and, as a result, may generate a more subtly nuanced understanding of Islam as it is lived from region to region. I am not convinced that an intelligent reader will not be able to follow the stories by my use of these Bangla spellings of what seem to be well-known terms, but hopefully it may also serve to slow down the scholar steeped in Persian and Arabic from jumping to conclusions about the "real" meaning of the terms. Where there are seemingly incomprehensible leaps of orthography, which do surface in the manuscripts from time to time, I have

3. Max Stille, "Poetics of Popular Preaching: *Waz mahfils* in contemporary Bangladesh" (PhD diss., Heidelberg Universität, 2016).

inserted a note of clarification. The term for apostle, *rasul*, will likewise give pause to those steeped in Arabic and Persian because in nearly all of the texts, which are predominately in *musalmāni bāṅglā*, the word will often be spelled রছুল, *rachul*, or রচ্ছুল, *racchul*. In a host of dialects in the eastern half of the Bangla-speaking region, the characters ছ, /ch/, and চ্ছ, /cch/, are pronounced much as the English *s*. Had the author written রসুল, *rasul*, the pronunciation would be "rah-shul," which is simply not what Bangla speakers say. Here the Arabic pronunciation has had a direct impact, its sonic dimension imported. It is important to note that in this monograph, the expression *musalmāni bāṅglā* is not used in the sometimes derogatory sense that some Hindu nationalists have used it and, I hasten to add, it is Bangla in spite of the efforts of some prominent scholars in the early twentieth century to pretend otherwise. The related term *dobhāṣī* has a centuries-long history that is as descriptive first, a term very deliberately used by authors to differentiate their writing by its incorporation of Urdu and Persian elements, which certain factions only later used derogatorily.[4] To imagine these terms negatively is to participate in a normative devaluation that reflects unwarranted prejudice or equally naïve sentiments of an imagined purity of language that has exclusively Sanskritic roots (which, of course, is an impossibility for this or any other North Indian vernacular).

Similarly, we must carefully consider the use of the terms Muslim and Hindu. Neither one of these terms was commonly used prior to the late eighteenth century, and they only took on an independent life (derived largely from English) in the mid-nineteenth century when identity politics emerged and turned the religious monikers of Muslim and Hindu into political identities of group participation. Prior to that period, we see মুসলমানি, *musalmāni*, as an adjective modifying the individual or the practice, and the occasional contrasting term হিন্দুআনি, *hinduāni*, or হিন্দুয়ানি, *hinduyāni*, which signifies "Indic," and on occasion হিন্দু, *hindu*, which as an adjective likewise generally means Indic, and as a noun usually signifies a person who participates in the traditional cultures of India. But মুসলমান, *musalmān*, to signify a nominal follower of Islam, gradually changes its semantic value as one enters the nineteenth century and begins to highlight the religious orientation. More often, especially in the early texts, one sees ethnic or regional markers (which today all too often tellingly signal, or are translated as, "Muslim"), words such as যবন, *jaban*, or যাবন, *jāban* (foreigner, lit. Ionian or Greek), তুরুস্ক, *turuska*,

4. Qazi Abdul Mannan traces the concept, if not the term, back to the thirteenth century; see Mannan, *The Emergence and Development of Dobhasi Literature in Bengal (up to 1855 AD)*, 2d ed. (1966; repr., Dacca: Bangla Academy, 1974). There is disagreement among some scholars regarding the origin of and the first use of the terms *musalmāni bāṅglā* and *dobhāṣī*, but in agreement with Mannan, for our purposes it will indicate Bangla composed for the *musalmāni* community that includes varying, but generally significant amounts of, lexical items derived from Persian and Hindustani/Urdu, and of course Arabic.

or তুরুস্কা, *turuskā*, and তুর্কি, *turki*, or তুর্কী, *turkī* (Turk), পাঠান, *pāṭhān* (Pathan, horse trader), কাবুলি, *kābuli*, or কাবুলী, *kābulī* (one from Kabul), and of course ম্লেচ্ছ, *mlec-cha* (babbler, that is, one who does not speak Sanskrit or its relatives, a term which also refers to Europeans and other ethnic and religious communities, and so forth, but frequently signifying the "uncouth" or "barbarian"). The terms "Hindu" and "Muslim," when capitalized, will only be used in this monograph when I intend the political categories they predominately signify today; otherwise, you should expect to see *musalmān/musalmāni* and *hindu/hinduyāni*, remembering that the latter designates traditional "Indic" as often as it signals *hindu* in orientation. Similarly, the terms Islam and Hinduism are only sparingly used, the latter especially signaling a new religious form which is essentially a response to the colonial experience and which imposes a romantic master narrative that does not match the lived reality of early modern Bengal and which begins to take shape at the very end of the period of these tales. Because the language is changing, there will be some slippage and unevenness in their use within the texts, which I will endeavor to make clear as much as I can determine it. To read the contemporary forms of the concepts of Muslim and Hindu automatically onto these older terms is to make a religious judgment that is not warranted and whose brutal binary reduction is bound to run roughshod over the often subtle distinctions.

Finally, Bangla rather than Bengali will be used throughout to designate the language (written বাংলা, sometimes বাঙ্গলা, which in technical transliteration would be rendered *bāṃlā* or *bāṅglā*). I recognize that this might be contested as overtly political, for the term Bangla is the official language of Bangladesh, but the language of these texts is, by its own election, pronounced "Bangla." This has the added advantage of once again reminding readers not to assume that the English term Bengali, with all its colonial associations, signifies the same thing. We will, however, use the familiar term Bengali to designate the Bangla-speaking region and its people.

Finally, it should be noted that in the translations, single quotations are used to mark the thoughts of the actor, with standard double quotation marks indicating audible speech.

CONVENTIONS REGARDING DATES

Nearly all of the dates in these materials are recorded in terms of the *bāṅglā śaka*, abbreviated BS, which generates an approximate Gregorian or civil calendar date by adding 593; in some instances the title page of the Bangla publication will indicate the precise civil calendar date, which will add 592 because of the slight shift in the way the beginning of the year is calculated. In a handful of references among the printed texts dedicated to Satya Pīr, the *śaka* designation requires the simple addition of 78 to approximate the Western date, and the *saṃvat* date generates the Western equivalent by subtracting 57. All non-Western dates will have the approximate Western equivalent added in brackets.

1

Heavenly Orchestrations

The World of the Legendary Pīrs *of Bengal*

I make obeisance to the spectacle of creation,
its parts strung together like a necklace.
I pay my deepest respects to Mohāmmad, Beloved of God.
With undivided attention I salute Satya Nārāyaṇ,
descended (avatār) *in the Kali Age.*
At the command of Āllā, he took birth in the world of men,
wondrously engendered from two different lineages.
He emerged from the womb of the unwed Sandhyāvatī
to tend the affairs of the kingdom of Mālañcā.
His right hand grips a staff,
a mesmerizing flute sparkles in his left.
His head is smothered with matted locks,
a brilliant dot blazes across his forehead;
a golden sacred thread hangs from his shoulder,
and a linked chain belt winds around his waist,
body swathed in a gleaming ochre-colored cloth.
He wanders back and forth from one region to another,
dressed in the garb of an ascetic sannyāsī,
assuming any number of guises and forms.
Who can fathom the wizardry of this holy pīr:
one life-giving heart, two distinct physical forms,
two different names, for two different communities.

—KṚṢṆAHARI DĀS, *BAḌA SATYA PĪR O SANDHYĀVATĪ KANYĀR PUTHI*

1.1. THE TALE OF THE BIRTH OF SATYA PĪR

Let our story begin with the narrative of the birth of the saint found in *The Great Story of Satya Pīr and the Virgin Girl Sandhyāvatī.*[1] With that laudatory opening and much much more, the author declares the plentiful benefits of paying respect to this *sūphī*[2] saint. After a rather urgent final personal disclaimer, the hagiographer segues into the story, which begins with a curious exchange among several of the significant occupants of heaven.

> Through his mysterious power, Bhagavān Satya Nārāyaṇ is my life's breath. With my mind focused, I pay obeisance to the feet of my *guru*. On my head I place and honor the names of my father and mother as I make a thousand prostrations. All of them together enable me to swim to the farther shore of this ocean of existence. May my *guru* helmsman safely guide me across; may he keep my failures of memory at bay, and grant me wisdom. May the fourteen syllables come together just right to create each metrical line of verse, and enable this hobbled poet to hurdle the mountain. Like so many prolix *brāhmaṇs*, may my writing hand wax like the moon, after which, waving a fan palm frond, may I calm and cool all those gathered to hear.
>
> Among the thousands of people present in this vast audience, Satya Pīr comes to those who call, whether orphans without means or those simply in need of direction. Should all present sing their praises publicly, Satya Pīr will send their troubles far away. When people serve him with respect, offering the custom due, Satya Pīr can become the refuge of every human being. May he grant me the power to sing this song of revelation, so that you too may spread its message. If my public audience

1. Kṛṣṇahari Dās, *Baḍa satya pīr o sandhyāvatī kanyār puthi* (Kalikātā: Nuruddīn Āhmad at Gaosiyā Lāibrerī, n.d.). What follows is a synopsis mixed with translated sections of the first thirty-nine of the printed text's two hundred twenty pages. The undated manuscript copy in my possession suggests a mid- to late-eighteenth-century composition, while, based on the layout, font, spellings, and metrical markers, the undated printed text has the appearance of a late-nineteenth-century production. I am indebted to the late Ābul Kālām Mohāmmad Jākāriyā in Dhaka for allowing me to copy the manuscript of the text from his personal collection.

2. *Sūphī* is of course roughly equivalent in sound and meaning to the word Sufi in English, but as will become apparent, the semantic field of this and other terms does not always perfectly map. I have chosen to transliterate all terms as they are written in Bangla. The names and epithets of all characters in the stories, as well as technical terminology, will be rendered in transliteration that reflects the orthography and in most cases the pronunciation of the Bangla in which it is written. Importantly, God will be rendered as it is written in Bangla, Āllā, rather than the more familiar Allāh used in transcriptions of Arabic and Persian. Other terms such as *phakīr* or *phakir*, *jāban* or *jaban*, *oli* (rather than *auliyā*), or *gājī* (rather than *ghāzī*), and so forth will become easily familiar. The point is to disrupt the assumption of the reader that the terms in Bangla automatically signal the same semantic range they invoke in Arabic, Persian, Sanskrit, or other languages. The differences in both denotation and connotation can at times be profound, so the transliteration of the Bangla term will serve to remind the reader that the conceptual world of Islam, while shared historically and transnationally, is neither uniform nor consistent through time or space. Please also consult the "Conventions Regarding Transliteration and Nomenclature" in the front matter for more of the problems of transliteration and the use of English terms.

feels that my song falls flat, I will be humbled, yet even by that uncommonly ordinary exercise of *dharma*, I may still help rescue many among them.

You [Satya Pīr] are a saint (*oli*). If this tale embarrasses you among the society of prophets (*nabī*), then I shall abandon your company and escape to some faraway place; may you have Āllā and the Prophet (*nabī*) eat my head, binding me head-to-toe a hundred times over. With just your two bare hands you are able to subdue Pṛthivī, the Earth Herself. Like a hundred expert warriors armed with bows, accompanied by thousands upon thousands of horsemen of all colors and stripes, you destroy one king's kingdom in order to put another king in his place.

The old king, Mādhāi,[3] his favored [queen] Priyāvatī, and their two princes, Śāmsundar and Dāmodar, were among those so chosen. Priyāvatī constantly fussed over her husband, ministering to his needs in both body and spirit. While the king, indeed, did have many fine qualities and served to protect *dharma*, as a rule he proved extremely mean-spirited toward *phakīrs*. Whenever one of the *phakīrs* of God Khodā appeared in the city, Mādhāi would chain him around the neck and imprison him in a cell. If the *phakīr* was deemed to cast an evil eye, he would be blown to bits by the royal cannons; then for thirteen days the king would drink only water and eat only rice in penance. Numerous *vaiṣṇavīs*[4] and ascetic *sannyāsīs* were always in attendance; they performed ritual *sevā* and *pūjā* worship, for which Mādhāi conferred gifts of great value.

The angel Jibril observed, "O Āllā, Guardian and Nourisher, this king who reigns in the Kali Age is a terrible sinner. He slays God-loving people (*momin*) and chops them to pieces. When he sees one of your *phakīrs*, he has him shackled round the neck, and the *phakīr* can be heard crying out for help in a loud voice, 'Āllā, Āllā!' Untold numbers of *phakīrs* have been securely detained in this way. Tell me Nirāñjan, Stainless One, why are they not being protected?"

Āllā spoke, "Give me a solution, a plan, my beloved Prophet (*nabī*). Whom might we dispatch, to descend and serve as my witness (*gāoyār*)?"

The Apostle (*rachul*) replied, "Āllā, Great Protector, Satya Pīr should descend as the *avatār* in this Kali Age. There is in paradise (*bhest*) a certain Cāndbibī, whose beauty is typical of a heavenly celestial nymph, a færie (*hurparī*). Send her down to take birth from the belly of that king's consort Priyāvatī. From the womb of that

3. He would later be called by the epithet *maidānav* or *mayadānav*, the Demon King. It is unlikely a coincidence that his name invokes that of one of the two willfully belligerent antagonists of Kṛṣṇa Caitanya (1486–1533) in Nabadvīp, Jāgāi and Mādhāi, who were redeemed by the intervention of two of Caitanya's closest companions, Nityānanda and Gadādhar, and subsequently became devout *vaiṣṇavs*; see Vṛndāvan Dās, *Caitanya bhāgavat*, edited with Bengali commentary "Nitāikaruṇākallolinī ṭīkā" by Rādhāgovinda Nāth (Kalikātā: Sādhanā Prakāśanī, 1373 BS [ca. 1966], 2.13. For an already somewhat dated translation of the tale, see Tony K. Stewart, trans., "The Rescue of Two Drunkards," in *The Religions of India in Practice*, ed. Donald S. Lopez, Jr., (Princeton: Princeton University Press, 1995), 375–88.

4. The way *vaiṣṇavī* is used in this text, it appears to be grammatically incorrect, but seemingly apposite in construction to *sannyāsī*, that is, a male *vaiṣṇav* or a *vairāgī* rather than a female worshiper of Kṛṣṇa or Caitanya. If we read female worshiper, then it likely signals that women of the king's family and court were highly learned, for *vaiṣṇav* women were often employed by the wealthy to educate daughters in reading, writing, poetics, and so forth.

comely virgin girl will Satya Pīr be born. He shall spring from the mixing of two different communities (*kul*) and will serve both publicly."

Āllā responded, "What a brilliant plan you have suggested, Apostle (*rachul*). But when he takes on a mortal human form, he must not enter into any marriage. Anything that happens after that, you report to me. Whatever shape he assumes in the ocean of worldly existence, he must retain my name."

Mohāmmad replied, "So it is decided; that is the strategy we will pursue. I will send Jibril to Cāndbibī."

And so the angel (*pherestā*) went to call on the Bibī.

While he was sitting there, exactly what kind of *karma* had Mohāmmad brought into play? For in the gateway to heaven he fashioned a venomous serpent with a physical bodily form, and then he had a frog sent as its meal.

Meanwhile Jibril called out, "Bibī, come! Your presence is requested. The honorable Prophet is calling you for a special cause. He would be most pleased were you to come right away," [which of course she did].

When she arrived and came upon Mohāmmad's conjured scene, Cāndbibī was stopped dead in her tracks.

The frog was weeping bitterly since it had fallen into the mouth of the serpent. It cried out, "Āllā, please forestall my imminent death!" The frog immediately appealed to her, "Bibī, hear my prayer. Please save me from the jaws of this serpent! If you do not, I am finished. I can only appeal to Āllā for justice."

But the serpent countered, "Listen, Bibī, consider my position. By the decree of the God of Fate, Bidhātā, has this meal been sent me. I have not eaten in more than a month. If the frog is destined to die to provide my meal, it is by the proclamation of Āllā."

The situation seemed intractable as each argued his case. Examining the conundrum from every angle, Cāndbibī reasoned through her options and finally resolved to act. Once decided, she promptly snatched the frog from the jaws of the snake and released it into the waters.

Thoroughly confounded, the serpent declared, "Cāndbibī, you have always been a paragon of virtue, so how could you steal the food right out of my mouth?" The snake continued his lamentation: "Because of your actions, I have been denied my life-sustaining meal."

[Cāndbibī] wasted no time in leaving and hurried on to the court of Āllā, presented herself, and made obeisance. Bibī spoke, "Pāk Nirāñjan, Pure and Stainless One, for what reason have you summoned me?"

Āllā replied, "Listen Bibī, here is why: you must go down to the demonic king Maidānav's home as the daughter of his queen, Rājarāṇī Priyāvatī. When you have taken birth in their home, you will become the royal princess Sandhyāvatī and from your womb will Satya Pīr take birth. I will come down as my own witness and become the embodied descent (*avatār*) of truth (*satya*)."

Cāndbibī replied, "Please listen, Āllā, Stainless One. How will I, a færie, be able to endure the excruciating pain of child bearing? In order for there to be a live birth, a fetus must grow in a woman's womb for ten months.[5] In the dark of night, the house

5. Pregnancies are traditionally measured as ten lunar months.

reverberates with her desperate and painful cries, 'Help! Save me!' The agony emanating from her womb is not to be endured by the frail likes of me. I am incapable of reproducing as that princess. Please do forgive me, Āllā, for challenging this. How and why am I to descend, Āllā? Why must I suffer the consequences of this singular entry to the world of ordinary human existence? Can you not please send someone else to the demon king's home?"

The Prophet replied, "You must go by the terms decreed. You will be gracious toward the Master and you will not disobey."

Turning then to Mohāmmad, Cāndbibī pleaded, "Please listen! What offense have I committed for you to condemn me to a mortal existence? Only those who are flawed and sinful must undergo birth as mortals. Who can send me to the land of mortals to become a *jābanā*?"[6]

By then the weakening snake, near death, had managed to catch up and wasted no time in lodging his complaint. "By what right could Cāndbibī have interfered and stopped me from eating? After more than a month I finally managed to land a frog morsel from the Dāmodar River. But Bibī plucked it right out of my mouth and sent it flying back to the deep." And with that pitiable lament, the now completely starved snake convulsed, writhed on the ground, and gave up its life.

[Mohāmmad then pointed out to Bibī], "This sin alone is sufficient to send you to hell. Only when you are born into a human clan will that sin and misery be atoned. After thirty-six years will your transgression be expiated."

As she listened to his words, Bibī lamented bitterly, "In the name of Āllā, what am I supposed to admit about this ersatz transgression of *karma?* I did not know what to do and for this ambiguous, if not deceptive, infraction you are going to dispatch me to the land of the mortals, to be touched, to be handled by a husband who comes from another social group (*jāti*)? I will become infamous in the whole of heaven."

The Prophet replied, "You *will* become the daughter of the king. But who has decreed that you are to be married? Whether for fame or infamy—that accrues to me. You are imagining miseries for no good reason. What Āllā brings about is for his own satisfaction and reasons. Now you must go and enter into the world of mortals."

Kṛṣṇahari Dās shares this conversation in accomplished meter. May the hero Satya Pīr fulfill your heart's desire.

Listen brothers to this gratifying tale. No one can fathom what Khodā does. What is sanctioned and what is nullified, or the way what is previously approved becomes prohibited—who can comprehend the full extent of divine power? Who can reckon what is sin (*pāp*) or what is merit (*puṇya*) in the divine economy? Why a sinner is destined to suffer while another prospers, why a person dies in one house and another lives—no matter how hard one tries, no one can fully explain it. Each individual suffers both sinful and meritorious qualities, and according to those tendencies will an individual habitually return. If a sin be committed while in heaven, then a return

6. Feminine of *jaban* or *jāban* (from *yavana*, lit. Ionian). A general term to designate people not originally from the subcontinent, today nearly always glossed as Muslim, but more accurately should be construed as an ethnic marker.

to the mortal world is in store. If a sin is committed in the world of mortals, then one falls into hell (*dojakh*). Listen carefully now to the natures of heaven and hell.

Has anyone actually seen heaven? What individual can speak of hell? As written in the Korān, there are seven hells. But what are the characteristics described by people who have witnessed heaven and hell? Listen carefully and I will tell you about heaven. Heaven is like the best of our worldly society—whether it is or is not, that *is* what people say. Just imagine, if you will, the one who enjoys the creature comforts, who gets to loll about on a fragrant bed of flowers, to be the one who sleeps in a house adorned with flower blossoms, and always eats ghee and honey. Who gets to own the horses? Who amasses and holds others' debts? Who becomes the merchant trader? He who has become king is the lord (*īśvar*) who takes the wealth of other people, the bounty of this earth, to enjoy for himself. It is said in the book that heaven is something just like that.

Now listen, good people, for now I will describe what is said about hell. Whether it is or is not, understand this *is* what people have authoritatively reported. No one there can see, like one who has fallen into the dark of a deep well. No one can discern whether it is night or day. Deaf and mute, not a sound can slip from anyone's mouth. One has neither legs nor arms, for all of one's limbs rot away. Fixated on begging for food, one must fast without end. To be mired in sin is to live at the foot of a scrub brush, scavenging as a dog or jackal. Understand that this is the nature of hell people describe.

Listen brothers all as I submit this before you. Focus your attention and listen to the pāñcāli tale of the saint.[7]

Cāndbibī continues to complain, especially among her closest companions, at which point the entire mechanism for her birth is explained by Mohāmmad, including the precedent that forty *bibīs* have previously been impregnated by flowers sent from heaven for the birth of special *pīrs*. So Cāndbibī descends, and Queen Priyāvatī duly becomes pregnant and gives birth to Sandhyāvatī, much to the joy of the king and his courtiers. A little more than twelve blissful years pass, and Sandhyāvatī blossoms into a stunning beauty. But one night she finds herself restless, inexplicably agitated.

Āllā has instructed Mohāmmad to interrupt Sandhyāvatī's sleep and reveal to her through her dreams that she is actually Cāndbibī, descended from heaven to bear the *phakīr* Satya Pīr. Mohāmmad then explains how, with her hundred companions, she will take herself to bathe in the River Ennar. There, immersed in the waters while bathing, a flower will float toward her and her alone, and it will impregnate her.

But before they can put the plan into effect, they have to get Satya Pīr to agree to the terms and conditions.

Āllā said, "My dear Messenger (*paygambar*), please put our plan into play, for the demon king Mayadānav is truly evil. Whenever one of my *phakīrs* goes to Mālañcā, he ends up chained by the neck and thrown in jail. As a result, the number of heralds

7. Kṛṣṇahari Dās, *Baḍa satya pīr o sandhyāvatī kanyār puthi*, 4–7.

to my majesty is diminishing everywhere on earth. In what fashion will my beloved son-as-witness (*beṭā gāoyār*) pulverize the king?"

The Prophet replied, "Revered Āllā-ji, you are the master of petitioners. There is no one who can fathom your miracle-working power. An ocean of mercy, you exercise dominion over the magic of creation (*māyā*). In your sight, the demon king Mayadānav is no more than a speck of a sesame seed. When you send Satya Pīr, Truth itself (*satya*) will be instituted through his descent (*avatār*)—he will be born from the womb of Sandhyāvatī. By following this unique expedient, two separate goals will be achieved. When the witness descends to miserable Mālañcā, the God (*devatā*) of the *hindu* will be the *pīr* of the *musalmān*. He will demonstrate how to serve both communities (*kul*). In the Kali Age, untold numbers of people are conversant with sin (*pāp*), but when they worship Satya, the Truth, their enlightenment will be effected and your majesty and glory will spread throughout the world (*saṃsār*). When that end is reached, may you quickly return him to heaven."

Listening to this plan of action, Āllā was exceedingly pleased. The Stainless One, Nirañjan, called and spoke to Jibril. Āllā said, "Listen carefully, Jibril, to what I say. Go fetch Satya Pīr to my dwelling."

No sooner had he received the command than off he flew. He called on Satya Pīr and escorted him to the presence of Āllā. When Satya Pīr arrived, he offered his profound salutations, "Why have you summoned me, you who are the treasure trove for supplicants?"

Āllā responded, "You must go once more to the world of mortals. The demonic king Mayadānav of Mālañcā perpetrates a reign of endless tyranny. I want you to fly down quickly and assume the task of spreading the noble ritual of revering God (*sevā*). Once you have initiated that ritual service in the city of Mālañcā proper, ensure it is instituted in each and every home."

Because it was the Pure and Stainless One, Pāk Nirañjan, who uttered these words, Satya Pīr replied, "Āllā, I humbly submit to your request. By all means dispatch me to earth, but I must admit that I am very much afraid to undergo the torments of the womb."

Āllā replied, "You will not suffer any of the burning pains of the womb. You will not even be born initially as yourself [in human form], but reproduced as a clot of blood."

Satya Pīr said, "Āllā, you are the great protector of all, please go ahead and send me down to earth. Whatever form you have me take in this birth, I will always be singularly devoted to your feet. In the Kali Age, so many people exist in misery—may they obtain their hopes and desires when they encounter me! May they be released from their dire straits and attain an exalted state of dignity! But tell me, how precisely am I to alleviate this suffering?"

Nirañjan, the Stainless, answered, "Go to earth, and any time you need, simply remember me, and you will succeed."

With that, Satya Pīr responded, "Whenever I fall into trouble, I shall take your name and by that alone may you rescue me."

Hearing this, Āllā promised, "The moment you start to utter my name, your worries will cease. He whom I do not allow to die cannot be killed. You will never suffer death in that earthly river of mortal life. You cannot be drowned, you cannot be

> burned by fire. Even if the moon or the sun were to attack you, you would not suffer death."[8]

Events follow the script as expected. When Sandhyāvatī and her friends splash in the river, Sandhyāvatī mysteriously refuses to come out of the water until she retrieves a most exquisite rose blossom. As it floats upstream, the flower will dodge and flee the grasp of any of the young women who reach for it, always pushing itself slightly out of reach—until, that is, it makes its way to Sandhyāvatī.

> The flower suddenly washed into her hands. In a single movement, Sandhyāvatī picked up that special blossom and sniffed its perfume. She breathed Satya Pīr right into her body, and he lodged in her womb. The flower instantly lost its brilliance, lost all color, withered, and died. Suddenly feeling queasy, she hurled the now wilted flower to the ground, but the flower flew from earth up to heaven like [Mohāmmad] in the night journey (*meyārāj*).
>
> *Listen now to the rest of the story of Sandhyāvatī. She finished bathing, returned to her group, and headed back to the capital city. Sandhyāvatī, the unmarried princess sans prince, had gotten pregnant. Accepting the command of my* guru, *I endeavor to make public this tale where Satya Pīr will fulfill every person's heart's desire. I grovel a hundred times over in salutation at the feet of Satya Pīr, for it is at your command that Kṛṣṇahari sings this song.*[9]

The servants are incredulous and then aghast as they try to hide Sandhyāvatī's increasingly obvious pregnancy. Eventually one serving girl informs the queen, who laments the stain on the family name. Sandhyāvatī herself is understandably confused. "I am an unmarried princess. How can I have gotten pregnant when I have never lain with a man? I cannot fathom this strange situation, but whatever is born from my womb will send me to hell, to Yam's perdition." She reconstructs the events at the river and realizes that she was impregnated the moment she inhaled the fragrance of the flower. "I cannot fathom Khodā's staging of this event."[10] Her mother seeks to have an abortifacient slipped into the goat's milk Sandhyāvatī drinks every evening, but Satya Pīr, neatly curled up in her womb as he is, divines her plan and calls on God to intervene. God, Satya Nārāyaṇ, sends Jibril, who communicates with Satya Pīr and, through the power of yogic scriptural utterances (*āgam śabda*), magically transforms the poison into a dense, sweet cream. The abortion never happens.

When Queen Priyāvatī is finally forced to tell the king, he goes crazy with all-too-predictable anger. He orders his constable to take Sandhyāvatī into the forest and abandon her. The constable is horrified, for it is too much like Rām banishing the pregnant Sītā to the forest. But banish her he does, and so, after tearful leave-taking and anguish, into the forest they go. Sandhyāvatī is allowed to take two

8. Kṛṣṇahari Dās, 13–14.
9. Kṛṣṇahari Dās, 16.
10. Kṛṣṇahari Dās, 17.

servants with her. On their way they cross the Nur River and go through Haripur, Dioḍi village, Lakṣmīpur, Jayantinagar, then Tripurā. Passing Kadalī Dikinī, they reach Nokāgrām. Jayantinagar is the village where Sandhyāvatī's brother Śāmsundar lives, but she refuses to visit him out of shame. They pass Thakāgrām, Kalyāṇ town, Dāmihāṭ, Śaṅkhapur, Sāpinī Pāpinī, and finally Bajarāśahar, until Sandhyāvatī can go no further. She asks the constable to erect a shelter there, but he refuses, pushing her forward. Finally, he abandons her on the banks of the Begavatī River.

Sandhyāvatī and her two servants camp out under the canopy of a massive tree for seven days and nights. Finding no food, they fast. Not a soul appears. At night, terrified, they lie down, their stomachs growling in hunger. At night the tigers prowl and growl, scattering the frenzied deer in every direction. Wild boars, oxen, and all manner of beasts tramp through the forest around them. Finally a female and male tiger couple, drawn by the irresistible smell of human flesh, creep forward for the kill.

> But Sandhyāvatī spoke first. "O tigress, I am emotionally overwhelmed, for I have come to the forest pregnant. Clamp your jaws around me and eat me so that you may put an end to my burning misery."
>
> The tiger muttered, "Then I think I am going to eat right now." But the tigress snapped and ordered him, "Stand back! Be still! It is not proper to eat pregnant prey."
>
> The tiger ignored her admonition, and with his tail swooped above his head, he pounced, jaws open, ready to kill.
>
> Satya Pīr called out to the tiger from the womb, "You have just forfeited your dotage! I am Satya Pīr. Anyone I curse is instantly turned to ashes."
>
> As soon as he heard the *pīr*'s clarion call, the tiger knew it to be true; he lowered his head in obeisance, and wrapped his tail around his own neck in submission. The tiger and tigress then slunk away, but soon a lion came to see the humans huddled at the foot of the tree. This lord among lions moved forward, ignoring the twenty slithering cobras that had also been attracted and were gnashing their fangs in anticipation.
>
> Satya Pīr called out, "Hey listen, you lord of lions! You may be the king of animals, you may be afraid of no one, and I am sure you can kill a monkey with one swipe of your paw to dine on his flesh. But know now that you are on the sure path of death and destruction. Know without doubt that a single blow from my hand will send you to hell, the abode of Yam!" Registering the menace of those truthful words, the lion king crouched down on the ground with grass between his teeth in surrender. He then jumped up and ran far away, fortunate to have preserved his life that day.
>
> After the lion had been driven off, some bears loped up in quest of a quick kill. The male and female bears circled the tree until Satya Bhagavān called out, "If you know what is good for you, you bears will leave now, otherwise you will be destined for death in Yam's house!" The bears, too, wasted no time in scampering away.
>
> *Till the tenth watch did this continue, as Kṛṣṇahari Dās mellifluously sings.*[11]

11. Kṛṣṇahari Dās, 27–28.

It takes the constable seven days to return to the king's court, where he describes the convoluted path they have followed, traveling from one river *ghāṭ* to the next, eventually to reach the Kul Forest where he left Sandhyāvatī. The king is pleased to have the business over and done with.

Meanwhile Sandhyāvatī and her two serving girls are wracked with hunger and thirst and, remembering the name of God, cry out for help. The Prophet alerts Āllā, who in turn consults with Bidhātā, the God of Fate, and then summons Jibril to descend in the guise of a watchman who seemingly just happens to stumble across them. Jibril provides them with food and water and swiftly returns to heaven.

From inside Sandhyāvatī's womb, Satya Pīr meditates on Lokmān Hākim, who in an instant miraculously materializes. He asks Lokmān to construct an impregnable royal palace with ten doors made of iron, each door lavishly decorated with rubies and precious stones, and each equipped with secure lock and key. The building should rise two full stories above the ground floor, and be replete with fresh drinking water and palm trees. He also instructs him to construct seven private bathing *ghāṭs*, and to provide for every want and need of Sandhyāvatī and her servants.

Lokmān Hākim diligently sets about his task, constructing the different buildings, including five- and nine-spired temples.[12] Celestial *gandharvas* arrive, and soon the grounds are teeming, seemingly populated by tens of millions. Even Indra with his *vidyādharis* visits from heavenly Indrapuri. The golden citadel is studded with rubies, pearls, and diamonds. When it is completed, after about a day, Lokmān Hākim takes his leave. A palanquin is sent for Sandhyāvatī and her servants, who are understandably overwhelmed at their opulent turn of fortune. The place is more lavishly appointed than anything ever seen in Bengal, including her father's citadel. And of course there is a *masjid*, an item not found on her father's palace grounds.

> *This is the way of Satya Pīr: he gives sons to the childless and riches to the poor, if you but worship him with respect.*

Sandhyāvatī's time has finally come, a dark night in the month of Māgh. In agony, she laments her inglorious fate for having innocently sniffed a flower.

> She eventually gave birth to a clot of blood. What can be said of the *pīr*'s promise? There were no arms, no legs, no head, no ears, no nose, no mouth. Ever so slowly did the clot ooze out, a quivering mass of congealed blood. This was how Satya was born.[13]

12. The *pañcaratna*, literally "five gems," is a typical construction for a temple in Bengal; it has a slightly arched pavilion with one spire (*śikhar*) on each corner, and a central elevated pavilion with a single spire (4 + 1). The *navaratna* or "nine gems" emerged in the seventeenth century, adding another level with four spires (4 + 4 +1). See David McCutchion, *Brick Temples of Bengal: From the Archives of David McCutchion*, ed. George Michell (Princeton: Princeton University Press, 1983).

13. Kṛṣṇahari Dās, *Baḍa satya pīr o sandhyāvatī kanyār puthi*, 32.

Sandhyāvatī laments the cruel work of fate, the double shame of being pregnant and then not delivering a child. "A woman without a child suffers a fruitless life—people will wonder: what kind of tree produces no fruit?"[14] She cannot understand, because everything has been so clear in her dreams that she would bear a son who would be a jewel among men. To be banished because of her pregnancy, which has turned out to be a strange event producing no child at all, angers and confuses her, fueling her grief.

After rehearsing *in extenso* her mind-numbing tragedy, Sandhyāvatī gathers her wits, takes her servant girls, and with resolve carries the clot of blood to the banks of the Begavatī River. Filled with sorrow and remorse, she hurls the mass into its swirling waters. As it begins to sink, a large female turtle rises from the depths and swallows the clot.[15] Sandhyāvatī bathes and heads back to her forest dwelling. The turtle swallows hard, and soon the clot is encased in a leathery egg, with Satya Pīr inside the egg inside her womb. Then Satya Pīr works some more of his magic, and after being ensconced in her belly for only ten watches (about four hours), he is hatched in the shallows, fully formed. He quickly scrambles across a shoal and onto a sandbank. As he looks on, the turtle is transfigured—she becomes a splendid heavenly nymph, a *vidyādharī*. Previously she was a *brāhmaṇ* widow, who, for the offense of eating raw meat, was transmogrified into a turtle, scavenging food on the banks and deep below the surface of the waters. But she also received a boon to ameliorate that offense: she was promised that she would hold none other than the Lord Nārāyaṇ in her womb, albeit for only a span of ten watches. With that promised act, she will be exonerated and dispatched to Vaikuṇṭha heaven—and Satya Pīr has made it so.[16]

14. Kṛṣṇahari Dās, 33.

15. Turtle is *kacchabinī*, a generic term which in this context points to sweet water riverine and estuary-dwelling turtles, which grow sufficiently large to swallow a mass the size of a newborn. At the time of the text's composition, it most likely referred to one of the six species of Batagur, all of which are nearing extinction today.

16. The turtle's role in serving as the vehicle for Satya Pīr's birth in the water invokes the image of the cosmogonic sequence of Dharma Ṭhākur as Nirañjan creating the universe out of the void (*śūnyatā*), with the turtle emerging from the primal waters. See Rāmāi Paṇḍit, *Śūnyapurāṇ*, ed. Cārucandra Bandyopādhyāy, with an introduction by Muhammād Śahīdullāh and Basantakumār Caṭṭopādhyāy (Kalikātā: Satīścandra Mukhopādhyāy from Basumatī Sāhitya Mandir, n.d. [preface dtd. 1336 BS (ca. 1929)]), *Sṛṣti pattan*, section 3, vv. 70–103, pp. 18–24. A more recent edition transcribes the text identically; see Rāmāi Paṇḍit, *Śūnyapurāṇ (śūnyapurāṇ, saṃjāt paddhati, dharmapurāṇ)*, ed. Bhaktimādhav Caṭṭopādhyāy (Kalikātā: Phārmā Ke El Em Prāibheṭ Limiṭeḍ, 1977), *Sṛṣti pattan*, sec. 3, vv. 70–103, pp. 74–76. For more on the association of the turtle with Dharma, see Āśutoṣ Bhaṭṭācārya, *Bāṃlā maṅgalkābyer itihās*, 6th ed. (Kalikātā: E. Mukhārjī āyāṇḍ Koṃ Prāibheṭ Limiṭeḍ, 1381 BS [1975]), 621–26. For a history of the speculation regarding the tortoise among worshipers of Dharma, see Frank J. Korom, "'Editing' Dharmaraj: Academic Genealogies of a Bengali Folk Deity," *Western Folklore*, 56, no. 1 (1997): 51–77.

As soon as the turtle is released to heaven, Satya Pīr encounters Khoyāj Jendā Pīr [Khijr], who dwells in those waters. Satya Pīr persuades him to accept him as his student (*murid*). As his teacher (*mursed*), Khoyāj coaches him for five years, after which Satya Pīr is ready to begin his new life's work.[17]

1.2. THE MARVELOUS TALES OF SŪPHĪ SAINTS

So begin the miraculous adventures of Satya Pīr, on his mission to meet the spiritual and worldly needs of those who petition and honor him, regardless of their religious orientation. He first goes to the courts of Mālañcā, and afterwards uses his wonder-working power to convince everyone from kings and cobblers to prostitutes and merchants that they share in a common humanity which prospers when the divine is properly acknowledged and suffers when the divine is denigrated. He preaches from the Korān and the *Bhāgavata purāṇa*, lecturing *imāms* and *brāhmaṇs* equally. His immaculate conception, effected through a flower sent to earth by God, signals that he lives a deservedly charmed life. Āllā promises that nothing can kill him, so he survives every peril, even when strapped to the mouth of a cannon, which is fired to no avail. The beginning of the story cues an expectation in the audience that eagerly enters Satya Pīr's fantastic world; it declares a dramatic mode familiar to nearly every inhabitant of the Bangla-speaking regions of the South Asian subcontinent (the region today comprised of the Indian states of West Bengal, northern Orissa, and parts of Assam, and the nation-state of Bangladesh). The sensational exploits of holy men and women of various religious persuasions, their interactions with gods and goddesses, *jinns* and angels, and a host of other celestial figures are woven into a common romantic thread. Though they circulate in a variety of slightly different but closely related literary and performative genres, these tales can be indexed generically as *kathā*, simply *story, tale, narrative*, or *fiction*, a vernacular storytelling form that has its roots in ancient Sanskrit literary traditions as much as in Persian and Arabic and related languages such as Avadhī, Hindavī, and what in colonial times was called Hindustāni, but now more recently in Urdu.[18] Like traditional heroic romances everywhere, they inhabit a world where the unthinkable is commonplace. They speak to surviving in the all-too-often hostile climate of Bengal, the vagaries of encountering jungly beasts and serpents, endemic disease, and the predations of unscrupulous rulers and their ever-present

17. Kṛṣṇahari Dās, *Baḍa satya pīr o sandhyāvatī kanyār puthi*, 33–36.

18. The *pīr kathās*, or stories of the *sūphī* saints, find expression in a variety of genres in addition to *kathā*, including *pāñcālī* (specifically indicated in the preceding passage), *pālāgān, jātrā, nāṭak, kissā, kāhinī*, and so forth; their forms and functions will be described as needed. Significantly, all of these forms are vernacular and half of them unique to Bengal, but one should resist automatically equating the forms directly to their analogues and homonyms in other North Indian languages, because the form and semantic field so designated may not always be identical.

merchants. But apart from the names, is there anything distinctly Islamic or even religious about this entertaining vignette of Satya Pīr's birth?

The author invokes Āllā and Mohāmmad, and the angel Jibril, which clearly frames the narrative in nominally Islamic terms. But Āllā is also called by the additional name Bhagavān Satya Narāyāṇ in a terminology that then and today would be instantly recognized as an epithet of the Hindu god Kṛṣṇa. So too the appellation Nirañjan, the Stainless One; commonly used to invoke Viṣṇu-Kṛṣṇa or Nārāyaṇ, it also equally serves as one of the most common appellations of Āllā in Bangla literature—a shared descriptor that would seem to capture commonly held notions of highest divinity as formless and pure. In the first lines following the various encomia and supplications, the homey colloquy in heaven (*bhest*) where Mohāmmad queries Āllā just as a minister might his king, jars the traditional images of Āllā's omniscience, his ninety-nine immaculate qualities, and his generally accepted formlessness. The exchange mimics a king's court. Immediately after their consultation, God summons Jibril and then dispatches him on his errands. That court is of course heaven, or *bhest*, but heaven is also called in this text by the common *vaiṣṇav* designation *vaikuṇṭha*. The actions of the characters in that special place likewise seem to challenge most Islamic descriptions of heaven, even veering away from what the author himself, Kṛṣṇahari Dās, shifting into a mildly homiletic mode, outlines in his comparison of heaven and hell. What about the traffic of celestial figures in and out of this courtly heaven? Is fetching a *houri* or *peri* (*hurpāri* as færie) a menial task one associates with an angel Jibril, presumably the archangel of the name who, according to the mainstream tradition, significantly shared the Arabic Qur'ān with Muhammad? Is the invocation of Prophet (*nabī*) and Apostle (*rachul/racchul*) sufficient to call the tale Islamic when Kṛṣṇa and Rām are likewise invoked? Is it within Mohāmmad's character, as we know it from the traditional Arabic *sirā* and *ḥadīth* texts, to devise a scheme wherein an exemplary, quality-laden færie would be tricked into committing such a minor, and certainly ambiguous, offense to warrant a thirty-six-year exile on earth? Where in the Islamic tradition do we hear of any character who, having gained heaven, returns to earth, save Mohāmmad's *mi'rāj*, which is explicitly invoked when the turtle that has borne Satya Pīr ascends to heaven? Indeed, as the author says, only God knows the mysteries of such action! How often do we hear of any heavenly figure, much less a færie, arguing with Jibril or with Mohāmmad about a divine decree? The argument Cāndbibī puts forward centers on the concept of the traditional Indic concept of *karma*, its consequences for rebirth, and who might expect to suffer negatively. What does Fate, especially delivered by the god Bidhātā, have to do with it? Who knew that at least forty other times God had sent down færies to give birth to special *pīrs* to do his bidding? And among those forty prior descents, was it normal for Āllā to send a færie into the womb of a *brāhmaṇ* queen, and not just as a færie, but as a *jabanā* or *musalmāni* woman? Impregnation from sniffing a flower is not an unknown trope in popular Bangla tales, but crediting Āllā with the instigation seems to put a new twist on it.[19] Can Sandhyāvatī's condition be considered an immaculate conception, or should we consider the nose just another orifice that leads to the womb, reminiscent of the varied ways in which the mythology of the *purāṇik* gods and goddesses of India fantastically procreate? Either way we must ask who, then, is the father. What does Āllā mean when he says he himself will come down as Satya Nārāyaṇ for his *hinduyāni* audience and as Satya Pīr for his *musalmāni* followers? Yet he has Satya Pīr fetched to make the descent in his place, but only with Satya Pīr's consent. Once in the womb, this special *pīr* speaks, commanding wild animals to proceed at their peril, which sends them packing, a variation of the widely accepted belief that *pīrs* and warrior *gājīs* talk to and control animals in the wild, the preferred home of these mendicants. But Satya Pīr also summons Lokmān Hākim, who executes his bidding without question. Are we supposed to understand that Lokmān Hākim is the same Luqmān of the Arabic Qur'ān, *surā* 31? How can Lokmān magically appear when called by Satya Pīr to construct a palace deep in the heart of a dense jungle in south central Bengal, and then do it in one day?

The text leaves us with many awkward questions unanswered if we attempt to resolve the actions of its characters with what we know of traditional Islamic history, or attempt to rectify the nature of divinity as described. To force the narrative into the genre classification that aligns with traditionally accepted Islamic religious discourses of history, theology, and law will inevitably do more violence than Procrustes himself could have engineered. *These stories fall outside the traditional strictures of history, theology, and law, and therein lies their secret power and a key to their interpretation.* Though the bulk of the narratives' propagation and circulation is the result of the performances of storytellers and performing troupes, oral literature, with its widely recognized modes of reproduction, maintains the fidelity of the tale. But the tales are not without their physical props and different modes of visual circulation, in both manuscript form and painted image.

Those who worship according to the prescribed ritual form of *sevā* or *pūjā* often sing the tales in the presence of images representing the various *pīrs*, *devs*, and *devīs* who control the powers of protection. But the exploits of these *musalmāni* luminaries and *hinduyāni* heroes and deities are at the same time extolled by singers of tales apart from formal worship.[20] Their narratives are illustrated in

19. One popular story (with multiple variants) tells of a king who has no sons, but one stunningly beautiful daughter who plucks a flower from the river and after smelling its fragrance finds herself pregnant; she escapes her father's wrath by fleeing to the forest where she meets a trader, who steals her away, but abandons her son, who is raised by a tigress. The boy eventually recovers his rightful kingdom as inheritance. See eight variants of the story in Ālamgīr Jalīl and Sāmīyul Islām, eds., "Āṭkuḍe rājār pālāgān o kissā saṃkalan," in the Bangla Academy journal *Lok sāhitya* 15 (Pauṣ 1385 [January 1979): 1–197. A variation of this trope will appear again in the story of Badar Pīr, in chapter 2.

20. It should be noted that there are several forms of textual performance that blur the distinction between chanting and singing. Mary Frances Dunham's analysis of *jārigān* highlights the performance

painted pictures called *paṭacitra* or *paṭs*, with sequential frames that function much like contemporary cinema storyboards. The visual narratives are produced by a hereditary groups of artisans—*paṭuās, paṭidārs, or citrakārs* in different parts of Bengal—who paint their tales frame by frame, originally on cloth, but much more likely now on paper. There is textual evidence of this practice of illustration dating back more than two millennia in South Asia, but no example exists today that is older than the mid-fifteenth century.[21] The *paṭ* illustrations are surprisingly mobile, and it is impossible to tell where certain themes and even painting techniques originated. Today the tales illustrated by these paintings—and the numbers of individuals practicing this art have diminished considerably—constitute much of the repertory of itinerant performers and troupes of actors who stage the dramas in open-air *jātrā, pāñcālī,* and *pālagān* performances.[22] Historically, the *paṭs* were deployed in those public performances to provide visual context for the actions being described and often enacted; fewer and fewer performances today

---

of semi-epic ballads, focusing primarily on the Shi'i martyrs of the Karbala narrative, and David M. Kane's analysis of the *sylheti nāgri* "melodic reading," called *puthi poṛā*, demonstrates the way texts form the classical romance and *sūphī* repertoires of *musalmāni* literature; see Dunham, *Jarigan: Muslim Epic Songs of Bangladesh* (Dhaka: The University Press Limited, 1997), and Kane, *Puthi Poṛā: "Melodic Reading" and Its Use in the Islamisation of Bengal* (London: Sylheti Translation and Research, 2017). For a related analysis of the preaching style of contemporary Bangladeshi *imāms*, including analyses of the tonal and melodic patterns adopted while code-switching during the public recitation of different texts and expository styles, see Max Stille, "Poetics of Popular Preaching: *Waz Mahfils* in Contemporary Bangladesh" (PhD diss., Universität Heidelberg, 2016).

21. Today the *paṭs* are of two basic types: *lotāipaṭ*, or scrolls (both vertical and horizontal registers), and *caukāpaṭ*, which are quadrangular in shape (squares or rectangles, usually with a central figure and surrounding registers). For a concise yet technically precise description and taxonomy of the styles of paintings in popular art, not only of the *paṭs* but of clay plates and pots in the same vein, see Nisir Hossain, "Folk Painting," in *Arts and Crafts*, ed. Lala Rukh Selim, Cultural Survey of Bangladesh Series 8 (Dhaka: Asiatic Society of Bangladesh, 2007), 499–510. With the kind permission of the British Museum, the cover and frontispiece of the current volume are taken from one of the oldest extant Bengali *paṭs*, c. 1780, as described by T. Richard Blurton, *Bengali Myths* (London: The British Museum Press, 2006), 67–72. The scroll itself is more than 42 feet long and contains 54 distinct registers, but is incomplete on both ends. Part of the scroll illustrates the stories of Satya Pīr, Mānik Pīr, the central portion that of Gāji Pīr, with several other as-of-yet unidentified tales. The image adorning the cover and the frontispiece of the current book are from this *paṭ*. For illustrations and contemporary ethnography of the tradition in West Bengal, see Frank J. Korom, *Village of Painters: Narrative Scrolls from West Bengal*, with photographs by Paul Smutko (Sante Fe: Museum of New Mexico Press, 2006), and more recently, Amitabh Sengupta, *Scroll Paintings in Bengal: Art in the Village*, foreword by Kapila Vatsyayan (Bloomington, IN: AuthorHouse, 2012). For the way the tradition has survived into the present, see David McCutchion and Suhṛdkumār Bhaumik, *Patuas and Patua Art in Bengal* (Calcutta: Firma KLM, 1999).

22. See the comprehensive ethnographies of indigenous theatre by Syed Jamil Ahmed, *Acinpakhi Infinity: Indigenous Theatre of Bangladesh* (Dhaka: The University Press Limited, 2000) and *In Praise of Nirañjan: Islam, Theatre and Bangladesh* (Dhaka: Pathak Samabesh, Losauk, 2001). See also the recent ethnography by Saymon Zakaria titled *Pronomohi Bongomata: Indigenous Cultural Forms of Bangladesh*, with a foreword by Tony K. Stewart (Dhaka: Nymphea Publications, 2011).

are illustrated in this way, though the technique stubbornly survives. The mobility of the paintings goes hand in hand with the itinerant troupe performances in such a way that laces together the disparate rural regions of the Bengali-speaking world into a common or shared cultural experience, the ongoing experience and physical instantiation of the shared cosmologies of the tales.

This convergence is further solidified by the written word, though not usually in the high literary mode of early Bangla belles lettres—another reason for the texts' easy dismissal—though there can be little doubt that many of the authors were acutely aware of and educated in those genres, especially when authors such as Bhāratcandra, Rāmeśvar, Kṛṣṇarām Dās, and Oyājed Alī also composed numerous literary texts. Many of the stories that constitute the central corpus of these performing troupes, the very tales illustrated by the *paṭuās*, date as far back as the late fifteenth century, though most extant today are the product of successive centuries. There are hundreds upon hundreds of such manuscripts housed in contemporary repositories in Dhaka University, the Bangla Academy, the Asiatic Society of Bangladesh, Calcutta University, the Baṅgīya Sāhitya Pariṣat, Viśva Bhārati in Santiniketan, and a host of other regional repositories in places such as Rangpur, Kumilla, and Chittagong. The stories in these manuscripts became the initial source for large numbers of inexpensive printed texts after the advent of the printing press in India in the early decades of the nineteenth century. By the mid- to late nineteenth century the stories of the gods and goddesses and *pīrs* and *bibīs* flourished in print, mass-produced by small presses, such as Īśāncandra Śīl, Viśvambhar Lāhā, and Akṣaykumār Rāy, while presses such as Siddikiyā Library, Gaosiyā Library, and Habibī Press in Calcutta, and Śulābh Jantra in Dhaka specialized in titles that would appeal to a largely *musalmāni* audience. Some new fictional tales in the romance genre, but only incidentally involving *pīrs* and other such figures, were composed as the corpus grew, some clearly for entertainment (in size and function roughly equivalent to the European novella), while others were more overtly didactic. Technically the didactic literature is rightly called *nasihat nāmā*, or "literatures of instruction," but the popular fictional romances that were generated in the same physical print form have also been folded into the genre, often as the antithesis of the former.[23] This blurring of genres is a sure indicator of the lackluster acknowledgement of the literature's worth by the colonial administrators who collected these titles for the National Library, Calcutta University, the Asiatic Society in Calcutta, and the India Office Library and the British Library's Oriental Collections in London—those collections yielding the bulk of extant

23. For discussion of the genre of *nasihat nāmā* as instructional literature, see Rafiuddin Ahmed, *The Bengal Muslims, 1871–1906: A Quest for Identity* (New York: Oxford University Press, 1981), 82–101; and Sufia M. Uddin, *Constructing Bangladesh: Religion, Ethnicity, and Language in an Islamic Nation* (Chapel Hill: University of North Carolina Press, 2006), 67–71.

titles today (and they represent only a fraction of what was published).[24] The *pīr kathā*, however, retained their distinct identity and remained true to the formulae of romance over the centuries.

It was the older stories, however, that endured, becoming "classics" by their popular repetition in performance and in print; that is, they are the tales that speak to generation after generation because the texts remain relevant and the stories sufficiently malleable to be revalorized, continuing to be meaningful, without having to introduce new features or change plots.[25] As testament to their durability, a substantial number of those tales of the *pīrs* are still reproduced in inexpensive chapbooks today, though somewhat less widely circulated than a century ago.[26] The classic tales of Baḍa Khān Gājī, Dakṣiṇ Rāy, Mānik Pīr, and Satya Pīr, among others, were printed and reprinted repeatedly for the better part of a century starting around the 1850s and, in this flurry of activity, set the stage for the emergence of new female heroines, such as Bonbibī and Olābibī. The greatest output in print peaked in the last decades of the nineteenth century and spilled over into the first two decades of the twentieth, a production level that curiously seems to have been in direct proportion to the amount of pressure brought to bear by the Salafists, Faraizis, and other Islamist reformers dedicated to eradicating their presence—certainly a circumstantial and statistical correlation worth noting, for it suggests these texts meant something to their audiences they were loath to relinquish. While this literary efflorescence peaked nearly a century ago, it still refuses to succumb to censorship, though the tools of suppression and the money available for it are far greater today. The narratives are numerous and widespread and, when compared to the mythology of their *hinduyāni* counterparts, are no less entertaining in their dynamic and often unpredictable twists of plot. The confluence of visual representation, public performance, and print circulation expresses a world that is distinctly Bengali, but also shares much with other vernaculars in the colonial setting.[27]

24. For the documentation by the India Office Library of this prodigious literature in the mid- to late nineteenth century, see Tapti Roy, "Disciplining the Printed Text: Colonial and National Surveillance of Bengali Literature," in *Texts of Power: Emerging Disciplines in Colonial Bengal*, ed. Partha Chatterjee (Calcutta: Samya, 1995), 30–62.

25. My understanding of the classic is very much conditioned by Frank Kermode's provocative essay; see Kermode, *The Classic: Literary Images of Permanence and Change*, The T. S. Eliot Memorial Lectures 1973 (Cambridge, MA: Harvard University Press, 1975).

26. For an introduction to these numerous productions, see Qazi Abdul Mannan, *The Emergence and Development of Dobhasi Literature in Bengal (up to 1855 AD)*, 2nd ed. (Dacca: Bangla Academy, 1974).

27. For a very nuanced reading of the ways in which educated Bengali Muslims fashioned identity through interaction with indigenous literary and cultural traditions, the analogue to the development of *bhadralok* culture, see Neilesh Bose, *Recasting the Region: Language, Culture, and Islam in Colonial Bengal* (Delhi: Oxford University Press, 2014). For other perspectives on the creation of Muslim identities, see again Ahmed, *Bengal Muslims*, and Uddin, *Constructing Bangladesh*. In a recent

Like their Hindu complements, which extol the material virtues of worshiping the goddess Caṇḍī or celebrate the great feats of the *nāth jogī* Gopīcānd, the tales of the *pīrs* and *bibīs* demonstrate the practical advantages of paying court to these holy figures: they are credited with increasing one's wealth, extending protection from disease, healing livestock, encouraging the resourcefulness of women to keep the world in order, and providing a counter to the many dangers of the jungle. For instance, Olābibī protects her followers from cholera and other water-borne diseases endemic to the swamps and waterways. A simple offering of rice powder mixed with banana, milk, cardamom, and sugar, called *śirṇī* or *śinni*, will satisfy Satya Pīr sufficiently that he will stave off penury, as our author promises in the opening to the tale quoted above. Indeed, if one is sincere and diligent in sharing with others the *pīr*'s efficacy, Satya Pīr can help one to amass great wealth. These popular figures mediate the vicissitudes of the world with a goodness and grace that invites, if not subtly induces, their listeners to strive for a better existence through their example. On the surface, the primary characters seem to be functionally equivalent to the various *hinduyāni* gods and goddesses and the ever-present *nāth jogī*, *sannyāsī*, or *vaiṣṇav* ascetic *vairāgī*. It is with these figures that they often interact through a kind of "exchange equivalence," which we will explore further.[28] Debabrata Naskar has mapped most clearly the sets of parallel figures that come into play in the southern reaches of the Bangla-speaking world, where most of these stories circulate.[29] In four chapters, he examines in turn: the song performances of the goddesses, the *devīpālā* (Śitalā, Manasā, Ṣaṣṭhī, Lakṣmī, Caṇḍī, Biśālākṣī, Nārāyaṇī, Durgā, and Santoṣī Mā); the tales of the gods, *devpālā* (Dakṣiṇ Rāy, Pañcānanda, Benākī, Cāṣīmahādev, Basanta Rāy, Śani, and Dharma Ṭhākur); stories of the matrons, *bibipālā* (Bonbibi, Olābibi, Āsānbibi, Sātbibi, Naybibi, Āorajbibi, Darbārbibi); and the tales of the *sūphī* masters, *pīr o gājī pālā* (Mānik Pīr, Baḍa Pīr Sāheb, Satya Pīr, Mādār Pīr, Pīr Gorācā̃d, Mobārak Gājī, Baḍa Khā̃ Gājī, Deoyān Gājī, Raktān Gājī, and Hajrat Jāber). These are the figures that populate the religious imagination of the Sunderbans. They are under-

---

dissertation, Epsita Halder has explored the ways the Karbala narrative was instrumental in defining *musalmāni* group identities and the ways the debates reverberated through the popular press, especially *musalmāni* periodical literatures; see Halder, "Of Blood and Tears: Tracing Self and Community in Karbala Narratives of Bengal (Late 19th to Early 20th Century)" (PhD diss., Jadavpur University, 2017), esp. chaps. 4, 5, and 6.

28. The concept of "exchange equivalence" can be found initially in Tony K. Stewart, "In Search of Equivalence: Conceiving Muslim-Hindu Encounter through Translation Theory," *History of Religions* 40, no. 3 (Winter 2001): 261–88. This essay has been twice anthologized, first in *India's Islamic Traditions: 711–1750* (with a faulty title), ed.. Richard M. Eaton (Delhi: Oxford University Press, 2003), 363–92; and again in *On Figuring Religions: Comparing Ideas, Images, and Activities*, ed. Subha Pathak (Albany: State University of New York Press, 2013), 229–62.

29. Debabrata Naskar, *Cabbiś parganār laukik devdevī: Pālāgān o loksaṃskṛti jijñāsā* (Kalakātā: De'j Pābiliśiṃ, 1406 BS [1999]).

stood to interact with one another, and people turn to them whenever they are in need of something that falls within the domain of their personal powers, regardless of overt religious persuasion. The distinctions of formal religion matter not at all; these figures help anyone to navigate the vagaries of basic survival.

With the way religion was politicized and conflated with ethnic and linguistic identities in the nineteenth century, ultimately culminating in the separation of India from Pakistan in 1947 (and which for different reasons led to the division of East Pakistan from West Pakistan to create Bangladesh in 1971), it is easy to see why today the perception of a functional equivalence of recognized Muslim holy figures with Hindu analogues would lead some to try to suppress the tales of popular *pīrs* and *pīrānīs*, *phakīrs*, *gājīs*, *dārveśes*, and *bibīs*. Consistent with fundamentalist impulses in theistic traditions around the world, starting in the mid- to late nineteenth century, reform-minded Muslims attempted to expunge anything deemed a local accretion, though these so-called "local" traditions have long roots in the Bangla-speaking world, in many instances stretching back to the fourteenth and fifteenth centuries, perhaps further (manuscripts simply do not survive in that climate, with the ravages of mold and mildew, white ants, and floods, so documentation is necessarily limited). The easy accommodation of yogic meditation and magic by *sūphī* practitioners, the similarity of devotional expression between the *vaiṣṇav* chanting the names of Kṛṣṇa in *kīrtan* or *jap* and the recitation of the qualities of Āllā in *sūphī jikir* (from the Persian *zikir*), and the gradual adoption of the Bangla language as a medium for Islamic discourse—these and many more parallel activities insinuated Islam into the culture of Bangla-speaking peoples over the last seven centuries,[30] to the point where no matter how zealous the effort, what is local can no longer be extracted without destroying what had grown into a very Bengali Islam. Yet in the nineteenth and twentieth centuries that kind of reform is precisely what was attempted, and that effort received reinforcement from unexpected sources.

With the emergence of the printing press in the colonial environment of the nineteenth century, the tales of the legendary *pīrs*, such as Satya Pīr and other popular figures, found vigorous competition in the form of inexpensive religious tracts prompted by the growing movements championing reform, many of which decried the general failures of *musalmāni* practitioners to be proper Muslims in the new sense of that term. The legendary *pīrs*, as well as those who had accepted guidance from a living *sūphī* teacher or *murśid*, soon found themselves attacked directly in many of these publications. These popular printed texts represented a new modality of public discourse within the Bangla-speaking community. Especially evident was the growing vitriol of Muslim reformers who published

30. Richard M. Eaton has mapped out many of these instances; see Eaton, *Rise of Islam and the Bengal Frontier*, esp. chaps. 3 and 10. See also M. R. Tarafdar, *Husain Shahi Bengal, 1494–1438 A.D.: A Socio-Political Study*, 2nd ed. (Dhaka: University of Dhaka, 1999).

tracts rife with diatribes against the inherent dangers of worshipping *pīrs* and *phakīrs*. Importantly, little distinction was made between *pīrs* who were living and those who were entombed, or, alternately, those whose existence was historically verifiable and those who seemed to function only in the realm of the Bengali *imaginaire*. Colonial scholars attempting to analyze these popular narratives conflated willy-nilly the historical with the legendary, treating them simply as variations, rather than as the distinct and divergent genres with the different histories they represent.

While foreign and local Orientalist and antiquarian scholars tended on the whole to be dismissive of all stories of this class of religious mendicants, always citing the claims of their miraculous powers and heroic feats as exaggerations aimed to dupe the gullible, the critique from the normative reform-minded factions was much more acerbic and sustained. For instance, one tract writer refers to the misguided worship of "fake" or "fanciful" *pīrs* (*mithya pīr*), and explicitly names Satya Pīr and Pāglāi Pīr as leading contenders to misguide the public.[31] Clearly the reputation of mendicant *pīrs* was in question, judging from the frequent charges of misconduct and hypocrisy,[32] but the critique of charlatan religious functionaries was not limited to Muslims. For instance, the great *vaiṣṇav* and district magistrate, Bhaktivinode Thakur founded the Gauḍīya Maṭh in the late decades of the nineteenth century precisely to make respectable the offices of *vaiṣṇav vairāgīs*, or mendicants, who had so sullied the title *vairāgī* in the eyes of the up-and-coming bourgeois communities who sought to modernize Bengali society.[33] Members of the Brahmo Samaj, the Hindu nationalist Arya Samaj, and the Ramakrishna Mission all took stands against religious frauds and poseurs.[34] Reform seemed to be on everyone's mind, but of course few could agree on what should constitute that reform.

Where there was antipathy towards *pīrs* during this period, it was far greater among the conservative factions of the Islamic community's self-proclaimed purifiers than among Hindus, especially *vaiṣṇavs*, who often saw the tales of the *pīrs*

31. Sāiyad Śāh Mohāmmad Āli, *Mithya-pīr* (Kochagrām, Dinajpur: by the author; printed in Kalikātā by Mohāmmad Reyājuddin Āhmād at Reyāul-Islām Press, 1325 BS [ca. 1918]).

32. Phajlar Rahmān, *Bhaṇḍa phakīr* (Kalikātā: by the author at Niu Sarasvatī Pres, 1321 BS [ca. 1914]).

33. For Bhaktivinode's role in reforming the *vaiṣṇavs* of Bengal and the founding of the conservative Gauḍīya Maṭh, see Jason D. Fuller, "Religion, Class, and Power: Bhaktivinode Thakur and the Transformation of Religious Authority among the Gaudiya Vaisnavas in Nineteenth-Century Bengal" (PhD diss., University of Pennsylvania, 2005). For a more traditional biographical reading in the subgenre of "life and times," see Brian D. Marvin, "The Life and Thought of Kedarnath Dutta Bhaktivinode: A Hindu Encounter with Modernity" (PhD diss., University of Toronto, 1996). For the ways the *bhadralok* communities seized on this sanitizing movement, see Varuni Bhatia, *Unforgetting Chaitanya: Vaishnavism and Cultures of Devotion in Colonial Bengal* (New York: Oxford University Press, 2017).

34. The references here are legion, too numerous to mention.

as a site of communal sharing. The *pīrs* served as a point of *equivalence*, both to Hindu deities and to various types of mendicants, in form and in function. As we have already suggested, reformers would see the *pīr kathā* as truly heretical, not Islamic at all, and some castigated the popular worship at the tombs of *pīrs*. One author named Garīb delivered a particularly scornful critique of the powerlessness of the dead *pīr* by arguing that if the *pīr* could not even keep the flies from swarming around the food offerings made at his tomb, how much help could he possibly be to the supplicant?[35] This technique of excoriation and mockery, which hinged on emotional sophistry, was not uncommon. Another popular tack that pushed the charlatan profile was to alert the unwary about ostensible religious teachers who were little more than thieves and scam artists, addicted to luxurious living, indulging their taste in elegant foods, milking the unwary of their hard-earned rupees.[36] Another author went considerably farther in his indictment by stereotyping *pīrs* and *phakīrs* as drug-addicted home-wreckers in this degraded Kali Age.[37] Using the shorthand label of the *mārphati* path, others took a more theological course by attacking as errant the *sūphī* practices that were designed to elevate the individual to a higher realm of consciousness, calling those practices a guaranteed way to perdition.[38] As Munsi Nachiraddin Chāheb and Adhin Mahāmmad Hādek Orephe argued in *Jālālātal phokrā*, it was because *mārphati* practices depended on the guidance of a human teacher, usually a *pīr* or *phakīr* serving as *murśid*, that any sober-minded practitioner would see the *sūphī* path as anathema to *śarīyat*. In that Islamist ritual economy, *śarīyat*, it was argued, was founded solely on God's guidance and was the only reliable recourse, whereas the fallible teachings of a mere human (mis)guided the devotee in the *mārphati* tradition. This jointly authored book especially condemned the mendicants' love of food and food offerings, and included an exceptionally pointed diatribe directed at the evil practice of tomb worship as the pathway to Saytān (replete with a drawing on page 13 graphically illustrating the results). Saytān, they allege, is said to corrupt the minds of the *phakīrs* by speaking to them through their meditation, so the belief in the sanctity

35. For this scathing critique of the alleged stupidity of tomb worship, see Garīb, *Iblich nāmār puthi* (Kalikātā: Śrī Akṣayakumār Rāy eṇḍ Kompāni, 1287 BS [1879–80 CE]), esp. the introductory pages, 2–4. Āhmad Śariph and Anisujjamān both consider the author of this *Iblichnāmā* to be Munśī Garībullāh, not Phakīr Garībullāh, who was the author of *Iusuph jolekhā*, *Jaṅganāmā*, *Sonābhān*, *Satyapīrer puthi*, and *Āmir hāmjā*, as cited in Garībullāh, *Śāh garībullāh o jaṅganāmā*, ed. Muhammad Abdul Jalil (Ḍhākā: Bāṃlā Ekāḍemī, 1991), 22–23.

36. For a vigorous warning against the corruption of bogus *phakīrs* and *pīrs* in this final cosmic age of degradation, see Ābbās Āli Nājir, *Kalir phakīrer khelā* (Lakpur: by the author, 1920); for a condemnation of the *bāuls* and other *fakīrs* as immoral and guilty of not practicing a legitimate or proper Islam, see Reyājuddin Āhmād, *Bāul dhvaṅsa fatwa* (Calcutta: Mohammadi Press, 1925).

37. Mahāmmad Āinaddin Sāheb, *Nachihate āhale kali* (Kalikātā: Phasih Uddin Ahāmmad, Mahāmmadī Lāibrerī, 1337 BS [ca. 1930]).

38. Munśi Mohāmmad Hāphej Ālī Deoyān, *Gupta māraphat bā nadhihate pherāun* (Kalikātā: Gaosiyā Lāibrerī, Nūruddīn Āhammad, n.d.).

of the *pīr* not only was grounded in the hubris of human ignorance, but was truly diabolical.[39] If it was so among the *pīrs* one encountered in person, how much more serious and damning the critique against the imaginal figures such as Mānik Pīr, Bonbibī, and others in the set of tales we are examining.

Subsequently, these conservative factions found their arguments paradoxically, albeit indirectly, supported by the authors responsible for writing the new histories of Bangla literature. These projects of establishing a nationalist secular literature, no doubt inspired by Dīneścandra Sen's *Baṅgabhāṣā o sāhitya*[40] and his subsequent *History of Bengali Literature and Language*,[41] reached their zenith in the first half of the twentieth century. The efforts expanded to multi-volume surveys like those authored by Sukumār Sen, whose text covered nearly three thousand printed pages,[42] and Asit Kumār Bāndhyopādhyāy, whose monograph was only slightly shorter,[43] to name two of the most influential among the many of that generation. The recovery of vernacular literatures, spurred by the nation-building projects associated with the emerging institutions of higher education and the literary academies for the preservation of manuscripts, and so forth, were overtly secular in conception, but in Bengal, heavily influenced by elite Hindu *bhadralok* ideals in their execution.[44] In these massive and highly influential projects, the tales of the *pīrs* were treated as little more than sources of rural amusement and diversion. "Derivative" was the dismissive characterization of nearly all *musalmāni* literary productivity, largely, I think, because the most sophisticated literary texts were Bangla versions of the heavily allegorical *sūphī* romances or *premākhyān*, a high literary form derived from Avadhī and Hindavī productions (*prem kahānī*) that hark back to the Persian *masnavī* story literatures. Sukumār Sen refused to include

39. Munsi Nachiraddin Chāheb and Adhin Mahāmmad Hādek Orephe, *Jālālātal phokrā* (Kalikātā: Āli Hāniphi, printed by Mūnsi Golām Māolā Chāheber Moratajabi Pres, n.d. [ca. 1878]). The date on the title page says 1847 BS, which is an obvious misprint (since that would indicate ca. 2440); the date of 1878 CE is provided by the Blumhardt catalogue, which often records the date of acquisition rather than the date of publication, so we can surmise publication would have probably been sometime in the mid- to late 1870s; see James Fuller Blumhardt, comp., *Catalogue of the Library of the India Office, Vol. II, Part IV—Bengali, Oriya, and Assamese Books* (London: Eyre and Spottiswoode, 1905). The reference to meditation as the entry point for Saytān begins on p. 41 of the text.

40. Dīneścandra Sen, *Baṅgabhāṣā o sāhitya*, ed. Asit Kumār Bandyopādhyāy, 2 vols. (1896; repr., Kalakātā: Paścimbaṅga Rājya Pustak Parṣad, 1986).

41. Dinesh Chandra Sen, *History of Bengali Language and Literature*, rev. ed. (Calcutta: Calcutta University Press, 1954).

42. Sukumār Sen, *Bāṅglā sāhityer itihās*, 7 bks. in 5 vols. (1347–65 BS; repr., Kalikātā: Eastern Publishers, 1383–88 BS [ca. 1976–1981]).

43. Asit Kumār Bāndyopādhyāy, *Bāṅglā sāhityer itibṛtta*, 4 Vols. [1365–80 BS [ca. 1958–63]; repr., Kalikātā: Modern Book Agency, 1373–90 BS [ca. 1966–1983]).

44. What has customarily been called the Bengal Renaissance might more rightly be styled the Bengal Hindu Renaissance, for Islam and Muslims were decidedly absent from the academic record of it.

his survey of the Bangla *premākhyān* in his multi-volume history of Bangla literature, preferring to keep their study separate in a small format one-hundred-fifty-page monograph titled *Islāmi bāṅglā sāhitya*, because in his estimation they were poor translations or unimaginative retellings, little more than clichéd copies of their refined forebears.[45] But stories of Satya Pīr and the other *pīrs* and *bibīs* who populate these tales are several times removed from those allegorical *premākhyān* in their literary quality, and distinctly spotty or even devoid of the allegorical dimension, which no doubt had the effect of marginalizing them even further since the formal allegory was considered to be a higher form of art.[46]

We might not unreasonably further observe that these early scholars constructing the first Bangla literary histories inherited an academic environment conditioned by colonial antiquarian and Orientalist scholars, foreign and local alike, who saw in such tales little more than syncretistic confusions of religion—Islam in unholy alliance with Hinduism—which rendered them both improper and illicit. Linguists, including the venerable polymath Suniti Kumār Caṭṭopādhyāy (in English, Chatterjee), saw the language as a mirror of religious incertitude. He considered the language of these texts to be confused, bastardized, and not proper *Bangla* at all, because it combined Persian (read: alien) elements with a

45. Sukumār Sen, *Islāmi Bāṅglā sāhitya* (Kalakātā: Ānanda Pābliśars Prāibheṭ Limiṭeḍ, 1400 BS [ca. 1993]).

46. Aditya Behl's study of the major texts of the Hindavī corpus, which flow out of the Persian tradition starting with ʻAṭṭār's *Conference of the Birds*, confirms just how fundamentally different those allegorical tales are from the set of tales in our study; see Behl, *Love's Subtle Magic: An Indian Islamic Literary Tradition, 1379–1545*, ed. Wendy Doniger (New York: Oxford University Press, 2012). In a study completed five decades ago, Mantajur Rahmān Taraphdār compared the Persian *masnavīs*, the Āvadhī and Hindavī *premākhyāns*, and the Bangla retellings of those same four stories found in Behl—*Candāyan (Lor Cānd), Mṛgāvatī, Padmavatī, Madhumālatī*—and contra Sen's position in *Islāmi bāṅglā sāhitya*, he found that the Bangla versions constituted new, creative retellings of their intertextual predecessors, not uninspired derivatives. In that analysis, it becomes clear that the overall sophistication and allegorical possibilities of those literary works mark them as fundamentally different from the *pīr kathās* of the current study; see *Bāṃlā romāṇṭik kāvyer āoyādhī-hindī paṭbhūmi* (Ḍhākā: Ḍhākā Viśvavidyālay, 1971). Thibaut d'Hubert's recent study of Ālāol's poetics underscores the sophistication of the Bangla romance of *Padmāvatī*, arguably the most accomplished of poets to re/create these allegorical romances; see d'Hubert, *In the Shade of the Golden Palace: Ālāol and Middle Bengali Poetics in Arakan*, South Asia Research (New York: Oxford University Press, 2018). Ālāol's use of high-register æsthetic theories from both Indic and Persian traditions contrasts dramatically with the register of the fictional *pīr kathās* of our study, which in some instances do look toward those æsthetics, but which are much more akin in spirit to the Urdu and Hindi traditions documented by Frances W. Pritchett; see Pritchett, *Marvelous Encounters: Folk Romance in Urdu and Hindi* (New York: Riverdale Publishing, 1985), and ʻAbdullāh Ḥusain Bilgrāmī, *The Romance Tradition in Urdu: Adventures from the Dastan of Amir Ḥamzah*, trans. Frances W. Pritchett (New York: Columbia University Press, 1991). For more on the Urdu *masnavīs*, see Anna Suvorova, *Masnavi: A Study of Urdu Romance*, translated from the Russian by M. Osama Faruqi (Karachi: Oxford University Press, 2000).

Sanskrit-derived (read: indigenous) Bangla into what became known as *dobhāṣī* (double- or two-language speech).[47]

The combined effect of these different pressures was to relegate the tales to the Victorian and Bengali *bhadralok* elitist (and even more recently, Marxist) curio cabinet of naïve folktales suitable only as entertainment for the masses, stories that came from and still belong in the kitchen. There was among the intelligentsia a palpable ambivalence about folklore and folktales, for they were indigenous, which was good for the emerging notions of nationalist identity, but they were considered naïve and childish, for some an embarrassing part of Bengal's cultural heritage.[48] The response, whose effects linger today, was to hide these tales from the official record of Bengal's religious and literary production, though after five centuries of circulation they continue to enjoy wide popularity and are performed regularly in dramas and public recitations, as noted above. The most deliberate corrective to the systematic omission of *musalmāni bāṅglā* in literary history was Āhmad Śariph's *Bāṅgālī o bāṅglā sāhitya*, which did not appear until 1983, more than a decade after Bangladesh's independence.[49] The foundational work that led to Śariph's project was undertaken by Muhammad Śahīdullāh,[50] Ābdul Karīm,[51] and Enāmul Hak.[52] These linguists, historians, and scholars of literature and religion realized that, while all manner of new *musalmāni* literatures could be generated in the high register of Bangla, *sādhu bhāṣā*, it was the older *pũthi* literature that captured the real emotional core of the Bengali Muslim community (*jātiya*), the *bhāv* or emotional core of its literary production.[53] They began the process of rehabilitating these and a host of other early *musalmāni* literary forms by establishing

47. Suniti Kumar Chatterji, *The Origin and Development of Bengali Language*, 2 pts. in 3 vols. (1926; repr., Calcutta: George Allen Unwin, 1975), 1:206.

48. In a rather remarkable essay, Giuseppe Flora traces this ambivalence and ambiguity across the late nineteenth to early twentieth centuries; see Flora, *On Fairy Tales, Intellectuals and Nationalism in Bengal (1880–1920)*, Supplement no. 1, Alla Rivista Degli Studi Orientali, vol. 75 (Pisa: Istituti Editoriali e Poligrafici Internazionali, 2002).

49. Āhmad Śarīph, *Bāṅgālī o bāṅglā sāhitya*, vol. 2 (Ḍhākā: Bāṅglā Ekāḍemī, 1390 BS [1983]); see esp. chap. 17. While there is no question that part of the mission of the Bangla Academy in Dhaka was to ensure a new Bangla literary world that included Muslim authors alongside Hindu and secular, it is perhaps notable that Ahmad Sharif was a self-described Marxist (personal communication, Dhaka, June 20, 1988).

50. Muhammad Śahīdullāh, *Bāṅglā sāhityer kathā*, in *Śahīdullāh racanābalī*, ed. Ānisujjāmān, 3 vols. (Ḍhākā: Bāṃlā Ekāḍemī, 1994), 2:1–504.

51. Abdul Karim, *A Social History of the Muslims of Bengal, down to A.D. 1538* (Dacca: The Asiatic Society of Pakistan, 1959). See also the pioneering sourcebook: *A Descriptive Catalogue of the Bengali Manuscripts in Munshi Abdul Karim's Collection*, comp. Munshi Abdul Karim and Ahmad Sharif (Dacca: The Asiatic Society of Pakistan, 1964). Karim identified numerous works of previously unknown *musalmāni* poets.

52. Muhammad Enamul Haq, *Muhammad enāmul hak racanāvalī*, ed. Mansur Musā, 5 vols. (Ḍhākā: Bāṃlā Ekāḍemī, 1398–1404 BS [ca. 1991–1997)]).

53. Halder, "Of Blood and Tears"; this is one of the central theses of Halder's dissertation.

an archive for manuscripts and for the mass-produced cheap print literature (*baṭ talā*).[54] Recently, Ābdul Khāyer Sekh completed a dissertation on this popular *puthi* or *pũthi* literature of the nineteenth and twentieth centuries, which surveys more than three hundred sixty such discrete texts.[55] Once widely popular, then repudiated in the face of criticism by the reformers and elites involved in the discovery of the vast Bangla literary heritage (without, however, losing their rural popularity), the texts had come full circle: the Bengali Muslim experience and identity of modern Bengal was captured in the sum of its distinctly religious narratives composed in the earlier *musalmāni bāṅglā*, reinstating the folk literatures that were the staple of the *musalmāni* population that was largely agrarian. And it is true, just as their critics pronounced, the tales are incredibly entertaining, but that entertainment value is not silliness or slapstick (though one will occasionally run across a vignette that would qualify, especially when the animals talk); rather, the humor likes to turn the-world-as-it-is-known on its head, raising an eyebrow at the pretensions of those in power, poking fun at hallowed institutions, indeed challenging even the gods.

We can identify fairly clearly many of the attitudes that contributed to the previous elimination from the official canons of Bangla literature and culture. But even these much-needed interventions do not address the question of the texts' raison d'être, their utility as religious and literary productions. Just what kind of cultural and religious work have these texts done, and have continued to do, that allowed them to thrive for centuries essentially unchanged? How have these texts managed to construct coherent worlds of meaning where *hinduyāni* and *musalmāni* characters share a common perspective? And what does it mean that they do? These and related questions will animate the remainder of this inquiry.

1.3. A PREGNANT AMBIGUITY

The story of Satya Pīr's birth at the beginning of this chapter provides some clues that can serve as a starting point for our investigation of the cultural work shouldered by these tales of *pīrs* and *bibīs*. As we have already seen, Satya Pīr's birth was anything but ordinary, and when things are out of the ordinary, there is often some hidden significance—the uncanny and marvelous are seldom gratuitous. When we talk of cultural work, we are not trying to articulate some goal-oriented agenda

54. Though he did not deem *baṭ talā* publications worthy of inclusion in his influential *Bāṅglā sāhityer itihās*, Sukumār Sen did write several short essays on these publications, mostly compilations of titles, illustrations, and presses; significantly he identified in excess of three hundred such publishers and printers. The essays were subsequently collected into a single volume by his son Subhadrakumār Sen. See Sukumār Sen, *Baṭ talār chāpā o chabi*, comp./ed. Subhadrakumār Sen, 1984; 2nd. ed. 2008 (repr., Kalakātā: Ānand Pābliśārs Prāibheṭ Limiṭeḍ, 2015).

55. Ābdul Khāyer Sekh, "'Musalmānī' pũthi sāhitya: Anusandhān o parjālocanā" (PhD diss., Calcutta University, 2015).

(which would, as we shall soon see, remove a text from the realm of the literary and relocate it in religious or political propaganda). Rather, I am keen to trace and explore the contours of these imaginative worlds, the world as these authors envisioned it might or could be. We can surmise that the rootedness of the text of *Baḍa satya pīr o sandhyāvatī kanyār puthi* in Bangla, with its setting in Bengal, would signal that the explorations are of local import—but the nature of that import may not be self-evident. Though this text and others depict an unusual, if not on occasion seemingly outlandish, cosmology according to accepted sectarian and even scientific standards today, I will argue that this represents a predictable exploration of possibilities that occur when the-world-as-we-know-it somehow seems unstable, shifting in directions that give one pause—*the tenor of these stories is one of uncertainty in changing times.* This is not to propose a direct causal connection, that every time the cultural climate shifts, fantastic tales ensue; rather, it is a particular response to a particular historical situation wherein a number of competing factions were laying claim to authority, often with no clear-cut arbiter of cultural standards, prompting exploration of alternatives. The alternatives carry with them concomitant shifts in moral sensibilities. This was the case in Bengal, especially from the fourteenth to the nineteenth centuries, a region rife with political strain from the shift from Sultanate to Mughal to colonial rule, and the constant influx of foreigners, many of whom brought a new vision of the world from across the seas. *Pīr kathās* emerge as culturally significant literary productions during these times of transition. So let us go back to our initial story of the birth of Satya Pīr and see how the author ruptures the expectations of the normal order of things and what some of the implications may be.

In Kṛṣṇahari Dās's opening, the conversation between Mohāmmad and Āllā centers on the need to send an "*avatār* for the Kali Age." This trope spins out of the classical *vaiṣṇav* construct of the *yugāvatār* or descent for the Age, which by the fifteenth century was a commonplace all across North India to indicate the need for the presence of God or some form of the divine to correct human excesses, to establish new forms of ritual practices that would be easier and more efficacious, and settle the world's uneasiness. Because of the obviousness and universality of the mechanism, no explanation is required for this religiously generic proposition: when the good of the world is under duress, God's intervention is required to reset the course of order. In this opening scene, Mohāmmad indicates that the form and the message will be different, which fits perfectly with the *vaiṣṇav* notion that each time God has to descend or send a celestial figure to earth, the remedy is novel to the situation, commensurate to the nature of the need. Mohāmmad makes clear that the way this *avatār* will differ from prior *avatārs* is his target audience: the single figure of Satya Pīr will serve a dual purpose by taking a dual form, appearing as Satya Nārāyaṇ to *hinduyāni* and as Satya Pīr to *musalmāni* constituencies. The dual form recognizes there are differences among the various communities, but its single source implies that the differences are superficial. With this approach, we should be wary of attributing contemporary notions of "identity" as most people tend to think of it today in a post-Enlightenment mode, and even more so as it informs contemporary "identity politics" in the subcontinent. When it does begin to skew in that direction—as is hinted in the late-arriving figure of Bonbibī—the stakes are quite different from the overt posturing we associate with the present categories of Hindu and Muslim in identity politics. So how might we interpret this action?

Theologically, there is no argument: the opening simply declares that there is only one God, Āllā, who will assume a dual form as Satya Nārāyaṇ (normally associated with the god Viṣṇu) and Satya Pīr (often assumed to be no more than a saint, though in this case Āllā explicitly declares that He Himself would take on this form, yet in the narrative Satya Pīr is mysteriously separate from him). The assertion of this ontology, which appears to be based on the widespread *sūphī* theological perspective of the unity of God (what could be technically construed as *waḥdat al-wujūd*) subtly underscores the Islamic leanings of the text, but no argument is made, no authority cited, and technical terminology (such as the Arabic phrase noted above) is absent—and this absence of Arabic or Persian technical jargon is an important feature of this and similar texts to which we will have occasion to return. So we must ask: if the text is not arguing for the identity of Viṣṇu and Āllā, but simply assumes it, what is the fuss about Satya Pīr assuming a dual form? In a statement that is repeated by different characters, Kṛṣṇahari Dās notes that dual form is an expedient device to ensure that the *avatār* for the Kali Age is heard: it is one's social standing, ritual orientation, modes of marriage alliance, and differences in commensal restrictions that distinguish people, one from another. This *avatār* for the Kali Age will not simply address the different communities in image or appearance, but will actualize the non-difference among them by quite literally taking birth in multiple communities (*kul*), but in the same form. So how does he do this if he is born of Sandhyāvatī?

Mohāmmad has designated the færie Cāndbibī to become Satya Pīr's mother, but Cāndbibī is already safely resident in heaven, *bhest*. She will have to descend to prepare the way, to be born of the queen Priyāvatī in the demonic *brāhmaṇ* king Maidānav's household. Before her rebirth, Cāndbibī herself wonders how she can be born a *jābanā*, that is, a female *musalmān*, from that parentage. Satya Pīr's mother—Cāndbibī as Sandhyāvatī—is, then, of mixed descent in this worldly birth, or so it would seem, except that she claims to retain her designation, that is, she self-identifies as a *jābanā*, which is not mixed at all. This is perhaps the first real indicator of what is at stake in this story, for apparently in our author's view, birth from a *brāhmaṇ* womb does not necessarily produce a *hinduyāni* child, in spite of the several thousand years of conditioning in South Asia regarding the nature of genealogy and birth. Does Sandhyāvatī, formerly the *jābanā* Cāndbibī, appear to be anything other than a *brāhmaṇ* princess? Already, long before the arrival of Satya Pīr, the boundaries between the various communities begin to dissolve. But whether Sandhyāvatī is both a *jābanā* and a *brāhmaṇ* seems moot when she finally gives birth. Satya Pīr seems to be signaling that the distinctions of social rank are artificial.

Sandhyāvatī gives birth, not to a child, but to a quivering mass of coagulating blood. She is understandably distraught, but assessing the situation with a kind of cool calculation—much as she did when confronted with the frog firmly gripped in the jaws of the serpent and pleading for its life—she reasons her way to a course of action. She takes the congealed mass and hurls it into the waters of the Begavatī River, just as she returned the frog to its natural habitat after prying it away from the jaws of the snake. On the one hand, it would appear that she has further compounded her serpent-killing offense in heaven, which damned her to thirty-six years on earth as a mortal. And remember, the author, Kṛṣṇahari Dās, in his descriptions of human action with respect to heaven and hell, observes that committing an offense (*aparādh*) in heaven sends one to earth, while doing the same on earth sends one to hell. One cannot but wonder how many more lives she will have to suffer for discarding the mass that was to be her son. The author is at pains, however, to note that individuals have predictable inescapable tendencies, so what they have done is what they are likely to repeat in the future—and here Cāndbibī seems to have been specially chosen to effect God's larger plan.

The frog that she liberates to the waters of the river was to be food for the snake, its release an apparent act of compassion for the animal that first appealed to her for mercy (the snake could only counter), so in spite of the karmic effect of her decision leading to the death of the serpent, there is some positive result in the rescue of the frog. In a curious inversion of her previous act, when she throws the oozing mass of preformed Satya Pīr—more of an embryonic mass rather than a fetus, based on the description, and not obviously alive—that splodgy mess becomes food for a turtle lurking in the waters of the Begavatī River. The potentially negative act inverts her action with the snake and frog with a positive result, though the author does not indicate that that was her intention. By turning the bloody mass into apparent food, Satya Pīr is rescued by the turtle, perhaps ameliorating what could well have been Sandhyāvatī's undoing. The turtle instantly gobbles up the mass, swallows it, and encases it in an egg, gestating it for ten watches (one watch, or *daṇḍa*, is calculated as twenty-four minutes). She lays the egg into the sands of a shoal, whence Satya Pīr emerges fully formed. As a result of that hatching, the turtle becomes his second mother, so at first blush it would seem that one of the communities Satya Pīr will be addressing is the animal kingdom, or at least the riverine ecology. But that turtle is not just any turtle; she has previously been a *brāhmaṇ* widow who was cursed to live as a turtle for the offense of eating the uncooked meat of a cow. In a predictable repetition of her previous act, she has just consumed the raw meat of the embryonic Satya Nārāyaṇ (who will eventually take on the form of a human, but whose ontological status is actually none other than God, Āllā). In this karmic economy, the turtle is granted a major reprieve of her sentence, with the promise that she will bear none other than God in her womb. As soon as she has fulfilled this duty by birthing Satya Nārāyaṇ, she will fly off to heaven, then called by the *vaiṣṇav* name of *vaikuṇṭha*—and that is precisely what happens. This, then, is the *avatār*'s second birth, ironically (perhaps?) literally making him twice-born, with one mixed *jābanā-brāhmaṇ* mother and one *brāhmaṇ* widow mother, each of whom in her own way abandons or orphans the fatherless Satya Pīr, leaving him to his own devices. The narrative sequence seems to suggest that the former *brāhmaṇ* widow has rescued the *jābanā* mother from further perdition by virtue of completing her pregnancy, but because of the nature of the birth—Satya Nārāyaṇ emerging from the egg buried in the sands—he not only comes from the wombs of two mothers of competing social status, but bears the marks of a chthonic hero, born of Mother Earth, Pṛthivī, as invoked in the author's opening.[56]

The familiar old saw that declares certainty of motherhood, but obscurity regarding the father, holds strangely in spite of the inversion that sees one offspring from many wombs rather than many offspring from a single womb, for each time, the identity and social standing of the mother is made clear. But most immediately for the narrative plot, Sandhyāvatī presents a problem, for in the eyes of her servants, her mother, and her father, she is very clearly pregnant (hence the mother), but unmarried, and therefore *prima facie* guilty of a premarital affair and about to issue a bastard. She of course protests her innocence, but no one else can know or believe that she is a virgin. Only she knows for certain that she has never even lain with a man; but who can believe that in the face of her pregnancy? Poignantly, the inchoate bloody mass to which she gives birth seems to beg the question, as she herself notes with bitter irony:

> I was born on earth to provide a womb, but I have not given birth to a son. This "child" has no eyes, no mouth, no arms, no legs. Concealed in my womb, it grew inside me for ten months. It left me indelibly stained for all the world and forced me to live abandoned in the forest. There is no father to come forward to acknowledge, for he could not acknowledge truthfully this rubbish born of my womb. Why has Fate, Bidhātā, written my *karma* this way, that I must live lost, deep in the forest, and for what? For whom?[57]

56. Mircea Eliade argued that in the case of chthonic cultural heroes, the Earth was the mother, and the remote Sky God the father. There is a strong resonance here because Āllā in heaven impregnates Sandhyāvatī via the rose, then she in turn, by inadvertently feeding the turtle, impregnates the turtle, who deposits the egg in the womb of Mother Earth, Pṛthvī, from whom Satya Pīr/Nārāyaṇ emerges fully formed. See Eliade, *Patterns in Comparative Religion* (1958; repr., New York: New American Library, 1963), 239–64. The mythic motif of the relay is also frequently noted by Eliade in a number of publications.

57. Kṛṣṇahari Dās, *Baḍa satya pīr o sandhyāvatī kanyār puthi*, 33.

The reader of this text will, of course, have the advantage of knowing what Sandhyāvatī cannot yet know, that her apparent stillbirth is actually Satya Pīr. She is understandably confused by the commonly noted amnesia that occurs when heavenly figures undergo birth in the world of mortals; she does not know who she "really" is. Prior to her birth on earth, she in fact astutely appraised the situation as singular—a *jābanā* born of a *musalmān*-killing king's wife—what we might imagine to be something akin to an existential crisis, except—as is often repeated in Indic tales—that she is oblivious to it once she has descended. She then questions the clarity of the instructions she received in the dream sequence, which impelled her to go to the river and refuse to leave until she retrieved just the right flower, since the result of that simple gesture of smelling the flower has proved so wrongfully fateful. Upon reflection, she is able to identify the precise moment of conception, but questions neither the method nor who is responsible. She feels mysteriously used, but to no end she can fathom. She observes, as many other narrators have routinely observed, "Who can know God's mysterious ways?" though the audience does already know.

While the audience for this story would be comfortable in the knowledge of Satya Pīr's descent from heaven, the question of his paternity remains obscure and hangs over the entirety of the Sandhyāvatī sequence of episodes. Is it God? Does divine insemination through the fragrance of a flower count as fathering? But Satya Pīr is already a fully formed, functional adult saint passing his time in the heavenly paradise of *bhest* before the descent, and he even observes that this will not be the first time he experiences existence on earth, his previous exploits having earned him that coveted place in heaven. So who, then, are his mother and father? Does it matter? Perhaps more importantly, one might not unreasonably ask how, precisely, a mortal (and to become a saint, one must presume that at some point Satya Pīr was mortal) can be reborn on earth. The operations of *karma* and rebirth, in fact, are commonly accepted in this text, for we may recall that the færie Cāndbibī herself argues that only by committing great offenses (*aparādh*) can one be reborn on earth. But Fate in the form of the god Bidhātā is also inextricably connected, and therefore blamed as well. From the references to reaping the fruits of *karma* and the characterization of the age being one of degradation, the Kali Age, the cosmology seems marked as a traditional Indic, and specifically Bengali, cultural view.

In the end, Satya Pīr, who is a recognized saint—one of the "friends of God," as they are known[58]—descends from heaven as the *avatār* of the Kali Age and is born directly from God's impregnation of an unmarried *musalmāni* færie in the form of a virgin girl born of a *brāhmaṇ* queen, and then born a second time from a turtle mother who is a cursed unmarried *brāhmaṇ* widow (both births magnifying Satya

58. See John Renard, *Friends of God: Islamic Images of Piety, Commitment, and Servanthood* (Berkeley: University of California Press, 2008).

Pīr's status as a twice-born (a twice-born twice-born!), yet from the perspective of those around him, twice a bastard, perhaps a not-so-subtle commentary on the "high esteem" in which *brāhmaṇs* are held. Earlier in *bhest*, Āllā told Mohāmmad that He Himself would descend, while the unnamed turtle reported that she too was to bear God, Satya Nārāyaṇ or Nirañjan, not just a saint. The quivering mass to which Sandhyāvatī gives birth is described in terms that hint of the famous passage in the *Śvetāśvatāra Upaniṣad* of the ultimate reality of *brahman* (n) assuming the characteristics of God, "grasping without hands, moving without feet, seeing without eyes, hearing without ears . . ."[59] If Satya Pīr is this ultimate reality as God, what of the paternity of Satya Pīr via the turtle mother? It would seem to be God working through Cāndbibī herself who impregnates the turtle, suggesting a transsexual paternity, which in turn conflates with gender the already-prophesied birth for two communities. That sequence at least raises the possibility that fathering is instrumental, that it is as much enacted as gendered; and in a karmic economy, gender is always situational because one may well have been another gender in a previous existence, which undercuts claims to blood lineage as the primary marker of identity. The multitude of ambiguities of parentage and genealogy for Satya Pīr cannot be insignificant. Satya Pīr's dual form is not simply an appearance, but the result of his multiple births from women of different social groups (*kul*), quite literally embodying the boundary-crossing his dual form was intended to address. He rises from within the ranks of those different groups, intent on appearing in whatever form is needed and appropriate to his followers. Here we get one of the first cogent statements of the future work of Satya Pīr: *he ministers to the needs of everyone, regardless of social standing—birth does not matter.* Importantly, he is of mixed parentage, born first of an unmarried *jabanā-brāhmaṇ* woman and then from a *brāhmaṇ* widow, both of whom abandon him immediately after birth, leaving him twice orphaned. This *avatār* for the age knows firsthand whereof he speaks and makes clear the object of his later ministrations. As the author Kṛṣṇahari Dās notes in his opening salutations:

> *. . . Satya Pīr comes to those who call, whether orphans without means or those devoid of guidance. Should all people present sing their praises publicly, Satya Pīr will send their troubles far away. When people serve him with respect, offering the custom due, Satya Pīr becomes the refuge of every human being.*[60]

What the Lord Nirañjan—as Satya Pīr and as Satya Nārāyaṇ—offers is not dependent on birth or social distinction, nor does it hinge on any sectarian or doctrinal

59. *Śvetāśvatāra Upaniṣad*, trans. Robert Ernest Hume, 3.19: *apāṇipādo javano grahītā paśyaty-acakṣuḥ sa śṇotyakarṇaḥ . . .* in *Thirteen Principal Upaniṣads: Original Sanskrit Text with English Translation*, trans. Hume, ed. N. C. Panda, rev. ed., vol. 2 (New Delhi: Bharatiya Kala Prakashan, 2012).

60. Kṛṣṇahari Dās, *Baḍa satya pīr o sandhyāvatī kanyār puthi*, 4.

stance: one need only respectfully petition God (regardless of form) to receive his aid. That in turn suggests that conversion per se is decidedly not at stake; God's good will and assistance is available to everyone regardless and is not affected by the various social strictures that are observed in Bengal's social world. Even offenses that center on food regimes, diet, and commensality do not stop one from successfully serving as an instrument of God's plan and, in the end, prove no bar to entering (in the case of the *brāhmaṇ* widow-cum-turtle) or reentering heaven (in the case of Cāndbibī-cum-Sandhyāvatī), whether that heaven is designated as *vaikuṇṭha* or *bhest.* And calling *bhest* by the *vaiṣṇav* name *vaikuṇṭha* would seem to be perfectly appropriate, for the etymology of *vaikuṇṭha* signals a place where people are devoid or separated from (*vi-*) their ignorance and anxiety (*kuṇṭha*), so people who worship God in whatever form find that as their reward. The breaking down of social distinctions and the futility of maintaining strict genealogical, commensal, and ritual purity will surface again and again as the first line of instruction in the *vade mecum* for personal conduct to allow access to Satya Pīr's helping hand. In laying out his divine plan of action, Āllā puts one final stipulation on Satya Pīr's descent as *avatār:* he will never be allowed to marry. Now it becomes clear why: for him to marry would perpetuate the social distinctions his dual form is designed to undermine—he must not choose sides and father children who would potentially recreate the distinctions he is attempting to efface. Why this is critical will become ever more apparent as we work our way through these cycles of adventure.

2

The Enchanting Lives of the *Pīrs*

Structures of Narrative Romance

One day Āllā was holding court and
Hāji Gāji Mahāmmad the Apostle took his seat.
A saint arrived from Makkā and Madinā
and they discussed the condition of the thirty-two worlds.
Khodā held forth there in the court and
with all gathered he considered
the possible means for salvaging the eon.
Hāji Gāji Sek Pharid suggested one possibility:
What if Mānik were to appear as the son of Badar?
Among hindu *clans he would be known*
as the True Form of Lord Nārāyaṇ;
In jaban *families he would be known*
as Mānik, the Ruby Whose Power Blazes Forth.

—ANONYMOUS, *MĀNIKPĪRER JAHURĀNĀMĀ*

2.1. THE MYTH-HISTORY CONUNDRUM

In the most comprehensive assemblage of hagiographical source materials about the *pīrs* and *gājīs* of the Bangla-speaking world, Girīndranāth Dās reported on the lives of thirty-one "historical" (*aitihāsik*) and eight "imaginary" or "fabricated" (*kālpanik*) figures. Among the *kālpanik*, he included Olā Bibi, Khūṅḍi Bibi, Trailokya Pīr, Bonbibi, Bibi Barakat, Mānik Pīr, and Satya Pīr.[1] He did not, however, explain how he derived this classification, which is drawn into question by

1. Girīndranāth Dās, *Bāṃlā pīr sāhityer kathā*, 1st ed. (Kājipāḍā, Bārāsat, Cabbiś Pargaṇa: Śehid Lāibrerī, 1383 BS [ca. 1976]), table of contents, vi–vii.

his inclusion of six different figures associated with Pīr Mobārak Baḍakhā̃ Gājī, which he indicated are simply alternate names for the same figure in East Bengal, but several of whose tales seem to be from demonstrably fictive as well as historical individuals.[2] His division of fabricated (*kālpanik*) and historical (*aitihāsik*) *pīrs* and *bibis* is simply one more variation of the *myth* vs. *history* paradigm that has been used to dissect the hagiographical narratives of exemplars, saints, and saviors in any number of religious traditions around the world, and its inconsistencies and arbitrariness are pervasive. But in addition, the connotation of the Bangla term *kālpanik* is inescapably despective, its semantic field a set of dismissive characterizations: "existing only in the mind," "falsely devised," "fabricated," "fictitious," "false," and "unreal,"[3] no doubt a residual effect of the scholarly attitudes so common during the last century. As Dās noted in the preface to the second edition of his text, the venerable literary historian Sukumār Sen prompted him to drop the distinction as artificial, for he argued it was impossible to tease out the *aitihāsik* from the *kālpanik* because the historical *pīrs*' tales strained credulity as much as the fictitious, and the stories of both were presented in a manner equivalent to well-known genres of Bengali Hindu mythology, such as the literary *maṅgal kāvya*. As a result, when Dās published the second edition of the text in 1998, he dropped the distinction in favor of a single combined list in strict alphabetical order.[4] Sen's advice was prescient, for the tales are indeed without exception hagiographical and there was no call to separate any perceived mythic bits from the historical. Even if the intention was to elevate the fictional or legendary figures to an equal status with the historical, the result was to subtly and efficiently move in the opposite direction, shifting all the historical figures into the same category as the legendary and setting up both to be dismissed—largely as a result of the miraculous content.

The point is not to criticize prior scholarship or speculate about possible motives, but to use this illustrative episode as a way of identifying why these hagiographical conundrums present so much difficulty to their interpreters—and perhaps why they have been so routinely ignored by scholars of Islamic traditions. Because contemporary historians and historians of religions have demoted the miraculous in the narrative events, they have understandably, one might unreflectively imagine,

2. Girīndranāth Dās, 224; the six include Mobārak Sāh Gājī, Baḍa Khā̃ Gājī, Barakhān Gājī, Mabrā Gājī, Gāji Sāheb, and Gājī Bābā.

3. See the entry for *kālpanik* in *Bangla Academy Bengali-English Dictionary*, ed. Mohammad Ali, Mohammad Moniruzzaman, and Jahangir Tareque (Dhaka: Bangla Academy, 1994), 127.

4. The second edition changed no text, but reordered the presentation to a strict alphabetical list; see Girīndranāth Dās, *Bāṃlā pīr sāhityer kathā*, 2nd. ed. (Kalikātā: Suvarṇarekhā, 1998), table of contents, 11–12; his explanation for the change can be found in the introduction (*bhūmikā*) on 14. Interestingly, the great Bangladeshi literary scholar Āhmād Śarīph categorizes the *pīrs* somewhat differently: "*kālpanik, aitihāsik evaṃ darveś pīr*," or "imagined, historical, and dervish"; see Śarīph, *Bāṅgālī o bāṅglā sāhitya*, 2:827–58 (chap. 15, sec. 2), which hints at his unwillingness to dismiss the miraculous altogether.

tended to shy away from these tales as legitimate sources of the Islamic experience in Bengal, and this holds especially for those narratives that depict the imaginative or fictional figures such as Satya Pīr, Bonbibī, and others already mentioned. By suppressing these tales by omission, scholars, such as the Orientalists previously noted, ironically find themselves supporting the same side of the evaluative curve as the conservative reformers who wish to do away with most of the tales and all that is associated with them. Regardless of how one classifies these tales, one effect of their omission is to produce an incomplete picture of how Islam came to occupy the place it does in Bengal, and how those stories functioned as part of that process of Islamicization, for as we shall soon see, they do, but in ways that will prove novel. To dismiss those stories is to level an a priori judgment that they have nothing to tell us, and part of that decision, one suspects, is based on a failure to recognize and take seriously the *genre* of the tales. Not surprisingly, the presence of the fantastic seems to have clouded all judgments and deflected analyses away from the religious and cultural work these tales have done and still do.

Most attempts to interpret these tales, when they are examined at all and not simply rejected outright, seem to be driven initially by European notions of history, which gathered momentum with the popularity of positivism in the late nineteenth century. Truth in the form of historical "facts" had to be separated from untruth, which was necessarily ahistorical "fiction" (in the negative sense in which that term is often used). For most scholastic approaches, and implicit in the blanket rejections by reformers, the question of historical veracity—did these things actually happen?—seems to drive a wedge into the narrative by dividing it between some kind of myth (in the popular sense of "falsehood" or counter to fact) and history, which forces an evaluative judgment, while begging the question of what criteria would be used to judge the difference.[5] Tzvetan Todorov usefully problematized the range of these approaches in his study of the genres of the fantastic in fiction—and I think his categories capture much of the sentiment of the scholarly approaches in question. He distinguishes three forms: the *uncanny*, the *fantastic*, and the *marvelous*. He argues that the way each narrative presents the unusual gives pause to both the *characters* in the fiction and the *reader* of the fiction. The parallel to the tales of the *pīrs* and *bibīs* is applicable, for it is ultimately as fictions that we will need to address these stories, though they are not of the type of fiction one suspects Todorov imagined. He writes, "The fantastic is that hesitation

5. Hippolyte Delehaye, S. J., one of the leading authors in the Société des Bollandistes whose mission is to produce hagiographies and evaluate the lives of saints and those under consideration for future designation as saints, produced a rather pointed negative critique of the pitfalls of this approach in his influential *Lés legendes hagiographique* in 1905; see the English translation of chapter 7, "Concerning Certain Hagiographic Heresies," in Père H(ippolyte) Delehaye, S. J., *The Legends of the Saints: An Introduction to Hagiography*, trans. V. M. Crawford (Notre Dame, IN: University of Notre Dame Press, 1961), esp. 224–25.

experienced by a person who knows only the laws of nature, confronting an apparently supernatural event." He insists that it is the *response* to, more than the depiction of, the miraculous that defines the genres. "The uncanny is the genre that persists when the reader resolves his hesitation and decides that the order of law is not violated; marvelous is when it is accepted as violated." The fantastic lies somewhere between the two.[6] Yet these responses do not seem to characterize the way miraculous stories have been received and accounted. The attribution of saints' miracles or extraordinary feats and the sometimes apparently contradictory tellings from multiple sources have a long tradition among Muslim scholars of being reported without choosing whether any given report is true, or which version is correct (the *ḥadīth* literatures are rife with such deflections). Whether it is uncanny, fantastic, or marvelous does not matter, for while the author may harbor private suspicions (which are seldom openly articulated), they leave the ultimate judgment to God, inserting formulaic phrases such as "God alone knows" or "only God can tell." This public disavowal of judgment (which expresses the author's suspension of both belief and disbelief) recognizes that the fantastic may not be what is really at stake from a religious perspective.

For most of the last two centuries, scholastic interpreters of a European bent have resolved the dichotomy by simply assigning the miraculous to a variety of alternate genres such as folk literature, mythology, popular legend, and so forth, without addressing the nature of the narrative qua narrative. In other words, they categorize in order to eliminate, relegating what they deem to be legendary or mythic material to a genre and discipline outside their declared purview, which allows them arbitrarily to ignore any story that presents difficulties for their interests. For every narrative they have approached in this way, scholars have, in effect, constructed two texts, but have given credence only to one, ceding the mythic or marvelous to those who deal professionally with them, to mythographers or folklorists, who, in turn, have routinely treated the tales ahistorically (which, given their criteria of evaluation, may appear on the surface to be appropriate) as part of a universal genre that ultimately hinges on cross-cultural comparisons, acknowledged or not.[7] When the scholarly interpreter has implicitly accepted or even argued for the dichotomy in terms of fact-versus-fiction (again in its popular sense), the litmus test for what is acceptable is one of historical truth of a variety

6. Each is constructed in the act of interpretation by the reader or auditor and teller, but there are distinctions of temporality generally not recognized. In structuralist terminology, marvelous is to the future as uncanny is to the past, while fantastic is in the present between the two. Tzvetan Todorov, *The Fantastic: A Structural Approach to a Literary Genre,* trans. Richard Howard, with a foreword by Robert Scholes (Ithaca, NY: Cornell University Press, 1975), 25, 41–42.

7. So many have adopted this comparative approach that one need only mention the leading names, such as Eliade with his morphological approach, Dumèzil with his tripartite Indo-European comparisons, Raglin, Rank, and Campbell's hero mythology, Lévi-Strauss's structural study, Propp's folktale motifs, and of course Stith Thompson.

that is generally recognized today as elusive at best. What these scholars have done, however, is to miss and misread the nature of the texts, to fail to recognize the special features of the narratives. To recover the texts from this awkward handling, our first step to restore their integrity as coherent narratives, and not break them into parts, is to recognize the *fictional* nature of these hagiographical narratives and see how the religious ideals they contain condition them into a special genre.

We shall see that the narratives demonstrate their own rigorous coherence of conception, which we shall endeavor to approach as a whole. We are not simply going to report the stories, but rather will use the tales themselves to open up distinct areas of inquiry as to their form and function, their cultural work. As will become clear, the narratives themselves have histories. They participate in a commonly shared realm of the Bengali *imaginaire*. And their histories, in turn, are bound to their reception by identifiable communities that circulate and perform these texts. The uses to which these texts are put, though not always immediately accessible, constitute another history in themselves,[8] but we must always take care to distinguish each of these propositions from the literal content of the stories. The stories appeal, which is why they endure, but the appeal, we will argue, is not just the entertainment they afford.

For well over a thousand years, much of the appeal of *sūphī* saints across the Islamic world can be found in their awe-inspiring and wondrous feats,[9] and South Asia has had more than a few examples, both predictably regular and wildly irregular in behavior.[10] As paragons of saintliness, *pīrs* are specially marked as the "friends of God," an epithet routinely designating *sūphī* masters.[11] Theirs is the discourse of *religious biography*, and the legendary or fictive *pīrs* and *bibīs* of Bengal participate in that discourse. While the reporting of miraculous elements is not a desideratum for hagiography, the pious practitioner is often elevated to saintly status by displays of the extraordinary, usually couched in terms of divine power, *karāmat*. Why it is important to place these tales in the larger category of religious biography and, more specifically, hagiography has to do with the stories'

8. One strategy for understanding this type of circulation and use will be suggested in the mapping of the literatures of Satya Pīr in chap. 6, this volume.

9. For instance, see Ahmet T. Karamustafa, *God's Unruly Friends: Dervish Groups in the Islamic Middle Period 1220–1550* (1994; repr., London: Oneworld Publications, 2004).

10. Simon Digby, trans., *Wonder-Tales of South Asia*, ed. Leonard Harrow (Jersey, Channel Islands: Orient Monographs, 2000; repr., Delhi: Oxford University Press, 2006). See also Raziuddin Aquil, "Miracles, Authority, and Benevolence: Stories of *Karamat* in Sufi Literature of the Delhi Sultanate," in *Sufi Cults and Evolution of Medieval Indian Culture*, ed. Anup Taneja, Indian Council of Historical Research Monograph Series 9 (New Delhi: Indian Council of Historical Research in Association with the Northern Book Center, 2003), 109–38. For stories from northern India, see Anna Suvorova, *Muslim Saints of South Asia: The Eleventh to Fifteenth Centuries* (London: Routledge, 1999); for our purposes, note esp. chap. 7, "The Warrior Saints," and chap. 8, "The Mendicant Saints."

11. See Renard, *Friends of God*; see also John Renard, *Islam and the Heroic Image: Themes in Literature and the Visual Arts* (Columbia: University of South Carolina Press, 1993).

connection to the religious truths they purport to represent. The miraculous powers displayed by the heroes and heroines and the ensuing events these displays precipitate always point to a single source, God, Āllā. That deferral is the single unfailing religious proposition common to all the tales. Miraculous displays, while often present in extremis, can be either necessary conditions or circumstantial by-products of the action, but not the point of these heroes' or heroines' life stories. The religious ideal to which these displays point is.

In a significant volume of essays that emerged from a multi-year project at the University of Chicago in the early 1970s, Frank Reynolds and Donald Capps made a significant move to break the hold of the crude myth-history distinction that had paralyzed the study of religious or sacred biography generally.[12] In place of the category of history, they proposed the *bios*, or life of the individual, without requiring that life to be about facts and dates; rather, the *bios* could be constituted by psychological experience or social role, to name only two alternatives to the more reductive notions of positivist history. The *bios* was the sequence of events that gave shape to the life-narrative as it had been conveyed. In place of myth, they argued for the much more complex *religious ideal*, which was the visionary configuration of the perfect religious figure whose life was shaped by and in turn itself shaped the theological truth and doctrinal directives they promoted. Reynolds and Capps proposed that the religious ideal conditioned the form of the life, *bios*, and in such a way that the two in their combination produced what they termed a distinct *biographical image*. This approach to the understanding of religious biography was generally articulated to displace the worn out and entirely predictable "life and times" (emphasis on contextual history) and "life and teachings" (emphasis on theology, religious abstractions, and mythology) that dominated most scholarly production and still does, and even more so in the popular press. For much hagiography, it is the religious ideal that becomes the primary interest or subject of the religious biography while the *bios* can languish as little more than a frame for it, the ostensible subject.[13] For the unwary, this displacement may not actually change the way the construction of religious biography is perceived; it is too easy to assume that the *bios* is a stand-in for history and the religious ideal a stand-in for the myth; but they are not apposite structural categories. But how might this help us understand better the fabulous tales of what I have been calling the fictional *pīrs* and *bibīs* of Bengal? In fictional stories, overt theology or doctrine tends to be absent

12. Frank E. Reynolds and Donald Capps, eds., *The Biographical Process: Essays in the History and Psychology of Religion* (The Hague: Mouton, 1976), see introduction, 1–33.

13. Tony K. Stewart, "The Subject and the Ostensible Subject: Mapping the Genre of Hagiography among South Asian Chishtīs," in *Rethinking Islamic Studies: From Orientalism to Cosmopolitanism*, ed. Carl W. Ernst and Richard Martin (Columbia: University of South Carolina Press, 2010), 227–44. This piece also traces the role of institutions, such as the *sūfī silsilā* and various literary forms (*maktūbāt, ishārāt, tazkirah*, and *malfūẓāt*) in the creation, transmission, displacement, and transformation of biographical images in the Indo-Persian context.

or implied, seldom made explicit except in the most general terms. As a result, we must approach the religious ideals embedded in these tales indirectly.

2.2. NARRATIVE BIOS AS AUTOTELIC FICTION

We have an admittedly special case of hagiography with this group of tales because the subjects are fictional. If the myth-history dichotomy is deemed to be irrelevant, how can we single out a group of *pīrs* and refer to them as legendary or fictional as opposed to historical? Again, it is the issue of the miraculous events that proves to be the red herring. The fictionality of these heroes and heroines has nothing to do with their miracles. And it is not just a matter of whether they appear in or are corroborated by the historical record outside of hagiography itself. Those *pīrs* whose existence can be confirmed in the Persian chronicles of courts and *silsilās*, in copper plate inscriptions, in East India Company records, and so forth are to be counted as historical (roughly equivalent to Girīndranāth Dās's *aitihāsik* category in the first edition of his monograph). But the category of legendary or fictive *pīrs* designates figures whose lives cannot be corroborated by any source outside literary narrative itself; but if this were the only criterion, we would be subject to the same charge of arbitrariness in making the distinction, for an argument from lack of evidence is always contingent, not definitive. We must also make clear that the stories and the characters are fictional, not "fictitious," "false," or "unreal," because their acts exist only in the realm of discourse. For instance, Gāji Pīr is a fictional figure who exists in a literary discourse, and while he, as a subject of that discourse, may be put to use by his creators and the audiences who hear of him, he himself remains in the realm of the fictional, and any reference to him is to his fictional world. There are a finite number of such figures in early modern Bengal, and it is clear that the authors themselves made this distinction, as Rādhāmohan Tarkālaṃkār Bhaṭṭācāryya tells us in his *Satya nārāyaṇ vratakathā*. In his opening salutations, he first pays obeisance to Viṣṇu and then Śiva, to the goddess in various forms including Gaṅgā, to the *nāgas* ensconced in the eight directions, to the stars scattered across the triple world, and to the places of crossing, pilgrimage sites. He honors Vyāsa as a small part or *aṃśa* of Viṣṇu, and Yam, the *yakṣas*, and everyone worthy now sheltered in Yam's abode. Ganeś is singled out, followed by other more specific forms of Viṣṇu and Śiva scattered across the subcontinent in places such as the Vindhya hills and the city of Kāśī. He then notes the *pīrs* who, as equivalent figures to the *hinduyāni* gods and goddesses, deserve his obeisance—and they are all, without exception, fictional.

> I have bowed down to the ranks of *brāhmaṇs*,
> grasping their lotus feet,
> for only after receiving their command
> have I undertaken to compose this new text.

In the accustomed manner, I circumambulate
and bow in full obeisance to Satya Pīr.
This illustrious Lord (*prabhu*) illuminates Makkā
in the company of Marddhagājī.
I fall at the feet of Darphā Khā̃ Gājī,
who resides on the banks of the Jāhnavī at the Triveṇī.
I make fair greetings to Baḍakhā̃ Gājī,
a village *pīr* who gallops on his Arabian steed
accompanied by a hundred tigers.
Just by remembering Satya Pīr is one relieved of all dangers.
This set of salutations now ends, leaving us enchanted.[14]

The figures named above constitute part of a set that also includes Bonbibī, Olābibī, and Mānik Pīr, and his father Badar Pīr.[15] Their texts are labeled generically *kathā*, which is "narrative" or "fiction." Importantly in Bangla, the stories of the exploits of Mohāmmad, Āli, Hāsān, and Husāin, as well as *sūphī* luminaries such as Śāh Jālāl, as a rule do not carry the genre marker of *kathā*, but use other terms denoting history, such as *itihās* or *sirā*. Though a figure like Badar Pīr may be inspired by some historical figure of the same name, a not uncommon conflation, the reader should be leery.[16]

14. Rādhāmohan Tarkālaṃkār Bhaṭṭācāryya, *Satya nārāyaṇ vratakathā* (Kalikātā: Prakāścandra Bandhyopādhyāy [Bhaṭṭācāryya] at Nūran Sen Press, 1814 *śaka* [ca. 1892]), 1–2.

15. There are a number of scholars who take these figures as a set. Part of the set-making seems to be geographical (Sunderbans); see Sanatkumar Mitra, ed., *Tigerlore of Bengal* (Kolkata: Research Institute of Folk-Culture, 2008), esp. the essay by Ashutosh Bhattacharya, "The Tiger Cult and Its Literature in Lower Bengal," 19–44. Inclusion also revolves around the control of tigers, which is of course a well-known power that sets apart *pīrs* and *phakīrs* from their other Indic counterparts; for instance, see the anthropological study of Tushar K. Niyogi, *Tiger Cult of the Sundarvans* (Calcutta: Anthropological Survey of India, 1996). In his report on conditions in the nineteenth century, Śaśaṅk Maṇḍal makes no effective distinction in the worship and following of these characters and Śitalā, goddess of smallpox, Olābibī, matron of cholera, and any of the *pīrs* and gods and goddesses; see Śaśaṅk Maṇḍal, *Britiś rājatve sundarban* (Kalakātā: Punaśca, 1995), 110–30, 150–56.; Sunder Lal Hora, "Worship of the Deities Olā, Jholā and Bōn Bībī in Lower Bengal," *Journal and Proceedings of the Asiatic Society of Bengal* 20, no. 8 (1933): 1–4. For a casual introduction to Bonbibī and Dakṣiṇ Rāy, see Sujit Sur, "Folk Deities of Sunderbans—Some Observations," in *In the Lagoons of the Gangetic Delta,* ed. Gautam K. Bera and Vijoy S. Sahay (New Delhi: Mittal Publications, 2010), 141–68. For insight into how this plays out in practice, see Sufia Uddin, "Beyond National Borders and Religious Boundaries: Muslim and Hindu Veneration of Bonbibi," in *Engaging South Asian Religions: Boundaries, Appropriations, and Resistances,* ed. Mathew N. Schmalz and Peter Gottschalk (Albany: SUNY Press, 2011), 61–84.

16. The complications of historical reconstructions make such connections tenuous at best. For example, Badar is often cited as one of the *pāñc pīr* or five *pīrs*, though the enumeration of those five is highly variable. He is also affiliated with the twelve *auliyās* or saints of Chittagong, but under the name of Badar Oyāliyā, Badr-i-Ālām, Badar Pīr, Pīr Badar, and Badar Śāh—though reports suggest these refer to more than a single figure. Different accounts of his arrival in Chittagong include riding on a fish (reminiscent of Khoyāj Khijir) or riding on a boulder (which appears in the tales of other figures

There is an important distinction: the stories that depict the lives of these *pīrs* are all fictions—which makes their protagonists fictional—while the stories-as-fictions themselves have extra-diegetic histories that we can, to a certain extent, reconstruct through different types of material evidence. Certain biographical information on the authors can be found in the signature lines of the texts, and the plethora of manuscripts, many of which are dated by the author or the time of copying, can be used to reconstruct at least the broad outlines of circulation and consumption. Then there are printed texts, which may or may not reflect what the original authors wrote, allowing us when we have corroborative manuscript evidence to see how stories may have been altered (usually only in minor details, as I have determined from a number of such comparisons), and the publication histories themselves speak to audience, class, and so forth (price indexes and the catalogue of other publications from that publisher). Finally, we can find intertextual evidence in several ways, including where the narrative appears in other traceable documents, such as the encomium provided by Rādhāmohan Tarkālaṃkār Bhaṭṭācāryya above, the appearance of figures and their stories in other narratives, or their persistence in visual images, which were mentioned in the first chapter.[17] Through these different means, we can document textual histories. But if we move our concern for history outside the frame of diegesis to an altogether different mode of discourse, then the narrative itself begs for a different set of hermeneutic tools. We must recognize that the terms of discourse for these narratives are literary, and the *bios* is a literary invention.

The linchpin is the nature of the narrative of the *bios* itself, for the bios is a type of *fiction*. Hayden White has already pointed in this direction in his analysis of historical narratives. Following Northrop Frye, White's now well-known argument is based on the adoption of tropes, literary conventions that shape the telling of the narrative that in turn dictates the narrative's emplotment. In White's scheme, narratives composed by historians tend to follow one of four predictable trajectories based on the author's desired outcome: metaphor emplots romance, metonymy emplots tragedy, synecdoche emplots comedy, and irony emplots satire.[18] But we are not dealing with historical narratives, which are automatically and necessarily second- and third-order syntheses of other materials. The tales of the *pīrs* and *bibīs* are not histories written as fictions; rather, we are dealing with primary narratives,

as well), and in the text below, he arrives surfing across the waters on his sandals. There are a host of references of this sort; see Asim Roy, *The Islamic Syncretistic Tradition in Bengal* (Princeton: Princeton University Press, 1983), 219–23. Anna Suvarova reports from her Persian sources the connection of Pīr Badr to Chittagong, to the *pāñc pīr*, and both versions of his arrival in Chittagong on a rock and on a fish; see Anna Suvorova, *Muslim Saints of South Asia*, 165–66.

17. See chap. 1, n. 21.

18. Among his many works, see Hayden White, *Metahistory: The Historical Imagination in Nineteenth-Century Europe* (Baltimore: Johns Hopkins University Press, 1973), and White, *Tropics of Discourse: Essays in Cultural Criticism* (Baltimore: Johns Hopkins University Press, 1978).

fictions that originate in and circulate through the Bangla-speaking world of the fifteenth to twenty-first centuries.

In a manner recognized to hold for any literary text, the hagiographical narrative of the bios-as-fiction creates its own unique, self-contained world that has an end and a purpose in itself; it is a self-referential world, hence *autotelic*. The stories can be detached from and read independently of context; that is, each text can yield a purely literary reading and all that the classification of fiction implies—and many of the tales of the *pīrs* and *phakīrs*, the *bibīs* and *pīrānīs*, and *devīs* and the *sādhus* and *jogīs* circulate just like that—one might even argue *primarily* like that—when delivered in *jātrā* or other performative modes. While the circumstances of a tale's creation and reception do impinge on that fictive world and condition it—the subject of the next three chapters—it is primarily by relying on unstated presuppositions regarding the way the world works, the presentation of images rather than arguments, that indirectly reflect the religious ideal, however vague and imprecise. Rather than thinking of the religious ideal as containing some fixed theological or doctrinal content, it can be better understood as a *perspective*, a way of understanding and operating in the world that, if followed through, would result in some utopian goal; this perspective and the cosmology it implies endorse ethical sensibilities that are imparted through action and deed. But because they are fictions, these narratives cannot articulate a religious ideal in explicit terms of precise sectarian doctrine or attempt to propose a theology, much less something that would qualify as systematic. Understanding why this is so will help us to uncover the work of these fictions and why they are so important to the people who circulate them.

In his study of genre, Tzvetan Todorov, following Northrop Frye, argues that one of the most important inherent structural features of the fictional narrative—whether fable, parable, myth, epic, or novel—is that the narrative is never subject to the truth test. Truthfulness will not arise precisely because the texts are in some basic way literary: the narratives are neither true nor false precisely because they are fictional.[19] This is quite a different proposition from the one most often adopted, which is to say that because they are fictions they are not true (fictitious, unreal; *kālpanik*); rather they are neither true nor false in the ordinary world of

19. Tzvetan Todorov predicates his entire argument about literary genres on this assertion. Todorov, *Genres in Discourse*, trans. Catherine Porter (Cambridge: Cambridge University Press, 1990), 3. With regard to the novel, which I think is also applicable here: "What exists, first of all, is the text, and nothing else; it is only by subjecting the text to a particular type of reading that we construct an imaginary universe on the basis of the text. The novel does not imitate reality, it creates reality" (39). See Northrop Frye, *Anatomy of a Criticism: Four Essays* (Princeton: Princeton University Press, 1957). Significantly, Edward S. Casey argues that the act of imagining is similarly complete in and of itself, and so is the content of that imagining, an observation congruous with the assertion of the fiction's autotelic nature; see Casey, *Imagining: A Phenomenological Study*, 2nd ed. (Bloomington: Indiana University Press, 2000), 171–91.

things, but instead, create their own realities. The first authors of the fictional *pīr* narratives, whether named or anonymous, had no need to declare the truth value of the narratives, though on occasion it is clear that they wondered whether they were conveying something acceptable, for one will occasionally encounter the disclaimer (so often heard among the purveyors of the *hadīs* literatures): "no one knows for sure," or "only God knows." Yet many of the narratives do contain overt, albeit unsystematic, statements about the nature of the divine, about occasional religious practices, and even hint at weak doctrine. What then is the nature of these pronouncements if they are not subject to normative truth tests?

Without any exception that I can locate, each of the stories of the *bibīs* and *pīrs*, the life narrative or bios, conforms neatly to the trajectory of the genre Western literary critics call *romance*. While romance is a widespread category, it is not at all unknown to India, which is to say that while there is no one Indic language genre category that can undeniably be translated as romance—with the possible exception of the early modern *premākhyān* or *prem kahānī*[20]—that type of tale lies at the heart of the Sanskrit epic *Rāmāyaṇa* and *Mahābhārata*, as well as the Persian *Shāh Nāmeh*, and is rife in the Buddhist story literature and in the literatures of every vernacular on the subcontinent. For those who tremble at the thought of using any term that is not indigenous—as if refusing to adopt anything other than an indigenous category actually clarifies our understanding—the term is not being deployed here to impute to these texts some ontological reality. Rather, the term is being deployed as an indicator of authorial strategy to help us understand *what these narratives do*, how stories that we call romance accomplish their work. The first step is structural, to identify the predictable markers of romance, then the next step will be to look at the process of narrative, and from that to determine the goal of this kind of writing, which I argue is quite the opposite of some doctrinal or theological assertion, but just as compelling, if not more so, in its persuasive effects on its audience.

Of the many studies, Frye's *The Secular Scripture*[21] gives us a good starting point because he is primarily concerned with the structure of the romance narrative.

20. See Behl, *Love's Subtle Magic*. As previously noted, the best comparative study of the Bangla *premākhyān* is by Mantajur Rahmān Taraphdār; see Taraphdār, *Bāṃlā romāṇṭik kāvyer āoyādhī-hindī paṭbhūmi*. See also Oyākil Āhmad, *Bāṃlā romāṇṭik praṇayopākhyān*, 6th printing (Ḍhākā: Khān Brādārs eyāṇḍ Kompāni, 2004); and Māhmudā Khānam, *Madhyajugīya bāṃlā sāhitya hindī suphī kāvyer prabhāv* (Ḍhākā: Bāṃlā Ekāḍemī, 1410 BS [2003]). Francesca Orsini has addressed this issue of vernacular names for romances in an essay titled "The Social History of a Genre: *Kathas* across Languages in Early Modern North India," *Medieval History Journal* 20, no. 1 (2017): 1–37. See also Orsini, "Texts and Tellings: *Kathas* in the Fifteenth and Sixteenth Centuries," in *Tellings and Texts: Music, Literature, and Peformance in North India*, ed. Francesca Orsini and Katherine Butler Schofield (Cambridge, UK: OpenBook Publishers, 2015), 327–58.

21. Northrop Frye, *The Secular Scripture: A Study of the Structure of Romance*, The Charles Eliot Norton Lectures, 1974–75 (Cambridge: Harvard University Press, 1976). Though Todorov used many of Frye's propositions about the structure of literary works, in *The Secular Scripture*, Frye is not willing to go quite as far as Todorov regarding the truth question because of the distinction he makes between

Briefly, according to Frye, the trajectory of the narrative is focused on the protagonist, male or female, who descends into some kind of confusion or illusion and then reverses that descent with a world-changing ascent. In this latter phase of ascent, the hero struggles to set the world right, addresses or overtly challenges morality and law, and counters with heroism the antagonist's negative counter response to the troubling moral situation. In all of our tales of *pīrs* and *bibīs*, that portion of the biographical image that is concerned with the religious ideal provides the resolution to these challenges to morality and law and is used to establish or reestablish a morally ordered world at story's end, or at least push the characters in that direction. Or, perhaps more accurately, the actions of the hero both create and investigate these ideals, which are often derived from nimble situation creativity prompted by the needs of the plot. These stories, however, are about action; there is little to no psychological or moral "development" in any character. Their public actions define them entirely, and problems are resolved accordingly.

Following Frye's narrative trajectory, the descent into illusion manifests itself in both personal and social confusion, trouble, war, or ignorance, all of which are characterized by meandering adventure, loss of identity, displacement of rightful role, and uncertain action that often leads to the underworld or some metaphoric equivalent. Vows and curses lead characters to descend into the darker realms of illusion and ignorance that routinely involve gender confusions, society with animals, deployment of extreme violence, and cunning deception in a world of fraud as tests of the hero's or heroine's fortitude. Once the hero or heroine recognizes the extremes of his or her alienation and divorce from what is good and proper, the struggle to make the world right signals the ascent. One can easily imagine the ascent as the heroes and heroines salvage what is left of their families or kingdoms to reestablish order. The themes are often of escape and survival. While in Frye's schema, the ascent often culminates in the leading character's own destruction, these resolutions tend to leave the world a better place, or, failing that, put into place the elements necessary to correct it after their own demise. It is, in Frye's terms, a predictably utopian outcome.[22]

Clearly in the tales of the historical *pīrs*, martyrdom provides one plotline that results in that final destruction of the hero. In Sufi hagiography, martyrdom is generally understood to be a self-sacrifice that leads to the further establishment and spread of Islam on earth; the protagonist gains as reward a coveted spot in paradise. This well-known and often idealized pattern is repeated throughout the Islamic world. But the fictional *pīrs* and *bibīs* of Bengal generally come to a less violent end, indeed, if any proper "end" is recorded, but never without going

---

myth and romance. He writes, "The anxiety of society, when it urges the authority of a myth and the necessity of believing it, seems to be less to proclaim its truth than to prevent anyone from questioning it" (16).

22. Frye, *Secular Scripture*, chap. 4, "Themes of Descent."

through a series of challenging adventures, often involving conflict, through which the hero or heroine establishes a pattern of action that leads to a more profoundly sound world.

To illustrate how these features are incorporated into the narratives, we will turn to a prolegomena of a larger work titled the *Mānikpīr jahurānāmā* of Jaidi or Jayaraddhi, which can be translated as "celebrating the glorious appearance (*jahurā*) of Mānikpīr." The text is a previously untranslated tale from an incomplete manuscript held in the library at Viśva Bhārati in Santiniketan, West Bengal, and transcribed by Pāñcānan Maṇḍal.[23] The date of the manuscript is 1817, and from internal evidence I would judge the composition to be not more than several decades earlier than that date, perhaps as early as 1780 or 1790. We do not know if the scribe is the author or some other. This particular piece illustrates the nature of these materials in their unedited form. Most of the so-called *musalmāni bāṅglā* texts that have made it into print have been subject to very inconsistent editing, starting minimally with seemingly innocuous standardization of spellings, but often intervening much further by the inclusion of paratextual apparatus in the form of dividing the unbroken text into chapters, giving titles to chapters, and even substituting modern words for older, and in some cases transposing couplets or the feet within couplets or rearranging syntax to a more easily read modern standard.[24] I can confirm, however, that Pāñcānan Maṇḍal presented the text "as is." Though the text is a fragment of a larger manuscript, it contains the discrete story of the descent of Mānik Pīr's father from heaven at the command of Āllā, and the exploits leading to the birth of his more famous son. It compresses the elements of romance noted above, which makes it ideal for illustrative purposes, but at the same time manages in a short span to convey the incredible complexity of a seemingly simple tale of the sort generally dismissed by those who have examined the history of Islam in the Bangla-speaking region. I have inserted limited explanatory footnotes and a few paragraph breaks, but the author's signature line (*bhaṇitā*) marks the ends of sections as he has created them. Those signature lines are italicized and in the author's own voice, though sometimes in the third person. I have refrained from smoothing out some of the precipitous transitions, or lack thereof, especially in dialogues where abrupt speech (not marked by tag clauses) is typical of a dramatic enactment on stage, specifically in this case the *jātrā* form; in other passages the speech is attributive. Where I have inserted a connecting or

23. Jaidi or Jayaraddhi, "Mānikpīrer jahurānāmā," in *Punthi paricay*, ed. Pāñcānan Maṇḍal (Śāntiniketan: Viśvabhārati, 1958), 305–18; MS no. 936, 12–1/2 folios, dtd. 1224 BS [ca. 1817], incomplete. Asim Roy summarizes the tale; see Roy, *The Islamic Syncretistic Tradition in Bengal* (Princeton: Princeton University Press, 1983), 241–45.

24. For the classic study of the nature and function of the various paratextual strategies, see Gérard Genette, *Paratexts: Thresholds of Interpretation*, trans. Jane E. Lewin (Cambridge: Cambridge University Press, 1997).

modifying word, I have adopted the standard convention of placing that word or phrase in square brackets.

I have also included what I consider to be significant Bangla words in parentheses. Many of these are, from the perspective of the study of religion, potentially technical terms, and their connection to their Arabic, Persian, or Sanskrit antecedents will be relatively obvious. So as we noted in the prefatory material, one will see Āllā as it is spelled in Bangla, *phakir* or *phakīr* rather than *fakīr*, *tapisvyā* rather than *tapasya*, and so forth. In many instances the scribe will spell the same word as many as four different ways, including the author's name as Jaidi, Jaiddi, Jayardhhi, and Jayaradhhi—and I have opted to retain those different spellings.[25] Clearly similar to the very incomplete anonymous manuscript cited in the epigraph of this chapter, the translation of Jaidi's *Mānikpīrer jahurānāmā*, or *The Tale of the Glory of Mānik Pīr*, follows here in its entirety as transcribed by Pāñcānan Maṇḍal.[26]

2.3 PROLEGOMENA TO THE *MĀNIKPĪRER JAHURĀNĀMĀ* OF JAIDI

One day Āllā[27] Sāheb took his seat in his *dargā* shrine and began to tell of the twelve saints (*āule*). Then Khodā asked who would take up his words and go to the earth to spread his fame and glory (*jahurā*). "That one who will be entrusted with the burden of the world, will in the Kali Age descend as an *avatār* named Mānik. He will speak to everyone about Haji, Gāji, Māhāmad, Rahim, Karim, Rasul, Paygambhar, Ijjat, and Mādār." Just then Badar, servant of Āllā, presented himself. "Merciful and gracious Lord, I will go spread the word (*jāhir*)[28] with your blessings. Send me to earth, if it pleases you. Āllā, please give me my instructions now." Then Āllā spoke of the many and great virtues of his servant Badar, but warned, "If you fall into the hands of a woman, she will distract your resolve." Badar responded, "Of that I am completely ignorant, please explain." When he [Āllā] was finished, he again enu-

25. It would be useful to refer to the "Conventions Regarding Transliteration and Nomenclature" in the front matter to see why and how the decisions for rendering this and the other texts were made.

26. See n. 23 above.

27. Throughout this manuscript, the word is frequently also rendered as *ārllā*, but this particular scribe routinely deploys the reph /*-r*/ to indicate the *japhalā* /*-y*/, producing *āllyā*; the geminate consonants, already doubled in pronunciation, are further exaggerated by the *japhalā* (here, *-ll- effectively becomes -lll-*) and, for this scribe, that *japhalā* also substitutes for a long final /*ā*/, which reasonably approximates the Arabic pronunciation. For reasons of recognition, I have chosen to retain a single spelling of Āllā; this is the only editorial intervention with respect to orthography that I have introduced. Orthography in manuscripts is highly inconsistent and often completely idiosyncratic to the scribe, and with the exception just noted, I have left the multiple spellings to convey something of the local nature of the text. The editor of the print edition, Pañcānan Maṇḍal, is to be lauded for his strict transcriptions in the volumes of the *Puṅthi paricay*, choosing a very light editorial touch.

28. The spellings *jāhir* and *jāhirā* (derived from Arabic *ẓāhir*) are used interchangeably, meaning "to make public" or "make known or manifest" the splendor of Āllā, often glossed as proselytizing or preaching.

merated Badar's many qualities; upon receiving this benediction, Badar begged his leave. Badar bowed his head to Āllā, seated in his court (*darbār*). Khodā's servant then gave precise instructions of his mission. Badar replied, "Khodā, may I suggest that I should go to the earth dressed as a *phakir mursid*." Āllā then furnished him with everything needed for the garb of a *phakir* with attention to every detail: the Summoner (*dāoān*)[29] received the rope-belt, tight-fitting pajamas for leggings, short cotton trousers, a staff, a robe, a horse Duldul,[30] and in his hand a crop of thorny bamboo. His face was covered with a strikingly handsome beard. He sported a necklace at his throat, a peaked hat on his head, and gems and jewels that glistened in the light. When he [Badar] put on his shoulder bag, Āllā opened his mouth in a wide smile of approval, and the Summoner gazed at the three worlds therein. His faithful follower (*momin*) affirmed to Khodā his commitment; then, prostrating himself before Āllā, he departed.

May the mother of the Master (kartā) *be blessed, finding riches everywhere.*[31]

With the names of Āllā resounding in his mouth, Badar Sāheb went. On his way to preach (*jāhirā*) in the city of Delhi, he first landed in the city of Lahore. In his *phakir*'s garb, he begged in the streets of Lahore. Muttering the incantation "*dām dām mādār*"—by the very breath of Mādār—he could cover great distances.[32] As soon as men and women heard the *phakir*, they would take out four cowries on a golden plate, "Oh Summoner *muni*, please take these alms, please accept them!" But the

29. The title *dāoān* refers to the person who calls out the *da'wa* (Arabic) or *dāoyā/dāoā* (Bangla), summoning people to join the *ummā*, the issuing of the invitation, which is a form of proselytizing, but with implicit intention to establish Islamic conventions of governance and law (Arabic *shari'a*), not just to invite individuals to participate. It will be translated as the Summoner throughout. From time to time the scribe will write *deoān*, which would be an alternate spelling of *deoyān* (from Persian *dewān*) rather than *dāoān*, but this title of minister or chief officer of state only distantly works if he is considered the minister of Āllā's court. For this author, however, this term and several other technical designations for the courts seem to function as honorifics as much as specific stations.

30. Coincidentally (?) Duldul is the same name as Alī's mount.

31. "Finding riches everywhere" is literally "finding gems in the mud."

32. The Sufi followers of Badī 'al-Dīn Madār were famous for their self-scrutiny (Arabic *muḥāsaba*) and self-contemplation (Arabic *murāqaba*), and silent forms of *dhikr/zikir* (Bangla *jikir*) including recitation of verses of the Qur'ān coupled with breath control (*habs-i dam*), which seems to be suggested here. For more on their practices and the ways scholars have reported on their apparent transgressive practices, especially the *malangs*, see Ute Falasch, "The Islamic Mystic Tradition in India: The Madari Sufi Brotherhood," in *Lived Islam in South Asia: Adaptation, Accommodation, and Conflict*, ed. Imtiaz Ahmed and Helmut Reifeld (New Delhi: Esha Béteille, Social Science Press, 2004), 256–72. For the more miraculous tales and local Bengali color, see the section on Mādār Pīr in Girīndranāth Dās, *Bāṃlā pīr sāhityer kathā*, 1st ed., 321–27, which also includes verbatim the entire section titled "Dām mādār o kālandar panth" in Sen, *Islāmi Bāṅglā sāhitya*, 143–47. The story he transcribes tells how Mādār Pīr engaged in a lively game of hide and seek with Baḍa Pīr when it was time to offer *śirṇi*, then how at the invitation of Āllā he was fetched by the angels Jibril and Ejrāphil to receive direct instruction from God. Āli, Bibi Phatemā, the two *imāms* Hāsan and Hosen and Hajrat Nabī, the Prophet, were all present. The section ends with a description of Mādār's unconventional habits and his penchant for meditation and silent recitation of the names. Sen cites his source as the *Śāh mādārer kāhinī*, collected by Chāyād Āli Khondkār, but unfortunately gives no bibliographic information nor was I was able to locate it.

Summoner replied, "I will not take any such alms." The devout (*momin*) servant of God (*bāndār*) said that he could never take alms in his hands unless he was [the donor's] spiritual preceptor (*mursid*). They contemplated over and again what the servant of God (*bāndā*) said. "Since the moment we were born, we have never known a proper preceptor (*mursid*)." The Summoner explained patiently what this entailed. "Chant three times 'Ed Āllā! Ed Āllā!'—only then will I accept alms from your hands, otherwise it would be counted an offense in the court (*darbār*) of Āllā." When they heard this, this servant of God (*bāndā*) became their preceptor (*mursid*). Everyone in the city of Lahore flocked to give him alms. Some brought tray upon tray, others platters full. Some said, "May we ever hold him in our hearts!" Some women found themselves weeping on account of the *phakir*. Others pleaded, "Let us accompany you!" The *phakir* comforted everyone there, "I am going to the city of Delhi to preach (*jāhir*)." And so it was that he left Lahore.

. . .

[small break in manuscript]

Śrī Śrī Durgā, Śrī Śrī Durgā, Śrī Śrī Durgā, Śrī Śrī Durgā,
Śrī Śrī Durgā, Śrī Śrī Durgā, Śrī Śrī Durgā
Śrī Śrī Nārāyaṇ Śrī Śrī Nārāyaṇ, Śrī Śrī Nārāyaṇ, Śrī Śrī Nārāyaṇ,
Śrī Śrī Nārāyaṇ, Śrī Śrī Nārāyaṇ, Śrī Śrī Nārāyaṇ[33]

. . .

[section of MS missing]

. . . mother held [him] in her heart. And so in this way Badar left Sāntipur and soon arrived at Sāhābājār, where he conversed with Golāmāli Sāheb. "I shall go to Cāṭigāñ [Chittagong] in order to make known the Divine's eminence." From there the Summoner crossed the rivers and not long after arrived at Saptagrām, the place where Gāṅgā Devī descended. Badar Mursid went to that place, and then he came to the landing *ghāṭ* of Triveni, a place where rishis [*risi*] and sages [*muni*] practiced their penance (*tapisvyā*), so stationary were they that reeds had grown up to cover their bodies. Hundreds of sages (*muni*) performed their austerities there. Some had restless eyes, while others had restless minds—and for that lack of concentration they had failed to gain the vision of Gaṅgā.

So then the *phakir* addressed the crowd. "Would you explain to me why you are sitting here stoically waiting?" Some said to themselves, "What is the lowly shaved head (*neḍiyā*)[34] talking about?" Another said, "We're undertaking austerities (*tapisyā*) for Gaṅgā, what's it to you?" As soon as he heard this snappy retort, Badar covered his ears with his hands and muttered, "Āllā! Āllā! What an awful and stupid thing to

33. The scribe's religious orientation is suggested by his choice of the names used to seal up the rupture of the manuscript with the vocative call to the goddess Durgā and the god Nārāyaṇ.

34. The term *neḍa* or *neḍā* is a shorn or tonsured individual, but *neḍe* is sometimes used to designate a *bauddha* or *vaiṣṇav* mendicant or, in a more vulgar tone, a *musalmāni* beggar; regardless of the specific reference, the tone is despective.

say! He who, in his mind, chants (*japi*) 'There is no God but God . . .'[35] will turn the tide. Seated in his aerial vehicle (*bimān*), Khodā will appear here. With an unsullied heart, call Gaṅgā! Pay heed to what I say. Or better yet, let me invoke [Gaṅgā] and may you behold for yourselves." When Badar spoke these words to these spiritual practitioners (*padri*),[36] it was like pouring ghee on a glowing fire.

"Where do you come from, *phakir*, what insignificant backwater? We have been seated here for twelve years performing our austerities (*tapasya*), so long that reeds have grown over our bodies. Still the mother of Brahmā has not yet appeared. From just what place, *phakir*, do you derive such overbearing self-importance?"

The Summoner retorted, "See for yourselves my manifest glory (*jāhiri*)!" Badar said this, flying into a rage. He sat on a tiger skin and began to practice a form of austerity (*tapisyā*) with great diligence.[37] May the power of the Lord ferry me across right now! Gaṅgā please show yourself, your elder brother is calling you!" As Badar uttered these words, he concentrated on Gaṅgā and soon Gaṅgādevī herself appeared, bubbling with pleasure. No sooner had they gained sight of Gaṅgādevī than they headed straight to Brahmalok as four-armed (*caturbhuj*) rishis (*risi*) and sages (*muni*). As he watched, Badar mulled over the spectacle. After watching the spiritual men (*pādri*) become four-armed, 'I shall see just how much virtue and power lies in those lotus feet.' He began to call out, "Hear me, hear me, Mother Gaṅgā!"

The lowly and poor Jaiddi sings through a boon granted by Gajamānīk, the one who shines like a magnificent ruby. Every one present who hears this tale will be blessed with wealth and sons.

Badar began to call out, "Gaṅgā, Gaṅgā." Devī did not normally come when a *jaban* called, but Badar wooed, "I want to see your face, to see your figure with my own eyes." Gaṅgā replied, "I'll show you, if you can survive the onslaught of my seven waves." When the Summoner heard this he experienced a nervous thrill. "With an appeal to Āllā I shall indeed withstand the seven waves!" Mother Gaṅgā then manifested herself in seven massive breakers. Seeing that enormous swell, Badar realized he was in dire straits, but he centered his mind, remembering the Creator (*kartā*). "Ed Āllā! Ed Āllā! Just this one time, this one time!" And so Badar called Āllā to mind with this chant and Āllā, seated in his aerial car (*bimān*), came to know of

35. The spelling is typical of the manuscript: the text reads *ilāhilerllā*, a shorthand for the Arabic *shahada*: *lā 'ilāha 'illāllāh, muḥammadun rasūlullāh*. It is precisely this kind of expression that is labeled pidgin Arabic and has reinforced the classification of these texts by literary scholars as doggerel and of no cultural or literary value, though in this case, with the scribe's propensity for using the *reph* to indicate a *japhalā* (n. 27 above), its pronunciation is much closer than an average reader might reckon: *ilāhilellā*. Unfortunately, that negative characterization fails to take into account the near impossibility of rendering Arabic or Persian in an accurate phonetic transliteration in Bangla.

36. The word *padri* or *pādri* is *pādari* or *pādarī*, technically a Christian clergyman or padre; it is not clear here if he means to be disrespectful of the sages or if he is using it as one more equivalent term for holy man, or more likely both, in a strategy of recognizing equivalence.

37. In addition to "diligence," the expression *ujā karya* invokes images of "reversing the tide," that is, going upstream, a typical yogic expression for a *tantrik*-style *sādhanā* that seeks to reverse the unfolding of the world in order to go back to the source of all creative power. The expression is adopted by *vaiṣṇav sahajiyās* and *nāth jogīs*. The use of the tiger skin for meditation is a classic image for *yogīs* in traditional India.

everything. Āllā immediately called out to the Wind, "You will summon Gaṅgā right away in order to tie her up in [Badar's] shoulder bag. Assuming the form of a white fly, the Wind flew with haste. When he reached Badar Mursid, his words tumbled out in a rush. But no sooner had he heard than Badar obeyed and opened up his shoulder bag. Gaṅgā Mātā towered above him in seven massive breakers, and those seven rollers swelled even higher, reaching a frighteningly enormous height. The tidal waves reached for the sky and bore down, violently shaking the land. Obediently and calmly remembering the Creator (*kartā*), he spread open his shoulder bag and impelled Gaṅgādevī to slip quietly inside. He carefully, purposefully cinched the pouch tight with a rope and Gaṅgā remained trapped in the bag. And in this way was the Bhāgirathi subdued.[38]

Badar then decided that he would now make known his majesty, just as the Creator (*kartā*) instructed. "Today I will plant jute along the river. I will draw attention (*jāhirā*) [to God's greatness] by planting the jute." By the clever intervention of Āllā did the plants sprout quickly. In a single day the sprouts popped out leaves. Within a mere seven days their stalks shot up, roots had grown, flowers blossomed, and their slender fruits emerged. Soon Badar was cooking this leafy vegetable along the river. "Take this, Āllā; I make the first offering to you, honoring my word."

Gaṅgā then pleaded, "Please release me. I now realize that you are indeed my senior, my elder brother from times past." Badar responded, "Gaṅgā, let me set one condition. If you promise you are now calmed and exhausted, I shall open the knotted mouth of the pouch and release you." When Gaṅgā acknowledged her submission and the mouth of the bag opened, the waters exploded out as if ignited by fire, and that watery deluge engulfed the Triveni. It was from that time that the river course was bent like a hunchback. Badar said, "Gaṅgā, I have released you, but Gaṅgādevī, I must now press one urgent request. O esteemed one, please transport stones to me here. I shall arrange to display His majesty here at the Triveni." Once she heard the Summoner's request, she could not avoid it, so she hauled stones from the Setubandha.[39] By the magical action of the Goddess Devī, the stones floated on the ocean's waters. One by one they floated all the way upriver until they reached that place.

When he finally caught sight of the stones, Badar was delighted and immediately summoned there Visvakarmmā, the celestial architect. Badar supplicated him, offering betel and flowers. "Over the next seven days and nights, please construct a building for a *masjid*." Visāi replied, "Badar, that will be sufficient for your request, but you must maintain darkness for all seven days and nights. I will not stay past the moment the dawn breaks the dark of night. No matter how far along the building construction has gotten, I will move out." Badar responded, "Visāi, what kind of talk is this? I shall call on the night this very day to ensure the nighttime prevails." And so the Summoner called the night and explained everything. Visvakarmmā began to construct the building. Two days passed smoothly in this activity, but Āllā, seated

38. Bhāgirathi is the name of one of the two headstreams of the Gaṅgā and the preferred name for the Gaṅgā in that part of Bengal.

39. This is the legendary land bridge of the *Rāmāyaṇa* epic that was believed to connect present-day Sri Lanka with the mainland of India.

in his aerial vehicle (*bimān*), began to express alarm that Visāi would erect a great building such that Makkā, Madinā, and heaven itself would be humbled in comparison. Considering all this, Āli was summoned by Khodā for the sake of honor: "Assume the form of a white crow and wing your way quickly." As soon as the Creator's (*kartā*) command registered, he moved with alacrity. Perching on a branch of a magnolia tree,[40] the crow began to caw rather raucously. On cue, dawn broke, blotting out the moon, and the Master Builder himself dropped his axe and scurried away, the structure only half completed.

When Badar saw Visāi flee, he began to call for Daphargā Gāji.[41] Soon Daphagā Gāji arrived in the presence of the esteemed Badar. "You stay put here at the Triveni where you will receive offerings of flowers and *sinni*.[42] I shall extol in song your glory and virtue throughout the world of humans. I shall place the [image of the] egg of the fabled *beṅgamā* and *beṅgama* birds[43] on your banner." And so Badar handed over the Triveni to Daphagā Gāji and with a light heart headed toward the city of Caṭṭigām [Chittagong].

The Summoner Badar moved on with clearheaded intention, his mind and heart unclouded by ambiguity. He surfed across the Gaṅgā on his wooden sandals, then along the way he held assemblies (*majlis*) for the next three days. The Summoner shared what was in his heart with the company of the faithful. Badar said, "O faithful *momin*, let me just explain one thing. I shall visit his highness, the Bādsā,[44] Sultan of Dilli." The faithful replied, "Do go and pay a visit to the honorable Bādsā." [And Badar replied,] "Afterwards I shall return and make known Āllā's magnificence in the city of Cāṭṭigā̃." With this plan in mind, the Summoner embarked.

40. Magnolia is *cā̃pā* (*Michelia campaka*) with its distinctive yellow and white flower, common to all of Bengal.

41. Spellings alternate between *daphargā*, *daphaga*, and *daphagā*. Daphargā Gāji would appear to be a variant spelling of Dafar Khān Gājī (Za'far Khān Ghāzī) at Triveni, where there is a *dargā* in his name. He is sometimes identified with Zafar Khān Gājī, a thirteenth-century warrior-saint from Murshidabad who was involved in the conquest of lower Bengal, but whether it is an attempt to use a historical *pīr* in the narrative or one who is modeled on the historical is impossible to determine. For more, see N. B. Roy, "Studies in Islamic History," *Visva Bharati Annals* 4 (1951): 70–84. I am indebted to Projit Mukharji for the reference. Further, see Muhammad Enamul Haq, *A History of Sufi-ism in Bengal* (Dhaka: Asiatic Society of Bangladesh, 1975), 196–97. The half-built mosque may be an oblique reference to the *dargā* of Dafar Khān Gājī (d. 1313) which, according to Haq, is located within an old temple on the site, which would be consistent with the structure erected by Viśvakarma in the tale.

42. The traditional offering to these *pīrs* is *sinni* or *śirṇi*, a mixture of rice flour, banana, jaggery or sugar, betal, and a mix of spices.

43. The *beṅgamā* bird is fabled because of its ability to speak; it appears in many popular tales, for instance, see Kavi Kaṇva, "The Fabled *Beṅgamā* Bird and the Stupid Prince: Kavi Kaṇva's *Akhoṭi Pālā*," in Tony K. Stewart, trans., *Fabulous Females and Peerless Pīrs: Tales of Mad Adventure in Old Bengal* (New York: Oxford University Press, 2004), 67–94.

44. The term is *bādsā*, and in this manuscript it is also spelled *badṣā*, *bādśā*, and *bādsva;* because of the Bangla phonology, all three are pronounced the same: baad-shah; English is generally Badshah. I have retained the different original different spellings throughout.

[Badar] went and presented himself in the court (*darbār*) of the Bādsā. In his dress as a *phakir*, the Summoner[45] carried a peacock feather fan.[46] He gave every appearance of the full moon in dark sky.[47] The Bādṣā then inquired after the Summoner, "Explain the reason you have come here to my court (*darbār*)." The *phakir* replied, "Bādsvā, please honor my request. I am only begging a small favor, promise me you will abide by it. First commit yourself, then I shall tell you." When the Minister (*ujir*) listened to this request, he immediately considered the implications. But when the Bādsvā heard, he was instantly ignited. [The Minister] took it up and threatened Badar in a blustery rage. "What kind of *phakir* are you? Where do you come from? Who do you think you are? How dare you speak to my Lord this way!" Badar retorted, "Bādsvā, I have no fear of you. Know now that your soon-to-be son-in-law is sitting here in your court (*darbār*)."

The Minister advised the Bādsvā to listen, "Have him bound and throw him into prison for three days." The Bādsvā was seething at the *phakir*'s words and with a violent outburst ordered the guard to do it. Hearing the Bādsvā's command, his personal security detail pummeled the *phakir*, some yanked his beard, and others verbally threatened him. Thinking about the welfare of the faithful, the Summoner devised a plan: 'Today I will humble the arrogance of this Bādsvā.'

Everyone was astonished to see the Summoner suddenly withdraw from sight. Sulking over the rebuke within the court (*darbār*), Badar, the Summoner, considering the faithful, disappeared into the forest. In a clearing where the undergrowth was trampled down, the Summoner took his seat, his mind at ease. He thought, 'With my retinue of tigers, I shall capture the Bādsvā's daughter.'

The poor and lowly Garib Jaidi sings: May you shower your grace! Grant a boon of wealth and a son for the ones in charge.

As his rage welled up again, Badar summoned all the tigers. Heeding his call, hundreds of thousands of tigers came forward in leaps and bounds. The tiger that led the streak was called by the name of Hum. Arriving with the tigresses, he proffered a royal salute. Then Kēd and Mēd arrived in the august presence of Badar. Gobāgā and Sobāgā ran with soaring leaps and bounds. Jaṭiyā and Maṭiyā came running with

45. When Badar is in the court of the *bādsā*, the scribe has titled him *deoyān*, minister or *dewan*, rather than *dāoān* (see n. 30 above). Because the function of the traditional *dewan* does not make sense for Badar, I take *deoyān* to be an alternate spelling of *dāoān* and have translated both terms as Summoner throughout.

46. Peacock feathers and fans and fly whisks made from them have long associations with royalty and sanctity in South Asia. It was not uncommon for many Sufis to carry peacock feathers, and they were a common sight in courts. It is not clear if the *beṅgama* bird egg mentioned a few lines earlier is a similar association with the ostrich egg in South Asian and Middle Eastern contexts. For more on this, see Nile Green, "Ostrich Eggs and Peacock Feathers: Sacred Objects as Cultural Exchange between Christianity and Islam," *Al-Masāq* 18, no. 1 (2006): 27–78, esp. 60–62. For contemporary use, see Samuel Landell Mills, "The Hardware of Sanctity: Anthropomorphic Objects in Bangladeshi Sufism," in *Embodying Charisma: Modernity, Locality and the Performance of Emotion in Sufi Cults*, ed. Pnina Werbner and Helene Basu (London: Routledge, 1998), 31–54.

47. *Badar*, of course, means "moon," an image that will play through the text.

the spirit and dignity of lions. The two brothers Cāndā and Cilya could leap a *yojana*—about five miles[48]—in leaps and bounds. Cāmar and Sāmar came along, running from house to house, and right behind them the tiger Kālā—the Black Death—sprang up and down. Taraṅgini, the Wavy One, rolled in like a swelling breaker, while Gigantic or Baḍa Humā plodded forward like a towering mountain. The pair Āblāk and Sāmlāk came running, and Nākesvari bounded with a single stride to the head of the frontrunners. Like the wind itself, the brothers Sonā and Dhanā breezed along. In but one single night they could traverse the distance ordinarily taking eighteen days. The four—Ud and Bud, Āmāne and Sāmāne—together came, running roughshod over anything that obstructed their way. Mātaāle and Sātaāle were accompanied by three hundred thousand others, and by the end twelve hundred thousand tigers came ready for a romping good play. One by one the Summoner received each of the tigers in the rally.

The poor Garib Jaidi sings, focused on Mānik the Emissary.[49]

Badar spoke, "Tigers, listen carefully to what I ask. Please enumerate to me the strengths and weaknesses of your many violent propensities." One by one all of the tigers of the rally offered their take. The tiger Hum stepped forward in the assembly and began to speak: "I always announce 'I have arrived, I am here' with a fittingly loud roar. The heavens, the world of men, and the nether world stand silenced by my call." A tigress then said, "Listen, Summoner, you who are a sage (*muni*), you need only give the command and I will turn the world upside down." Gobāgā and Sobāgā then spoke. "Let us elaborate our style. In the murky waters of the marsh thick with arum we lie in wait. Just when men squat down there to piss we leap and fall on their necks, then drag them away." Ked and Med spoke: "Listen, Summoner, to our techniques. We grab our humans by the nape of the neck and drain them of their blood—glub glub—in one long swallow." The tiger Jaṭe lamented, "One time I crouched along the edges of the marsh, after jumping from a large *jiuli* tree.[50] I landed in a bog of those prickly seed pods of the castor oil plant[51] that were floating right in the middle of a cast of crabs. Just as I lunged for the neck [of a human], the crabs' claws ripped open my scrotum." Sobāgā added, "O Summoner, hear my submission. One day I showed up at Kājipāḍā, and as I was waiting under the eaves of the house to hunt, [someone] threw out the excess water from boiling rice and scorched my face." Jaṭiyā and Maṭiyā spoke in turn. "Listen, revered Summoner, two of my paws' claws got snagged deep in the arm of a man." The tigers Cāndā and Cile spoke: "I was cheered when I located the home of a bard, a public narrator of popular tales. On the day I landed up at the home of that versifier, I found the door bolted and could not

48. Some calculate the *yojana* as a fraction under five miles, while others calculate it closer to eight or nine miles, clearly a long distance here.

49. Emissary is *deoān*, the same title given Badar (see n. 30 above). When the term is used with Mānik, I have translated it as Emissary to distinguish from his father Badar.

50. Also called *jikā*, a large deciduous tree used for timber (*Odina woodier* or *Lannea grandis*); its flowers are used in Ayurvedic medicine for *vattha* disorders and have anti-inflammatory capabilities.

51. The castor oil plant (*Ricinus communis*) has prickly fruit pods that hold three seeds, the poisonous seeds of course being the primary interest in the plant for its medicinal oil.

open it, so I climbed onto the roof when, all of a sudden, someone rammed a red hot poker—a prickly stick, sharp as a needle—right up my anus. Listen, O Summoner, Sage (*muni*), when I jumped, I fell and it hurt! The ground was really hard!"

Cāmare and Sāmare, Ghaṛa and Ghaṛe—each of these four tigers agreed, "I am capable of running nonstop for about five miles." The tiger Kālā, the Black One, then said, "I am Kālā of the Sea. Know that my weakness concerns the resounding crack of thunder—when it booms the hair bristles on my neck and I freeze, I cannot open my eyes, paralyzed I cannot move a muscle." Nāpāne and Jhāpāne spoke: "Listen carefully. At the first sniff of a human we are spooked and flee helter-skelter." The pair of Taraṅgini and Ṣuraṅgini laughed, "We crouched down on some pieces of lumber being joined by a carpenter. On the opposite side of the road a number of people were passing by. Of course our greedy desires got the better of us, so we raced toward them. We roared ferociously as if engaged in a great hunt, but truth be told, it was because our nut sacks had stayed put, hard snagged on one of the carpenter's pegs!" The senior tiger, Baḍa Hum spoke. "Once when I called my sister, my roar caused a poor pregnant woman, huddled in a dark corner, to abort." When the two tigers called Abalā and Sāmalā were summoned, they flew like the wind, a swift death. The tiger Nākeśvari boasted, "Listen O sage (*muni*) Summoner, I can turn your world completely upside down!" The two brothers, Sonā and Dhanā, reported the following: "In a single night we can cover the distance [a human] needs eighteen days to cover." The four brothers Ud, Bud, Āmāle, and Sāmale promised, "There is no protection, no escape for any human who lives in the forest. We move from house to house breaking down all the doors. Do understand that these are qualities of us four brothers."

The tigers Mātāle and Sātāle were joined by three hundred thousand others. And altogether twelve hundred thousand made a show of their prowess while romping in fun. The Summoner was filled with pleasure to see the gathering, and then this devoted servant addressed Cādā and Cile once again. Badar said, "Tigers all, please honor my command. Fetch the daughter of the Bādsvā from the palace!" The tigers Cādā, Cile, Hum, and Nākeśvari all spoke: "We will bring [princess] Dudbibī and place her at your feet." No sooner had they received the order than they left as a group. They soon had the dwelling of the Bādsvā in their sights. The dark of that night was ink-thick all around. The tigers easily leapt on top of and then over the wall, and they soon entered inside the great palace residence. The princess Dudbibī was sleeping in her own room all alone. Lamps were lit all around as far as one could see. A mosquito net of delicately thin decorative gauze was draped from the four posters of the bed. Deep in sleep, Dudbibī remained blissfully innocent. Each of the four tigers lifted up one of the legs making a four-bearer litter. All four jumped in unison to the top of the wall; the Bādsvā's daughter, still deep in sleep, registered nothing. The princess was stretched out on the bed like a ruby gemstone. The tigers seemed to make the bed float in the air as they entered the forest where Badar sat serene. They brought Dudbibī and placed her there within his view. The Summoner pulled up the mosquito net. To his mind's utter confusion, [it was as if] two moons had risen in that one spot. The Summoner gazed on the stunning countenance[52] of

52. The letter য়, /ẏ/, in য়ুরত, /*ẏurat*/, is an obvious and not uncommon orthographic miscue for ষ,

the Bibī with his own eyes. Badar whispered to her over and over, "Wake up, sit up," but the Bibī lay completely insensate, lost in her sleep. As he gazed intently, Badar was befuddled, inexplicably bewildered.

The Bibī [awoke] and, nonplussed, alertly said, "Tell me, just who are you? And why have you brought me into the forest?" The Summoner replied, "Listen carefully to our situation. When I was in the court, the Bādsvā humiliated me. For that reason I summoned all the tigers to capture you. Now you must marry me and all will be well." Wits about her, Dudbibī replied, "I have one stipulation. In the Tretā Age I was devoted to Rām Nārāyaṇ. After that I lived in Gokul as a cowherdess (*gupini*). In the home of Nanda and Nandini, I always fed [Kṛṣṇa] butter. Assume your four-armed form and show it to me. I promise that if you can do that, I will marry you." Badar instructed her, "Bibī, please do as I request: close your eyes and you will behold that very form." Bibī closed her eyes and experienced a thrill. Casting off his garb as a *phakir*, Badar assumed the form of Lord Rām. He held a bow in his left hand and an arrow in his right, while Lakṣmana held a royal parasol above his head. When the daughter of the Bādsvā beheld this, she was astonished. Then Badar in turn transformed into the *avatār* Kānāī, holding the conch, discus, club, and lotus. He then held a garland of wildflowers and played the flute with Balarām at his side; he stood beneath a *kadamba*[53] tree, revealing himself to be Kṛṣṇa. Rippling with pleasure, Bibī draped a garland over his neck, and the couple solemnized a *gandharva* style marriage of mutual consent.[54] The night passed, and in the morning the sun rose on the happy couple.

The lowly Jaidi sings, meditating on the gem Mānik. Badar's actions will make them both happy, while the princess's mother will be calling out in a panic, "My child, my child!" over and over, her heart trembling with fear.[55]

When the dawn broke through the night, the *kokil* bird[56] sang, and the mother of Dudbibī stirred from the bed. One by one every resident was questioned, but

/ṣ/, so ষুরৎ, /*ṣurat*/; that, in turn, is a common enough scribal misspelling of সুরৎ, /*surat*/, where ষ, /*ṣ*/, is written for স, /*s*/, which means "form, figure, shape, face, countenance," but importantly with its homophone সুরত, /*surata*/, hints at the double entendre of "amorous or sexual pleasure, arousal, intercourse." That arousal is precisely the pitfall about which Āllā warns Badar in heaven before descending. He is smitten with a single glance.

53. The *kadamba* (previously classified as *Nauclea kadamba*, but now *Neolamarkia cadamba*) is a fast-growing fir tree with distinctive orange globular flowers, long associated with Kṛṣṇa, who plays his flute beneath it; it is sometimes called *haripriyā* or "beloved of Hari (Kṛṣṇa)." In the following passage, the *padma* and *kamal* names for lotuses and the *kadamba* appear to be used synonymously by this author.

54. According to *The Laws of Mānu* (3.21–42), the *gandharva* style is one of the eight classical Indic forms of marriage consisting of a consensual agreement where the woman chooses the man, signaled by the exchange of garlands in some private trysting place and requiring the permission of no one else. Citations reach back in to the early *Grihya sūtra* literatures and epics. See Wendy Doniger, trans., *The Laws of Manu*, with an introduction and notes by Wendy Doniger with Brian K. Smith (London: Penguin Books, 1991), 45–47.

55. This line does not scan.

56. *Kokil* is a generic name for black cuckoo, of which there are no fewer than twenty species in

Dudbibī was not in her room or anywhere else in the palace. The Bādsvā lamented, "Oh my, alas, what has happened to my little girl?" [Queen] Dhanbibī slapped her head and rolled around on the ground in grief. The Bādsvā then called his advisors and went to meet them. "Go throughout this land and beyond. Search her out among all peoples." And as soon as they heard his command they dashed in all directions, but nowhere was the precious daughter of the Bādsvā to be found. In each and every town they searched, house to house, but were bewildered to discover not a single trace of her. At this point, the king's minister suggested to the Bādsvā, "You should enter into the forest and search every part of it." When he heard the minister's advice, the king's spirits were raised. They equipped themselves from the stores of the city: Turkish horse carts, hundreds upon hundreds of thousands of elephants assembled, matched with assorted musical tumult, all accompanied by pike-wielding infantry. They lumbered along until they finally entered the forest.

The precious daughter of the king registered the sound of their entry and worried in her heart of hearts. Dudbibī warned, "O Summoner, take heed of the looming shadow. For my sake my mother and father have entered into the forest. Here comes my father with his minister. Tell me quickly what subterfuge I can adopt to distract him!" Badar quickly replied, "Bibī, listen carefully to what I say: We two shall assume the guise of Rām and Sitya."[57] And so Badar became Rām and the Bibī transformed into Sitya on his left, two moons of incomparable beauty rising in the midst of the forest.

When he witnessed this, the Bādsvā contemplated the prospects. "How is it possible that we now see Rām and Sitya in the forest? Speak out, my minister, explain this, for I am unable to fathom it! Where has Dudbibī disappeared? Who could have stolen her away?" At that moment Badar the Summoner spoke. "Close your eyes and you shall see straight away." Heeding this instruction, the Minister and the Bādsvā closed their eyes and the forms of Badar and Dudbibī were suddenly and surprisingly revealed. The Bādsvā queried, "My precious daughter, what is this all about? How, why did you leave the palace and enter the forest?" Dudbibī responded, "Daddy, do you not understand what has just transpired? In birth after birth Badar has been my husband and lord. He arrived at your court in order to marry me, but you not only insulted him publicly, but bound him and threw him in prison. Because of that insult, the Summoner retreated into the forest. He sent tigers to fetch my bed, and here in the forest the two of us joined together in a *gandharva*-style marriage. Consider this and then do what you think is right." The Bādsvā replied, "My precious daughter, listen to my counsel. Marry in great joy and come along with me." When the Bādsvā spoke these special words to the couple, a thrill coursed through Bibī and she returned to her familiar hereditary home. Badar, Dudbibī, and the Bādsvā returned together to their homeland, their joy reflected in the reverberating sounds of the musical instruments at play.

---

the Bangla-speaking world, mostly resident; the male is extremely vocal. Given the context of stealing Dudbibī's bed, there seems to be a vague allusion to the *kokils*' habit of placing their eggs in the nests of other birds, pushing out the original eggs.

57. This scribe's use of the *japhalā* to substitute for a final /ā/ causes *sitya* to be pronounced *sitā*.

Life returned to energize [Dudbibī's mother] Dhanbibi's body, and everyone from the town came to watch the spectacle. A great joy arose as if Rām and Sitya had arrived home in Ẏajaddhya.[58] The Bādsvā then addressed the minister, "Please call the judge (*kāji*) and the *marllā*[59] to perform a proper wedding ceremony as quickly as possible." It was only then that Āllā, sitting in heaven (*bhest*), became aware of it, so he dispatched Hāji Kāji Muhammad (*mahārmmad*).[60] Accompanied by Rahim, Karim, and Sek Phakorān, the judge soon arrived near the city of Dirlli (Delhi). Badar, as *mursid*, sat on a royal divan. All the town's inhabitants thronged around to have a look at the Bādsvā's new son-in-law. With a stentorian tone, the Bādsvā called out, "Minister, minister! Summon the judge quickly to make the wedding of my precious daughter official!" And so the letters of invitation were sent through the realm and beyond. Any number of other Bādsvās came to the city of Dirlli. As they were arriving, the Bādsvā spoke to his wife Dhanbibī: "Waste no time in calling all of the women from all parts of the city!" When she heard this, she interrogated her precious daughter Bibī Dud. "How did your mind come to be smitten, charmed by a *phakir?*" Then the young woman explained in great detail and concluded, "When you examine your heart you know that 'God is singularly great.'"[61] "Listen carefully, my darling child, let me explain. I had planned to arrange your marriage to the son of a Bādsvā, a prince." She consoled her mother, "Listen mother: Āllā, the jewel of virtue, presented him to me."

Eventually Dhanbibī was satisfied and set about making the customary ritual preparations consistent with their social status (*jāti*). After receiving permission from the Bādsvā, the *morllā* was called. Four *morllā*s came, each carrying the *Ketāb Korān*. Opening the *Ketāb Korān*, they performed their calculations and concluded that it was Khodā's action that brought about this union.

The lowly Jaidi sings focused on Mānik, while Badar will pray to behold a son.

. . .

The Dark Lord, Kālā

Listen to the name, the virtues of the Dark Lord
heard in home after home.

58. *Ẏajaddhya* is Ayodhyā, the famous home of Rām and Sītā. This scribe routinely prefaces words beginning in অ, /*a* or *ɔ*/, with the addition of the on-glide য়, /*ẏ*/, interchangeable with homophones জ, /*j*/, and য, /*y*/, producing *ẏajarddha*. This scribe uses the reph /*-r*/ to signal a *japhalā* /*-y*/, to produce *ẏajaddhya*. Because this scribe routinely uses the *japhalā* /*-y*/ with the final geminate consonants to substitute for a final /*ā*/ (n. 27 above), we read *ẏajaddhyā*. So *ẏajaddhyā* > *ajaddhyā* > *aẏaddhyā*, and because the following high vowel turns the inherent vowel /*a* or *ɔ*/ into /*o*/, we end up with the pronunciation of *ayoddhyā*, which is of course *ayodhyā*.

59. The word for *mullah* is spelled three ways: *mollā*, *mallā*, and *marllā* (but pronounced *mollā*).

60. It appears that Hāji and Kāji are titles for Muhammad, spelled predictably here as *mahārmmad*, but understood as *muhammad*.

61. The text reads slightly differently from that noted above (n. 36): *ilāhilelelrllā*, which with the *japhalā* shift produces *ilāhilelelallā*, with one extra syllable that may be a scribal inconsistency but does allow the line to scan.

I shall write Kālā's own name
on the trailing edge of my sari.
Who brought to this land
a moon so dark,
that in dancer's disguise has pilfered
the honor of this virtuous wife?
How inauspicious the moment
I dipped my foot into the Jamunā's waters.
At the foot of the *kadamba*, bent in his careless pose,
he played mischief with his flute.

Phakir Guñjar contemplates his worthless body—
a hollowed out dead tree
whose leaves have dropped off
and floated away.

. . .

As the Bādsvā sat with everyone in the court gathering (*majlis*), the four *mallās* arrived from heaven (*bhest*). The legal affairs were settled under a tree in the midst of a plantain forest in which Badar sat perfectly calm and content on a flayed skin, impervious to everything,[62] while the judge and the *morllā* had him read the *kalmā*.[63] Hāji Gāji Sek Pharid, the theologian, sat down. Submitting themselves before Khodā, each in quick succession disavowed any future divorce and, with eyes cast down, were then bound together by the marriage contract. The Bādsvā formally made over Dudbibī to Badar.

62. These few couplets are obscure. A traditional Bengali wedding marks off a sacred space by setting up plantain trees (often small saplings or even single plantain leaves stuck in mud mounds or pots) on each of the four corners; but one can imagine the wedding could take place in a plantain forest, as is clearly indicated here (*kadalī ban*). I read *māmṛā* [*māmṛā* < *māmlā* < *mokaddamā* < *makaddamā*] as "legal affairs." But *māmṛa* can also be read as *māmṛi*, which indicates a scabrous, dried flesh, or a place where skins are tanned, with the verb *karā*, which would indicate *maṛamaṛi*, the flaying of skin—the flayed skin of a tiger is precisely what *jogīs* and other mendicants use for meditation. The second reading is contextually more difficult to construe and would normally call for the application of the general principle of *lectio difficilior lectio potior*. The image, however, seems to be foreshadowed in the last line of the poem above, the body as dried-up trunk, which here is doubled sitting on the flayed skin. The plantain is often used to designate a woman's thighs, and the plantain forest is a sign of immersion in the sensual world, especially sexual, which was the troubling period for the *nāth jogī* Gopīcānd and other characters in Bangla literature of the period. Badar was warned by Āllā to be wary of that pitfall and here he now is, initially appearing to be impervious to the charms of his bride. For Gopīcānd's adventure, see Bhābanidās, "Gopīcāndrer pāñcālī," in *Gopīcāndrer gān*, ed. Āśutoṣ Bhāṭṭācāryya, 3rd ed. (Kalikātā: Kalikātā Viśvavidyālay, 1965), 273–324. Contextually, however, the king has just ordered that all the necessary legal documents be gotten in order to validate the marriage in the eyes of the court and according to Islamic custom, and in the very next verses the *mullahs* comply. So I have chosen to read the word both ways—were the text more orthographically sound, the decision might be clearer.

63. *Kalmā* is *kalimā;* whether one or all six is not indicated

When the night gave way to morning, the pair were favorably disposed and comfortable with one another. They strung up a screen of cloth and then played among the flowers strewn on the bed. Bibī would hurl flowers at his feet and then steal them back, while the Summoner flung flowers at Bibī's head. And in this way the two consummated their marriage, passing the night with joyful hearts in the pleasures of making love. [The maidservant] Mukil richly adorned Dudbibī's body; she wore with glamour the eight types of ornaments. They passed so many days savoring the joys of making love that Badar had forgotten everything else, totally distracted by this delectable gifted lover in his lap. This sensuous woman stupefied him like the God of Love, Smara, a seductress who shot love arrows from the corners of her eyes.

And so it was that many years passed with no thought of his austerities (*tapisvy*) ever entering Badar's mind until late one night a reminder appeared to him in a dream. Three times he recited, "Ed Āllā, Ed Āllā." [Then he said,] "That I needed to spread the glory of God has not entered my thoughts of late." The Summoner then called for Dudbibī. "I shall go to the city of Caṭṭagāñ to spread word of his greatness (*jahurā*). You must stay here in your beloved's home and I will join you at the end of the next age when you are again young!" Listening to these words Bibī smiled sweetly, but pulled a cloth over her head signaling her distress. "O Summoner, you have gone crazy. You do not know love. You are going to cast off a nubile woman for the sake of spreading the word! If a bee did not drink the sweet nectar of a lotus, understand that that lotus would have bloomed in vain. Consider how the sun lavishes its love from hundreds of thousands of miles away, and sitting in the waters the day-blooming lotus opens up at the sun's touch. For no reason at all, a storm blows the leaves and petals off of flowers in the garden, and similarly, for no reason at all, a voluptuous wife has to live bereft of her lord and husband. Listen, O Summoner, how shall I manage to pass the time, to survive?" Then Bibī called her maidservant Mukil and confessed her troubles.

The lowly Jaidi sings thinking of Mānik—Badar will be gracious upon seeing the boy.

. . .

Hey, stitch fine garlands with consummate care,
as the ruby (*mānik*) is carefully strung in the heart.
All five flowers rest on a single branch, so which flower will bloom?
What twenty-bud [garland] can be stitched with no thread?
How can you sew a garland made of rubies (*mānik*) and gemstones?
Is it possible for a lamp immersed in water to disperse the dark of night?
O how will I recognize that particular flower?

Phakir Guñjar sings, contemplating this hollowed,
dessicated trunk, shedding a single petal that floats away.

. . .

In response to what the Summoner had announced, the maidservant responded, "A woman's youth does not last very long. At twelve she enters the sudden rush of puberty, at fourteen she blossoms, at sixteen she becomes the stuff of poetry. At eighteen she is still someone's sister, but at twenty she is a mother. At twenty-five the beautiful woman enters old age."

The Summoner was incensed by the maidservant's cheeky observations. "My words mark the beginning of my mission to bear witness." After handing over Bibī to the care of Mukil, he now undertook in earnest his mission in the city of Cāṭigāñ.

Though Bibī had wailed and wept and put up a fuss, Badar went away undeterred in pursuit of his ascetic cause. He pulled his mendicant's robes around his neck and wore golden sandals. In his gatherings (*majlis*) lasting some four *daṇḍas*—about an hour and half—he cinched his loincloth around his waist and with great sincerity performed his prayers (*namāj*). He assumed the name of Gaṅgā Badar when he began his preaching (*jahurā*). He left there and went his way in this image, and he soon appeared on the *ghaṭs* of Cāṭṭigāñ. Establishing himself by the edge of the river, the skin of a tiger for a seat, with singular concentration the Summoner recited silently the attributes of God.[64] He then repeated over and again the formulaic *ilāhilelellā*, which made Āllā, sitting in his aerial vehicle (*bimān*), aware of his action. Right then Khodā suffered a fit of sneezing; he coughed violently, expelling a camphor phlegm which he spat into a flower he had picked up in his hand. He concentrated, and suddenly an insect the color of gold emerged from the lotus's stem. Āllā said, "Go, tiny insect, I give you this boon! You will become the prince, son of Dudbibī, with the name Mānik."

Just at that time Dudbibī saw the blood of her period, but she brooded that her groom was not at home. One, two, then three menstruations ensued, then a fourth. Acil, the maidservant, discretely spoke to the Bādsvā, with appropriate bowing and greetings. "[Dudbibī] must go to the river to bathe. The entire distant of one *yojana* will be screened with cloth. Dudbibī wants very much to go to cleanse herself." The Bādsvā was satisfied with what he had been told and he called the minister quickly to arrange the stretching of the cloth.

Meanwhile Āllā, seated in his aerial car (*bimān*), looked deep in his heart of hearts and realized that Dudbibī was set to go to bathe after her period. Khodā spoke, "Flower blossom, cross over the river to the place where the saint (*āuliya*) Badar is practicing his penance (*tapisvy*)." Saying "Go!" he threw the flower into the stream, and it floated on and on till it approached the city of Delhi (*dirlli*).[65]

Badar was sitting on his tigerskin doing his penance (*tapisvy*). Right at that moment, at the command of Āllā, he spotted the flower and lifted it up in his hand. The Summoner was somehow very gratified to see it. He began to muse, 'Dudbibī used to dress beautifully and adorn herself with flowers. But alas, what can I do? You, flower, are inappropriate for my chosen garb. But as I have said to you already, it

64. The text reads *ekmane kare deoān āllāre saṅaran* [< *smaraṇa*], which rather than a simple "remembering" is the silent recitation of the attributes of God in *jikir* consistent with Madāri practice, as noted above (n. 32).

65. At first blush, it appears the narrator has forgotten where Badar is, or there is a missing verse or two, or Badar went to Delhi after Chittagong, or perhaps the narrator meant that he went to Delhi all along; based on usage, I am inclined to see Delhi as the place where heaven is connected to earth, serving as one portal to India, while later in the text it does appear that Badar has only been in Chittagong since departing.

would be beautiful on Dudbibī's outfit.' And mumbling in this manner, he threw the flower back into the stream. "By the graciousness of Āllā, take yourself to the town of Cāṭṭigāñ! I swear by the name of the Creator (*kartā*) that when Bibī picks up a *kadam* flower,[66] it will be this one and no other that goes into her hand!"

Back in that place, Dudbibī went to have her bath, and she was merrily perched on the banks of the river with her maidservant. Someone massaged her body with oil and turmeric, another brought fragrant tamarind fronds and fenugreek to massage her scalp. She was thoroughly enjoying herself playing in the water with Mukil when, at that very moment, a flower floated straight up to her. Bibī said, "Whoever is able to capture that flower will be made beautiful and honorable enough to adorn the house of Khodā." Under the order of Āllā to go to no one else, it was quickly lifted by the hand of Dudbibī. When she looked at the lotus blossom[67] she experienced a bliss, but then sadly remembered that Badar was no longer at home. Dudbibī quickly then returned to her quarters and had herself dressed in her various ornaments and jewelry. Even though it was at the very end of the day, she dressed herself immaculately, and her wavy hair fanned out just like a peacock's spread tail. Around her neck she draped a necklace of coral called a "hundred goddesses," and her face glowed like a full moon. She added more layers of elegant clothes, scented herself with expensive perfume, and chewed forty betel nuts with coquettish delight. Over her breasts she pulled a tight-fitting bodice that dazzled like the glow of a rising sun. Bibī wrapped herself in a diaphanous shawl by the name of *kuṅāṭhuṭi*, twenty-two yards in length but which was so fine that it could be compressed in its entirety in one's fist. When she was finished dressing, the maidservant spoke, "When the husband is not at home, there is no reason to dress up, no reason for this finery. When that woman whose husband is out of the country dresses up in her own home, the flowers groomed by the gardener drop without prompting. When a bee does not come to sip the intoxicating nectar of the blooming lotus, know that that is inauspicious, a woman in her youth wasting without a man. A woman in her youth lies awake for four watches of the night, listlessly passing the time while her husband is in another land." When the maidservant had gone on prattling such profundities, Bibī was suddenly overwhelmed that the son-in-law, her husband, was not home. Now she was beside herself and wept inconsolably. Feeling hurt and deprived, Bibī retired to her private quarters. When she stretched out on her raised bed, she silently muttered three times "Ed Āllā." In her heart she thought over and again of Badar the Summoner, and that lotus flower Bibī pressed hard against her heart.

Cruising in his aerial car, Āllā understood exactly why she did this, so he called out over and over again, "Saytān, Saytān!" At Āllā's divine command Saytān presented himself. "Go quickly and enter into Badar's body!" Receiving this divine order, Saytān wasted no time in going, and in the middle of the night, he entered into the

66. The *kadam* or *kadamba* (*Neolamarkia cadamba*) has a globus head flower, red orange in color, with a diameter of about two inches with a sweet fragrance; as previously noted, it has a long history in Indian culture and is associated with the love play of Rādhā and Kṛṣṇa. The lotus and *kadamba* seem to be interchangeable in this passage, connoting simply "beautiful flower."

67. Lotus is *kamal* (*Nelumbo nucifera*).

body of Badar [to incite him]. In their dreams, the couple looked at one another. In that year, their paths . . . [rest of verse illegible]. Their clothed bodies pressed hard together, their faces were mouth to mouth. In their dreams that night the couple embraced. They kissed, they hugged, and they coupled in sexual intercourse. [First four syllables illegible] . . . was the lotus Bibī held in her hand. The insect crawled out of the lotus stem up her nostril and seated itself in the hundred-pedaled navel lotus to take birth. Mānik had entered Dudbibī's womb; Bibī's sleep was interrupted, and she began to fret. She groped frantically all over the bed, then wailed, "You came to me and then disappeared!" And this is the sad situation that transpired for these two. Then Bibī called out for her maidservant and began to tell her. The maidservant began to lecture her, "You weep for no good reason. What you see in dreams never comes true in reality." And so the night passed, the sun brought the dawn, and the post-menstrual bathing healed Bibī completely.

By the boon of Mānik does poor Jaidi sing: O Mānik, shower mercy on him who narrates this tale.

Mānik began to grow, and Dudbibī was content and comfortable. One, two, three, four, and then five months passed. At six months Dudbibī began to roll around on the ground [from the pains], and when the maidservant finally noticed the telltale signs of her belly, she cried out in alarm. After the seventh and eighth months, all the maidservants worried that when the Summoner learned of it, he would be furious. When nine months had passed, there was much concerned discussion and gossip, so they came to a decision and called Visvakarma there. There was one resourceful, indeed wily servant girl who would instigate a conflict between Āllā and Visāi.[68] "Listen Visvakarma, please construct a body-shaped hollow copper vessel, and I will give you fine garments, ornaments, and fifty gold coins." As soon as he received the commission, Visāi eagerly went his way. In his workshop he stoked the mighty fire of his furnace, refined and cast the copper into a casket, and covered it with a silver lid. Then Visāi forged a golden hinge and bolt. He presented the vessel to the Bibī,[69] who gave him the eight kinds of ornaments and various and sundry other forms of wealth. Visāi took his leave and then departed for his own home.

After the ninth month had been endured, the tenth month had at last arrived.[70] As Mānik lay curled comfortably in the womb, he decided, 'I will not make it difficult for mother Dudbibī to give birth.' The day for delivery finally arrived, and right on time the young Emissary was born with a blooming of flowers and fruits. He did not cry, he did not throw an arm-waving tantrum, he remained deathly still—he appeared to be stillborn.

Meanwhile the young serving girl had floated the copper vessel on the river.

I will sing of the virtues of Mānik, reflecting on them in my heart. May Badar and his assembly shower mercy on our heads.

68. Visāi is Visvakarmma. The text indicates conflict, but the action suggests collusion in the saving of Mānik. The manuscript is incomplete, so that mystery will remain unresolved.

69. This Bibī is the maidservant, not Dudbibī; the maidservants were apparently hiding Dudbibī's pregnancy from her parents and planned to take remedial measures.

70. See chap. 1, n. 5.

"Where will I find another miserable wretch like me with a stillborn baby?" Bibī had begun to weep uncontrollably, striking her head with her fists. "Where will I ever see again that golden color so beautiful? My Mānik, the young Emissary, was floated on the river's waters." Experiencing insufferable pain, Dudbibī cried out in agony.

In his copper casket, the Emissary Mānik floated away on the waters. But Āllā, ensconced in his cruising aerial car (*bimān*), caught sight of it. He Himself sat aboard the casket as the helmsman, and it sailed on as if it were a thirty-two oared ocean-going galley. In this way did Mānik the Emissary head to the settlement of Dip.[71] After twenty-one days, the boat managed to reach shore. There lived a gardener named Madu, and his garden was perched on the banks above the river. His garden had no blooming flowers because the land was completely parched—it had been twelve years since it had produced fresh young buds. It was nighttime when the young Emissary first touched the banks, and instantly all manner of flowers in a rush of wild colors miraculously burst forth. When it was morning, the cowherds were headed to graze the cows when they were unsettled by the fragrance of the masses of flowers. There were white Arabian jasmines, royal jasmines, milkwoods, and oodles of fragrant tuberoses; there were blossoms of coral jasmine and other plants like it, there was Spanish jasmine and the like. There was jungle flame, mahogany, magnolia, screwpine, amaranth, and cobra's saffron. Sacred basil was spread across the place and everywhere sprouted lotuses.[72] The cowherds plucked various colors and types of flowers, then in the pandemonium they all yelled to the gardener Madu. When he heard the commotion, the gardener and his wife hurried out: "Your flower

71. An alternate reading for *dip sahar* would be "a city on an island" with *dip* < *dvīp* (island); but the way cities have been designated throughout the text, e.g., *dirlli sahar*, suggests that *dip* is the name of the city.

72. Taken in order, Arabian jasmine is the name in the United States; *mallikā* (*Jasminum sambac*) has small white flowers, very fragrant. Royal jasmine, *malatī* (*Jasminum grandiflora*) is one of the most common forms of jasmine in South Asia. The designation *ṭagar* is milkwood, but can be of the pinwheel or crêpe jasmine variety. Tuberose is *gandharāj* (*Polianthis tuberosa*); it has long stalks and, as the name suggests, tube-like flowers that are extremely fragrant. Coral jasmine or night-blooming jasmine, *śiuli* (*Nyctanthes arbortristis*), has five- to eight-petaled white flowers, each with a distinctive orange red center; it blooms in the autumn. I read *eiuli śiuli* as "coral jasmine and plants like it," since *eiuli* appears to be only a reduplicative form and not a specific flower designation. Spanish jasmine, *jāti*, is another version of royal jasmine (*Jasminum grandiflora*) with the synonym of *cambelī*. Likewise, another jasmine, *juti*, is *jūthī*/*ẏūthī*, most likely from *jūhī* (*Jasminum auriculatum*), but it is extremely difficult to differentiate from Spanish jasmine, so the pair *jāti juti* can also be read as a reduplicative form which elicits the same meaning, "Spanish jasmine and the like." Jungle flame or jungle geranium, *raṅgan* (*Ixora coccinea*), has dense rounded clusters of scarlet flowers. Mahogany is *piyāṅg* (< *priyāṅg*) (*aglaia Roxburghiana*). Magnolia is *cāñpā* (*Michelia campaka*), with its distinctive yellow and white flower. Screwpine is *ketuki* (< *ketakī*) (*Pandanus tectorius*). Amaranth is *parijātā* (*Amaranthus caudatus*) with its distinctive red or magenta drooping flowers; the authorities, however, are not in agreement, some indicating it is the coral tree of paradise (*Erythrina fulgens*), which also bears very similar vividly red, small flower clusters. Cobra's saffron or Indian rose chestnut is *nāgeśvar* (also *nāg keśar*) (*Mesua nagassarium*), an enormous tree up to thirty meters tall and two meters in diameter with reddish bark and flowers with four white petals and reddish-orange stamens. Sacred basil is *tulsi* (*Occimum tenuiflorum*). Lotus is *śatadal* (*Nelumbo nucifera*), not indicating whether day- or night-blooming.

gardens have all miraculously bloomed!" When Madu the gardener heard this from the mouths of the ruffians, the couple raced up to the flower gardens to see for themselves. They systematically scrutinized the gardens, working in opposite directions. The bees buzzed noisily in one particular place, and they searched and searched but could find nothing, then suddenly Madhusudan spotted something lodged in the tall marsh grass. When the gardener noticed the copper casket, it piqued his curiosity, and he blurted, "Oh me, oh my, let's waste no time in hauling this away!" Thinking it might be rubies (*mānik*) and other gemstones, they lugged it home. Once inside the house, they opened the lid and gazed, mesmerized—they were dumbfounded. Their eyes were riveted to the beautiful baby Mānik, a ruby indeed. Then they began to hatch a plan, considering all the angles.

I, lowly and poor Jayarddhi, sing with my mind fixed on Mānik—may he shower blessings on him who narrates.

When they saw the baby boy, they were filled with delight, for the god Bidhātā, Fate, had made them both infertile. The gardener said, "Mālini my dear, let me tell you what you should do. Bind a water bag around your stomach and make a point of going specifically to the house of Sẽgatini. They will surely feed you the ceremonial *sādh* dinner.[73] Then, as soon as you can, return home. Afterward that, I will go to the home of the midwife Hirā." Without wasting time, the Mālini tied a bag of water around her waist; she visited her friend's house and ate the *sādh* meal. She crooned with genuine affection; then she quickly asked the question, "Friend, my dear friend, how many days have passed?" "Nine months have elapsed and now the tenth month has arrived." She continued, "I had had this wish to visit you, my friend, to have my *sādh* meal." Saying "May you be well! May you experience good!" they proffered their blessings. They fed her the ceremonial foods and presented her with gifts. The woman took her leave and hurried back to her own home.

[She continued the act:] "Aiee, the child, I'm dying from the pain, Gardener, feel my head!" The gardener dutifully called the neighbors as his wife continued her complaints, "Umh, umh, I'm dying. Quick, call Hirya [the midwife]." The gardener then sent for Hirya, with a feeling of sheer delight. As soon as Hirya heard, she came running as quickly as an old woman could. In the thick dark of night no one could see clearly as Mānik lay among the fruits and flowers on the floor, crying.

Mānik descended (yavatirnya) *in the home of the gardener Madu. May the Hindus chant "Hari, Hari!" for this ranking official among those devoted servants of God* (mamin). *By the boon of Mānik does the poor and lowly Jayaraddhi sing: May He direct his grace to him who narrates.*

So it was in this way that Mānik began to grow up. One, two, three, four, five days passed, and on the fifth day, oil was given away and the customary rituals were

73. The *sādh* dinner is a ceremonial occasion, usually served by relatives or close friends anywhere from the seventh to late in the ninth month of pregnancy (based on the traditional ten-month gestation); today it includes special dishes, such as cooked fish head, fried banana, and a bitter curry, completed by rice pudding. The food is followed by a showering of gifts, the whole event very much like a baby shower.

performed.[74] On the sixth day the gardener performed the *seṭerā* ritual to propitiate the Goddess Ṣaṣṭhī, while on the sixth day the gardener's wife performed the formal *pūjā* worship to her.[75] And so Mānik, full of virtues, made it through to the seventh day. On the eighth day, eight cowries and eight fried cakes were given away, and these were accompanied by gifts of silver and gold. On the ninth day the mothers of both the gardeners performed the *nattā* ritual for the boy's welfare.[76] On the twenty-first day, another Ṣaṣṭhī *pūjā* was performed with great thrill and excitement: [they offered] twenty-one heaps of parched rice and twenty-one bowls of milk. To look on the face of their son gave them untold pleasure. One, two, three months passed, then through four and five; in the sixth month he was ritually fed solid food.[77] In this way did Mānik start to grow.

One, two, three years, then the fourth came and went. Five, six, seven, and then eight years did Mānik manifest his glory. Then the ninth and tenth years passed until Badar had performed his austerities (*tapisvy*) for a full twelve years. Badar performed those austerities (*tapisvy*) in the name of Āllā, then finally one day [he remembered] the lady Dudbibī and decided to go home. Memories of his beloved flooded his mind and his heart became unsettled, so he broke off his austerities (*tapisvy*) and returned to his home place. He had golden sandals on his feet, and he carried a long staff. Know that he wasted little time as headed for the town of the Ṣultān Rājā. The rooms of the gardener were close by the seat of the Bādsā, and being weary, he took a room there and settled down for a short rest. Meanwhile Dudbibī had gone to the lake, where she caught sight of the *phakir*. She immediately inquired of the gardener's wife. "Listen carefully, madame gardener, please take this seriously. Tell me truthfully, where did that *phakir* come from?" The gardener's wife replied, "Bibī, I have no idea. Why not go and ask the Summoner yourself?"

The extraordinary beauty of the Summoner filled Bibī's vision, "Listen O Summoner, hear me!" as she called him repeatedly. Badar replied, "Beautiful woman, hear my story; listen carefully. For these last twelve years I have been performing austerities (*tapasvi*) on behalf of Āllā. On account of my beloved wife, my . . . [damaged MS ends].

. . .

74. Commonly on the fifth day the parturition room is ritually cleansed, local women bring gifts of grain and money, sweets are distributed, and the barber and midwife are paid. The details here are scanty, so the oil may be a substitute for the gifts by local women. Neither the word *pācuṭe* or any of its possible variants appears in any of the dictionaries consulted.

75. Ṣaṣṭhī is the goddess of child bearing and rearing, and on the sixth day she is said to write the fortune of the child on its head. Monthly *vrats* or domestic ritual vows are also performed to maintain her protection. For translations of the *vrats* of Ṣaṣṭhī, see Tony K. Stewart, trans., "The Goddess Ṣaṣṭhī Protects Children," in *The Religions of India in Practice*, ed. Donald S. Lopez (Princeton: Princeton University Press, 1995), 352–66; see also June McDaniel, *Making Virtuous Daughters and Wives: An Introduction to Women's Brata Rituals in Bengali Folk Religion* (Albany: State University of New York Press, 2003), 39–84.

76. This ceremony is to celebrate the birth of a son (i.e., etymologically, a grandson; < *naptya*).

77. This ritual, normally called *annaprāśan*, the "offering of first rice," is simply called here *bhojan*, or "eating."

2.4 EXPLORING THE ROMANCE OF MĀNIK PĪR'S BIRTH

Following Northrop Frye's characterizations, the short tale of Badar Pīr found in the opening to Jaidi's *Mānikpīrer jahurānāmā* contains many of the key essential, and just as many minor, elements of the structure of romance, though the story does not take us through the entire life of Badar Pīr on earth. Other manuscripts telling the exploits of Mānik Pīr suggest that the point reached in our example is very close to the end of Badar's assigned role as popularly conceived. Frye argues that to characterize a narrative as romance is really to recognize its special mental landscape, a contrast between the world's heroes and villains. Typical of this perspective is the axial orientation of the idyllic world above, a world of happiness, security, peace, innocence, a domain aligned with spring and summer, with flowers and sunshine, contrasted with the world below, a painful landscape of separation, loneliness, humiliation, a world of darkness.[78] This binary functions as a constant contextual frame for the action. In the opening to this tale, Badar Pīr is summoned by Āllā to his court within heaven and commissioned to descend to earth to prepare the way for the arrival of Mānik Pīr by summoning people to recognize and accept the glory and sovereignty of Āllā, about which they have been slack. The movement from the idyllic world of heaven to the less-than-ideal world of humans is the first step in this descent, a meandering journey that will actually take several stages.

When he comes to earth, Badar initially knows fully well who he is and what he is about, but he is warned of the pitfalls of sensuality, the attraction of women, about whom he is admittedly ignorant. This warning from Āllā functions as an indirect curse. Curses operate analogously to vows in the way their damning power is directly proportional to the moral purity of the offended party, impelling action and event. Here Āllā's warning foreshadows the ever-devoted Badar's descent into the sensual realm, a realm that replaces clarity of vision and mission with illusion and loss of memory, but an experience necessary to the larger need of effecting Mānik's birth. Early on, Badar's boldness with respect to the Gaṅgā gets him momentarily in trouble. A short while later the offense he takes at the Bādsvā's rudeness leads him to escape into the jungle, that is, away from the ordered world of culture into the wilds of nature. True to Frye's depictions, Badar enjoys society with animals,[79] specifically the tigers, who jump at his wizard-like command. While he does not resort to physical violence, he does perpetrate a different kind of violence when he orders the tigers to steal the Bādsvā's daughter as she sleeps innocently on her royal bed.[80] The tigers' potential for violence is accentuated by the

78. Frye, *Secular Scripture,* 53.

79. Frye, 115.

80. This is a common trope that can be traced at least as far back as the story of Qamar al-Zamān; see Ulrich Marzolph and Richard van Leeuwen, with Hassan Wassouf, "Qamar al-Zamân and Budûr,"

comic relief they provide in their whining complaints about what a tough life they live as their would-be victims retaliate, striking at their genitalia, and so forth (one can imagine how this would go over on stage, as this piece was likely performed).

The real loss of identity for Badar that comes with this descent[81]—which may be better understood in terms of his loss of mission—takes hold when he is smitten the moment he sets his eyes on Dudbibī. That infatuation will provide the biggest test of his mettle. In Frye's structure, entry into the forest is dreamlike, and the entering takes on an erotic quality so that the surrounding forest becomes itself a sexual personality.[82] Badar Pīr's forest soon gives way to a plantain forest that results in marriage, and as previously noted, the plantain forest is synonymous with infatuation with the sensual, especially the sexual. Even the marriage comes in two stages, the first in the forest in *gandharva* style when Dudbibī consents to the tryst, taking the decision away from Badar who wants it, but will not force it, choosing rather to reveal to her the inevitability of it based on her correlative confirmation of inevitability should he meet the test of displaying his forms as Rām, Nārāyaṇ, and Viṣṇu. Then, after their retrieval by Dudbibī's father, their liaison is subsequently made official according to Islamic custom and in the eyes of the law and God, with the blessings of the king and queen. This now-official marriage and entry into the world of royals inducts Badar into the throes of domestic obligation, farther and farther away from his function as a *pīr* performing a mission directed from Āllā Himself, yet ironically his lapse into sensuality serves God's plan. That a divinity often directs or occasionally impels the action is not at all atypical in this type of tale, according to Frye[83]—but I would hasten to add that this kind of intervention is so frequent that the gods and demigods should be seen as simply active characters rather than the force behind the deus ex machina that populates Western fictions as an extraordinary and timely one-off event.

Frye notes that in the narratives of romance the loss of identity—forgetting who you are and why you are there—is often accompanied by, or the result of, gender or identity confusions.[84] In Badar and Dudbibī's story there is no direct gender confusion, but there is illusion regarding identity when Badar shows Dudbibī his multi-armed forms of Nārāyaṇ, and then the two together show themselves to be

in *The Arabian Nights Encyclopedia,* 2 vols. (Santa Barbara: ABC Clio, 2004), 1:341–45. See also the introduction to Mīr Sayyid Manjhan Shattārī Rājgīrī, *Madhumālatī: An Indian Sufi Romance,* translated with an introduction and notes by Aditya Behl and Simon Weightman, with Shyam Manohar Pandey, Oxford World's Classics (New York: Oxford University Press, 2000), xxxi–xxxii, cited as Story 167 in Richard F. Burton, trans., *A Plain and Literal Translation of the Arabian Nights Entertainments, Now Entitled the Book of the Thousand Nights and a Night,* 4 vols. (London: Kama Shastra Society, 1885–86), 3:212–348, 4:1–29.

81. Frye, *Secular Scripture,* 129.

82. Frye, 104.

83. Frye, 107–8.

84. Frye, 105–6.

Rām and Sītā when her father arrives. Dudbibī does not recognize Badar until he has her close her eyes to see the truth, the truth in some kind of undefined apparitional way that points to the primacy of the heart in determining such matters, rather than outward appearances. Similarly, the Badshah does not recognize Badar or his own daughter until Badar has him close his eyes to see the truth, an inversion of the process Badar uses to reveal himself to Dudbibī: the king, with eyes wide open, sees Sītā and Rām, who are visible only in the mind's eye of Dudbibī and Badar. This murky set of revelations in this apparent subterfuge both discloses identities and at the same time confuses and conflates, exhibiting a kind of cunning that ameliorates a potentially disastrous encounter with both Dudbibī and the Bādsvā. The first revelation to Dudbibī allows Badar to avoid violence; the second revelation to the Badshah averts the latter's likely violence.

Dudbibī similarly adheres to the typical pattern of heroines. She is high born, a princess, who is virginal and chaste, that virginity one of the primary concerns of the upper echelons of society.[85] Once married to Badar she remains faithful, that fidelity being the primary currency of the romantic heroine. As Wendy Doniger has noted in comparing Damayantī to Penelope, the issue in these types of tales is "his identity and her fidelity, the two qualities that are implicitly equated and essentialized: where he must prove who he is, she must prove that she is his."[86] This dual expectation is part of the currency of romance and no less so here. Though Dudbibī seems to acquiesce rather quickly to the circumstances of her kidnapping—not only by agreeing to marry Badar, but actively choosing him as her mate—that quick consent actually confirms the true extent of her fidelity, which stretches over æons: in the Tretā Age when she was Sītā with Rām, in the Dvāpara Age when she was a *gopī* with Kṛṣṇa (though the text does not identify her explicitly as Rādhā, it only implies it by analogy with Sītā—perhaps reflecting the author's knowledge of Rādhā's status as unmarried in most retellings), and now in the Kali Age where she has been reunited, this time with Badar Pīr as her spouse. She is not only faithful, she has maintained a serial fidelity that speaks of karmic rebirth. How Dudbibī's fidelity is proved after getting pregnant, however, is never revealed. Significantly, the knowledge appears to be kept from her parents by the active intervention of the maidservants, though it is not explicitly spelled out. Those maidservants are no doubt devoted to Dudbibī, but equally watchful of their own well-being, as the actions of the one devious maidservant suggest. The audience, of course, knows how Dudbibī got pregnant, so no explanation is neces-

85. Frye notes that virginity signals that "she is not a slave," which would resonate in the Indian context; Frye, *Secular Scripture*, 73.

86. Wendy Doniger, *Splitting the Difference: Gender and Myth in Ancient Greece and India* (Chicago: University of Chicago Press, 1999), 167; this passage is also quoted in Alf Hiltebeitel, "Listening to *Nala* and Damayantī," in Hiltebeitel, *Rethinking the Mahābhārata: A Reader's Guide to the Education of the Dharma King* (Chicago: University of Chicago Press, 2001), 222 and n. 18.

sary. Indeed, that subterfuge by which the maidservants disguise her pregnancy makes possible the removal of the child Mānik to safer grounds for, no doubt, the Bādsvā would have taken drastic steps to protect his and his kingdom's honor—a variation of the classic royal threat to the birth of the hero.

Badar Pīr's birth (that is, his descent from heaven) hardly conforms to the myth of the birth of the hero, as Rank and others have outlined it, but his son Mānik's does, with some distinctively South Asian twists.[87] His mother, Dudbibī, is of royal stature, a princess, impregnated directly by Āllā's intervention when, by producing camphor phlegm, he impregnates the lotus flower, a standard symbol for both the vulva and the womb, which in turn generates an insect. The insect in turn impregnates Dudbibī through her nostril, thereby protecting her erstwhile virginity (though presumably she had already consummated her marriage), virginity here really suggesting her fidelity—she did not have sexual relations with a man. The impregnation, however, does miraculously flow through Badar when he intercepts the flower, speaks directly into it—invoking the long-standing image of the *guru* initiating the student through the overtly sexual whispering of the seed syllable *mantra* (the tongue as phallus) into the ear (as vulva)—and through the creative and coercive delivery of a command in the name of Āllā, sends it on its way with instruction to fall only into the hands of Dudbibī. It is insemination by relay: semen as phlegm, into a flower womb, which bears an insect and is again inseminated by the word, the insect then entering the nasal cavity as vulva, and seating itself in the hundred-petaled lotus of her yogic interior landscape. Mānik's paternity is as opaque as Badar's and Dudbibī's identities in the forest.

Mānik's miraculous conception—miraculous because Badar has been gone many months, as Dudbibī's multiple periods attest—results in a birth typical of heroic figures all over South Asia: the newborn is sentient in the womb, decides to appear without fuss, and makes not even a single sound after he is dropped, his mother mistaking that silence for stillbirth. That in turn plays directly into the hands of the maidservant who, appearing to be protecting her mistress or possibly simply being mischievous, secretes the baby away and deposits it into the copper vessel and floats it on the river, the vessel corresponding to Rank's and Frye's basket or boat[88]—but the text seems to suggest that her deviousness lies in enlisting Viśvakarma to do her bidding, which would seem initially to derail the divine plan for Mānik by removing him from the royal household. Certainly the Bādsvā would have made her and her compatriots pay for their deception as much as Dudbibī, so the lowborn maidservant becomes Mānik's and Dudbibī's accomplice, looking after everyone's best interest, regardless of apparent ambiguous intention. Āllā intervenes, and Mānik reaches a safe haven. The earth, which

87. Otto Rank, *The Myth of the Birth of the Hero: A Psychological Interpretation of Mythology*, trans. F. Robbins and Smith Ely Jelliffe (New York: Robert Brunner, 1952).

88. Frye makes this explicit; *Secular Scripture*, 148. Rank illustrates this trope throughout his text.

had not remarked Mānik's birth with any special omens, miraculously blossoms fully when he reaches his new home—his second birth—where he is raised by the low-status gardener Madu and his wife. Curiously, in the signature line or *bhanitā* of the section narrating the gardeners' subterfuge of the second birth, the author uses the term *yavatirnya* (from *avatār*, descent) to describe Mānik's coming down to earth. Since he was already descended in his birth to Dudbibī, we might surmise that the term is not being used in quite the same technical way as the *vaiṣṇav* notion of theophany, but more as appearance. Of course, the hero being high-born but then cast into the wilderness to be raised by simpler peasants is one of Rank's most common hero birth motifs and typical in romance literatures worldwide. The gardener and his wife raise him for twelve years—to the age of puberty—when his erstwhile proxy "father" Badar Pīr returns to take a room in the same house. And here the manuscript of Jaidi's *Mānikpīrer jahurānāmā* breaks off.

The predicament of Dudbibī's pregnancy is the result of the hero Badar's return to his mission. Frye observes that once the hero recognizes the extremes of his alienation and his divorce from what is good and proper, his struggle to make the world right signals the ascent.[89] After indulging in the sensual benefits of marriage, Badar wakes up to his forgotten mission, reaffirms his resolve, and departs, abandoning his young wife—but was not his matrimonial bond to Dudbibī good and proper? Though Dudbibī is abandoned and left to her own devices to manage the pregnancy, the trajectory of the narrative of this incomplete story points to a reunion that will demonstrate Dudbibī's fidelity to Badar, thus successfully fulfilling her function as heroine. On the surface, it appears that Badar may have interrupted the original plan—he was specifically sent by Āllā to father Mānik—but in fact his action allowed God himself to intervene in a way that removed the carnality of the impregnation and guaranteed Mānik's extraordinary status as a friend of God, resolving the tension between the asceticism requisite for Badar's religious calling and his erotic function as progenitor of the savior of the Kali Age.[90]

89. Frye, 129–33.

90. Wendy Doniger has traced this now well-known ascetic-erotic trope through the range of Hindu and other mythologies, starting with Śiva; see Wendy Doniger (O'Flaherty), *Asceticism and Eroticism in the Mythology of Śiva* (New York: Oxford University Press, 1973), and Doniger, *Śiva: The Erotic Ascetic* (New York: Oxford University Press, 1981).

3

Subjunctive Explorations

The Parodic Work of Pīr Kathā

Gāji and Kālu landed up on the shore of the ocean,
but there was no boat moored there, not even a dinghy.
The two boys sat on the beach pondering their plight.
Together they prayed to resolve their problem:
"Please show your mercy to us, O Stainless Nirañjan!"
In response to Gāji's call, a disembodied voice called out:
"Throw into the ocean that staff you hold in your hand!
It will magically mutate into a boat,
and by my grace will you be guided across."
Heeding these miraculous words from the sky,
Gāji immediately hurled his staff into the ocean
while meditating on the Stainless Nirañjan.
The staff that was cast immediately morphed into a boat.
Giddy with satisfaction, the two brothers climbed in.
They pushed off and floated out into the deep waters.
The pair crossed from one region to the next, where
they finally beached on an island in the Sundarban forest.
Śāhā then called all of the tigers scattered
through the mangrove swamps of the Sundarban.
They came, and each and every one made obeisance,
dropping in submission before the person of Gāji.

—SĀYEB MUNSĪ ĀBDUL OHĀB, *GĀJI KĀLU O CĀMPĀVATĪ KANYĀR PUNTHI*

3.1. NARRATIVE STRATEGIES IN FICTIONAL HAGIOGRAPHY

We can affirm from the unabridged translation in the last chapter that the *Mānikpīrer jahurānāmā* of Jaidi conforms to the generally accepted structure of romance, even in the truncated form of the manuscript which leads up to but does not include the life of Mānik Pīr, its proper subject. As a first step, the rather mechanistic catalogue of motifs is useful to confirm the narrative's participation in the semantics of the genre as outlined by Jameson.[1] It does not, however, address how the story might be expected to execute its mission. To help us move from mode to structure, which points to authorial strategy, Frye instructively contrasts realism with romance: "In realism the attempt is to keep the action horizontal, using a technique of causality in which the characters are prior to the plot—'given these characters, what will happen?' Romance is more 'sensational,' moving from one discontinuous episode to another, describing what happens to the characters 'externally.' The logic of realism is 'hence' and the logic of romance is 'and then.'"[2]

Taken as a whole, Jaidi's tale conforms to the "and then" structure of romance as we meander with Badar Pīr across Bengal and parts of North India, not to mention heaven. But the "and then" strategy is much more pronounced in the considerably longer story of Satya Pīr penned by Kṛṣṇahari Dās, the *Baḍa satya pīr o sandhyāvatī kanyār punthi* with which we started the first chapter. The text presents discrete episodes, which are at best only loosely connected, and which are sufficiently self-contained that—with one exception, the transition from the story of the prostitute to that of Jasmanta the merchant (as we shall see below in chapter 6)—they could be presented in just about any order, especially those that constitute the second half of the book. The only transitions are statements on the order of "*And then* Satya Pīr went to see Main Gidāl," literally articulating the logic of the genre. Much of the changing geographic locale is fictional, though not all, so tracing the arc of his movement does not plot a particularly recognizable passage through contiguous space or measured time; rather, it is his movement itself that establishes the temporality that signals the ongoing segments of his mission, each ordeal completed only to be displaced by yet another circumstance in need of intervention, which by the end of the book is left hanging, incomplete.

The early episodes that take place in Mālañcā, whose king Satya Pīr has been explicitly sent down to chastise, occupy more than half of the book; then we see Satya Pīr interacting with and instructing a number of different figures across this fictional Bengali landscape. Structurally, as the number of episodes multiplies—there are ten altogether in the second section—the narratives become increasingly

1. Frederic Jameson, "Magical Narratives: Romance as Genre," *New Literary History* 7, no. 1 (Autumn 1975): 136–37.

2. Frye, *Secular Scripture*, 47.

attenuated, condensing the formula of confrontation and resolution in a manner that suggests the concept of "and so on and so forth"; once the formula is established, it is left to the receiver of the text to fill in the gaps, which by that time are nearly completely predictable. Not surprisingly, this massive text has no concluding episode that closes out Satya Pīr's work on earth. In his last recorded encounter, his intervention with king Main Gidāl, he successfully stops the ruler from sacrificing young boys to the goddess Kālī. The king has had a dramatic change of heart—the details of how this came about are not recorded—and he recognizes the sanctity of Satya Pīr, proffers his favored offering of *sinni*, and, says the text, remains true to this new morality for as long as he lives. In the last lines, the author writes: "The episode of Gidāl has come to a close. May Satya Nārāyaṇ be merciful to all who can taste its beauty. May those who have listened be rescued by their own changed virtues. This book has finally come to an end, composed through the strenuous efforts of Kṛṣṇahari Dās."[3] This open-ended finale does not provide closure, subtly suggesting that Satya Pīr continues his work in the Kali Age and that there are more stories to be told.

Jameson argues persuasively that both the *semantic mode* and the *syntactical structure* combine to reveal the work of romance, which will require mediation by some magical element,[4] and magical elements abound, often launching each episode in a long succession. Each exhibition of fantastic acts, sometimes in a cluster, resolves conflict and settles the point, which is always some variation of the greatness of God, Āllā, and the power of the friends of God, peppered with quick lessons in morality that connect social-class-specific concerns to a larger, universal ethic. Barbara Fuchs characterizes the succession of these episodic events in the syntactical structure as the *segmented narrative*, wherein each plot is interrupted to advance the others,[5] a strategy that is aptly demonstrated in Badar Pīr's adventures, as translated in the preceding chapter. In Fuchs's terms, this displacement of one narrative by the next, the episodic structure becomes "a textual template for productive longing" which delays resolution or consummation, the delay itself paradoxically producing the text.[6] Each new undertaking is interrupted, redirecting the protagonist's action to another task. In Jaidi's *Mānikpīrer jahurānāmā*, Badar is sent to prepare the way for Mānik, but gets caught up in his preaching. He starts to build a *masjid*, but leaves it unfinished when stalled by God, so he installs another *pīr* to establish a *dargā* there. He marries the princess who will be the mother of Mānik, but fails to impregnate her before heading into the wild to practice his austerities. Then, sometime after forfeiting his celibacy to her in a

3. Kṛṣṇahari Dās, *Baḍa satya pīr o sandhyāvatī kanyār punthi*, 220.

4. Jameson, "Magical Narratives," 137–42.

5. Barbara Fuchs, *Romance* (New York: Routledge, 2004), 57–58.

6. It is precisely the ability of this episodic structure to expand or contract to fit the performance or needs of any particular telling that makes the genre so appealing to performers and the audience.

dream, he interrupts his physical austerities and heads back home—and the rest we can only imagine, since the manuscript breaks off.

Though we cannot follow Badar's tale any further from the manuscript at hand, there is another manuscript that starts about where Jaidi's text ends, with a slight modification to the identity of the characters. In Munsī Mohāmmad Pijiruddīn's *Mānik pīr kecchā*,[7] Badar is not the father of Mānik, but his foster father, the position of Madu the gardener in Jaidi's narrative. Badar is Badarjinda Śāh, suggestive of high religious status, but actually a merchant, who finds Mānik and takes him home to his wife, Churāt Bībī. Soon after Mānik's arrival, Badarjinda Śāh goes off on a trading venture and returns only after twelve years. He finds a young man sleeping in the same house with his wife and predictably is outraged at being the cuckold. Without inquiring, and ignoring all attempts by his wife and son to explain, he bundles Mānik into a large chest, bolts the lid, and sets it ablaze, where it burns for three days. By the intervention of Jibril, sent by Āllā to protect Mānik, the young man is kept safe, steps out of the chest, respectfully but forcefully chastises his foster father for his irrationally unjust treatment, and leaves home to begin his own set of heroic adventures as a *jindā pīr* to do the work of God. The reader is made to understand that Mānik, having emerged unscathed from these trials, is now prepared to undertake his mission.[8] The trials of this preparatory period leading to departure can take many forms, but it is also not unusual for these tests to be formulaic, though their resolution may be improvised differently.[9]

7. Munsī Mohāmmad Pijiruddīn, *Mānik pīr kecchā* (Kalikātā: Gāosiya Lāibrerī, n.d. [ca. 1872?]; see Tony K. Stewart, trans., "The Tales of Mānik Pīr: Protector of Cows in Bengal," in *Tales of God's Friends: Islamic Hagiography in Translation*, ed. by John Renard (Berkeley: University of California Press, 2009), 312–32; see also a summary in Dineshchandra Sen, *The Folk-Literature of Bengal* (Calcutta: Calcutta University Press, 1920), 113–24.

8. A recent high-end comic book version of the birth of Mānik follows the same story line as Pijiruddin's *Mānik pīr kecchā;* see Saswat Ghosh, comp., "The Birth of Manik Pir," in *Folk Tales from India: The Sunderbans*, vol. 1, with illustrations by Dipankar Bhattacharya (New Delhi: Vivalok Comics, 2003), 7–11. The text also includes another story similar to one from Pijiruddīn's tale, "Kinu Ghosh and Manik Pir," 12–15.

9. While Mānik Pīr is widely recognized by name, other manuscripts and print editions of his stories are not easily found. Sen summarized the story of Dukhe/Dukhī/Dukhīya in Phakīr Mahammad's *Mānik pīrer gīt;* see Sukumār Sen, *Islāmi bāṃlā sāhitya*, 62–70. Syed Jamil Ahmed has given an English summary and an insightful reading as a tale of subaltern resistance, following Scott; see Ahmed, "Manik Pir as a Subaltern Trickster: Grandiloquent Tales of Extra-Scriptural Imagination," *Depart Magazine*, 9th issue, accessed December 2, 2018, at www.departmag.com/index.php/en/detail/189/Grandiloquent-tales-of-extra-scriptural-Imagination. Beyond a transcription of an excerpt regarding Mānik's skill as a veterinarian in Girīndranāth Dās's reference work, I was unable to locate the *Mānik pīr gān* of Satyen Rāy, though I translated that one passage in Stewart, "The Tales of Mānik Pīr," 314; see Girīndranāth Dās, *Bāṃlā pīr sāhityer kathā*, 1st ed., 418. Roy has provided a summary of another wonderful tale of Mānik and Īsā (= Jesus) who kill a boy for his liver to resurrect another young boy, then go and resurrect the liver donor—it is from a manuscript in the Jaynagar Manuscript Library by Shaikh Hābil titled *Mānik pīrer gān*; see Roy, *Islamic Syncretistic Tradition in Bengal*, 245–48.

While romances in any language are going to have culturally relevant obstacles, the array of challenges fall into recognizable sets that have shaped our understanding of the Quest in hero stories.[10] We can illustrate this with another of the *pīr kathās* (which we shall examine in more detail below) through the perilous trials in the opening sections of the story of Gāji, his brother Kālu, and the maiden Cāmpāvatī. The tale closely mirrors Mānik's own experience: Gāji has decided to begin his mission as a *pīr*, so he informs his father that he is abdicating his future kingship. His father, the king Sekander, is furious and refuses to grant permission to leave. We take up the story when Gāji is twelve years old, as told in *Gāji kalu o cāmpāvatī kanyār puthi* by Abdul Ohāb (Wahab).[11]

Śāhā Sekandar sent for Gājī and spoke to him. "I want you to rule, my child, to sit on the throne in court. To see you deliberate and judge affairs would fill my eyes with tears of joy." Gāji replied, "Listen carefully to what I have to say, dear father. I have no desire whatsoever to rule."

When he heard this, Sekandar Śāhā rebuked him in anger, "Why else were you born on this earth, you unworthy, disobedient son?" to which Gājī replied, "Listen father, please pay attention as I try to explain to you. Do not lecture me about assuming your kingship. I have turned away from that and put behind me this endless intoxication with power and wealth. What pleasure would come my way from the managing of riches and people? When I die to this world, not even the tiniest shred of cloth will accompany me. I will become a *phakir* and pay my respects only to him who imagined and fabricated this universe we call creation. I will become a *phakir* and bow only to him who, with but a tiny word, brought this world into existence." Sekandar Śāhā desperately tried to reason, "Listen my dear child, abandon this notion of becoming a *phakīr* and dedicate yourself to ruling." But Gāji was already a *jindā pīr* and would not listen to his father's argument. When Sekandar Śāhā heard him announce publicly "I will become a *phakir*," he seethed with anger. He issued the order for the executioner to put Gāji to death.

As soon as his courtiers received the order, an executioner was brought. He had decided in advance the way Gāji was to die. The executioner swung the curved blade of his *talwar* sword across Gāji's neck to decapitate him, but Gāji fixed his heart and mind on the Lord Khodā, and He, Āllā, showered his beneficence upon him. Not even a single hair on his head was grazed as Gāji remained serene. Ten times and more did the *talwar* rain down its blows, but Gāji's body never suffered a wound.

10. The worldwide hero and Quest tales are well documented, so not enumerated here. For the hero cycle in Indian narratives, see Véronique Bouillier and Claudine Le Blanc, comp., *L'usage des héros: Traditions narratives et affirmations identitaires dans le monde indien*, Bibliothéque de l'École Pratique des Hautes Études Sciences Historiques et Philologiques Tome 343 (Paris: Librairie Honoré Champion, 2006).

11. Sāyeb Munsī Ābdul Ohāb, *Gāji kālu o cāmpāvatī kanyār punthi* (Kalikātā: Munsī Ābdul Hāmād Khān; repr., Kalikātā: Śrīmahāmmad Rabiullā at Hāmidīyā Press, Es Rahmān aṇḍ Sans printer, 1315 BS [ca. 1908]), 6–10.

Witnessing this, Sekandar Śāhā screamed his anger: "Fit out ten of the biggest most dangerous bull elephants!" The mahouts heard and quickly brought ten such elephants. The Śāhā described precisely what he wanted the mahouts to do: "Stir up the elephants quickly to make them trample Gāji." The mahouts heeded his order and drove the elephants hard. The elephants first wrapped their trunks around Gāji and repeatedly hurled him against the river bank, each time ramming their tusks into his body. The elephants mangled and gored him, over and over and over, but Gāji remained unperturbed, his mind serenely fixed on Āllā. They pulverized and impaled Gāji's body absolutely to no avail; rather, it was they who suffered broken tusks, and when the distal pads of their feet were split, they were left crippled. The elephants made obeisance to Gāji's person and threw off their mahouts who, in a mad dash, barely managed to escape. Though Sekandar Śāhā witnessed this marvel, he once again boiled in a rage.

He then gave the order, "Build a fire pit and stoke it to an inferno, be quick!" The second they heard, his attendants hastened to dig that fire pit. Sekandar ordered them to hurl Gāji into the pit, and the moment they received that directive, they wasted no time in mobbing Gāji. When the flames were roaring high, into the pit they launched him. As he flew deep into the belly of the fire, Gāji's heart remained pure and calm as he remembered his Lord, Prabhu. With his hands pressed together in respect, Gāji called out to the Lord God, Master Creator, Prabhu Kartā, "Please send water to me, for I am your obedient servant." Suddenly cascades of water deluged him as the fire raged all around. Gāji sat calmly in the midst of that fire until after three days it burned itself out. When Sekandar saw this, he thought his eyes were playing tricks on him; he thought to himself, 'My son possesses some kind of magic or sorcery.'

Still not pacified, he issued the order to fetch ten massive boulders to bind Gāji to those massive rocks. "Ah, cast him into the depths of the ocean so that he surely sinks." When they received the decree, they bound Gāji and heaved him into the sea. As he sank into the ocean depths, Gāji meditated on Nirañjan, the Stainless One: "O Lord, Prabhu, come quickly to the aid of your lowly servant." The Lord God, Master Creator, felt compassion for Gāji. The shackles on his limbs sloughed off and by the grace of God, Prabhu, the boulders floated. Gāji perched himself quickly on top of the rocks, and not too much time later he made his way back to the town of Bairāṭ. When they saw Gāji, everyone was flummoxed and filled with awe.

Sekander Śāhā met Gāji and said, 'You have one more chance to convince me that you are a *phakir*." The Śāhā then picked up one tiny needle and cast it far out into the ocean, after which he beckoned to Gāji and commanded, "Go and fetch that needle!" When he heard this Gāji shivered at the prospect. He eventually made his way to the shores of the ocean. Gāji appealed to God: "Listen, O Lord Prabhu, you are an ocean of mercy. The Supreme Lord, Param Īśvar, you can rescue any and every one. O Lord Prabhu, filled with grace, please hear my petition offered at the tomb of a saint. How will I be able to retrieve the needle from the ocean depths?" And in this fashion did Gāji Śāhā meditate.

At the express command of the Lord Prabhu, Khoyāj arrived there. Khoyāj Khejer said to Gāji, "Tell me what is troubling you." Gāji replied, "Please tell me who you are, then I will tell you my tale of woe." Khoyāj Khejer then revealed his identity, and as soon as he heard the name, Gāji made obeisance, offering *sālāms*. He knelt down, clasped Khoyāj Khejer's feet, and then detailed all of the troubles that made him suffer so. Khoyāj consoled him, "My son, be at peace." The Pīr then called on Śura and Āśvari.[12] They arrived, their bodies the size of mountains. They bowed in obeisance, making *sālām*, and inquired of their calling. Khoyāj Khejer spoke, "Listen to our predicament. Śāhā Sekāndar threw a needle into the ocean and I need you to retrieve it. It is to execute this task that I have summoned you." No sooner had they heard than Śura and Āśuri descended into the waters. They drew the waters up and stored them up in the mountains.[13] The ocean was drained dry and only sand was left, so Śura and Āśvari dug, but could not locate the needle. They returned to Khoyāj and spoke to him: "Although we dug and mined the sand, we could not locate the needle anywhere in the ocean floor." So the Pīr took himself into meditation and then understood. "Just as Śāhā Sekāndar threw the needle into the ocean, along came a man of the sea, a merman, who picked it up and then headed onward to the underworld city of Pātālanagar. He gave the needle to his young daughter, a færie, so she could fix up her hair, and so into her hair she wove it." Khejer then instructed them, "Śura and Āśvari, go back again. The needle is pinned in the hair of the young færie who lives in Pātāla; bring it back here straight away." When the two celestials (*dānav*) received the command, they headed for Pātāla at once and just as quickly returned with the needle. After Khoyāj vouchsafed the needle into the hands of Gāji, he departed.

Gāji then took it and eventually made his way to his own quarters, whereupon he immediately placed the needle into the hand of his father. Sekāndar looked hard at the needle and contemplated its meaning. Feeling quite gratified, indeed overwhelmed, he embraced Gāji and kissed his lotus face hundreds of thousands of times. Sekāndar spoke. "My dear son, treasure of my heart, I have caused you much grief and suffering. Do not hold a grudge against me for all the suffering, for you cannot possibly fathom what I intended. Look, my beloved son, I have on my tongue a poison pill. Had you died, I would have swallowed the poison. That poison would have eaten up my life right then and there. I take an oath before God, Khodā, to confirm the truthfulness of what I say. Listen, son, to what I now tell you. You are the one and only son I have in these three worlds. You must rule the kingdom with the aid of your ministers and confidants. When I look at you my heart and life are refreshed. My treasured son, you are the lamp that lights my lineage. Please honor my request and rule the kingdom with pleasure and ease. After I have died, only then should you become a *phakir*. I beg you to honor my wishes and calm my heart." And so in this way did Sekāndar make his various arguments and pleas.

Gāji gave no reply and remained with his head bowed. Gāji then properly gave *sālām* to his father as the king, after which he sought out his mother, Ajupā, in the women's apartments. He grasped the feet of his mother in deep obeisance and

12. The names of these two appear to be versions of the Sanskrit *sura* and *āsura*, the feminine of the latter being *āsuri*, thus demigods and antigods. The conjunct /v/ *bɔphalā* is not pronounced, but rather doubles the consonant to which it is joined, so *āśvari* and *āśuri* (as it is spelled a few lines later) are pronounced in much the same way. Subsequently they are referred to as *dānavas*, often glossed as demons, who are foes of the gods but obviously here under the control of Khoyāj Khejer.

13. The line can also be read as "They stacked the waters up like a mountain."

then, with tears streaming from his eyes, he buried himself in his mother's bosom. Seeing her Gāji like this, she broke down in loud lament. "In spite of the wretched misery that has been written on your forehead, my child, you are the defender of the ignorant and the wealth of those bereft. You are the life of my life, the jewel of this wretched woman. Your father has tortured you unmercifully, what more can I say? Please do not leave this house for the world—stay here with me in my quarters day and night! Just to look at you soothes my eyes." The winsome Ajupā then took Gājī to her lap and tenderly fed him specially prepared dishes. When the day came to a close and darkness fell, Ajupā pulled him close and they lay down together.

When she lay on the couch, the queen eventually drifted off to sleep, and as soon as her guard was down, Gājī Śāhā quickly got up. Crying softly to himself, Gājī began to reflect privately on his sad plight: 'In this king's world my father has inflicted great misery on me. I cannot describe the horrors my father has committed. To stay under his dominion is impossible, so this is my vow: I will abandon this land and wander across the world, and in the name of Āllā, I will become a *phakir*.' Gājī then dressed himself in a traditional mendicant's robe woven with gold thread, and cinched a chain of gold around his waist. Gājī picked up a golden staff in his hand and slipped his feet into golden sandals. He pulled a woven bag onto his shoulder and wrapped prayer beads around his ankle as protection against all troubles and fears. After hastily dressing in his *phakir*'s garb, he reverently honored his mother's feet.

Ābdul Ohāb tells of his remorse: Dear mother, your son is now a phakir.

. . .

The entertainment value in this passage is found in part in the formulaic nature of the succession of ordeals, each one insurmountable until the last, about which even Gājī despairs. The critics are right when they say these tales are indeed amusing, but that entertainment is hardly the end of it. The production and circulation of these lengthy tales bespeak a skill with language and composition in an environment where the majority of the population could neither read nor write. The prolific seventeenth-century author Kṛṣṇarām Dās, who composed the more than two-thousand-line story of Dakṣīṇ Rāy in conflict with Baḍa Khān Gājī in his *Rāy maṅgal*, also composed *maṅgal kāvyas* dedicated to Kālikā, Ṣaṣṭhī, Śītalā, and Kamalā, covering another six thousand lines.[14] The Mahārāj of Bardhamān in the early eighteenth century awarded the title Kaviratna, or "Jewel of Poets," to court poet Ghanarām Cakravartī, author of one of the most popular poems dedicated to Satya Nārāyaṇ, variously titled *Satyanārāyaṇ itihās* or *Satyanārāyaṇ*

14. Kṛṣṇarām Dās, *Kavi kṛṣṇarām dāser granthāvalī*, ed. Satyanārāyaṇ Bhaṭṭācāryya (Kalikātā: Kalikātā Viśvavidyālay, 1958). Haridev also composed a *Rāy maṅgal* and a *Śitalā maṅgal*; see Haridev, *Haridever racanāvalī: Rāy maṅgal o śītalā maṅgal*, ed. Pañcānan Maṇḍal, Sāhityaprakāśikā vol. 4 (Śāntiniketan: Viśvabhāratī [1466 BS (ca. 1959)]).

ras sindhu;[15] he also composed the weightiest of all the *Dharma maṅgal* texts,[16] the figure Dharma who is associated on occasion with Satya Pīr. Śekh Khodā Bakhś composed the tale of Gājī, his eventual wife Cāmpāvatī, and his half-brother Kālu, which in the earliest known manuscript dated to about 1750,[17] stretched to more than eighteen thousand lines in fifty-eight *pālās* or sections, the manuscript made up of 664 folios; critically edited by A. K. M. Jākāriyā and published by the Bangla Akademi, it covers 307 imperial octavo double-columned pages. In that same printed edition Jākāriyā included the full edited text of Kavi Hālumīr, titled *Baḍo khā̃n gājīr kerāmati*, which itself covers more than eleven thousand lines.[18]

These *pīr kathās* can not only be imposing in size, their vocabulary can be uncommonly formidable, and their diction not always but often artful. Kṛṣṇarām routinely switches from a narrative Bangla to a formal register when portraying Dakṣiṇ Rāy's direct speech, but shifts registers altogether to a patois we might characterize as pidgin or *kichiri* Hindustani when portraying Baḍa Khān Gāji's tirades.[19] In some instances the authors formally employ *alaṃkār*—an æsthetic standard that is often deemed little more than linguistic pyrotechnics or tricks of the trade, but which even then attests to the technical skill of the author and which is a prerequisite for generating literary expression that invokes the carefully orchestrated experience of emotion (*ras*, Skt. *rasa*). One good example is the *cautriśa* embedded in the *Satyanārāyaṇer puthi* of Caitanya Prasād Poddār Mahāśay, which begins each line with the next consonant in alphabetical order, and in this example, includes further alliteration of that initial character within the same line.[20] Other authors make more than passing attempts to manipulate the standard elements of *rasa* theory in their depictions of the emotional palette

15. Ghanarām Cakravarttī, *Satyanārāṇa ras sindhu*, ed. Praphullakumār Bhaṭṭācāryya and Kālīpad Siṁha (Barddhamān: Barddhamān Sāhitya Sabhā, 1353 BS [ca. 1946]), and the considerably older but also nicely edited Dvija Ghanarām, *Satyanārāyaṇ itihās*, ed. Mahendranāth Ghoṣ (Kalikātā: Bhabanīpur Orieṇṭāl Pres, 1292 BS [ca. 1885]).

16. Ghanarām Cakravarttī, *Dharma maṅgal*, ed. Piyūṣkānti Mahāpātrā (Kalikātā: Kalikātā Viśvavidyālay, 1962).

17. Ābul Kālām Mohāmmad Jākāriyā, ed., *Bāṅglā sāhitye gājī kālu o cāmpāvatī upākhyān* (Ḍhākā: Bāṃlā Ekāḍemī, 1396 BS [1989]), introduction, 77–80. Khodā Bakhś was born in 1698–99.

18. Ābul Kālām Mohāmmad Jākāriyā, ed. This volume includes an introduction of 113 pages as well as the tales of Śekh Khodā Bakhś (1–307) and Kavi Hālumīr (309–510).

19. Baḍa Khān Gāji's speech is always colorful, but for one of the more invective-laden, ear-blistering rants, see Kṛṣṇarām's "Rāy maṅgal" in *Kavi kṛṣṇarām dāser granthāvalī*, 197–98, vv. 373–86.

20. Raghunāth Cakravartī, *Satyanārāyaṇer puthi*, ed. Caitanya Prasād Poddār Mahāśay, 2nd ed. (Noyākhālī: Yogendramohan Poddār, 1315 BS [10 August 1908]), 18–21. The introduction states that the book was published in memory of the author's older brother, Lalitmohān Poddār, but was actually composed by the publisher's father, Caitanya Prasād Poddār Mahāśay, who was not acknowledged on the title page. See also the *cautrīśā* by Rādhāmohan Tarkālaṃkār Bhaṭṭācāryya, *Satya nārāyaṇ vratakathā*, 8–9.

familiar to Bangla speakers, from anger and astonishment to friendship and love.[21] For instance, in Sāyeb Munsī Ābdul Ohāb's version of *Gājī kālu o cāmpāvatī kanyār punthi*, which we just quoted, he takes ninety couplets (*payār*) to explain Gāji's trials—his father's attempt to behead, maul, burn, and drown him, and then provide as final proof of his sainthood an impossible test that could only be passed by a miracle. It is a barebones description of the action, and the emotional tenor is flat—anger on one side and anguish on the other.

In Śekh Khoda Bakhś's *Gājī kālu o cāmpāvatī*, the same episode stretches through four chapters (*pālā*) covering just over a thousand lines of text (444 *payār*, 49 *tripadi*).[22] Khoda Baks details the long and angry arguments of the king, who feels publicly humiliated at the repudiation of kingship by Gājī and vows to bend him to his will. The blow-by-blow accounts of the torments are explored in detail, including such things as naming and describing the elephants deployed to trample and gore Gājī, the most magnificent being the mythical Airāvata (the name of Indra's mythical white elephant, often depicted as having multiple trunks and tusks), whom, because of his ghastly effectiveness in battle and execution, Khoda Bakhś nicknames the Yam Avatār, the Incarnation of Death. The agony and anxiety Gājī feels at his father's unwarranted outrage, and his steadfast commitment to the command of Āllā to become a *phakīr*, is played out in the most desolate, gut-wrenching terms. Āllā's compassion is equally moving as he worriedly orders Jibril's intervention, and his request of Khoyāj Khijr to come to Gājī's aid stirs the passions. In terms of classical æsthetic theory, not only are the foundational emotional attitudes (*bhāvas*) clearly established, the contributing factors (*vibhāva*), the ensuing entailments (*anubhāva*), and the involuntary physical responses to the emotional situation (*sāttvika bhāva*) are mindfully present and in some instances skillfully portrayed. In a manner consistent with literary strategies in early modern Bangla, Khoda Bakhś switches from the more pedestrian couplet (roughly equivalent to modern prose) to the more elegant *tripadi*, or three-footed metrical form, in order to pause the narrative and explore the more intimate emotional worlds of the King, the Queen, and Gājī. In these small emotion-laden vignettes—traditional *tripadi* for intimate emotions and the more lively three-footed *lācāḍī* meter for the more raucous, such as anger—he opens up the characters' interior landscapes as they attempt to cope with Gājī's impending abandonment of the courtly

21. The history of *rasa* theory dates back to Bharata; see Sheldon Pollock, trans., *A Rasa Reader: Classical Indian Aesthetics* (New York: Oxford University Press, 2016). In Bengal, nearly every author followed its application to the world of devotional *bhakti* as articulated by Rūp Gosvāmī; see Rūpa Gosvāmin, *Bhaktirasāmṛtasindhu*, edited with Bengali translation by Haridās Dās, with the commentaries "Durgasaṃgamanī ṭīkā" of Jīva Gosvāmin, "Artharatnālpadīpikā" of Mukundadāsa Gosvāmin, and "Bhaktisārapradarśiṇī ṭīkā" of Viśvanātha Cakravartin, 3rd ed. (Mathurā: Haribol Kuṭīr from Śrī Kṛṣṇajanmasthān, 495 GA [ca. 1981]).

22. Śekh Khoda Bakhś, "Gājī kālu o cāmpāvatī," in *Bāṅglā sāhitye gājī kālu o cāmpāvatī upākhyān*, ed. Ābul Kālām Mohāmmad Jākāriyā, 81–99.

life, which would generate the desired æsthetic *rasa*, the distilled and unsullied experience of emotion that lies at the heart of accomplished South Asian literary productions. The emotional impact as well as the richness of both physical and even psychological detail, which remains consistent throughout the text, marks this tale as a high literary achievement. Recognition of the emotional intensity of the passage is confirmed by the early-twentieth-century production of the drama *Śāh gāji kālu gītābhinay* by Mahāmmad Kārim Bākhs,[23] whose narrative closely follows that of Khodā Bakhś. The author indicates that, while certain factions at that time condemn the use of song to celebrate *musalmāni* themes, he finds the emotion-laden passages of a number of these narratives too compelling to ignore.[24] Make no mistake: by indigenous æsthetic standards, not all of these tales are up to the mark set by Śekh Khodā Bakhś, but as will become apparent, some tales are simplistic and others not, yet these *pīr kathā* are anything but naïve; they are performing a cultural work that, as will become apparent, is nontrivial.

The formulaic nature of this set of ordeals is of course part of the craft of the storyteller and too often casually denigrated as lacking in originality by those who fetishize novelty as a vital component of serious literature, rather than addressing what the sequence might signal. What becomes clear is that the young Gājī could not be killed by any of the standard executions of the ancient world—beheading, trampling, burning, drowning—nor could he be stymied by the impossible task of recovering an infinitesimally small needle in the infinitely large ocean. The author makes clear that he was favored by God, already a *sūphī* saint following a path similar to that taken by other pious figures across the world and in different religious traditions. The type is immediately recognizable. True to his measure as a friend of God, like Mānik Pīr, Gāji retains the controlled restraint of filial piety in spite of the horrible ordeals—a trait that indexes both humility and self-discipline. That contrast of the wrathful father who, engrossed in the wielding of worldly power, wrongly punishes his son, juxtaposed against the meek respect and submission that the son returns in the face of such torments, encapsulates the recurring tension found in some form in virtually all romances, the tension between evil and good. Not surprisingly, this specific tension likewise surfaces in many hagiographical accounts worldwide: the vagaries of the ordinary world of householders, of kings and courtiers, which stand in fundamental conflict with the religious calling. As a fictional romance-as-hagiography, the tension between worldly and religious pursuits is perhaps the most common form in which each text expresses its religious struggle.[25]

23. Mahāmmad Kārim Bākhs, *Śāhā gāji kālu gītābhinay, pratham khaṇḍa* (Jāiyānpur, Rājśāhī: by the author, printed in Kalikātā by Śrī Bimalcaraṇ Cakrabartī at Nāgendra Ṣṭīm Priṇṭiṅg Oyārks, 1326 BS [ca. 1919]).

24. Mahāmmad Kārim Bākhs, 1.

25. The concept of romance-as-hagiography was recognized by Delehaye; see Delehaye, *Legends of the Saints*, 3–4.

3.2. ENTERTAINING ENCOUNTERS THAT SHAPE THE RELIGIOUS IDEAL

The tales of the fictional *pīrs* clearly fit the entertainment mold easily enough, but equally importantly, they are hagiographies in the treatment of their heroes and heroines—hagiography easily arguable as a subgenre of romance. As hagiographies, they must treat the religious ideal in connection with the *bios* of the protagonist.[26] While the succession of tales marks them structurally, the plot of each distinct episode, which usually takes the form of an encounter with those of different moral or social practices, often traces the development and maturation of the *pīr* or *pirānī* in both personal and religious terms. The growth frequently involves the discovery of the limits of the hero's or heroine's powers and the ethic of their deployment, while the mission tends to explore a world that often turns out to be considerably more complex than the *pīr* or *bibī* may have first imagined. The growth, however, is seldom depicted in psychological terms through any form of interiority, though shifts in the antagonists' moral landscape are not unusual but are, in fact, often the point.

In Jaidi's *Mānikpīrer jahurnāmā*, Badar descends from heaven (*bhest*) fully capable of delivering God's message yet still learning just how that might be executed in the world of Bengal. He fumbles through one encounter after another in a manner that, in spite of the fabulation, hints at a slightly more realist depiction as defined by Frye ("given these characters, what might happen"), on occasion producing completely unexpected outcomes. The effect is to generate a sympathy with the hero Badar, which in turn inclines the listener to pay attention to his religiously oriented action. Through this series of adventures, Badar discovers the nature and limits of his power, which is of course ultimately and always the power of Āllā channeled productively through this servant of God. While trying to cope with each new challenge, Badar is often stymied by the nagging persistence of his own foibles, which often enough place him in precarious situations that require rescue from above, as his encounter with the goddess Gaṅgā entails. He displays extraordinary control over the physical universe in his encounter with the *jogīs* who are performing their austerities at the Triveṇi; they cannot conjure Gaṅgā, so he manages to effect it for them, but only as a demonstration of his *karāmat* or spiritual power once he has been insulted. As a rule, *karāmat* is only marshaled to persuade someone who is skeptical or insulting. Insults require remediation or punishment, while a show of respect reaps rewards. In this encounter, it might appear counter-intuitively that he has rewarded the *jogīs*' insults with the goal they sought—and in fact he does—but he facilitates their ascent to the formless

26. Tzvetan Todorov has observed that works do not have to manifest a category or any category, but can manifest several because the categories are intellectual abstractions: they are constructed, while the works are empirical realities. Todorov, *Fantastic*, 22.

brahman, the neuter principle of cosmic unity, which is in the salvific economy of Islam a punishment because they lose their identities and remain outside of heaven. When Badar subsequently decides to find out what this Gaṅgā meditation is really about, he comes face to face with the extraordinary power of the goddess and barely manages to contain her, but contain her he does, corralling her into his mendicant's shoulder bag, courtesy of instruction from an oracle, that is, a voice from the heavens (*ākāśbāṇī*), which gives him instruction through a white fly. While the personal piety of Badar is a necessary precondition to make him a worthy receptacle for it, it is only by remembering God (*jikir, smaraṇ*) that he can manifest the personal power of *karāmat*. When he releases Gaṅgā, it is on the condition that she assist him in bringing the stones to build a mosque (*masjid*). For the goddess to float the stones from the Setubandha on the southern tip of the subcontinent would surprise no one familiar with the mythology of the goddess, but in the cycle of tales dedicated to *phakirs* and *pīrs*, the ability of Badar to harness Gaṅgā to the business of building a *masjid* in a swampy delta area where there is no natural rock bespeaks an extraordinary power that could only be generated by Āllā. Similarly, when the familiar mythological figure Viśvakarma stipulates in his contract to build that *masjid* that he will only work for one night and will stop the moment the sun appears, Badar again demonstrates his control over the physical world and stops the sun from rising. It is at this point that Āllā feels compelled to intervene out of an ostensible concern that the completed structure will be more extraordinary than anything in Mākkā, Medinā, or indeed heaven, which really suggests that Badar has overreached the use of his powers and has to be curbed. The *masjid* remains unfinished as he moves on to other tasks.

The narrative strategy of interrupting one decisive action to commit to another course allows Badar as protagonist to demonstrate his growing understanding of the ways of the world, where and how his God-derived powers can be deployed, and how he comes to embody and convey the religious ideal, a function of nearly every hagiography. The succession of episodes plays out a narrative that ultimately results in the utopian outcome, or at least its promise and vision. Badar's God-given assignment is instrumental to a larger mission; he is to herald the coming of Mānik and to facilitate his descent, but the meandering nature of his efforts—almost all of which result from losing his focus as he discovers and rediscovers why he is there—are almost comical in their repeated misdirection, as he is rescued and nudged back on track time and again by the interventions of Āllā. While on the surface some of Badar's actions appear to be a form of comic relief, likely in anticipated contrast to the work of his son Mānik, they lay a foundation for understanding the world as envisioned by the author Jaidi, that self-contained reality that operates according to its own set of rules. In other narratives, the comic element may be played down, but the work of the protagonist generally accomplishes the same thing.

The molding of Satya Pīr's character in the opening section of the *Baḍa satya pīr o sandhyāvati kanyār puthi*, which covers nearly sixty percent of the text, is a somewhat more causally connected set of events than the apparently haphazard peregrinations of Badar. Satya Pīr's birth, instruction, and then focused mission on chastising the king of Mālañcā tell the story of a *phakir* finding his way from heaven to earth and then testing his powers through the exercise of a situational creativity. Though the outcomes of Satya Pīr's encounters are relatively predictable, they are not without improvisations that attest to his wit, and more importantly, that mark growth, if not character development (Badar, for instance does not appear to have any psychological growth, but Satya Pīr does show signs of psychological maturity in the first section—though it should be noted that no *pīr kathā* functions as a fully developed Bildungsroman). Satya Pīr remains in focus and with far fewer digressions than Badar Pīr, but he still has to receive direct instruction about the nature of the world he is to explore and to test through personal experience the limits of what he can do. Like Mānik and Gāji, his (apparent) father, the king, attempts to kill him while he is still in the womb when Satya Pīr's mother is abandoned in the jungle (another method of execution parallel to Mānik's and Gāji's, but indirect, though the threat to the unborn or newborn child is common in hero mythology). While still in that idyllic state of the womb, he wards off sure death by successfully taming wild animals, a hallmark of *sūphī pīrs*.[27] He saves the life and eventually the honor of his mother, initiates the release of a *brāhmaṇ* widow to heaven, and as soon as he assumes his fully human form, seeks out Khoyāj Jendā Pīr or Khoyāj Khijir, the elusive and ancient *pīr*, former guide to Alexander in his search for the fountain of eternal life, and who reigns over Bengal's waters.

Satya Pīr takes instruction from Khoyāj, then after five years visits his mother to reveal to her his survival and reassure her of her instrumental function in his mission, which he then formally launches. Through that mission he quietly establishes a protocol of proper religious action which corrects misperceptions and errors of belief among those he encounters, of course especially first countering the nefarious actions of the ignoble King of Mālañcā, whose execrable treatment of *phakirs* prompted Satya Pīr's descent. It is through actions such as these, often heavily symbolic, that Jaidi and other authors of these fictional hagiographies shape the broad outline of the religious ideal. Interactions with people, with opponents and the wayward, demonstrate the truth of Satya Pīr's calling, not preaching per se; or if he does preach, the authors simply tell us he preached, but do not provide the content apart from his pointing out small-mindedness and bigotry based on social issues, such as matrimonial exclusion, purity and pollution, and sartorial transgressions. Humiliation as a function of power drives many of the lessons he metes out. The contours of the religious ideal are never formulated in explicit theological or doctrinal terms, but are rather signaled through images and actions. Even the

27. In an interesting structural inversion, these fictional *pīrs* and *bibīs* often resort to the company and counsel of wild animals, taking the jungle or forest as their natural habitat for practicing their spiritual goals, while the civilized urban worlds are for them a kind of godless wilderness filled with conflict.

occasional overt interjections of the narrator—for instance the short observations about the reputed nature of heaven and hell that Kṛṣṇahari Dās inserted in the birth narrative of Satya Pīr—tend to take the form of a very generalized and generalizable instruction in morality rather than theology. Even the lessons from the most famous teacher of teachers, Khoyāj Khijir, to the just-manifest Satya Pīr are conveyed in the most general terms. The simple report of Khoyāj Khijir's role as teacher of Satya Pīr, the image that establishes the latter's significant relationship to the ageless *shaykh*, signals a superior religious achievement, for only the most extraordinary *sūphī* saints have over the last millennium had the privilege of being instructed by Khijir.[28] Instruction is reported, but seldom with more than the simplest religious or ethical propositions that are short on specific content. There is a reason this is so.

3.3. THE *PĪR* IN A SUBJUNCTIVE WORLD

We have argued that the fictional narratives of the *pīrs* are not subject to the truth question, but as Pierre Macherey has argued, the autotelic nature of the fictional narrative does establish reflexively its own truth,[29] and in that sense each of these narratives is of necessity true, but according to its own standards (the same can be said of myth). In the case of the narratives of the fictive *pīrs*, this means that the worlds they inhabit are ones of the authors' own making; they cannot portray directly the ordinary world of things, but can only mimic. These narratives can only give the impression of reality. Macherey writes:

> The autonomy of the writer's discourse is established from its relationship with the other uses of language; everyday speech, scientific propositions. By its energy and thinness literary discourse mimics theoretical discourse, rehearsing but never actually performing its script. But in that evocative power, by which it denotes a specific reality, it also imitates the everyday language which is the language of ideology. We could offer a provisional definition of literature as being characterised by this power of parody. Mingling the real uses of language in an endless confrontation, it concludes by *revealing* their truth. Experimenting with language rather than inventing it, the literary work is both the analogy of knowledge and a caricature of customary ideology.[30]

28. Hugh Talat Halman enumerates more than a dozen of the great Sufi saints who received instruction from the ageless al-Khiḍr (as he is known in Arabic), including al-Bisṭāmī, al-Ḥallāj, al-Jīlānī, Ruzbihān Baqli, Ibn 'Arabi, and others; see Halman, *Where the Two Seas Meet: The Qur'ānic Story of al-Khiḍr and Moses in Sufi Commentaries as a Model of Spiritual Guidance* (Louisville: Fons Vitae, 2013), 195–247. The Alexander story is in the following chapter of Halman, 248–58.

29. Pierre Macherey, *A Theory of Literary Production*, trans. Geoffrey Wall (London: Routledge, 1978), 44. On 45, he continues: "The writer is able to create both an object and the standards by which it is to be judged." He adds, "The text alone has a truth, which it alone can express" (47).

30. Macherey, *Theory of Literary Production*, 59; emphasis in the original. The implications of this argument are extended for several more pages, 59–65.

Following Macherey, fictional writing cannot then articulate overt theology or advocate specific doctrines; were it to do so, it would become simply normative propaganda and not fiction at all. Fictions can only operate with partially formed or incomplete *simulacra* of ideologies, or in the case of the *pīr kathā*, of theologies and doctrines. A dogmatic or doctrinal position would be characterized as a Bakhtinian *monologic*, speech aimed at the listener in an attempt to close out alternatives, ossifying the narrative through a propagandistic discourse of ideology (not its simulacrum), seeking to limit, to control potential meanings.[31] But the fictional tales of the *pīrs* do not participate directly in that theologically or doctrinally conditioned world; rather, they *comment on it.* By virtue of their fictional quality, they are *dialogic* in character, inviting participation by the listener, who will in that interaction be provoked to imagine the world incompletely described, and that incompleteness or the disruption of expectations compared with the known world impels the imagination to exploration. The language it adopts is itself recognizable, but orients itself toward the listener with a specific conceptual horizon, toward the specific world of the listener, where it introduces new elements, sometimes totally novel, into his or her discourse.[32] This marks the subjunctive quality of these fictions, inviting the listener or reader to explore possibilities that are closed off in the familiar religious discourses of history, theology, and law; to investigate and invent meaning is one of the most important functions of all fiction.[33] The activity is *dialogical*, for it addresses the listener in a heteroglossic environment, where multiple communities operate within overlapping discursive realms, where different conceptual horizons are brought into interaction through suggestion. The protagonists of these stories operate in worlds of possibilities, often indeterminate realms that do not offer a systematic statement of what should be, but what might be. This fictional world is inevitably a partially constructed world (since no fiction can go so far as to address systematically how a complete world should look).[34]

31. M. M. Bakhtin, *The Dialogic Imagination: Four Essays*, ed. Michael Holquist, trans. Caryl Emerson and Michael Holquist (Austin: University of Texas Press, 1981), 270–71.

32. Bakhtin, 282–91.

33. For those unfamiliar with this commonplace, in a standard reference J. Hillis Miller writes about the essential nature of fiction generally: "The human capacity to tell stories is one way men and women collectively build a significant and orderly world around themselves. With fictions we investigate, perhaps invent, the meaning of life. . . . Narratives are a relatively safe or innocuous place in which the reigning assumptions of a given culture can be criticized. In a novel, alternative assumptions can be entertained or experimented with—not as in the real world, where such experimentations might have dangerous consequences, but in the imaginary world where, it is easy to assume, 'nothing really happens' because it happens only in the feigned world of fiction." Miller, "Narrative," in *Critical Terms for Literary Study*, ed. Frank Lentricchia and Thomas McLaughlin, 2nd ed. (Chicago: University of Chicago Press, 1995), 69.

34. In a very compelling and sophisticated comparative analysis of the nature of ritual, a quartet of prominent scholars—taking their cue from J. Z. Smith—argue that one of the underlying features of ritual is its subjunctive mode, in the sense that it offers an ideal world in contrast to the world of

Because fiction establishes its truths with images, rather than philosophical propositions about the nature of reality, it is through the manipulation of images that we will discover the real nature of this exploratory dimension. We can often spot the moment the author moves the protagonist from the indicative to the subjunctive when the listener's expected norms of conduct are violated, when symbolic social hierarchies are transgressed, when the action moves into the realm of the fantastic or the marvelous, or when customary cosmologies and cosmographies seem to be conflated or abandoned.

Jaidi makes no attempt anywhere in the *Mānikpīrer jahurānāmā* to articulate an overt theology or cosmology, but the world Badar navigates often meanders through unrecognized realms and brings together the unexpected. In the very opening lines the author locates Āllā in his heaven (*bhest*), in his court (*darbār*), to which he enjoins Badar to undertake the mission to prepare the way for a new descent, the *avatār* for the Kali Age: his name will be Mānik. The spatial orientation of heaven on the order of a Sultanate or Mughal court positions Āllā in a manner not normally encountered in the mainstream theological literatures of traditional Islam. The invocation of the concept of *yugāvatār* or *avatār* for the age immediately signals the adoption of a fundamental, but generic *vaiṣṇav*-inspired cosmology. That soteriological function of *avatār*, which has a long history in the *vaiṣṇav* traditions stretching back to the centuries prior to the Common Era, is appropriated for a message tailored to this last age of humanity, as is always necessary—the *avatār* redefines *dharma* (morality, truth, and so forth) according to the needs of the age, and in this Badar and his son Mānik conform to expectation.[35] This *avatār* will "speak to everyone about Haji, Gāji, Māhāmad, Rahim, Karim, Rasul, Paygambar, Ijjat, and Mādār." In the same way the *avatār* concept is invoked as a generic commonplace—in spite of its long elaboration theologically in the *vaiṣṇav* tradition of the nonfictional world—there is no explicit content regarding the work, the names of these figures being sufficient to invoke a set of standards and moral sensibilities; yet in their contentless generality they leave the impression of being apposite to and functioning in some way sympathetically with

---

everyday things, that ideal world being the world *as it should be*. That seems to eliminate any possibility, however, for open-ended exploration of what else might be, which is the form of the subjunctive I see at work in these fictions; precisely because they are fictions, they cannot offer genuine alternatives, but rather can only explore *possibilities*. See Adam B. Seligman, Robert P. Weller, Michael J. Puett, and Bennett Simon, *Ritual and Its Consequences: An Essay on the Limits of Sincerity* (New York: Oxford University Press, 2008), esp. chap. 1, "Ritual and Subjunctive." I am indebted to Nancy G. Lin for bringing this to my attention.

35. One of the great innovations of the *Bhagavad gītā* was the redefinition of *dharma*. Having previously subsumed the concept of *ṛta* as the ordering principle of the cosmos, but extending the sense of order to the moral world, the *avatār* from this point forward redefines *dharma*, making it mutable to the needs of the current age. See Kṛṣṇa Dvaipāyana Vyāsa, *The Bhagavad Gītā in the Mahābhārata*, trans. J. A. B. van Buitenen (Chicago: University of Chicago Press, 1981), chap. 4.

the preexisting standards. Later, when Mānik is actually born, the author in his signature line writes: "Mānik descended (*yavatirnya*) in the home of the gardener Madu." Given the conventions of this scribe, *yavatirnya* is *avatirnya*, which is more conventionally *avatīrṇa*, descended, what *avatārs* do, that is, "cross over" (Sanskrit root *ṭr-*) and down (prefix *ava-*). Both Badar and Mānik, as we know from other texts, meet the forecast of future action inherent in the concept.

Jaidi is hardly alone in appropriating the idea of *avatār*. Satya Pīr is named as the *yugāvatār* in several hundreds of manuscripts, and it is not unusual to see even Muhammad so characterized.[36] Though Badar Pīr is not declared to be the *avatār* of the age, but only the herald, when he meets Dudbibī and she indicates that because of her prior births she can only marry some form of the god Nārāyaṇ, he accommodates her through a miraculous serial revelation visible in her mind's eye which reveals him to be precisely those *avatārs*: she recognizes him as Nārāyaṇ, sporting four arms, then as the *avatār* Rām with Lakṣmaṇ and her as Sītā, and after that as the *avatār* (the word is explicitly used) Kṛṣṇa while she is one of the cowherd women or *gopīs*—each form paired with an identity she has already declared for herself. It is likely to be no coincidence that the name Dudbibī is the "lady of milk," invoking the image of a *gopī*, and the name Badar means "full moon," invoking one of the most common adjectives used to describe Kṛṣṇa and his effulgent beauty, a subliminal suggestion that brings into question the real nature of Kṛṣṇa as God and the cowherdesses as his lovers.

Badar reveals his form as Nārāyaṇ in progressive serial permutations when he instructs Dudbibī to shut her eyes, but later he reverses the process by presenting the figures of Rām and Sītā to the Bādsvā, who, when he shut his eyes, sees they are none other than Badar and Dudbibī. The presence of multiple realms of perception, the unseen realm suddenly seen, challenges the listeners' assumptions about the ordinary world of things—a cosmological issue that will have ramifications for Mānik's advent, indeed our readings of a number of these tales. In the context of the *avatār* of the age, which Badar's revelations confirm, it is clear that the cosmological cycles of the four ages are assumed to be operational. It also signals that some form of reincarnation or transmigration is at work, which in turn implies the laws of *karma*—but that is not explored explicitly as a law of the universe, but implied through offhand remarks. It is a given that is acknowledged by just about everyone, even Mohāmmad, who in the episode with Cāndbibī engineers the latter's karmic retribution to execute God's plan to send Satya Pīr to earth to alleviate the sufferings of the many saints, the friends of God persecuted by the King of Mālañcā. Karmic retribution seems to be little more than an immediate causality; for instance, when the Bādsvā insults Badar, he immediately loses his daughter;

36. See chapter 6 of this volume for the details of this expansive literature of Satya Pīr, which features him as the *yugāvatār*. For some of the other appropriations, see Stewart, "Religion in the Subjunctive."

and when the *jogīs* meditating at the Triveṇi cast aspersions on Badar, he instantly demonstrates his superior power by giving them the vision they seek, which triggers their immediate disappearance as they assume multi-armed forms and fly off to the realm of their choosing.

Just as comfortably, Fate is invoked by any number of characters, usually through the expression of having one's situation, usually misery, written on the forehead, which is how the god Bidhātā sets each human life in motion in Bengal, visiting shortly after birth. Bidhātā has made both the gardener and his wife infertile, so the recovery of the baby Mānik is a delight beyond measure, and they dutifully perform the *pūjā* to the goddess Ṣaṣṭhī on the sixth day, during which time Bidhātā is sometimes assumed to deliver his prognostications—seeking the protection of the goddess helps to ensure that it is a positive fate that is indelibly inscribed on the child's forehead. The familiar architect of the universe, Viśvakarma, in this narrative becomes little more than a mercenary craftsman available to anyone with worldly wealth or power to coerce him into cooperation, hardly the noble helpmate of the gods. These and many other simple assertions about the makeup of the cosmos suggest a novel universe, which easily accommodates *musalmāni* and *hinduyāni* constructs in interaction with one another. From a strictly traditional Hindu or Muslim perspective, no such world exists—it is a subjunctive world, a suggestive incorporation of features from both.

The power of Badar Pīr as controller of the natural world is demonstrated over and over again. Using the Mādāri method of quick transport through a mystical utterance, he moves effortlessly around the country and later disappears from the jail where the Bādsvā had imprisoned him. His marvelous control of tigers and his ability to converse with them is one of the telltale marks of the power of the *pīr*. But in each of these displays of his *karāmat*, he invokes the memory of Āllā through *jikir* or repetition of the qualities of Āllā, or remembrance (*smaraṇ*), one of the *vaiṣṇav* equivalents to *jikir*, the real source of his power. The author does not reveal the content of those practices, but simply reports their practice and efficacy.

The ambiguity of Mānik's conception is nothing short of miraculous. The seed, in the form of phlegm transmogrified into an insect in a flower, not only suggests that Āllā has a body that is afflicted in the same manner as humans (he coughs or sneezes, phlegm is expelled)—clearly bypassing the lengthy debates within Islam regarding his corporeal reality (e.g., hand of God, throne)—but it also suggests that Āllā is somehow the father of Mānik. Mānik would then be half god, half human, much as the Pāṇḍava heroes of the *Mahābhārata* with their split parentage (again the *vaiṣṇav* connection). But the flower and its insect do not travel directly to Dudbibī, but appear to be modified or possibly even activated by the touch of Badar, who subsequently orders the flower in the name of God to travel upstream to Dudbibī. Reminiscent of the act of spawning (or the activity of reversing the flow of semen in some Bengali *tantrik* yogic practices), it at least places Badar in the line of transmission as *one* of Mānik's fathers, minimally a surrogate father, along with Madu the gardener as foster father. The insect has been explicitly given the boon by Āllā that "You will become the prince, son of Dudbibī, with the name Mānik," which subtly suggests that Āllā has only created the means by which Dudbibī will become pregnant, but that it is not his own seed (it is, after all, snot, but it is his bodily substance nonetheless—and any bodily substance shed from a god or goddess is capable of generating life, a commonplace in the mythology of the subcontinent). But after Dudbibī intercepts the flower, she dresses and ornaments herself in a manner fitting for her wedding night. Once prepared, she and Badar meet one another in their dreamworld, another rupture of the ordinary world of things. For this dream connection to be made, however, the ascetic stalwart Badar needs prodding, so Āllā requests Saytān to enter his body and incite him. When he does, Badar is roused out of his meditations, or more appropriately aroused by thoughts of Dudbibī that plague him until they meet in that dream. Dudbibī is clearly already prepared to receive Badar, the power of her longing and her nubile young body poised to procreate, as her maid Mukil has observed more than once, whereas Badar, who has been practicing his austerities, needs a nudge of encouragement to respond, but in the age-old tradition of South Asia asceticism, his seed would be especially potent. Saytān, of course, is famous in the *musalmāni bāṅglā* literature for his constant work inciting humans to indulge their bodily cravings, instigating fornication, profligacy, inebriation, and violence, among other forms of infamous behavior.[37] But Saytān here functions in a manner very similar to the way the *apsarasas* interrupt the meditations of *yogīs* in classical mythology, though he incites the base instincts, rather than presenting the mendicant with an immediate body for gratification. The result leads Badar to enter the same dreamworld as Dudbibī, and in that dreamworld the text explicitly declares that they do what lovers do and conclude by having sexual intercourse. That would then seem to remove doubts about Mānik's parentage, for having a human who was half-god would be difficult in any Muslim context, no matter how fictional, yet the impregnation is still miraculous, having been effected in a dreamworld.

37. There are several texts in Bangla carrying the title of *Iblis nāmā* or *Iblich nāmā* in which Iblis/Iblich or Saytān has a colloquy with Muhammad, describing all the things that he does to incite humans to behave in ways contrary to God's injunctions. See Garīb, *Iblich nāmār puthi* (Kalikātā: Śrī Akṣaykumār Rāy eṇḍ Kompāni, 1287 BS [ca. 1880]); Śrī Jān Ārāmullā, *Iblich nāmār puthi* (Kalikātā: Viśvambhar Lāhā, 1284 BS [ca. 1877]); and Nanā Gājī, *Iblisnāmā*, ed. Khandkār Mujāmmil Hak (Ḍhākā: Khośroj Kitāb Mahal, 1390 BS [ca. 1987]). For more on Iblis and Saytān and the ways they are deployed rhetorically (for they are not automatically synonymous), see Peter J. Awn, *Satan's Tragedy and Redemption: Iblīs in Sufi Psychology*, with a foreword by Annemarie Schimmel, Studies in the History of Religions (Leiden: E. J. Brill, 1983), and more recently, Whitney S. Bodman, *The Poetics of Iblīs: Narrative Theology in the Qur'ān*, Harvard Theological Studies 62 (Cambridge, MA: Harvard Divinity School, 2011).

3.4. IRONY AND PARODY IN *PĪR KATHĀ*

It is easy to see why someone schooled in the mainstream perspectives of traditional Islam would find the world of Badar Pīr to be zany at best, for there is little room in those traditional constructions for other deities, however demoted, for notions of transmigration, nor for God to send insects down to impregnate a princess with his special *pīr*, and so forth. It is equally easy to see how someone might interpret this as some form of syncretism—local gods and goddesses blended into the mix of angels, færies, and the Prophet—without taking into account the tale's fictional quality or what syncretism really suggests.[38] Both of those responses hinge on a failure to understand what these fictions do: *fictions allow authors to explore worlds of their own making, freed from the strictures of the legislative authority of theology, law, and history laid down by the mainstreams of Islamic traditions.* Whether it is deliberate or simply part of the art of storytelling, these narratives invariably test-drive ideas that may run counter to the prevailing perspectives which, by virtue of this effort, must not be completely satisfactory in their totalizing rejection of the Bengali world into which Islam entered. Where the discourse of the mainstream Islamic traditions attempts to impose a different cultural standard, to legislate the monologics of cosmology, ritual practice, theology, and social organization, these fictional tales by contrast emerge more organically and internally; the domains they depict are Bengali-inspired worlds, replete with a proximate Bengali geography and recognizable Bengali customs that elude such imposed strictures. As such, these fictional *pīr kathās* parody the depictions found in other mythologies or fictions (religious and semi-epic), for example especially the *maṅgal kāvyas* dedicated to the various goddesses and stray gods (actually poaching on the domain of Dharma Ṭhākur), and they likewise parody the *vaiṣṇav* mythology of Kṛṣṇa and Rādhā, of Viṣṇu and his many forms. But the parodies are not just of written or oral texts, but of the discursive regimes of religious orientation, including simulacra of doctrines and all manner of ascetic and sectarian practitioners that populate the local landscape, *vairāgīs*, *sannyāsīs*, *padres*, and of course *nāth jogīs*, *śaivas*, and *śāktas* of various ilks. In addition to a specific text or mythology, the object of the parody can be as general as a cultural norm, that is, any of the conventions of cultural expression. Reiterating Macherey and Bakhtin, I observe that *when a fictional narrative mimics a precursor discursive text or convention, it inevitably provides a critique of that which it parodies.* It is in

38. My critique of syncretism and the argument for why it is a problematic concept—primarily because of the inevitably negative entailments of the metaphors used to characterize it—was provoked initially by the important work of Asim Roy and can be found in Tony K. Stewart and Carl Ernst, "Syncretism," in *South Asian Folklore: An Encyclopedia*, ed. Margaret A. Mills and Peter J. Claus (London: Routledge, 2003). Its later expansion can be found in the previously cited essay, Stewart, "In Search of Equivalence."

this critique, both positive and negative, that we begin to uncover how the narratives function and why they remain popular to this day.[39]

A finished literary work (since nothing else can be added) disturbs and reveals the gaps in prevailing ideologies, and in this case, the stories of the fictional *pīrs* function radically differently from their counterparts, the ever-accumulating tales of the historical *pīrs*. The expansion of fantastical material in the latter can at times blur the distinction (as we earlier noted in the struggles of Girīndranāth Dās in *Bāṅglā pīr sāhityer kathā*), leading to the conflation of what are essentially two distinct genres. The tales of the historical *pīrs* are directly involved in and document the propagation of Islam and therefore function in discourses that can only be mimed by the fictional *pīr kathās*. Not surprisingly, then, the hagiographies of prior historical *pīrs* themselves also serve as potential objects of parody by the fictional tales.

It is no accident, I think, that these fictional tales first emerged just after the great movement toward vernacularization was underway in Bengal,[40] the fertile period given official impetus by Sultān Husāin Shāh, who commissioned Bangla translation-cum-retellings of the great Sanskrit epics; soon Bengalis were enjoying Kṛttibās's *Rāmāyaṇ* and Kāśīrām Dās's *Mahābhārat*,[41] among a host of other retellers, the preponderance of which subsequently prompted Saiyad Sultān to write the great narrative of the line of prophets culminating in Mohāmmad in his *Nabīvaṃśa*.[42] This was also the moment when the *gauḍīya vaiṣṇav* literatures

39. While Bakhtin, Macherey, and Genette pointed me in this direction, my fuller understanding of the mechanics and use of parody closely follows Linda Hutcheon, whose comprehensive theory of parody most directly addresses its articulation, function, and pragmatic result. Her structural, semiotic, and post-structuralist approaches resonate strongly with my own approaches to these literatures, and so much of what I argue about parody is much more completely explored in her monograph that is now three decades old but endures as the standard. See Hutcheon, *A Theory of Parody: The Teachings of Twentieth Century Art Forms* (Urbana: University of Illinois Press, 1985; repr., 2000).

40. Sheldon Pollock's work on vernacularization has prompted numerous new studies of the process; among other works, see Pollock, *The Language of the Gods in the World of Men: Sanskrit, Culture, and Power in Premodern India* (Chicago: University of Chicago Press, 2006); and Pollock, ed., *Literary Cultures in History: Reconstructions from South Asia* (Chicago: University of Chicago Press, 2003).

41. The numbers of manuscripts of these two texts are legion; *Catalogus Catalogorum of Bengali Manuscripts* [*Bāṃlā puthir tālikā samanvay: Saṅkalak o samapādak yatīndramohan bhaṭṭācāryya*], comp./ed. Jatindra Mohan Bhattacharjee (Calcutta: Asiatic Society, 1978). There are multiple authors over the next few centuries.

42. Saiyad Sultān, who had no connection to any court, explicitly observed that the stories of Rām and Kṛṣṇa were widely circulated in the vernacular Bangla, but because Bengalis did not know Arabic, and only certain elites knew Persian, few knew the stories of Muhāmmad well. He explicitly states that in an effort to remedy this he composed the *Nabīvaṃśa* in the local language; Saiyad Sultān, *Nabīvaṃśa*, ed. Ahmad Sharif, 2 vols. (Dhaka: Bangla Academy, 1978), 2:479. For a comprehensive study of this text, see Ayesha A. Irani, *The Muhammad* Avatāra*: Salvation History, Translation, and the Making of Bengali Islam* (Oxford University Press, forthcoming), which is a much more focused study based on her encyclopædic dissertation "Sacred Biography, Translation, and Conversion: The

began to flourish and the vast array of *maṅgal kāvyas* were beginning to round out. It was a time of vernacular innovation and literary efflorescence, which is critical, for *parodies must have precursor discursive texts of note to execute their work.* Linda Hutcheon persuasively argues that it is in just such periods of cultural sophistication that parody prospers.[43] There would be a resurgence of *pīr kathās* again in the nineteenth century with the advent and circulation of the stories of Bonbibī and the proliferation of tales dedicated to Satya Pīr, coincident with the so-called Bengal Renaissance, which affected both Hindu *bhadralok* and Muslim authors, but in different ways. Before visiting those, there are important aspects of the mechanics of parody that we must understand before we return to the tales of Badar Pīr and of Satya Pīr to illustrate.

Where Hutcheon observes that parody thrives in periods of cultural sophistication, the reason is that the parodist must rely on the competence of the reader, listener, or viewer to recognize and interpret the parody.[44] No text can function as a parody unless its audience recognizes it as such. In the high literary world, a parodist as a rule is not going to waste time on obscure productions;[45] but the parody of a *pīr kathā* is not so much concerned with a specific text as it is with the ethos embodied in genres, the forms of traditional Indian mythology, the structures of a caste-based world, and so forth. Margaret Rose notes in this regard that "it is not a function of fiction to offer verifiable statements of the world—for the naïve reader to take as true—but to lead the reader to interpret the fiction as, in its turn, an interpretation of the world of the reader."[46] In this more generalized form of parody, that is, where in most instances no specific literary text is named, the *pīr kathā* can easily function as the univocal, so-called entertainment for the masses, while for the more literarily, and in this case, religiously aware recipients, the text, or parts of it, can be understood to deliver a multivocal commentary on the reader's world, but only in part rather than in whole. Not every aspect of the parody need be registered by any one recipient for it to still be parodic; in fact, it would be unlikely that any two readers would have the exact same response. This variability of readings may well also account for a text's ability to function parodically through different eras, as the target understood by one reader may

Nabīvaṃśa of Saiyad Sultān and the Making of Bengali Islam, 1600–Present" (PhD diss., University of Pennsylvania, 2011).

43. Hutcheon, *Theory of Parody*, 19.

44. Hutcheon, 19. See also Margaret A. Rose, who writes, "The parodist creates a situation whereby the reader must also relate to himself as an object of the author's discourse if he is to understand the status of other objects represented in the fiction. He must, that is, see his own world through the image of himself, the reader, in the text before him, as a part of a fiction which, as he himself, has taken on a different form than in the world of objects." Rose, *Parody//Meta-Fiction: An Analysis of Parody as a Critical Mirror to the Writing and Reception of Fiction* (London: Croom Helm, 1979), 62.

45. Hutcheon, *Theory of Parody*, 57.

46. Rose, *Parody//Meta-Fiction*, 86.

well have shifted a century or two later, that ability to be revalorized being part of its enduring quality.[47] The tales of Satya Pīr and of Gājī and Kālu would appear to demonstrate such shifts as their audiences changed, accelerated perhaps because of the tendency of parody to escalate its presence as certain culturally preferred "vogues in handling conventions are getting worn out."[48] And it is important here to recognize that parodies are always context-specific, taking forms that are unique to their historical moment, characterized by their interactions with prevailing authoritative discourses;[49] but they should not be seen as parasitic or always negative. They can be value-neutral, they can deliver bitterly scathing critiques which ridicule, or they can elevate a prior discursive text as a standard of contemporary measure. But regardless of the tack, parody dramatizes difference.[50]

The genre of parody (operating intertextually on the structural level) depends on the mechanism—the rhetorical trope—of *irony* (operating intratextually on the immediate semantic level) to deliver its critique of a prior discursive text. Hutcheon argues:

> On the semantic level, irony can be defined as a marking of difference in meaning or, simply, as antiphrasis. As such, paradoxically, it is brought about, in structural terms, by the superimposition of semantic contexts (what is stated / what is intended). There is one signifier and two signifieds, in other words. Given the formal structure of parody . . . irony can be seen to operate on a microcosmic (semantic) level in the same way that parody does on a macrocosmic (textual) level, because parody too is a marking of difference, also by means of superimposition (this time, of textual rather than of semantic contexts). Both trope and genre, therefore, combine difference and synthesis, otherness and incorporation. Because of this structural similarity, I should like to argue, parody can use irony easily and naturally as a preferred, even privileged rhetorical mechanism. Irony's patent refusal of semantic univocality matches parody's refusal of structural unitextuality.[51]

47. This is analogous to Frank Kermode's notion of the "classic"; see Kermode, *Classic.*

48. Hutcheon, *Theory of Parody*, 36, quoting Northrop Frye, *Anatomy of a Criticism* (New York: Athaneum, 1970), 103.

49. Simon Dentith, *Parody* (London: Routledge, 2000), 163–64; Hutcheon, *Theory of Parody*, xi, xiv.

50. Hutcheon, *Theory of Parody*, 60–61.

51. Hutcheon, 54; for the exploration of this semiotic function, see Hutcheon, chap. 3. The *locus classicus* for interpreting literary irony is Wayne Booth, *A Rhetoric of Irony* (Chicago: University of Chicago Press, 1974); for our purposes, see esp. chap. 4, "Essays, Satire, Parody." It should be noted that much of Linda Hutcheon's analysis of irony and irony's role in parody is in conversation with Booth; see Hutcheon, *Irony's Edge: The Theory and Politics of Irony* (London: Routledge, 1994). Booth's insistence on determining authorial intention has unfortunately tended to sideline his other arguments about irony that still stand; by arguing that irony is a trope and not a genre, Hutcheon demonstrates how irony is the tool that energizes the genres of parody and satire, so she shifts much of her focus onto the pragmatics of the activity (away from the syntactic and toward the implications of the semantic).

Parody thus involves one signifier, two (or more) signifieds, the former the work of the author, the latter the work of the author and the recipient together, for the encoded second message must be decoded by the recipient for parody to work. Parody requires a critical distance from its target to be effective, and the irony on which it depends generally operates through inversions. In Wayne Booth's terms, the pleasure of irony and parody comes from the awareness of the ambiguity of duplicity, for both author and reader or auditor.[52] It can and does challenge the acceptance of narrow, doctrinaire, or dogmatic views of any particular group, which in the fictional *pīr kathā* would be aimed at both the *hinduyāni* cultural norms that the followers of Islam encountered in Bengal and the attempts by *sharī'ā*-bound *mollās* and other conservative *musalmāni* factions to impose the restrictive history-theology-law regimes. This resistance to strictures appears readily in the hierarchical society of early modern Bengal, and is further exacerbated with the divisions that mark the colonial period; Muslim reformers in the nineteenth century were especially targeted by the resurgence of *pīr kathās* in print, and it is at this same time that Hindu reformers became fixated on hagiography again, especially that of Caitanya, which tied into their critique.[53] As Simon Dentith notes, "Strongly stratified societies, for example, where separate classes live in relative social isolation, are very likely to produce mutual parodic characterisations of the social layers, whose manner of speech and writing are very strongly marked by class."[54] Our concern, however, is specifically with the *pīr kathās* and not with earlier *hinduyāni* or later Hindu and colonial forms of parody—which were certainly prevalent—or with parody generally. We have noted that the narratives of the *phakirs* circulated widely and still do today, but we cannot know just how much of the parodic double-voiced content was recognized as parody, though one suspects that average nonliterate audiences would have gleaned more than they are credited for. It is naïve to think that the nonliterate recipient would only hear the text as entertainment, for it is often precisely in the entertaining bits that the parody is on display; if they laugh, it is for a reason, and that reason will often be the parodic content. In high literary modes the explicit uncovering of parody would likely trend within elite circles[55]—and we have already commented upon the sophistication of many of the writers—but because the parodies tend to be fragmented or piecemeal, rather than a tightly focused sustained commentary on a precursor, there will often be an indirect or stealth quality to it and not everyone

52. Booth, *Rhetoric of Irony*, 127; also cited in Rose, *Parody//Meta-Fiction*, 89.

53. For this multi-faceted resurrection of the hagiographies of Caitanya, recovering the sixteenth-century texts that write of him as God, the writing of new hagiographies make Caitanya into a cultural hero, a romanticized swadesi nationalist, while others make him out to be modern reformer, and even a humanist emphasizing secular notions of privatized religion. See Bhatia, *Unforgetting Chaitanya.*

54. Dentith, *Parody*, 30–31.

55. Hutcheon, *Theory of Parody*, 27.

will register it. But if we can see these tales as parodies from this distance, then it is safe to assume that others did.

3.5. MIMESIS AND PARODY IN THE TALE OF BADAR PĪR

The opening of Jaidi's *Mānikpīrer jahurānāmā* presents Āllā in heaven holding court with twelve of his saints in a manner that mimes the gods gathering round in Indra's court to discuss what to do when the world is teetering on the brink of disaster; in various instances, the latter send down an *avatār* of Viṣṇu, or they band together, each providing a weapon to Durgā to slay a demon, or come up with some other novel solution to the problem at hand. As a result of Āllā's consultation with the saints, Badar Pīr is magically summoned. After presenting himself he is outfitted with the appropriate garb and provided with the necessary accoutrements, the signs of his position, given instructions, and sent down to earth to prepare the way for Mānik, who will become the *avatār* of the age, the *yug avatār*. The descent is not by a god or a goddess, but a *phakir*, one of the friends of God; he is not divine, and Mānik, who will follow as the *avatār*, will likewise be a *pīr*. When Badar prepares to depart, he looks into Āllā's mouth and sees the universe, mimicking the well-known act of Yaśodā with the baby Kṛṣṇa or the baby Viśvambhar (Kṛṣṇa Caitanya) and his mother Śacī, and miming a variation of Arjuna's experience with Kṛṣṇa at Kurukṣetra. There can be no mistake that Āllā is God.

Badar begins his mission in Dilli (Delhi) and Lahore, charming everyone with his presence, the women especially smitten with his personal charisma, begging to accompany him, much as Kṛṣṇa might have expected—the reference not made explicitly, but set up by the notion of *avatār*, or descent from heaven—and here Āllā's instruction about avoiding women, coupled with Badar's ascetic practices, signals that he is the structural opposite of the gallant cowherd Kṛṣṇa, inverting the expectation of the *avatār*.

Badar's encounter with the *jogīs* clearly mocks their ineffectual practices, but it is not altogether clear what types of *jogīs* they are, though one might suspect a kind of generic *tantrik* or *nāth* ascetic known for their *haṭha* yogic disciplines. The *jogīs* boast that they have remained transfixed for twelve years, sufficient time for the reeds and grasses to grow from them, but to what end? Badar Pīr conjures the goddess Gaṅgā in an instant and the *jogīs* suddenly ascend to the heavens and sprout additional arms, suggesting just how easy it is for a *pīr* to effect the transformation of humans into *hinduyāni* gods. It is equally reasonable, though, to read the images the other way: the *jogīs* were actually gods posing to test Badar Pīr with their insults and challenges, and he simply saw right through them and returned them to their heavenly domains. Either reading ends at the same place—a demonstration of Badar's superior power. But, utilizing kinship status as older brother to Gaṅgā (the *jogīs* refer to her as mother, Mā Gaṅgā, thereby establishing Badar's relation to them as uncle to nephews), Badar invites her presence, to which she responds that she does not normally acknowledge the call of a *jāban*. When she does arrive, she very nearly overwhelms him before he is advised by the wind (magically transformed into a white fly summoned by Āllā) to capture her in his shoulder bag. The commentary on the power of the goddess hardly needs elaboration. Badar further underscores his God-given powers by speeding up the growth of fruits and vegetables he planted along the Gaṅgā's banks—a wry commentary on his fecundity in relation to Gaṅgā, especially as they are growing in the waters of the Gaṅgā—and then offers first fruits to Āllā, a gesture that would be familiar to gods and goddesses used to receiving *pūjā*. Though Gaṅgā is powerful enough to float giant boulders from Setubandha up the coast to Bengal in order to provide raw materials to fashion a *masjid*, that divine power is easily commandeered by the *pīr*, another not-so-subtle message. Similar is Viśvakarma's plight. Badar summons him to build the *masjid*, but he attempts to wiggle out of the project by agreeing to work only one night. Doing the work of God, Badar is not to be deterred, so he stops the sun from rising, impelling Viśvakarma to continue to work, though eventually Āllā intervenes lest Badar's action upset the balance between heavenly *bhest*, sacred Mākkā, and earth.

Badar's trip to Dilli is to secure the daughter of the Bādsvā as his wife, to which the king predictably objects and moves to punish him—kings punishing *phakirs* is, as we have seen, a recurring theme. The request to marry a king's daughter, regardless of the family's religious orientation, is always met with fierce rejection if not outright violence—the mixing of social stations (ascetic *phakir* with a worldly princess, who can be *musalmāni* or of caste, either *kṣatriya* or *brāhmaṇ*) marking key tensions that ripple through this *pīr kathā*. Taking the bride by stealth or by outright battle is, of course, one of the traditional Indic techniques for marriage, and here, as we have already noted, the author takes a page from the Arabian Nights where tigers, rather than færies, secrete Dudbibī out of the palace on her bed, which they deposit in the forest.[56] The marriage proper is not, however, effected by the stealth capture as one might expect, but by Dudbibī's consent. It is in the *gandharva* style, one of eight recognized forms of traditional Indic marriage, but—and here is where the inversion comes in—while her father is convinced by his vision of the divine couple to bless the marriage, that marriage cannot be considered official—nor will it satisfy Dudbibī's mother—until it is confirmed in a manner

56. Here and in other stories, the tigers that assemble from the forests at Badar's summons provide comic relief as they whine about how tough their lives have become since humans have started encroaching on their forests, an interesting environmental observation. In works as early as Kṛṣṇarām's *Rāy maṅgal* in the late seventeenth century, the tigers are shown to exhibit great bravado, scaring people to death, but whining and crying about their plight in dealing with the seemingly endless advance of humans into their territory; see Kṛṣṇarām Dās, *Rāy maṅgal*, in *Kavi kṛṣṇarāmdāser granthāvalī* (secs. 14–17, pp. 186–95, vv. 237–337), where scores of tigers, male and female, are quoted by name with their complaints.

consistent with the dictates of the local application of Islamic custom, which perforce supersedes local custom.

The four *mollās* who consult their almanacs and calculate the auspiciousness of the union, its sanction by Āllā, and the proper time for it to take place clearly mimic the ubiquitous South Asian *brāhmaṇ* wedding astrologer. The Korān is deployed in much the same way as locally prevalent *jyotiṣa śāstra* (astrological texts), so this activity can also be read as a form of technical one-upmanship, for the Korān was fairly routinely used for bibliomancy, for divination and prognostication of such affairs as weddings and personal concerns. No details are provided in the text of this *kathā*, of course, but there were bibliomantic texts routinely employed during the period of Sultanate and Mughal ascendancy in South Asia, such as *Fa'l-i Qur'ān* (Divination by Qur'ān).[57] The tenor of this parody is playful and not aggressive, for it points to the ways Islamic practices found analogues in traditional South Asian ritual forms, while also signaling that a Korān-based prognostication was necessary to validate the decisions that led to the *gandharva* marriage agreement.

Dudbibī's decision to acquiesce to Badar's request for marriage is based on the revelation of their conjoined identities in past lives. We have already noted the invocation of the mechanism of karmic transmigration, but the specific trope is reminiscent of a common South Asian lovers' story of the ideal husband and wife finding one another in life after life, as attested throughout the epic and *purāṇik* texts for gods and goddesses and in literary works such as Somadeva's *Kathāsaritsāgara*, for various celestials and humans.[58] Badar's display of multi-armed forms, followed by Rām and then Kṛṣṇa, is easily read as revealing his identity to her, and hers to him. But remembering that a fiction cannot produce an authentic theological statement, only its simulacrum, the expression is of necessity vague. Her eyes are closed and she sees Badar as Viṣṇu, Rām, and Kṛṣṇa, with her as the matching counterpart, an expression that could be read several ways:

57. The recognized Persian genre of such texts is *fāl* or *fāl-nāma*. *Fa'l-i Qur'ān* (Divination by Qur'ān) by Sadr Jahan and Jacfar al-Sadiq (880 AH; ca. 1480) contains circular diagrams with topics to be explored, including marriage, that are coordinated with another circular table of random numbers, which then together index a selection of thirty *suras* from the Korān; each *sura* bears fifteen possible interpretations which are narrowed to the one correct reading by a different combination of those original numbers. Similarly, elaborate tables of prognostications were added as codices to the Korān, which would be used in relation to certain letters of the alphabet. The letter would be determined by randomly opening the Korān, counting seven lines down, then identifying the seventh letter across, whose significance would be determined by the table to formulate an answer to the question; for descriptions and color images, see Francesca Leoni et al., *Power and Protection: Islamic Art and the Supernatural* (Oxford: Ashmolean Museum, 2016), 21–25. Seeking guidance from God on specific issues (*esteḵāra*) was usually regarded as a licit use of the Korān, but not using it as a device for augury (*tafa''ol*); Īraj Afšār, "Fāl-nāma," *Encyclopædia Iranica* (New York: Bibliotheca Persica Press, 1999), 9:172–76.

58. Somadeva Bhaṭṭa, *Tales from the Kathāsaritsāgara*, translated with an introduction by Arshia Sattar, with a foreword by Wendy Doniger (London: Penguin Books, 1994).

identity (they are not different from the figures represented), similarity (they are "like" the figures represented), or all true lovers make the divine pair (the Kṛṣṇa and Rādhā principles and their analogous sets are found in all couples, a generic *tantrik* reading). Regardless of how one parses the revelation of images, the god complex in all its forms is displayed by Badar Pīr, who is himself not a god, for there is only one God. Either way, the ancient Indic gods are reduced from their supreme stature and possess no greater power or status than this friend of God. Just as easily, one can apply the permutations to the Bādsvā, who sees the true love of his daughter for Badar and so "sees" Rām and Sītā. But what the father "sees" is the image of the faithful wife, Sītā, not the unmarried *gopī* (not named, but implied to be Rādhā), a gentle suggestion about what constitutes a proper liaison (the *gandharva* marriage more fitting for Rādhā, but the confirmed and validated marriage according to Islamic custom more appropriate to Sītā, which is of course what he and his wife insist is proper). What he saw was what he wanted to see, a liaison that could not be censured by the social customs of the court.

The convoluted manner of Dudbibī's impregnation has already been noted, but the idea of Āllā guiding a particular individual apart from the Prophet to set right the affairs of the populations of India can only point to the recurring activity of the *avatārs* of Viṣṇu, but the *avatār* is not a god. There is no need to rehearse the sequence again, but the obvious reference to the ascetic practices of Badar Pīr being broken in much the same way as the *apsarasas* disrupt the meditations of the *sādhus* of old (our first reading) must be modified to account for the role Saytān, whose nefarious activities are routinely associated with indulging the appetites for self-gratification. Under the direct command and control of Āllā, Saytān actually enters the body of Badar to stir his virility, but Badar's arousal and sexual activity is not illicit because its object is his wife, nor has he broken his ascetic celibacy because the love-making occurs during the enchantment of a dream sequence, not in his waking state.[59] With the actual impregnation coming from the God-commissioned insect crawling into Dudbibī's womb through her nose, her chastity is likewise preserved, quite an inversion of the *apsarasas* impelling the ascetic to actually spill his seed, by which he retrogresses and loses his power, no longer a threat to the gods. The union of Badar and Dudbibī in their dreams is generative to the work of God. The apparent commentary on the difference between licit and illicit sexual activity among ascetics is provocative.

The rest of this prolegomena to the work of Mānik Pīr follows the simple outlines of Quest mythology, as already noted. But there is one last feature that confirms the parodic reading: the two poems inserted in the middle of the narrative. It is a commonplace in Bangla narratives in the premodern period to insert poems or songs as ways of capturing succinctly a fundamental point. Similar to the way

59. It should be noted that the text does not use the word *naphs* (Arabic *nafs*) or base instincts, though by way of the action implies it.

the author switches to the three-footed *tripadi* meter to explore more thoroughly the intimacies of profound emotion, the inserted poem or song can go a step further and reveal or provide a commentary on the underlying meaning or point of the story. Sometimes these insertions punctuate, on occasion they anticipate reversals or turning points, at other times they simply illustrate. The first poem inserted just after the marriage has been sanctioned by the *mollās'* calculations is titled "The Dark Lord, Kālā."

> Listen to the name, the virtues of the Dark Lord
> heard in home after home.
> I shall write Kālā's own name
> on the trailing edge of my sari.
> Who brought to this land
> a moon so dark,
> that in dancer's disguise has pilfered
> the honor of this virtuous wife?
> How inauspicious the moment
> I dipped my foot into the Jamunā's waters.
> At the foot of the *kadamba*, bent in his careless pose,
> he played mischief with his flute.
>
> *Phakir Guñjar contemplates his worthless body—*
> *a hollowed out dead tree*
> *whose leaves have dropped off*
> *and floated away.*

In the first surface reading, the title refers to Kṛṣṇa, and the epithet of moon-faced is common enough. He is the cowherd lord who lures the maidens (*gopīs*) to nighttime trysts—the pose of three breaks (*tribhaṅga*), his signature stance as he plays the flute, bent at the knee, waist, and neck—asking the *gopīs* to give up their love, their bodies to his seemingly insatiable appetites. But he has disappeared, leaving the *gopī* to ponder her fate, to ponder her decision to cuckold her husband. She has written Kṛṣṇa's name on the *añcal*, the very trailing end and edge of the sari where the village women keep their valuables tied in a knot, but by writing his name along the edge, that name—when it is written or uttered, manifests the aural dimension of Kṛṣṇa's ontology and therefore makes him present, in much the same way uttering his name in *jap* wraps the mutterer in his aural protection—frames her, embraces her every time she pulls her sari over her head, ironically in a gesture of modesty, emblematic of the predicament for these women who risk everything for this fleeting pleasure. The mood of abandonment and wanting is the well-recognized experience of *viraha*, the exquisite pain of lovers when they separate, but we only witness the woman's agony for an absent Kṛṣṇa. Since a poem generally focuses on one of the basic experiences of love, the expression of *viraha* is expected as the dominant trope of one's relation to the fickle Kṛṣṇa.

According to the *vaiṣṇav* æsthetic classification of Rūp Gosvāmī's Sanskrit *Bhaktirasāmṛtasindhu*, the *gopī's* fundamental emotional platform (*bhāva*) is the supreme love (*prema*), which is experienced as erotic engagement (*śṛṅgāra rasa*). In this poem, she exhibits three of the thirty-three transitory emotions (*vyābhicāri*), which are passing indicators of the depth of emotion. She shows hints of shame (*vrīḍā*) for her actions, coupled with a stronger sense of grief (*viṣāda*) over the resulting loss, which seems to be both for her loss of Kṛṣṇa and for her unrecoverable loss of innocence and her standing as a properly faithful wife. The underlying emotional tenor is one of anxiety (*cintā*), fearing what she cannot admit to herself, her unresolved desires, yet unable to maintain a pique or anger because of the depth of her love.[60]

Traditionally, the signature line or *bhaṇitā* is the point where the author inserts himself into the poem's narrative, sometimes retaining his name as a man (and nearly all authors in this tradition are male) but in his assumed identity as the *gopī*'s confidante. Phakir Guñjar's name means the buzzing or humming of bees, the bee famous for hovering over and licking the nectar of the lotus (with its culturally obvious sexual associations), and he plays the role of a woman too in order to aid those who love Kṛṣṇa. In this role s/he presents a sympathetic ear, proffers advice or words of encouragement; s/he often vicariously identifies with the *gopī's* plight and berates Kṛṣṇa for his callousness, his fickleness, and so forth. Here s/he seems to be an older woman, most likely a duenna or traditional go-between messenger (*dūtī*) who arranges trysts for her younger friend and Kṛṣṇa. Her lament, however, is from the perspective of one who is no longer able to participate directly in the games of love, whose body has dried up and is no longer ripe for love play, whose beauty has long disappeared like the leaves from a dead tree. Her *gopī* friend is clearly still young and desirable enough to have attracted Kṛṣṇa, who has granted her entry into his endless play (*līlā*). Phakir Guñjar can only participate vicariously, his reportage providing an experienced perspective born of great longing.

The technical flaws in this poem, however, signal a parodic inversion and mark the poem as the work of a poet either not steeped in the *vaiṣṇav* æsthetics of *bhaktirasaśāstra* or, more likely, deliberately subverting the standards. The emotional content of the poem does not display any of the expected indicators (*anubhāva*) by which emotion is conveyed or any of the excitants (*vibhāva*) that prompt the manifestation of emotion, nor does it demonstrate the involuntary responses (*sāttvika bhāva*) to the experience of the emotion. Rather, the poet's heroine talks about the *image* of Kṛṣṇa, which elicits little other than the generalized notion of *viraha*, the searing pain of separation. *Viraha* is perhaps the most

60. As previously noted, the foundational text for devotional æsthetics of *rasa* is Rūpa Gosvāmin's *Bhaktirasāmṛtasindhu*. For the experience of *prema* as erotic love (*śṛṅgāra*), see Rūpa Gosvāmin, *Bhaktirasāmṛtasindhu* 3.4.1–36; for the transitory emotion of grief (*viṣāda*), 2.4.13–20; for shame (*vrīḍā*), 2.4.113–17; for anxiety (*cintā*), 2.4.1136–39.

common emotional depiction of early modern poetry and song in the Bangla-speaking region, and it remains so to this day. Contemporary religious commentators are quick to liken this experience of the lover's absence as a metaphor of the soul yearning for God, a sentiment that clearly resonates in *sūphī* circles as well. But the signature line at the end of the poem ruptures the mood, rather than enhancing it, because it can be read as self-pitying, an attitude that has no place in supreme love (*prema*), nor does it offer hope, only despair where there is no place for the erotic. This mixing of messages would be considered a fatal flaw, and in the vocabulary of the devotional æsthetes within the *vaiṣṇav* tradition, the poem would be characterized as inauthentic and artificial.[61] But can it be any other way?

This song is integrated into a fictional narrative and therefore is itself fictional, rather than expressive of devotion.[62] This particular poem does not appear to exist outside this manuscript. There is no recognized author (*padakartā*) by the name of Phakir Guñjar found in any of the exhaustive compilations of either *musalmāni* authors writing on *vaiṣnav* themes or the myriad of *vaiṣṇav* authors; the numbers of authors run into the hundreds and the poems into the thousands.[63] But whether

61. It is important to note that this is not an arbitrary value judgment, for there were very exacting measures the *vaiṣṇav* traditions followed to evaluate the quality of literary production. In the hagiographical tradition surrounding Kṛṣṇa Caitanya (1486–1533), the inspiration for the *gauḍīya vaiṣṇav* tradition in Bengal, the ultimate arbiter of the devotional æsthetic was Caitanya's companion in Puri, Svarūp Dāmodar. According to the hagiographies, Svarūp screened every poem, every play, every song to be presented to Caitanya. At one point he censured an unnamed Vaṅga *brāhmaṇ* for writing a flawed drama that depicted inauthentic and artificial emotions, and while the erstwhile dramatist was allowed to stay in the company of devotees, his writings were never read out. In the *Caitanya caritāmṛta* of Kṛṣṇadās Kavirāj, Svarūp is reported to have said, "In the words of indifferent poets there is seeming *rasa* (i.e., the experience of the emotion of love), and it gives me no joy to listen to opposition to the truths. Those who cannot discriminate between *rasa* and that which seems like *rasa* can never gain the shore of the sea of devotional perfection." For the whole story, see Kṛṣṇadās Kavirāj, *Caitanya caritāmṛta*, ed. Rādhagovinda Nāth, with the commentary *Gaurakṛpataraṅgiṇī ṭīkā* by the editor, 3rd ed., 6 vols. (Kalikātā: Sādhanā Prakāśanī, 1355–59 BS [ca. 1948–52], vol. 5, bk. 3, chap. 5, vv. 87–149. For a translation based on the Rādhāgovinda Nāth edition, see Kṛṣṇadāsa Kavirāja, *The Caitanya caritāmṛta of Kṛṣṇadāsa Kavirāja*, trans. Edward C. Dimock, Jr., ed. Tony K. Stewart, with an introduction by the translator and the editor, Harvard Oriental Series 56 (Cambridge: Department of Sanskrit and Indian Studies, Harvard University, 1999), 3.5. In another passage Svarūp deduces the devotional worthiness of Rūp Gosvāmī from a single Sanskrit *śloka* the latter had composed. This was, of course, the same Rūp Gosvāmī who later composed the previously cited text of the *Bhaktirasāmṛtasindhu*, which became the standard for devotional æsthetics; *Caitanya caritāmṛta*, 3.1.69–82.

62. It is important to note that the corpus of poems in praise of Rādhā and Kṛṣṇa were not and demand not to be read as fictions as we understand fiction, even though the subject matter is what many scholars term mythological. These compositions are held within the tradition to be a form of *revelation*, what the poets saw of the eternal *līlā* or play of Kṛṣṇa, either in meditation, dreams, or in their mind's eye. They are then primary documents that serve as a confirmation of the theological position of the group.

63. For *musalmāni* authors writing on Kṛṣṇa's love play, see Jatīndramohan Bhaṭṭācārya, comp./ed., *Bāṅgālār vaiṣṇavbhāvāpanna musalmān kavi padamañjuṣā* (Kalikātā: Kalikātā Viśvavidyālay, 1984).

the poet existed or not is moot because the text is incorporated into a fictional narrative; we have to treat the poet not as a writer of *vaiṣṇav* poetry, but as an allographic figure parodying *vaiṣṇav* poetry, whether the putative author is Jaidi himself, Jaidi's *guru*, or some other unknown figure.

A second reading of the poem, however, suggests how this poem may function to articulate a different parodic message. It suggests a deliberateness on the part of the author Jaidi for inserting this poem the way he did—and because it is the reader or listener who must determine if the product is parody, that determination points to or implies (but may not directly identify) authorial intent.[64] The name for Kṛṣṇa in this poem is Kālā, which is *not* a common epithet for Kṛṣṇa. *Kālā* means black, and *kṛṣṇa* likewise means black, but generally that inky blue-green-black; both indicate dark or darkness, hence the translation of the Dark Lord. But *kālā* as a noun also means Time and Death personified, with unpleasant, indeed dreaded associations.[65] Kṛṣṇa as the moon-faced one is generally referring to a full moon with its brilliant luminescence, but a dark full moon is an oxymoron and does not invoke the positive associations of the epithet of moon-face. If it is truly a dark moon, then there is no moon; it is absent, and suddenly the darkness seems portentous, if not sinister. The cowherd maiden as heroine pines for something that no longer remains: a lord who abandons his lovers and friends. A black moon is absent. The moment of committing to the play of that fickle and unfaithful lord might now seem truly inauspicious indeed—it is not an empty lament, for this shadowy figure pilfered the one thing any woman in the world of romance can claim for her character: fidelity, which here would include virginity. The tone is ominous and bleak. As a critique or parody of the prevailing *vaiṣṇav* theologization of the poetry, the message subtly hints that the *vaiṣṇav* way is itself a potential death trap; to use profane love as a model for love of the divine is dangerous.

Phakir Guñjar's signature line initially looks to be that of a time-worn woman consoling the young *gopī* and wishing herself into her place, but now reduced to

---

For the most comprehensive *vaiṣṇav* collections, see Vaiṣṇav Dās, comp., *Padakalpataru*, ed. Satiśacandra Rāy, with an introduction by the editor, 5 vols., Sāhitya Pariṣat Granthāvalī, no. 50 (Kalikātā: Rāmakāmal Siṃha for the Baṅgīya Sāhitya Pariṣat, 1322–38 BS [ca. 1915–31]). See also Rādhāmohan Ṭhākur, comp., *Śrīpadāmṛtasamudra*, ed. Umā Rāy, with the Sanskrit commentary "Mahābhāvanusārinī ṭīkā" by the compiler (Calcutta: Calcutta University Press, 1391 BS [ca. 1984]).

64. Hutcheon, *Theory of Parody*, 40, 55, 93.

65. The form *kālā* invokes images of Kālī, who in this literature was often depicted as a bloodthirsty goddess requiring human sacrifice. See also the compelling passage in the *Bhagavad gītā*, which was chosen by Oppenheimer to express the horror of the first nuclear experiment, which he quotes as "Now I have become Death (*kāla*), the destroyer of worlds." For a detailed account of the history of this moment, see James A. Hijiya, "The Gita of J. Robert Oppenheimer," *Proceedings of the American Philosophical Society* 144, no. 2 (June 2000): 123–67. Van Buitenen's translation reads *kāla* as Time rather than Death: "I am Time grown old to destroy the world, embarked on the course of world annihilation." Kṛṣṇa Dvaipāyana Vyāsa, *Bhagavad Gītā in the Mahābhārata*, 11.32a, "*kālo 'smi lokakṣayakṛt pravṛddho lokān samāhartum iha pravṛttaḥ*," 116–17.

vicarious participation. That reading would result from the expectation provided by the figure of the duenna in thousands of well-known poems, but the line ruptures the mood of the *vaiṣṇav* sensibility and hints at something else altogether. By retaining the title of *phakir*, the author signals that he is a mendicant, his body dried up to the sensual world of *rasa*, the basis for the *vaiṣṇav* æsthetic, but which hints at Badar's state. Indeed *rasa*, the distilled experience of love, is tasted, for the literal meaning of *rasa* is sap or juice; not surprisingly, *rasa* also retains an association with semen. As the signature line signals with the image of the dead tree trunk, Phakir Guñjar through his own austerities seems to have abandoned the sensual world, his body desiccated, his *rasa* dried up, just as Badar Pīr did after he left his wife to pursue the mission assigned by Āllā that opened the tale. What is suggested seems again to be the age-old tension between the spiritual exercise of celibacy and the draw of sensual life, whether for self-indulgence or for procreation. It places the control of the *sūphī* ascetic in opposition to the hypersensual indulgence of the *vaiṣṇav* devotee (a not uncommon critique over the last six centuries among many detractors of the *vaiṣṇav* path). Phakir Guñjar's sapless trunk drops one last leaf, foreshadowing the action of Badar Pīr when he drops the flower into the waters to find Dudbibī. It bespeaks a disciplined control, and points to the nearly immaculate conception of Mānik that could only be effected by Āllā Himself by dispatching Saytān to enter Badar's body to arouse the passions. The tension between an ascetic religiosity and a sensual world shadows the worlds of *pīrs*.

That friction between the ascetic demands of the mendicant and the impulse to lawful procreation are captured in the precise moment that Badar Pīr picks up the flower that contains the insect sent by God to inseminate Dudbibī. Consistent with the subjunctive nature of the narrative, which is suggestive rather than overdetermined, there is a well-known *ḥadīth*, with the gradation of *ḥasan* that states, "In this world, women and perfume have been made dear to me, and my comfort has been provided in prayer."[66] Badar has been practicing his remembrance of God, *jikir* (*smaraṇ*), for four months after leaving his wife. The flower—as all the flowers in the story are—is fragrant, but in this case redolent with the touch of Āllā. The beauty of the flower and its perfume interrupt Badar's prayers with memories of his wife. He is momentarily distracted, but weighing the significance of its interruption, he sends it to his wife in the name of God and then

66. Sunan An-Nasâ'I, *The Book of Kind Treatment of Women*, chap. 1, "Love of Women," 3391, trans. Nâsiruddin al-Khattâb, comp. Imâm Hâfiz Abû Abdur Rahmân and Ahmad bin Shu'aib bin 'Ali an-Nasâ'i, edited and referenced by Hâfiz Abu Tâhir Zubair 'Alî Za'î (Riyadh: Darussalam, 2007), 4:191. Additional variants are attested in Wensinck, A. J. and J. P. Mensing, comps., *Concordance et indices de la tradition Musulmane*, Les Six Livres, al-Dārimī's *Le Musnad*, Mālik's *Le Muwatta'*, and Aḥmad ibn Ḥanbal's *Le Musnad*, compiled with an introduction by A. J. Wensinck, vols. 1–8, 2nd ed. (Leiden: E. J. Brill, 1992), 1:405.

resumes his recitations. Āllā Himself has to rouse him from his reveries by the dispatch of Saytān. This allusion to the *ḥadīth* confirms the parodic use of a critical Islamic truism, not in citation that would be appropriate for legal and theological discourse, but through the invocation of images, the semantic currency of fiction.

The second poem by the allographic Phakir Guñjar is much more opaque than the first, but seems to anticipate the next installment of the tale, the adventures of Mānik Pīr. The translation I have provided is provisional because the language is oblique with allusions rather than clear referents:

> Hey, stitch fine garlands with consummate care,
> as the ruby (*mānik*) is carefully strung in the heart.
> All five flowers rest on a single branch, so which flower will bloom?
> What twenty-bud [garland] can be stitched with no thread?
> How can you sew a garland made of rubies (*mānik*) and gemstones?
> Is it possible for a lamp immersed in water to disperse the dark of night?
> O how will I recognize that particular flower?
>
> *Phakir Guñjar sings, contemplating this hollowed,*
> *dessicated trunk, shedding a single petal that floats away.*

The author is clearly playing on Mānik's name, which means "ruby," and the contrast of flowers strung into a garland that will wilt versus the difficulty of stringing a garland of indestructible jewels points to a potential reading—how can the indestructible Mānik be created in a world of flesh and blood? Because of the placement of the poem as Badar is about to take his leave for the city of Cāṭigāñ, it likely presages the miraculous process of Mānik's conception. In traditional Bengal's yogic and Islamic traditions, creation itself is strung, an image with ancient associations.[67] Given the role of stringing in creation, the act of stitching that thread could be interpreted as the act of procreation, but the riddle—how can a fully formed (twenty-bud) garland be stitched with no thread?—suggests the impossibility of impregnating Dudbibī while Badar is absent. Following that image, what then is the thread? Recalling the lines—"The insect crawled out of the lotus stem up her nostril and seated itself in the hundred-petaled navel lotus to take birth. Mānik had entered Dudbibī's womb"—invokes the possibility of the five petals strung on a single branch referencing the *cakras* of *yoga* in the subtle body.[68] Mānik lodges himself in the hundred-petaled lotus, which traditionally suggests

67. Going back as far as the Vedas, David White explores the stringing of creation and the following of those strings as part of the yogic mastery of the universe; see White, *Sinister Yogis* (Chicago: University of Chicago Press, 2009).

68. See Shaman Hatley, "Mapping the Esoteric Body in the Islamic Yoga of Bengal," *History of Religions* 46, no. 4 (May 2007): 351–68.

the point of enlightenment *mukti*, or by analogy in the *sūphī* path, the highest state of ecstatic experience called *fanā* (Arabic *fanā fi allāh*), which is actualized in the fourth stage (Arabic *maqāmāt*) known as *mārphat* (Arabic *maᶜrifa*), the four stages often aligned with the *cakras.*[69] More simply, as the *avatār* of the age, Mānik will save humanity. The lamp immersed in the waters would seem to allude to Badar's physical location away from Dudbibī, but also his immersion in his ascetic practices (*tapisya*), which drowns sexual passion the same way water extinguishes the candle. What the reader of the poem is about to learn is that Badar overcomes this paradoxical situation through the dream meeting. Recognizing the flower would then suggest Dudbibī's predicament when she spotted the very flower that Badar had sent on its way upstream. Gañjar Phakir's contemplation of the single dropped petal seems to ruminate on the oddity of the *pīr* being dead to the world (shriveled, dried up), yet magically capable of reproducing, giving us in the process a second reading of the signature line of the first poem: Gañjar Phakir contemplating how Badar Pīr would send the impregnating flower to Dudbibī. It is nothing short of miraculous.

The hermeneutic difficulties this poem poses, however, may well rest on its deployment of a "twilight language" (*sandhya bhāṣā*), which is common to the esoteric *tantrik* traditions utilized deliberately to obfuscate the layers of meaning, and this includes some Bengali *sūphī* texts. In these esoteric poems, the metaphors often index technical terminology involving physiology, stages of ritual *sādhanā* (practice), and so forth, but these technical terms cannot automatically be read as a consistent code because, like parody itself, they are always context dependent.[70] One might anticipate in this passage a possible critique of the recherché *tantrik* groups, such as *nāths* and *sahajiyās*, the latter a *vaiṣṇav* orientation known for sexo-yogic practices—but that would, I think, be a too easy capitulation, and we have no evidence beyond a vague use of riddles and terminology which are not in the least definitive, especially since the terms are not in common with the poetic and didactic expressions of those groups.[71] Finally, and very seriously, we cannot rule out the possibility that the apparent technical expressions are a kind of pidgin mumbo jumbo, a parody of twilight language, which would, I suppose, make it doubly opaque, well-nigh impenetrable. In much the same manner as the gesture

69. Among the many texts I have examined that articulate these stages are the anonymous "Yoga kalandar," Hājī Muhammad's "Surat nāmā" [alt. Nur jamāl], and Āli Roja's "Āgama," all of which can be found in Āhmad Śariph, ed., *Baṅglār sūphī sāhitya* (Ḍhākā: Baṃlā Ekāḍemī, 1371 BS [1964]), on 87–116, 171–91, and 336–43, respectively.

70. For more on the mechanics of *sandhya bhāṣā* and the problem of deciphering the technical language and the epistemological hurdles one faces in attempting to interpret these texts, see Tony K. Stewart, "The Power of the Secret: The Tantalizing Discourse of Sahajiyā Scholarship" in *The Legacy of Vaiṣṇavism in Colonial Bengal*, ed. Ferdinando Sardella and Lucien Wong (London: Routledge, 2019).

71. For the full range of such groups that have been identified in Bengal, see Shashibhusan Dasgupta, *Obscure Religious Cults*, 3rd ed. (Calcutta: Firma KLM, 1969).

toward linguistically unviable Arabic versions of the *shahāda*, which still manage to signify something in that direction, these riddles may not indicate a specific content, but true to their fictional quality, allude to a type of understanding that would always be obscure to the reader or listener, but would be immediately identifiable as part of an esoteric discourse of *sūphīs* and other ascetic groups—expressions intended to mystify because ordinary readers or auditors could never be expected to understand. True to their subjunctive dialogical function, the poems engage the reader or listener, demanding interaction, pushing the imagination to places that it might not ordinarily go. Without the rest of the text, we can only speculate, but that, I think, is precisely what this text intends to make us do.

The story of Badar Pīr, father of Mānik, which constitutes the prolegomena of Jaidi's *Mānikpīrer jahurānāmā*, can be easily read on two levels. The surface narrative points initially to ways in which Islamic perspectives might be expressed in terms of the prevailing *hinduyāni* cosmology that is predominately *vaiṣṇav* in its vision. Āllā and the various traditional Bengali gods and goddesses range through the heavens and around earth, mixing with *avatārs* of various sorts, and with *jogīs*, *pīrs*, *phakirs*, *peris*, *phereśtās*, the *nabī*, and other celestial traffic. The activity is subjunctive in exploring how it all may fit, and it invites the reader to try to imagine how the traditional world of Bengal might accommodate a *musalmāni* outlook. But a closer reading reveals that time and again the naïve perspective of the first reading gives way to a more stringent critique of that traditional Bengali world and its features which are shown often to be artifices. The parodying of the generic *vaiṣṇav avatār* theory, the mocking manner in which Badar Pīr manhandles Gaṅgā and harnesses her to his work, suggest a different world order. Badar's assumption of the identities of Viṣṇu, Rām, and Kṛṣṇa reveals just how limited those gods are, or more importantly, just how powerful this friend of God can be. In this particular text, it may appear that the traditional gods and goddesses have been recognized with equal status to Āllā, but the second reading makes clear that something else is being suggested. This text does not just explore how an Islamic perspective might be incorporated into the preexisting Bengali cosmology, but quite the other way around. Through its symbolic imagery, a generalized Islamic cosmology is made to stretch and bend to incorporate an Indic or *hinduyāni* world, to appropriate it for its own ends. Importantly, there is a subtle shift of register: yes, the various gods and goddesses certainly exist, but no, they are not the equivalent of Āllā, for he has no peer, he alone is God. The traditional gods and goddesses are not even as powerful as the *pīr* or *phakir*; they are hierarchically shifted into a lower cosmological register and made subservient to Āllā and those who people his court in heaven. As Booth persistently asked in *A Rhetoric of Irony* how a reader knows when a statement is ironic, here we have the confirmation: the *repeated* shift from the gods being equivalent to Āllā to everything being subordinated to Āllā, and the appropriation of a *hinduyāni* world into a *musalmāni* cosmology substantiates the reading. As the adventures of Badar multiply to extend the narrative, the broad strokes of this new cosmology emerge in a grand exploration. This exploration is one of the most important functions of fiction: to investigate and invent meaning in ways that are safe from the strictures of institutional, doctrinaire thought, and here the exercise intimates how the old world order is not displaced, but incorporated into a larger, necessarily vague and incomplete, fictional, but very generically Islamic, cosmological vision.

The exercise in establishing a seeming equivalence of cosmologies and then adjusting it to reflect the "real" structure to be Islamic, speculates and then explores ways that Islam might accommodate and incorporate a Bengali cultural legacy that is primarily *vaiṣṇav* and *śākta*. In this newly constructed world, then, one must rethink what "conversion" might actually mean, if an Islamic cosmology could be stretched to accommodate and then appropriate a *vaiṣṇav* or *śākta* perspective. It hints that there would be no radical break with prior tradition, rather a displacement and reordering, for while doctrine in this scenario may only be a faint impression of the rigorous prescriptions of theology and law, the general perspective on the world is preserved on both sides. In this exercise, it is possible to see how Islam might be made understandable and palatable to its Bengali audience and how that understanding could then be transformed, displaced, and ultimately replaced by an emerging Islam. That new cosmology carries with it expectations, and adjustment to moral sensibilities, wherein the traditional Indic social structure is undercut and a new order put in its place, one where action, not birth, determines standing. While recognizing the limits of fiction to participate directly in that discourse, that the author has something of this in mind seems to be attested in one of his signature lines just at the moment of Mānik's appearance, when he writes, "Mānik descended (*yavatirnya*) in the home of the gardener Madu. May the Hindus chant 'Hari, Hari!' (*hari bol*) for this ranking official among those devoted servants of God (*mamin*)." The expression *Hari bol!* is perhaps the most common affirmation of religious commitment on the part of *vaiṣṇavs* in Bengal, specifically the *gauḍīya vaiṣṇavs* who are the majority *vaiṣṇav* community in the Bangla-speaking world; it is used to affirm and sanction any religious activity they may undertake, it is a mark of auspiciousness, and a way of proclaiming their confederacy. That the author considers his audience may well include those of *vaiṣṇav* persuasion gently links the text back to its context, its historical moment.

That the author may have had an audience in mind that would be familiar with the *vaiṣṇav* habit, if not *habitus*, of uttering the name of Hari at auspicious moments reminds us that we have characterized the text of Badar Pīr (and those like it) as a religious biography, explicitly a hagiography, the life of a saint. But Badar's story is a *fictional hagiography*, which has several unexplored complications. It may seem odd to characterize any hagiography as a parody, because the whole point is to deliver a message in the service of religion, but the structure of hagiography lends itself to just such deployment. As previously noted, I have argued that the narrativized life, the *bios*, is not generally the primary subject, but the "ostensible" subject, of religious biography.[72] The "real" subject is the *religious ideal*, which is what turns biography into religious biography. In its most basic form, this bicameral structure of religious biography—one life, but two messages (*bios* and religious ideal)—is conceptually parallel to the most basic structure of parody, which in semiotic terms, Hutcheon has characterized as one signifier and two signifieds. Provocatively, Booth uses the same terminology to describe the workings of irony: a "real" subject and an "ostensible" subject. The hagiographical form would seem to be well suited to the task of delivering a parodic critique. Read as hagiographies, the fictional quality of these *pīr kathās* does not change the operational structure, but does place them in a unique position. The historian cannot demythologize the *bios* because there is no history to find; the figure represented in the narrative slips beyond the vanishing point of a history. Similarly, because it is a fiction, the religious ideal can only be presented as a simulacrum, unsystematic, vague assertions presented through images and actions, but not by explicit argument; it too slips beyond the vanishing point of theology at the opposite end of the spectrum. The *bios*, then, functions as a pure parody of the lives of saints and the adventures of gods and goddesses in Bengal, and the religious ideal is a parody of all manner of religious practices and cosmologies relevant to Bengali culture. In the guise of entertainment, these *pīr kathās* deliver stealth critiques. While by most modern literary interpretive standards, contra Booth, it would be impossible to determine authorial intention; but the fact of the parody's existence points to a historical context that lies outside the text's narrative. It is hard to imagine that the author did not deliberately take aim at precursor texts.

Though we have argued that the narrative of Jaidi's *Mānikpīrer jahurānāmā* must be understood to be autotelic, creating its own reality, that autonomy does not mean independence of production;[73] that is, the text is always a product of a particular time and place, in this example Bengal, likely the mid- or late eighteenth century. When it provides a parodic commentary on prevailing ideologies or theologies, it depends on that context in the ordinary world of things and directs that critique to an audience who must be familiar with the shapes and images of the story for it to be comprehended. The text must use a language of rationality rooted in that context if it is to be understood, if its critique is to be accessible. Jaidi did not write *Mānikpīrer jahurānāmā* in a vacuum, and that context alone puts limits on what he might have imagined or pushed his reader and listener to imagine—so we now turn to the *conditions of possibility* for any of the fictive hagiographies of the *pīrs*, the limits operating in the realm of the *imaginaire*.

• • •

72. Stewart, "Subject and Ostensible Subject."

73. Macherey, *Theory of Literary Production*, 53.

4

Mapping the *Imaginaire*

The Conditions of Possibility

Bonbibī said to Śājaṅgali,
"Whenever anyone in this forest calls me Mother,
I must fly to their rescue.
You do not understand the responsibility
and implications of wielding the power of barakat.
In the low-lying lands of the eighteen tides,
I am the mother of each and every one."
—MOHĀMMAD KHATER, *BONBIBĪ JAHURĀ NĀMĀ*

4.1. THE REALITY OF THE BENGALI *IMAGINAIRE*

As a starting point to better understand the work of the narratives of the fictive *pīrs*, we accepted Todorov's and Macherey's argument that the worlds constructed by those stories are completely self-contained. This remove exempts the tales from evaluation according to the discourses of everyday reality, that is, from the world of truth or falsity. The worlds they depict legislate for themselves all that one needs to know to apprehend the story being told; and of necessity those worlds so constructed are always incomplete, yet fictional worlds are neither incomprehensible nor completely alien to those who produce and consume them. The landscapes, though sometimes truncated and finessed, invoke place-names that are often familiar—Lahore, Delhi, Chittagong, the Sundarbans—though their connection with those historical places is proximate at best. While there are some places cited for which no historical evidence attests to their existence, such as the realm well known to Hindu mythology as Pātālnagar, the land of the *nāgs* that lies underneath the surface of the earth, there are just as many of these tales that draw quite explicitly on the local geography and history. Bairāṭ is one such site, associated with Śāh Sekander, father of Baḍa Khān Gāji; the coincidence of the name suggests Sekandār Śāh of the Ilyas Shāhi dynasty, who controlled the fort at Bairāṭ in the second half of the fourteenth century. The place-names alternate between an intimate familiarity with the Bengali landscape and fantasy, or perhaps invoking names of places that no longer exist, but the effect is to place distance between the protagonists' various exploits rather than signal some more profound notion such as establishing the borders of a kingdom or a sustained strategy of provocation and control. In more than a few instances, the enumeration of places marks a physical displacement and temporality, the greater the number of places invoked in sequence, the greater the distance in time and space.

The types of figures the tales depict are likewise familiar, no matter how incompletely they are drawn; in fact, the plots depend on the audience understanding the stereotypes they invoke: kings or *bādśās*, various ministers and courtiers, and of course the retinues of *pīrs*, *phakirs*, *bibīs*, *sannyāsīs*, *śāktas*, *śaivas*, *vaiṣṇavs*, *vairāgīs*, *nāths*, *padres*, *turuskas*, *jabans*, *kābulīs*, and so on. While some figures invoke names that resonate with historical figures, such as the famous Śāh Sekandar, the allusion remains just that, an allusion, which temporally translates as "a long time ago." While it is tempting—and this has been done more than a few times by scholars in the last century—these fictional figures should not be construed as depicting historical figures per se. There has been and still is a cottage industry of this type of construal (called euhemerism) that attempts to read mythology and fictional narratives as depicting actual historical events in the world of ordinary things, whereas I wish to argue the opposite: if indeed there is a connection at all, at best a particular historical figure may have provided an inspiration for a character.[1] But the fictional characters do have a special kind of reality and I follow Amie L. Thomasson, who argues that fictional characters are "artifactual," that is, real abstract objects that have been created by their authors

1. The figure of Mukuṭ Rājā in the story of Gāji, Kālu, and the king's daughter Cāmpāvatī provides a good case in point. In an unpublished essay, Benjamin Costa, citing Satiścandra Mitra, reported that Mukuṭ Rājā could be identified as a historical figure known as Mukuṭ Rāy from the village of Lāujāni in Jessore District, somehow identified with the narrative's own depiction of Mukuṭ Rājā's town, which is called Brāhmaṇānagar. His source depicts the historical Mukuṭ Rāy as a zealous *brāhmaṇ* during the reigns of Husāin Śāh and his son Nusrat Śāh of the early sixteenth century, but includes all manner of reportage of the protagonist's conversations with Husāin Śāh about the persecution of Hindus by Muslims (though the author fails to note that those terms were not operational in any significant way at that historical moment), all of which seems to have driven the identification far beyond the evidence in order to recast the narrative in more convenient political terms relevant to the time of Mitra's writing; see Benjamin Costa, "Literature of the Tiger-Cult in Bengal (*Raymangal* et al.)" (unpublished typescript), 2–3; for the specifics, he cites Satiścandra Mitra, *Yaśohar-khulnār itihās*, 3rd ed., vol. 1 (Calcutta: Dasgupta, 1963), 429–33; and for the issue of general historicity of Haridev's *Rāy maṅgal*, he cites the introduction *Haridever racanāvalī: Rāy maṅgal o śītalā maṅgal*, ed. Pañcānan Maṇḍal, 129.

and thereby exist as such.[2] Fictional characters are real in the realm of discourse, just as the fictional landscapes are real. Like the general geography, the flora and fauna invoke the familiar topography of Bengal. But in the same way that seemingly official titles often signal generic "court functionaries" or just "the court" rather than precisely distinguished offices, the flora and fauna are often generic. For instance, in the story of Badar Pīr the same flower is called a *padma* lotus and a *kadamba*, two entirely different flowers, but their function was simply to designate the flower dropped by Āllā and then passed along by Badar Pīr as a vehicle for the conception of Mānik Pīr. There is no need to assign such apparent inconsistencies to some scribe's mistake or ignorance or some other equally baseless speculation;[3] importantly, that kind of consistency is not required by these narratives.

The stories, however, are made comprehensible precisely because of their contexts, their framing, which is generated and shared by the people who compose and consume them. Those authors were very real, they lived in a Bangla-speaking world, the Bangla texts they wrote and circulated were and are very real, and there had to have been something in their historical situation that stimulated them to generate those imaginary domains. *The content of the narrative defines its own reality, and that reality need not automatically conform to the world of ordinary things though it does depend on that world for comprehension.* That is an important distinction. The texts' meanderings and explorations—which are often in a subjunctive mood—allow the reader or listener momentarily to escape the discursive strictures of history, theology, and law found in mainstream *musalmāni* society, yet it is against that backdrop that they were generated; indeed, one could easily argue that is precisely the backdrop that made them necessary. They open a space that is not regulated in the ways of those discourses; but that space itself does in fact have strictures.

We seem to have reached an impasse by granting the narratives their autotelic status; there would appear to be an unbreachable gulf between the story-as-fiction and the author in a particular historical moment. It is through understanding the nature of their discourse that these narratives can be properly situated and analyzed for their cultural work. In part, the impasse is a function of the narrative's ontology; that is, characterizations about their "reality" are actually attempts to address their status vis-à-vis that of "things" in the ordinary world. The narratives-as-fictions

2. Amie L. Thomasson, "Fictional Characters and Literary Practices," *British Journal of Aesthetics* 43, no. 2 (April 2003): 138–57; and for a more extended analysis, see Thomasson, *Fiction and Metaphysics* (Cambridge: Cambridge University Press, 2008).

3. There are seldom sufficient manuscripts to apply the principles of stemmatology necessary for a critical edition, and scribal conventions were not standardized at the time most of these texts were composed. This is, of course, quite apart from the concept of the critical edition which operates on the assumption that there was an original text that can be recovered or largely so, a staple of western scholarship that fetishizes the "original" as inherently more valuable or important, whereas my experience with Bangla texts is that fidelity to an original yields to imperatives of utility and actual use.

stand quite apart as language-dependent and language-mediated realities, a product that *takes its reality purely from discourse*. In evaluating the reality of fictions, epistemologist Nicholas Rescher observes that "discourse alone underwrites no workable distinction between fact and fiction"; rather, *context* is required, which is a standard of measure that lies outside of discourse. "As far as the discourse itself is concerned, a statement's fictionality—like its truth or falsity—is altogether invisible: it is something that cannot be extracted from the statement itself and generally requires us to look beyond discourse as such." As a result, fictions create trouble for theorists because the fiction's internal truth does not correspond "with fact *tout court*, but rather pivots on an oblique, story-mediated correspondence with fact."[4] Narratives-as-fictions take on a different ontological status when talking about "possible worlds."

> What possible world theory needs at this point is not bold metaphysics but ontological minimalism (not to say common sense). As far as we mere humans are concerned, the only possible worlds there are are those embodied in fictions: worlds imaginatively projected through supposition, assumption, or hypothesis. No one knows—or can know—of a possible world that is not realized through the mental artifice of envisioning a scenario of some sort. Neither I nor anyone else can offer an example of a possible world for which there is not a real-world author, a living, breathing producer who conjures up some possibility by a *coup d'esprit*. All of the possible worlds at our disposal are fictional constructs arising from the suppositional thought work of the living, breathing individuals who project them by way of imagination. Accordingly, the question of the ontology of possible worlds does not call for transcendental metaphysics but for a deflationary account that sees such worlds as thought-artifacts produced by and only available through the mental operations of real-world individuals by means of supposition, assumption, hypothesis, or the like.[5]

He goes on to point out that "there are, strictly speaking, no fictional fictions: there are no fictions unless real people really make them up."[6]

4. Nicholas Rescher, "On the Ways and Vagaries of Fiction," in *Nicholas Rescher Collected Papers*, vol. 14: *Studies in Epistemology* (Frankfurt: Ontos Verlag, 2006), 89–90.

5. Rescher, 79–80.

6. Rescher, 80. Rescher extends the observation on 93: "A fictional world has no independent ontological status of its own; such status as it has it derives from the real-world actualities of the fictional work at issue." He goes on to say, "Since fictions are thought-projected products of the mind, then insofar as there are fictions there must be minds that think them up. The circumstance that fiction involves intent means that only real authors can produce real fictions. . . . While there is no reality to fictions as such, there certainly are fictions in reality. Like everything else, works of fiction have to exist in the real world in order to exist at all. Fictions have no actual reality in themselves; their only reality is the thought reality projected through the creativity of their authors and the receptivity of their readers." And on 96: "There are no fictional (unreal) things; there are only (real) people's thoughts (ideas, beliefs, assertions) about such things that position their ontological *locus standi* on discourse alone."

The reality of these texts as products of people does complicate, but also actually augments, the simple proposition that the worlds they produce are autotelic. The texts themselves are historical products that take the form of books or performances, and the content of their stories cannot be fully isolated from their genesis. Fictions retain their autotelic status but do maintain some kind of connection to what Macherey calls a "pretext."[7] These texts and their stories do not come into existence *ex nihilo*; rather, they are given birth within specific *contexts*—linguistic, literary, religious, ethnic, geographic, historical—that together *somehow* give them shape. The creators of the tales are constrained by these various contexts, which means that the tales themselves are not produced indiscriminately and without constraints. They serve to critique prevailing cultural norms, wittingly or not, in the manner of all fictions. There can be no question about the reality of that critique because many of these stories are parodies, which means they automatically target a real-life precursor text or event, whether by imitation (mimesis) or some trenchant, often ironic, assessment.

The blanket proposition that the creators of these tales can simply make up anything they want is actually misleading, because *there are limitations on what they can imagine, historically grounded limitations that are both restricting and enabling.* I argue that these limitations define the discursive parameters of the *imaginaire*, which is the realm within which the imagination operates. From this perspective, the discursive arena of any text is the *imaginaire*. This is radically distinguished from Jean Paul Sartre's use of the term wherein *l'imaginaire* was construed as a special act of consciousness; his concept is closer to what I consider in English the "imagination," though they do not map precisely.[8] Nor is it the "social imaginary" as described by Charles Taylor.[9] Rather, as I am using the term, the *imaginaire* constitutes a metaphorical "space" where the imagination is exercised, where imagining can be actualized, the result taking the form of a concrete cultural product, such as the production of a text. I am not proposing to explore the act of imagining, which is a phenomenological inquiry that falls well outside the scope of these observations; rather, I am concerned with the *space* within which the imagination, as it pertains to these texts, operates. Not insignificantly, Casey argues that imagining can only take place in what he calls an *imaginal space*, though the nature of that space is in his reckoning pure possibility; I am arguing here that we can in the production of texts identify certain of the parameters that define that

7. Macherey, *Theory of Literary Production*, 46, 95, and passim.

8. See Jean-Paul Sartre, *The Imaginary: A Phenomenological Psychology of the Imagination*, trans. Jonathan Webber, revised by Arlette Elkaïm-Sartre (London: Routledge, 2004); Sartre's original text from the 1940 Gallimard edition was simply titled *L'imaginaire*. Similarly, Jacques Lacan's use of the term *l'imaginaire* focuses on the image of the body; see Lacan, *The Four Fundamental Concepts of Psycho-Analysis*, ed. Jacques-Alain Miller, trans. Alan Sheridan (London: Hogarth Press, 1977).

9. See Charles Taylor, *Modern Social Imaginaires* (Durham, NC: Duke University Press, 2004). Taylor builds on the theories of Jürgen Habermas and Benedict Anderson.

space, parameters that both enable and limit possibility.[10] As a locus of human thought, the *imaginaire* is itself structured; it is always historically grounded to particular times and places and, as a result, has observable restrictions and an observable horizon. We might best think of the *imaginaire* as the "realm of possibility" for an author to create some kind of text (whether literary, analytic, scientific, or extended to other cultural forms that are architectural, legal, and so forth). For a text to take shape in this discursive space, a language or languages must be chosen to express the workings of the imagination, and that automatically places strictures on the production, for language inevitably structures thought and determines audience.[11] Similar to language patterns within the *imaginaire*, historical context likewise dictates other structures of authority that place limits on what can be imagined. Culturally grounded accepted practices of expression help to define and thereby limit various modes of discourse, whether social and legal systems, science, theology, or simply what passes as common sense (and here we start to approach Taylor's usage, though in a different modality). At the same time, these constraints should not just be seen as limiting, but *enabling*, for they provide frameworks within which the imagination can be exercised and which define the boundaries against which the imagination can push and expand, can think new thoughts.[12] It is seldom possible to envision a world that runs completely counter to prevailing forms—changes can be wrought, but the structuring itself is seldom,

10. See Casey, *Imagining*, esp. 52, 120. For his phenomenological analysis of space, see Casey, *Getting Back into Place: Toward a Renewed Understanding of the Place-World*. 2nd ed. (Bloomington: Indiana University Press, 2009). For a critical rundown of the various theoretical approaches to the ways the imagination, imaginary, and fiction intersect, see Wolfgang Iser, *The Fictive and the Imaginary: Charting Literary Anthropology* (Baltimore: Johns Hopkins University Press, 1993).

11. Among the first theorists to assert the notion of the thought-structuring nature of language were Sapir and his student Whorf, though today most consider them to have overstated their position regarding the unthinkability of certain concepts in other languages, though after a rather thorough dismissal, their proposals on key points seem to be receiving a grudging rehabilitation among contemporary scholars. See Edward Sapir, *Culture, Language and Personality*, ed. David G. Mandelbaum (Berkeley: University of California Press, 1949), and Benjamin Lee Whorf, *Language, Thought, and Reality* (Boston: MIT Press, 1956). For an interesting but somewhat saucy critique and partial rehabilitation, see Guy Deutscher, *Through the Language Glass: Why the World Looks Different in Other Languages* (New York: Picador, Henry Holt, 2010), esp. chap. 6, 129–56.

12. Anders Schinkel, wrestling with Reinhart Koselleck's notions of conceptual history, places the imagination between experience and expectation. He writes, "So the space of experience is also (and if Koselleck did not intend it this way, I will include the meaning myself) the space within which experience may occur; it sets the *limits of possible experience*." That space, which Schinkel leaves unnamed, appears to be a direct analogue to the space within which the imagination itself works, what I call the *imaginaire*, a discursive realm which sets the conditions of possibility for the imagination. Koselleck's formulation, which is heavily conditioned by Dilthey, does not actually lay out what those limitations are or how they come into play. See Schinkel, "Imagination as a Category of History: An Essay Concerning Koselleck's Concepts of *Erfahrungsraum* and *Erwartungshorizont*," *History and Theory* 44, no. 1 (February 2005): 42–54.

if ever, outside of these constraints. At the same time, with each new formulation the shape of the constraint itself can and does shift, often subtly and imperceptibly, and usually in gradual processes,[13] even in major paradigm shifts that are not quick and are often very messy.[14]

This is not to propose some new form of intellectual history but a pragmatic approach to understanding the creative force of these fictional tales of *pīrs* and *bibīs* and how they relate to their historical moment. It is especially focused on what kinds of conversations their authors had with prior authors that prompted them to formulate the tales they did and to what end. In a sense, we are talking about the double-voice of Bakhtin's dialogic process,[15] as authors and their fictional actors give voice to different perspectives, their conceptual worlds in connection to their consumers. The creative exercise of the imagination to produce the content of the narrative situates the fictional product in the context of the author's own historical time and place, yet in connection to the literatures that have preceded it. The author straddles the divide, one foot in the world of ordinary things, and the other in the narrative. The causality and intentionality of the author as divined from the narrative, however, are elusive at best, and any attempt to discern some one-for-one correspondence between an author and his or her fictions lands us automatically in the world of conjecture. But if the fictions are suspended in this realm of the *imaginaire*, and through that suspension connect through the author to the world of ordinary things, how do we map in consistent ways the nature of that suspension? What are the threads of connection? The answer inches us closer to answering what kind of cultural work these texts have been performing for their consumers, which is to move the locus of our inquiry to the fictions' effects on the world of everyday reality.

Some years ago, while mining bibliographical entries for intertextuality, I came across a small article by Jonathan Culler titled "Presupposition and Intertextuality,"[16] in which he articulated a generalizable set of propositions that would help situate any literary form. Upon reflection I have come to realize that these propositions apply much more broadly to virtually any configuration of cultural production across any discourse, from legal and the judicial structures, to architectural trends, religious rituals, and theological or philosophical texts. Culler's observations are not proposed as the basis of a system of interpretation, but rather isolate four features that any hermeneutic exercise should or could productively analyze to place texts into an imaginal landscape, in that process producing their intellectual or

13. Foucault's observations about the nature of historical intellectual shifts are germane here.

14. Thomas Kuhn, *The Structure of Scientific Revolutions* (Chicago: University of Chicago Press, 1962).

15. Bakhtin, *Dialogic Imagination*, 324–25 and passim.

16. Jonathan Culler, "Presupposition and Intertextuality," *Modern Language Notes* 91 (1976): 1380–96.

even cultural history. These four features constitute some of the threads that connect the textual product to its various contexts; they help define the conditions that allow for the production of any specific text and can, then, once isolated, guide its interpretation. The fictional texts dedicated to the *pīrs* do not come into existence in a void, though their provenance may often prove fugitive. Following Culler, we can identify two forms of presupposition—*logical* and *pragmatic*—and two forms of intertextuality—*explicit* (or overt) and *implied* (or covert)—that will situate these texts. These factors will in part define a text's generative context, identify at least some of its historical conversation partners, and point to its implied audience, inviting that audience to understand the text according to its own standards of production and consumption. They serve as *constraints* on what can be envisioned by these authors in locatable historical settings, and they serve equally as *opportunities* for these authors to improvise and innovate. This allows us to uncover the terms of a text's initial creation (how it represents "the present"), and, when those texts themselves become one of the conditions of possibility for some future text, we can through these same four features evaluate how the text has been repurposed. As a result, this type of exegesis will allow us to address fruitfully the relationships of seemingly disparate fictional (autotelic) narratives across centuries by different authors and their audiences. These connections may, on the surface, seem to compromise the autotelic status of the narrative, but because they operate on the level of discourse-to-discourse, independence is retained.[17]

17. A nascent version of the application of intertextuality and presupposition appeared in Tony K. Stewart, "Popular Sufi Narratives and the Parameters of the Bengali *Imaginaire*" in *Religion and Aesthetic Experience: Drama—Sermons—Literature*, ed. Sabine Dorpmüller, Jan Scholz, Max Stille, and Ines Weinrich, Transcultural Research–Heidelberg Studies on Asia and Europe in a Global Context (Heidelberg: Heidelberg University Press, 2018), 173–95. The text can also be accessed in HTML format online at DOI: 10.17885/heiup.416.

It should be noted that Gérard Genette's terminology for *transtextuality*, most completely developed in *Palimpsests*, provides a brilliant technical classification scheme for the parts of a text and the relationship of one text to another, but would still require further elucidation to address Culler's notions of logical and pragmatic presupposition. Genette narrows Kristeva's first use of the broad term *intertextuality* to quoting, plagiarism, and allusion. Genette's *metatextuality* can be both a form of overt and covert intertextuality as I have used it following Culler—and parody is the most common modality. *Hypertextuality*, as the overlay of one text (*hypertext*) or another text (*hypotext*) through transformation and imitation, does not really operate in any significant way in these *pīr kathās*. *Paratextuality* entails all elements of textual production that exceed the narrative proper— title pages, prefaces, chapter divisions, postscripts, publication encomia, and so forth—elements which are noted when relevant but which are not part of the immediate analysis. And *architextuality* is the genre classification that is a function of reader expectations, which in the *pīr kathās* would be the general features of the romance, with which we have earlier dealt. See Gérard Genette, *Palimpsests: Literature in the Second Degree*, trans. Channa Newman and Claude Doubinsky, foreword by Gerald Prince (Lincoln: University of Nebraska Press, 1997); for the extended analysis of paratext, see Genette, *Paratexts*; for more on architexts, see Genette, *The Architext: An Introduction*, trans. Jane E. Lewin, foreword by Robert Scholes (Berkeley: University of California Press, 1992).

Logical Presupposition. Every discursive arena is governed by a set of *logical presuppositions*, that is, *rules for conducting discourse.* These include such things as what constitutes a rational argument, how to draw a proper inference, or what is allowable as a "fact" or proof. So the formal nature of logic, such as the mathematical basis of the syllogism, would be included here. It also includes other sources of authority which serve the community in setting the rules for these logical, or at least acceptable, arguments, for instance the role of revelation versus reason in traditional Islamic legal systems, resulting in the liberal application of ratiocination among the inheritors of the *mu'tazilah* traditions, or the absolute denial of anything suggesting local cultural preferences or opinions by the conservative Hanbalite school of law. The *imaginaire* is the realm within which the adjudication of these rules takes place—and, as will become apparent, no one standard ultimately prevailed in any community, regardless of sectarian or social orientation. Because the logical rules of discourse and their contexts were not uniform, language users constantly negotiated among them, often defining and redefining the same terminologies. This negotiation becomes critical when new terms are introduced into the lexicon, such as the Persian or Arabic technical vocabulary which often yields new forms in their crossover to the target language of Bangla. Cosmology is the root of all logical presuppositions (and vice versa), which means that all theological propositions and assumptions automatically fall under this heading, however general; so too such propositions as the laws of physics and cause and effect, for instance, the traditional Indic law of *karma*, which is prevalent throughout these *musalmāni* productions. One of the most important features of these cosmological propositions is the ethical sensibilities they engender, as we shall soon see. The same would apply for the assumptions that govern science, mathematics, and practical applications, such as legal codes, and related bureaucratic and institutional regulation, regardless of provenance.

Pragmatic Presupposition. Every discourse takes certain identifiable shapes by assuming certain structures that Culler labels *pragmatic presuppositions*. As already noted, the first obvious but often overlooked pragmatic issue is language—that the stories of the *pīrs* and *bibīs* were composed and circulated in the vernacular Bangla declares a particular audience that stretches beyond the discourses of law and theology, which operated primarily through Persian and Arabic, or among the Hindu populations through Sanskrit. In literary issues, the choice of textual genre also signals a type of discursive activity that further defines its audience and the issues to be adjudicated; the choice of genre underscores how authors and even communities choose to present themselves. That authors most commonly choose to utilize the *kathā* in *pāñcālī* form to describe these extraordinary exploits of the *pīrs* and *bibīs* already situates the tales in discernible patterns of reproduction and consumption—they are often publicly performed (the texts often include information on musical expression) rather than studied as chirographic or printed texts.

Further, genre is not limited to the outward literary form, but can also be formulated diegetically within the tales themselves. So we can extend this concept of shifts to include structured modes of discourse that populate the narratives. For example in the *Mānik pīrer kecchā* of Munsī Mohāmmad Pijiruddīn Sāheb, the antagonist presents himself initially as a merchant, so the mode of discourse is replete with its own set of rituals and structured venues that intersect with the expectations of trade and protocols of domestic and foreign courts; but when the same character assumes his persona as both householder and itinerant *pīr*, he abruptly shifts to a completely different sets of standards commensurate to that mendicant's calling.[18] The choice of genre or the switching of diegetic frames of authority within the narratives, signals authorial perspectives which reflect historical expectations of discursive negotiation. *In other words, the choice of form conditions expectations in the audiences as much as when the genre for delivery is chosen.*

Overt or Explicit Intertextuality. Many texts, with their incipient vision of like-minded community, frequently explicitly invoke precursor texts; and it is worth remembering that *text* can be more broadly construed as any prior source of recognizable authority as long as it is explicitly named. These precursors signal an *overt intertextuality, an invocation that provides a context for the current story without having to spell it out.* In practice, the naming of another text invokes a prior discursive realm associated with that text, but camouflages the vagueness of detailed content, leaving audiences with the sense of knowing more than what is actually stated, allowing them to fill in blanks according to their own understanding of the applicability of that textual content to the current narrative. Through this, overt intertextuality also serves to obviate, or at least lessen, the need to justify claims through other more explicit means, though references are often bound to the justification of logical presuppositions, as noted above. By invoking the precursor, its power and prestige are directly associated, if not immediately connected, to the present. There are obvious explicitly cited texts, such as the Arabic Qur'ān and the Sanskrit *Bhāgavata purāṇa*, in many of the tales of the *pīrs* and *bibīs*, whose authority is invoked to shore up the position of various characters, to signal affiliation, or even to eliminate dissent by placing the narrative situation in the larger context of prior cultural constructs. The explicit invocation of a text clearly aligns an overtly religious text with tradition, but in a literary text, the invocation points to a more general orientation that acknowledges but does not necessarily promote an explicit perspective on cosmological or other religious issues.

When a protagonist or antagonist encounters any gods or goddesses, such as Nārāyaṇ, Gaṅgā, or Śitalā, or encounters other celestial-ranging figures, such as the Prophet, Phātemā, Jibril, or even Āllā himself, those connections can qualify as

18. Stewart, "Tales of Mānik Pīr: Protector of Cows in Bengal," 319–20.

overt intertextuality if the figure's role in a text-specific event is easily identifiable. But if the divine figure in question is not indexed to a discrete event, but rather is invoked more generally, the reference fades into the grey area between explicit and implicit intertextuality or should be understood to function as an implied intertextuality. I do not wish to draw a hard and fast line between these two forms of intertextuality, because ultimately they depend on the background and perception of the recipient to make the connection; what may be an obvious reference to one reader or listener may completely slip by another.

Implied or Covert Intertextuality. A significant amount of the discourse defining the world of these early modern narratives hinges on *unstated* invocations of precursors, an *implied* or *covert intertextuality. Working through a rhetoric of association, these intertextual connections tend to be vague and often open-ended, pushing the recipient to determine what correspondences are relevant.* Perhaps the most common form is the appearance of a character or event from a prior text. A fictional character from one story may suddenly intrude into another, or in another variation, some historical character may show up in a fictional episode. These appearances are forms of analepses, which are often depicted as, but certainly not limited to, flashbacks; they directly connect the narrative to the plot of a prior tale though that tale is not named. For instance, in the opening sections of the *Baḍa satya pīr or sandhyāvati kanyār puthi* noted in the first chapter above, immediately following Satya Pīr's rather extraordinary birth from the turtle in the river waters, he submits to the mysterious figure of Khoyājā Jendā Pīr or Khoyājā Khijir,[19] with whom he spends the next several years receiving instruction to prepare him for his mission. Khoyājā Khijr is widely associated with safety on the waters and is the patron *pīr* of fishermen and sailors, so one is not surprised to see him appear to the newborn Satya Pīr on the sandbanks of the river. That association with water is likely to be the extent of the connection for most. But for the more astute auditor of this text, Khoyājā Khijir will be recognized as (Arabic) al-Khiḍr, the ageless and enigmatic saint who is considered to be the most accomplished of all of the "friends of God." As a teacher, his instruction is often puzzling to all but the most extraordinarily accomplished *sūphī* adept. His story can be found in the Korān (Arabic Qur'ān, *surāt* 18 *al-Kahf*). In that story, Musā is showing signs of an incipient hubris regarding his abilities as a prophet, so Allāh sends him to al-Khiḍr to demonstrate the profundity of his ignorance of the larger mysteries of the cosmos. In that encounter, three distinct problems are presented, the solutions to which in each case seem completely counterintuitive to Musā. Musā amply demonstrates his impatience and his inability to follow simple instruction without question, which further underscores his inability to see the truth that

19. It should be noted that in *Baḍa satya pīr or sandhyāvati kanyār puthi,* his name is spelled Khoyājā, while in the *Nabīvaṃśa* noted below it is spelled Khoyāj.

al-Khiḍr could see. That story of al-Khiḍr's instruction was, in turn, recorded and amplified by any number of authors compiling the tales of the prophets in Arabic. Of particular interest here are the version recorded in the thirteenth-century collection *Qiṣaṣ al-Anbiyā'* or "Stories of the Prophets" by 'Abd Allāh al-Kisā'i and the subsequent *'Arā'is al-Majālis fī Qiṣaṣ al-Anbiyā'* or "Lives of the Prophets" by Aḥmad Ibn Muḥammed al-Thalabī,[20] both of which Saiyad Sultān seems to have followed in his sixteenth-century Bangla retelling of the tales of those in the lineage of Mohāmmad, the *Nabīvaṃśa*.[21] For the learned, then, that simple reference to Khoyājā Jendā Pīr imparting esoteric instruction to Satya Pīr linked the tale back through a host of other texts to the Korān/Qur'ān itself, though no text is actually named.

Allusions to both mythical and historical figures provide a rich background through this rhetoric of association, for instance when a king is compared to Rām or when a historical figure is cited to set a tone. The heroine Lālmon in the famous tale *Lālmoner kāhinī* of Kavi Āriph is married to a young prince named Husāin Shāh, invoking the historical figure of the Sultanate king of the same name and all that his enlightened reign stood for.[22] The invocation situates the text historically because it had to have been composed after that legendary kingship to be effective. It also signals what most Bangla speakers see even today as an accommodating cultural perspective, for Husāin Śāh (r. 1494–1519) proved a champion of Bangla literature by commissioning the translation of such texts as *Rāmāyaṇa* and *Mahābhārata* into Bangla,[23] celebrating non-*musalmāni* culture—and any number of scholars have casually made that connection. As the hallmark of this reign, wherein communal conflict was minimal, some scholars have actually proposed that Lālmon, Husāin's daughter (conflated with the heroine Lālmon), was responsible for introducing the worship of Satya Pīr, who as the amalgamation of Nārāyaṇ

20. Muḥammad ibn 'Abd Allāh al-Kisā'i, *Tales of the Prophet* [*Qiṣaṣ al-anbiyā'*], trans. Wheeler M. Thackston, Jr., Great Books of the Islamic World, ed. Sayyed Hossain Nasr (Chicago: Kazi Publications, 1997); and Aḥmad Ibn Muḥammed Al-Thalabī, *Lives of the Prophets* [*Arā'is al-Majālis fī Qiṣaṣ al-Anbiyā*], trans. William M. Brinner (Leiden: E. J. Brill, 2002).

21. Saiyad Sultān, *Nabīvaṃśa*, 1:670–87. For a complete translation of this passage, see Saiyad Sultān, "Curbing Moses' Hubris: Khoyāj Khijir's Instruction to Musā in the Bengali *Nabīvaṃśa* of Saiyad Sultān," trans. Tony K. Stewart and Ayesha A. Irani (typescript). Other possible sources include texts by Juwayrī and Bal'amī; for more on the full extent of the intertextual relationship of these texts to the *Nabīvaṃśa*, see Irani, *Muhammad* Avatāra.

22. Kavi Ārif, "The Wazir's Daughter Who Married a Sacrificial Goat," in *Fabulous Females and Peerless Pīrs: Tales of Mad Adventure in Old Bengal*, trans. Tony K. Stewart (New York: Oxford University Press, 2004), 29–50.

23. Dating from the period, see Kṛttibās, *Rāmāyaṇ*, ed. Harekṛṣṇa Mukhopādhyāy, with an introduction by Sunitikumār Caṭṭopādhyāy (Kalakātā: Sāhitya Saṃsad, 1386 BS [1979]), and Kāśīrām Dās, *Mahābhārat*, ed. Maṭilāl Bandhyopādhyay, re-edited by Dhīrenda Ṭhākur (Kalakātā: Tārācā̃nd Dās eṇḍ Sans, n.d. [1988?]. These two texts are the most popular Bangla versions of the great epics and have appeared in a myriad of print editions since the early nineteenth century.

and Khodā was and is cherished as Nirañjan, the Stainless. Yet if one looks at the actions of the Husāin Śāh in the *Lālmoner kāhini*, he is the opposite of everything people associate with that *sultān*: brash and imperious, impatient, easily seduced, not to mention having his head lopped off because of his uncontrollable sexual urges. That wayward head is subsequently reattached by Satya Pīr as a direct result of Lālmon's devotion, wherein the text explicitly invokes Behulā, the heroine of the *Manasā maṅgal*, whose devotion brings her husband Lakkhindar back to life.[24] Later Lālmon herself rescues him from the clutches of a witch who had transmogrified him into a ram for her personal pleasure, a variation on the salvific fidelity of Behulā. Yet, the invocation of Husāin Śāh as the historical figure stands.

Mixed forms of intertextuality can occur with completely different referents. For instance, in the opening section of the *Mānikpīrer jahurānāmā*, the hero's father Badar Pīr marries the princess Dudbibī. Prior to the wedding, when the four *mullahs* determine the astrologically precise time for the event, they deploy the Ketāb Korān, which allows them to ascertain Āllā's authorization for the marriage.[25] As previously noted, using the Korān for divination was common across South Asia, but the image of them huddled around their text mimicked their *brāhmaṇ* counterparts who would consult their Sanskrit astrological texts (*jyotiṣa śāstra*) prior to a wedding. The act signaled to the audience that these functionaries were performing the marriage properly according to a culturally relevant prescription—for any audience, regardless of religious practice, would instantly recognize that act in equivalent terms. The explicit intertextual reference to the Korān/Qur'ān combined there with the implicit intertextual reference to accepted marriage practices.

Not coincidentally, parody will almost always utilize the full set of permutations of presupposition and intertextuality, for its power depends on elaborate mimesis. The replication of the form of prior texts or sets of texts (in the larger sense of the concept) will deploy both implicit and explicit intertextual connections, while the rules that govern the action narrated in the tale itself, the plot, will of necessity share presuppositions with its textual predecessor—a significant moment when those autotelic narratives can prove vulnerable to external modification by another later narrative operating within a shared discursive arena. But shared discourse does not automatically signal identical situatedness; rather, those presuppositions can just as easily become the grounds for a critique, the assertion of difference in the mimesis of the parody. That mimesis, however, has a double

24. For an English translation of the basic tale, see Ketakā Dāsa, "The *Manasā Maṅgal* of Ketakā Dāsa," in *The Thief of Love: Bengali Tales from Court and Village*, trans. Edward C. Dimock (Chicago: University of Chicago Press, 1963), 195–294. For an analysis of Behulā's actions, see Tony K. Stewart, "The Process of Surface Narrative: Corpse Worship," in *Sarpa-saṃskṛti o manasā*, ed. Añjan Sen and Śekh Makbul Islām (Kalakātā: Baṅgīya Sāhitya Saṃsad, 2012), 181–94.

25. Jaidi or Jayaraddhi, *Mānikpīrer jahurānāmā*, 313; see also this volume, chaps. 2 and 3.

effect, for while it functions to relate the text to its precursor text/s, it also ironically preserves the precursor's place in the world of the *imaginaire*, fixing it ever the more firmly in the shared discourse—it is a relationship of structural dependence. As a precondition of comprehensibility, mimicry, whether positive or negative, ensures the stability of the newly created work as well as that of its parodic object. By anchoring itself to what has preceded it, the parody's own effectiveness will depend heavily on the continued relevance of the precursor in an expanded discursive arena, pushing the boundaries of what might be imagined and, as we shall see, shifting the direction of it.

4.2. THE *BONBIBĪ JAHURĀ NĀMĀ* OF MOHĀMMAD KHATER

To demonstrate briefly how these features might be useful for understanding the world of a particular text and how it connects to prior texts in this discursive realm of the *imaginaire*, we will examine the tale of Bonbibī. The saga of Bonbibī is a late-nineteenth-century production, considerably later than all the other texts in this set of fictional stories of *pīrs* and *bibīs*. The origins of the tale are bit fuzzy, but the earliest recorded text is by Bayanuddīn, which was printed in 1284 BS (ca. 1877).[26] The text we will examine was composed a mere three years later in 1287 BS (ca. 1880) by Munśī Mohāmmad Khater Sāheb as the *Bonbibī jahurā nāmā*.[27] This version of the story has become synonymous with the Bonbibī cycle and has been reprinted with ongoing editorial interventions, some changes as simple as modernizing spellings, but more substantively adding paratextual assertions attributed to the author.[28] The last rendition of the tale was composed by Mohāmmad Munśī

26. Munśī Bayanuddīn, *Bonbibī jahurānāmā* (Sisvādaha: by the author, 1284 BS [ca. 1877]), cited by Sarat Chandra Mitra, "On a Musalmāni Legend about the Sylvan Saint Bana-bibī and the Tiger-Deity Dakshiṇa Rāya," *Journal of the Department of Letters* 10 (1923): 156. For a revised edition of Bayanuddīn's text, see Munśī Bayanuddīn, *Bonbibī jahurānāmā* (Kalikātā: Āfājuddin Āhāmmad, from 337–2 Upper Chitpur Road, 1327 BS [ca. 1920]).

27. The earliest edition of the text I could examine was Munśī Mohāmmad Khater Sāheb, *Bonbibī jahurānāmā* (Kalikātā: Śrī Rāmlāl Śīl at Niu-Bhikṭoriyā Pres, 1325 BS [?] [ca. 1918?]).

28. The most popular reprint that has flooded the market in the last few decades is Munśī Mohāmmad Khater Sāheb, *Bonbibī jahurā nāmā: Nārāyaṇīr jaṅga o dhonā dukher pālā* (Kalikātā: Nuruddīn Āhmmad at Gaosiyā Lāibrerī, 1394 BS [ca. 1987]), which was followed by multiple reprints. That reprint also serves as the basis for Munśī Mohāmmad Khater Sāheb, *Bonbibī jahurā nāmā: Nārāyaṇīr jaṅga o dhonā dukher pālā* (Kalikātā: Nuruddīn Āhmmad at Gaosiyā Lāibrerī, 1401 BS [ca. 1994]), a digitally typeset edition which is virtually identical to the old hand-set reprint version of 1394 BS, but with some careless misreadings of the original text that in several instances change the tenor of the text, whether intentionally or not. A later edition is Mohāmmad Khāter Sāheb, *Bonbibī jahurānāmā: Nārāyaṇīr jaṅga ār dhonā dukher pālā* (Kolkātā: Ji Ke Prakāśanī, 1409 [ca. 2002], reprint 1416 [ca. 2009]). See also the retelling by Samir Rāy, *Banbibī o nārāyaṇīr pālā* (Kāśīnagar, Cabbiś Pārgaṇas: n.p. 1990).

in 1305 BS (ca. 1898),[29] but has not enjoyed the same popularity as Khater's account. All three versions tell essentially the same story with differences primarily in emphasis, phrasing (often paraphrasing of the prior work or works), minor elaborations of combat engagement, and the greater or lesser unraveling of emotion.[30] The story has also taken life in popular dramas, all-night recitations, and other performance genres.[31] Not coincidentally, following Amitav Ghosh's masterful retelling of the tale in the novel *The Hungry Tide*, Bonbibī's saga has now become inextricably linked to the environmental issues at stake in the Sunderban.[32] The popularity of the story has likewise generated a number of articles holding up the narrative as an example of religious tolerance and secularism (which in the current Indian context often refers to the social recognition of pluralism),[33] a position that will be challenged in the next chapter.

. . .

29. See the new edition: Muhammād Munśi, *Bonbibī jahurā nāmā kanyār punthi* (Kalakātā: Osmāniā Lāibrerī, 1393 BS [ca. 1986]).

30. See Sujit Kumār Maṇḍal's summary of the print history: Sujit Kumār Maṇḍal, ed., *Bonbibir pālā* (Kalakātā: Aṇimā Viśvās Gaṅgcil, 2010), 12–13; as he indicates in note 3, he dates all three texts based on arguments put forward by Girīndranāth Dās, Sukumār Sen, Gopendrakṛṣṇa Basu, Āśutoṣ Bhaṭṭācāryya, and Ābdul Karim Sāhitya Viśārad.

31. In his introduction, Sujit Kumār Maṇḍal brilliantly traces the movement of the tale through various performance genres (*kecchā*, *pālā*, *ekani*, *nāṭya gīt*, and *jātrā*) and their relationship to printed texts, both prior texts and those generated as a result of performance; Sujit Kumār Maṇḍal, *Bonbibir pālā*, 1–51. The volume contains transcriptions of the *Bonbibir 'Ekani' pālā*, *Bonbibir pālā*, and *Dukhe jātrā*. Śaśāṅk Śekhar Dās provides a good overview of the place of Bonbibī in Sunderban culture, including the *Bonbibī jahurā nāmā* and other performance forms, as well as insights into the language and use of the tiger in legends; see Dās, *Bonbibi* (Kalakātā: Loksaṃskṛti o Ādibāsī Saṃskṛti Kendra, Paścimbaṅga Sarkār, 2004, reprint 2018). This text is almost entirely derivative of a much more expansive dissertation, which also includes extensive texts; see Dās, "Bonbibi o grām bāṃlā" (PhD diss., Calcutta University, 1989). See also Girīndranāth Dās, "Loknāṭya bonbibi pālā evaṃ ekai viṣaye duṭi ādhunik nāṭak," *Lokśruti: Loksaṃskṛti viṣayak ṣānmāsik patrikā* 10 (1399 BS [1993]): 83–85.

32. Amitav Ghosh, *The Hungry Tide* (London: HarperCollins, 2004). Ghosh's retelling is delightfully broken up for the purposes of his narrative, leaving the reader anxious to pick up the thread, a gentle labor which adds to the dramatic tension. The Bonbibī entries on the web, blogspots, Facebook, and small texts or pamphlets are too numerous to register, though it should be noted that a number of them synoptically retell the story, for instance see Baren Gaṅgopādhyay, *Bonbibīr upākhyān* (Kalakātā: Nāth Brādārs, 1978), with many responding to Ghosh and the environmental concerns for the Sunderbans. Similarly, the print literature on the environment frequently cites the story; on the whole there is significant repetition in these short tracts.

33. See Ipshita Chanda, "*Bonobibir Johurnama:* A Method for Reading Plural Cultures," *The Delhi Journal of the Humanities and Social Sciences* 2 (2015): 51–62; Shatarupa Bhattacharyya, "Localising Global Faiths: The Heterodox Pantheon of the Sundarbans," *Asian Review of World Histories* 5, no. 1 (January 2017): 141–57; Sonali Roy, "Hindu-Islamic Folk Goddess in Bengal: Bonbibi," *The Appollonian* 4, nos. 1–2 (March–June 2017): 66–74.

The Three Episodes of the Bonbibī jahurā nāmā[34]

A *phakir* named Berāhim is married to Phulbibī, a woman who cannot conceive, a predicament which causes much agony for both. Phulbibī advises Berāhim to make their plight known to *rachul*, the Apostle, whose grace will surely resolve the issue. So Berāhim goes to the Prophet's tomb in Madinā where he humbly petitions for children. Rather than answering directly, the Prophet promises Berāhim he will ask Phātemā, who is resident in heaven (*behest*), why they have had no children.[35]

> With these words Berāhim was consoled and Hajrat himself took off for heaven. When she saw him, Phātemā inquired of the Prophet, "Tell me, my beloved one, why have you come to see me in person?"
>
> Hajrat replied, "O Mā, the reason I have come is this: Why is the house of Berāhim bereft of children?"
>
> Phātemā replied, "Please be seated and wait. The Korān is right there on the throne so I will look it up." And with these words Bibī went to consult the Korān. She soon returned and announced to Hajrat Nabī, the Holy Prophet, "It records that there will be two offspring in the house of Berāhim. But they will not be born of Phulbibī. He must couple with another woman in marriage, then he will have children. Go and give the news to Berāhim."
>
> As soon as he heard, the Prophet returned to his dwelling in Madinā. Remaining invisible, he relayed this to Berāhim in a disembodied voice. "Long have you been beloved of me, an immaculate learned saint (*sāi*). But there will be no children from Phulbibī's womb. Understand that what is required is for you to join together with another in marriage. From her womb will be born a boy and a girl." When he heard this Berāhim was thrilled. He made a thousand *sālāms* in obeisance before *rachul*, the Apostle. Then he took his leave and headed back to his home. Berāhim reported to Bibī all the intelligence that he had gleaned.[36]

Not surprisingly, Phulbibī is furious and tells him to ignore the oracle, but he persists. So as appeasement, she extracts from him a promise that he will grant her one wish, which she will hold in reserve. He agrees. Finally, with her permission,

34. Because of its ubiquity, I am using the hand-set reprint of Khater's 1394 BS [ca. 1987] edition. The initial tale of Bonbibī and Śājaṅgali growing up, visiting Madinā and then coming to the Sunderban where they defeat Dakṣiṇ Rāy's mother, Nārāyaṇī, corresponds to pp. 1–17 in the 1394 BS [ca. 1987] edition and 1–16 in the 1401 BS [ca. 1994] digital imprint; the second tale of Dhonāi and Dukhe corresponds to 18–43 in the 1394 BS [ca. 1987] edition and 16–39 in the 1401 BS [ca. 1994] digital imprint.

35. The visit to the tomb of Muhāmmad mimics a quintessential popular *sūphī* practice in the Bangla-speaking world and the Indian subcontinent of the early modern period. For the early history of the construction, veneration, and multiple controversies around Muhāmmad's tomb, see Leor Halevi, *Muhammad's Grave: Death Rites and the Making of Islamic Society* (New York: Columbia University Press, 2007). For a general overview of tomb veneration in Islamic South Asia, see Annemarie Schimmel, *Islam in the Indian Subcontinent* (Leiden-Köln: E. J. Brill, 1980), esp. chap. 4.

36. Munśī Mohāmmad Khater Sāheb, *Bonbibī jahurā nāmā*, 3–4.

Berāhim heads to Makkā, where after searching he comes to the home of one *phakir* named Śāhā Jalil, who has an eligible daughter, Golālbibī. Their marriage is soon arranged.[37]

The couple are married according to custom. Predictably, Phulbibī is mad with jealousy.

> God then determined it was time for the great event of the birth. Āllā summoned Bonbibī and Śājaṅgali, both of whom were residing in heaven, and issued this command: "You will be born to a Bibī named Golāl in the home of Berāhim."[38]

And so they descend into the womb of Golālbibī with the express mission of establishing their auspicious domain in the low-lying land of the eighteen tides where Gāji and Rāy exercise their power.

Phulbibī waits until Golālbibī is about to deliver, then demands her husband keep his promise: the boon she begs is that he abandon Golālbibī in the forest. Berāhim protests but sees no other recourse, for he is an honorable man and cannot break his promise. So Berāhim takes his pregnant second wife Golālbibī and abandons her in the forest.

Golālbibī's cry of distress generates sympathy among the wild animals who come to her aid, tending her as she gives birth to twins: a girl first and then a boy. Understandably distressed, Golālbibī feels incapable of surviving with two children to feed, so after consideration, she abandons her newborn daughter. The wild animals of the jungle—especially the deer—take it upon themselves to raise this little girl, and so she grows into her role as Bonbibī, Mistress of the Forest. After some years, Bonbibī manages to catch up with her brother, Śājaṅgali, who has also survived, and together they soon travel to Madinā, where they become the students or *murids* of one of the descendants of Hāsen.[39] After they have mastered their studies and become themselves accomplished *murśids*, they visit the grave of Phātemā to ask her blessings before launching out into the world. There an oracle, a disembodied voice, directs them to go to the land of the eighteen tides, or the Sunderbans. Before departing, they visit the tomb of the Prophet (*nabī*), where

37. A translation of the wedding section can be found as Munśī Mohāmmad Khater Sāheb, "Bonbībī, Protectress of the Forest," trans. Sufia Mendez Uddin, in *Tales of God's Friends: Islamic Hagiography in Translation*, ed. John Renard (Berkeley: University of California Press, 2009), 301–11.

38. Munśī Mohāmmad Khater Sāheb, *Bonbibī jahurā nāmā*, 5.

39. This is likely Hashim, Mohammad's paternal grandfather. See ibn Isḥāq, *The Life of Muhammad: A Translation of Isḥāq's Sīrat Rasūl Allāh*, trans. A[lfred] Guillaume (1955; reprint: Karachi: Oxford University Press, 1967), 3: "Muhammad was the son of 'Abdullah, b. 'Abdu'l-Muttalib (whose name was Shayba), b. Hashim (whose name was 'Amr), b. 'Abdu Manaf (whose name was al-Mughira)." This identification is based on the opening of Sāyeb Munsī Ābdul Ohāb, *Gāji kālu o cāmpāvatī kanyār punthi*, 1: "Born in the house of Ābdullāh, Ābdul Mataleb was his grandfather, and his father was named Hāsem. His father in turn was Mānnāph, dear to the hearts of all in the community and foremost leader among the Prophet's lineage."

they praise him as "the *guru* of all mendicants (*phakirs*)"[40] and request his imprimatur in their quest to establish the *khelāphat* in that swampy place. His sanction comes in the form of a special headdress, which they accept; they make their obeisances and leave. These headdresses allow them to cover great distances in a flash, and so they end up in the Sunderbans.

When they reach the edge of the swamplands, they are warned of a powerful landlord named Dakṣiṇā Rāy,[41] who controls the fabulous wealth of the place: timber, honey, beeswax, and salt. When they enter the region and Śājaṅgali pauses to give the call to prayer, the sound rolls across those low-lying islands like thunder. Dakṣiṇā Rāy is intimidated by the power of this call, so he quickly orders his second, Sanātan, to investigate. He has immediately realized it was not the voice of his friend Baḍa Khān Gājī, with whom he made peace after a lengthy battle. Sanātan reports back: he has espied a young man and a young woman, both dressed in black cloaks, offering praise to Āllā with hands upraised and their staffs firmly planted in the ground, laying claim to the place in the name of Āllā. Rāy is furious that they did not first approach him for permission to enter his lands, so he summons his army of shape-shifting ghouls (*pret*) and hungry ghosts (*bhūt*) and prepares to show them who is in control. Rāy's mother, Nārāyaṇī, presciently intervenes and advises him not to fight a woman because, even should he win, there will be no victory, but should he lose, the humiliation will be permanent. Rāy concedes and generously allows his mother to fight as his proxy: let a woman fight a woman. Nārāyaṇī gathers her army:[42]

> Hungry ghosts (*bhūts*) emerged from the cremation grounds, appearing as so many messengers of death (*kāl duts*), more than one hundred fifty-six thousand issued forth from secret places. Witches (*ḍākinī*), all fierce viragos, numbered three hundred sixty million and fanned out over the land of the eighteen tides screaming "Kill! Kill!" Once they were assembled, Nārāyaṇī prepared her battle dress, covering herself with glittering ornaments of war. Arming herself with a myriad of weapons, she vainly sashayed down the road atop her royal chariot, confident of victory.[43]

Her hordes advance on Bonbibī and Śājaṅgali from all sides.

The twins are worried, but the elder sister Bonbibī reassures her brother that he need only call on Āllā for protection. He again belts out the call to prayer, which rattles Nārāyaṇī's skittish legions, causing them to scatter in all directions. Bonbibī's own booming roar (*huṃkār*) paralyzes the rest of the demonic masses, and she rains destruction down upon them. Nārāyaṇī rallies and lets fly her arrows, but Bonbibī always sees them coming, so with the *kalemā* wet on her lips, those arrows

40. Munśī Mohāmmad Khater Sāheb, *Bonbibī jahurā nāmā*, 13.

41. This printed text throughout writes Dakṣiṇā Rāy, rather than Dakṣiṇ Rāy found in Kṛṣṇarām's *Rāy maṅgal*.

42. Munśī Mohāmmad Khater Sāheb, *Bonbibī jahurā nāmā*, 15.

43. Munśī Mohāmmad Khater Sāheb, 15.

pass through her body as if she were made of mere water. Nārāyaṇī unleashes her most fearsome weapons: the *ṣaṭcakra*, the *gadācakra*, and finally the ultimate *dharmmacakra*. They roar through the air like angry missiles, but again Bonbibī tastes the *kalemā*, plants her staff, and the fiery weapons fizzle out. Nārāyaṇī then strikes hard at Bonbibī, but she remains untouched as the gleaming sword turns into harmless flowers by the grace of Phātemā. Bonbibī and Nārāyaṇī proceed in hand-to-hand combat for the rest of the day, neither one getting the upper hand, until Bonbibī feels herself giving way. She petitions Khodā for help from his perch in heaven, and through an intermediary he grants her the additional power (*barakat*) she needs. "The *barakat* that was to be found in heaven, Khodā summoned and commanded to descend to the aid of Bonbibi."[44] With this reinforcement of power, Bonbibī mounts and then sits on the chest of Nārāyaṇī, squeezing from her the very breath of life until she capitulates and begs for mercy.

> "Spare me my life, please do not kill me. I will ever be your loyal servant. Through the region of the eighteen tides, all those who exercise power will become your loyal and obedient followers. From this day forward you rule as *rājā* and we are your subjects. You have become the master. Please pledge to forgive and protect us and we will be your loyal vassals. We will flawlessly execute your every order." As she listened to this prayer of heartfelt contrition, being naturally beneficent, Bibī did not crush and dismember her, but spared her.[45]

Nārāyaṇī ingratiates herself with Bonbibī, whom she diligently serves. After that, when Śājaṅgali gives the call to prayer with Dakṣiṇā Rāy present, all the inhabitants of the forests respond with gifts. Bonbibī is heard to say, "Sister, listen to what I decree: We will divide up and share the land of the eighteen tides. No one need ever suffer again. Now go back to your own homes."[46] In this manner, Bonbibī assumes control of the low-lying land of the eighteen tides. She marks a number of locales as her own, where she begins the production of honey and beeswax. She imposes order and consigns responsibility for clearly demarcated regions to other vassals; Dakṣiṇ Rāy is made responsible for maintaining the area of Kẽdokhāli.[47]

Everything works smoothly until a trader named Dhonāi arrives to collect honey and wax. Dhonāi and Monāi are two brothers from Bārij Hāṭi in Huglī who trade in goods from the low-lying lands of the eighteen tides. The months of spring are the ideal time to collect honey, and Dhonāi has convinced his reluctant brother that the latter needs seven boats to take advantage of the opportunity. As he outfits and then mans his boats, Dhonāi finds he is one hand short, so he importunes his

44. Munśī Mohāmmad Khater Sāheb, 16. It is interesting to note that *barakat* here is personified and given explicit instruction.

45. Munśī Mohāmmad Khater Sāheb, 16.

46. Munśī Mohāmmad Khater Sāheb, 17.

47. Vivalok Comics faithfully retells the first half of the *Bonbibī jahurā nāmā;* see Saswat Ghosh, comp., "Banbibi," in *Folk Tales from India: The Sunderbans*, 22–27.

young, and quite poor, nephew Dukhe in an effort to recruit his help. Dukhe's widowed mother is initially opposed, for she has no one else to look after her. Dhonāi's assurance that he will keep Dukhe safely on board the ship at all times, coupled with the prospect of his amassing substantial wealth, is persuasive, but when he follows with a pledge to arrange Dukhe's marriage to his own daughter upon their return, she entrusts Dukhe to his care. She advises him that if he ever finds himself in trouble, he need only silently think on Bonbibī and she will come to his aid.

Dhonāi, with Dukhe on board, heads south, but when the ships enter the low-lying regions, they bypass the area controlled by Dakṣiṇā Rāy without stopping. Honey and beeswax are everywhere abundant, so they excitedly anchor and go ashore; Dukhe remains on board as Dhonāi has promised his mother. But Dakṣiṇā Rāy has detected their presence, and he observes to his brother Biṣam Rāy:

> Take a look, brother, Dhonā has come into our territories without offering me *pūjā* worship or the offering of rice balls. He is trying to evade me and steal the honey. But when he reaches Goḍakhāli, I will trick him instead. I will conceal the beeswax and honey so that he can find none of it. He will get his just desserts unless he performs a *pūjā* with a human sacrifice (*narabali*)." As he was saying this, Dakṣiṇā Rāy's anger began to build, and he headed off to Goḍakhāli, where he camouflaged all the beeswax and honey.[48]

When Dhonā arrives, he greedily surveys and sees honey everywhere, but when he draws near, it mysteriously disappears. After three days of searching in vain, he begins to suspect the trick of some deity, so he repairs to his boats and frets about his venture. That night . . .

> Dakṣiṇā Rāy came and spoke to him in a dream. "Why, Dhonā, are you lying here in my territory asleep, going without food? Tell me, what misery has befallen you?"
>
> He remonstrated with a certain petulance, "Just who are you appearing here? Make yourself known!"
>
> When he heard this, Dakṣiṇā Rāy explained the matter this way: "I am the one who creates the honey and the beeswax in these swamps and forests. A sage, *muni*, who was a strong-willed arbiter of justice was the chief in the low-lying regions. I am his son, Dakṣiṇā Rāy."
>
> Dhonā replied, "If you are indeed really the great lord of this low-lying land, then why can I not find any beeswax or honey?"
>
> Rāy responded, "O Dhonā, it has been many long days since anyone offered me human sacrifice in worship. Should you manage to perform a human sacrifice for me, I will fill your seven ships with beeswax."
>
> But when he heard this demand, Dhonā could only exclaim in distress, "Ah, fie!" It was as if the sky itself had shattered and fallen on his head. He quickly improvised, "The only people I have brought with me are lowly. Tell me, how can I supply some-

48. Munśī Mohāmmad Khater Sāheb, *Bonbibī jahurā nāmā*, 21.

> one suitable? I do not want your beeswax and honey. We will row our boats back to our own land."
>
> Rāy heard him out, then his anger rising, he retorted, "All of the sailors that fill your boats I will feed to the crocodiles, and then we will see just how you flee back to your homeland."[49]

Dhonāi is hapless and helpless, and Rāy presses him to hand over Duhke, no one else; but Dukhe overhears what is happening, and he closes his eyes and meditates, calling three times to Bonbibī. His call of distress shakes her throne, and she tells Śājaṅgali:

> "Whenever anyone in this forest calls me Mother, I must fly to their rescue. You do not understand the responsibility and implications of wielding the power of *barakat*. In the low-lying land of the eighteen tides I am the mother of each and every one."[50]

Bonbibī responds to Dukhe's call by assuming a magical created form (*māyārūp*). She instructs the astonished Dukhe that when Dhonāi starts to hand him over to Dakṣiṇā Rāy, he should call on her just as he has done.

So Dhonāi takes his ships to the appointed place of Kēdokhāli to collect the honey and beeswax, which Dakṣiṇā Rāy has loaded with the help of his demonic hordes (*deo dāno*), reminding Dhonāi of their bargain. Dukhe grows increasingly terrified as the time draws near, and so he laments:

> "Tomorrow the boats will cast off and my uncle will return to his home. He will surrender me to Dakṣiṇā Rāy to be mauled to death. Dakṣiṇā Rāy will shapeshift himself into a tiger, a man-eater, and eat me. By that act of handing me over, my uncle will have made himself a rich man, returning home triumphantly."[51]

As expected, at the first opportunity, Dhonāi offloads Dukhe, casts off his boats, and heads back to Bārij Hāṭi, leaving Dukhe to fend for himself. Dakṣiṇā Rāy, "that son of a *rākṣas* demon, assumed the form of a tiger and advanced in order to eat Dukhe."[52] Dukhe calls out for Bonbibī, but before she can arrive, he expires, dying of fright. Śājaṅgali has accompanied Bonbibī, so assessing the situation, he sprinkles Dukhe with magic water and blows on his face. He soon revives.

Śājaṅgali spots Dakṣiṇā Rāy and gives chase. As they cross the waterways, Dakṣiṇā Rāy calls out to his crocodiles and sharks to attack Śājaṅgali, but he dispatches them by the hundreds with seemingly little effort, flinging them by the tail to their deaths. Rāy flees to the shelter of his friend Baḍa Khān Gāji, who consoles him but points out that what he has unwittingly done was to pick a quarrel with Bonbibī, who is extending her personal protection to Dukhe. He also reminds

49. Munśī Mohāmmad Khater Sāheb, 21.
50. Munśī Mohāmmad Khater Sāheb, 22.
51. Munśī Mohāmmad Khater Sāheb, 26.
52. Munśī Mohāmmad Khater Sāheb, 27

Dakṣiṇā Rāy that his own mother Nārāyaṇī, acting as his proxy, has submitted to Bonbibī after her defeat, which makes him subservient to Bonbibī as well. Right then Śājaṅgali catches up with them, but Baḍa Khān Gājī himself steps forward to intervene, cooling him down. Śājaṅgali is nonplussed; he cannot understand how a god-fearing *gājī* warrior can be friends with a demon (*rākṣas*) like Dakṣiṇā Rāy, sufficient to mediate on his behalf. As they face off, Bonbibī's own summons rings insistently in their ears, so the three of them hurry to her with hands pressed together in supplication. Turning to Baḍa Khān Gāji, she demands to know who he is and how, if he is indeed a true saint (*oli*) of Āllā, can he shelter this demon *rākṣas*. Gājī explains that he is the son of a king, Śāhā Sekandār, and that in a previous battle, he, Baḍa Khān Gāji, defeated Dakṣiṇ Rāy. In the aftermath of that battle, he has graciously allowed Rāy to share power in the region. Pressing on, Baḍa Khān then reminds Bonbibī that Dakṣiṇ Rāy must be considered her *de facto* son because she has defeated his mother Nārāyaṇī in battle, after which Bonbibī has tendered Nārāyaṇī her protection and grace—and a share in managing the land. That act of compassion has made Nārāyaṇī's offspring her own. Bonbibī acknowledges the truth of it, and so a second rapprochement is achieved. Bonbibī then declares that Dukhe enjoyed her protection as if he were her own little brother, so she commands Baḍa Khān Gāji to be a brother to Dukhe and provide him with wealth should the need ever arise.

Dhonāi is unaware of what has transpired as he flees home. When he arrives, embarrassed but feigning grief with a long face, he informs Dukhe's mother that the poor boy has been eaten by a tiger. Such is her grief that she becomes blind and deaf. She cannot imagine how Dukhe could have died, for she explicitly instructed him to take refuge in Bonbibī, who would always protect her lowly devotees. His mother's heartache is so great that Bonbibī soon comes to hear of it, so she makes arrangement to send Dukhe home from the low-lying regions. She instructs him not to fear tigers, for he will travel under her protection. She also advises him not to chastise Dhonāi, for had Dhonāi not acted in the duplicitous manner that he did, Dukhe "would never have met her, would never have gotten her *darśan*."[53] So she dispatches him to his homeland, mounted on the back of a magical crocodile named Seko,[54] with the promise that he will soon marry Dhonāi's daughter.

The giant crocodile uses his supernatural powers to traverse the swamps and rivers to their destination in less than the twinkling of an eye. Finally on dry land, but still overwhelmed with the emotion of it all, Dukhe strikes out to look for his mother. When he finds her, blind and deaf, Dukhe calls on Bonbibī once

53. Munśī Mohāmmad Khater Sāheb, 33.

54. *Seko* means arsenic. The presence of naturally occurring arsenic in the ground waters of the whole of the southern Bangla-speaking region on both sides of the border is a discovery of the very late twentieth century, its sudden appearance blamed on deep tube wells. So this reference, which is seemingly and appealingly prescient, has to be read as a coincidence, barring some other corroboration.

again. This time she materializes in the form of a white fly and instructs him to touch his mother's eyes and ears while reciting Bonbibī's name. It works. After his mother has recovered, she advises her son to don a mendicant's garb and visit seven villages to beg food and spread the story of Bonbibī's compassion. With the food he collects, his mother prepares a feast for the village, and Bonbibī's fame spreads far and wide. Afterwards, Dukhe decides to visit the local judge (*hākīm*) to lodge a legal complaint (*nāliś*) against Dhonā for his actions in the Sunderbans. His mother discourages him because it would be so costly, but he insists they can afford it because Baḍa Khān Gāji has promised to supply him with seven carts of riches in his time of need. So he summons Baḍa Khān, who keeps his promise and takes him to a place where the carts are buried, then disappears. But when Dukhe tries to dig, the ground will not yield, and he feels somehow deceived. Right then, seven miscreants come along, frightening Dukhe, so he flees, and they in turn greedily dig up the carts. When they open the lids of these treasure chests, nests of writhing serpents are stirred and rise up, hissing their danger. Their improvised plan aborted, the thieves convince themselves it has all been a trap, so they decide to take revenge. They deposit the chests at Dukhe's mother's house, fully expecting the poisonous snakes to kill her and her son, but when Dukhe opens the chests, there is nothing but piles of gleaming treasure.

Now, of course, Dukhe and his mother need a proper dwelling to store that wealth, so he calls out for Dakṣiṇā Rāy, who instantly sends him a consignment of three lakh pieces of cut timber. Being inexperienced in business matters, Dukhe does not know how to procure carpenters and handymen, so he calls on Bonbibī again and explains his deficiency. She shows herself in a dream to one resourceful man named Jadurāy and instructs him to locate Dukhe and assist. He does: he hires and manages all the necessary help to build a lavish compound: day laborers, carpenters, guards and the rest of the requisite constabulary, female servants, rent collectors, and so forth. Thus Dukhe, though low-born, has "become famous throughout the region as a wealthy land-owning *caudhurī*."[55] He has houses built for widows, clears roads, constructs ponds, and turns the region into a profitable *jamidār*'s estate with untold numbers of satisfied tenants, for by Dukhe's decree they pay no taxes.

Witnessing this transformation from a safe distance, Dhonāi grows increasingly worried.

Everyone by now has come to pay respects, curry favor, and attend on Dukhe—everyone except Dhonāi, so Dukhe has him summoned. Dhonāi is understandably terrified, but when he is put before Dukhe, the latter forgives him, for he notes that it was Dhonāi's perfidious act of abandonment that proved a felix culpa, leading to his meeting with Bonbibī and his becoming a *caudhurī*. Dhonāi goes away certain

55. Munśī Mohāmmad Khater Sāheb, *Bonbibī jahurā nāmā*, 39.

that Dukhe will eventually get even, so this time it is Dhonāi who calls on Bonbibī for help. Attentive to those who call on her—even scoundrels such as Dhonāi—she appears to him in a dream where she scolds him for his stupidity. "Listen, Dhonā, you imbecile. If you really want to avoid being chastised at the hands of Dukhe and escape with your life, then gift him your daughter in marriage."[56] Desperate, Dhonāi does as instructed, proffering his daughter Cāmpā to Dukhe, who happily accepts her. A magnificent wedding soon follows and thousands upon thousands of people from every social rank are in attendance. A number of *mollās* and *kājis* are summoned, and the latter consult the Korān for approval of the wedding before performing the nuptial rituals. Afterwards, Dhonāi and Dukhe are reconciled. In his euphoria, and remembering his own plight as a poor boy, Dukhe forgives all of his farmer tenants their taxes for the next three years. Dukhe then escorts his bride home to his mother, who gives her blessings. When summoned, Bonbibī appears once again as a white fly to offer her grace to Dukhe's bride, Cāmpā, so they may live a good life.

• • •

4.3. THE SEMIOTIC CONTEXT OF BONBIBĪ'S TALE

Even a cursory run at the connections made in this abbreviated rendition of the *Bonbibī jahurā nāmā* proves formidable. The text is suspended in a web of intertextualities and exhibits presuppositions about the basic structure of the universe that will resonate with the texts to which it connects. We can be brief while making the point, so I will employ a shorthand to summarize the connections: logical presuppositions (LP), pragmatic presupposition (PP), explicit or overt intertextuality (E/OI), and implicit or covert intertextuality (I/CI). A number of these items may seem obvious, but because virtually no basic exegetical work has been performed on this text, this approach will at least remove some of the arbitrariness of this interpretive exercise, as it will when applied to any text or set of texts.

The title declares the genre as *jahurā nāmā*, which is a form of *kathā* (fictional story), that genre subset specifically celebrating the glories of the appearance or manifestation (*jahurā*) of a celestial figure (PP); in this case, it details how Bonbibī establishes her preeminence in the Sunderban and how Dukhe makes her even more famous and thereby the object of worship. The *jahurā nāmā* clearly patterns itself (through mimesis, therefore parody) on the *maṅgal kāvya*, one of the most ubiquitous forms of early modern Bangla literature (I/CI) which celebrate the auspicious appearance or activities (*maṅgal*) of the goddess, such as Caṇḍī, Manasā, Durgā, Śitalā, and others, including two male deities, Dharma and Dakṣiṇā

56. Munśī Mohāmmad Khater Sāheb, 41.

Rāy.[57] The Bangla of the text is somewhat Persianized (PP), aimed obviously at a *musalmāni* or, more likely as will become apparent, a later Muslim audience as the communities grow apart.[58]

The text assumes a basic tripartite cosmography (LP) with a heaven (*behest*) that serves as residence for Āllā, Mohāmmad, Phātemā, and others (I/CI),[59] including the heroine Bonbibī and her twin brother Śājaṅgali. In his paramount role as the Prophet, the chief religious functionary, Mohāmmad is styled the *guru* of all *phakirs*, the moniker *guru* acknowledging the cultural context (I/CI). He also has preternatural abilities, such as invisibility, marking him as an extraordinary celestial figure; while not in evidence in the Nārāyaṇī story, in the Dukhe story Bonbibī has assumed similar celestial abilities. This of course mimics the powers of the gods and goddesses in the *maṅgal kāvyas*. Heaven is somewhere "up there" above or apart from earth, but includes communication gateways through the tombs of Mohāmmad and Phātemā at Madinā. The pristine original Korān sits on its throne in heaven, the tale seeming to take a position on that long-standing debate about its status (LP; E/OI); it is also explicitly used in divination, making it parallel to the brāhmaṇical use of astrological texts (I/CI). From his place in heaven God, that is Āllā/Khodā, observes and intervenes in the world, establishing what appears to be a fairly routine traffic between heaven and earth, a manner that imitates *purāṇik*-style descents (*avatār*) (LP, I/CI). Interestingly, and a good example of terminological imprecision—or perhaps a genuine misunderstanding of the nature of Mohāmmad—the author refers to Mohāmmad as Khodā, a name that one would expect to be exclusively reserved for Āllā; it suggests an understanding of divinity through the notion of *avatār*, which is used for Mohāmmad, but one cannot rule

57. For a survey of the corpus of *maṅgal kāvya*, see Āśutoṣ Bhaṭṭācāryya, *Bāṅglā maṅgalkāvyer itihās*.

58. Jawhar Sircar argues that the *maṅgal kāvya* texts were a brāhmaṇical effort to claim the allegiance of lower-caste groups and so-called *ādibāsis* or aboriginal tribes by formally appropriating low-caste goddesses and gods in direct response to Muslim proselytization; see Sircar, *The Construction of the Hindu Identity in Medieval Western Bengal? The Role of Popular Cults* (Kolkata: Institute of Development Studies, 2005), 81–95. While Sircar's argument suffers from reading back the contemporary categories of Hindu and Muslim, his contention may well be supported for, at the same time the *maṅgal kāvyas* were being created, new texts on *dharma* obligations were aimed explicitly at the lower-caste groups; see Theodore Benke, "The *Śūdraśiromaṇi* of Kṛṣṇa Śeṣa: A 16th Century Manual of *Dharma* for *Śūdras*" (PhD diss., University of Pennsylvania, 2010). I am indebted to Donald R. Davis, Jr., whose unpublished paper titled "The Evolution of the Legal Subject in Classical Hindu Law" (typescript) draws attention to this development that saw a proliferation of such texts between the fifteenth and nineteenth centuries. Kumkum Chatterjee's take on the function of the late *maṅgal kāvya* genre suggests a slightly different audience, a much more elite consumer in a Mughal-inflected court setting; see Chatterjee, *The Cultures of History in Early Modern India: Persianization and Mughal Culture in Bengal* (New Delhi: Oxford University Press, 2009), chap. 3, "Performance Narratives and the Mughal Factor," 90–122.

59. There is no need to elaborate the intertextual connections invoked by such well-known figures.

out the possibility of a Christian perspective being appropriated, considering the nineteenth-century date of the text.

In this cosmography there is a special place called Yam's abode, where non-*musalmāni* dead go, and from its depths (and notably its locational marker is "down") *bhūts*, *prets*, *ḍākinis*, *joginīs*, *rākṣasas*, and all manner of unseemly demonic figures can be conjured from the earth via the cremation grounds and graves (LP). This particular universe admits of no explicit Indic goddesses or gods—though *pūjā* as a preferred form of worship is noted (I/CI)—but the populations do include the full range of lesser celestial figures just noted and the generic *deo*, which suggests generic godlings or antigods with special powers (LP). The chief antagonist of the first episode is Nārāyaṇī, mother of Dakṣiṇā Rāy, who commands those ghoulish minions and who herself has special powers (LP). The secondary antagonist of the Dukhe story cycle is Dakṣiṇā Rāy, in this text not quite a god (as we will see, he is in the *maṅgal kāvya* bearing his name) but the son of a *muni* or seer, though still possessing extraordinary powers. He is adept at shape-shifting, whereby he assumes the form of a man-eating tiger, and has the ability to control sentient beasts, including tigers, crocodiles, and sharks (LP). His man-eating is couched as human sacrifice or *narabali*, hinting at popular stories about worshipers of various forms of the goddess who is commonly reputed to need human sacrifice, representing the most fearful manifestations of Indic deities (LP, I/CI).

Bonbibī receives special care authorized by Khodā in order to survive in the forest and complete her mission, another example of God's intervention in the affairs of the world (LP). She and her twin brother are learners (*murids*) who must go to Madinā and Makkā to gain initiation and become themselves capable teachers (*murśids*), invoking prevailing *sūphī* institutional structures (I/CI). With this knowledge, they are able to understand the disembodied voices or oracles from the inhabitants of heaven (Mohāmmad, Phātemā); to draw on the power of Khodā himself through meditation, especially on his name, a special *sūphī* power associated with recitation or *jikir*; and, in the case of Bonbibī, to be a worthy recipient of the power of *barakat* (LP, I/CI). As the recipient of *barakat*, Bonbibī has additional powers and responsibilities, including being able to hear anyone who calls on her as mother and to assume other forms, such as the white fly, in order to minister to her devotees; she uses this *barakat* to generate the tactical power of *kerāmat* necessary for her to perform miracles. Her use of the *kālemā* as a *mantra* (perhaps conflating its recitation with *jikir*) to invoke celestial power likewise acknowledges the local cultural context (LP, I/CI).

Cultural background is evident through the invocation of a number of administrative, legal, and socioeconomic systems that were operational in the Bengal of the times. Dukhe, for instance, decides to file a legal case against Dhonāi and goes to the *hākim*, but at great expense (I/CI). When Dukhe becomes rich enough he becomes a *caudhurī*, head of a community and landlord, with all of the various functionaries he is required to hire to run his estates, which paints a fairly detailed picture of prevailing policing, land revenue, and taxing systems (I/CI). Dhonāi takes his boats into the Sunderban for trade, specifically after honey and beeswax, and Dakṣiṇā Rāy dispatches three hundred thousand pieces of cut timber, all three commodities obviously part of established trade networks to plunder the Sunderban during this same period (I/CI). All of these implied intertextualities reference complex administrative systems associated with the Mughal settlement of Bengal, so they strongly suggest a temporality that is never stated explicitly, but remains consistent and assumed to be familiar, and at the time of writing seem very much still to be in place with only a different government in power. Social rank is paramount, but expressed in terms of lineal relations, not caste (LP, I/CI). Conflict is generated over insults that do not acknowledge relative rank and spheres of influence and power, and are smoothed over by the establishment of proper kinship and marriage relations, features of Bengali culture that imbricate religion but do not depend exclusively on it; relative prestige cuts across communities (I/CI). This feature is perhaps the most commonly shared perspective when all the stories of fictive *pīrs* and *bibīs* are compared, and it is significant that, here and in a number of other stories, one finds the *sūphī* tendency to emphasize the familial relationship within the lineage, and perhaps the more general Islamic insistence on the rhetoric of brotherhood.

Finally, there are several significant explicit intertextual references that signal to the audience certain expectations. Apart from the Korān already mentioned—deemed the source of all knowledge, now and in the future—the story of the *Rāmāyaṇ* frames the opening sections, without being made explicit (I/CI), but with sufficiently precise analogies that there can be no mistaking it (E/OI). Berāhim promises the barren Phulbibī that he will honor any request she might make as appeasement for taking a second wife, a promise she holds in reserve, just as Daśarath promises the same to one of his wives, Kaikeyī, for her aid in his time of need. The latter uses her promise to exile Rām and Sītā in the forest, and Phulbibī uses her pledge to have Golālbibī abandoned in the jungle. Golālbibī is pregnant with the twins, just as Sītā is pregnant with Lav and Kuś when banished by Rām toward the end of the *Rāmāyaṇ*. In both instances, the twins are saved, but in the case of Bonbibī, she is abandoned a second time because her mother, Golālbibī, cannot see how to raise both, so she opts for the boy—a commonly held Bengali cultural preference regardless of religious orientation (LP). The tigers and deer and all the other animals of the Sunderban raise Bonbibī and become her real family, which she subsequently nurtures in her role as mother of all the inhabitants of the low-lying lands of Āṭhārobhāṭī.[60]

60. Jalais explores this series of relationships based on Bonbibī as mother, Dakṣiṇ Rāy, Baḍa Khān Gāji, and Dukhe as brothers, and everyone in the Sunderban under Bonbibī's protection through kinship; see Annu Jalais, *Forest of Tigers: People, Politics and Environment in the Sunderbans* (London: Routledge, 2009), chap. 4, "Is Salt Water Thicker than Blood?," 65–108.

Dakṣiṇā Rāy is an analeptic figure in this story whose own tale was told several centuries earlier (E/OI). His battle with Baḍa Khān Gāji, who also appears as another analeptic figure, is the subject of explicit inquiry by both Śājaṅgali and Bonbibī separately (E/OI). Baḍa Khān is acknowledged by Bonbibī to be a recognized saint (*oli*) with a formidable set of powers, including the ability to conjure wealth on demand (LP, I/CI). Śāh Sekandar, who is introduced when Baḍa Khān answers Bonbibī's question about his origins, makes a third analeptic figure. We have already noted how his name invokes the Ilyas Śāhi dynasty of the thirteenth century. But because the conflict between Dakṣiṇā Rāy and Baḍa Khān Gāji is central to Bonbibī's assertion of power in the region, let us take a look at the two tales that speak to that conflict, the reasons for it, and how the conflict is ultimately resolved. The web of connections that suspends the *Bonbibī jahurā nāmā* is about to become even more complicated.[61]

4.4. THE *RĀY MAṄGAL* OF KṚṢṆARĀM, PRECURSOR TO THE TALE OF BONBIBĪ

The earliest adventures of Dakṣiṇ Rāy[62] and Baḍa Khān Gājī predate the *Bonbibī jahurā nāmā* by several centuries. Not only does their prior interaction provide a backdrop to her story, but the resolution of her own conflict with Nārāyaṇī, Dakṣiṇ Rāy's mother, is conditioned by the issues of symbolic kinship established in the first tale, as the narrator openly declares. We see the effect of the precursor narrative again in the second Bonbibī tale, Dukhe's adventure, when the eminent Baḍa Khān stops the execution of Dakṣiṇ Rāy by reaffirming kinship relations that would forbid a violent outcome. That precursor narrative was not singular, however, for the tales of Baḍa Khān Gāji and Dakṣiṇ Rāy circulated in four roughly parallel trajectories, three of which connect to different features of Bonbibī's story.[63] The earliest extant version of the conflict between Dakṣiṇ Rāy and Baḍa Khān Gājī can be found in the opening tale of the *Rāy maṅgal* of Kṛṣṇarām, which dates to the late decades of the seventeenth century (ca. 1684).[64] This text is the most likely candidate for the explicit intertextual reference in the *Bonbibī jahurā nāmā* to the outcome of the conflict because in the next oldest extant *Rāy maṅgal*, that

61. For the culture of the indigenous communities (*ādibāsī*) and the literatures, tales, and performances that circulate in the Sunderbans, including analyses of the language; see Raṇajit Kumār Bāuliyā, *Sundarban añcaler ādibāsī saṃskṛti o sāhitya* (PhD diss., Calcutta University, 2010).

62. Note the spelling of Dakṣiṇ Rāy in this text.

63. For a survey of these texts, including a comparative analysis of features, see Āśutoṣ Bhaṭṭācāryya, *Bāṅglā maṅgalkāvyer itihās*, 922–38. For the most concentrated study of all the texts of Dakṣiṇ Rāy, including the *Gāji kālu o cāmpāvatī kanyār puthi* covered in the next chapter, as well as the ritual processes practiced today and the emergence of ancillary figures, see Amarkṛṣṇa Cakravartī, *Dakṣiṇeśvar dakṣiṇrāy: Ek laukik debkalper anupam rupkathā*, ed. Debabrata Bhaṭṭācārya (Kalakātā: by the editor at De Buk Sṭor, 1412 BS [2005]).

64. Kṛṣṇarāmdās, *Rāy maṅgal*, 165–248.

of Haridev, there is no overt hostility.[65] Haridev's text was composed in the early decades of the eighteenth century, and in it he tells a story that seems to have already accepted the brokered peace between the two antagonists, choosing to eschew reports of conflict in favor of a more benign, prearranged alliance: not only does Dakṣiṇ Rāy acknowledge Baḍa Khān Gājī as his brother—another kinship connection that determines status—the latter also enjoys equal favor from Īśvar to rule the Sunderban mangrove swamps, even though Dakṣiṇ Rāy was a demigod in the lineage of Śiv. As a brilliant example of Fuch's notion of Romance as a segmented narrative, the plot of Haridev's tale constitutes a meandering mythic replay of the exploits of Dakṣiṇ Rāy's genealogy involving a seeming myriad of gods and goddesses and other heroic and celestial figures in a concatenation of vignettes that eventually leads to the birth of Dakṣiṇ Rāy on earth, and then quickly moves on—Dakṣiṇ Rāy's connection to Baḍa Khān Gāji occupies only a fraction of that text.

A later text by Rudradev, which exists only in a lengthy fragment, tells a slightly different version of the all-out war between Baḍa Khān Gāji's band of *phakīrs* and Dakṣiṇ Rāy's eighty-four tigers.[66] While the etiology of the conflict is missing from the fragment, the contours of the exchange between the principals is parallel to that of Kṛṣṇarām's *Rāy maṅgal*, but many more *phakirs*—some of whom are already familiar to us—are explicitly named, including Mānik Pīr, Gorācā̃dā Pīr, Dapharkhā̃, Badar Pīr, Śalemānā, and Dāyānā Gāji.[67] After a seesaw slaughter of both tigers and *phakīrs* through the deployment of a multitude of magical weapons by both sides, and by the predations of crocodiles and swarms of wasps, the war is a standoff after seven days. Famously riding his husking pedal, Nāradā is dispatched from the heavens by Brahmā, Viṣṇu, and Śiv to broker a peace, which he does; Baḍa Khān acknowledges Dakṣiṇ Rāy as his older brother and shares power over the land.[68] Then the manuscripts breaks off and picks up with a later episode of the *bāuliya* named Ratā and his encounter with Dakṣiṇ Rāy.

Fortunately, the oldest extant text of Kṛṣṇarām is complete and provides a sustained and unified narrative of the incredibly destructive conflict of Baḍa Khān and Dakṣiṇ Rāy, which occupies more than a third of the overall text. Kṛṣṇarām's *Rāy maṅgal* is easily the most literarily sophisticated of all the stories about Rāy and Gājī, so it is worth pausing for a moment to comment on its linguistic challenges. Written in a colorful earthy language that captures the rough obscenities one might well imagine to be common among warriors and others involved in

65. Haridev, *Rāy maṅgal*, 1–172.

66. Rudradev, "Rāy maṅgal: Rāy gāji yuddha, ratā bāuliyā puṣpadatta baṇik pālā," in *Dvādaś maṅgal*, ed. Pañcānan Maṇḍal, Sāhityaprakāśikā, vol. 5 (Śāntiniketan: Viśvabhāratī, 1373 BS [1966]), 121–48.

67. Rudradev, 134–35.

68. Rudradev, 136–39.

grueling manual labor far from the culturally sophisticated urban centers favored by most aspiring rulers, the author sensitively depicts dialectal differences to signal status, rank, and ethnic background. Perhaps most notably, Dakṣiṇ Rāy's diction is in a high register worthy of a deputy of the king's court, his pronouncements delivered in a formal, cultivated style, while Baḍa Khān Gājī speaks in what we might term a cruder (to the Bengali ear) pidgin Hindustani, which points to his non-Bengali origins. His speech is a free mixture of Persian and Hindustani words, and neologisms formed from their roots or from Hindavī and Avadhī (but notably there seems to be no early Oḍiyā or identifiably Maithili lexicon I could discern), and it is laced with the most obscene invectives imaginable, signaling a considerably less cultured discourse than that of Dakṣiṇ Rāy. The communication between the Gājī and his tigers produces yet another unique dialectical register, a kind of "tiger-speak," for lack of a better term, rippling with rude, sexual, and scatological humor. In this remarkably supple handling of a Bangla that has not yet managed the stability of diction it achieves in the late nineteenth and early twentieth centuries, Kṛṣṇarām pushes the virtuosity of the elite composers of the *maṅgal kāvya* genre of his generation and subsequent periods.

The frame narrative of Kṛṣṇarām's story begins when Dakṣiṇ Rāy visits the poet in a dream and importunes him to compose the story of his devotees, the merchant Devdatta, who was jailed and nearly killed on his trading voyage, and the adventures of his son of twelve years who sets off at Dakṣiṇ Rāy's urging to find the father he has never seen. Kṛṣṇarām conveniently reports that in that dream, Dakṣiṇ Rāy criticized a prior poet, Mādhav Ācārya, for failing to tell his tale with the dignity and respect it deserved, making Dakṣiṇ Rāy the butt of jokes by many a country bumpkin.[69] When Kṛṣṇarām pleads ignorance of the proper narrative, Dakṣiṇ Rāy assures him of how it will progress and renders an impromptu précis of the entire narrative to get him started. Kṛṣṇarām begins in the first person:

. . .

12 Listen, everyone, how this strange and wonderful tale came to be composed and made famous in wide circulation. 13 From the name alone the region of Khāspur Parganā proves a delight, and therein Viśvambhar Baḍiṣyā constitutes the eastern portion. 14 I was passing through there on a Monday in the month of Bhādra [August-September] and at night lay down to sleep in the barn of some cowherder. 15 Toward the end of the night I saw in my dream a great man mounted on the back of a tiger.[70] 16 Massive of girth, he gripped a stunningly heavy draw-weight bow. He introduced himself as Dakṣiṇ Rāy, the Lord of the South: 17 "Do write my auspicious

69. This is the only known reference to Mādhav Ācārya's text, which is not to be found in any catalogued manuscript collection. There is a report of another text which is unattributed and could not be located; see Satyanārāyaṇ Bhaṭṭācāryya, ed., *Rāimaṅgal* (Bardhamān: Sāhitya Sabhā 1363 BS [ca. 1956]).

70. At times Dakṣiṇ Rāy rides a horse; at other times, he rides a tiger.

tale using the theatrical style of *pāñcālī* so that it will be broadcast far and wide through the Āṭhārobhāṭī, the Land of the Eighteen Tides. 18 Previously one Mādhav Ācārya composed such a song, but it did not suit me and failed to do its proper job as a work of art. 19 Merchants never gamed with dice on any cremation ground as he claimed—he bamboozled rustic farmers, misled them, and now his song is popularly recited. 20 Nearly all singers are ignorant of my story and so repeat the familiar; they perform songs that extol others in their all-night vigils. 21 The salt workers and mat weavers are reduced to hysterics when they hear his farcical comedy, with all its jokes and banter. 22 But no longer. Should any person fail to appreciate your poem in the proper manner, my tigers will slay every member of his lineage."

23 When I heard this grave pronouncement, I grew apprehensive in the extreme, and quickly placed my hands together in the sign of humility and spoke, bringing to his attention that 24 "I know virtually nothing of your feats, your character. How can I, ignorant as a child, compose properly your tale in song?"

25 Rāy smiled and spoke in gentle reassuring words. "By my grace will the song be unsurpassed and complete. 26 If you are diligent and mindful, you will discern it all. Listen carefully. I will tell you everything you need to compose my tale. 27 One day some time ago, following carefully the words of a sage, the brilliant sun king Prabhākar performed the ritual service of Lord Sadāśiv, who granted him the boon that he would become his son. 28 It was I [Sadāśiv] who became his son, and it was I who cleared the forests and established a viable kingdom. 29 I married the daughter of Dharmaketu;[71] then, and by the power of *yoga*, [my mother and father] left behind their bodies and the couple took themselves to Kailās.

30 "So by virtue of that boon, Hara, Śiva himself, became the Lord of the Southern Regions, but first and only in disguise did he accept the food offerings of *pūjā* in the settled areas. 31 Then he dispatched Kālu Rāy to the city of Hijali, for there the king, that man-lion among men, failed to recognize and honor me. 32 I slew his son and then restored him to life, whereupon the king dutifully lavished me with honor and respect by making the requisite sacrifices of offering.

33 "There was a merchant, Devdatta by name, who hailed from Baḍadaha, but for many long days he had been held prisoner in Turaṅga, the City of Horses. 34 Paying heed to my words of guidance, his son Puṣpadatta made ready seven hardy boats and pushed off in search of him. 35 Along the way he accosted the king not realizing who he was; the king did not recognize him either and started to hack him to pieces. 36 As he was about to die, that merchant's son focused his thoughts on me; at the moment of his crisis I went to protect him. 37 With tiger in tow, I attacked, raining down mighty blows. I slew King Surath and all of his many soldiers. 38 The Queen appeared and importuned me with solemn hymns of praise, and suffused with feel-

71. There is an allusion, if not a deliberate connection to Kālketu, the first of the heroes of the *Caṇḍī maṅgal*, because Kālketu's father is Dharmaketu, which would make Dakṣiṇ Rāy his brother-in-law. The text and the story are not explicitly named. See Kavikaṅkan Mukundarām Cakravartī, *Caṇḍīmaṅgal*, ed. Sukumār Sen, rev. ed. (Naẏ Dillī: Sāhitya Akādemī, 2007), esp. bk. 2; for translations of this and all *Caṇḍī maṅgal* passages, see Kavikankan, *Chandimangal of Kavikankan*, trans. Edward Yazijian (New Delhi: Penguin India, 2015), which follows the Sen edition.

ings of compassion, I gave her back his life. 39 Then they married their daughter Ratnāvatī to the young merchant [Puṣpadatta], and so the father and son returned to their own land. 40 Puṣpadatta was one valiant hero: he constructed a citadel for me and, within it, a palatial abode. He then routinely performed my worship with due diligence. 41 So make known in my auspicious *maṅgal* escapades such as these."

42 *And so Kṛṣṇarām has composed the* maṅgal *of Rāy in the* śaka *year 1608.*[72]

With that frame narrative set, Kṛṣṇarām launches the saga of Dakṣiṇ Rāy and his followers. A Bengali merchant named Devdatta undertakes a trading voyage at the behest of his local king to supply the accoutrements of kingship the courts demand. His wife is four months pregnant, and though she begs him to delay his departure, the king is impatient. Prior to departure, his wife's pregnancy is attested before *brāhmaṇs* at the insistence of his mother, a document that will prove valuable for all concerned. Devdatta, however, is not a terribly fortunate merchant, and when he reaches his southern destination, his ships laden with goods for trade are confiscated and he is summarily jailed for trespass, among other charges. Some twelve years later his son sets out to find him.

The young boy-merchant is named Puṣpadatta, and he badgers the king until the latter grants permission for the trip, but Puṣpadatta needs ships built. Seven brothers, traditional woodcutters of the Sunderban region, chop and rick wood in an abundance never before witnessed, certainly enough for the seven ships Puṣpadatta requires. In their euphoria over the extraordinary stand of trees they are felling, they mindlessly destroy one particular tree that is the favored of Dakṣiṇ Rāy, Lord of the Āṭhārobhāṭī, made up of the low-lying lands of the eighteen tides. He sets his tigers on them with instructions to slay six of the brothers, but not devour their bodies, and to spare the eldest; so they break their necks and drink their blood before abandoning the six corpses. The surviving brother nearly commits suicide, but Dakṣiṇ Rāy appears before him and explains why his brothers have been killed. Dakṣiṇ Rāy proposes that if this unfortunate man will make a sacrifice of his only son, he will revive his brothers. Following the old Bengali saw that sons can always be replaced, while brothers cannot, he reluctantly agrees to the bargain. After the sacrifice, where he slices through his son's torso at the waist and offers his flesh, Dakṣiṇ Rāy is appeased and restores the brothers and the son to life with the express instruction to sing of his magnificent glory, which they dutifully do. And so the story of Dakṣiṇ Rāy's greatness spreads.[73]

72. Kṛṣṇarām Dās, *Rāy maṅgal*, sec. 2, pp. 166–68. *Śaka* 1608 is approximately 1686 CE. The *śaka* date is embedded in a riddle called *hēyālīmūlaka śloka*, frequently based on astrological signs, but sometimes on other known "sets" of things (e.g., *kar* = hand = 2); so here the code is *vasu* = demigods (8), *śūnya* = nul or void (0), *ṛtu* = seasons (6), and *candra* = moon (1).

73. There is a similar story in Rudradev's *Rāy maṅgal* wherein the *bāuliyā* Ratā is forced to sacrifice his son to Dakṣiṇ Rāy for not properly worshiping him prior to entering the forest to cut wood. His son is unfazed and volunteers, and so: "With the right intention forming in his heart, he grasped his son's hair in his left hand, and slew him with the three-pointed sword. Recognizing Ratā's devotion . . ."

When the time comes for Puṣpadatta to have his ships constructed, he has the timber he needs, so he advertises widely for skilled shipwrights. From his celestial chariot Dakṣiṇ Rāy summons Viśvakarmmā and Hānumān, who, in disguise, apply for and receive the commission. They construct the vessels in the blink of an eye. The ships are loaded with goods for trade, all described in lavish detail, and Puṣpadatta sets off after receiving the blessings of his mother, who as the ideal wife, *satī*, is an ardent devotee of Dakṣiṇ Rāy, whom she petitions to watch over her son. Off the young merchant goes in quest of the fabled land of Turaṅga to find his father.

As Puṣpadatta moves slowly through the meandering distributaries of the Bhāgirathī River in lower Bengal, deeper and deeper into the swampy byways of the Sunderban's mangrove forests, he witnesses what is for him a strange form of worship, a *pūjā* in which the locals pay their respects to mounds of earth, usually crowned by clay pots. Puzzled, he asks his much older and experienced captain why they are worshiping in this way.

> 168 The helmsman began, "Brother, there is definitely a reason. Since you are not aware of it, I will tell you, but you must listen carefully. 169 You must have already heard of Baḍa Khān Gājī, a *pīr* who appears in the flesh, and Dakṣiṇ Rāy, Lord of the Āṭhārobhāṭī, the Land of the Eighteen Tides. 170 Previously those two had been fast friends, then a conflict between them escalated into an all-out war. 171 Each of the two lords wanted complete suzerainty over the same vast domain, so the two brothers pursued their dispute on all fronts. 172 The Gājī struck Dakṣiṇ Rāy's expansive chest, and he was felled, but just as promptly sprang back up, his body a trick of the illusory nature of creation, *māyā*. 173 Then Baḍa Khān hacked through Rāy's now-raised neck and that phantom head bounced to the ground. And so it went. 174 Finally God, Īśvara himself, broke up the stalemate and these two giant figures afterwards became fast friends. 175 Since that event, worship has been directed toward the waterpot, the severed head [of Dakṣiṇ Rāy]; but in some places, his arresting image sits astride a tiger. 176 Wherever a settlement is associated with the name of Baḍa Khān, the established practice is to erect a mound of earth. 177 No image is fabricated; only contemplation will impel him to fulfill the supplications of his devotees. 178 The jurisdiction of the entirety of Āṭhārobhāṭī lies with Dakṣiṇ Rāy; and Gājī's jurisdiction lies therein by virtue of being the Lord's close friend. 179 With a single combined worship are the two figures truly satisfied. One can see them appear together in the same place as brothers."[74]

Intrigued, the young boy wants to hear the cause of the conflict between Baḍa Khān Gājī and Dakṣiṇ Rāy, which constitutes the third nested frame of Kṛṣṇarām's narration. The conflict turns out to be the result of an insult, born of ignorance, by

---

Unfortunately, we can only speculate if his life was restored because the manuscript once again breaks and does not pick up the rest of the story, but moves on to Puṣpadatta's adventures; see Rudradev, *Rāy maṅgal*, 140–42.

74. Kṛṣṇarām Dās, *Rāy maṅgal*, sec. 10, p. 180.

a merchant named Dhanapati. Rāy rules by virtue of being one of the demi-gods, born of the legendary King Prabhākar and wife Līlāvatī, daughter of Dharmaketu, and now controller of much of the land and resources of the region.[75] On a trading voyage that had to traverse Dakṣiṇ Rāy's region, just as Puṣpadatta is now doing, Dhanapati stopped to perform *pūjā* worship to an earthen mound at one of Rāy's shrines along the route. The innocent but ignorant trader failed to pay any, much less commensurate, respect to Baḍa Khān Gājī, the prominent warrior saint who lived as Dakṣiṇ Rāy's brother in the forest with his band of tigers. When the tigers reported back that they had lost face, the prestige of Baḍa Khān Gājī was completely undone in the region as a result of the favoritism shown by the merchant. The Gājī was inconsolably angry and sought revenge on both the merchant and Dakṣiṇ Rāy, who had allowed this to transpire without intervention.

183 While Dhanapati the merchant was pursuing his seafaring trade, by the intervention of Fate, he laid up at one particular landing. 184 He had spotted the special waterpot of Dakṣiṇ Rāy on the shore, and, knowing he was the special boon-born son of Hara, Śiv, he made a generous offering of fragrant flowers 185 and varieties of ornaments studded with gems. Who else could lavish so much? Finishing his service of worship, he begged leave with his hands pressed together in respect. 186 But he unwittingly failed to pay his respects to Baḍa Khān Gājī, and soon he was surrounded by great hosts of *phakirs*. 187 The naïve merchant felt he was being threatened and grew angry, driving them away from the premises. 188 He boarded his ship and set sail for Siṃhala, while the *phakirs* went together to complain to Gājī Pīr.

189 Situated in that particular village was a sanctum for Gājī, and the city and its markets were appropriately resplendent. 190 "Respected sir, you no longer seem to give proper attention to the administration of the region. 191 Some merchant fellow paid his respects in worship of Dakṣiṇ Rāy and departed, but he ignored you altogether. We consider this an egregious offense. 192 The bumpkin Bāṅgālī does not know to fear. He attacked us and drove us from our rightful place. 193 We cannot show our faces to the people out of our shame. We will no longer consider ourselves *phakirs*; we spit on that title."

194 Right then a tiger by the name of Kālānal spoke up. "When I went out to hunt, I received none of the usual deference, or the run of the territory. 195 The tigers of Dakṣiṇ Rāy always deferred and allowed us to snatch the prized head, but now when they hear your name [Gājī], everyone simply casts knowing looks. 196 The mat weavers, the salt manufacturers, and the woodcutters now recognize no one else save Dakṣiṇ Rāy. 197 I had just eaten one nobody salt miner, when in a rage three swifts of twenty tigers each came roaring after me. 198 Seeing the situation, I began to calculate how the importance and stature of this lordly Baḍa Khān had declined, for the *pīr* is no longer recognized or revered in Āṭhārobhāṭī, the Land of the Eighteen Tides. 199 This anger festers because everyone accepted your authority."

. . .

75. Kṛṣṇarām Dās, sec. 2, pp. 166–67.

202 In the presence of all gathered there, Gājī cursed the merchant. 203 "This daughter-fucker has fled! Now what are you going to do? The bastard will be totally lost. 204 Can you not just hear Dakṣiṇ Rāy wail when he is bound and hauled back here? Only then shall I again be considered a true warrior-saint, a *gājī*." 205 Thus Khān instructed them to crush the ears of [Rāy's] servants. "I have to see for myself quickly what kind of Śaytān he is. 206 Every day his bare fists pummel people into bloody submission. He seizes their land and produces with a flourish a document that testifies to his ownership, that claims it as his property."

207 Then he ordered them, "Be quick, go to [Dakṣiṇ Rāy's] house, search him out. It will take all of you together to corral him and pound his enormous body to a pulp!" 208 With these words he exhorted and aroused the *phakīrs* gathered there. In a breathless, unruly mob they sped off to initiate the quarrel. 209 They destroyed everything in [Rāy's] dwelling, then hurled what was left into the brackish waters. With the help of the tigers, they destroyed the carefully crafted icons. 210 Someone laid hold the *brāhmaṇ* priest, ripping off his sacred thread. They jostled him to the ground and with a swarm of fists battered him senseless. 211 This army of *phakīrs* deliberately polluted his food: "Your *jāti*,[76] like your body, is stripped, and now all you can wear is a beard, you daughter-fucker!"[77]

A tiger among Dakṣiṇ Rāy's entourage has been witness to the melee and reports back to his master, who is puzzled and outraged at the same time. Cautioning against immediate punitive retaliation, an elder statesman among his tigers is sent to sound out the Gājī and ascertain the real root of the trouble. The emissary counsels Gājī, "As yet no one has openly broken from the other. What is the point of this treachery, this rivalry? Should conciliatory words be uttered, all will be well."[78] But the Gājī cannot be mollified and rejoins with a volley of imprecations laced with the most vulgar of obscenities. The conflict, now inevitable, escalates quickly. Rāy gathers all his tigers and sets out to destroy Baḍa Khān. First routing a group of *phakīrs*, Rāy scatters all the tigers, who suddenly decide that this fracas is none of their affair. Then he finds the Gājī.

365 When suddenly the two sovereigns appeared, they began to heap abuse on one another. Rāy was first to scream insults at Gājī. 366 "Previously you fell at my feet—do you not remember that? But when you started to eat meat, you became high and mighty, so who is that chum to you now? 367 You snatched away the mercenary *brāhmaṇ*'s whore-daughter,[79] and that act makes you little more than a common

76. *Jāti* is "birth" or station, often wrongly translated as caste, the latter an imported construction. The language implies that only the beard—that is, to join the ranks of *musalmāns*—can cover his shame, now that he is symbolically and literally stripped. But importantly, the motivating factor for this forced change of status is not ideological, therefore not a religious "conversion" as the term is understood today, but about honor and social standing and pollution.

77. Kṛṣṇarām Dās, *Rāy maṅgal*, sec. 11, pp. 181–83.

78. Kṛṣṇarām Dās, sec. 12, v. 226, p. 184.

79. This reference suggests the marriage of Gāji with Cāmpāvatī, the daughter of *brāhmaṇ* king Mukuṭ Rājā, which is detailed in the various versions of the *Gāji kālu o cāmpāvatī kanyār puthi*, the

highwayman. 368 Were there a real *pīr* standing here, he would receive an offering of *śirni* from me; I would have brought proper food for him to eat—but instead this one runs after tits and cunt. 369 If you had managed to take possession of my army of tigers just now, then you would be the master-in-control and I would be like the thief. 370 Just as ants sprout wings in order to [swarm in reproductive frenzy and] die, you go and destroy the sacred room that houses my worshipful image. 371 If you will relent in these despicable actions, I will make nothing more of it. You are not normally considered to be a nasty or particularly evil man, so return to your good standing now. 372 If you take refuge in me, then I will be mollified and suffer you protection."

Kṛṣṇarām now relates how the Gāji replied in the rising flush of his anger.

373 "What kind of infidel are you, you lowlife bastard? Listen carefully to my pronouncements, you dunce, you filthy vulture. 374 What do you do here in the jungly wild besides smoke your hookah and get intoxicated? Are you really such an ignoramus that you can only spew deprecations from your pumpkin-chariot?[80] 375 You really do not have a clue about the *pīr* Baḍa Khān Gāji. [Just as] Khodā, God Himself has given the coral tree[81] to this world as proof of the good things in life, 376 who has blessed you with such a kingdom with its abundant flowing rivers? Tell me, have you paid no heed to that great opportunity and benefit? 377 If there is no sense of honor or propriety in the gush of big-talk you aim in my direction, then you will be made to show respect after I have chastised you. 378 All of the prosperity you previously enjoyed as a result of your various offices will disappear like so much wet smoke belching from your water pipe. 379 Are you listening, whoremonger, to this rehearsal of your death? The Lord Gosāñi is the essential reality of the totality of creation, you daughter-fucker. 380 Everyone will ignore your cry for help, Dakṣiṇ Rāy, they will not offer even the tiniest dried up tit to suck. 381 If you desire your own well-being, make yourself scarce, scamper away like a scared cat. 382 With a power like a raging river, we swept away your icon, utterly collapsing your thatched hut. 383 The tiger Kālānal tried to stop me, but this outrageous and treacherous action has serious consequences. I will shackle this jacket-wearing Bāṅgālī dog and humiliate him. 384 According to the custom in the Bhāṭi, he must make some token offering. 385 Whenever and whatever thing gets produced here, half is yours, half is mine—it is a simple agreement. 386 It is written that the act of hoarding and loaning money is an abominable practice, while the calculation of the debts of the poor will be forgiven."[82]

---

earliest extant version somewhat later than this text. That story will occupy our attention in the next chapter.

80. The pumpkin-chariot (*kaduratha*) refers to the bowl of the hookah.

81. In the Bangla-speaking world, the coral tree (*mādāra*) is *Erythrina variegata*, sometimes called the flame tree or the tiger-claw, with its distinctive red claw-like flowers. It is a special favorite for gardens and attracts a variety of nectar-seeking birds. The intertextual reference is likely Qur'ān 55, *Sūra al Raḥmān*. (Note: the English name for the coral tree is a coincidence with the reference to coral in the *sūra*.)

82. The implication being that Dakṣiṇ Rāy engages in such activities as a *zamandar*. This prohibition against usury and related practices is one of the few intimations of Islamic law, and a direct intertextual reference to Qur'ān 2.275–81, *Sūra al Baqara;* see also 3.130–31, *Sūra al 'Imrān;* 4.160–61; and 30.39–40, *Sūra al Nisā.*

387 Unable to tolerate further the Gāji's outrageous behavior, Dakṣiṇ Rāy interrupted and began to speak. 388 "Who are you, where are you from, and just what are these customary rules? You act as if you own the world, but in the village you have no respect. 389 The more I forgave you out of our previous affection, the greater your arrogant swagger has grown, it swells bigger and bigger. 390 Just as the sinner's heart and mind are submerged in sin, that haughtiness in the end must reckon with Yam, the lord of death. 391 When a lowly person grows too big and waves his fist at the sky in defiance,[83] every imaginable form of misery and anguish accrues, for Lachmi[84] will have fled. 392 You should prepare yourself to meet a similar destruction: die or take flight and escape with your life to someplace far far away. 393 However many tigers have accompanied you, I will rip them to shreds, and devour them morsel by tiny morsel. 394 [Your tiger] Khān Dāṇḍā suffers you to mount his back. Hold that pose as this arrow is loosed. 395 As he soothingly addresses him as *beg*, the honorable one, the arrow called *siṁhaduḥkh*, the "scourge of lions," streaked forward.[85] The new razor-sharp arrow escaped with a zipping hiss. 396 It split the blaze on the tiger's forehead like a crack of lightning. The *pīr's* tiger tumbled to the ground and writhed in the dirt. 397 Baḍakhā̃ staggered up, his most noble mount gone. He called to his tigers, "Hey, gather around me!" 398 But they vanished, scattered here and there; who would stay and get mixed up in this kind of exchange? They blended in and disappeared into the throng of Rāy's congeries.[86]

The two mighty figures exchange as many imprecations as they do blows, the insults flying as fast as the missiles from their celestial weapons and bows. As he fervently meditates on the Prophet, *paygambar*, doom seems to fall upon the Gājī, for his chest is split open. His body slumps to the ground, lifeless, but his prayer to *paygambar* has been rewarded and he heals himself with a new body, the old one still lying on the ground.[87] Śiv's trident has proved ineffective for Rāy. The *pīr* taunts him: "You son of a stinking Bāṅgāli jackal, you hide behind your women's skirts, but now you are found out, there is no going back. You will find no protection

83. Literally "tries to beat the sky."

84. Lachmi is Lakṣmī, the goddess of wealth and good fortune.

85. In this construction—*balite balite bege siṃhaduḥkh bāṇ*—the author has skillfully captured the seamless action of Dakṣiṇ Rāy notching his arrow and letting it fly as he addresses Baḍa Khān ironically as *beg*, or "revered one" or "your highness." The term */bege/* is a noun in the first foot, while it serves as the verb for the second foot.

86. Kṛṣṇarām Dās, *Rāy maṅgal*, sec. 18–19, pp. 197–99.

87. This is the only example among the many tales of the fictive *pīrs* where the warrior saint is slain—but significantly, he is not really slain in the traditional sense, because he is instantly revived (this is not, however, a point of theological contention or a position that requires explanation apart from what the text tells us). This avoidance of death is a feature that sets apart Baḍa Khān Gāji and the other fictional *pīrs*, *phakirs*, and *bibīs* from the more historically famous, whose fame as *gāji* was partially predicated on their martyrdom, and whose tombs become the focal site for the development of a religious community. See, for instance, Shahid Amin, *Conquest and Community: The Afterlife of Warrior Saint Ghazi Miyan* (Hyderabad: Orient Blackswan, 2015).

there."[88] Unknown to Rāy, the *paygambar* has bestowed on Gājī the power to strike a blow that never fails, for Yam, the Lord of Death himself, dwells in his sword's diamond-sharp edge. After using magical incantations to round up and slay all of Rāy's tigers, he advances toward his foe and, with a calculated deliberation, raises his sword for all to witness as he severs Rāy's head from his body. That head falls to the ground with a deafening thud and rolls still in the dirt. The earth herself staggers and tilts under the weight, and the gods are startled. Suddenly the Supreme Lord, Īśvar, personally appears to mediate and end the dispute.

416 Half of his head was black,
a tuft of hair pulled to one side,
  wildflower garland and rosary looping his forearms.
Half of his body was a dazzling white,
the other half the deep indigo of rainclouds,
  Korān in one hand and *Purāṇa* in the other.[89]
417 The exact same vision
was beheld by both men
  and both fell and grasped his feet.
That lord of the universe lifted them up,
placed one's hand in the other, and made them to understand
  they must establish a formal pact of friendship.
418 "Suzerainty over this Bhāṭi land
lies entirely with Dakṣiṇ Rāy,
  so why have you kicked up a fuss, Pīr?
Who does not show you honor and respect?
Is there anywhere you are not loved and honored?
  Your name and standing are famous across the world.
419 "You and Rāy are one and the same.
In this matter only knuckleheaded barbarians
  see you as different and suffer all manner of misery for it.
There is one essential truth in all this:
whatever else you may see,
  it is only the play of apparent forms.
420 "Baḍakhā̃'s magically created body[90] will
from its grave emanate a charismatic power, *kerāmat*,
  that will allow people to gain their desires.

88. Kṛṣṇarām Dās, *Rāy maṅgal*, section 20, v. 409, p. 200.

89. The image is consistent with that of the combined form of Satya Pīr and Satya Nārāyaṇ, which had already been made popular in Bengal more than a century prior to this text.

90. Magically created (*māyā*) body or form (*ākār*); except in explicit vedāntic passages, *māyā* in Bangla nearly always refers to the magic or wizardry of creation, and only in that sense is it illusory. When Baḍa Khān Gāji is killed and when Dakṣiṇ Rāy's head is lopped off, the poet makes clear that the ontological reality of these two is in no way affected, i.e., it is simply the play of the created world.

Wherever the name of the *pīr* is invoked,
that locale is designated an official court where
any decree or settlement can be registered in his name.
421 "May everyone worship in *pūjā*,
the King of the Southern Regions
in the form of a pot, a sign of his shaved head.[91]
Then his story and fame will proliferate
to every imaginable spot on earth, and
images (*mūrti*) will reside in all those places."[92]

. . . .

426 "Now Dakṣiṇ Rāy
is the overlord of all the Sunderban *bhāṭi*.
Kālu Rāy has Hijuli as his special domain.
Sāheb Pīr has free reign in all areas.
Everyone must bow their heads to him.
No one should show him any disrespect."
427 The god, Dev Bhagavān,
disappeared after delivering these words.
Who has the power to fathom the magic of his *māyā*?
His words are not to be foresworn,
as every human in every home recognizes—
and acknowledging that, they show proper honor and respect.
428 *When the good and virtuous merchant heard this,*
he made his obeisance in an attitude of loving devotion
and took a flower as the leftover offering, prasād.
Kavi Kṛṣṇarām notes that
finding the winds favorable,
he boarded his boat and shoved off.[93]

The remainder of the tale traces Puṣpadatta's adventures further south in finding his father. At each place they stop, the helmsman recites the local lore, such as the wonders of Puri and Orissa[94]—in the midst of which the poet pointedly opines that, based on what the protagonist observed in Puri, all distinctions of social ranks will eventually be leveled in the Kali Age: *jabans* and *brāhmaṇs* and the rest of the *varṇas* will be merged into a single society.[95] When they encounter the Setubandha, the helmsman narrates the tale of Rām, Sītā, and Rāvaṇ.[96] As

91. A sign (*māyā*, not the head itself) referencing his shaved head (*muṇḍa*) which takes the form of a waterpot; see above, vv. 166, 175.

92. There seems to be a conflation of the traditional Sanskrit concepts of *pratimā* (copy, sign) and *mūrti* (manifestation).

93. Kṛṣṇarām Dās, *Rāy maṅgal*, sec. 21, vv. 416–28, pp. 201–3.

94. Kṛṣṇarām Dās, sec. 23, vv. 449–63, pp. 204–6.

95. Kṛṣṇarām Dās, sec. 23, vv. 455–56, p. 205.

96. Kṛṣṇarām Dās, secs. 24–25, vv. 464–85, pp. 206–8.

they continue south, the merchant's fleet soon encounters a menagerie of strange creatures—monstrous crabs with snapping claws threatening the boats, tides of blood-sucking leeches, gargantuan raptors that menace the ships until scattered with cannon shot, and leviathans sufficiently large to swallow the ships but thwarted only by invoking Garuḍa, Viṣṇu's avian mount, to come and save them. Fatefully they arrive at the treacherous Kālidaha where Dakṣiṇ Rāy generates a vision seen only by the merchant and no one else and which will prove fateful:[97] On a sandbank in the middle of the ocean there is a magnificent palace of gold wherein sit Nārāyaṇ and his wife Nīlāvatī. They are attended by hundreds of different types of birds, a multifarious profusion of arresting and fragrant flowers, and around them deer, buffalo, tigers, and humans share the idyllic space, where peacocks play with serpents and elephants mix with lions. All around an ethereal music wafts to which celestial figures dance. The merchant is stunned and in his euphoria vows to share this incredible vision with anyone who will listen, while the taciturn helmsman, who sees nothing at all, remains mute, figuring it to be a phantasm.

When they reach their trading destination, the young merchant explains his mission to the local king—to find his lost father and then to trade—and then foolishly trumpets his encounter with the apparition in the middle of the sea. Intrigued, but detecting a scam, the king promises him half his kingdom and the hand of his daughter, Ratnāvatī, should he be able to verify the claim, but incarceration should he not—an agreement they formally certify in writing.[98] Needless to say, the naïve Puṣpadatta lands in prison with a death sentence, his boats brimming with trading goods confiscated. As he languishes in prison, a large stone on his chest, the young Puṣpadatta meditates on Dakṣiṇ Rāy, who eventually feels his prayers. He dispatches his tigers, led by Lohājaṅga Rūp Rāy and Balāki, to terrorize the king and aid the merchant. Swarms of hornets, wasps, and bees likewise wreak havoc and a major war ensues with much bloodshed. Finally Dakṣiṇ Rāy himself arrives and confronts the king, whom he slays.[99] His grieving queen bargains with Dakṣiṇ Rāy to offer worship to him and to give her daughter's hand in marriage to the merchant in exchange for her husband's resurrection. Dakṣiṇ Rāy's conditions are met and he brings the king back to life,[100] along with all his slain soldiers and courtiers. The young merchant finally recovers his father from deep within the prison, barely alive. A joyous reunion ensues. Puṣpadatta convinces his father that

97. Kṛṣṇarām Dās, sec. 28, vv. 508–24, pp. 210–11.

98. Kṛṣṇarām Dās, sec. 32, vv. 581–85, p. 215. It should be noted that in Rudradev's tale, Puṣpadatta demonstrates a different kind of naïveté upon reaching the strange shores of the southern king. He ignores the advice of his helmsman and is enticed ashore by a bevy of incredibly beautiful women who seduce him with promises of supersensual sex and other delights . . . but alas, once again the manuscript breaks off, this time completely. See Rudradev, *Rāy maṅgal*, 143–46.

99. Kṛṣṇarām Dās, *Rāy maṅgal*, secs. 38–39, vv. 725–45, pp. 227–28.

100. Kṛṣṇarām Dās, sec. 40, vv. 749–52, p. 229.

he is indeed his son when he produces the letter of surety attesting paternity as sworn before *brāhmaṇs*, who have recorded his testimony that his wife was indeed pregnant at the time of his leaving.[101]

Subsequent to that reunion, the young merchant is married to the princess. After basking in the joys of married life and the riches of kingly favor, he eventually realizes he needs to return to Bengal. In riddles he tells his bride that he must return to his ancestral home and asks if she can possibly leave her loving family. She replies that Sītā went with Rām into exile, Damayantī did not resist when Nala had to escape, and Draupadī left without sorrow.[102] After a long and emotional preparation for farewell, they take their leave, laden with riches. Working their way back up the coast, they stop at Setubandha, then at Puri—where the narrator again inserts his own voice into the narrative and comments that rice *prasād* from Jagannāth is routinely distributed to all without discriminating among social groups (*varṇa*).[103] They reach the mouth of the Gaṅgā and move upstream until they are close enough to home for Puṣpadatta to send a messenger by land to his mother. Upon docking, Puṣpadatta pays his sailors handsomely and distributes alms to the needy. His father is reunited with his mother. Ratnāvatī is received as the proper daughter-in-law, who through a ritual dice match extracts from Puṣpadatta a vow never to marry another, ensuring his fidelity.[104] Puṣpadatta then meets the king, providing him with extraordinary riches as appropriate, while narrating the tale of his adventures which were successful because of the intervention of Dakṣiṇ Rāy, whom they all subsequently worship.[105] Afterwards, with the help of Viśvakarmmā, he builds a palace for Ratnāvatī and himself, and they install an image of Dakṣiṇ Rāy seated on a tiger, whom they worship with *pūjā* and animal sacrifices.[106]

. . .

4.5. THE NEW WORLD ORDER OF THE SUNDERBANS

One does not have to look far to see how the author Muhāmmad Khater drew on the *Rāy maṅgal* to craft the tale of the *Bonbibī jahurā nāmā*. The raison d'être of both the *maṅgal kāvya* and *jahurā nāmā* genres is to make known the advent of the heroic figure, to inculcate appropriate behavior as directed by that hero or heroine, and to instigate a sanctioned form of worship. In this, the *jahurā nāmā* positively parodies the genre of *maṅgal kāvya*, the shared goals of the genre binding them

101. Kṛṣṇarām Dās, sec. 41, vv. 765–807, pp. 231–34.
102. Kṛṣṇarām Dās, sec. 46, vv. 860–67, p. 238.
103. Kṛṣṇarām Dās, sec. 50, v. 920, pp. 242–43.
104. Kṛṣṇarām Dās, sec. 52, vv. 948–50, p. 246.
105. Kṛṣṇarām Dās, sec. 53, vv. 956–62, p. 247.
106. Kṛṣṇarām Dās, secs. 53–54, vv. 868–73, pp. 247–48.

in many of their pragmatic presuppositions. Both portray conflict that pits divine will against human foibles, and resolutions that bring human conduct into alignment with divine plans. In both narratives, the mechanisms that trigger conflict hinge on the unwitting failure to pay proper respect to the presiding powers that govern the Sunderbans. Dakṣiṇ Rāy's failure to intercede with the merchant who has failed to show respect to Baḍa Khān Gāji results in the latter desecrating Rāy's images and polluting his *brāhmaṇ* priests. The result is armed combat. Similarly, the hapless woodcutters who inadvertently violate the sanctity of Dakṣiṇ Rāy's favored tree precipitate severe retribution that is eventually redressed. When Bonbibī and Śājaṅgali enter the Sunderban, they too violate the boundaries without permission as they establish their small foothold in the name of God after their departure from Medinā. That transgression culminates in Bonbibī's battle with Nārāyaṇī, mother of Dakṣiṇ Rāy. In the second tale of the Bonbibī cycle, the near disaster sparked by the greedy merchant Dhonāi, who tries to slip past Dakṣiṇ Rāy's home territories without paying his due, prompts the battle between Śājaṅgalī and Dakṣiṇ Rāy over the anticipated, but never executed, sacrifice of Dukhe. Disrespect cannot be allowed to go unpunished; honor becomes a means of establishing relative standing and rank, which is translated into socially recognizable hierarchical kinship terms.

The *Bonbibī jahurā nāmā* does not automatically follow all the contours of the *Rāy maṅgal* or *maṅgal kāvya* formulas. Though the role of merchant centers much of the narrative, the resolution of his fortunes is inverted, but it is worth remembering that following structuralist principles, an inversion is still mimetic. Following the well-attested formula for the *maṅgal kāvya* romance, prosperity eventually accrues to the merchants in the *Rāy maṅgal*. Puṣpadatta and his father Devdatta, whom he rescues, both benefit by virtue of their devotion, and both benefit from the dual devotion of their wives to their husbands and to Dakṣiṇ Rāy. In the *Bonbibī jahurā nāmā* the tables are turned; while the avaricious merchant Dhonāi is denied his profits, he is eventually spared by the grace of both Dukhe and Bonbibī, and at least some of his wealth is not taken away. But it is Dhonāi's nephew, Dukhe, the youngest, poorest, and socially lowest individual on the voyage, who ultimately reaps the greatest benefit from the commercial voyage to the Sunderbans, benefits Dhonāi never intended for him to receive, including the hand of his own daughter rashly promised when he was desperate to recruit one more crew member. The mechanism for effecting the aid of Rāy or Bonbibī is perfectly parallel: meditate on them with earnest devotion, which will draw their attention and give them the opportunity to intervene. One of the recurring points of these texts is that worship of the *pīrs* and *bibīs* is an effective way to satisfy worldly needs, often in the form of wealth, which they are reported frequently to supply when someone calls on them with even the simplest devotion. The message is not without its ambiguity, though, for even the double-crossing Dhonāi in the end gains Bonbibī's help, but only when he is cornered, with all his other options exhausted. In that vexed predicament, perhaps because all of his other possible courses of action are eliminated, his prayers of desperation produce the positive aid he seeks. One cannot but be reminded of the grudging way that Cāṇḍo, devotee of Śiva, grudgingly proffers worship to Manasā, goddess of snakes, in the *Manasā maṅgal*, perhaps the most widely circulated of all the *maṅgal kāvyas*. Up to that point in the Dukhe story the receiver of the text is led to believe that the protector's mercy can only descend if the intentions of the protagonists are honorable and pure with respect to Bonbibī and what she represents, but just as in the defeat of Nārāyaṇī earlier, supplication alone, regardless of how it is brought about, suffices to wrap oneself in Bonbibī's protection, which is itself an extension of Āllā's bestowal of power.

The key sequence in the *Rāy maṅgal* for the *Bonbibī jahurā nāmā* is undoubtedly the death match. In that protracted battle, Baḍa Khān, a saint (*oli*) and warrior *pīr* (*gāji*), demonstrates a power throughout that is equal to, but eventually proves to be greater than, that of Dakṣiṇ Rāy, who is himself a demigod, in the lineage of Śiv through the *muni* Prabhākar. In the end, each slays the other, but it is Baḍa Khān Gāji who ultimately prevails, rising from his dead body to lop off the head of Dakṣiṇ Rāy. His prayer to *paygambar*, the Prophet, has granted him invincibility, which ultimately gives him the advantage. Only when God, designated in the text as Īśvar, descends does the fight stop and the two enemies are forced into a truce of friendship. Dakṣiṇ Rāy is left to be the de facto administrative ruler of the Āṭhārobhāṭī region, the low-lying lands of the eighteen tides, while Baḍa Khān Gāji freely roams the entire area with an even greater power, for not only is he not confined geographically, but everywhere he goes, his presence constitutes an official, albeit mobile and temporary, court for any legal hearing or registry; so too do his various tombs or *dargās* come to function more permanently. Previously the two had been reckoned brothers, and Īśvar has reimposed that relationship. All those resident in the Sunderban are instructed to honor them both equally, though the text does not stipulate which one is elder and which junior. In terms of privilege, Baḍa Khān Gājī emerges as the senior of the two. But the *Bonbibī jahurā nāmā* alters decidedly the balance of power away from the two "brothers" in favor of Bonbibī.

Recall in the Bonbibī story, Dakṣiṇ Rāy's mother Nārāyaṇī serves as his proxy but is bested in battle with Bonbibī. After her defeat, Bonbibī shows mercy when Nārāyaṇī begs for her life, but the condition of course is that all people in the Sunderban have to switch their allegiance and become vassals of Bonbibī. By virtue of his mother's defeat, Dakṣiṇ Rāy is made into a vassal of Bonbibī, so everyone who counts as his subject likewise comes under her power. Similarly, that battle establishes Bonbibī's superiority over an entire army composed of hungry ghosts, witches, goblins, and the like, sending an unmistakable message about the hierarchy of the cosmos. Bonbibī's God-given power leaves no mistake—remember, she requests the help directly of Āllā, as opposed to Baḍa Khān Gāji's power, which derives from the Prophet. Bonbibī's power and prestige are predicated on a new cosmic order, changing the basis of a key logical presupposition found in the *Rāy maṅgal*; the *Bonbibī jahurā nāmā* asserts that Āllā alone is in charge.

In the second tale of the *Bonbibī jahurā nāmā*, wherein Dakṣiṇ Rāy is being beaten directly by Śājaṅgali but is saved by the intervention of Baḍa Khān Gājī, the new social order is again asserted, instantiating the rehierarchizing of the cosmos. Not quite as accomplished as his twin sister, Śājaṅgali seems a bit nonplussed when Baḍa Khān Gāji stands up for Dakṣiṇ Rāy; he cannot imagine how a revered and powerful *musalmāni pīr* could intercede on behalf of a bloodthirsty demon, a *rākṣas*. But as his temper flares and he is castigating Baḍa Khān for being sympathetic to this infidel, Dakṣiṇ Rāy attempts to explain Śājaṅgali's relationship to them both, but with little success. Before the issue is settled, Bonbibī summons all three of them for an audience and, not insignificantly, they respond immediately and appear before her, an act of submission that already acknowledges her privilege. Then the same query is rehearsed regarding Baḍa Khān Gāji standing up for Dakṣiṇ Rāy. The critical moment occurs when Baḍa Khān Gāji explains to Bonbibī that after Dakṣiṇ Rāy's defeat the two of them are sharing power as brothers, that Rāy is a *brāhmaṇ*, not a *rākṣas*, and that Nārāyaṇī's defeat at her hands makes them all her children. At that point in the text, the *Bonbibī jahurā nāmā* unmistakably invokes the intertextual connection with the *Rāy maṅgal*, for the outcome of the conflict found in the alternate tale of Gāji, Kālu, and Cāmpāvatī is not about brothers as equals, as we shall soon see.

The cosmos operational in the *Rāy maṅgal* is clearly *purāṇik* and invokes such figures as Viśvakarmmā and Hānumān, Rām and Sītā and Rāvaṇ, and Nārāyaṇ and consort Nīlavatī. But the *Rāy maṅgal* cosmology only partially maps onto that of the *Bonbibī jahurā nāmā*. In both texts, fate is tied together with notions of *karma*, as it is in virtually every early modern Bangla text regardless of religious or other orientation. But the gods and goddesses—the *devs* and *devīs*—are absent in the Bonbibī text. In Bonbibī's world only the sinister dimensions of the traditional Indic cosmos seem to operate, the demonic extra-human characters figuring into the narrative: ghosts, demons, goblins, witches, and so forth, and the one apparent godling, Dakṣiṇ Rāy, requires a human sacrifice—the accusation a convenient misreading of Kṛṣṇarām's report of the many men slain by Dakṣiṇ Rāy, though in every case he revives them as a result of the interventions of the women who then institute his worship (a common *maṅgal kāvya* trope).

Explicit references to Rām and Sītā are missing in the Bonbibī text, but it is clear that the author played on the audience's knowledge of the story, which we might not unreasonably speculate suggests that to name them explicitly (an overt intertextual reference) would somehow validate them, and the *Bonbibī jahurā nāmā* seems deliberately to avoid all such explicit recognition. Both texts propose separate realms of heaven and earth, though in the *Rāy maṅgal* traffic and communication seem to be one-way (heaven to earth), while the Bonbibī text allows for two-way traffic, with portals to heaven active, especially in Medinā and through tombs more generally. Both share in the assumption that God, however conceived, actively intervenes on earth to set the good of the world back on course. But the nature of highest divinity in the *Rāy maṅgal*—as revealed when Īśvar descends to arbitrate the conflict between Dakṣiṇ Rāy and Baḍa Khān Gāji—is radically apart from that articulated in the Bonbibī text. In the *Rāy maṅgal*, Īśvar as Dev Bhagavān is a combined form of a *musalmāni* and *vaiṣṇav* divinity, half white, half black, carrying the Korān and *Bhāgavata purāṇa.* Semiotically the two parts are equal, just as Dakṣiṇ Rāy and Baḍa Khān Gāji are equals as brothers. This image of Īśvar is one to which the *Bonbibī jahurā nāmā* does not subscribe: the sole divinity is Khodā, Āllā. Here the similarities of cosmic order diverge dramatically, and all forms of Indic divinity—and, by the time the Bonbibī tales were circulated, more accurately Hindu divinity—are rehierarchized under a single and singular God, Āllā. This shift in cosmology will turn out to be highly significant and consistent with the tenor of the other tale of Baḍa Khān Gāji and Dakṣiṇ Rāy, the *Gāji kālu o cāmpāvatī kanyār puthi*, to which we now turn.

. . .

5

Manipulating the Cosmic Hierarchy

A Practical Act of Conceptual Blending

This daughter of the king was an accomplished scholar of the sacred texts,
so she deployed the astrological treatises to run her calculations.
She concluded that whether in heaven or on earth,
whether above ground or below, wherever they were to appear,
Gāji would be her husband, her svāmī.
Campā breathlessly spoke, "Get up, my lord, do not cry,
for you are indeed my husband, my svāmī, *the life of my life.*
You are the one who is my husband, and I am always your wife,
just as Śiv and Pārvvatī could never be separated . . .
Though I am a virgin brāhmaṇ *girl and you are a* machalmān,
I will present you to my father straight away."

—SĀYEB MUNSĪ ĀBDUL OHĀB, *GĀJI KĀLU O CĀMPĀVATĪ KANYĀR PUNTHI*

5.1. THE *GĀJI KĀLU O CĀMPĀVATĪ KANYĀR PUTHI* OF ĀBDUR RAHIM

The alternate version of the story of Baḍa Khān Gāji begins with the tale told by Khodā Bakhś, known simply as *Gāji kālu o cāmpāvatī.*[1] As previously noted, the earliest known manuscript dates to ca. 1750 and is a voluminous text of fifty-eight chapters and more than eighteen thousand lines. The oldest extant manuscript of the *Baḍo khā̃ gājīr kerāmati* by Kavi Hālumīr, who also self-identified as Mīrā

1. Ābul Kālām Mohāmmad Jākāriyā, ed., *Bāṅglā sāhitye gājī kālu o cāmpāvatī upākhyān*, introduction, 77–80; the text is found on 1–307.

Chaiyad Hālu, dates to ca. 1823 but was likely composed earlier.[2] This tale follows closely the narrative of Khodā Bakhś but truncates the story to less than two-thirds of Khodā Bakhś's original. After the advent of printing in Bengal in the mid-nineteenth century, a heavily abridged version of the story was circulated by multiple authors, the most popular version being that of Ābdur Rahim. There is no evidence of a manuscript tradition for Ābdur Rahim's work, the author likely having taken it to print from its inception; the earliest edition I have seen is dated 1282 BS (ca. 1875).[3] An edition that is not dated but appears to have its origins in the late nineteenth or early twentieth century is titled simply *Gājikālucāmpāvatī*.[4] This version from the Hāmidīyā Lāibrerī may well be the source, or one of the earliest reprints of the source, of which there have been a multitude of reprints by different publishers over the last century.[5] The primary difference between the earliest edition and the popular reprint is basically paratextual: the author has inserted some information regarding the melodic content (*rāg*) of a particular song, the expansion of the refrains used in performance (usually from one line to two or three), and the very occasional aside embedded in the signature line. The narrative substance, however, is not changed. Ābdur Rahim's text is less than five thousand lines and the other texts, such as that of Ābdul Ohāb, even shorter.[6] The most significant excision of material from these shorter versions is the opening story of Gāji's older brother Julhās, which covers just under a quarter of Khodā Bakhś original story; otherwise the versions are simply abridged, but not significantly modified, though a close textual comparison would undoubtedly reveal subtle differences in cosmological construction and slightly different sets of intertextual invocations and the use of rhetorical devices. In 1326 BS (ca. 1919), Mahāmmad Karim Bākhs from Rajshahi adapted the Gāji and Kālu story for the performance genre known as *gītābhinay*, a drama built around songs. It was titled simply *Śāhā gāji kālu gītābhinay*. In the preface he puzzles over the current Islamic prohibition against song, since *ghazals* are so popular, and seems mystified by the criticisms he

2. Ābul Kālām Mohāmmad Zākāriyā, introduction, 81; the text is in the same volume, 309–510.

3. Ābdur Rahim, *Gājikālu o cāmpāvatī kanyār puthi* (Mayamansiṃha: Prīṇṭār Śrī Ābdur Rahim at Rahimni Jantra in Mahakumā Kiśor Gañj, 1282 BS [ca. 1875]). There is at least one known immediate reprint to be found in the British Library dated 1283 BS (ca. 1878).

4. Ābdur Rahim, *Gājikālucāmpāvatī* (Ḍhākā: Ābdul Latiph and Ābdul Hāmid at Hāmidīyā Lāibrerī, Cak Bājār, n.d. [ca. 1890s?]); this text also appears in dated editions from 1904 and 1919, but with a slight adjustment of the title to *Gājīkālu o cāmpāvatī*. This is essentially the same text as the source of the popular reprint just noted.

5. The most popular edition today is Ābdur Rahim, *Gājikālu o cāmpāvatī kanyār puthi* (Ḍhākā: Hāmidiyā Lāibrerī, 1961); see the reprint, Munśī Ābdur Rahim Sāheb, *Gājikālu o cāmpāvatī kanyār puthi* (Kalikātā: Gaosiyā Lāibrerī, printed by Nuruddīn Āhmmad, 2001). Because it has been frequently reprinted without changes and is still on the market, this 1961 imprint will be cited with any variations from the earliest edition duly noted.

6. Sāyeb Munsī Ābdul Ohāb, *Gāji kālu o cāmpāvatī kanyār punthi*.

received for earlier songs he composed about the life of Mahāmmad and his family. He goes further to lament that the two *baṭ-tolā* press versions of the story composed by Maulvī Ābdul Jābbār Sāheb, titled *Gāji* and *Gāji boi*, are unsatisfactory and no longer followed by people because of the dated language; so he informs readers that he composed the *gīitābhinay* in a modern idiom and has included some mythical anecdotes to keep up the interest of the audience. The overall drift of the narratives again follows Khodā Bakhś.[7]

Because of the late composition of the *Bonbibī jahurā nāmā*, we cannot know which version of the Gāji, Kālu, and Cāmpāvatī story was indexed intertextually. The texts are sufficiently close in their structures, each one a paraphrase of the other, that the overall effect should be more or less the same. There are of course many oral versions of this set of tales that still circulate today,[8] as attested in the volumes of the journal *Lok Sāhitya* and in the popular theatre.[9] Without any further guidance, then, and for considerations of space, we shall look at the most popular printed version, that of Ābdur Rahim, which serves as a distillation of the entire tradition.[10]

7. Mahāmmad Karim Bākhs, *Śāhā gāji kālu gītābhinay, pratham khaṇḍa* (Jāiyānpur, Rājśāhī: by the author, printed in Kalikātā by Śrī Bimalcaraṇ Cakrabartī at Nāgendra Ṣṭīm Priṇṭiṅg Oyārks, 1326 BS [ca. 1919]). Unfortunately, only the first part is available (if indeed the rest of the text was finished). In his cast of characters he indicates that Gāji was named Dārabuddin prior to his renunciation as a *jindā pīr*. I have been unable to locate the two texts by Maulvī Ābdul Jābbār Sāheb he mentions.

8. For a rich analysis of the various song cycles of Gājī circulating in the Sunderban, see the recent publication, Jāhāṅgīr Hosen, *Dakṣiṇbaṅger aitihyabāhī loknāṭya* (Ḍhākā: Mohammad Śāh Ālam Sarkār at Samācār, 2014); see also the compilation, Khondkār Riyājul Hak, ed., *Gājīr gān*, Bāṁlā ekāḍemī phoklor saṃkalan, no. 66 (Ḍhākā: Śāmsujjāmān Khān, Parikālak, Gobeṣaṇā Saṃkalan o Phoklor Bibhāg, Bāṃlā Ekāḍemī, 1402 BS [1999]).

9. Anonymous, "Cāmpāvatī kainyār pālāgān—Part 1," *Lok sāhitya* 1 (Āṣāḍh 1370 BS [ca. 1963]): 55–104; "Cāmpāvatī kainyār pālāgān—Part 2," *Lok sāhitya* 2 (Āśviṇ 1370 BS [ca. 1963]): 127–75. This tale has been partially translated: see Anonymous, "*Campavati Kainyar Palagan:* Anonymous Muslim Folk Poem of Bengal," trans. Edward C. Dimock, Jr., Learning Resources in Bengali Studies (New York: Learning Resources in International Studies, 1974 [circulated in mimeograph]). Gāji also has additional tales in his cycle; see "Sonāi kanyā," in "Caṭṭagrām gītikā—part 4," *Lok sāhitya* 57 (Āṣāḍh 1399 [1993]): 1–101. For popular theatrical performance today, see Syed Jamil Ahmed, *Acinpakhi Infinity: Indigenous Theatre of Bangladesh*, esp. 181–241, 310–311, 329–32; Syed Jamil Ahmed, *In Praise of Nirañjan: Islam, Theatre and Bangladesh*, 68–165; and Saymon Zakaria, *Pronomohi Bongomata: Indigenous Cultural Forms of Bangladesh*, esp. part 4, chap. 5, 57–68.

10. The comic book version of this tale, found in the same volume as the Mānik Pīr and the first half of the Bonbibī story, represents a version of Gāji's marriage to Cāmpāvatī that only vaguely follows the lines of the other narrations I have found; see "Bada Khan Ghazi" in Saswat Ghosh, comp., *Folk Tales from India: The Sunderbans*, vol. 1, with illustrations by Dipankar Bhattacharya (New Delhi: Vivalok Comics, 2003), 32–41.

5.2. GĀJI'S LOVE FOR CĀMPĀVATĪ AND THE CONFLICT WITH DAKṢIṆĀ RĀY[11]

As Ābdur Rahim begins his tale, Śāh Sekandar of Bairāṭ town is as strong as the vaunted Rostam and able to defeat the Sistani rulers Nurimān and his son Śām. Tribute pours in from rulers far and wide, except for the *kṣatriya* king Bali. They clash, and Bali has to hand over his daughter Ājupā to become Sekandar's wife. They soon have a son, Julhās, who one day gets lost in the forest and lands in a magnificent underworld kingdom ruled by Jaṅga Bāhādur. That king has a daughter, Pā̃ctolā, whom he desires to have married. Considering her beauty and the wealth she brings with her, Julhās consents to be her groom, and so there he settles, forgetting all about his family. Meanwhile, Sekandar and Ājupā are heartbroken, but the astrologers realize that Julhās is not only alive but happily married in the citadel of Pātālnagar, which lies beneath the earth's surface. Ājupā's grief prevails unabated until one day at the seashore, a large chest floats up, which she has her servants retrieve. Inside is a six-month-old boy, whom she adopts: she calls him Kālu. It is not long until Kālu has a younger brother, for Ājupā is pregnant again, this time with Gāji.[12]

Gāji and his half-brother Kālu are inseparable as they grow. Sekandar is keen to have Gāji become king, but Gāji refuses. We have already seen Ābdul Ohāb's rendition of this set of ordeals to which Sekandar sets Gāji for his refusal.[13] After enduring unimaginable tests, Gāji resolves to abandon the world of kings and become a mendicant *phakir*, for he is already a *jindā pīr*. It takes little for him to persuade Kālu to join him. Not long after they set out, they face a huge expanse of water that they see no discernible way to cross, so they petition the Stainless Nirañjan, Khodā, who instructs Gāji to throw his staff into the water to transform into a boat. He does and it does. They cross the waters into a new wild land, the Sunderban.[14] When they reach the shore, they erect a *cillākhāna*[15] for prayer, *jikir* recitation, and meditation. Gāji's power (*kerāmat*) is such that in no time all the tigers have become Gāji's disciples. Wherever in that world they decide to go in their boat, the tigers row while a crocodile serves as the helmsman, his tail the tiller. Soon Gaṅgā, Durgā, and Śiv watch over him, for the two goddesses are his

11. It should be noted that in Ābdur Rāhim's text he spells the antagonist's name Dakṣiṇā, whereas Kṛṣṇarām spells it Dakṣiṇ.

12. Ābdur Rahim, *Gājikālu o cāmpāvatī kanyār puthi*, 1–5.

13. See the translation of Sāyeb Munsī Ābdul Ohāb, *Gāji kālu o cāmpāvatī kanyār punthi*, 6–10 in this volume, chap. 3. The episode can be found in Ābdur Rahim, *Gājikālu o cāmpāvatī kanyār puthi*, 6–8.

14. The image from the scroll painting held in the British Museum that serves as the frontispiece of this volume illustrates this scene.

15. A special venue set aside for forty days of prayer, *jikir*, and meditation.

aunts, while the queen of the færies and her following plus all the *jinns* together become his disciples.[16]

After some indeterminate time, they grow restless and set out to visit other settlements. As they walk, they encounter a young boy that Gāji, but not Kālu, knows to be Khoyāj Khijir; Kālu rudely dismisses him, much to Gāji's consternation. Eventually they arrive at Cāpāinagar, ruled by one *hinduyāni* king named Rām, and as soon as they begin to chant the qualities of God in *jikir*, they are driven out. Khodā again intervenes to provide them sustenance, while ensuring that the town burns for his devotees' mistreatment; *jinns* capture Rām's queen, spirit her across the river to a *masjid*, and hold her prisoner. The king is understandably distraught and, under orders, the astrologers soon divine the reason for the kidnapping. Suitably chastised, the king brokers a peace with Gāji and Kālu, recites the *kālemā*, and has his wife restored. In no time, the king sets about building a *masjid* in Cāpāinagar.[17] Then Gāji and Kālu move on.

After some time the two mendicants encounter woodcutters, from whom they beg food. The woodcutters are unfortunately beyond poor, but they are respectful of *pīrs*, so they pawn their tools and soon spread a feast for the two *phakirs*.[18] Deeply gratified, Gāji then detours to visit his aunt Gaṅgā, who supplies him with vast riches to bestow on these loyal woodcutter devotees. Gāji summons the færies, who clear-cut the land and build a city they name Sonāpur, the City of Gold. The first construction is a *masjid*, followed by a massive central market, which is soon peopled with hundreds of merchants, while grand houses are built for all the new inhabitants. As if that were not enough, Kālu goes into meditation and, just for that simple act of submission, Khodā rains gold on the inhabitants.[19]

Gāji's charisma attracts everyone, but even more a group of six færies from the land of Kukāph who are roaming nearby. They have meandered their way to Sonāpur, which they immediately liken to Rāvaṇ's magnificent citadel in Laṅka. They soon begin to debate who is more beautiful, the *pīr* Gāji lying there asleep on his cot, or the twelve-year-old princess Cāmpāvatī, whom they previously espied in the opulent city of Brāhmaṇānagar. They both make the færies equally mad with love. They first compare Cāmpāvatī's beauty to that of a *devatā*, goddess, or at least a celestial *kinnara*, but eventually claim it rivals that of Jolāykhā.[20]

16. Ābdur Rahim, *Gājikālu o cāmpāvatī kanyār puthi*, 8–11.

17. Ābdur Rahim, 11–15.

18. The comic book version of this has Mānik Pīr and Gājī Pīr together arriving at the village, but the trajectory of the narrative is more or less the same; see "Murad Kangal," in Ghosh, comp., *Folk Tales from India: The Sunderbans*, 16–19.

19. Ābdur Rahim, *Gājikālu o cāmpāvatī kanyār puthi*, 15–17.

20. Jolāykhā is one of several spellings of Zulaykhā of the famous romance with Yūsuf. For the popular Bangla version, see Śāh Muhammad Sagīr, *Iusuph jolekhā*, ed. Muhammad Enāmul Hak (Ḍhākā: Māolā Brādārs, 1408 BS [2001]). For an analysis of the text, see Max Stille, "Metrik und Poetik der Josephsgeschichte Muhammad Sagirs" (Master's thesis, Ruprecht-Karls-Universität Heidelberg,

The city of Brāhmaṇānagar, ruled by Cāmpāvatī's father, is opulent with gold, and its only residents are *brāhmaṇs*. The king's security guarantor, his *gõsāi*, is one Dakṣiṇā Rāy, whose physical stature is astounding, his strength as prodigious as his appetite for good food. Apart from the protection afforded by Dakṣiṇā Rāy, Cāmpāvatī herself is sequestered in ornate chambers surrounded by three hundred guards. Because of the safety provided by Dakṣiṇā Rāy, the king prospers with his extended family of brothers and wives. Feeling somewhat impish and thirsting to quench their curiosity, the færies decide to fly the sleeping Gāji on his cot to the bedroom of the sleeping Cāmpāvatī. When they are placed together they match perfectly—they have two bodies, but together make one person. The fickle færies, distracted by the abundance of flowers and food they glimpsed in the gardens, slip out to sup, leaving the couple alone. Cāmpā is lying naked, and when Gāji rolls over, his hand touches her breast. Her body is suddenly aflame. Flustered and confused by her inexperience, she quickly dresses, but as she gazes at the young man's beauty, she knows him to be the thief of her young love. Cāmpāvatī knows deep down that she has found her mate, but they are both soon dismayed because their different social standing (*jāti*) dims any hope of a future together. In Brāhmaṇānagar, Dakṣiṇā Rāy is famous for eating *jabans*, so though they are betrothed, tragedy looms.[21] As they puzzle over their doom, Gāji confesses:

> "Your youthful beauty makes me indifferent to all else. Listen my dear, my beloved, I am unable to remain still. . . . my life is in your hands, what more can I say? Because you are the daughter of the king, you know fully all the scriptures (*śāstras*). Look in your astrology (*jyotiṣa*) books to forecast our fortunes." Then Śāhā Gāji wept, the tears from his eyes washing over his face. So the ever-pure *satī* Cāmpāvatī fixed the chalk in her hand. She wrote their names together and began to run her calculations. When she had finished the astrological reckoning, the young lady stared hard at what the God of Fate, Bidhātā, had written. A single thread bound and knotted Cāmpā to Gāji. Sāheb Gāji would ever be ruler of her heart. Apart from Gāji, she would have no other husband in this world. Her heart began to ache as she registered the implications: 'I am a *brāhmaṇ* by birth, he is a *jaban*. How will it be possible for me to be married to him?'[22]

But realizing that what is written cannot be done in vain, she takes heart; they are strung together on a single garland, just as Gaurī was to Hara. So she resolves to take the chance. She offers herself to Gāji, but he refuses to consummate their betrothal until they are properly married. "Whenever you feel your heart leading

2011). See also Ayesha A. Irani, "Love's New Pavilions: Śāhā Mohāmmad Chagīr's Retelling of *Yūsuf va Zulaykhā* in Premodern Bengal," in *Jāmī in Regional Context: The Reception of ʿAbd al-Raḥmān Jāmī's Works in the Islamicate World, ca. 9th/15th–14th/20th Century*, ed. Thibaut d'Hubert and Alexandre Papas (Leiden: Brill, 2018), 692–751.

21. Ābdur Rahim, *Gājikālu o cāmpāvatī kanyār puthi*, 18–26.

22. Ābdur Rahim, 26.

you to immoral action, meditate hard on my form and you will develop love for Nirañjan. Then your act will generate two results at once: you will gain me and you will also gain Khodā."[23] He then teaches her how to perform *jikir*, the recitation of the attributes of God. She symbolically washes his feet with her floor-length hair and then they sit, she on the left, their bodies emanating a splendid effulgence. They exchange rings, exchange their chewed betel as lovers do, and eventually fall asleep. The færies suddenly realize it is nearly dawn and rush back to the princess's bedroom, only to find the couple exhausted and fast asleep—so they pick up Gāji, who is still lying on Cāmpāvatī's cot, and fly him back to the *masjid*.[24]

The next morning, each awakes mystified. Cāmpā goes nearly mad in her despair, and only after long days of probing does her mother Līlāvatī pry out her story: Cāmpāvatī confides that she is "dying while still living" (*jiyante marichi*).[25] It is a foreign (*bideśi*) thief who has stolen her heart, and now she is burning with love. Her mother counsels that only the Creator determines one's fate, so she must persevere. As instructed, Cāmpā remains lost in meditation on Gāji's beautiful form. Gāji, meanwhile, is likewise afflicted, waking up to discover his Cāmpāvatī gone, but he has confirmation that they were indeed together: her ring and her bed. He is inconsolable. He decides to abandon Sonāpur to everyone's objection, but he instructs his followers simply to meditate on him and he will make himself present. As he leaves in the company of Kālu, he encounters a multitude of good omens, and along the road he finally reveals to his half-brother Kālu that he has met Cāmpāvatī. Kālu chides him for his emotional behavior:

> "You are the *phakir* of Āllā, and *hindus* and *musalmāns* alike honor a *pīr*. When I hear this kind of blather slip from your mouth, what fault would you have accrued by assuming the kingship? How can you embrace renunciation (*phakirī*) under this false pretense, in name only, when you have failed to renounce lust, anger, greed, and the allure of creation?"[26]

And so they argue: Kālu points out the existential danger of being attracted to a woman, while Gāji counters how, by losing himself in her, he will gain Khodā, much as he has advised Cāmpāvatī that when she thinks of him, she will find God, too. Finally Kālu realizes the futility of arguing, and they set off in search of Cāmpāvatī. After traveling for three years and three months, they eventually reach the city of Brāhmaṇānagar; but before entering, they stop in a nearby village named Kāntapur. Overwhelmed by the city's opulence and hearing that Dakṣiṇā

23. Ābdur Rahim, 27.

24. Ābdur Rahim, 29.

25. Ābdur Rahim, 31. This phrase is a common trope among ascetics, *jogīs*, *tantriks*, and modern figures such as the *bāuls* of Bengal.

26. Ābdur Rahim, 39.

Rāy is its protector, Kālu argues that they should not be bothered, that Cāmpāvatī must have already forgotten Gāji—but Gāji will have nothing of it.

As Cāmpāvatī languishes in her palatial quarters, mad from being separated from Gāji, her sleep is uneasy.

> At the command of the Lord (*prabhu*), an angel (*phereśtā*) came and appeared to her in her dreams. The angel settled above her head and spoke to Cāmpā. "The agony that plagues you is about to be relieved. Listen, listen carefully. Cāmpāvatī, your brother-in-law and your husband have arrived at the banks across the river. They have settled by the river at the northern *ghāṭ* and they have vowed in their heart of hearts that come tomorrow, if they gain sight of you, they will enter the city. If they do not, then they will leave, and Śāhā Gāji has himself declared that he will never take your name again."[27]

So, she arranges to go to the river to bathe.

She enters the waters and, as she searches the opposite bank, she catches and fixes Gāji's gaze. When her auntie tries to hasten her to return, she gradually confesses all that has transpired. The girls in her retinue then do what potential in-laws and friends always do: they flirt and joke and do everything silly to get Gāji's attention. Cāmpāvatī separates herself and, in deliberate gestures, washes her hands, her feet, her face, then sensuously her breasts, before undoing the knot in her hair and letting it spread on the water. As she immerses herself up to her neck, Gāji signals that he will soon come to get her. As she returns home, Cāmpā visits the temple of Caṇḍī, whom she summons for a boon: Caṇḍī identifies Gāji as her sister's son and promises that Cāmpā will soon have him as her husband, though a *jaban*. As she leaves, Caṇḍī stops to chat with her nephew Gāji and reminds him that fate cannot be averted—he will have Cāmpā—but he must watch out for the rest of the women who will cling to him like leeches lest he get lost in their feminine attentions.[28]

Gāji grows impatient and finally dispatches Kālu to act as matchmaker. Kālu bargains with the ferrymen, Chirā and Ḍorā, who warn him he must have a death wish as a *jaban* to try to enter Brāhmaṇānagar. Finally, they will agree only if Kālu gives them a hefty sum of gold, which he immediately produces through the power of *kerāmat* after meditating on *Āllā*. When he reaches the palace, he finds Mukuṭ Rājā holding court with his seven sons and nine sons-in-law, listening to recitations of the *Bhāgavata purāṇa* and *Mahābhārata*. Suddenly they are interrupted by Kālu reciting "*lā-ilāhā . . .* " Mukuṭ Rājā is furious and summons a guard to dispose of the *phakir*, but Kālu manages to make known his request: that Gāji wishes to marry Cāmpā and that the goddess Caṇḍī has promised it will be so. The king seethes and turns to his ministers, who confirm that Cāmpā has been mad for love

27. Ābdur Rahim, 42.
28. Ābdur Rahim, 43–46.

of him. In high dudgeon, the king dispatches him to prison in shackles while Kālu objects that he is only the messenger. Then the king takes an axe to Kālu's bed in Cāmpā's quarters, but Cāmpā manages to hide behind the skirts of her sisters-in-law and escapes her sure death.[29]

Gāji senses that the plan has gone terribly awry, so he flies to the Sunderban forests and summons the tigers—some ninety-three hundred altogether—and returns to Kāntapur. Embarrassed that the townspeople are calling him a magician for his ability to control the tigers (not to mention their fear), he whispers *bismillā* and blows it across the tigers and transforms them into rams and ewes. The townsfolk want to buy them, but he refuses and heads for the ferry landing. He tries to bargain with Chirā and Ḍorā to cross, but they refuse until he offers a couple of rams, and naturally they choose the largest: the tigers Khāndeoyārā and Bedābhāṅgā in disguise. The ferrymen tie up the rams and take Gāji and the rest of the still-disguised sheep across to Brāhmaṇānagar. Meanwhile, one of the færies reports to their queen how Kālu is incarcerated in Brāhmaṇānagar, and so they fly to the *masjid* to retrieve Cāmpā's cot that Gāji has inherited from their fateful nocturnal machinations and wing it to him in Brāhmaṇānagar to serve as an impromptu throne; then they join his forces.[30]

Back in Kāntapur, Khāndeoyārā and Bedābhāṅgā pretend to be rams by eating grass and water, but when they are sized up for a meal and tied to a stake for slaughter, they butt and knock the ferrymen's old mother and everyone else silly. The two rams regain their tiger forms and terrorize everyone. Battered, but very much alive, the ferrymen realize that this is the work of the *phakirs* they insulted, and they vow always to transport any *phakir* for free in the future. The two tigers bound across the river in a single leap and then lope easily till they find Gāji and the others, where they share their tale to the amusement of all. But Gāji has waited long enough.[31]

> Amidst a tumult of roars, the tigers leaped here and there as if they were the monkey hordes bounding about Laṅkā.
>
> With menacing grunts and growls the tigers moved quickly. Gnashing their canine fangs, they moved with alarming fervor. There were a great many houses in Brāhmaṇānagar, and they surrounded each and every one without exception. In fanned ranks, some systematically scouted every lane and ghat, while others patrolled back and forth, growling menacingly. The tigers had surrounded the town in its entirety without the residents even registering their presence. At sunrise, water pot in hand and emerging into the lanes with their usual deliberation, the townspeople made for the thicket. But as soon as they came out they saw the lines of tigers. Flushed with fear, they screamed madly and beat back to their houses. All

29. Ābdur Rahim, 46–49.
30. Ābdur Rahim, 49–53.
31. Ābdur Rahim, 53–55.

the *brāhmaṇs* headed to the river to fill the golden water pots they toted, but when they encountered the tigers they screamed "O Mother! O Mā!" and, filled with terror, they fled, flinging away in every direction those precious gold vessels. Everyone was rattled, quaking with fear. The cowherds kept their cows in the sheds. None of the townsfolk who had slipped out of their homes made it as far as the bushes; they all had to return. So they shat and pissed into whatever cooking pots—large or small—they had, and once those began to overflow, they tossed them outside. The very ground split open from the tigers' roars. All the many *brāhmaṇs* and *brāhmaṇīs* shuddered and shook. One cried out "Stay away, stay!" and another shrieked, "It got me!" Another howled, "Oh Bābā, I'm about to die!"

Someone managed to slip away and inform the king. "Brāhmaṇanāgar has become godforsaken because you have incarcerated that *phakir*. His brother, the Gājī, a *jindāpīr*, has come. He controls untold hundreds of tigers and he has dispatched them; they are eating all the cows and water buffaloes wherever they catch them. That Śāhā Gājī is sitting on a jewel-studded lion's throne, with golden pennants waving on the standards in all four corners. A ruby-studded canopy is draped above his head and the færies attending languidly wave their yaktail fans. Go quickly and meet that Gājī, you erstwhile king, otherwise those tigers will eat all of our heads!"

The king responded, "Say no more about the matter. With Dakṣiṇā Rāy present, what is to fear? As soon as Dakṣiṇā Rāy hears this he will slay that *phakir* along with all his tigers."[32]

But once he sees, the king, too, is terrified. To placate Dakṣiṇā Rāy, he sends many mountains of the best of foods, and only then does he approach, weeping and grasping his champion's feet. In a gush of words the Rājā conveys that his social standing (*jāti*), indeed his very life, is on the verge of destruction. Then he relates the circumstances: the arrival of Kālu with the marriage proposal, Kālu's incarceration, and the arrival of Gāji with his thousands of tigers. Hearing him out, Dakṣiṇā Rāy chuckles and promises to slay the *phakir* and his tigers. Donning his armor, he picks up his massive club and strides out to engage in battle.

As he stepped forward he heard someone sneeze to his left. Flies buzzed around and one landed directly on his eye, and as he moved on some insect bit him on his little finger. He also encountered a woodcutter hauling a pile of wood, and three times he heard someone behind him call out, "Don't go, stay!" Next he happened upon a corpse; he watched it materialize right in front of him as if by magic. As he considered all these omens, each one ill, he realized he should not sally forth, but he could not turn back for the shame of it. So he plunged ahead, his mind gripped with worry. As he passed by different houses, women ululated auspiciously, some sounded conches, blew horns, and clapped small hand cymbals, while some made hollow *bom bom* sounds by thumping their cheeks. . . .[33] It was at that moment that Dakṣiṇā Rāy saw for himself hundreds of thousands of tigers leaping and bounding here and

32. Ābdur Rahim, 56–57.

33. This gesture is deemed a prophylaxis against the evil eye.

there. For every one tiger the warrior encountered, seven more seemed to appear. His throat constricted, choking off his voice. Terrified, Dakṣiṇā Rāy began to shake violently. The great warrior worried: 'All alone, what can I do? If I raise my club to slay one tiger, ten or twenty more will come one-by-one to lay hold of me.' Worrying along these lines, the great warrior withdrew from battle and then in shame retreated to the river bank.

Taking a seat at the edge of the river, the valiant warrior cried out plaintively, calling to Mother Gaṅgā. As a result of his call, Gaṅgā floated to the surface and, as soon as he saw her, Dakṣiṇā Rāy made respectful obeisance. Blessing him, the goddess Devī then asked, "Tell me, great warrior, why have you summoned me?"

Dakṣiṇā Rāy whined pitifully as he spoke. "Listen, my dear Mother, how shall I put it? Mukuṭ Rājā . . . today will witness the loss of his social standing (*jāti*) as king: a *phakir* has come who wants to marry his daughter. I did not realize the *phakir* commanded so many tigers and they have completely surrounded and held hostage Brāhmaṇānagar city. If you are compassionate, supply me with crocodiles, and then I will be able to find out just how much of a *phakir* he really is."

Gaṅgā queried, "Tell me now, great warrior, speak! What is the name of this *phakir* and in what region is his family home?"

Dakṣiṇā Rāy replied, "Listen my good woman, his name is Sāheb Gājī. I have heard that his family home lies in the western regions in the city of Bairāṭ. His father's name is Śāhā Sekāndar, and Bali's daughter, Ajupā, is his mother. This is what some have said, but I do not know for sure."

Gaṅgā returned, "Then there can be no doubt about it—that *brāhmaṇ* has already lost his social standing (*jāti*). Listen up, Dakṣiṇā Rāy, you clearly are not aware, but I know for certain that Gāji is my sister's son. He is my own flesh and blood and no stranger to me. My affection for him is even greater than for my own son. Both Āllā and Durgādevī watch over him. Who has the power to thwart his marriage to Cāmpā? Were all the people in the world to come together as one, they would not be able to defeat Gāji in battle. You must make Mukuṭ Rājā understand: 'You must join your daughter and Gāji in marriage!'"

Dakṣiṇā Rāy listened and then spoke, "Why did I even bother to call on you, Mother? If I flee out of the fear in my heart, people will laugh, and the tigers will ambush me from all sides and devour me. It is not my desire to ensure either victory or defeat. Please be merciful and give me the crocodiles so I might simply fight with honor."

Gaṅgā said, "I will not provide you with crocodiles, for Gāji would become annoyed and would rebuke me."

Whining, Dakṣiṇā Rāy then replied, "What good will come from protecting a Turk (*turuk*)? Will a Turk ever offer *pūjā* to you? You are without compassion, Mother, and that is my misfortune. If you do not gift me the crocodiles, then right here and now, in your presence, I will kill myself." And declaring that, he picked up his club and raised it to beat himself senseless.[34]

34. Ābdur Rahim, *Gājikālu o cāmpāvatī kanyār puthi*, 57–59.

Gaṅgā capitulates at the threat of his suicide and summons the crocodiles from the underworld of Pātāl.

> The crocodiles floated up from Pātāl until ten thousand crocodiles broke the surface. Utterly thrilled, Dakṣiṇā Rāy led them away. The crocodiles knocked down the trees, clearing the forest canopy as they plodded forward; their stomachs abraded numerous channels through the swamps. So the great warrior headed to the battlefield with his crocodiles in tow while the Rājā sat in his rooftop gazebo to watch it all unfold. "Look at that, the Gõsāi has brought me crocodiles. Now the *phakir* will round up his tigers and flee."
>
> But as soon as they spotted the crocodiles, the færies went to Gāji and informed him, "Look, your aunt, Gaṅgā Māsī, has armed him with crocodiles."
>
> "My good aunt only mouths her blessings—she cuts the root of the tree while pouring water on its leaves." As Gāji squatted on the ground letting the news sink in, Dakṣiṇā Rāy sallied forth, brutishly aggressive. He set the crocodiles on the tigers, which proceeded to chomp their way through them. Right then Gāji shouted at the top of his voice, "All of you tigers join ranks, and rip the heads off those crocodiles!" Just as the Gāji ordered, the tigers immediately charged and the pitched battle with the crocodiles began. At the roaring of the tigers the town of Brāhmaṇānagar quaked in fear, all the *brāhmaṇ* women there convulsed with terror. Dakṣiṇā Rāy, too, was unsettled and shaking in fear, while tears leaked steadily from the eyes of the hapless Mukuṭ Rājā. Amidst the steadily increasing roars, the tigers crouched, dropping their tails, then pounced on the backs of the crocodiles. With loud shrieks born of battle they bit down hard with their long carnassial fangs, but neither fangs nor claws could pierce through their leathery hides, the dermal armor of those crocodiles. The bodies of the crocodiles were as tough as ironwood, so the tigers' normally effective gnashing bites and lacerating swipes of their razor claws went for naught. They were shocked when their teeth cracked and their claws broke off; they were rendered powerless, completely enervated. The bellowing of the bull gators and guttural hissing of their mates rolled across land. They snagged the tigers by paw and limb, clamping down hard their jaws. Some suffered bones broken, others had their skulls crushed. Rattled, the tigers retreated best they could. Dakṣiṇā Rāy gave chase screaming, "Kill them, kill them all! Today you must break their bones and eviscerate these tigers."[35]

The tigers are terrified and flee, pleading with Gāji Sāhā to intervene. Gāji assesses the predicament and meditates hard on the sun to heat the battleground like a furnace, scorching the crocodiles and drying up the mud in which they coolly wallow. It is too much, and the crocodiles break ranks.

> [They] fled helter-skelter back to the underworld city of Pātāl while all Dakṣiṇā Rāy could do was lament in shame. His doom was falling about him as the tigers circled. The valiant hero began to wail. In a quandary he fretted, "What recourse do I have? This danger follows me wherever I go; who can help me escape? I now understand that this fate was written on my forehead. My death is to come at the hands of the

35. Ābdur Rahim, 59–60.

phakir's tigers. If I flee to save my life, everyone will laugh at me, and King Mukuṭ, the ruler of the earth, will have to eat ashes in shame."

Devastated by worry, what did the valiant warrior then do? Through meditation, he brought his earnest grieving to the attention of the goddess Caṇḍī.

With sincere devotion the warrior called out, "Where are you, Mother Bhavānī? O Mother of Ganeś, please rescue this devoted subordinate. O Durgā, the destroyer of all afflictions, where are you? Please Mother, grant me protection in the shade of your feet."[36]

Durgā is moved by her devotee's stentorian call and comes careening down from the heavens in her chariot. He petitions her for hungry ghosts, ghouls, and assorted demonic creatures to defeat Gāji.

Caṇḍī replied, "Listen, my dear child, bring the war to a close. It is indelibly written that Gāji will have Cāmpā. You must tell this to Mukuṭ Rājā and make him understand—'You must make over your daughter in marriage to Gāji!' Gāji is my nephew, my sister's son, and I am his aunt, his Māsī. If your king does not arrange this wedding, then I will flood all of Brāhmaṇānagar and there will be no one left alive to light the lamps for the ancestors of their lineages. Gāji is my son just the same as Kārttik and Ganeś; he is my kin, descended from my sister; he belongs to no one else. . . . Now go and tell Mukuṭ Rājā that if he desires a propitious outcome, then he must give his daughter to Gāji. He is a puffed-up king with enormous hubris and vanity, but he is not even qualified to be the servant of a king. The daughter of Bali Rājā is Gāji's mother and Bali is the crest jewel of all kings, so there can be no fault at all for making that marriage alliance. One could not buy with hard cash such a quality son-in-law."[37]

Just as he did with Mā Gaṅgā, Dakṣiṇā Rāy whines and then threatens suicide at Caṇḍī's feet, coercing her reluctantly to relent, so she conjures the legions: demons, hungry ghosts, ghouls, and witches without number. Invisible to the tigers, they rain down boulders on the confused tigers, who are soon maimed and weakened, so they plead with Gāji.

Hearing them out, Sāheb Gāji began to search with his mind's eye, and in this meditation the *pīr* fathomed the truth deep within his heart: Durgā had provided spirits, demons, hungry ghosts, and ghouls. So Sāheb Gāji immediately began to recite the *kālemā*, which he blew in four steady streams in each of the four directions he gazed. Instantly the bodies of the ghosts began to burn, and wherever he looked, the ghosts became visible. Flames shot out in their direction and the naked demons ran roughshod over one another to escape the burning fires. They spotted a way out through the northeast quadrant of the sky, and they set in motion their chariots. Many of the

36. Ābdur Rahim, 60.
37. Ābdur Rahim, 60–61.

> demons managed barely to escape with their lives, leaving a flummoxed Dakṣiṇā Rāy sick with worry.[38]

Sensing his imminent death, Dakṣiṇā belts out a blood-curdling scream. Primæval in its terror, the sound concusses the tigers, who slump down insensate, sends the færies scurrying, causes the earth to quake, and makes pregnant women abort. Through it all Gāji sits, alone, silent, unperturbed in his meditation.

> Dakṣiṇā Rāy immediately advanced toward him. With a roar the great warrior ran forward to slay Gāji, which prompted Śāhā Gāji to pick up his ascetic's staff in slow and deliberate movement. The *pīr* addressed the staff, "For him whose face you now see, go and conquer Dakṣiṇā Rāy!" Reciting the *bismilla*, he flung the staff. The staff growled as it advanced and feinted this way and that, before it lunged directly at Dakṣiṇā Rāy's chest. The flurry of blows from the staff sent blood spurting from his face. The staff leaped up, cracking his hard head again and again—one second a blow to his nose and mouth, the next second a thrashing of his neck and shoulders. It attacked him so swiftly and relentlessly from so many different angles, it was as if a snake had coiled around him. The valiant warrior succumbed to the rain of blows and slumped hard to the ground. No matter what he did, he could not fend off the staff's blows. Eventually, through sheer determination of will, he managed to pick up his massive club. He raised the club and struck hard at the staff, and the staff splintered, snapping in two. Picking up one piece in each hand, he carried them to the river where he flung them into the depths. . . .
>
> Meanwhile, Dakṣiṇā Rāy took his club in hand and, seething with a newfound strength of anger, moved forward to slay Gāji. Sāheb Gāji had just gotten up, but when he looked all around, he saw no one at all who could help. As he puzzled over whom he might deploy as proxy, he happened to look down, and his eyes fixed on the wooden sandals on his feet. Then Śāhā Gāji coolly commanded his sandals, "Go forth and engage Dakṣiṇā Rāy in battle!" The sandals let out a battle cry, flew up, and promptly hammered Rāy's head. They thumped his noggin—*dhum dhum, dhum dhum*—this way and that, they smacked him silly on his nose and across his mouth. One second they would soar high into the air and the next second they would plummet, pummeling his body. The valiant warrior soon fell, writhing on the ground in agony. Time and again the wooden sandals flew up and down in the same mechanical rhythm as womenfolk pounding fried paddy. Exhausted and war-weary, Rāy slumped to the ground. At that critical moment of weakness, Śāhā Gāji approached, scimitar in hand. He sat on Rāy's chest and lopped off both of his ears. Crying "Rām, Rām," the valiant warrior covered his bleeding ear holes with his hands. After that Gāji was set to slit his throat with his sword, but Rāy cried out, begging over and over, "Have the mercy of God, Khodā! Don't slit my throat or chop me up! You have cut off my ears and that is humiliation enough. Grant me your sovereign protection and do not execute me. I will attach myself to you as your personal servant. I will go right now and tell Mukuṭ Rājā that he must give Cāmpā to you in marriage."[39]

38. Ābdur Rahim, 61–62.
39. Ābdur Rahim, 62–63.

Sāheb Gāji does not harm him further, but binds his wrists, drags him by his magnificent topknot, and ties it to the palanquin. Slowly the færies return, ingratiating themselves with Gāji for the shame of having fled. Gāji is mollified. The tigers gradually recover their wits and gather, praising Gāji for their good fortune in his vanquishing the valiant Dakṣiṇ Rāy. Then, licking his chops, one says,

> "Now we will divvy up his body into parts. We will all eat until our bellies are full to bursting!" The tiger Beḍābhāṅgā quickly claimed, "For my share, I want his liver." Khāndeoyārā chimed, "The heart and lungs are all mine."
>
> Dakṣiṇā Rāy could not but overhear and he quaked in mortal fear. He tried to raise his hands and beg Gāji directly, "Please do not butcher me and feed me to the tigers. I will go right this minute to arrange Cāmpā's wedding." When he heard this proposal, Sāheb Gāji smiled knowingly and the færies averted their faces as they giggled. Smiling, Gāji told all the tigers, "I'm not going to give you Dakṣiṇā Rāy to eat because he has given his word that he is going to arrange my wedding with Cāmpā." And hearing this promise, the tigers broke into gales of laughter. Gāji remained with those tigers and færies sharing their feelings of joy.
>
> *What did Mukuṭ Rājā do when Dakṣiṇā Rāy was defeated and bound? Listen carefully everyone: Mukuṭ Rājā cried, "Alas I am dead, aargh, aargh! What has happened? How could it come to this?" Indeed, just how could such a valiant warrior be defeated?*[40]

. . .

5.3. GĀJI'S MARRIAGE TO CĀMPĀVATĪ AND THE ASCETIC TREK

The hubris of the *brāhmaṇ* king Mukuṭ Rājā, coupled with the unwise counsel of his ministers—none of whom register the magnitude of Baḍa Khān's power in defeating Dakṣiṇā Rāy—lead him to assemble his own army to oppose Baḍa Khān Gāji. They assure him that the batteries of cannons and the regiments armed with European rifles will prevail. Desperate to defend his rank (*jāti*) and clan (*kul*), the king succumbs to the bad advice of his courtiers:

> "There is no need to worry, great souled one, what can a single *phakir* do by himself? You have so many regular soldiers—thirty million, seven hundred in number, and one million, two hundred thousand fusiliers and archers. You have three hundred thousand warriors mounted on elephants and cavalry on horseback. What strength does the *jaban* have that will enable him to wage war on you? Volleys of musket shot and arrows will lay waste all the tigers. We can organize this in the blink of an eye." The king's nerves are calmed, and he soon orders everyone, "Let's not delay this task a moment longer. When the *phakir* is captured, I will haul him to the Caṇḍī temple and sacrifice him like a goat."[41]

40. Āhdur Rahim, 63–64.
41. Āhdur Rahim, 64.

As soon as he gives the command, the mahouts muster their elephants, musketeers and archers mount, drums resound, cymbals clang, women trill their ululations, and the earth quakes at the tumult. Watching it all, Kālu, still in chains in his cell, advises the passing king to relent and give his daughter in marriage to Gāji, but of course his advice is met with a fusillade of deprecations, to which he adds the pledge to double the promised sacrifice to Kālī by offering both brothers. He assembles his army and surrounds Gāji and his tigers.

Gāji simply sat still with his tigers and færies huddled around him. The fusiliers and archers completely surrounded them from all directions. Then the Rājā commanded everyone, "Fire each and every weapon at once!" and they discharged all their arrows and shot, the echo of which rattled the earth. The leaves on the trees and whatever else had the misfortune of being in that open field were incinerated by the unparalleled force of those projectiles. They discharged whatever amount of shot and arrows they had and the smoke that ensued shrouded the earth in darkness. The obscuring haze lingered about an hour. Mukuṭ Rājā triumphantly called out to everyone, "All the *phakir*'s tigers have been slain and the danger averted." The name of Lord Hari rang forth in jubilation, and he said, "Now let us go home." Within moments of the enemy's unguarded fallback, tigers materialized en masse, standing smartly in neatly organized ranks. Not a single tiger had been killed. The færies, too, gathered around Śāhā Gāji, foremost among the living.

When Mukuṭ Rājā took in this sight, he hands flew to his cheeks, stunned with disbelief. Completely unhinged, he wailed and whined, "Now I understand that this *phakir* truly knows some magic spells (*mantra*). Twelve lakhs of gunshot and arrows were discharged needlessly, without effect. I brought along thirty million soldiers to engage him, yet not even a single one of the *phakir*'s tigers was slain. I cannot engage this *phakir* in battle any further. I have come here with false and misguided hopes only to lose my life." And uttering these words the Rājā turned tail and fled, gripped in mortal fear. Gāji calmly summoned his tigers and said, "The Rājā and all the soldiers with him are slipping away. Hem in all the soldiers and kill them now!"

And so the tigers fell onto the backs of the soldiers and began to massacre them fang and claw. As their own brutish anger welled, they erupted like a conflagration embodied, and they chased down and slew thousands upon thousands of soldiers. Everyone feared for their lives and scattered. The tigers toyed with them, dancing around them. Anyone who heard a tiger's deep-throated growl of "*hāu hāu*" expired of his own accord, falling dead in his tracks without even being touched. The thundering roars of Khāndeoyārā, Beḍābhāṅgā, and Kālkuṭ even made the *nāgs* of the underworld city of Pātāl shiver. Amidst the grunting sounds of close engagement, the tigers savagely and efficiently killed—they butchered all the elephants and horses there were, and slaughtered so many hundreds of thousands of soldiers that they soon lost count. Routed, the soldiers scattered, running helter-skelter wherever they could. As Mukuṭ Rājā scrambled to slip away, he flung off his turban and the *cādar* cloth that wrapped his upper body. He rushed into his house and made fast the doors and shutters. The tigers searched for more humans but could find no more. When those tigers had vanquished the entire army of enemy soldiers, they returned to Gāji elated.

Listen carefully to the report of what Mukuṭ Rājā did next.
He possessed a well that revived the dead.[42]

That night after the battle, Mukuṭ Rājā fetches water from that magic well and sprinkles his dead soldiers and their mounts, who immediately spring back to life ready to engage. This same scenario plays out every day for eighteen days, which takes a mounting toll on the increasingly weary tigers. Faces maimed, fangs and claws broken off, they are utterly exhausted, so they turn to Gāji for guidance. Gāji takes himself into meditation and sees in that vision the magic well, so he dispatches the tiger Beḍābhāṅgā to slay a cow and bring its flesh. The færies fly over the well and drop the bloody meat into it, polluting it so that its life-giving magic is negated.

The next day's battle is as gruesome as those that have preceded it, the tigers ripping apart the armies while the færies rain down destruction from the skies. Of Mukuṭ Rājā's thirty million men and twelve lakhs of elephants and horses, not a single living thing survives. When the dead bodies fail to revive, it hits him and he cries out:

"That *jaban* has thrown the flesh of a cow into the well. Ah, aargh, where can I go? What else can I do? No one can protect me when the tigers come to eat me."

Chattering away in his fear, what did he do? He ran as quickly as his legs would carry him to the cool confines of the palace. Once inside he fixed the iron doors fast so that the tigers could not break in.[43]

But of course the tigers are not to be denied. They kill all the sentries, break open the prison, and free Kālu, who rides the tiger Khāndeoyārā back to an emotional reunion with Gāji. When they have calmed down, Gāji sends Khāndeoyārā and Beḍābhāṅgā to fetch the king. The tigers then bound through the palace, amazed at its opulence. They break into a barricaded room and find all of Cāmpā's aunts there and decide to have some fun, for, as Khāndeoyārā observes, "They are the soon-to-be in-laws of Sāheb, so we should joke with them."[44] But his joking literally frightens the piss out of them, their clothes flying as they scramble to escape. The tigers then move to another room where they find Cāmpā and her mother Līlāvatī, to whom they bow out of familial respect, then go off to find the king. One of the tigers places him on his back and takes him to Gāji. Speaking through Kālu, Mukuṭ Rājā submits without reservation to Gāji, promises to recite the *kālemā*, and hands over his daughter in marriage. Gāji releases Dakṣiṇā Rāy to Mukuṭ Rājā and then dismisses all the tigers and the færies.

The wedding is duly registered with a qualified legal official (*ukil*) and celebrated in a manner befitting royalty. At the moment that Gāji and Cāmpāvatī

42. Ābdur Rahim, 65–66.
43. Ābdur Rahim, 67.
44. Ābdur Rahim, 68.

retreat to consummate their marriage, the sisters-in-law play jokes which utterly break the romantic mood: they mix bitter foods with sweet, they substitute cow dung for tobacco in the water-pipe, and so forth. Gāji firmly calls their hand and lectures them that their pranks make clear they do not understand the subtleties of the techniques of making love as found in the *rati śāstras*. They flee in embarrassment. Then Cāmpā and Gāji dive into a sea of love-making bliss.

Meanwhile, outside, Kālu frets to himself:

> "My brother has been bound by the magical lure of this world. I have no power sufficient to cut through this web. It is false to say he became a *phakir* in the name of Āllā. If he was secretly harboring all this desire, why did he give up his kingship and become a *phakir* in the first place?"[45]

Gāji catches Kālu weeping for him, and queries him. Kālu replies:

> "I cry on account of you, brother. You have been ensnared in the net of the bewitching allure of this world. This magical illusion is a man-eating ogress (*rākṣasinī*): know her to be woman. Whoever plays at love with her, engrossed in the affairs of this world, loses everything. This man-eating monster, woman, consumes all his wealth down to his moral capital. You land neither on this side or that side, but remain firmly stuck in the middle. Let me illustrate, so listen with all your body and mind: If a woman has two husbands, tell me in all seriousness, to whom will she be committed? Your heart has the capacity for only a single love (*prem*). Will you give it to a woman or will you give it to Khodā. If now you produce a son, the enchantment of the created world (*māyā*) will soon engulf you altogether. Gazing at that child's face, your love for Khodā will be disrupted, troubled, lost. When your ship is berthed secure in the dock, would you scuttle your goods, your capital, by throwing everything overboard? Listen to this story from the words of the Korān: The virtuous woman Maryam was the beloved mother of Īsā. Her heart brimmed with her love for Khodā. So singular was her focus that she completely forgot herself in her constant attachment to the Lord. He sent down færies (*hur*) from heaven (*beheśet*) bearing divine fruits and other delightful comestibles, which the færies fed her. As a result, Īsā was later born. She was consumed with affection when she held Īsā in her lap, especially when she would lift him up and place her breast in his mouth. Then the Lord's words echoed down from heaven: 'It has been many days since you called out to me in your singular love, but now that you have a son, you have quite forgotten me. My dear, your love is split; you cannot abide both. . . .' Listen brother Gāji, what else can I say? Who has the power to make someone understand what is already well known?"[46]

45. Ābdur Rahim, 72.

46. Ābdur Rahim, 72–73. The story of Maryam as conveyed here is not found in the Qur'ān. In Qur'ān 3.37, there is a reference to provisions or food being made available to Maryam by God's intervention, and again in 19.25–26 when Maryam is standing giving birth, she holds onto a palm tree and is instructed to shake it in order to receive ripe dates to refresh her in her pains.

Gāji demurs but decides to prove to Kālu that he has not lost sight of what is important and tells him to prepare to leave first thing in the morning. And they do. But Cāmpāvatī in her wisdom senses something wrong and realizes Gāji is about to leave, so she remonstrates that she, too, should go, lest her father sacrifice her to Caṇḍī after they have all given up their *jāti* and recited the *kālemā*. She dresses as a *yoginī*. Finally Kālu convinces Gāji to relent, and she is allowed to join them.

It is not long before Gāji complains to Kālu that having Cāmpāvatī is a burden, for people look and wonder just what kind of a *phakir* he could possibly be when he keeps a woman. So for the next three years as they wander through the countryside, Gāji blows on Cāmpāvatī and transmutes her into a flower which he stuffs in his bag, or he turns her into a ring that he wears on his finger. Then at night, when it is time to cook, he blows on her three times and transforms her back into the woman she is so that she can do the needful, then he repeats the process again the next day. The routine wears thin. So one morning Gāji blows on Cāmpā and turns her into a tree, a night-blooming jasmine.[47] To say she is distraught would be an understatement:

> "Alas, my cruel and pitiless lord, where are you going? I am a weak and defenseless woman. I made love to you, I donned the garb of a *vaiṣṇavī*, a female renunciant, and I abandoned my mother and father, everyone, when I came with you. Now you abandon me in a foreign land, and are heading off where? Will you please explain how this can be called the *dharma* of love (*prem*)?"[48]

Now stranded, Cāmpāvatī continues to bemoan her fate and chastise Gāji for his indifference, until he stifles her and accuses her and all women of being conniving, perfidious, and self-serving by entrapping men to do their bidding. He reminds her that he promised Khodā that he would never abandon her and so he promises to return. He and Kālu then leave and travel all over Khodā's creation.

The adventures pile up. One day they cure a man with elephantiasis; on another they conjure the presence of Gaṅgā for a group of *jogīs*, who are amazed that she appears at the call of a *jaban*. They are so grateful for the sight of the goddess that they construct a bejeweled *masjid* in her honor.[49] Then the pair decide to go to Pātālnagar, guided by Basumati, Mother Earth herself. There Gāji and Kālu are united with their elder brother Julhās and his wife Pā̃ctolā, as they enjoy the

47. *Śeuti* > *śeuli*, also known as *śephālī*, a member of the *olea* (olive) family: *Nycanthese arbor tristis*, coincidentally the name in Latin, means "sad night-blooming tree," making it strangely apropos of Cāmpāvatī's predicament. The alternate name is Coral jasmine, which can grow to a height of ten meters, with a gray or gray-green flaky bark. The flowers are fragrant with a five- to eight-lobed corolla of snowy white petals, and a brilliant orange-red pistil, clusters of which can be as few as two and as many as seven. Very aromatic, it is often used in garlands and medicinally as well.

48. Ābdur Rahim, *Gājikālu o cāmpāvatī kanyār puthi*, 75–76.

49. Ābdur Rahim, 76–78. This is a reprise of Badar Pīr's encounter with the *jogīs* (chap. 2, this volume).

opulent hospitality of Pā̃ctolā's father, Jaṅga Rājā. For the first time, the brothers are united. They soon decide to return to their parents' home in Bairāṭnagar. Their journey backtracks through every place Gāji and Kālu traversed en route, including a special pause to release Cāmpāvatī, who is still trapped in her tree.[50] Finally they arrive amidst fanfare befitting the return of the three prodigal sons. The daughters-in-law meet their mother-in-law Ājupā Rāni, and Śāh Sekandar is overjoyed. The whole adventure is recounted once more in abbreviated form, and they all settle in to enjoy their new life.[51]

. . .

5.4. REVISIONS TO THE HISTORY OF BAḌA KHĀN GĀJI AND DAKṢIṆ RĀY

We have already commented on the intertextual positioning of all three of the *Rāy maṅgals*, which are largely *purāṇik* in their connections, both overt and covert. Like the *Rāy maṅgals*, the Gāji and Kālu narrative links itself intertextually to any number of prior texts, some classical Indic epics, especially *Rāmāyaṇa*, including the allusion to Ahalyā, but also *purāṇik* figures such as the tales of Gaurī and Hara. A description of Śāhā Sekandar opens the narrative of the *Gāji kālu o cāmpāvatī kanyār puthi*, where he is reputed to be as strong as the legendary Persian warrior Rostam, and easily able to defeat the prior Sistani rulers, Nurimān and his extraordinary son, the warrior Śām, all of whom are central to the epic Persian narrative of the *Shāh nāmeh* of Firdausī.[52] These pre-Islamic paladins and kings, Rostam in particular, signaled just rule and impeccable defense of kingship that was itself held as a standard throughout the Mughal world. They were champions of an often irrepressible *bazm* and *razm*, feasting and fighting, as the two poles around which ancient Persian royal culture was articulated,[53] echoes of which percolate through the Gāji narrative.

During the wedding sequence, when Gāji invokes the traditional *rati śāstras*, or manuals that address the business of the physical and emotional dimensions of love and romance, it explicitly recalls sources for the earlier *premākhyāns* or love

50. The allusion is clearly to Rām freeing Ahalyā, Cāmpāvatī's sin being to share Ahalyā's gender which, as Gāji rather acerbically noted, made women the origin of the torments of men and the distractor of ascetics.

51. Ābdur Rahim, *Gājikālu o cāmpāvatī kanyār puthi*, 78–83.

52. Abolqasem Ferdowsi, *Shahnameh: The Persian Book of Kings*, trans. Dick Davis, with a foreward by Azar Nafisi (New York: Penguin Books, 2016).

53. Dick Davis, *Epic and Sedition: The Case of Ferdowsi's Shahnameh* (Washington, DC: Mage Publishers, 1992). In describing the Urdu *dāstān*, a storytelling genre akin to the *pīr kathā*, Frances W. Pritchett, quoting 'Abdul Ḥalīm Sharar, notes that "the *dastan* consists of four arts: *razm* (war), *bazm* (elegant gatherings), *ḥusn o 'ishq* (beauty and love), and *'ayyārī* (trickery)"; 'Abdullāh Ḥusain Bilgrāmī, *Romance Tradition in Urdu*, 15 (translator's introduction).

narratives (*prem kathā* or *prem kahānī*) in Persian, Hindavī, and Avadhī. After the invocation of the Qamar al-Zamân episode from the *Arabian Nights*, Cāmpāvatī's beauty is compared first to a goddess, a *devatā*,[54] then to a celestial nymph, a *kinnara*, but ultimately is seen to rival even that of Jolāykhā, the heroine of the original Korānic adaptation of the Biblical narrative, the expanded Arabic and Persian romance, Yūsuf and Zulaykhā, one of the most popular and most often retold romances across the Islamic world. The sequence of comparisons is telling, for Jolākhyā's beauty is not only matchless but the peak of perfection, standing above that of Indic goddesses and celestial nymphs. The narrative structure of the *premākhyān* lends itself to esoteric (*batin*) allegorical interpretation in the hands of skilled *sūphī* teachers, and Ābdur Rahim seems to have been conversant with those strategies, for the narrative trajectory of his Gāji tale is similar to the tales of *Madhumālatī* and *Mirigāvatī* and could in the most general terms be subject to a similar allegorical reading:[55] the hero Gāji receives a glimpse of his future reward when he is carried by the færies to Cāmpāvatī's bedroom (lover/God), then they are separated; he then explores the far reaches of the earth in search of her, overcoming one obstacle after another (the stages of *sūphī* practice, *mokāms*) before marrying her, then prompted by his half-brother Kālu, an ascetic, he struggles to find an even higher truth that transcends worldly love. The parallels pretty much end there without much subtlety. Overall, the allegorical esoteric reading is sufficiently weak compared to its Hindavī counterparts that one would be hard-pressed to argue for the analogy. More likely, the vague similarity of form should be considered a parody. This is to say that, in spite of its surface similarities, the concerns of this and the related texts of the fictional *pīrs* in our study are different from those of the extended narratives of the Hindavī *premākhyāns* and Persian *masnavīs*, and it is a mistake to equate them.[56] But Kālu's comparison of Gāji's love for Cāmpāvatī in his critique of Maryam's love for Īsā hints at the pragmatic positioning of the text in moving to establish the position of a proper *sūphī* path vis-à-vis a generic Christianity, a move that will resonate later with Bonbibī's tale. Similarly, the perfidy of both of Gāji's aunts—the Indic goddesses Gaṅgā and Caṇḍī—sends a mixed message about the strength of their kinship to Gāji as opposed to their inability to refuse their devotees, in spite of their protest that fate has decreed the outcome. Interestingly, the brothers together personify the three viable paths to salvation: Gāji represents the explorative nature of the *pīr* who lives in the world, the step-brother Kālu represents the more constrained version of *sūphī* asceticism who is in the world but not of it, and Gāji's older brother,

54. There is an allusion in the name of the heroine to the Śākta goddess Cāmpāvatī, but it is difficult to determine if this was a deliberate choice.

55. For comparisons, see Mīr Sayyid Manjhan Shattārī Rājgīrī, *Madhumālatī*, and *The Magic Doe: Quṭban Suhravardī's Mirigāvatī*, trans. Aditya Behl (New York: Oxford University Press, 2012).

56. See chap. 1, n. 46.

Julhās, the married prince, represents the more straightforward commitment to mainstream *śāriat.*

In appropriating the precursor of Gāji, Kālu, and Cāmpāvatī, Mohāmmad Khater's Bonbibī narrative inherits a vast web of intertextual connections that create a literary and cultural context for Bonbibī's own story, validating that tale in ways that the narrative alone could never accomplish—and the tilt in the Bonbibī narrative is increasingly toward an Islamic cultural heritage. Khater's invocation of the *Rāy maṅgal* and the *Gāji kālu o cāmpāvatī kanyār puthi* gives the *Bonbibī jahurā nāmā* instant credibility through its multiple intertextual references, which create a kind of literary pedigree and indirect imprimatur. Khater's text appropriates the power of the precursors (for our purposes Ābdur Rahim's Gāji Kālu tale synecdochically represents multiple versions of the saga dating back two centuries); he effectively conflates the *Rāy maṅgal* precursor with the Gāji narrative precursor by deployment of select features from both texts in a way that leaves the reader imagining a unified narrative, much as I had imagined when I began this study. Details are glossed and every reader of the Bonbibī story already knows the outcome of the conflict of Baḍa Khān and Rāy. As Linda Hutcheon has argued, the parodic text mimics the prior text and in so doing preserves it, but she does not comment on the way that appropriative mimicry can alter the memory of the prior texts or even conflate them, which is what has happened here.

Bonbibī's narrative appropriation generates several noteworthy effects. It arrogates to itself the continuation of the story of Dakṣiṇā Rāy[57] and Baḍa Khān Gāji, who are in the end divested of their overbearing, notably patriarchal, power in the Sunderban mangrove swamps, a leadership they are forced to concede to Bonbibī. Mohāmmad Khater self-consciously situated the Bonbibī narrative temporally in the wake of the earlier conflict—how far back this was imagined to have occurred we cannot determine, but both protagonists are still active in his narrative of Bonbibī. Khater exercised his power as a later author to reshape the prior narrative by highlighting only those parts he wished to emphasize. *This "continuation" was, in fact, a completely new and independent story in its own right, but by virtue of the intertextual references, left the impression of a continuing story.* Since Bonbibī emerges as the ultimate controller of all the inhabitants of the Āṭhārobāṭi—human and animal—she naturally controls whatever they control. The receiver of the tale is left to understand implicitly that she can control the tigers, which variously constitute the followers and army of Baḍa Khān in both prior tales, and of Dakṣiṇ Rāy in the *Rāy maṅgal* (he does not command tigers in the Gāji and Kālu cycle). Today virtually everyone who has heard of Bonbibī is acutely aware of her power over tigers, her ritual *pūjās* reflect the tiger's omnipresence, she is sometimes depicted in images straddling a tiger mount, and her command of them is invoked to ensure

57. Mohāmmad Khater's Bonbibī tale also writes Dakṣiṇā rather than Dakṣiṇ, which is used by Kṛṣṇarām.

safe ventures for honey collectors, wax makers, salt manufacturers, woodcutters, and so forth—anyone, really, who dares to venture into the mangrove swamps of the Sunderban. Yet, so complete is her appropriation of the prior narratives, it is ironic that nowhere in the text of the *Bonbibī jahurā nāmā* does she actually command tigers. Everyone simply imagines she does by virtue of her command of Baḍa Khān Gāji and Dakṣiṇā Rāy, over whom she has authority.

In the *Bonbibī jahurā nāmā*, Mohāmmad Khater clearly invokes the outcome of the battle between Dakṣiṇā Rāy and Baḍa Khān Gāji from the oldest Gāji text, Kṛṣṇarām's *Rāy maṅgal*, where they end up as power-sharing brothers, one in a fixed abode, the other itinerant throughout the entire Āṭhārobhāṭi lands, an outcome confirmed by Rudradev's incomplete *Rāy maṅgal*. Nor does that image conflict with the presentation in Haridev's *Rāy maṅgal* that revels in the brotherly affection of the two. That choice, though, forced Mohāmmad Khater to finesse, that is, to *ignore* the outright victory of Baḍa Khān in the Gāji, Kālu, and Cāmpāvatī cycle, for that outcome could never be construed as closely consanguine, even symbolically. In that version, Dakṣiṇā is humiliated in defeat; he is unceremoniously bound head, hand, and foot, and suffers the final indignity of Baḍa Khān cutting off his ears before sparing his life. No brothers there. But curiously, in the Dukhe episode—the second of the two Bonbibī stories—Dakṣiṇā Rāy is forced to seek the protection of Baḍa Khān to avoid being slain by Śājaṅgali, this time affirming Baḍa Khān's superior position over Dakṣiṇā Rāy (no modifying term, such as "elder" brother, is needed). This authorial move invokes the victory of Baḍa Khān in the *Gāji kālu o cāmpāvatī kanyār punthi*; then, just as conveniently, a few couplets later, Bonbibī summons all the male protagonists and—after the plea by Baḍa Khān which invokes Bonbibī's symbolic and very real position of matriarchal authority over the entire region of the Sunderban—she declares Dukhe, Dakṣiṇā Rāy, and Baḍa Khān all to be mutually supporting brothers. This choice is all the more striking because the fixing of kinship relations to resolve conflict in the *Gāji kālu o cāmpāvatī kanyār puthi* is far more extensive than in the earlier *Rāy maṅgal*. As I can personally attest in my initial reading of these tales, a careful but casual reading would not initially reveal the ambiguities of Mohāmmad Khater's convenient selection of intertextual references, for in both precursor tales, Baḍa Khān and Dakṣiṇā Rāy fight, both somehow survive, both subsequently somehow share in the rule of the region, and that final outcome seems to gloss over any equivocation. But significantly, using kinship to adjudicate the relative ranking of *musalmāni* and *hinduyāni* figures, or the *musalmāni* saint with the *hinduyāni* king, displaces the traditional Indic notions of *varṇa* or caste markers of identity. It is the rhetoric of Islamic brotherhood, or more specifically *sūphī* fraternity, that prevails, and with the addition of Dukhe, the socially oppressed emerge as coequal.

Comparing the logical presuppositions regarding the construction of divinity, once again we find Mohāmmad Khater choosing between the two precursors. He clearly avoided any reference to, or even vague acknowledgement of, the form of divinity described in the *Rāy maṅgal*, the combined form of God, Īśvar or Dev Bhagavān, that served those who followed the Korān as well as those who followed the *Bhāgavata purāṇa*. Notably, but without being explicitly named, the manifestation of that unusual iconic form in the *Rāy maṅgal* appears to be a version of Satya Pīr, that is, Satya Nārāyaṇ fused with Āllā, both characterized as the stainless one, *nirañjan*. Khater unambiguously favored the divinity articulated in Ābdur Rahim's Gāji and Kālu tale. There was no notion of graded forms of divinity, so it would be wrong to speak of the highest divinity; rather, Khodā or Āllā were the names given to the sole divinity, and there was no second and certainly no compromised or combined form. In this cosmological system, the author posited a universe that was ruled by one God, whose revelation, the Korān, could be used as a source of all knowledge past and future; no other beings, earthly, celestial, or otherwise were considered divine—including the full range of *nabīs*, *olis*, *pīrs*, *bibīs*, *jinns*, *paris*, *vidyādharīs*, *kinnaras*, *phereśtās*, and demonic figures of *jogīs*, *bhūts*, *prets*, *rākṣasas*, *ḍākiṇīs*, and so forth. The familiar gods and goddesses, *devs* and *devīs*, such as Hara, Gaurī, Caṇḍī, and Gaṅgā, were made to function in a lower register that in effect reduced their seeming divinity to a kind of limited supernatural power, greater than ordinary humans, but certainly not as great as that of the *pīrs* or *gājis* who were their superiors. That marks an aggressively rehierarchized cosmos with respect to celestial figures and heroic religious functionaries, a downward displacement for indigenous Indic divinities.

The universe's cosmography is roughly equivalent in all three sets of tales. After Āllā sends Bonbibī and Śājaṅgali to earth to carry out their missions, physical access to heaven (*bhest*) itself is denied in the Bonbibī narrative. Access is available only through the proxy intercessions of Mohāmmad and Phātemā via their *dargās*, which are presented as homologues of the court of heaven and therefore create a conduit, but which at the same time insulate the protagonists from direct contact. The same holds for Berāhim when he seeks aid for offspring at the *dargā* of Mohāmmad. In the Gāji and Kālu tale, too, *bhest* is the abode of God, but is not accessible to any of the characters. So while we see that the Bonbibī tale acknowledges a similarly basic structure of the universe as its two explicit precursor texts—a heaven, earth, and underworld—the way the characters navigate that cosmos offers three slightly different perspectives and, in the Bonbibī tale, only Mohāmmad can fly to heaven, much as he did in the fabled *mi'rāj*.[58]

58. There are several moments in the narratives that invoke the *mi'rāj*, an event that has served any number of important social and theological functions for different groups of Muslims historically. Among the many possible citations, see the especially provocative and wide-ranging set of narratives in Christine Gruber and Frederick Colby, eds., *The Prophet's Ascension: Cross-Cultural Encounters with the Islamic* Mi'rāj *Tales* (Bloomington: Indiana University Press, 2010); for immediate relevance, see especially Ayesha A. Irani, "Mystical Love, Prophetic Compassion, and Ethics: An Ascension Narrative in the Medieval Bengali *Nabīvaṃśa* of Saiyad Sultān" in *The Prophet's*

All three sets of texts presuppose the interventions of Āllā, who manifests supernatural power to shape affairs in the world; the mechanism to elicit such help is prayer or meditation, sometimes aided by recitation of the qualities of God in *jikir* to assist in one's ability to concentrate. As we would expect from fiction, the passages that portray these pleas for help can only be characterized as generic, for there is no finely tuned doctrinal or theological prescription, only the simulacrum of a ritual injunction. Still, it is notable that once Bonbibī and Śājaṅgali are given the imprimatur of Āllā as a result of their training, and become properly qualified *murśids*—signaled by their special hats and their ability to traverse great distances by the utterance of a simple *mantra*—they tend to tap directly the source of power, Āllā; they do not work through some mediator such as Phātemā or Mohāmmad. Later, in the story of Dukhe, Bonbibī herself becomes just such a meditator for all the inhabitants of the Āṭhārobāṭi, the result—as she famously lectures Śājaṅgali—of the responsibility and obligation that accompanies the gift of Āllā's *barakat*, which he has dispatched to her in her moment of crisis battling Nārāyaṇī. She has ascended to a higher power that allows her to shape-shift, to materialize whenever and wherever she is needed as she discharges her moral responsibilities to her devotees. Power, then, is portrayed as proceeding from heaven to earth, from Āllā or the Prophet, directly to Baḍa Khān Gāji and Kālu, and later Bonbibī and Śājaṅgali, and then being dispersed accordingly. But in the *Rāy maṅgal*, Dakṣiṇ Rāy, who participates in divinity directly through his birth, receives no such support, save an ultimately ineffective trident from his Lord Śiv. Worse yet for him, in the *Gāji kālu o cāmpāvatī kanyār puthi*, he has to take himself physically to the portal of Pātālnagar on the banks of the river to solicit the help of the goddess Gaṅgā, who reluctantly extends her aid in the form of crocodiles, coerced by his threat to commit suicide to expose her as unwilling to help her devotee. Similarly, he is made to travel to the portal of Mount Kailās to solicit the aid of Caṇḍī, who in a reprise of the previous interaction between goddess and devotee likewise only reluctantly provides him with the sinister army of ghouls, ghosts, witches, and so forth.

Readers would be hard-pressed not to notice the difference: couched in devotional terms, this Dakṣiṇā Rāy's sources of power require wheedling and threats and a potentially antagonistic relationship with the goddess based on an implied exchange economy (devotion/worship or threat for help/power in the world), and in the end produce results of limited value; while the relationships based on kinship prevail. It may well be that Dakṣiṇā Rāy's efforts amount to a veiled critique of the practice of pilgrimage (*tīrtha*), which produces merit, but of limited utility in the real world compared to the power of the *gāji*. The further reconfiguration of the nature of Dakṣiṇā Rāy into a *rākṣas* in the Bonbibī narrative highlights his impotence. He becomes a shape-shifter who transforms into a tiger to accept

Ascension: Cross-Cultural Encounters with the Islamic Mi'rāj *Tales*, edited by Christine Gruber and Frederick Colby (Bloomington: Indiana University Press, 2010), 225–51.

offerings of human sacrifice, implying that he requires the blood of humans to maintain his position, an ominous and very low life-form that is irredeemable and beneath human status, a deliberately inverted reading of the numerous episodes in Kṛṣṇarām's *Rāy maṅgal* where Dakṣiṇ Rāy slays men and boys when he is not properly worshiped, but always restores their lives when appropriate propitiations are made.[59] He undergoes a similar transformation in the Ratā episode in Rudradev's later *Rāy maṅgal*, which signals rather ambivalently a shift in Rāy's status, since the *maṅgal kāvyas* were as a rule celebratory of the triumph of their subjects. In the greater cosmic hierarchy, this demotion from godling to bloodthirsty *rākṣas* demon renders him increasingly pathetic while transforming him into a personification of malevolence, considerably beneath the exalted status he enjoyed in the earliest texts and his appreciable, but diminished, status in the Gāji and Kālu cycle. Ultimately Bonbibī consigns and confines him to the small Kēdokhāli region of the Āṭhārobāṭi, in effect curbing his influence altogether and keeping him locked into an area where he can do little harm, but where he is allowed to save face. The slippage of Dakṣiṇā Rāy's place in the world of cosmic power is significant, and we will argue that it was a move that resonated with the emerging polarization of communities into Muslims and Hindus that was crystallizing in the later decades of the nineteenth century, when the deployment of the Bonbibī text in its extramural application to real-life situations was a pressing pragmatic attempt to change the world of the reader, to effect social change.[60] Following Hutcheon again, the treatment of Dakṣiṇā Rāy in the Bonbibī narrative signals a slip from the parodic connection of one text to another, or simply discourse to discourse, to the more overtly pragmatic, sometimes satiric, politics of the text deployed to effect social change, connecting its discourse directly to the world of ordinary things.

Kālu, who is a protégé of Dakṣiṇ Rāy with his own small domain in the Āṭhārobāṭi according to the *Rāy Maṅgal*, seems to have switched, for he becomes the adopted elder half-brother of Gāji in the *Gāji kālu o cāmpāvatī kanyār puthi*, where he plays a truly pivotal role as an accomplished *pīr*. His luster seems to have come from his affiliation with Gāji, though he exhibits an independence of thought and action that makes him a significant figure, more conservative and ascetic in nature. Since these tales are fictions, can we even assume any connection based on the similarity of name from one text to another? Given the paucity of named characters, and the obvious way characters are invoked in later texts, the choice does not seem to be an accident, yet there is precious little to draw from

59. Kṛṣṇarām Dās, *Rāy maṅgal*, e.g., 167–68, vv. 31–32; 168, vv. 33–38; 169–72, vv. 53–79; 227–28, vv. 725–45.

60. For understanding the pragmatics of the text, I tend to follow Wolfgang Iser, whose many works on reception theory have shaped my thinking, but perhaps most succinctly in his early essay outlining in brief the underpinnings of his functionalist approach; see Iser, "The Reality of Fiction: A Functionalist Approach to Literature," *New Literary History* 7, no. 1 (Autumn 1975): 7–38.

the two roles, since he disappears altogether in the Bonbibī story. It does suggest, however, that Kālu has switched allegiance, and his later function as half-brother is perhaps code to indicate a change that he is now Gāji's *sūphī* confrère, a shift that subtly signals the new order in the Gāji Kālu tale; but Kālu's absence in the Bonbibī narrative remains enigmatic unless it serves as a critique of the futility of the ascetic's path, which was certainly under fire in Bengal at the time of the text's composition.

Just as noticeable as the absence of Kālu is the nearly total lack of humor in the *Bonbibī jahurā nāmā*, a significant structural feature of the first two tales of the cycle (which is, of course, among the pragmatic presuppositions related to genre). That marks a significant departure in style. In the first two tales, the tigers provide a raucous interlude of comic relief at several points midway through each episode involving the conflict of Dakṣiṇā Rāy and Baḍa Khān Gāji. In performance terms, one can easily imagine the utility of the comic relief as the tigers complain bitterly about how tough life has become there in the low-lying lands of the eighteen tides, now that humans have encroached into the territories they once ruled without interference. So too the battering of the crone when the two tigers are disguised as ewes in the Gāji and Kālu story and their later kidding of Dakṣiṇā Rāy whom they threaten to eat. The tiger humor clearly functioned to expose and stereotype prototypical human behavior—compassionless greed, exploitation of natural resources, and so forth. When the half-white half-black Īśvar descends to broker the peace between Baḍa Khān and Dakṣiṇ Rāy, he warns the tigers in an aside that in ten years' time they might not find enough food to feed their cubs (which may have been the first environmental risk assessment in Bangla literature, composed in 1684), the tigers providing a contrast in style to reckless patterns of human consumption. But why did humor disappear from the *Bonbibī jahurā nāmā*, which had frequently and explicitly declared intertextual connections and whose cosmology operated according to shared presuppositions found in prior texts? While we can only speculate—who can ever know how any author has made decisions about his or her narrative?—we have already seen evidence that the Bonbibī text was riding on the margins, crossing the line where fiction serves religious ideology, where the narrative begins to yield some of its fictional qualities and starts to become, in Macherey's terms, a vehicle for religious propaganda. *This raises the possibility that humor itself in these early modern Bangla texts may be indexical of the subjunctive*, especially when the stories were parodies and then used satirically,[61]

61. David L. Curley has convincingly explored the important role of humor and satire in his study of Kavikaṅkaṇ's *Caṇḍī maṅgal*; importantly, he deploys the literary critical perspectives of Kenneth Burke and Wayne Booth to analyze specific episodes, especially the treatment of gender. See Curley, *Poetry and History: Bengali* Maṅgal-kābya *and Social Change in Precolonial Bengal* (New Delhi: Chronicle Books, 2008), esp. chaps. 1–3.

for humor seldom seems to be part of the prescriptive monologic of theology, history, and law. While the text of the *Bonbibī jahurā nāmā* articulates a general *sūphī* image of the world, it is a very conservative one in spite of the protagonist being female and Phatemā in *bhest* functioning as the arbiter of fate as translated through the divination of the Korān. In comparison to the *Gāji kālu o cāmpāvatī kanyār puthi*, which is an obvious parody of the *Rāy maṅgal*, the Bonbibī text is all seriousness about establishing hierarchies of power that coerce and impose a *shari'a* form of conduct on all human and animal inhabitants of the Āṭhārobāṭi. The new manifestations of power in the Bonbibī narrative eliminate all ambiguity regarding the hierarchical nature of divinity entertained in the earlier texts. The *Bonbibī jahurā nāmā* seems to have been bent on changing the order of things in the social world.

5.5. CONCEPTUAL BLENDING TO FASHION A NEW COSMO-MORAL ORDER

In an article nearly two decades ago, I proposed that as Islamic practices gradually took hold in Bengal, the use of local Bangla terminology was not a naïve form of syncretism, but rather represented an attempt, mainly by *sūphī pīrs*, to translate concepts from Arabic and Persian into the local vernacular in a simple effort to convey an alien religious system to a new audience.[62] In that article I argued that one effective way of conceptualizing this process was to use formal literary translation theory as a hermeneutic strategy to tease out the instances of conceptual crossover. This strategy has the advantage of highlighting historical shifts that in nearly all studies of what is generally called the Islamization of Bengal simply collapse or blur. Following the writings of *musalmāni* practitioners, we can see an initial phase wherein the local vernacular is used almost exclusively, with only a few key terms introduced from Persian and Arabic. But we can document how, as the centuries wore on, authors created a new Bangla vocabulary of technical terms imported from Arabic and Persian to increase the precision of their formulations, especially noticeable in technical manuals for yogic-style instruction, practical manuals of *śāriat*-based ritual, and theological and metaphysical pronouncements. At some point—and no scholar writing on the subject today seems to agree when this happened—a new register of the language, which we now term *musalmāni bāṅglā*, with its heavy reliance on Persian and Urdu terms, came to dominate *musalmāni* writing in the vernacular.

I proposed several lower-order forms of translational moments, using various formal literary equivalences as a guide. Literal or formal translation was common enough, but was of limited utility for higher-level concepts and abstractions.

62. Stewart, "In Search of Equivalence."

More often documented were refraction theory and mirroring, argued perhaps most concisely by André Lefevre,[63] and by many others adopting similar metaphors which recognize the exclusion of some meanings and the intrusion of other meanings—sometimes disjunctive—to produce an imperfect, slightly fractured, or distorted transformation from source to target language. Many of the attempts to translate Islamic concepts into Bangla follow this technique, which results in the equivalences we have repeatedly noticed in our examples in the literature of the fictional *pīrs*, where Indic gods and goddesses find their equivalent among the *pīrs* and *bibīs*, where the *masjid* is counterpoised to the *mandir*, where the recitation of the names and attributes of Āllā in *jikir* is equated with the *vaiṣṇav* practice of *jap* or *kīrtan*, in which the practitioner recites the names of Kṛṣṇa, and so on.[64] Dynamic equivalence, for the likes of those who imagine some kind of divine inspiration in the process, as Eugene Nida popularized in his translations of the Bible,[65] provided a perspective that took into account equivalences that might dramatically shift the tenor of the translation, thereby potentially introducing profoundly new meanings into the formulations, but which still convey the "message," a technique that would only work with a religious tradition that deemed its "message" inspired, universal, and thereby exportable to any language.

On the highest level, the complexity of translation moves from key terms and concepts to *shared metaphoric worlds*, which lie in the *domain of the intersemiotic*. Let me quote the relevant passage from that article.[66]

> Linguistic activity which embraces more than equivalent concepts to include larger structures for negotiating the exigencies of the world moves us into more complex acts of appropriation and assimilation that are required to transcend the purely interlingual. Roman Jakobson refers to this as the highest level of complexity, the category of the intersemiotic.[67] On the intersemiotic level of translation we find an interchange and interpolation of ideas among mythologies, between rituals that are (to a certain extent) mutually observed, and even in the fixing of translational equivalents among the parts of extended theological systems. At this stage, which is the

63. André Lefevre, *Translating Poetry: Seven Strategies and a Blueprint* (Assen: Van Gorcum, 1975); he subsequently expanded his strategies through a series of articles, references to which can be found in my original analysis.

64. These equivalences also yield to Ludwig Wittgenstein's analysis of family resemblance; see Wittgenstein, *Philosophical Investigations*, German text with English translation by G. E. M. Anscombe, P. M. S. Hacker, and Joachim Schulte, rev. 4th ed. (Chichester: Wiley Blackwell Publishing Ltd., 2009).

65. Eugene Nida, *Towards a Science of Translating* (Leiden: E. J. Brill, 1964); see also Eugene Albert Nida and Charles Russell Taber, *The Theory and Practice of Translation* (Leiden: E. J. Brill, 1969).

66. Stewart, "In Search of Equivalence," 282–84. Footnotes in this passage are in the original article.

67. Roman Jakobson argues that translation is "intralingual" within different parts or dialects of the same language, "interlingual" or between different languages, and finally "intersemiotic" between different cultural signification systems; see Roman Jakobson, "On Linguistic Aspects of Translation," in *On Translation*, ed. Reuben A. Brower (Cambridge, MA: Harvard University Press, 1959), 232–39.

most vexing type of translation—a cultural translation—an entire conceptual world is understood in terms of another, not just in its single terms or phrases. Because these worlds are not identical, yet admit to be being understood in terms of direct or implied comparison, they are extended, complex metaphorical constructs, which can be conceived as "shared" or "emergent" metaphorical worlds (and we might even argue that to call it translation is itself a metaphoric leap). Linguistically, the impulse behind this analysis is what Gideon Toury has called "polysystem theory," which attempts to extend the processes of translation to the cultural, intersemiotic level, wherein different features of culture participate in increasingly complicated, often disjunctive, systems of discourse.[68] Polysystem assumes that no single mode of discourse or cultural construct can account for the varieties of lived experiences or types of exchanges within which people routinely operate, and that people comfortably shift from system to system, often without reflection, depending on the situation. The system in operation is context-dependent, the domains of meaning are not limited to exclusively verbal significations, and the application of them necessarily imprecise, if not inconsistent. Translation, then, will shift from purely linguistic to symbolic and other forms of cultural expression in ways that are not naively arithmetic; different modes of translation will embody greater and lesser degrees of conformity in the same complex act, so that depending on what is being emphasized, the various dimensions of cultural expression will be more or less translated into their equivalents. If in our examples each expression of religiosity attempted by these precolonial authors is understood to participate in a range of semiotic systems, then its translation will likewise reflect these multiple referents as well. A theological term could conceivably imply then certain ritual actions, cosmological expectations, political allegiances, and so forth, in an ever-spiraling complication as one attempts to account for the encounter of one religious culture with another through a shared language, and its metaphoric and symbolic systems.

It must be remembered, however, that what is sought is not the precise equation of the parts of one symbolic or semiotic system with another in clear one-to-one matches. Rather, this overt use of an apparently alien terminology and conceptual system is an attempt to establish the basis for a common conceptual underpinning so that the matching systems and their parts are demonstrated to be coherently conceived, or at least rectifiable—hence the possibility of equivalence—while almost certain to remain inconsistent in their particulars.[69]

68. Gideon Toury, *In Search of a Theory of Translation* (Tel Aviv: The Porter Institute for Poetics and Semiotics, 1980); see also Edwin Gentzler's critique of polysystem theory in *Contemporary Translation Theories* (London: Routledge, 1993), 105–43. A slightly different approach that seeks to quantify discretely the complex levels of translation that account for the rich cultural context can be found in the "variational" model as described by Lance Hewson and Jacky Martin in *Redefining Translation: The Variational Approach* (London: Routledge, 1991). In this model, the highest level of intersemiotic translation involves the isolation of multifaceted "homologons" that lead to more tightly controlled paraphrastic constructions. This seems to be a promising model for translators to conceptualize what they do, but less useful descriptively in conceptualizing the problem as I have described the encounter of religious traditions.

69. I am here following the lead of George Lakoff and Mark Johnson, who argue in their work on

At the time of that writing, I could envision such a sharing of metaphoric worlds, but had not found a good example until reading the Bonbibī narrative when I realized that many of the processes Pramod Talgeri had described in his introductory essay to the volume *Literature in Translation*—as a movement "from cultural transference to metonymic displacement"—do by analogy describe precisely the activity undertaken by author Muhāmmad Khater.[70] His shift of intertextual references from a commonly recognized set of traditional Indic sources, such as the epics and *purāṇas* and *maṅgal kāvyas*, to the Korān, the *Shāh nāmeh*, and other *musalmāni* sources signaled a departure from the previously shared contours of the *imaginaire*, that is, the discursive arena, we saw constructed by earlier texts. His move was neither vague nor arbitrary when he appropriated all prior cosmologies and enfolded them within the world of Bonbibī and her brother Śājaṅgalī. What the author of the *Bonbibī jahurā nāmā* did was to perform an act of *conceptual blending* wherein two preexisting cosmologies were brought together with a profoundly different end result from that found in any other text—and to interpret that process, I suggest following the basic strategy outlined by Gilles Fauccioner and Mark Turner in *The Way We Think: Conceptual Blending and Mind's Hidden Complexities*.[71]

There is a very significant displacement that occurs in the translational exchange economy of these fictional *pīr kathās*. In the *Rāy maṅgal* of Kṛṣṇarām, a traditional Indic world of gods and goddesses acknowledges and admits into its realm the figure of the *pīr*, in the person of Baḍa Khān Gāji. Dakṣiṇ Rāy, the hero of the tale, has previously tolerated Baḍa Khān Gāji, who is clearly depicted as an outsider (by speech and act), then is forced to recognize his power and claim to the land when they fight to a standoff—each killing the other and each revived. This rapprochement and elevation of Baḍa Khān Gāji occurs when their battle is interrupted and peace forced upon them by the appearance of an *avatār* of Īśvar in the conjoined form of Satya Nārāyaṇ and Satya Pīr, a joint image of divinity that reflects both *hinduyāni* and *musalmāni* interests. They are made to break off enmities and share

metaphor in everyday speech that the mechanics of this process can be envisioned as seeking the "coherence" of conceptions without worrying about the consistency of the details of the expression, image, or symbol being manipulated; see Lakoff and Johnson, *Metaphors We Live By* (Chicago: University of Chicago Press, 1980).

70. Pramod Talgeri, "The Perspectives of Literary Translation: From Cultural Transference to Metonymic Displacement," in *Literature in Translation: From Cultural Transference to Metonymic Displacement*, ed. Pramod Talgeri and S. B. Verma (London: Sangam, 1988), 1–11; a number of other essays in that volume are germane here.

71. Gilles Fauconnier and Mark Turner, *The Way We Think: Conceptual Blending and the Mind's Hidden Complexities* (New York: Basic Books, 2002). For more on the workings of this model, see Fauconnier, *Mappings in Thought and Language* (Cambridge: Cambridge University Press, 1997); Fauconnier and Turner, "Metonymy and Conceptual Integration," in *Metonymy in Language and Thought*, ed. Klaus-Uwe Panther and Günter Radden (Amsterdam: John Benjamins, 1999), 77–90; and Todd Oakley, "Conceptual Blending, Narrative Discourse, and Rhetoric," *Cognitive Linguistics* 9 (1998): 321–60.

rule as brothers, reinterpreting a *hinduyāni* hierarchical relationship of social superior (Dakṣiṇ Rāy over Baḍa Khān) to a consanguineous relationship of shared parentage, that is, as brothers, a resolution that reorders traditional Indic hierarchies. As a result, a traditional Indic cosmology has stretched to embrace and accommodate in part a *musalmāni* cosmology by equating Āllā with Nārāyaṇ, with Muhāmmad and the *pīrs* and *bibīs* variously equated with the *devs* and *devīs* of the pantheon, sometimes symmetrically and at other times less so. The move is not an isolated event; for instance, in a related text we have not previously discussed, and which was likely written slightly later than Kṛṣṇarām's *Rāy maṅgal*, Rāmāi Paṇḍit's *Śūnya purāṇ* spells out this move from a hierarchical *hinduyāni* perspective when he equates the Indic god Dharma with Satya Pīr. Dharma takes the form of a *jaban* wearing a black hat, while Brahmā becomes Muhāmmad, Viṣṇu becomes a messenger or *pekāmbar*, Śūlapāṇi [= Śiva] becomes Adam (*adamph*), Gaṇeś becomes the warrior-*pīr* (*gājī*), Kārtik becomes the magistrate (*kāḍī*), and all the sages (*muni*) become mendicants (*phakīr*); Nārada becomes a religious leader (*śek*), Purandar becomes a scholar (*malanā*), Caṇḍikā Devī becomes Hāyā Bībī [= Eve], and Padmāvati becomes Bībīnur [lit. Lady of Light = Phātemā].[72] The traditional Indic divinities are prior but are identified, that is, "translated" into their new forms as *musalmāni* figures, while the supreme Lord Dharma appears to be equated with Āllā. The *hinduyāni* cosmos stretches to embrace the *musalmāni*.

In the *Gāji kālu o cāmpāvatī kanyār puthi* of Ābdur Rahim, that accommodative Indic cosmology is shifted slightly: Dakṣiṇā Rāy, a godling, is made subservient to Gāji, who, by virtue of that victory, triumphantly marries the daughter of the *brāhmaṇ* king Mukuṭ Rājā. Gāji is also declared to be the nephew of both the goddesses Gaṅgā and Caṇḍī, incorporating Gāji through family relation directly into the pantheon. In this emerging cosmology, Āllā is the supreme divinity. We have noted a similar move in the prolegomena to the *Mānik pīrer jahurā nāmā* of Jaidi, in the actions of Pīr Badar, who manifests the forms of Viṣṇu and Kṛṣṇa, who tames Gaṅgā and imprisons her in his shoulder bag, and so forth. The *hinduyāni* pantheon shifts downward in relation to its *musalmāni* counterpart. By the time of the *Bonbibī jahurā nāmā* of Muhāmmad Khater, we witness a significantly further downward displacement in the register of traditional Indic forms of divinity: preexisting celestial figures there are only recognized in the realm of ghouls, demons, vampires, and the like, all negative forms. In this new configuration, which appropriates the cosmologies of the *Rāy maṅgals* and similar texts, and the Gāji and Kālu tales, Āllā and Āllā alone is divine. Bonbibī displaces the goddesses

72. Rāmāi Paṇḍit, *Śūnyapurāṇ*, ed. Cārucandra Bandyopādhāy, 233–36. For an earlier transcription of the same text based on fewer manuscripts, see Rāmāi Paṇḍit, *Dharmapūjā bidhān*, ed. Nanīgopāl Bandyopādhyāy, completed by Yogīndranāth Rāy Bāhādur, Sāhitya Pariṣad Granthāvalī no. 56 (Kalikātā: Rāmakāmal Siṃha from Baṅgīya Sāhitya Pariṣat Mandir, 1323 BS), 263–65. For more on this process, see Stewart, "Religion in the Subjunctive," 29. Other equivalences can be found in Saiyad Sultān's *Nabīvaṃśa*, but more for purposes of criticism.

that populate the *maṅgal kāvya* literatures and emerges to rule the land, including Dakṣiṇā Rāy, his mother Nārāyaṇī, and Baḍa Khān Gāji, who is chastised for being friends with Dakṣiṇā Rāy. As a result, the traditional Indic cosmology of the *Rāy maṅgal* and the equivalence-seeking cosmology of *Gāji kālu o cāmpāvatī kanyār puthi* are both completely appropriated by, subsumed within, and reordered in an emerging *musalmāni* cosmology that grants only the lowest recognition and status to traditional Indic celestials.

In all three texts, we see three distinct conceptual blends under construction. When Baḍa Khān Gāji enters the domain of Dakṣiṇ Rāy's Sunderbans, he is grudgingly accepted, the cosmo-moral order he represents accommodated within the Indic world of the *maṅgal kāvya*–extolled divinities. A short while later, in the cycle of Gāji, Kālu, and Cāmpāvatī, the direction of appropriation, the new conceptual blending of orders, reflects the *musalmāni* appropriation of Dakṣiṇ Rāy's world and its *brāhmaṇ* king. Though Gāji prevails, and Āllā is declared the highest God, there are other divinities who populate the cosmic order as powerful beings in their own right. Divinity for Gāji, who is superior to these gods and goddesses, is even hinted, not only by his subjugation of Dakṣiṇ, now written Dakṣiṇā, but through the lineage of his mother Ājupā, who is sister to Gaṅgā and Caṇḍī (whether they are literally Gāji's aunts, or assumed, that relationship is immaterial, for kinship is established). Both Kṛṣṇarām's text and Ābdur Rahim's text incorporate all figures still a part of Āllā's creation into a new configuration, seeming to move toward what we might rightly style a popular version (that is, a simulacrum) of the well-attested *sūphī* concept of *waḥdat al-wujūd*, the Unity of Being.[73] But in the third conceptual blending, which produces a new cosmology articulated by Muhāmmad Khater, we read hints of the rejection of *waḥdat al-wujūd* that had allowed a place for traditional Indic gods and goddesses—they are nowhere to be found in the *Bonbibī jahurā nāmā*. With this shift away from *waḥdat al-wujūd*, we find evidence of a hardening of sectarian identities which seems to anticipate, if not signal, the emergence of exclusive categories of Hindu and Muslim that have come to mark the identity politics that started in earnest in the mid-nineteenth century, just prior to and during the wide circulation of Bonbibī's tale. Though not overtly sectarian or doctrinal, the stories still point to a gradual shift in perspective—and it is hard to imagine that that shift was not registered by the stories' audiences. In Fouconnier's and Turner's terms, each text represents a conceptual blend, so that in their schema, the *Rāy maṅgal*'s blend functions as Input One and *Gāji kālu o cāmpāvatī kanyār puthi*'s blend functions as Input Two; combined, they contribute to the new, more complex conceptual blend depicted in the *Bonbibī jahurā nāmā*.[74]

73. For a quick survey of the concept and its origins, including relevant bibliography, see Alexander Knysh, "Waḥdat al-Wujūd," in *The Oxford Encyclopedia of the Islamic World* (New York: Oxford University Press, 2009), 510–11.

74. See Fouconnier and Turner, *Conceptual Blending and the Mind's Complexities*, esp. pt. 1, 1–168. Each conceptual blend represented by all three texts is actually a complex blend that involves

The new conceptual blend signaled that the *Bonbibī jahurā nāmā* parodied, indeed satirized, the *maṅgal kāvya* and its *hinduyāni* world—as noted in the previous chapter, even its name, *jahurā nāmā*, functioned as a translation of the name of the genre, *maṅgal kāvya.* But that parody turned the traditional Indic world completely on its head, which could hardly have been clearer than in the outcome of the second story in the Bonbibī cycle, the tale of the innocent and hapless child Dukhe. A number of the central stories of the *maṅgal kāvya* celebrate the exploits of oceangoing traders, and notably, the early modern Bangla term for trader in these texts is *sādhu*, which means "virtuous," "honorable," and "respectable," the exact same name used for holy ascetics and mendicants. In many of the *maṅgal kāvyas*, it is these *sādhu* merchants who are instrumental in establishing the worship of the glorified goddess or god, which in Kṛṣṇarām's text is the semi-divine Dakṣiṇ Rāy, Lord of the Southern Regions. In the Bonbibī narrative of the child Dukhe story, we may well finally see the significance of the slight name change wherein Dakṣiṇ becomes Dakṣiṇā—spelled throughout the Bonbibī narrative with a feminine ending. Like *dakṣiṇ*, *dakṣiṇā* also means south or southerly, but its primary meaning is the *gift* or *donation*, especially that made to an officiating priest; it can also occasionally mean *reward.* In this text, Rāy is no longer the refined figure depicted in Kṛṣṇarām's *Rāy maṅgal*, rather he is transformed into a bloodthirsty *rākṣas* demon who demands human sacrifice; he can be bought for the appropriate fee. Enter the greedy *sādhu* merchant, whose name Dhonāi is a homophone of the word for *wealth* or *riches.* When he offers the child Dukhe, Dhonāi colludes in this sacrificial economy by paying the transactional *dakṣiṇā* fee to Dakṣiṇā Rāy; in return, Rāy promises to allow Dhonāi to plunder the land, which will result in the accumulation of vast cargoes of honey, wax, and lumber, the Sunderban commodities that were famous for generating obscene wealth. The indictment was anything but subtle: with its gods and goddesses suspect, the old brahmānical order was immoral, corrupt to its core and could no longer be tolerated in a world that turned its face toward the one true God as Bonbibī proposed.

. . .

interactions with two prior generic structures which represent *hinduyāni* cosmology and *musalmāni* cosmology, whose elements are manipulated to generate a new conceptual blend; see esp. 59–67 and the visual plotting of figure 4.1 on 62, which partially captures this complex movement of ideas. It should be further noted that individual moments in these texts can yield multiple complex blends involving such issues as analogy, space, time, cause-effect, category, and so forth (all of the issues suggested in our consideration of presuppositions and intertextualities at work in the *imaginaire*)—but that is an inquiry that would constitute a full-length monograph of its own. My initial efforts in this regard suggest that it would, however, produce a much more finely grained analyses of the creative, subjunctive explorations embodied in these works. That model of conceptual blending, in turn, has promising implications for tracing historical changes, as this example makes clear. In addition to its relevance to both Toury's and Talgeri's positions, this approach would be useful in modeling some of the mechanisms of Koselleck's arguments about conceptual history.

6

Pragmatics of *Pīr Kathā*

Emplotment and Extra-Discursive Effects

In the Kali Age people reap misery as the fruit of their actions.
Recognizing that, the Lord created a way to alleviate the suffering.
For the express purpose of saving all peoples, that Great Protector
manifested himself in this world, wearing the garb of one who begs for food.
The Lord Himself extended his immanent dominion across the earth.
He appeared as Satya Pīr, the perfection of all phakīrs.
Listen one and all and be glad at heart, for your misery will flee,
your afflictions will disappear, and happiness will to you accrue.
Dvija Ghanarām has composed this sweet song—
Now Lord, may you quickly fulfill every heart's dreams and desires.

—GHANARĀM CAKRAVARTTĪ, *SATYANĀRĀYAṆ RAS SINDHU*

6.1. FROM LITERARY EMPLOTMENT TO SOCIAL DISCOURSE

It would have been easy to have ended this book with the conclusions of the last chapter, marking the subtle shift in the tenor of the narratives of the fictional *pīrs* and *bibīs*. The literatures of Satya Pīr taken by themselves—and they constitute the largest block of stories dedicated to a single figure—not only confirm this transformation but demonstrate how the tales enter the political world of the last two centuries. In a sense, the tales of Satya Pīr serve as bookends to the *pīr kathās*; they are the earliest of the fictional *pīrs* to emerge in the manuscript archive, and they actively span the centuries with new stories being generated up to the present. Especially notable is the upsurge of activity that occurred with the advent of inexpensive printing in the decades of the late nineteenth and early twentieth centuries. While the figure and image of Satya Pīr is common in all the tales, when examined collectively they tend to aggregate into at least three separate emplotments. Each of these emplotments was favored by a different audience with very little overlap, the appeal in each instance alerting us to their deployment in the world of ordinary things, not just operating intradiscursively. While maintaining a strong parodic position in their intertextual and presuppositional elements, discourse to discourse, some have been and can be used to confirm outlooks that we associate today with the broad, but still generic, categories that embody the identity politics of the last two centuries. *This is where the autotelic narrative emerges from its isolation in discourse to critique the existing society.*

These fictional tales are hagiographies and share in all of the features of the hagiographies of their historically verifiable counterparts, except for the curious fact that the *bios* is fictional and therefore the religious ideal can only resemble in broad outline any particular dogmatic or theological position that might have been articulated by the *pīrs* of history. That imitation does not mean that the religious ideals to which they point are not truly religious; as we have already observed, by virtue of the constraints of fiction, they can only articulate generic notions of religion, while their religious orientation or commitment must be conveyed through symbolic images, the actions of their characters, and of course the texts and the associations they invoke as precursors. To invoke the precursor is to engage with its presuppositions, positively or negatively, to share or share in part its positions on key cosmological and pragmatic issues, which inevitably formulate an ethical position. As a result, these parodies mimic, for better or worse, the beliefs and practices that are associated with those other texts in the ordinary world of things. *A simulacrum of religious tradition is still a simulacrum of some thing that exists in the world of ordinary things, and therein lies their connection.* Because of this, the stories of Satya Pīr could be pressed into the service of sectarian interests.

We started by treating these *pīr kathās* as pure fictions in order to escape the irresistible urge to treat them as source documents for history (which would inevitably strip them of their miraculous phantasmagoria in the name of demythologizing). Treating them as fictions has allowed us to see some of the mechanics of how they operate, the function of those miraculous elements, and the critical cultural work of commenting on—and in that commentary, critiquing—Bengali culture and religion, its actors and its rituals, as they might occur in the ordinary world. It is through that commentary and critique that the narratives of the *pīr kathās* rightly cross over from their apparent narrative isolation and enter the ordinary world of Bengali religious life, with the self-appointed, express task of influencing their readers to a particular perspective. In formal semiotic terms, the *semantics* and *syntactics* with which we have been concerned to this point move now to the possible effects these tales have on their readers, how they may be deployed to make a difference in the world, that is, to their *pragmatics*. Because of the vast range of stories dedicated to Satya Pīr—easily the largest block in the set of fictional *pīr kathās* in manuscript and print—just through the tales themselves, we can see emerge the contours of a social history that complicates the exclusive Hindu-Muslim binary that the modern world has accepted as the norm.[1]

There are a number of ways these tales could persuade people to look at the world differently. Individual events and the emergence of outright victors in specific episodes point the way. Manipulating the plot toward an optimistic and ultimately favorable end is precisely what the genre of romance tends to do. But as Barbara Fuchs observes, the technique is incremental, and repetition is what pushes the point. The tales displace overt religious argument in favor of symbolic maneuvering of characters and the repositioning of social relationships that point to a resolution of the conflicts that, when strung together, constitute the plot. For instance, in the opening lines of Kṛṣṇahari Dās's *Baḍa satya pīr o sandhyāvatī kanyār puthi*, the author laments the sad state of Āllā's emissaries being harassed and tortured by the malevolent king Mādhāi, which prompts Satya Pīr's descent from heaven. Unremarkable in itself, this simple situation not only invokes analogues from other tales—the scenario of persecution a common enough trope for other religious narratives in Bengal—but also establishes the frame for the plot. The simple setup alerts the reader to the imagined contours of the proposed cosmos, with a heaven above and the possibility of traffic between the celestial and terrestrial realms, and of Āllā's determined interventions on earth. But to effect that goal of neutralizing Mādhāi, Satya Pīr must build his credibility through a series of lesser encounters that ultimately end in a demonstration of power or *kerāmat* that convinces Mādhāi of the folly of his ways. The cosmography, the nature of cause and effect or *karma*, the efficacy of meditating on the names and qualities of Āllā are all propositions that not only associate the text with other narratives that have approached the same situations in Bengal, but the mechanism by which Āllā chooses to intervene in the affairs of earth appropriates and redirects the *purāṇik* notion of the degradation of the ages, which in turn precipitates divine interference as a corrective in the form of *avatār*. Enter Satya Pīr, who in the simplest rationale for the *avatār*, declares, "I will appear in the form of *satya* (truth) to dispel *asatya* (untruth). Unrighteous people will bear the brunt of my appearance when I manifest myself in the form of Satya Pīr."[2]

1. Farina Mir's brilliant social history of the role played by popular or folk literatures in the Punjab, especially the centrality of the Hīr Ranjha romance to the shaping of a unique Punjabi cultural sensibility—that is, the pragmatics of those texts in circulation—provides a model for emulation that our current foray can only hint at for Satya Pīr and Bengal; see Farina Mir, *The Social Place of Language: Vernacular Culture in British Colonial Punjab*, South Asia Across the Disciplines (Berkeley: University of California Press, 2010).

2. Anonymous, *Satyadever pāñcālī*, Bengali MS no. 874H, Dhaka University, complete, 10 folios, dtd. 1218 BS [ca. 1811], folio 3b, lines 7–8. See also Anonymous, *Satyadever pāñcālī*, Bengali MS no. 3688, Dhaka University, complete 18 folios, dtd. 1239 BS [ca. 1832], folio 5b, lines 1–2. A later manuscript of the same text, also anonymous but attributed to Jaymuni in the catalog, follows the wording verbatim

With hard manuscript evidence in hand, it is clear that as early as the sixteenth century the narratives of Satya Pīr were the first to appropriate this broad (read generic) theological concept among the fictional *pīrs*. It would seem to be no accident that the first of these tales of Satya Pīr began to circulate in the same time frame as the advent of the *gauḍīya vaiṣṇav* movement inspired by Kṛṣṇa Caitanya. In the sixteenth and seventeenth centuries *vaiṣṇavs* sometimes popularly portrayed *musalmāns* as responsible for, or at least symptomatic of, the ills of the Kali Age;[3] but the Satya Pīr storyline turned that perspective on its head and argued that the *sūphī* beliefs and practices promoted by *pīrs* and *phakirs*, by *pirānīs* and *bibīs*, offered a more equitable alternative that made life in this world, and salvation for the next, available to everyone regardless of gender, ethnic background, or social rank. That emplotment directly countered much of the appeal of the *gauḍīya* form of *vaiṣṇav* practice that itself tended to reach across caste and, if one accepts the rhetoric, even sectarian lines.[4] The *kathās* of Satya Pīr likewise rallied against caste-oriented exclusions from religious practice, while requiring no overt doctrinal or dogmatic positioning to resolve the issue. On the popular level, the *gauḍīya vaiṣṇav* writers and the authors of the *pīr kathās* seemed to be aiming at similar audiences, but the latter ultimately claimed a considerably wider reach. While these *pīr kathās* as romances may not have directly changed the way their audiences committed themselves to religious issues, at the very least they gave pause—they invited the reader or listener to join them in exploring alternative worlds, that subjunctive dimension essential to their construction. But early modern India's incredibly rich regional linguistic diversity, its competing modes of traditional indigenous and imported modes of governance, and different types of competing discursive modes of authority vying for dominance affected the production of these fictions and the resources from the real world on which those fictions drew. As part of the symbolic currency of the tales, ethnic-cum-social distinctions abounded, such as traditional caste markers (e.g., *brāhmaṇ*, *kayastha*, and so forth) which were juxtaposed with labels based on geographic origin (e.g., *turuska*, *jaban*, *bāṅgāli*, *kābuli*, and so forth), each of which indexed stereotyped or expected modes of behavior, commensality, ritual obligation, and so forth. The interactions of these differently designated characters were a constant negotiation of asymmetrical standards. Similarly, holy men

---

except to insert Satyadev in place of Satya Pīr; see Anonymous [attributed to Jaymuni], *Satyadever pāñcālī*, Bengali MS no. 1316, Dhaka University, complete, 12 folios, dtd. 1273 BS [ca. 1866], folio 3b, lines 7–8. One might easily see this as the harbinger of the eventual instantiation of the exclusive categories of Hindu and Muslim that came to dominate the literature by the end of the nineteenth century.

3. Tony K. Stewart, *The Final Word: The Caitanya Caritāmṛta and the Grammar of Religious Tradition* (New York: Oxford University Press, 2010), 60–62, 114; Fuchs, *Romance*, 57–58.

4. The hagiographical materials dedicated to Kṛṣṇa Caitanya routinely extolled the way his message reached across sectarian lines, including to those who followed *śaiva*, *śākta*, and *musalmāni* practices. See Stewart, *Final Word*. For nineteenth- and twentieth-century developments that explicitly target not only those groups but Christians as well, see Bhatia, *Unforgetting Chaitanya*.

and women, key technicians of the sacred, navigated landscapes of multiple religious orientations in which they exhibited different types of power in and over the created world (e.g., *pīr, pīrānī, bibī, phakir, shaykh, mollā, sannyāsī, vairāgī, nāth, jogī, pūjārī, purohit, padri,* and so forth), while the invocation of superhuman figures defined the nature of the cosmos and the powers within that were relevant to the religious traditions so indexed (e.g., *nabī, avatār, jinn, pari, phereṣtā, kinnara, vidyādharī, dev, devī, āsura, ḍākini, piśācī, bhūt, pret*), and of course in a similar way, the names and forms of God (e.g., Āllā, Khodā, Bhagavān, Nirañjan, and so on). The unique network of choices made by each author to suspend the narrative in this imaginal context dramatically demonstrated the complications of the narrative itself, but also helped to give it shape and impart its perspective on a number of critical issues without having to articulate them in so many words. The specific invocation or mere allusion to another text—such as the *Bhāgavata purāṇa* or the Korān—and the accompanying pragmatic presuppositions relieved the story in question from having to lay out all the parts of its own constructed reality. In this intricate economy of selected precursors, much of the appeal of these tales seemed to lie in the way they creatively mediated the competing standards of authority they called into use. Until the late nineteenth century, these early modern tales hinged on negotiating these differences; after that, we begin to see much more clearly and firmly instantiated positions.

Many of these negotiations only come to light when we isolate the intertextualities and the presuppositions for any given story, as proposed in chapters 4 and 5; but if we follow those leads simplistically as purely mechanistic operations, they are likely to produce but a crude set of propositions. If we use them as a starting point, we can provide consistently measurable elements across multiple stories—each new connection enriching the texture of the work's background. This approach avoids at least some of the vagaries and limitations of relying solely on the interpreter's personal insight for guidance regarding the relationships of these tales. When these connections are traced back from our current text to each precursor, and then to the precursors' precursors (and even further), the broad strokes of these constructed worlds—and what really seems to matter to the authors who make them—become significantly more fine-grained, more focused, defining the conditions through which they emerge in the *imaginaire*. With this kind of mapping, linking generations of texts, authorial choices can be better understood beyond the intuitions we tend to follow without always knowing why, when we have sensed a particular slant or view toward ideological or religious possibilities that may not have been explicitly declared in the narrative proper. That "sense" of the story's direction, I argue, is largely our response to the author's manufacture of a rich semiotic domain that both directly and indirectly references the world of ordinary things and the prior discourses found through other texts. Uncovering the intertextual connections and presuppositions of any text locates it within a discursive arena—and tracing that web of connections reveals where changes in outlook have occurred.

We have to assume that each author deliberately chose his precursor texts; in some instances the precursor provided a complete morally ordered universe that required no modification. But more creative authors would pick and choose from a variety of precursors—as we saw in the Bonbibī narrative—constructing in the process a new conceptual blend. While every plot set up some kind of conflict for resolution, it was often only through the narrative's relationship to its precursors and the parodies of those texts that the full impact of what that resolution meant could be made clear. We witness just such a move in the prolegomena to the *Mānikpīrer jahurānāmā*, where Badar reveals first to Dudbibī and then to her father that he is a true friend of God by virtue of his masterful power that enables him to manifest the many forms of the panoply of *vaiṣṇav* gods. The structure of *avatār* has already been invoked with Badar's descent, and the apparent input source is *purāṇik*, but when combined with the second input of a world where Āllā and Āllā alone is divine, the resulting blend is something new, but not without its ambiguities regarding what constitutes a sense of unique identity for Badar or for the gods. In this new blended space, are these *vaiṣṇav* divinities ontologically stable identities, or are they to be understood as appearances or apparitions? The narrative of Badar parodies *purāṇik* mythology, including the portrayal of the feeble attempts of yogic *sādhus* to attain *mokṣa*, which does not just diminish the prominence of gods and goddesses in *purāṇik* cosmology, but by mocking and trivializing its object draws their very reality into question. Similarly, Muhāmmad Khater's Bonbibī tale shares pragmatic presuppositions from two inputs—the *Rāy maṅgal* and the *Gāji kālu o cāmpāvatī kanyār puthi*—in a way that for the reader conflates the two texts into a single blended narrative in order to establish a different sort of cosmic hierarchy from that found in either of its two precursors. What becomes clear is that this kind of clever manipulation served a purpose, which in these examples hinged on the reordering of the hierarchies of cosmic and worldly power, promoting a world where Āllā alone was Lord. That message made each particular fictional narrative relevant to the ordinary Bengali world of lived history, and here we bump into the pragmatics of the texts' use. These feats of conceptual blending generated possible new structures for the cosmos and the places of humans in it; they found a way, sometimes seemingly willy-nilly, to accommodate a Bengali *purāṇik* world within a generic Korānic framework. That was and is a subjunctive creativity at work.

We have sufficient numbers of Satya Pīr texts to trace and generalize *longue durée* tendencies of common narrative trajectories that point to real-life utility in the world of their readers. As noted in the preface, there are more than seven hundred fifty extant manuscripts[5] and several hundred print editions,[6] composed

5. The bulk of the manuscripts are listed in *Catalogus Catalogorum of Bengali Manuscripts*, comp./ed. Jatindra Mohan Bhattacharjee, vol. 1 (Calcutta: The Asiatic Society, 1978).

6. The British Library has perhaps the largest collection of such tales, though many can be found in the various repositories in Kolkata, Santiniketan, and Dhaka.

by more than a hundred different authors. New tales continued to be produced well into the twentieth century and still circulate today. The reach of Satya Pīr's narratives is transregional, far greater than any of the other *phakirs* and *bibīs* we have encountered. Found across every region of the Bangla-speaking world, these stories have also taken life in Assamese, Oḍiyā, and Sanskrit.[7]

In the late sixteenth century, perhaps sooner, Satya Pīr entered the Bengali imagination with the first known works by Phakīr Rām, Ghanarām Cakravartī, Rāmeśvar, and Ayodhyārām Kavi.[8] A number of seventeenth- and eighteenth-century texts related new exploits, but it was in the period of easy access to inexpensive printing and the concomitant creation of great entrepreneurial fortunes—the mid-nineteenth to early twentieth centuries—that this literature burgeoned into one of the most prolific in Bangla. Satya Pīr not only survived the transition period from early modern to colonial times, but his appeal expanded from the rural, largely agrarian, communities to urban dwellers in the metropolises of Calcutta and Dhaka, where the bulk of his tales were published.[9] The religious exploits of Satya Pīr did not initially champion a single group of people or practitioners. In spite of perceived differences in his audiences today, he was and still is accessible to all; his wide embrace provides stability to different people of all social classes with common basic needs.

7. The initial conception of the basic divisions of texts into three types was first published in Tony K. Stewart, "Alternate Structures of Authority: Satya Pīr on the Frontiers of Bengal," in *Beyond Turk and Hindu: Rethinking Religious Identities in Islamicate South Asia*, ed. David Gilmartin and Bruce B. Lawrence (Gainesville: University of Florida Press, 2000), 21–54. This chapter depends on that original analysis, but the concept of emplotment is expanded and the number of references to printed works has been augmented substantially, as have the summaries of texts.

8. Sen, *Bāṅglā sāhityer itihās*, vol. 1, pt. 2, p. 471. For Ghanarām's text see the nicely edited version, Ghanarām Cakravarttī, *Satyanārāyaṇ ras sindhu*, and the considerably older but also nicely edited, Dvija Ghanarām, *Satyanārāyaṇ itihās*. An early edition of Phakīr Rām's text is Phakīr Rām, *Satyanārāyaṇ pā̃cālī* (n.p., 1270 BS [ca. 1863]); a reliable and more easily accessible edition is *Śrīśrīsatyanārāyaṇer phakīrāmī kathā: pujāpaddhati o śabdārtha sambalitā*, ed. Raghunandan Śatapathī (1382 BS [ca. 1975] reprint: Bānkuṛa: Vikrampur Jagadbandhu Catuṣpaṭhī, 1978). The only version of Ayodhyarām I have found is Kavicandra Ayodhyārām Rāy, "Satya nārāyaṇ kathā," ed. Vyomakeś Mustaphī, *Baṅgīya sāhitya pariṣat patrikā* 8, no. 1 (1308 BS [ca. 1901]): 61–72. Arguably the best and most carefully edited version of the many editions of Rāmeśvar can be found in his collected works; see Rāmeśvar, *Satyanārāyaṇ vratkathā*, in *Rāmeśvar racanāvalī*, ed. Pañcānan Cakravarttī (Kalikātā: Baṅgīya Sāhitya Pariṣat, 1964), 509–28.

9. Richard M. Eaton argues that based on his reading of the *Nabīvaṃśa* of Saiyad Sultān, Bengalis were the first to introduce the idea to the Muslim world that Adam was the first and premier cultivator; see Eaton, *Rise of Islam and the Bengal Frontier*, 308, n. 6; but Ayesha Irani convincingly argues that the likely source of the story for Bengal is the account found in Muhammad ibn 'Abd Allāh al-Kisā'ī's' *Ṣāḥib Qiṣaṣ al-Anbiyā'* which Saiyad Sultān was only translating into Bangla; see Ayesha A. Irani, "Sacred Biography, Translation, and Conversion: The *Nabīvaṃśa* of Saiyad Sultān and the Making of Bengali Islam, 1600–Present" (PhD diss., University of Pennsylvania, 2011), 284, n. 1065.

As literary narratives, the textual materials for glorifying Satya Pīr range from sophisticated poetic productions of the royal courts of the eighteenth century to more rustic oral performances designed to be improvised and delivered by itinerant bards or in touring dramatic troupes. Occasionally an author would insert a cogent exegetical comment in the signature line (*bhanitā*) of a section that provided a guide to the reader on how to interpret what was being conveyed, but the touch tended to remain light. Very occasionally, the author as the omniscient narrator would interrupt the narrative with an observation, usually of greater sociological than theological import, inserted extradiegetically into the narrative frame—and we see this increasingly in the print editions, which raises the question of editorial intervention. Some nineteenth- and twentieth-century publishers clearly seized the opportunity to editorialize in ways that begin to tilt the fictional narrative in the direction of what Macherey calls ideological or religious propaganda. As I have noted elsewhere,[10] the advent of printing religious texts in Bengal provided editors with the opportunity to alter the text from what was found in the manuscripts. But when I compared Satya Pīr manuscripts one to another, especially the older manuscripts, I found overall a strong fidelity of transmission, and in the move from manuscript to printed versions, the texts have, on the whole, suffered only a relatively benign form of intervention—more often in the direction of shifting the tenor by substitutions of nomenclature (e.g., interchanging the names of heaven between *golok* and *bhest*) and the modernizing of spellings or the insertion of punctuation—but I hasten to add that these shifts do not align consistently with what one would expect today given the cleavage of Muslim from Hindu, for often the author's name suggests a background opposite to the expected substitution (e.g., Satya Pīr for Satya Nārāyaṇ or Satya Dev). But the possibility of editorial intervention always looms, especially when there is disagreement among manuscript sources or the use of incomplete manuscripts. Overall, the structures of the stories remain more or less intact from manuscript to print and successive print editions. Because we have such a sizable number of texts at our disposal, we can identify larger trends without recourse to arguments based on a single document or isolated lexical difference of the type that haunts the hermeneutics of Biblical texts or other traditions overwrought about critical editions, but with few sources.

In order to produce a workable, statistically sufficient sample of story types, more than a third of the manuscripts and nearly all of the printed literature available

10. Stewart, *Final Word*, esp. 159–60, 270. Guidelines for editing texts and collating multiple manuscripts were not standardized until around the turn of the twentieth century when, after the publication of some texts of dubious manuscript origin, the Baṅgīya Sāhitya Pariṣad (Bengal Literary Academy) took steps to ensure greater precision and ethical scrupulousness in the rendering of manuscripts into print, a trend that has been widely embraced. Till then, and even today in the inexpensive *baṭ-tolā* editions of texts, editors were free to omit passages they found offensive or problematic or simply did not like, and would appear to have felt few qualms when inserting new material or changing readings to adjust the perspective.

have been analyzed. In order to maximize the use of manuscripts, I generally read only complete versions of texts and no more than three versions by any one author, and I surveyed as many authors as possible, starting with the oldest texts available. I attempted to maintain a balance of authors that appeared to represent the general distribution of *hinduyāni* and *musalmāni* names, but the latter especially proved misleading, for the names do not necessarily reflect the author's religious orientation, confirming the inappropriate assumption that "naming" means "belonging" as it is often assumed to do in the new world of identity politics. The tales of Satya Pīr tended to group according to the three basic sets of emplotments that were determined by a combination of the manifest identity of Satya Pīr and his direct role (or absence) in the plot; the social standing and vocation of the protagonists other than Satya Pīr; the nature and direction of instruction; the occasional overt religious point or more general moral of the story; and the audience for which the stories were apparently intended but which can be determined only partially. That audience is where the pragmatics of the texts becomes visible.

Vaiṣṇav Emplotment. Through the mechanism of the *avatār* of the Kali Age, the earliest emplotment seems to have followed the age-old tradition of subsuming important religious figures in the style formally outlined by Kṛṣṇa in the *Bhagavad gītā* (chapter 4). I say "seems" because there was some slippage with respect to both terminology and the apparent identities of characters and what those identities portended. Satya Pīr in this emplotment was another form of Viṣṇu who descended to right the decaying moral order by establishing a new form of *dharma* that is simple and geared to the limitations of people in the Kali Age. He disrupted normal expectations by taking on the form of a *musalmāni phakir*. He was a figure of local power.[11] As far as one can tell from the names of the authors, and often reinforced by the sometime ambiguity of references to *musalmāni* figures or the simple equivalence of key concepts and institutions (e.g., *mandir* and *masjid*), the origin of this first emplotment is generally *hinduyāni* in orientation, conforming to a classical Indic prospect. The overall outlook of this set of texts demonstrates a strong affinity with the various *maṅgal kāvyas* dedicated to Dakṣiṇ Rāy, especially that of Kṛṣṇarām, which we examined in chapter 4, but perhaps with less

11. Some scholars have been inclined to associate him with the historical *pīr* Ḥusayn ibn Manṣūr al-Ḥallāj (d. 922) as the True Pīr, the *pīr* who is *satya*. This popular story is asserted by the editor in Kavivallabh, *Satyanārāyaṇ punthi*, ed. Munsī Abdul Karim, Sāhitya Pariṣad Granthāvalī no. 49 (Kalikātā: Baṅgīya Sāhitya Pariṣad by Rāmkāmal Siṃha, 1322 BS [ca. 1915]), 7, and then repeated frequently in the secondary literature as "hearsay." The most explicit connection is proposed by Louis Massignon in his translation of Husayn Ibn Mansûr Hallâj, *La Passion de Husayn Ibn Mansûr Hallâj*, new ed., 2 vols. (Paris: Gallimard, 1975), 2: 299–302. The same thin documentation goes for Satya Pīr's identity as the son of the daughter of the famous ruler of Bengal, Husain Shāh (r. 1493–1519), which is frequently repeated; for the earliest citation, see Sen, *Folk-Literature of Bengal*, 100, where he credits manuscripts of Kavi Āriph and Śaṅkarācārya.

subtlety. All of the tales revolve around the ordeals of indigence and its reversal, the tribulations of generating wealth, and with that wealth, a general weal. They take a formulaic order that begins with the poor *brāhmaṇ*, followed by the tale of the woodcutters, and finally with a merchant's tale.[12]

Emplotment of Gendered Creativity. The second emplotment drew on a prior knowledge of Satya Pīr, but hardly demonstrated any strong religious orientation beyond a very simple devotion to the figure who can be called by either name: Satya Pīr or Satya Nārāyaṇ, epithets which were seamlessly interchanged. Where the first emplotment focused on the elimination of penury as a prerequisite of living a moral life, and secondarily equated the creation of wealth with the general benefit of the family, this second emplotment emphasized the creative responses by individuals to life's vagaries, very much as the classic genre of Romance would demand. Significantly, a large number of these tales placed women in the pivotal role of heroic protagonist, so traditional gendered roles were not fixed, but enacted, modifying the simplistic formula of Romance wherein women had to be faithful while the men were heroic. Satya Pīr's interventions depended on the personal commitment of the heroine (or the occasional hero) to improvise ways to align personal action with a dharmically defined moral order, to exhibit patience in the face of seemingly intractable problems, and to exhibit a gritty determination to succeed, only turning to Satya Pīr when personal resources had been exhausted. Satya Pīr tended to be found residing in an ethereal Mecca, and the protagonist could conjure him with a heartfelt call of his name (in some cases *jikir*, but generally much less elaborately). With his support the protagonists survived the machinations of power-mad kings, malevolent *jogī* magicians, and the perils lurking in the swamps of Bengal, where they were often pitted against *bhūts* and *prets* as well as disciplined sepoys, and in one case even a rogue rhino. Antagonists tended to be transparent manifestations of something akin to the embodiment of the early Christian seven deadly sins (though sloth enjoyed but a cameo appearance). The adventures were mad, but the moral was clear: when you needed help most and did not know what else to do, you demonstrated your devotion to Satya Pīr and all would be well.

Musalmāni Emplotment. The third emplotment embraced a decidedly *musalmāni* outlook, emerging in the early eighteenth century, at least a century later than the *hinduyāni* trilogy. Satya Pīr functioned as a moral exemplar in order to make the world safe for *sūphīs* and their followers, to wake up the society of *brāhmaṇs*

12. I am reminded that as the number of these texts proliferated in the early twentieth century, William James's notions of pragmatism hinged on the elimination of penury as the foundation of a moral life; see James, *Pragmatism: A New Name for Some Old Ways of Thinking* (New York: Longmans, Green, 1907), esp. chap. 1.

and kings (and *brāhmaṇ* kings), and all the other figures of questionable moral standing famous for oppressing or taking advantage of the general population. The world depicted in these tales was not one particularly favorable to *pīrs* and *phakirs* and the *musalmāni* population in general, so Āllā intervened by sending down Satya Pīr. There was a subtle but marked shift, however, in the language that was used to describe the relationship of celestial and terrestrial figures and their place in the cosmos. The stories pointed to a popular, that is, nontechnical or generic form (a simulacrum, of course) of the *sūphī* concept of "unity in being" (*waḥdat al-wujūd*) to describe the nature of this created world. This cycle of tales was very much in harmony with the various texts dedicated to Gāji, Kālu, and Cāmpāvatī, and to Mānik Pīr. There was a new cosmic order being promoted and one that no longer proposed a simple equivalence of all forms of divinity with Āllā and Viṣṇu somehow equal, for in these tales they were not. The new order envisioned only one God, Āllā, with all other so-called divinities demoted to secondary status as celestial figures. It was a new world order heralded by Satya Pīr.[13]

The situations described in the *vaiṣṇav* literature of Satya Pīr constituted a fairly limited narrative domain, using small numbers of fixed character types, in a finite set of possible fictional predicaments, whose primary complications were generally permutations of a much smaller set of underlying themes, for example turning to Satya Pīr to get rich, to be rescued from trouble, or both. These underlying themes, however, were not always approached the same way, but the plots hinged on narrative codes that determined the outcomes of the various emplotments.[14] In the case of Satya Pīr, and in much of the popular religious literature of South Asia, the narrative codes did not simply shape the literary fiction, they had a much more immediate connection to everyday life, that is, their perspectives had relevance to the way people lived and came to understand how they should conduct themselves, how they might better survive, in a world that was opaque or did not always reveal itself in easily discernible features. The most common narrative codes reflected the following strategies to model the interaction between *vaiṣṇav* and *musalmāni* (and, by the mid- or late nineteenth century, Hindu and Muslim) characters, which we will elucidate for each emplotment: they included movements toward *recognition*, *accommodation*, *alliance*, *legitimation*, *appropriation* or *incorporation*, and *subversion*. Here is where the practical consumption of these fictions clearly

13. These tales did not, however, assert the strong position taken in the Bonbibī narrative, which appeared to include an incipient reformist sense of *tawḥīd* that edged toward, if not actually crossed over to, Macherey's notions of religious propaganda as noted in the last chapter. For a summary of the history of the concept of *tawḥīd*, see Tamara Sonn, "Tawḥīd," in *The Oxford Encyclopedia of the Islamic World* (New York: Oxford University Press, 2009), 5:332–41.

14. I have adopted the notion of narrative code from Gérard Genette; see Genette, *Narrative Discourse: An Essay in Method*, trans. Jane Lewin (Ithaca: Cornell University Press, 1980).

spilled over into the lives of individuals, precisely because their fictional depictions did, in fact, not only have roots in, but were directed immediately toward, negotiating the everyday culture of Bengal and the interactions of people with the religious opportunities afforded them. They reflected the way actors marshaled competing structures of authority, or pitted one against the other, to modulate the power of survival represented by the protagonist, Satya Pīr, or his devotee. This is a vital function, because when we identify and recover these narrative codes we can see some of the logic by which different people could and did think differently about the same contingent existence, interacting with the same figures in the same settings, but using different standards of measure. Narrative codes served as indexes to the actors' response toward different forms of authority, which allows us to recognize different systems of signification, often reinforced through intertextual references, both overt and implied (e.g., the Satya Nārāyaṇ story in the text of the *revā khaṇḍa* of the *Skānda purāṇa* and of the *Bhaviṣya purāṇa*), or to other cultural institutions (e.g., the tomb or *dargā* as *sūphī* center), that are used to reinforce the orientation, but which also generate the basic contours of the logical presuppositions governing the action. Finally, because these individual items or subsets of alternate signification often stand in metonymic relation to the basic narrative code in the context of the narrative itself—they are often freely mixed and matched as elements in the story—their differences will ultimately reveal that the structures of authority are considerably more complex and subtly nuanced than the basic contemporary political identities of Hindu and Muslim could ever recognize, and they often actively imbricate what are today thought of as either exclusively Hindu or Muslim attitudes and acts.

In short, the identification of narrative codes within the three emplotments refines our ability to differentiate the protagonists' actions and orientations—different ways of thinking about and negotiating the way power is wielded in the world—far more dynamically than the assignment of monolithic labels, such as Hindu or Muslim, which have a flattening effect suitable to a propagandistic monologic. This is not to say that individuals who preserved and propagated these tales of Satya Pīr today would not be cognizant of the signification of the categories Hindu and Muslim, but those categories operate on a different level of experience most often associated with the symbolic posturing appropriate to the larger public sphere, and in that sphere they maintain a kind of consistency of image that everyone recognizes in the identity politics of today (e.g., the rules of public propriety, severely delimited ritual and symbolic action and dress, and so forth). But in the case of Satya Pīr, it would be wrong to read back into the early narratives those kinds of political distinctions, for they were not the signal markers by which people negotiated the private vicissitudes of daily experience on the frontiers of early modern Bengal—and as we have seen, this would also hold for the tales of Dakṣiṇ Rāy and Baḍa Khān Gāji, Bonbibī, Mānik Pīr, Badar Pīr, and others. While those stark distinctions of Hindu and Muslim play large in today's political world, the categories were incipient but not yet fully formed in the older materials, and, as will become apparent, when invoked could be used as a foil to expose the ignorance of their improper application. Conflating the categories that today are understood to be mutually exclusive is a subjunctive exploratory move that at least continues to question, if not directly critique, the utility of those formations—and none of the *pīr kathās* can escape that repurposing today.

What bound together all three of the Satya Pīr narrative emplotments was the common improvisation necessary to negotiate an often difficult or compromising environment using locally available sources of power, obviously the *pīr*, but also committed or reluctantly reoriented (converted) kings, and especially their entrepreneurial merchants. The environment of their setting was always some kind of frontier, so these are generally read as narratives of survival, and, as Eaton has clearly shown, the land of Bengal where these stories proliferate has for centuries been conceived in just such terms.[15] The frontier, however, is plural and shifting, for they were geographic, political, economic, and religious—and the stories of Satya Pīr addressed them all, sometimes in conjunction and at others in different combinations. In these narratives, the frontier was an arena of human action that lay beyond the circumscribed limits of what was familiar, beyond what constituted the predictably settled world of "tradition." Therein lay much of the stories' interest and mystery, if not reason sufficient in itself to question the use of the larger categories of Hindu and Muslim which so often blur in these socially ill-defined areas. These tales documented journeys into the unknown, where dangers were manifold, not so much because they were inherently threatening, although the tales are littered with episodes of real danger to the protagonists, but often simply because the modes of action that were considered normal did not always hold true in a land that was unfamiliar. Yet, for many of the people who listened to the tales of Satya Pīr, that shifting frame of reference described their Bengal precisely: it was a land of constantly renegotiated values, of improvisation, of attempts to impose stability in a physical environment that challenged human intervention. And so it is still perceived today. As a frontier it was a place where the social, political, and economic stakes were often high, with commensurate rewards for success or failure. In this formulation we discover part of the secret of Satya Pīr's social mobility and appeal. *Meeting the needs of the frontier has allowed Satya Pīr to endure, for his pragmatic approach to the problems of the world is one that has favored innovation and compromise in the pursuit of basic human needs, especially the elimination of penury and the quest for social dignity.* His are the tales of survival in a contingent environment, and for many in Bengal, that is the commonplace of experience.

15. Eaton, *Rise of Islam and the Bengal Frontier*, esp. chaps. 8–9.

6.2. THE VAIṢṆAV *AVATĀR* OF THE AGE

In the first emplotment, Satya Pīr deals directly with the most pragmatic concerns of basic survival, especially the generation of wealth—people accept that he wields a power to make their lives better, and that is good no matter how it is labeled. In more dire circumstances, he protects the innocent and reestablishes a proper social and just order. Rather than articulating a new form of religiosity, he simply appears to each individual in a form she or he can recognize as legitimate: Satya Pīr or Satya Nārāyaṇ, with no distinction between them. One early-twentieth-century author neatly summed it up, though his audiences would hear this message differently depending on their orientation:

> No matter if one is rich or poor,
> no matter *hindu* or *jaban*,
> each and every one is rescued.
> Should any human being facing disaster,
> remember Satya Nārāyaṇ
> with heart-felt devotion;
> the Lord of Heaven himself
> will direct compassion toward him
> and make all disasters disappear.
> Any time one might fall sick,
> but remembers Satya Nārāyaṇ,
> the gods' own physician Dhanvantari appears.
> When disaster grips one in fear,
> he suffers misery no more
> when he seeks the refuge of His name.
> Listen brother, *hindu* peoples
> call on Satya Nārāyaṇ,
> while the *jaban* calls on Satya Pīr.[16]

To enjoy the benefits of this general weal does not require group participation to be valid—so the direction of these emplotments in no case suggests formal religious commitments, but aims at the individual. To turn one's attention to Satya Pīr is a matter of individual opportunity or convenience. The stories of Satya Pīr tell their listeners to recognize the accessibility of a coercive power to ensure one's health and economic stability, if not be the direct source of riches. These are the oldest stories and still the most widely circulated today.

Manuscript evidence dates this oldest cycle of Satya Pīr narratives to the early or mid-seventeenth century and in astonishing numbers by Bangla manuscript

16. Prāṇkiśor Ghoṣ, *Śrīśrīsatyanārāyaṇer punthi*, ed. Kumudkānta Devśarmmā (Kalikātā: Aśīm Kumār Ghoṣ at Jayaguru Prakāśālay, 1375 BS [ca. 1968]), 34.

standards.[17] The three tales that make up the cycle have ossified into a fixed set and sequence and today account for the overwhelming majority of manuscripts and printed texts: the cycle always begins with the story of the poor *brāhmaṇ*, then the tale of the woodcutters, and finally the merchant's adventure. Ghanarām Cakravarttī writes in his *Satyanārāyaṇ ras sindhu*:

> Pay your respects to Satyadev daily and with a serious intent, for all great and respectable people throughout the world serve him. In this day and age he descended in the form of a *phakīr* named Satya Pīr, the repository of all powers sufficient to grant every wish. . . . For the express purpose of saving people, that great protector of the world manifested himself on this earth in the garb of a poor mendicant who begs his food. . . . In the dress of a *phakīr*, the Lord wanders—Mathurā, Gokul, Gayā, Govarddhan Mountain, the lands of Aṅga, Vaṅga, Kaliṅga, Utkal, Gauḍa—pointedly determined to spread his *pūjā* worship. Previously, when a *hindu* heard the words *pīr* and *sinni*, he tended to turn away in the oblivion of ignorance, so it was that he first appeared to a *brāhmaṇ* of highly respected rank. Once his power was revealed, the *pūjā* spread, and when they saw its effectiveness, many more people performed the worship. Woodcutters made up the second group to enjoy the benefits; and thirdly, the merchants found all their desires fulfilled. Merchants especially well understood both the pitfalls of gaining and the dangers of losing wealth, so for this reason his majesty became renowned, spreading from region to region. If I tell his story in a way that gives people the knowledge to tread the prescribed path, then all who listen will be everywhere rescued from this ocean of tribulation. To promote this *pūjā* worship among *hindus* and *jabans*, Satyadev descended (*avatār*) assuming the bodily form of a human.[18]

The outward form of the *pīr* is semiotically rich, an explicit visual metaphor in the way he combines key marks of a public *musalmāni* and *vaiṣṇav* allegiance. Deliberately flaunting his position through this mixed sartorial code, it is not unusual for Satya Pīr to approach significant religious figures of any community while carrying the Korān and *Bhāgavata purāṇa*. The overt symbolism produces multiple variations of the form of divinity that descended to break up the feud between Dakṣiṇ Rāy and Baḍa Khān Gāji in Kṛṣṇarām's *Rāy maṅgal*. Deliberately conflating signs that would today be considered disjunctive endlessly amuses or

17. All of the early authors tell some version of the same cycle. There are many other manuscripts in private hands in collections whose catalogues had not been included when Jatindra Mohan compiled his monumental *Catalogus Catalogorum*, but based on the latter, the authors with the highest numbers of extant manuscripts, including complete and incomplete, dated and undated, are: Rāmakṛṣṇa Dvija—82; Phakīr Rām Kavibhuṣaṇ—61; Viśveśvar Dvija—42; Rāmeśvar Dvija—35; Rāmbhadra—18; Śaṅkarācārya—17; and Vallabh Kavi—11. The oldest of the dated manuscripts to survive are Śaṅkarācārya dtd. 1062 BS [ca. 1655] × 2, 1102 BS [ca. 1695]; Phakīr Rām dtd. 1086 BS [ca. 1679], 1093 BS [ca. 1686], 1095 BS [ca. 1688]; Rāmeśvar Dvija dtd. 1087 BS [ca. 1680]; Vidyāpati dtd. 1090 BS [ca. 1683]; Gaṅgārām Kavi dtd. 1097 BS [ca. 1690].

18. Ghanarām Cakravarttī, *Satyanārāyaṇ ras sindhu*, 2–3.

annoys characters in the narratives—a clear indication that the authors deliberately counted on this effect, and played on these symbolic currencies. This play has a very serious side, for the narrative strategy of conflation serves to create momentary confusions among the characters that predictably elicit spontaneous, unreflective responses of ridicule and invective. These outbreaks create an opening for Satya Pīr to instruct the naïve in a way that is all the more compelling by virtue of the extreme situation he manipulates by playing on their prejudices, hubris, and ignorance to demonstrate the inappropriateness of those perspectives to the more basic business of living, or at least the need to question their commonplaces. To the delight of the listener or reader, he is not above resorting to more brutal magical persuasions to make his point. The content of those biting symbolic homilies varies dramatically, depending on the author's proclivity, for the narratives are anything but uniform in this regard. Apart from these occasional and short opportunities to lecture or preach a basic morality—the content is understandably theologically thin, nearly devoid of doctrine altogether, but frequently contains a biting critique of prejudicial religious practices and class or caste bigotry—most of Satya Pīr's messages emerge through the resolution of predictable dramatic situations.

Variations in the tales reflect the creativity and skill of the poets, rather than differences in plot or message. The frame narrative which sets up the classic trilogy of tales provides some opportunities for improvisation, though authors do have greater latitude to diversify the obstacles thrown in the path of the merchant before he gains success, that tale being always the longest and most elaborate of the set. As we shall see, the merchant's tale clearly shares the same impulse that drives the *maṅgal kāvya* genre as a whole—the establishment of the deity's worship and evidence of its benefits—and the earliest versions of the tale were being composed when the *maṅgal kāvya* was approaching the zenith of its popularity. The complete cycle functions to establish the worship of Satya Pīr as Satya Nārāyaṇ for the whole of society, from the highest-ranking *brāhmaṇs* to the lowest classes who clear the land, including indigenous communities, and those in between, the merchants and kings. Occasionally, but only in extremely elaborate productions, we find a fourth tale about the king variously named Tuṅgadhvaj or Vaṃśadhvaj, who encounters cowherders worshipping Satya Pīr but refuses the offer of *śinni*, an act that results in the death of all one hundred of his sons; he sees his error, worships with sincere devotion, and their lives are restored.[19] While we might not

19. One of the earliest texts of the genre includes the Sanskrit text from the *Skanda purāṇa*, with the standard stories of the poor *brāhmaṇ*, the woodcutter, and the merchant, and the concluding the tale of King Vaṃśadhvaj appearing in the *revā khaṇḍa*; see Vyāsadeva, *Satyanārāyaṇa nāmaka granthaḥ*, Sanskrit text edited by Rājacandra Rāya, Bengali translation by Dharmadās Mukhopādhyāy (Kalikātā: Kāśīnāth Śīl at Jñānoday Yantra, 1268 BS [ca. 1861]). See also Rāsvihāri Sāṃkhyatīrtha, *Satyanārāyaṇ vrat kathā*, edited with Bangla translation by Rāmdev Miśra (Murshidabad: Rāmdeva Miśra for Haribhaktipradāyinī Sabhā of Baharampur at Rādhāramaṇ Press, 1315 BS [ca. 1908]); that abbreviated tale covers only three pages, 53–55. See also Meghnāth Bhaṭṭācāryya, *Satya nārāyaṇ vratkathā* (Kalikātā:

unreasonably speculate that the merchant's tale was always the driving impulse since it is always so much longer than the other two, the addition of those two abbreviated tales of the poor *brāhmaṇ* and the woodcutters, even the cowherder's tale, was necessary to signal Satya Pīr's extension of help to all active parts of society on the frontier.

Ghanarām gives us the opening for identifying the narrative codes common to this set when he notes that Satya Pīr lacked the *recognition* among those major groups that constituted traditional *hinduyāni* society. The frame for recognition was made possible by *vaiṣṇav avatār* theory. He is a descent (*avatār*) of Viṣṇu Nārāyaṇ in *purāṇik* terms. Parenthetically, it should be noted that there are a very small number of texts that also include a connection to the uniquely Bengali deity Dharma Ṭhākur, such as Phayajullā's *Satya pīr pāñcālī*[20] and Rāmāi Paṇḍit's *Śūnyapurāṇ*.[21] The reference to Dharma Ṭhākur does not seem to compete with his identification with Nārāyaṇ, but as one would expect in these tales, the theological niceties are avoided; in other terms, from a narratological perspective, the association does not change the trajectories of action, but from a theological perspective, this loose association may represent a frame of reference that simply seeks *equivalences* among other figures of divinity. This is not idle speculation since at least one of the authors, the same Ghanarām Cakravartī, is known to have also composed a *Dharma maṅgal*[22] in addition to his Satya Pīr text already quoted. Put another way, the equivalences seem to efface sectarian distinctions, while subtly projecting the underlying reality based on a traditional Indic pantheon, while the *musalmāni* forms are simply new guises for this Kali Age.

Although the nature of that *avatār* can vary, Satya Pīr is generally accorded the status of *yugāvatār*, Nārāyaṇ's incarnational descent for the Kali Age. The logic of this characterization is quite predictable, for this is one of the earliest propositions and one that is explicitly invoked in the Satya Pīr tales a position that derives from *Bhagavad gītā*, as we have seen repeatedly in other stories. Nārāyaṇ promises to descend whenever the *dharma* has languished, and to assume a form conditioned by the needs of the people of that age (*yug*). Once Satya Pīr is recognized, he is

Saṃskṛta Pres Ḍipajiṭorī, 1306 BS [ca. 1899]), who calls it the *Vaṃśadhvaj gop saṃvād*, a variation on the theme of the hunt and encounter with Satyadev; the text by Rāmgopāl Rāy likewise includes the extra tale titled *Vaṁśadhvajoddhār*; see Rāmgopāl Rāy, *Satyamaṅgal bā satyanārāyaṇ dever vratkathā o pūjāpaddhati* (Kalikātā: Jayakṛṣṇa Caudhurī, 1835 *śaka* [ca. 1913]), 31–35.

20. *Satya pīr pāñcālī* of Phayajullā, discussed in Girīndranāth Dās, *Bāṃlā pīr sāhityer kathā*, 453–54. My copy of Phayajullā's text with title page missing—the only copy I could locate anywhere—is badly printed, with ink and dirt clogging the type face so that characters are smudged or altogether indecipherable, the bleeding through the cheap paper obscures text on the recto and verso, and of course large holes abound in the text courtesy of white ants. As a result, I can only partially confirm Das's observation, but I have found his reporting to be generally very reliable.

21. Rāmāi Paṇḍit, *Śūnyapurāṇ*; see chap. 5, n. 71.

22. Ghanarām Cakravarttī, *Dharma maṅgal*.

easily understood to be present to help right the *dharma* of the Kali Age, each new telling incorporating him into a familiar Indic world, completing the process of *accommodation*. The opening frame narrative of the three tales gives us explicit clues to the different strategies by which authors sought to accommodate Satya Pīr into that familiar framework through a series of overt intertextual references that link him to *purāṇik* and epic tales.

Many of the stories begin with Nārāyaṇ asleep on Śeṣa, coiled on the primal ocean of milk or alternately holding forth in his heavenly court. Nārada—that celestial gadfly who is just as responsible for stirring up problems as he is for coming to everyone's aid—journeys to Nārāyaṇ's presence to alert him to the malaise that threatens to engulf civilization on earth. After an exchange of traditional greetings, Ṇārada invites Nārāyaṇ to survey the situation for himself and determine an appropriate response. As Nārāyaṇ wakes up to the full extent of *dharma*'s decay, Nārada prods him to descend in a form people will understand, and because foreigners alien to the traditional brāhmaṇical homeland (*madhya deś*) are everywhere in power, would it not make sense, he reasons, to play on that familiarity for this particular descent, that is, to assume a form recognized as originating from the religious world of those in power? The prologue closes when Nārāyaṇ takes the advice to heart and descends in the form of Satya Pīr, overtly a *pīr*, but in reality none other than the celestial Viṣṇu Nārāyaṇ (those texts that omit the prologue and join the action *in medias res* generally start here). Even for those tellings that do not explicitly provide this narrative frame to justify the descent, it is implied, for it everywhere replicates the *purāṇik* premise of the *avatār*, as Harimohan Śarmma perhaps most eloquently states in a very high *sādhu bhāṣā* register.[23] In what would appear to be an effort to provide a clear *purāṇik* authority and Sanskritize the story, Rādhānāth Mitra composed a text in 1889 called simply *Satyanārāyaṇ*, in which he uses the Nārada visit to frame the tale, exhorting good people, especially *brāhmaṇs*, to discipline their conduct and worship, which Nārāyaṇ recognizes is deteriorating in the Kali Age. He refers repeatedly to the *revā khaṇḍa* of the *Skanda purāṇa* as his source, and he includes the tales of the poor *brāhmaṇ*, the woodcutters, and the merchant, whose wife Līlāvatī and daughter Kalāvatī play much larger roles than in most versions. He also adds the fourth tale, titled "Vaṃśadhvaja," in a synoptic telling of the encounter of the king with the cowherders. *Not once does he mention Satya Pīr*, the only example in this vast literature I have seen where the name Satya Pīr has been systematically eliminated. Everyplace one would expect to see Satya Pīr, he substitutes Satyadev. Nowhere does he propose that *śirṇi* should be the offering of choice—no variant of the word is used—but rather it is a somewhat

23. See Harimohan Śarmma, *Satyakathā* (Ḍhākā: Harimohan Basāk at Ḍhākā Giriś Pres, 1277 BS [ca. 1870]).

more complicated concoction offered as part of a *Satyanārāyaṇ vrat*, which he details in the opening section and then repeats throughout the text.[24]

On occasion, Yudhiṣṭhīr replaces Nārada as the one who alerts Nārāyaṇ to the disaster that awaits the earth if he does not take action; for instance, see the explicitly titled tale by Dvāraknāth Pāl: *Satyanārāyaṇer pāñcālī: Kṛṣṇa yudhiṣṭhīr saṃvād o kalāvatār upākhyān.*[25] In the tale told by Dvija Rāmdhan, the frame is suggestively complicated when Nārāyaṇ seems to be distracted with Lakṣmī's presence while the earth is in decay.[26] In a twentieth-century version of the tale by Dhīrendra Nāth Mukhopādhyāy, Satya Pīr is paired with Śani or the Evil Eye, which is not surprising given the generally somber tone of the state of the world, and with Trilakṣya Pīr, whose own textual tradition is extremely truncated to a single vignette about a devotee who attempts to pay homage to all three hundred thousand (*trilakṣya*) *pīrs* who have taken action to help alleviate the ills of the world, only to discover that to worship one is to worship them all—and they are all manifestations of Nārāyaṇ.[27] Finally, one author, Surnāth Bhaṭṭācāryya, writing in the early twentieth century, noted that the popular versions of the cycle as told by Rāmbhadra and Śivrām were outdated and did not really speak to the modern condition; so in addition to retelling the three tales, he "updated" the accompanying *pūjā*, and even included songs, which are interspersed throughout the text. Writing in a very Sanskritized highfalutin *sādhu bhāṣā* form of Bangla, he notes that regardless of religious persuasion—Hindu, Muslim, Christian—we are all humans and we share the same basic laws and moral imperatives, so his approach was to attempt to rectify the theological slant to reflect that extended universalism.[28] In his exercise, we see encapsulated in a single text how the narratives of

24. Rādhānath Mitra, *Satyanārāyaṇ*, 2nd ed. (Kalikātā: Sāradāprasād Mukhopādhyay, 1889).

25. Dvāraknāth Pāl, *Satyanārāyaṇer pāñcālī: Kṛṣṇa yudhiṣṭhīr saṃvād o kalāvatār upākhyān* (Ḍhākā: Lachman Baśak at Ḍhākā Bāṅglā Press, n.d. [1285 BS (ca. 1878)]). For the same type of frame, see Dīnhin Dās, *Śrīśrīsatyanārāyaṇer pāñcālī: Līlāvati o kalāvatī upākhyān*, ed. Sītānāth Basāk, 72nd printing (Kalikātā: Sītānāth Ādarśa Lāibrerī, 1979); that the copy I have is in its 72nd printing suggests something of the popularity of these small texts, which cost between fifty *paiśa* to several rupees. Dvija Rāmbhadra likewise uses Yudhiṣṭhīr to initiate the action; see Dvija Rāmbhadra, "Satyadev saṃhitā," ed. Vyomakeś Mustaphī, *Baṅgīya sāhitya pariṣat patrikā* 8, no. 2 (1308 BS [ca. 1901]: 131–36.

26. Dvija Rāmdhan, *Satya Nārāyaṇer punthi* (Kalikātā: Rāju Pāblikeśans, n.d.); interestingly it is Satyadev who instructs the author in a dream to compose the text (pp. 4–5).

27. See Dhīrendra Nāth Mukhopādhyāy, *Śani satyanārāyaṇ o trilakṣadever pāñcālī* (Kalikātā: by the author, 1319 BS [ca. 1912]). A slightly different version of the tale can be found in two manuscripts: Anonymous [Harinārāyaṇ?], *Trilakṣya pīrer pāñcālī*, Bengali MS no. 74, Dhaka University, complete, 3 folios, dtd. 1246 BS [1839]; and Anonymous [Harinārāyaṇ?], *Tinlakṣya pīrer pāñcālī*, Bengali MS no. 1313, Dhaka University, complete, 3 folios, dtd. 1259 BS [ca. 1852].

28. Surnāth Bhaṭṭācāryya, *Śrīśrīsatyanārāyaṇ vratkathā* (Kalikātā: by the author at Bi. Pi. Emer Pres, 1321 BS [ca. 1914]); the observations about the need for updating, etc., are found in the introduction, pp. 3–6. It is interesting that he names Rāmbhadra and Śivrām as popular authors because over the printing history of the cycle, Śaṅkarācārya and Rāmdev have emerged as the most oft-printed tellers of the tales, perhaps suggesting a change in popularity or preference for style over the last century.

Satya Pīr were deployed in such a way that they could cross the gap from discourse to the everyday world through the ritual process. The key was the promise of positive outcomes in the world of ordinary things for anyone who would perform the *pūjā* to Satya Pīr. As a result, the three-story cycle became a staple *kathā* of the ritual *vrat*, which now women in many households of Bengal routinely conduct. The telling of the story in the context of ritual would improve one's lot.

The *vrats* are relatively simple rituals performed within the household, usually by women (with children attending), and are primarily designed to look after the general weal of the family, the obvious reason why Satya Pīr or Satya Nārāyaṇ was incorporated into the monthly cycle.[29] The explicit ritual instruction for worshiping Satya Pīr emerged during the frenzy of printing in the late nineteenth and early twentieth centuries. Unlike the tales of the other *phakirs* and *pīrānīs* we have examined, the instruction is explicit, but simple in nature. Characters within the narrative will, in times of need or as a result of their thankfulness for Satya Pīr's help, make a simple offering of *śirṇi* (alt. *śirṇi*, *śinni*, *sinni*). But beyond an occasional vague suggestion, instruction on how to make it and offer it falls outside the narrative proper; as we might expect of these tales, the offering is simply noted. The explicit ritual instruction tends to be found in a paratextual apparatus that is appended to the narrative, as either a preface or an appendix in print editions, which is to say that apart from the general directive in the narrative to offer *śirṇi*, the ritual instruction lies outside the narrative and frames it; it is through that paratextual apparatus that the narrative eases into the world of action. One author, Bidubar Ghoṣ, would appear to be one of the first to include instruction on how to do the *pūjā* of the *vrat* in the body of the text, integrating directly into the narrative some of the material that in most manuscripts was paratextual.[30] This manuscript

29. The truncated story of Satya Pīr or Satya Nārāyaṇ is found in virtually every compilation of women's household *vrats*, with publications, often anonymous, running in the hundreds since the nineteenth century; for a particularly well executed example, see Vasantakumār Dāsī, *Meyeder vratkathā bā vrat māhātmya*, edited by Rākhālcandra Dās (Kalikātā: Mahendranāth Kar at Mehendra Lāibrerī, n.d. [1340 BS (ca. 1933)]). *Vrat* literature, which is often connected with the visual dimension of the ritual process, is considerable; see Sudhir Ranjan Das, *Folk Religion in Bengal: A Study in Vrata Rites* (Calcutta: S.C. Kar, 1953); Eva Maria Gupta, *Brata und Ālpanā in Bengalen* (Wiesbaden: Franz Steiner Verlag, 1985).

30. Encased in a single wrapper in the collection, there are two manuscripts of this text, virtually identical with respect to content, but radically different in construction. The first (MS 747A) is produced in the traditional manner of loose-leaf pages in the elongated landscape orientation. The second (MS 747B) is a high-end production, written in a careful hand on machine-milled watermarked paper, the individual leaves stitched together along the left and which are oriented, not in the traditional manuscript landscape orientation, but in portrait on the order of a western printed book, approximately 8vo. The binding edge laces together individual leaves, rather than a folded signature, which suggests mimicry of print without knowledge of the technology. Significantly this second work is titled *Satya nārāyaṇ pustak* (that is, "book," rather than *pāñcālī*, which is employed in the body of the text itself). Curiously the authorship of the text would seem to be a joint work, possibly started by Bidubar Ghoṣ

seems to have anticipated the move toward printing as the norm for the emergence of the *vrat kathās* that are routinely performed in the household.

The most common instruction indicates a generic *pūjā* as its model, but one that does not require the offices of a *brāhmaṇ* to perform; it can be and is done by people of all social ranks and religious orientation. In one printed edition from 1909, the cover declares: "This edition includes a *pūjāpaddhati* (ritual instruction) which is not abbreviated. Even children can see it and learn how to do the *pūjā*. Women will be able to prepare precisely everything they need to perform the *pūjā*."[31] Rice or rice-flour, sugar, thickened milk, banana, and betel are formed into a ball and offered in a manner that anyone familiar with devotional *pūjās* would recognize. The worship is aniconic; no image is used to receive the offering, though occasionally a small dais or simple stool might be set as the focal point. On occasion a sacred space is first demarcated by inserting sticks or banana stalks (originally arrows) into the ground at the four corners. The formulaic reference for the dais is a golden *āstānā*, which designates the stand, the haunt, or the abode of the *pīr* (which is also a term occasionally used to reference a *pīr*'s tomb). Not infrequently, the dais is spelled *āsthān* or *āsthānā*, which—considering the overall literacy of the authors—can be read not as a spelling mistake but as a playful neologism that conveniently conflates the *pīr*'s place of residence (*sthān*) or the threshold of access to the *pīr* or, more explicitly, the *pīr*'s tomb (both from Persian *āsitāna*), and the devotee's "confidence," "faith," or "allegiance," signaled by the term *āsthā*. Once the *śinni* is offered, the leftovers (sometimes called *naivedya*, but unlike in other *vaiṣṇav* contexts, seldom *ucchiṣṭa*) are consumed as *prasād*: ingestible grace, food transubstantiated by the touch of the divine. Regardless of what the leftovers are called, the offering has to be made with sincerity to be effective, and if so the *pūjā* is capable of effacing any number of different offenses (*aparādh*).[32]

While the benefits are consistent with the idea of *prasād*, these technical terms (*naivedya*, *ucchiṣṭa*, *prasād*) were not used regularly until certain authors began the process of Sanskritizing the ritual. Rāmdev Miśra, the well-known and highly productive second series editor and publisher of *gauḍīya vaiṣṇav* texts on behalf of the Haribhaktipradāyinī Sabhā in Murshidabad in the early twentieth century, reproduced the sanctioned edition of the Satya Nārāyaṇ cycle originally compiled and written by Rāsvihāri Sāṃkhyatīrtha, which included twelve full pages of

---

and completed by Niṣākar Ghoṣ—but that is speculation based on the initial appearance of Bidubar in the first signature line (*bhaṇitā*) and Niṣākar in the remainder; the attribution in the catalogue distinguishes the two as separate authors. Niṣākar Ghoṣ, *Satyanārāyaṇ pāñcālī*, Bengali MS no.747A, Dhaka University, complete, 12 folios, n.d. Bidubar Ghoṣ, *Satya nārāyaṇ pustak*, Bengali MS 747B, Dhaka University, complete, 12 folios, dtd. 1265 BS [ca. 1858].

31. Śyāmcaraṇ Kaviratna, ed., *Satyanārāyaṇ o śubhacanīr kathā*, 2nd ed. (Kalikātā: by the editor through Gurudās Caṭṭopādhyāy at Bengal Medical Library, 1315 BS [ca. 1909]).

32. Gaurīśaṅkar, *Satyanārāyaṇ pustak*, Bengali MS no. 1584B, Dhaka University, complete 19 folios, dtd. 1726 *śaka* [ca. 1804], folios 18a–b.

instruction for the preparation and offering of *śīrṇi* (he understandably uses the high or *sādhu* form of the word). This instructional text extended the number of ingredients to twenty-eight, but when the compounds are analyzed, the full number is forty-three discrete elements—the extreme opposite of the advertisement indicating that even children can learn it. He also integrated other features into the ritual instruction in Sanskrit (*pūjāpaddhati*): worship of the nine planets (*navagraha*) and a eulogistic *stotra* to them, worship of the five deities (*pañcadevatā*), and then *satya nārāyaṇa* worship proper, and accompanying poetic eulogies (*stava*).[33] A decade later Rāmgopāl Rāy's version contained twenty-two detailed pages for performing the offering.[34] In a book that is undated, but appears to have been published in the 1970s, Ratneśvar Tantrajyotiṣaśāstrī devoted fifteen pages to the offering of the *pūjā*, including illustrations of thirteen hand gestures (*mudras*), a feature nowhere else encountered in the scores of texts consulted, but not surprising given his professional titles.[35] In these dramatic expansions one can see the hand of reform-minded élites, seeking to Sanskritize the worship of Satya Pīr to make it conform to that Satya Nārāyaṇ worship found more widely in North India, while eliminating all *musalmāni*-related terminology, but not the structure of the story or the naming of the protagonist himself as a *phakir* or *pīr*.[36] It is interesting to note that this impulse toward Sanskritization and the appropriation of the *pūjā* to Satya Pīr and Satya Nārāyaṇ in the *vrat* cycle seems to be the culmination of simple assertions about how the devotee's diligence would open the way to heaven itself. The manuscript of Satyānanda's *Satyar pāñcālī*, dated 1765—a book that I have not been able to locate in print—advised in the concluding verses of the narrative that should one worship Satya Nārāyaṇ as described, one would certainly gain *vaikuṇṭha*, heaven.[37] Another unpublished anonymous manuscript written fifteen years earlier indicated clearly that "if you do not worship Satya Nārāyaṇ, you go to hell (*narak gaman*)."[38] In the above-mentioned manuscript, Bidubar Ghoṣ

33. Rāsvihāri Sāṃkhyatīrtha, *Satyanārāyaṇ vrat kathā*. In the introduction Rāmdev Miśra indicated that the text had originally been published under the name of Rāmnārāyaṇ Vidyāratna, who was the series' first editor and who was still alive, the attribution of which he was now correcting in the second version by giving full credit to Rāsavihāri Sāṃkhyatīrtha.

34. Rāmgopāl Rāy, *Satyamaṅgal bā satyanārāyaṇ dever vratkathā o pūjāpaddhati*); see n. 19 (above).

35. Ratneśvara Tantrajyotiṣaśāstrī, ed., *Śrīśrīsatyanārāyaṇ o śubhacunī pūjāpaddhati* (Kalikātā: Puṣpa eṇḍ Koṃ., n.d.).

36. For the Sanskrit versions and an analysis of their *pūjā*, see the chapter titled "Examples of Occasional *Pūjās*: *Satya Nārāyaṇvrata*" in Gudrun Bühnemann, *Pūjā: A Study in Smarta Ritual*, De Nobili Research Library Publications, vol. 15 (Vienna: Institute for Indology, University of Vienna, 1988), 200–13. For a contemporary version of the story and an account of the *pūjā*, see Anoop Chandola, *The Way to True Worship: A Popular Story of Hinduism* (Lanham, MD: University Press of America, 1991).

37. Satyānanda, *Satyar pāñcālī*, Kṛṣṇakanta Rāy Collection, Bengali MS no. K-67, Dhaka University, complete, 17 folios, dtd. 1171 BS [ca. 1765], folio 17a.

38. Anonymous, *Satyanārāyaṇ pustak*, Kṛṣṇakanta Rāy Collection, Bengali MS no. K-434, complete, 8 folios, Dhaka University, dtd. 1157 BS [ca. 1750], folio 8a, line 9—folio 8b, line 1.

and Niṣākar Ghoṣ explained that one needed a proper priest or *purohit* to perform the *pūjā*, and signaled in general terms the negative impact of not performing the worship. But apparently merit will accrue simply by copying the manuscript, for the scribe wrote in the more elaborate of the two manuscripts that "he transcribed the text in the home of Gaura Candra Sen in the western reaches of Ḍhākā *jelā*. He wrote for the welfare of his relatives in Ḍhākā, Śrīhaṭṭa, and in the West."[39]

In keeping with this move toward Sanskritization, by the early twentieth century, the most common overt intertextual references were to the previously noted *Bhaviṣya purāṇa* and *Skanda purāṇa* (*revā khaṇḍa*), which are cited as the sources of the trilogy of tales.[40] Some authors simply referred to these sources, but others included the relevant passages in Sanskrit.[41] Both of these Sanskrit *purāṇas* are among the most malleable in the tradition, with some additions and emendations to the texts appearing well after the sixteenth century, about the time the Satya Pīr narratives began to circulate. The lateness and the lack of a fixed text, especially in the case of the *Bhaviṣya purāṇa*, opens the distinct possibility that the stories circulated first in Bangla, then subsequently were incorporated into the *purāṇik* text, before being reintroduced in Bangla. While that speculation exceeds the ambit of this current inquiry, whether or not it is so does not matter, because the authors who took this tack of referring back to one or the other of these *purāṇas* were attempting to domesticate the story into comfortable *purāṇik* idiom. *Legitimation* follows *recognition* in the process, so the by-then familiar form of the mendicant *pīr* or *phakir* was made suitable to reveal a new *dharma* that would unite the *jaban*

39. Bidubar Ghoṣ, *Satya nārāyaṇ pustak*, Bengali MS 747B, folio 12a.

40. In the manuscript of the *Satyanārāyaṇ pustak*, the anonymous author indicates the source of the story as the *Brahmā purāṇa*, which is the only such attribution I found in the literature. I was unable to locate any such passage in standard editions of the *purāṇa*. See Anonymous, *Satyanārāyaṇ pustak*, Kṛṣṇakanta Rāy Collection, Bengali MS no. K-434, folio 8b, line 2. For the definitive work on the history of the *purāṇas* and *upapurāṇas* and their construction and dating, see Ludo Rocher, *The Purāṇas*, in *A History of Indian Literature*, ed. Jan Gonda, vol. 2: *Epics and Sanskrit Religious Literature*, fascicle 3 (Wiesbaden: Otto Harrassowtiz, 1986); the *Skanda* and *Bhaviṣya* are both classified as *upapurāṇas*. See the pioneering work on *upapurāṇas*, R.C. Hazra, *Studies in the Upapurāṇas*, 2 vols. (Calcutta: Sanskrit College, 1958). It should be noted that at the same times the *Skanda* and *Bhaviṣya purāṇas* added this later material, the worship of Satya Nārāyaṇ was becoming increasingly popular across northern India.

41. Many include the Sanskrit text and/or translations or retellings of the *revā khaṇḍa* of the *Skanda purāṇa* and the section of the *Bhaviṣya purāṇa*; see also Rāmeśvar Bhaṭṭācārya, *Satyanārāyaṇ*, ed. Rādhāvallabh Śīl (Kalikātā: Hindu Press, 1276 BS [ca. 1869]); Īśvarcandra Kar, *Satya nārāyaṇer pāñcālī* (Bariśāl: Denovandoo Kar at Satya Prakāś Yantra, 1930 *saṃvat* [ca. 1872]); Rāmkānth Nyāyapañcānan Bhaṭṭācāryya, *Bāṅgālā pāñcālī kathā: Revā khaṇḍokta satyadev vrat kathāmūlak*, ed. Rasrañjan Sen Gupta (Kahliśākoṭ, Bariśāl: n.p., 1322 BS [ca. 1915]); K. Sadānanda, *Pāñcālī satyanārāyaṇ kathā* (Kāśī: Raghunandan Prasād at Bhavanna Tulsī Pustakālay, 1929), n.b., the text is Bangla in *nagari* script; Candrakānt Sarkār, *Satyanārāyaṇ nāmak granthaḥ arthāt vratprakāś o mahimā varṇan*, ed. Rajanīkānt Sarkār (Kalikātā: Umeścandra Madak at Jñān Dvīpak Pres, 1281 BS [ca. 1874]); Rāmeśvar Śarmma, *Satyanārāyaṇ* (Kalikātā: Nṛtyalāl Śīl, 1281 BS [ca. 1874]); Rādhāmohan Tarkālaṃkār Bhaṭṭācāryya, *Satya nārāyaṇ vratkathā* (Kalikātā: Prakāścandra Bandyopādhyāy at Nūtan Sen Pres, 1819 *śaka* [ca. 1897]).

with the *vaiṣṇav*. This is the final act of *appropriation*, wherein the new object of religiosity is fully incorporated into the existing *vaiṣṇav* cosmological and theological structures. As counterintuitive as this move to incorporate the *jaban* Satya Pīr must have been to some, the strategy was grounded in an unassailable logic; that is, it must have been made to conform to expectations in a way that was undeniably appropriate to the *vaiṣṇav* conception of, or at least orientation to, the world. That is precisely where the narratives begin.

The process of legitimation starts by having an experienced *brāhmaṇ*, who serves as the representative of traditional society—in a manner symptomatic of the degradations of the Kali Age, a society that has failed to support him—recognize the form of Satya Pīr by affirming his "true" identity as Nārāyaṇ. From this simple beginning the *pīr*'s form is gradually valorized throughout the whole of brāhmaṇical society, which is "documented" in the set of three stories—and that set is the overwhelming favorite form for the practicing *vaiṣṇav*.[42] Nearly three-

42. There are both pre- and early colonial authors whose texts have seen print, several of them regularly, all telling the same basic trilogy. Bhāratcandra's version of the tale is considered especially elegant though short. Among the many, see Bhāratcandra Rāy, "Satyanārāyaṇ vratkathā," in *Bhāratcandra granthāvalī*, ed. Vrajendranāth Bandyopādhyāy (Kalikātā: Baṅgīya Sāhitya Pariṣat, 1357 BS [ca. 1950]), 391–96; Bhāratcandra, "Satyapīr vratkathā," in *Bhāratcandra racanāsaṃgraha*, ed. Kṣetra Gupta and Viṣṇu Basu (Kalikātā: Bhaumik eṇḍ Sans, 1974), 430–35; and the inexpensive popular edition, Bhāratcandra, "Satyapīr kathā," in *Bhāratcandra granthāvalī*, ed. Kṣetra Gupta and Viṣṇu Basu (Kalikātā: Basumati Sāhitya Maṇḍir, n.d.), 1–3. Others include Dvija Aśvinīkumār, *Śīśrīsatyanārāyaṇer pāñcālī: Pūjāpaddhati, dhyān, pranām, phardamālā evaṃ daridra brāhmaṇer upākhyān sambalita* (Kalikātā: Subhāṣnāth Pustakālay, n.d.); the synoptic text by Dvija Dīnarām, *Nārāyaṇer dever pāñcālī*, ed. Abdul Karim, *Baṅgīya sāhitya pariṣat patrikā* 12, no. 4 (1312 BS [ca. 1905]): 189–92; the elegant and literarily sophisticated text by Dvija Raghunāth, "Satyanārāyaṇer punthi," ed. Satiścandra Rāy, *Baṅgīya sāhitya pariṣat patrikā* 24, no. 1 (1324 BS [ca. 1917]): 21–38; Dvija Rāmkṛṣṇa, *Satyanārāyaner pustak*, ed. Vīrcandra Cakravarttī (Ḍhākā: Ḍhākā Giriśyantra, 1283 BS [ca. 1876]); Dvija Rāmkṛṣṇa, *Satyanārāyaṇer pāñcālī* (Kalikātā: Aruṇoday Ghoṣ, 1281 BS [ca. 1874]); another short text by Dvija Viśveśvar, "Satyanārāyaṇ pāñcālī," ed. Vrajsundar Sānyāl, *Baṅgīya sāhitya pariṣat patrikā* 8, no. 3 (1308 BS [ca. 1901]): 193–200.

More recent mid-nineteenth- to twentieth-century works in the same vein include: Rājcandra Rāy, trans., *Satyanārāyaṇ nāmak granthaḥ* (Kalikātā: Jñānoday Pres, 1268 BS [ca. 1861]); Raghunāth Cakravartī, *Satyanārāyaṇ punthi*, ed. Caitanyaprasād Poddār (Kalikātā: Eṇ. El. Śīl Pres, 1277 BS [ca. 1870]); Raghunāth Cakravartī, *Satyanārāyaṇ punthi*, ed. Caitanya Prasād Poddār Mahāśay, 2nd ed. (Noyākhālī: Yogendramohan Poddār, 1315 BS [ca. 1908]); Rāmdayāl Bandyopādhyāy, *Satyanārāyaṇer pāñcālī*, 2nd ed. (Ḍhākā: Brajdās Bābājī at Giriś Pres, 1279 BS [ca 1872]); Kaliprasād Dattaja Mahāśay, *Satyanārāyaṇ grantha* (Ḍhākā: Jagadānanda Basu at Ḍhākā Giriś Yantra, 1281 BS [ca. 1874]); Īśāncandra Rāy, *Satyanārāyaṇer pāñcālī*, 1st ed. (Kalikātā: Akṣay Kumār Rāy eṇḍ Koṃ. n.d. [1876]); Baṇkim Bihāri Majumdār, *Satyanārāyaṇer kathā* (Kalikātā: Bhavanīpur Somaprakāś Pres, 1284 BS [ca. 1877]); Golokcandra Sengupta, *Satyanārāyaṇ pāñcālī* (Midnapur: Nibaraṇcandra Dāsgupta at Hari Sabhā Pres, 1319 BS [ca. 1912]); Kālīpada Devśarmma, *Śrīśrīsatyanārāyaṇer pāñcālī* (Ḍhākā: by editor at Bāherak Hari Sabhā, 1327 BS [ca. 1920]); Rām Śāstrī, ed., *Śrīśrīsatyanārāyaṇ vratkathā bā satya nārāyaṇer pāñcālī* (Kalikātā: Kṛṣṇa Bhaṭṭācāryya at Vāṇī Pustakālay, 1327 BS [ca. 1920]); Śivacandra Sen, *Satyanārāyaṇer pāñcālī*, ed. Nibāraṇcandra Basu (Ḍhākā: by the editor at Bhikṭoriā Pres, 1328 BS [ca. 1921]); Śyāmākānt Tarkapañcānan, ed., *Satyanārāyaṇ vratkathā* (Vārāṇasī: Vāmārañjan Ṭhākur, 1330 BS [ca. 1923]);

quarters of all manuscripts and printed texts are devoted to the three-step narrative precisely because its effectiveness lies in its progression, each story creating greater expectations for the next, as all parts of society are invited to follow Satya Pīr. Of all the renditions, the two versions attributed to the Bengali poets Śaṅkarācārya and Rāmeśvar[43] prove most popular and are frequently printed together.[44]

The third tale, that of the merchant, the analogue to the popular *maṅgal kāvya*, seems to have created the greatest traction and was often composed and published as a stand-alone work, the two most sophisticated and powerful versions composed by famous Vikrampūr poet Lālā Jaykṛṣṇa Sen, the *Harilīlā*, and the *Satyanārāyaṇ punthi* of Kavivallabh.[45] Not surprisingly, it is this trilogy which

---

Premnāth Bhaṭṭācāryya, comp., *Satyanārāyaṇ pāñcālī: Līlāvatī o kalāvatī upākhyān sambalitā*, 2nd ed. (n.p.: by the editor at Bāndhav Press in Utrāil Kumuk Bhavan, n.d.).

43. Of the two, Rāmeśvar most often appears separately; the most reliable single-author edition is Rāmeśvar Bandyopādhyāy, *Satyapīrer kathā*, ed. Nagendranāth Gupta (Kalikātā: Kalikātā Viśvavidyālay, 1336 BS [ca. 1929]); see also Rāmeśvar, *Satyanārāyaṇ*, ed. Trailoknāth Datta, 2nd ed. (Kalikātā: by the editor, 1283 BS [ca. 1876]); Rāmeśvar, *Rāmeśvarī satyanārāyaṇ pāñcālī*, 5th ed. (Khāñtāi: Madhusudān Jānā, 1330 BS [ca. 1923]); Rāmeśvar, *Śrīśrīsatyanārāyaṇer pāñcālī: Līlāvatī, kalāvatī o daridra brāhmaṇ upākhyān (pūjādravya o pūjāpaddhati sambalita)*, ed. Paśupati Caṭṭopādhyāy (Kalikātā: Jenārel Lāibrerī, n.d.); Rāmeśvar, *Śrīśrīsatyanārāyaṇer pāñcālī: Pūjāpaddhati, dhyān, praṇām, pharddamālā, evaṃ darīdra brāhmaṇ upākhyān*, ed. Tīrthanāth Bhaṭṭācāryya Kāvyatīrtha (Kalikātā: Oriyeṇṭ Lāibrerī, n.d.); and Rāmeśvar, *Śrīśrīsatyanārāyaṇ o subacanī vratkathā bā pāñcālī*, ed. Śrīmantu Cakravartī (Kalikātā: Māyā Lāibrerī, n.d.).

44. These two texts are available in multiple *baṭ-tolā* editions and have been printed together as many times as they have been issued separately. I have personally examined more than fifty such publications. Typical among them is Śaṅkarācārya and Rāmeśvar, *Śrīśrīsatyanārāyaṇer pāñcālī: Līlāvatī kalāvatī daridra brāhmaṇer upakhyān (pūjādravya, pūjāvidhi, dhyān o praṇām sambalita)*, ed. Gaurāṅgasundar Bhaṭṭācāryya (Kalikātā: Rajendra Lāibrerī, n.d.). With usually only relatively minor variations, see the previously cited Śaṅkarācārya and Rāmeśvar, *Śrīśrīsatyanārāyaṇ o śubhacunī pūjāpaddhati*, ed. Rateśvar Tantrajyotiṣaśāstrī (Kalikātā: Puṣpa eṇḍ Koṃ., n.d.). Many of the texts are nearly identical, suggesting the nature of *baṭ-tolā* printing; see Śaṅkarācārya and Rāmeśvar, *Śrīśrīsatyanārāyaṇer pāñcālī: Līlāvati, kalāvatī o daridra brāhmaṇ upākhyān*, ed. Avināścandra Mukhopādhyāy and Sudrendranāth Bhaṭṭācāryya (Kalikātā: Śrī Kārttik Candra Basu at Kalikātā Ṭāun Lāibrerī, 1360 BS [ca. 1953]); Śaṅkarācāryā and Rāmeśvar Bhattācāryya, *Śrīśrīsatyanārāyaṇer pāñcālī: Līlāvatī, kalāvatī o daridra brāhmaṇer upākhyān*, ed. Paṇḍit Śrī Kālīprasanna Vidyāratna (Kalakātā: Akṣay Lāibrerī, n.d.); Śaṅkarācārya and Rāmeśvar, *Śrīśrīsatyanārāyaṇer pāñcālī: Līlāvati, kalāvatī o daridra brāhmaṇ upākhyān* (Kalikātā: Rāmnāth Dās at Tārācāñd Dās eṇḍ Sans, n.d.). Anonymous texts are often by either Śaṅkarācārya or Rāmeśvar, and sometimes based on both. One scholarly edition includes the story by Bhāratcandra in addition to Rāmeśvar and Śaṅkarācārya; Priyanāth Ghoṣāl, ed., *Śrīśrīsatyanārāyaṇ: Trividha kathā* (Kalikātā: by the editor at Ripon College, 1910).

45. Lālā Jayakṛṣṇa Sen, *Harilīlā*, ed. Dineśacandra Sen and Basantarañjan Rāy (Kalikātā: Kalikātā Viśvavidyālay, 1928); the text was finished in 1772 (p. 7). See also Kavivallabh, in his aforementioned *Satyanārāyaṇ punthi*, which was composed earlier in the eighteenth century (p. 15). Both of these texts are substantially larger than the standard trilogy taken as a whole. David Cashin has included a translation of Vallabha's *Satyanārāyaṇer punthi* in his chapter on "The Cult of the Pīr"; see Cashin, *The Ocean of Love: Middle Bengali Sufi Literature and the Fakirs of Bengal*, Skrifter utgivna av Föreningen för Orientaliska Studier no. 27 (Stockholm: Association of Oriental Studies, Stockholm University, 1995), 251–82.

forms the basis for incorporation into the monthly *vrat* cycle of the wider Hindu households of Bengal.[46]

One particularly enterprising scholar, Priyanāth Ghoṣāl Jñānvinod, produced a scholarly labor of love that captures the entire process of *recognition*, *legitimation* through Sanskritization, and *appropriation* in a single volume motivated by a reformer's zeal. In the introduction to his 1903 publication titled *Satyanārāyaṇ vratvyavasthā, pūjāpaddhati o pañcavidha māhātmyakathā*, he deplores the poor quality of the *vrat kathās* and endeavors to clean up the textual tradition and improve the *pūjā* (as we noted above). He claims to have consulted numerous unpublished manuscripts and prefers the narrative style of the tale in the *Bhaviṣya purāṇa*, but he then composes his own new version of the trilogy based on the skeletal outline of Rāmeśvar, declaring his preference for Rāmeśvar over Śaṅkarācārya because of the latter's use of obviously Hindi words. He seems to be associating what he calls Hindi words with Urdu—evidence of that late-nineteenth-century move to identify languages as indices of religious identity—so apparently in his outlook, Bangla is purely Hindu, while Hindi (Urdu) marks the speaker as Muslim.[47] This text of some 122 pages includes Sanskrit texts of the *purāṇik* accounts of Satya Pīr and the author's own Bangla translations of those, in addition to his own composition.[48] So in this vast array of manuscripts and publications, the texts range from the simplest crudely printed and abbreviated retellings to elaborate productions that would tax all but the most assiduous *brāhmaṇ*. The basic trilogy can be summarized as follows.

The Brāhmaṇ's Tale

The tales begin with the saga of the old *brāhmaṇ* who has been reduced to utter penury. He lives in Vārānaṣī, that center of traditional piety, but cannot even beg a day's worth of alms to feed his wife and himself. He is distraught over his prospects

46. For translations of different versions of these three tales from the *vaiṣṇav vrat kathās*, see Tony K. Stewart, trans., "Satya Pīr: Muslim Holy Man and Hindu God," in *Religions of India in Practice*, ed. Donald S. Lopez, Jr., (Princeton: Princeton University Press, 1995), 578–97. There are four selections in order: "Salutations to Prepare for the Ritual," from Dvija Rāmbhadra, *Satyadev saṃhitā*, 131–36; "Satya Pīr Described," from Bhāratcandra Rāy, "Satyanārāyaṇ vratkathā," in *Bhāratcandra granthāvalī*, 440; "The Story of the Poor *Brāhmaṇ*" and "The Woodcutters' Tale," from Śaṅkarācārya, *Satyanārāyaṇer pāñcālī*, ed. Gaurāṅgasundar Bhaṭṭācāryya, Baṭ-tolā edition (Kalikātā: Rājendraī, n.d.); and "The Merchant's Adventure," from Kavicandra Ayodhyārām Rāy, *Satya nārāyaṇ kathā*, 61–72.

47. As we have seen, language marks the creation of discrete Muslim and Hindu identities in the nineteenth and early twentieth centuries. See Ahmed, *Bengal Muslims*; Bose, *Recasting the Region*; and Halder, "Of Blood and Tears."

48. Priyanāth Ghoṣāl Jñānvinod, *Satyanārāyaṇ vratvyavasthā, pūjāpaddhati o pañcavidha māhātmyakathā* (Kalikātā: Peṭrik Pres, 1310 BS [ca. 1903]). Another scholar notes that he prefers Rāmeśvar because his language is sweeter and more melodious (*sulalit*), so he has cleaned up the infelicities of the *baṭ-tolā* editions (p. 1) and included the Sanskrit text of the *Skanda purāṇa*; see Śyāmācaraṇ Kaviratna, *Satyanārāyaṇ o śubhacanīr kathā*, preface.

because the downward spiral conspires to keep him from being productive as a priest, for the poorer he becomes, the less likely his employment in his calling. When his prospects dim to the point where he can no longer offer a viable service to the competitive world of that metropolis, he finds himself in the unthinkable horror of being pushed to the very edges of civilization, east into the wilds of Bengal.[49] In this pitiful state, he is approached by Satya Pīr, who holds out one last alternative. "Offer *śinni* to me," he commands, "and your wishes will be fulfilled." Ever polite and sorely tempted, the *brāhmaṇ* resists the cry of his stomach and refuses to jettison what he considers to be the last remnants of his dignity as a *brāhmaṇ*, demurring on the grounds that Satya Pīr is *jaban* and such worship would be improper. Satya Pīr acknowledges the *brāhmaṇ*'s piety and instructs him to pay close attention. He gently suggests to that good but poor *brāhmaṇ* that he must never be fooled by outward appearance, for Satya Pīr is really none other than Nārāyaṇ himself. The *brāhmaṇ* is skeptical and asks for proof, which Satya Pīr provides by displaying his four-armed form (and even a less common six-armed form) as Viṣṇu, the form of Satya Nārāyaṇ. "Satya Pīr," he explains, "was but an *avatār*." Having witnessed it with his own eyes, the *brāhmaṇ* happily acknowledges the revelation, proffers the *śinni* precisely as instructed, and in an instant grows wealthy, all to the extreme pleasure and benefit of himself, his wife, and others around him. In every version of the story he does, in fact, live quite comfortably ever after.

. . .

The Woodcutters' Tale

Numerous woodcutters inhabit the same area as the *brāhmaṇ*, and it falls to them to clear land for cultivation and provide wood for fuel in this expanding economy. They have grown accustomed to passing the old *brāhmaṇ* beside the road as they made their daily trips deep into the forests. When the *brāhmaṇ*'s fortunes abruptly change, they are astounded, for the transformation is miraculous and rapid; overnight he has become successful and highly esteemed. Naturally, they want to know the source of his good fortune, and when they inquire, the *brāhmaṇ* proves himself worthy of Satya Pīr's trust. Being ever grateful to that mysterious *pīr*

49. It is interesting that the eastern reaches of the delta region have always provided last-ditch moneymaking opportunities for poor *brāhmaṇs*, for the dearth of *brāhmaṇs* in the region puts their services at a premium; even Kṛṣṇa Caitanya made the journey when his family was in financial straits; see Stewart, *Final Word*, 50. Being momentarily itinerant in the region does not seem to overly affect the status of the *brāhmaṇ*, but residence in the region during this period does seem to compromise status, for most of Bengal sits outside the boundaries of *madhyadeś*, the traditional brāhmaṇical homeland, and therefore lies beyond the reaches of civilization, a barbaric frontier. It is, then, the ideal place for a *pīr* to exercise his power.

who has so dramatically secured his fortune, he does just as he has been instructed and shares the secret. He is blunt: "Sincerely worship Satya Pīr with *śinni*, and you too will become rich." Not slow to recognize the opportunity, the woodcutters follow the injunction and within a very short time they become custodians of fabulous wealth. Their success allows them to build large fortresses on the tracts of land they clear, their estates expanding rapidly, while the frontier they are taming recedes further east and south. Inevitably, their success brings more land under cultivation and makes it fit for habitation by traditional brāhmaṇical society, for not only is it cleared but it is filled with moral people, including law-abiding kings to rule, and *brāhmaṇs*, like the one who shared his secret, to ensure propriety.

. . .

The Merchant's Tale

As the settlements develop in Bengal, local rulers require certain royal items, both luxury and symbolic, to assert their status and claim to power, that is, simply to be recognized as chieftains of these new lands. To bring the requisite and rare goods to court, each ruler finds himself in need of reliable merchants, who themselves, if they are successful, will become fabulously wealthy and powerful in the process. Procuring these unusual items, however, entails great risks, for their sources invariably lie beyond the seas; any trading venture is perilous, and the risk is compounded exponentially by traversing the ocean waterways. Through their own devices or with the financial backing of the king, the merchants set off to adventures only imagined by ordinary people. Their ships would glide effortlessly through the familiar waters of Bengal, out into the Bay of Bengal and the Indian Ocean. When they dare to venture away from land, they cannot but suffer events unique to the tricks of the deep seas, for instance, the report of Dayāl, who records "a tomb of marble floating on the sea with girls dancing around it to the musical accompaniment of celestial *kiṃnaras*, exquisitely situated in the middle of the ocean, deerskins were spread like carpets on the surface of the waters, with four *phakīrs* pronouncing their *namāj* facing West."[50] Because of such reports and with a practical estimate of their own limitations, they more often prefer to hug the coast as they work their way south. They stop periodically at cities and lands of decreasing familiarity until they reach the furthest outposts of civilization: Kaliṅga, then the Draviḍa region, and even the isle of Laṅka, which in the legacy

50. Sukumār Sen, *Bāṅglā sāhityer itihās*, vol. 1, pt. 2: 474–75; the text quoted is Dayāl's *Śaṅkara gadya pālā*, Bengali MS B-7484, Bāṅglā Bibhāg, Kalikātā Viśvāvidyālay. The merchant Śrīmanta likewise sees the extraordinary image of the goddess Abhayā Caṇḍī, in the form of a Kamalekāminī, a moon-faced maiden sitting on a freshly opened lotus, effortlessly engorging and then vomiting out an elephant over and over again; see Kavikaṅkan Mukundarām Cakravartī, *Caṇḍīmaṅgal*, 249–52, secs. 433–36 (the *pālā* to be performed on the night of the seventh day).

of the *Rāmāyaṇa* is always populated by demons and monsters, who predictably protect great wealth.

To offset the dangers, the merchants turn to Satya Pīr, for the creator of instant wealth can likewise be counted on to watch over its acquisition. Thus Satya Pīr comes to be the protector of merchants and travelers in general. To ensure this success, the merchants promise to worship Satya Pīr to a degree commensurate with their acquired wealth. But if wealth and good fortune can be created at a stroke, so too can those precious commodities be lost and destroyed; a failure to maintain that promise to worship Satya Pīr will only result in disaster. Sometimes it is the merchant who refuses to give alms to Satya Pīr when the latter comes in disguise, or it is the merchant's accompanying son, whose greed causes one of them to withhold the worship, which in turn precipitates the ship's foundering or lands one of them in jail. In those vile dungeons they may languish for years with no hope of escape until they belatedly remember the offense to Satya Pīr. Equally disastrous is the negligent action of the merchant's wife who has remained at home, or more frequently it is the action of the selfish daughter-in-law, who offends Satya Pīr so that success is denied even as the ships sail back into view after years abroad, sinking in the estuary as they come to dock. The variations are many, but the theme is relentlessly driven home: *if you fail to make good on your contractual promise to worship Satya Pīr in exchange for his protection, you are doomed.* But here, when the worship is properly discharged or the mistakes are acknowledged and corrected with appropriate humility, the merchant enjoys success with fortunes reversed: the chieftain receives the goods he desires to maintain his status as a right and just ruler of the land, the merchant accrues wealth and status for his reliable delivery, the merchant's wife and daughters-in-law receive appropriate protection of their fidelity in the merchant's absence, and the society as a whole confirms the validity of its attempt to maintain stability and order—all because Satya Pīr is widely worshiped. In short, *dharma* prevails, everyone prospers, and, say the stories, if you pay attention, you, too, can prosper.[51] The emphasis on humility and sincerity is central to all the stories, suggesting a leveling of social distinctions and an indirect parodic critique of *brāhmaṇs* in particular, who are nearly always depicted as arrogant, self-centered, and insincere. It is, perhaps, no accident that in early modern Bangla, the word for merchant was *sādhu*, which

51. Sukumār Sen ignores the woodcutters' tale while declaring the merchant's tale to be an unimaginative recapitulation of the *Dhanapati khullana* in the *Caṇḍī maṅgal*; Sukumār Sen, *Bāṅglā sāhityer itihās*, vol. 1, pt. 2: 471. The merchant's tale is indeed sufficiently close to be called a variant, but the question of historical or aesthetic priority—that is, whether Satya Pīr's story or Caṇḍī's story is earliest and/or the model—is never considered, largely, one suspects, because on account of the monumental stature of the text of the *Caṇḍī maṅgal*, its priority is assumed, just the opposite of my own reading wherein numerous authors develop the idea which the *Caṇḍī maṅgal* ultimately epitomizes.

meant adjectively: good, honest, virtuous, excellent, righteous, honorable, respectable; as a noun: holy man or, alternately, trader.

. . .

These three tales should be already familiar as part of the stock and trade of the *pīr kathās* as a whole, for we have seen Gāji Pīr intervening for the benefit of *brāhmaṇs* and rewarding woodcutters. Dakṣiṇ Rāy confers benefaction on woodcutters as a result of their hospitality and work in the Bonbibī tale. Like Satya Pīr, Badar Pīr displays his multi-armed form of Viṣṇu to Dudbibī as living proof of his divine calling. And in a tale not included in this set of essays, but which I have translated elsewhere, Mānik Pīr not only helps woodcutters but inverts the story of the briefly noted Tuṅgadhvaj episode when he kills the sons of the cowherd for not paying their respects, then restores them to life when their wives intervene and do the needful by proffering *śirṇi*.[52] Finally, recall the hapless merchant Puṣpadatta, who, while in search of his father in the *Rāy maṅgal*, witnesses the fabulous scene in the middle of the ocean, the reporting of which lands him in jail in Kaliṅga—that entire episode reminiscent of the merchant's tale common to all tellings of the Satya Pīr trilogy.

Of all the communities in early modern Bengal we can call religious, it should not surprise us that the *vaiṣṇavs* (and later *bāuls*) were the ones to appropriate a figure who was clearly "foreign" or *jaban*, for they alone could justify the action through the mechanism of their ever-expanding *avatār* theory, which could and often did claim virtually any popular figure as its own. As becomes apparent through the other narrative types, the *vaiṣṇav* model of God's descent, the *avatār*, and the Islamic institution of the *pīr* can be allied not only because the respective images of the holy man—*pīr* and *phakir* (sometimes *dārveś*) and *vairāgī* and *sannyāsī*—coincided so conveniently as images of the embodiment of power, but because there was a basic theological compatibility that undergirded both conceptions of divinity to which they referred, and this consonance would generate apposite orientations toward authority that would prove their coherence in the narratives of Satya Pīr.

Like the *vairāgī*, the *pīr* did not prescribe for the public the esoteric practices he reserved for adepts like himself, but proposed simpler and more popular forms of piety appropriate to ordinary householders. Much of his guidance fell into the adjudication of everyday problems, marital issues, arbitration of disputes, and the curbing of individual vices, such as greed and parsimoniousness, and so forth. The image of divinity associated with these simpler prescriptive rituals and instructions would run the full gamut of experiences, just as they do in the *vaiṣṇav* order. Not only were the institutional structures of the *pīr* and *vairāgī*, then, analogous

52. Stewart, trans., "Tales of Mānik Pīr: Protector of Cows in Bengal."

in a general way, but their operational and theological underpinnings were closely equivalent, and that is borne out in comparisons of both general and historically specific issues of theology, such as the nature of the godhead and the injunctions to ritual practices. While it may be easy to speculate in purely intellectual or theological terms why these two traditions might be inclined to find mutual alliance, it was their operational dimension that bore out the practicality of it—and that allowed the *vaiṣṇavs* to appropriate the image of Satya Pīr with virtual impunity—in fact, one might even argue, with a very unsurprising anticipation if not expectation of its inevitability. The trilogy not only told the story of this process; the stories themselves served the process.

Given the similarity of the functions of the *vaiṣṇav* and *sūphī* spiritual guides and the theological parallels they represented, it was ultimately the fact that Satya Pīr was a mythic or fictional figure that effectively eliminated any possible challenge to the narrative's veracity, for no historical documentation of the *pīr*'s life and teachings aligned him with any particular sectarian group.[53] This independence of the narrative from historical verification dramatically aided the process of appropriation by enabling the *vaiṣṇav* to sanitize it. In this, Satya Pīr's image was plastic and malleable in the manner of a *purāṇik* figure and, indeed, he quietly slipped into the *purāṇas* as another form of Nārāyaṇ. This same kind of plasticity likewise extended to the use of the narratives, for it enabled them to be applied to a wide range of generic situations, again quite apart from any explicit historical event. Each of the *vaiṣṇav* episodes deals tacitly, if not explicitly, with generalized processes of *reclamation*—geographical and cultural—making habitable a land that has been off-limits to *brāhmaṇs* and therefore problematic for establishing a proper brāhmaṇical society.[54] Because of its lack of specificity, the nature of that rehabilitation could be adjusted to the user's immediate

53. The only historical *pīr* or *musalmāni* figure that I can find being appropriated by the Bengali *vaiṣṇav* traditions is the *jaban* Haridās, whose stories percolate through the hagiographies of Kṛṣṇa Caitanya, though the historicity of some of his tales is very much in question; see especially the tales in Vṛndāvan Dās, *Caitanya bhāgavat*, 1.11, and in Kṛṣṇadās Kavirāj, *Caitanya caritāmṛta*, 3.3 and 3.11. For translations, see Tony K. Stewart, "The Exemplary Devotion of the 'Servant of Hari,'" in *The Religions of India in Practice*, ed. Donald S. Lopez, Jr. (Princeton: Princeton University Press, 1995), 564–77. There were, however, large numbers of *musalmāni* poets who wrote *vaiṣṇav*-style lyrics on Rādhā and Kṛṣṇa; see Jatīndranāth Bhaṭṭācārya, *Bāṅgālār vaiṣṇavbhāvāpanna musalmān kavir padsaṃjuṣā*; and Edward C. Dimock, "Muslim Vaiṣṇava Poets of Bengal," in *Languages and Areas: Studies Presented to George V. Bobrinskoy on the Occasion of His Academic Retirement* (Chicago: University of Chicago Press, 1967), 28–36.

54. Ronald B. Inden argued that in previous centuries the genealogical histories included several mythic episodes for the royal importation of *brāhmaṇs* with proper Vedic knowledge to people the land and make it properly habitable; the last of these kings faded into the historical figure of Ballāl Sen. See Inden, *Marriage and Rank in Bengali Culture* (Berkeley: University of California Press, 1976), 49–82. It should be noted that *hinduyāni* Bengal has been, including in the myths, a two-*varṇa* society, composed of *brāhmaṇs* and *śūdras*, and in that frame, it is easy to see where *jabans* fit.

circumstance. The progress documented in the trilogy of *vaiṣṇav* tales curiously paralleled the historical events of the settling of Bengal. As the Gaṅgā shifted steadily to the east, the limits of what defined the traditional heartland or *madhya deś* of brāhmaṇical culture could be extended, but only if brought under proper control. Making good use of the available powers, one agent of that *vaiṣṇav* domestication became the generic *pīr*, for the *pīr* could actually do what *brāhmaṇs* themselves could not: inhabit a wild land and tame it. Though some question the stereotype, ironically, the *pīr* has often been depicted as the very same agent for analogous processes of Islamization, for a number of scholars over the last half century have argued that the *sūphī* guide—as *pīr* or *phakir* or *shaykh*—was often the first to enter new regions to make Islam available to the local population—sometimes converting but, perhaps much more often and more effectively, simply making familiar what initially might have seemed alien—so that the land might be brought into the line of traditional Islamic culture. Bengal was no exception. The same figure of the *pīr* served two religious orientations in nearly exactly the same capacity.

Therein may lie the most important reason for *vaiṣṇavs* to appropriate the *pīr*'s image, for by doing so they not only unquestionably acknowledged the presence of Islam as a legitimate social organization and religious option in the region, bowing to the reality of *musalmāni* presence, but they also acknowledged that the *pīr* worked as an effective source of local power. It was an act of a pragmatic *Realpolitik* in that the *vaiṣṇavs* adopted a stance toward their rulers' culture and religion that did not try to wish away the reality of that rule but attempted to adapt to its presence and co-opt its power by appropriating it: they took the *pīr* as one of the most effective tools for spreading the example of Islam and then revalorized the *pīr*'s image to their own ends. It should come as no surprise, however, that even though Satya Pīr was embraced, the embrace was not unmitigated or unconditional, because the *vaiṣṇavs* did not elevate him to the level of their adored Kṛṣṇa or Caitanya, but by the late nineteenth and early twentieth century absorbed him into the lower strata of the brāhmaṇical hierarchy, placing him squarely in the women's ritual cycle of the *vrat*, which was dominated nearly exclusively by lesser images of divinity, especially the household goddesses, such as Ṣaṣṭhī, Lakṣmī, et al., who were (and still are) petitioned to make life easier and more fruitful; interestingly Olābibī, the matron of cholera and other waterborne diseases, and Bonbibī both often find themselves similarly incorporated. But Satya Pīr, whose stories were circulating before those of the *pīr kathās*, proved his worth by doing much of the "dirty work" of making the land habitable and ensuring the wealth and weal of the family—the mundane role of lesser celestials—and in that proved his expediency. In spite of the "official" recognition, he was destined to remain a ubiquitous but marginal figure at the lower end of the *vaiṣṇav* and brāhmaṇical world.

6.3. GENDERED WITNESS TO SATYA PĪR'S POWERS

In the tales that deploy the second emplotment, Satya Pīr provides courage and moral support for the protagonists who are befuddled by their predicaments, which tend to be attributed to the fruits of past *karma* or, just as often, simply the inexorable machinery of fate. When these heroines and heroes attempt on their own to resolve the issues they confront, when they exhibit patience, commit to a dharmically defined moral order, and demonstrate an improvisational creativity in the face of repeated obstructions—only then, with resources exhausted, do they turn to Satya Pīr with a heartfelt summons to which he graciously responds. He tends to hover in the background, but where and how is not always clear. On occasion he is said to fly in from Makkā, a misty ethereal sacred location where he dwells with other friends of God. Sometimes he descends directly from *bhest*, heaven, and at others simply magically materializes out of thin air. His interventions are, for the most part, *enabling* rather than resolving, for he adjusts the situations to help the protagonists, his devotees, to restart their quest on their own, leaving them to their own devices to take advantage of the opportunities he presents. He does not simply fix things; rather, he encourages his devotees to utilize their own resources to benefit those around them before themselves.

Most of those stories, with perhaps one or two exceptions, seem to have originated in the nineteenth century, and the numbers of manuscripts are virtually nil, which suggests that most of the productions moved straight to print. The protagonists of these tales, generally more often women than men, provide direct witness to the fruitfulness and virtue of devotion and the responding power of Satya Pīr. They share the narrative code of the demand for *recognition* of the *pīr* found in all the tales, but focusing primarily on the outcomes, on the *efficacy of worship* and the benefits that will accrue, regardless of social standing or orientations toward the divine. They can be read as essentially nonsectarian, for they require no one to alter any preexisting allegiances. One could predict that the final rewards of worship are gendered—the female protagonists' fidelity to their husbands proves their worth and enhances the social standing and wealth of their husbands, while, as a result of the heroines' actions, the males garner great riches and beautiful princesses for wives and co-wives and even gain control of entire kingdoms filled with unimaginable wealth. But the plots often undercut expectations of gender, championing the independence, the education, the morality, and the self-determination of women. These eighteenth- and nineteenth-century tales fully illustrate Judith Butler's now widely accepted argument that gendered roles are not assigned, but *enacted* sometimes deliberately and at others as necessity demands.[55] When the

55. Among a host of publications refining the argument that the performance of gender creates gender, see Judith Butler, *Gender Trouble: Feminism and the Subversion of Identity* (New York: Routledge, 1990).

naïve and hapless men nearly inevitably become incapacitated or even killed, the women step forward to do what the men cannot—they fight with swords, negotiate royal support, sleuth the sources of problems in ways that outfox even the wiliest constables, and receive rewards from kings for service and valor. I have located a dozen of these tales, eight of which can be found in full translations in *Fabulous Females and Peerless Pīrs*. In that volume, there are three tales by Kavi Kiṅkar or Kiṅkar Dās: *Rāmbhāvatī pālā*,[56] translated as "The Unwilting Garland of Faithfulness"; *Śaśidhar pālā*,[57] as "The Bloodthirsty Ogress Who Would Be Queen"; and *Matilāler pālā*,[58] as "The Mother's Son Who Spat Up Pearls." Others in the anthology include: Kavi Kaṇva's *Ākhoṭi pālā*,[59] translated as "The Fabled *Beṅgamā* Bird and the Stupid Prince"; Dvīja Kavibar's *Bāghāmbarer pālā*,[60] as "The Disconsolate Yogī Who Turned the Merchant's Wife into a Dog"; Gayarām's *Madanamañjarī pālā*,[61] as "The Princess Who Nursed Her Own Husband"; and Rasmay's *Manohar phāsarār pālā*,[62] as "The Erstwhile Bride and Her Winged Horse." The lead story in that anthology is Kavi Āriph's *Lālmoner kāhini*,[63] trans-

56. Kiṅkar Dās, *Rambhāvatī pālā: Satyanārāyaṇ pāñcālī*, 4th ed. (Khāñtāi: Madhusudan Jān at Nihār Press, 1331 BS [ca. 1924]).

57. Kiṅkar Dās, *Śaśidhar pālā: Satyanārāyaṇ pāñcālī* (Khāñtāi: Madhusudan Jān at Nihār Press, 1322 BS [ca. 1915]).

58. Kiṅkar Dās, *Matilāler pālā: Satyanārāyaṇ pāñcālī* (Khāñtāi: Nihār Press, 1322 BS [ca. 1915]).

59. Kavi Kaṇva [= Kavi Karṇa], *Ākhoṭi pālā: Satyanārāyaṇ kathā* (Manuscript no. 59B, Dhaka University Library, 14 folios, complete, dtd. 1273 BS [ca. 1866]); the scribe used a *baphalā* (v) in lieu of a *reph* (4) throughout, hence the unusual spelling of Kaṇva rather than Karṇa. Bishnupada Panda edited a version of the text which shows many discrepancies when compared to the original manuscript; see Kavi Karṇa's "Satyanārāyaṇ ākhoṭi pālā" in Śrī Kavi Karṇa, *Pālās of Śrī Kavi Karṇa*, comp./ed./trans. Bishnupada Panda, 4 vols., Kalāmūlaśāstra Series, vols. 4–7 (New Delhi: Indira Gandhi National Centre for the Arts and Delhi: Motilal Banarsidass, 1991), vol. 1 (KS Series, vol. 4): 1–93. After publishing my translation of the *Akhoṭi pālā* in *Fabulous Females and Peerless Pīrs*, I found two more versions of this same text, but attributed to Rāmeśvar; see Rāmeśvar, *Ākhoṭi pālā*, in *Rāmeśvar racanāvalī*, ed. Pañcānan Cakravartī (Kolkata: Baṅgīya Sāhitya Pariṣat, 1371 BS [ca. 1964]), 536–49; and Rāmeśvar, *Ākhoṭi pālā: Satyanārāyaṇ pāñcālī*, 3rd ed. (Khāñtāi: Madhusudan Jān at Nihār Press, 1924).

60. Dvīja Kavibar, *Bāghāmbarer pālā: Satyanārāyaṇ pāñcālī*, 10th ed. (Kāñthāi: Nihār Press, 1322 BS [ca. 1915]).

61. Gayārām, *Madanmañjari pālā: Satyanārāyaṇ pāñcālī* (Khāñtāi: Madhusudan Jān at Nihār Press, 1334 BS [ca. 1927]).

62. Anonymous, *Manohar phāsarār pālā: Satyanārāyaṇ pāñcālī*, 10th ed. (Kāñthāi: Nihār Press, 1313 BS [ca. 1906]); the attribution as anonymous is unfortunate because after I had translated the text for the volume, I discovered the text was by Rasmay; see Rasmay, *Galakāṭā phāsyarār pālā* (Bengali MS no. 214. Dhaka University Library, 17 folios, complete, dtd. 1264 BS [ca. 1857]). It should be noted that the Nihār Press editor took liberties with the text, emending a few sections, including sanitizing a couple of passages for what appear to be prurient interests.

63. Kavi Āriph, *Lālmoner kāhinī*, ed. Girīndranāth Dās (Gokūlpur, Cabbiś Pargaṇās: Śrīmati Karuṇāmayī Dās, 1984). This version is virtually identical to two printed editions from the mid-nineteenth century; see Āriph, *Lālmoner kecchā* (Kalakātā: Sudhānidhi Yantra, 1274 BS [ca. 1867]), and Āriph, *Lālmoner kecchā* (Kalakātā: Viśvambhar Lāhā, 1276 BS [ca. 1869]). There are at least a dozen

lated as "The Wazir's Daughter Who Married a Sacrificial Goat." In many respects the story of Lālmon serves as a prototype for these tales and is likely the oldest of the stories that comprise this grouping. It is also the most popular, seeing frequent printings. The story goes like this:

The Adventure of Lālmon

Lālmon is the daughter of the king's chief minister, but she is being raised as a boy because of the minister's frustrated desire for a son. She is sent to school disguised as a boy and becomes literate in the usual branches of knowledge, including literature and mathematics and other subjects typical of royal training. A young prince named Husāin Śāh finds himself frequently enjoying the company of his gifted classmate until one day, as he is walking down the street, he looks up and sees that she is not a boy at all. She is standing at her window, combing out her long hair, exposing her budding breasts. He is immediately smitten and presses her to agree to marry him on the spot for his instant gratification. She refuses unless there is a witness, but strangely enough, there is no one around to do the needful. Husāin is impatient, his desire now little more than unmitigated lust, so he determinedly importunes her and presses her to capitulate. Worried that should she yield, he will, in spite of his promises, just as quickly abandon her, she meditates on Satya Pīr to come to witness Husāin's promise of fidelity and support. Satya Pīr magically appears from his abode in Makkā. Husāin, angered by this unwelcome intrusion, picks up a pen that is sitting on Lālmon's writing desk and, with a volley of vile imprecations, hurls it at Satya Pīr. Satya Pīr unhesitatingly counters with a curse that Husāin will be fated to lose his head, then stands as Lālmon's witness. After he leaves, the two consummate their betrothal. As was nearly always the case in palaces, the word is soon out and Husāin realizes that both his father and the minister will take him to task for his lack of restraint, so he and Lālmon bolt just before the guards arrive. Dressed as soldiers, they ride deep into the forest. Brigands surround them and they fight back-to-back as well as any trained *laskār* soldiers might. They slay the disorganized highwaymen, but counter to Lālmon's counsel, Husāin spares one young servant. When they are finally able to sleep, that young boy picks up Husāin's sword and lops off his head. Lālmon quickly dispatches the lad, but the deed is done.

Lālmon cradles Husāin's severed head in her lap and weeps as she meditates on Satya Pīr. The extraordinary nature of her lamentation brings the wildlife of the forest to a complete standstill. The animals realize she is just like the famed Behulā

---

more reprints and other editions over the next several decades. There is another retelling that circulated in the early decades of the twentieth century, but not since; see Chaiyad Hāmjā Sāheb, *Chahi baḍa lālmon* (Kalikātā: Hāji Āijaddīn Āhmad eṇḍ Sans at Gāouchiyā Lāibrerī, 1344 BS [ca. 1937]); and what appears to be an earlier imprint, Chaiyad Hāmjā Sāheb, *Chahi baḍa lālmon* (Kalikātā: Śrī Rāmlāl Śīl at Niu-Bhikṭoriyā Pres, n.d.).

of the *Manasā maṅgal*, who floated down the river with the dead body of her snake-bitten husband, Lakkhindār, in pursuit of a miracle of revival.[64] The animals of the forest empathetically fast to multiply the urgency of her appeal to Satya Pīr for help. Satya Pīr is moved by the anguish, and he flies again to Lālmon's side. He grants her wish, reattaches Husāin's head to his lifeless body, and revivifies him. Balance and harmony are restored to the forest, and Lālmon nurses Husāin till he regains his strength. Off they go. They camp deep in the forest to escape detection, tethering their royal steeds to the trees. As soon as they have dismounted and settled, Husāin strikes for the nearest town to secure food. On the way, a woman gardener, a garland weaver, sees him and from visage and comportment recognizes instantly that he is a royal. She quickly spruces up her appearance, sprinkles a magic spell on one of her garlands and, using all of her feminine charms, beckons him to come closer. Husāin, of course, cannot resist the allure of her exposed breasts and, when he leans forward for a better look, she slips the magic garland over his head and turns him into a ram. He is ensorceled. She tethers him to a post in her yard and keeps him as breeding stock. At night she returns him to his manly form so that she can have her pleasure, but keeps him mute, only to transmogrify him back into a ram the next day, transformations that soon become routine.

Meanwhile, Lālmon, alarmed at Husāin's failure to return, is set to search when a party of the local king's scouts discover her hideaway—because she is dressed as a *laskār*, to them she appears as a soldier of unknown allegiance suspiciously in possession of what, by the look of them, could only be royal horses. They haul her to jail as a horse thief without recourse to a hearing. As she languishes in jail—and Husāin continues to service his new mistress—a rogue white rhino goes on a rampage, terrorizing the kingdom, destroying crops, and killing peasants. For the one who can kill it, the king offers a handsome reward, including half of his kingdom and the hand of his daughter in marriage. Lālmon overhears the guards discussing it, and so, still dressed as a *laskār*, she bribes her way out of jail. With a little help from Satya Pīr, she tracks and slays it, quickly cutting off its horn and tongue. Other bounty hunters soon arrive and begin taking ears and other parts of the rhino hoping to prove they have slain it, but the king knows that the real destroyer of that beast will possess the horn and tongue—and so when Lālmon, still in *laskār*

64. One of the most widely circulated versions of Behulā's tale is by Ketakādās; see Ketakādās Kṣemānanda, *Manasā Maṅgal*, ed. Jatīndramohan Bhaṭṭācāryya (Calcutta: Calcutta University, 1949), and Ketakādāsa Kṣemānanda, *Manasāmaṅgal*, ed. Bijanbihārī Bhaṭṭācārya (New Delhi: Sāhitya Academy, 1977). For a retelling of Ketakādās's tale, see Ketakā Dāsa, "The Manasā Maṅgal of Ketakā Dāsa: Behulā and Lakhindar," in *The Thief of Love: Bengali Tales from Court and Village*, trans. Edward C. Dimock (Chicago: University of Chicago Press, 1963), 195–294. For an unabridged French translation of the story as told by Bipradās, see Vipradāsa, *La victoire de Manasā: Traduction française du Manasā Vijaya, poème bengali de Vipradāsa (XVe)*, trans. France Bhattacharya, Collection Indologies 105 (Pondichéry: Institut Français de Pondichéry, École Française d'Extrême-Orient, 2007). For an analysis of Behulā's actions as a ritual of *tantrik* revivification, see Stewart, "Process of Surface Narrative."

drag, presents the horn and tongue to the king, he proclaims that *laskār* the winner of the purse, including the gift of his daughter's hand. Lālmon plays along.

The union is made official, but much to the distress of the young princess Māhtāb, Lālmon refuses to consummate their marriage. Lāl tells her that after one month she will reveal all, but to be patient. Māhtāb, of course, has no choice, and perhaps out of embarrassment remains silent. During that month Lāl, who is now running much of the kingdom, devises a strategy to locate her wayward Husāin. She orders the construction of a *masjid*, with a promise of free food and celebrations to last for weeks, rightly figuring that when the word spreads everyone in the kingdom will eventually show up for the festivities. Sure enough, the garland weaver arrives with Husāin in tow, but he is still magically rendered dumb. He does manage to scribble a message to Lāl on the wall of the *masjid* using the gum of smoked tobacco he finds on the ground. That message is just what she was hoping to see, and see she does.

Soon Lāl rounds up the garland weaver witch and her ram and has them hauled into the palace. When instructed to turn her ram back into the man Husāin, the garland weaver laughs and pointedly replies that she can no more do that than a horse thief can run the country. Finally, under threat of death, she complies, and for her trouble is instantly dispatched, her mutilated body unceremoniously thrown into a ditch. After Husāin has regained his form, Lāl reveals to her astonished audience of king, queen, and bride the truth of her gender ruse. The king is flummoxed by his gaff, the princess humiliated, and Husāin astonished at this turn of events. The king is not sure what to do, but the young princess immediately determines a course of action: because she is married to Lāl and Lāl is married to Husāin, she will assume the role of second wife, but will not be Husāin's sexual partner; she will remain as the devoted companion of Lālmon, since it is to her she was betrothed. So, by the interventions of Lālmon, aided by Satya Pīr, Lālmon wins a wife, and the randy prince Husāin inherits a second kingdom and now a second wife. He returns home to succeed his father with dominion over a now expanded territory. Everyone dutifully followed Lālmon's lead in worshiping Satya Pīr as the guarantor of all things good.

. . .

The story attests to the power of the *pīr* to aid his devotees through every trial and tribulation, but the devotee must be bold and enterprising in utilizing the aid proffered. There is no theological positioning in these tales: God is seldom, if ever, positively identified, unlike in the trilogy where Nārāyaṇ and Āllā are asserted to be equivalent, with Āllā taking the form of Satya Pīr. Nor does God intervene—that is the work of Satya Pīr. But because the texts tend to be noncommittal regarding the identification of Āllā and Nārāyaṇ, nor do they assert the supremacy of Āllā—which, as we shall see, is the dominant trope in the third set of tales—the audiences for this second form of emplotment are free to read or hear the attribution as they see fit, and it is in this sense they effectively circulate as nonsectarian, openly malleable in orientation. It would not be unreasonable to suspect that the near total absence of even the most rudimentary religious sentiment beyond the enacted examples of the benefits of worshiping Satya Pīr was the reason these tales were often characterized as simply entertainment. But the more likely underlying explanation was that, because Satya Pīr is never the protagonist—rather, his devotees are—they must prove themselves worthy of his aid, and when they do, benefits accrue. It is the *instrumentality* and *efficacy* of the *pīr* that is demonstrated over and again.

Sharing in this second emplotment is a set of stories by a poet who composed tales in a dialectical form of Bangla mixed with Oḍiyā: Kavikarṇa (seen above as Kavi Kaṇva). The stories circulated in a set of sixteen tales, but editor Bishnupada Panda, who published a four-volume work with his selection of the preferred sixteen tales, indicated in the introduction that nineteen tales can be found among the various editions of his works.[65] The tales tend to feature men as the protagonists and are marked by plots with minimal transitions and speech that is often abrupt, suggesting planned oral performance (or, conversely, suggesting its origins in public performance prior to transcription).

We have already seen nearly every trope and twist of plot to be found in these tales, and the reader can draw the connections. Both the intertextual references and the cosmological structures tend to reference a classical Bengali world. Satya Pīr's punishments and rewards favor the swift and dramatic, in an economy of brutal chastisement and retribution, usually indicated by seemingly intractable conflicts, balanced at the extreme opposite end of the spectrum by his magnanimity and beneficence, which inevitably translate into wealth and weal. These extremes mirror in their diegetic expression the radical endpoints of the two characteristics that in *vaiṣṇav* circles define the nature of Nārāyaṇ's or Kṛṣṇa's divinity—omnipotent lordship (*aiśvarya*) balanced by his loving sweetness (*mādhurya*) or, just as easily, can point to the analogous qualities of Āllā that bracket his traditionally eulogized ninety-nine qualities—awesome majesty (*jalāl*) and sublime beauty (*jamāl*). In effect, the cosmos was then sufficiently neutral to require no explicit commitment to a preferred form of divinity, which had the effect of shifting the focus almost entirely onto the action. In most of these tales there is an ebb and flow of predicaments and resolutions typical of Romance, but I have located one text, published by Nihār Press, composed in a very heavily Oḍiyā-inflected Bangla, that

65. The tales include: Śrī Kavi Karṇa, *Pālās of Śrī Kavi Karṇa* (vol. 4): "Satyanārāyaṇ ākhoṭi pālā," "Satyanārāyaṇ pālā," "Madansundar pālā"; (vol. 5): "Marddagāji janma pālā," "Marddagāji vibha pālā," "Padmalocan pālā," "Guḍiā śaṅkar pālā," "Vidyādhar pālā," "Śrīmanta saudāgar pālā"; (vol. 6): "Abhinnamadan pālā," "Herācānd pālā," "Phāśiyārā pālā," "Kaṭhuriyā pālā," "Kiśormohan pālā," "Lakṃaṇkumar pālā," "Durjan siṃha pālā"; (vol. 7): "Satyanārāyaṇ janma pālā," "Candrāji vibha pālā," "Nīlasundar pālā," "Daś avatār pālā," and "Hīrāmohan pālā."

starkly captures the link between the rewards that accrue from devotion to the *pīr* and the disasters that follow for ignoring him. With no author credited, the text of the *Nalanīler pālā* straddles both gendered forms of the tales that constitute this second emplotment. One young man, Nal, faithfully and patiently pays his respects to Satya Pīr and reaps the rewards; his twin brother Nīl scoffs and refuses to commit, and Satya Pīr discretely arranges for his education in the vagaries of worldly life. But it is the king's scheming wife who has created the problem and her faithful and brilliant daughters-in-law who resolve it. The story goes like this.[66]

The Tale of Nal and Nīl

King Vīrbhadra of Surāṭ Nagar has two wives, both gorgeous, both childless. They long for at least one son. Following the advice of their *paṇḍit*, together they go to petition Śiv, and along the way they pass a *pīr*, hunched down in his tattered mendicant's garb. He has not eaten for three days. He begs food with the promise to fulfill their desires; but in response, the younger queen angrily rebuffs him, while her elder co-wife responds more compassionately and unhesitatingly lays at the feet of the *pīr* all of the jewelry she has on her person.

When they pray at the Śiv temple, Hara reveals that it is that old *pīr*, named Satya Pīr, who is the giver of sons. He predicts that the elder will have twins because of her beneficent act of giving to the *pīr*. He also foretells that the younger will be punished for her lack of charity; she will remain barren. Then he advises them both to offer *śirṇi* to the *pīr*. The younger queen is distraught, rightly fearing she will soon be sidelined by the good fortune of her senior co-wife. As predicted, in no time the elder queen is pregnant, and ten months later she delivers twins. The king makes all the appropriate donations to *brāhmaṇs* and so forth, and the older queen dedicates the two boys to Satya Pīr for protection. As they celebrate, the jealous younger queen slips poison into the food of her senior, who realizes too late the perfidy. She knows she is dying, and the king's distress mirrors Rām's grief when Sītā is stolen away by Rāvaṇ. Moments before her death, the queen hands the care of her twins to her co-wife and instructs her to name them Nīl and Nal—and with that final breath, a chariot descends from *vaikuṇṭha* (heaven) to whisk her away. But the king grows suspicious of the obsequiousness of the surviving wife, a behavior previously uncharacteristic, so as a precaution he consigns the boys to the care of his constable for rearing.

The Constable raises the boys with diligence and pride. He has them educated in the forms of knowledge appropriate to their station. When they reach twelve, he returns them to the king and is handsomely rewarded. The younger queen had hoped to have a son of her own, but these two boys stand first in the line of kingly succession, so she schemes to remove them. One day the boys rambunctiously

66. Anonymous, *Satyanārāyaṇ pāñcālī: Nalanīler pālā*, 6th ed. (Kāñthāi: Jatīndranāth Jānā at Nīhār Press, 1340 BS [ca. 1933]).

chase a bird into their stepmother's apartment. Sensing an opportunity, she hides the bird in the folds of her sari, and when the boys burst in, she accuses them of entering her private quarters with salacious intent. She surreptitiously inflicts wounds on her body that would pass as the result of a violent sexual assault. She demands that the king punish them or else she will commit suicide, which would lay the guilt on the king, making him complicit.

> Just look at my body, clawed all over by the nails of those boys—your sons! How can this be permitted in a dharmic world? The servants can attest to my pitiful condition. If you, as the head of this kingdom, allow these boys to go unpunished, be sure that no good will come of it. If this violation of my person is allowed to stand, then your kingdom is doomed.[67]

Angry, unsettled, and unsure, the king summons his courtiers and friends, and on their advice decrees that the boys present an abomination to his lineage and threaten the stability of the kingdom. He orders them taken to the jungle and executed and instructs the guards to return with their blood so the queen can expiate their unholy transgressions by bathing in it.

Their guardian the Constable is aghast at the sentence because he does not believe the accusations. The boys protest their innocence, but the king charges the Constable to carry out the sentence. With no way to countermand the king's order, he sets out to do as told. When they reach the forest, he raises his sword above their heads, but his arm freezes mid-swing. One of the boys has called Satya Nārāyaṇ, who materializes, seething with anger. Sensing the violation, a darkness settles over the forest. The enervating roar of the tigers knocks the Constable senseless, allowing Satya Pīr to spirit the boys away. When the Constable finally awakens, Satya Pīr instructs him to slaughter a goat and catch its blood, and that will serve as ostensible proof of the boys' execution. Not long after, the young queen bathes herself in a blood ecstasy. She can finally imagine that her own son will become king. Meanwhile, the boys' adventures are just beginning.

> The *pīr* abandoned the boys in the thick of the jungle and vanished. As the boys hunkered down at the foot of a massive banyan tree, they pondered their plight. Nal spoke while Nīl listened. "Satya Nārāyaṇ saved us. Come, let us perform a *pūjā* to worship Satya Pīr. He will surely drive away any danger."
>
> Nīl listened to his brother's words and replied softly, "You are proposing that we give worship to a *jaban devatā*? How is it possible for a *hindu* to do such a thing? If we worship a *hindu devatā* like Śiv, we will be protected against all harm. If we worship Ambikā, Caṇḍī, and Mahākālī, our suffering will come to an end. In the Tretā age, Rām Raghumaṇi worshiped the Parvvata Nandinī, and by that he was able to destroy Rāvaṇ of Laṅkā and rescue Sītā. Who can even begin to fathom the endless

67. Anonymous, *Satyanārāyaṇ pāñcālī: Nalanīler pālā*, 16.

> glory and majesty of *hindu devatās*? Go ahead and perform your worship, but do not expect me to follow suit."
>
> At Nīl's pronouncements, Nal was dismayed, but went about the business. He set up a small dais, *āsthānā*, in the lap of the banyan tree's roots. After gathering fruits and flowers, he installed the *pīr* at the base of the banyan tree. He pressed the palms of his hands together and cried out loudly, "Lord, Prabhu, please grant your protection!"
>
> At these words, the *pīr* acknowledged the great qualities of Nala: "Today I will bestow upon you a great honor and opportunity. Harbor in your heart no doubts. You are destined to become the Lord of Kings, Rājeśvar."[68]

Nal keeps watch while Nīl sleeps, but he soon grows thirsty—the thirst, of course, instigated by Satya Pīr—so he carefully leaves fruits and edible roots next to the place of worship and sets out to find a sweet water stream. The river traverses a kingdom called Nāgeśvar, whose ruler is named Candraketu. Candraketu's only issue is female, and she is of marriageable age, but she has been cursed: every prospective groom will fall dead with the first touch of her hand. The king despairs of ever finding a groom.

Worried over his daughter's prospects, Candraketu summons his trusted bull elephant to search the world over for a suitable boy. Satya Nārāyaṇ contrives to cross paths with the elephant and promises to furnish the object of the king's desire. Together with the elephant, he heads to the river where they espy Nal, radiant with the marks of royalty. The elephant ceremoniously wraps his trunk around Nal and gently lifts him onto his back. Deed accomplished, Satya Pīr vanishes, while the elephant returns to Candraketu with his prize. Candraketu wastes no time in arranging the wedding. Rather than killing Nal, the daughter's touch has the opposite effect: it renders his body immutable, no longer subject to any kind of decay. The princess's curse is annulled, the king is thrilled, and Nal is soon conducting affairs of state as the crown prince.

Meanwhile Nīl wakes to find his twin gone, and he fears the worst there in the wild. A horse from the royal stable of Candraketu mysteriously winds up tethered to a tree near the place where Nīl had been resting. Soon soldiers appear and apprehend him as a horse thief. In jail, bound hand and foot, and with a stone placed on his chest, Nīl's spirits run the gamut of despair and puzzlement. The entire farce is, of course, the result of the *pīr*'s magical meddling. Thoroughly befuddled, Nīl slips into the delirium of sleep, only to encounter Satya Pīr in a vision. Satya Pīr offers him a way out: "Offer *śirṇi* to me, or you will die in this prison." In his abject condition, what can he do but agree? Satya Pīr promises to deliver him in three days.

Now the king needs sandal and wood apple timber for his monthly sacrifices, so he requisitions more from a trader named Bāṅgāl. When the stars and planets align favorably, the merchant's crew pushes off, but the boat refuses to budge. The

68. Anonymous, *Satyanārāyaṇ pāñcālī: Nalanīler pālā*, 22–23.

merchant fetches the king's astrologer, who turns out to be none other than Satya Nārāyaṇ. Working his calculations, he instructs the king to produce the horse thief languishing in prison. The moment he sets foot on the boat, it lunges into the waves. They head to Siṃha Island.

The king of Siṃha Island is, appropriately enough, named Siṃhabāhu. His daughter Līlāvatī possesses an electric beauty. As the merchant arrives at Siṃhanagar, the king's daughter is to choose her groom from among a host of suitors, so the place is crawling with kings and princes. Just as she passes the gawking Nīl in his tattered rags, Satya Pīr makes him appear breathtakingly beautiful to her mind's eye. Līlāvatī does not hesitate to choose him, and they quickly exchange garlands to the outrage of all present, including her father the king.[69] Humiliated, the king rebukes her, and confines her and her new husband to house arrest. Satya Pīr intervenes, claiming Nīl was his personal servant, so the king, seeing an easy way, releases them to return with Bāṅgāl to Candraketu's kingdom, which is now being ruled by Nal. Bāṅgāl, cleverly sensing an opportunity, plots to push Nīl overboard en route and then offer the princess as a gift to the king. Nīl soon finds himself unceremoniously bobbing in the water. As anticipated, Nal is smitten with Līlāvatī's beauty, but she resists his offer of marriage until she can complete her Ūṣā vow, a *vrat* to the goddess. She decrees that she must keep to her room for nine months and lay eyes on no man; if her vow of chaste seclusion is not honored, she promised to commit suicide. Not wishing to court disaster, Nal agrees.

Meanwhile, Satya Pīr, the Prime Mover, plops into the water and takes the form of a log, to which Nīl clings.[70] After a full month, addled from sun and surf, he washes up on shore in a bleak and barren garden, which miraculously bursts into bloom. Wonderstruck, the gardener goes to investigate and stumbles across a young man curled up asleep in the roots of an *aśoka* tree. At her touch Nīl awakes. She manages to coax him home where she nurses him back to health, a tonic for her own childless condition.

When Līlāvatī is about to conclude her Ūṣū *vrat*, the king summons his most knowledgeable *brāhmaṇ* priest to explain the vow. The *brāhmaṇ* is stumped: there is nothing like it in the Veda or the *purāṇas*, he proclaims, so he cannot possibly

69. This is an inversion of the story of Nala and Damayantī in the *Mahābhārata*, wherein the gods conspire to marry Damayantī by taking on his appearance, but which she sees through because the gods, though identical in every way to him, hover slightly above the ground while he is firmly planted on it, so she knows it is he. For a lively translation of the Nala and Damayantī story, see "Nala" in *The Mahābhārata*, trans./ed. J. A. B. van Buitenen (Chicago: University of Chicago Press, 1975), vol. 3, bk. 3 (32a), 319–64.

70. Given its Oḍiyā inflection, the allusion here seems to be to Jagannāth, who is known as the *dāru brahmā*, the *brahmā* in the form of wood, combined with the well-worn metaphorical trope of God providing the raft by which an individual might navigate across the river of life or *saṃsār*. In some forms of Oḍiyā *vaiṣṇava* theology, Jagannāth inhabits the void, *śūnyatā*, the ocean in which Satya Pīr now floats.

predict what it means. He proposes that the king load his most trusted elephant with riches and let it roam through the land to reward anyone who can explain; imposters will reveal themselves and be executed for their greed. The man who can unravel the puzzle of the vow will clearly possess an arcane knowledge, and the elephant will bring him to the palace to reveal all.[71] Eventually, the elephant passes by the gardener's house, and when Nīl hears the wager, he understands. He gifts the elephant's riches to the gardener and, looking wan and emaciated, heads to the palace. His twin brother Nal does not recognize him, for through his tribulations Nīl has lost his royal luster. Curiously, Nīl, too, fails to recognize Nal. As the time approaches, the excitement rises; even the seas swell in anticipation of the end of this unusual Ūṣā *vrat.*

Everyone who is someone is present. Līlāvatī immediately spots him and, as rehearsed, he takes his place and begins his tale, a reprise of his life—how his mother died, how he and his brother were falsely accused, how he was whisked away to the forest where his brother disappeared, how he was apprehended as a horse thief, and how his escape was engineered. He narrates how he fatefully landed up on Siṃhala and managed to win the princess in a *svayaṃvar* bride choice. Then, after being cast out of the king's palace and en route to Candraketu's land, the merchant pushed him overboard. He tells how he clung to a buoyant wooden plank that luckily floated by, and how he eventually washed up on the gardener's beach. Līlāvatī confirms it. As the story unfolds, it gradually dawns on Nal that this man is none other than his own brother, whom he once nearly had killed as a horse thief. They are soon reconciled. Nal quickly orders the merchant jailed with the same stone on his chest that Nīl suffered.

Nal and Nīl together worship Satya Pīr and then send a messenger to Līlāvatī's father, Siṃhabāhu, to join them. In thanks, they lavishly worship Satya Pīr to spread his fame. Siṃhabāhu will bring Nīl and Līlāvatī back to Siṃhala Nagar, where he will install them as the rightful rulers. Nal and Nīl then send for their father Vīrbhadra. In his grief-stricken condition, having lost his wife and his two sons, he has ceased to care about life, but when he learns that both of sons have survived and each has a princess for a wife, he finds hope. Reunited, he and his sons and everyone in the kingdom worship Satya Pīr.

. . .

Nal and Nīl's saga very unsubtly distills the message into its starkest binary: *worship Satya Pīr and prosper, fail to worship and suffer.* The coercive quality of Satya

71. This release of the elephant with its challenge and reward seems to be a structural inversion of the traditional *aśvamedha* or horse sacrifice wherein an aspiring king, seeking to assert sovereignty over a particular territory, would release a horse, with proclamation attached, but accompanied by an army. At the end of the year, the horse would be escorted back and the territory it had traversed would be, ipso facto, subject to the king because no one had succeeded in killing it. Here the peregrination is in search of the hero-king, and no one else would dare to assert that identity.

Pīr's intercession bluntly moves the male figures into a place of submission, but the optative interventions he offers his female leads, such as in Lālmon's story noted above, again apply. It is Līlāvatī's prescient realization that prompts her to initiate a new *vrat*, that of the goddess Ūṣū, which is an Oḍiyā variant of Uṣas, Dawn, attested frequently in the *Ṛg veda*. Uṣas is closely allied with *ṛta*, the principle of cosmic and moral order, and is naturally associated with the Āśvins, the twins, who in their form as horses or men with horse heads pull the sun's chariot. Consistent with the impulse behind this cycle of tales, it is with the help of Satya Pīr that Līlāvatī has been empowered to take matters into her own hands. She figures out what no one else yet knows, so by undertaking her vow she will reveal the two men as *twins*, which will correct the horrible miscarriage of justice perpetrated by the younger queen by restoring both rightful heirs to their kingdom. It will at the same time expiate the sins of the father for having wrongly ordered their execution—precisely the kind of moral order the goddess Uṣas would engender. With the connection to the Āśvins (who are identified with horses), it is hardly a coincidence that Satya Pīr uses the ruse of the royal horse to cause Nīl to be suspected of thievery.

This second emplotment deploys the narrative code that touts the efficacy of worshiping Satya Pīr or Satya Nārāyaṇ. Female protagonists reason and work their way toward a happy resolution that judiciously calls on Satya Pīr's aid—knowing when and how to utilize his extraordinary power—while many of the male protagonists seem to require more brutal instruction and even coercion before they learn. In the same way women are instrumental in insinuating the worship of Satya Pīr through the *vrats* that constitute the trilogy of the first emplotment, more often than not it is the women in this second emplotment who are responsible for slipping the worship of Satya Pīr into everyday life, who explore the prospects of tapping alternate forms of power that open the Bengali cosmos to accommodate what was initially a non-Bengali form of religiosity. But it is the third emplotment that inverts the trope of a simple accommodation of the *sūphī pīr* into a *hinduyāni* cosmology: the traditional Bengali cosmology finds itself incorporated into a larger *musalmāni* cosmos that displaces the easy equivalences of the other two emplotments.

6.4. THE SIGNIFICANCE OF SATYA PĪR IN *MUSALMĀNI* TERMS

The tales of Satya Pīr that are *musalmāni* in their provenance and orientation take a decidedly different tack to the power of the *pīr* and the dynamics of interacting with the local populace. The overarching perspectives transform a traditional Indic cosmological frame to a *musalmāni* one. With that shift, no time need be spent justifying Satya Pīr's existence, as was necessary for the *vaiṣṇavs*, for *pīrs* are already part of the everyday *musalmāni* world. Nor is there any attempt to equate

Satya Pīr with a *sannyāsī* or *vairāgī* or *jogī*, even though the authors routinely refer to these figures in ways commensurate with the analogues of the *phakir* and *pīr*, and in so doing draw upon the association of their underlying signification systems. Because the form of the *pīr* functions in Bengal's culture as a source of local power and moral fortitude, any *pīr* would be an obvious choice for literary interest. But relating Satya Pīr's triumphs as a way of celebrating his superiority is clearly subsumed by the larger interest of proving or confirming that he is worthy of a following in the first place. Much of that message is communicated semiotically through the changes in his physical image, the conflation of *vaiṣṇav* images of divinity and suggested ritual practices with the accoutrements and *phakirī* customs of *sūphī* mendicants.[72] Examining these images in some detail will help us to uncover the art of *incremental realignment*, that is, conditioning the audience to changes that will ultimately invert the cosmological relationships. Often displayed in order to elicit some kind of confrontation, these semiotically rich images manipulate the encounter with divinity experienced by the antagonists and, at the same time, subtly manipulate the reader's emotional world in ways that might influence behavior.

These triumphs of Satya Pīr are not always narratively sequenced as they are in the *vaiṣṇav* trilogy, nor are they ordered for consumption in any way similar to the incorporation of his tales into the *vrat* cycle. Most are independent or only loosely related to others, but the liveliest coordinated group can be found in one expansive collection composed in the late eighteenth or early nineteenth century, the *Baḍa satya pīr o sandhyāvatī kanyār punthi* of Kṛṣṇahari Dās,[73] with which we started this book. It is structured in the form of an anecdotal hagiography of the generic religious hero and constitutes the largest single text telling the tales of Satya Pīr. The author's name might suggest an overt *vaiṣṇav* orientation; he conveys that his father is named Rāmdev, his mother Pañcamī, but importantly his *guru*'s name is Mohāmmad Sarkār—the name of his *guru* telling of the text's perspective.[74] Here

72. A number of scholars have come to recognize the obviousness of the partnership of *pīrs* and *vaiṣṇavs*, an image patterned after that of Satya Pīr; see Ajoy Kumār Ghoṣ, "Viṣṇupurer pir sthān," in *Bā̃kuḍār khoyālī: Jaṅgalmohal saṃkalan*, ed. Arabinda Caṭṭopādhyāy (Pratāpabāgān, Bā̃kuḍā: E. Ṭi. Pres, 2014), 125–43.

73. Girīndranāth Dās includes a summary of Kṛṣṇahari Dās's *Baḍa satya pīr o sandhyāvatī kanyār punthi;* see Dās, *Bāṃlā pīr sāhityer kathā*, 469–92. Unfortunately, the subtle textures of the narrative are completely lost as he simply reports the action, especially conflict, which not-so-generously changes the text to fit into his stark Hindu-Muslim binary. See also the second revised edition: Dās, *Bāṃlā pīr sāhityer kathā*, 2nd ed (Kalikātā: Suvarṇarekhā, 1998), 347–62. For a rare synoptic article that includes references to Kṛṣṇahari Dās's text, see Kānāi Lāl Rāy, "Satyapīr," in *Bāṃlā Ekāḍemī Patrikā*, ed. Mohāmmad Hārun-ur-Raśid (Śrāvaṇ-Āśvin 1399 BS [ca. 1992]), 71–82. It should be noted, however, that his Kṛṣṇahari Dās references are to Muhammad Śahīdullāh's *Bāṃlā sāhityer kathā*, which can now be found in Śahīdullāh, *Śahīdullāh racanābalī*, ed. Ānisujjāmān, 3 vols. (Ḍhākā: Bāṃlā Ekāḍemī, 1994), 2:1–504.

74. Kṛṣṇahari Dās, *Baḍa satya pīr o sandhyāvatī kanyār punthi*, 59–60.

we have confirmation that names do not automatically signal religious orientation even as late as the eighteenth and early nineteenth century as they are assumed to do today.

Kṛṣṇahari Dās's lengthy tome opens by invoking the glory of Āllā and the Prophet and describing the wonders of *bhest* (heavenly paradise). Because a certain *brāhmaṇ* king named Maidānava, a worshiper of Kālī, has been persecuting *pīrs* and *phakīrs* indiscriminately, Satya Pīr is sent down—recall the convolutions of his birth that were described in chapter 1. More than half of Kṛṣṇahari Dās's lengthy volume is taken up by the quest of Satya Pīr to prepare himself, finally meet, and eventually triumph over King Maidānav—the primary raison d'être for the *pīr*'s descent.[75] After the *pīr*'s emergence from the turtle's egg, he disappears into the jungly forest and only after five years returns to his mother. Almost immediately after his birth, he encounters Khoyājā Khijir. We must assume that Satya Pīr is fully formed and intellectually and emotionally accomplished (having lost little or nothing between the time he was summoned by God and when he descends[76]), so he begs Khoyājā to accept him as his *murid* or student. Khoyājā quickly disappears, but Satya Pīr demonstrates his eligibility and patience by trailing him for more than a week, guided only by the sound of the Khoyājā's anklets. They traverse through all seven levels of the underworld, eventually landing in the underground realm of Pātāl where Khoyājā begins his instruction in earnest.[77] The young *pīr*'s tutelage constitutes one of the lengthiest passages about Khoyājā Jendā Pīr in early modern Bangla literature, as far as I have been able to determine, exceeded only by the recapitulation of the Korānic tale told by Saiyad Sultān's *Nabivaṃśa*.[78]

Khoyājā Khijir, often simply called the Green One, is regularly invoked as the guide and protector of boatmen and fisherfolk along the coastal waterways and out into the Bay of Bengal.[79] He is an enigmatic figure whose first mention is in the Qur'ān (18.60–82), where he is known as al-Khiḍr in Arabic. Since his original notice, he is said to be found "where the two seas meet."[80] In the Korānic

75. Kṛṣṇahari Dās, 1–134.

76. This is different from traditional *vaiṣṇav* divinity, whose characters undergo some kind of amnesia in order to descend to earth and only gradually discover their identity as divine.

77. Kṛṣṇahari Dās, *Baḍa satya pīr o sandhyāvatī kanyār punthi*, 35–36. The spelling here is Khoyājā, while in other texts and traditions, Khoyāj.

78. Saiyad Sultān, *Nabīvaṃśa*, 1: 670–84; for translation, see Stewart and Irani, "Curbing Moses' Hubris."

79. Pīr Badar shares these duties as protector of seamen, especially those operating toward the south along the coasts of Chittagong and further to the east into southeastern Asia; recall Badar Pīr's base of operations as recounted above in chapter 2. There is a festival known as *baḍo bhāsān*, which is performed at the end of the month of Bhadra to ensure the purity of the waters of the rivers and is done in devotion of Khoyāj Khijir and/or Gaṅgādevī; see Anonymous, "Baḍo bhāsān," *Lok sāhitya* 51 (Phālguṇ 1397 BS [February 1991]): 1–184.

80. Halman, *Where the Two Seas Meet*. The reports that follow here document al-Khiḍr's place in the commentarial tradition.

passage, it is in order to curb Musa's growing hubris that God sends Moses to al-Khiḍr to receive instruction. As possessor of the most esoteric knowledge of the saints, al-Khiḍr attempts to instruct Musā, but in three discrete episodes, al-Khiḍr exposes the limits of Musā's capacity to comprehend the inscrutable esoteric domains of the religious insight reserved for the most accomplished of prophets (*nabī*), apostles (*paygambar*), and saints (*auliyā*). He succeeds primarily in exposing Musā's habit of impatience, whereupon al-Khiḍr dismisses him for not following his instruction. As the ultimate *murśid*, al-Khiḍr is the teacher of teachers.[81] Traditions associated with Alexander, including the *Iskandarnāma*, tell that al-Khiḍr drank from the fountain of life and so became physically immortal.[82] By virtue of that physical immortality, he is said to have continued to guide extraordinary *sūphī* masters through successive centuries.[83] Appearing in the earliest *ḥadīth* literatures of al-Bukhārī and Muslim, the *tafsīr* commentaries attest to his continued presence and his initiation of key saints, including Rūzbihan Baqlī, Ibn ᶜArabī, Rūmi, and Ḥāfiẓ, among others.[84] In the larger Islamic traditions, the rare intervention by al-Khiḍr signals the elevated status of the accomplished *pīr* who becomes his disciple or *murid*; the same holds for his rare appearances in the stories of *pīrs* in Bengal. A similar association, though not as forcefully articulated, is suggested for Gāji Pīr when he and Kālu meet Khoyājā Khijir in the guise of a child and Gāji immediately recognizes him and pays his respects, while Kālu does not. For the receiver of these stories, the presence of Khoyājā Khijir signals a level of accomplishment of these heroic *pīrs* that validates them completely. That Khoyājā Jendā Pīr initiates Satya Pīr and then gives him instruction for five years places Satya Pīr among the most accomplished in all of God's creation.

When Satya Pīr follows Khoyājā down beneath the surface of the world into Bali's domain, and trails every step of the way by the Lord of Death, Yam, he

81. For a much more comprehensive study of al-Khiḍr and the spread of his tales, see Patrick Franke, *Begegnung mit Khiḍr: Queellenstudien zum Imaginaren im traditionellen Islam*, Beiruter Texte und Studien 15 (Stuttgart: Franz Steiner Verlag, 2000).

82. When Alexander and al-Khiḍr have been journeying through the Land of Darkness for four months, al-Khiḍr accidentally drops something from his hand, and when he reaches for it, his hand brushes against a source of water. The water tastes of honey and he realizes instantly that it is the fabled water of life. He orders the army to stop right there so they will not lose the site while he sends for Alexander, but when Alexander returns, the fount has disappeared. See Anonymous, *Iskandernamah*, trans. Minoo S. Southgate (New York: Columbia University Press, 1978), 57–58. See the three appendices of that volume for Khiḍr's discovery of the waters of life in the Persian Alexander romances, in the Pahlavi literature, and in the work of Persian and Arabic historians, including Firdausi.

83. Franke traces the controversy in the twentieth century of the historicity of al-Khiḍr, specifially regarding his longevity and his classification as saint or celestial figure; see Franke, *Begegnung mit Khiḍr*, 306–70.

84. Halman, *Where the Two Seas Meet*, 195–247; for a more expansive narration of al-Khiḍr's role as teacher of God's friends, that is, as *murśid* to numerous *sūphī* saints throughout history, see Franke, *Begegnung mit Khiḍr*, 175–264.

demonstrates his heroic resolve. There he receives direct instruction and promise of help from the Waters, from the Wind, and from the Earth, granting him control of each by simply calling on Nirāñjan, at the foot of whose throne lies heavenly Golok Vṛndāban. He is then advised of the nature of his birth, how he, as a *phakir* of Āllā, was born to Devī Sandhyāvatī in the family of King Maidānav of Mālañcā.[85] Khoyājā instructs him in the use of the *kalemā* and *bichmillā* as tools to destroy obstacles and achieve his goals. Once armed with that secret knowledge, Satya Pīr is ready. Khoyājā initiates him into more advanced metaphysical issues. "Khoyājā said, 'Listen, my child, to the nature of the stainless Nirāñjan's form (*rūp*). His name (*nām*) and essential nature (*svarūp*) constitute the complete godhead (*pūrṇa brahmā*). Should anyone claim to see Khodā in any other form, they do not attain salvation, for he has no identifiable marks (*dhvajāgajā*). He has no form (*rūp*).'"[86] When Khoyājā has taught him what he needs to know, Satya Pīr is directed to visit his mother before beginning his work. Five years have passed.

Because his mother has never seen him, he first presents himself in a dream as a saint (*oli*), before arriving in person. She is understandably nonplussed and suspicious. So she puts him to the test: after he performs *jikir* of the prophet and Āllā, he suckles her breasts, which triggers a thick flow of creamy milk—an effect only a son could produce.[87] Then Dharmarāj, Yam, appears from the seventh underworld and confirms that he has not died and is indeed her son.[88] She has a hard time believing it until he explains how the turtle encased him in the egg and gestated him and how Khoyājā took him in and taught him. Then he says, "I can tell you now my name, who I am: I, Satya Nārāyaṇ, am Satya Pīr."[89]

Though she has her opulent dwelling, without family support Sandhyāvatī has suffered there in the forest, so to help make up for it, Satya Pīr decides to improve her living conditions. He visits the settlement of Jhāḍakhaṇḍa, controlled by one Basanta Rājā. Appearing in his mendicant's garb, he provocatively begs one of the king's protected royal geese as alms. Basanta Rājā takes umbrage and orders the constabulary to drive away this nuisance of a *pīr*. Having engineered the confrontation, in retaliation Satya Pīr then steals—and that is the way it is expressed—Basanta Rājā's subjects. To effect this, he appears in a dream to the prominent figure Cānd Khā̃, to whom he reveals himself as Satya Nārāyaṇ. He commands Cānd Khā̃ to lead the subjects of Jhāḍakhaṇḍa to Sandhyāvatī's forest abode, to clear the land, and to build a city around her palace appropriate to her station.

85. Kṛṣṇahari Dās, *Baḍa satya pīr o sandhyāvatī kanyār punthi*, 36–37.

86. Kṛṣṇahari Dās, 37–38. *Dhvajāgajā* is gender marking by the presence of the penis.

87. Satya Pīr proposes a similar test to prove maternity when Śīlāvatī's son, Motilāl, has been switched by the midwife for a stillborn; see Kiṅkara Dāsa, "The Mother's Son Who Spat Up Pearls," in Stewart, trans., *Fabulous Females and Peerless Pīrs*, 140–42.

88. Kṛṣṇahari Dās, *Baḍa satya pīr o sandhyāvatī kanyār punthi*, 43–44.

89. Kṛṣṇahari Dās, 45–46.

Cānd Khā̃ is convinced, but no one else is, so they refuse to budge. Realizing muscle will be required, Satya Pīr summons the goddess of diseases, Rogeśvarī. He instructs her to afflict Jhāḍakhaṇḍa with leprosy to persuade the inhabitants to join him. She readily agrees and does. Appearing in a bright flash as the fearsome goddess Cāmuṇḍa, she unleashes leprosy and a score of other dread diseases that within five days lay waste to much of the population. With fevers sweeping through the residents of every part of the city, *bhūts*, hungry ghosts, patrol the carnage. Bodies are covered with blood that has boiled to the surface of the skin of unfortunates; others fall, dotted with suppurating abscesses, while still others find their bones extruding their skin. The agony is unimaginable. With so many dying, Cānd Khā̃ finally persuades those remaining survivors to flee and to build the city of which he has dreamed. In no time the settlement of Jhāḍakhaṇḍa is bereft of its entire population.[90]

Their trek through the jungle seems endless as they weather tigers and other beasts of prey. It is so wild that they encounter no other humans. When they finally reach Sandhyāvatī's compound—constructed by Viśvakarmma years earlier—they see that it rivals the celestial capital of Indrapurī. They rejoice at finally having reached their destination, realizing it has not been just a dream; so they apply themselves to clearing the land and constructing a proper city. They settle their new urban space with *brāhmaṇs*, *sannyāsīs*, oil pressers, gardeners, garland weavers, farmers and ploughmen, blacksmiths, traders, physicians, weavers, cotton carders, and cowherders. Sweet-makers, perfumers, conch carvers, and gold- and silversmiths all settle. Sekhs and Saiyads come in numbers, Pāṭhāns too. Some Europeans, Mughals, and Khāns find their places. The markets are packed with different merchants, their flood of wares covering every imaginable need. And of course there are instrument makers, drummers, and musicians of all types. Ḍoms and Namaśūdras dot the banks of the river, beside leather workers, brickmakers, boatbuilders, ferrymen, and untold others, even the occasional madman or epileptic. Altogether there are thirty-four social ranks (*jāti*) that make the city complete.[91]

That night Satya Pīr enters the dreams of Basanta Rājā and chides him for not giving the goose as alms. He reveals that in retribution, it was he who lured away his subjects. Basanta Rājā sends his chief of police, who confirms its truth. Enraged, he orders his soldiers to pursue Satya Pīr, to sack Sandhyāvatī's new urban paradise, and force his lost subjects back to Jhāḍakhaṇḍa. The first of his warriors to confront Satya Pīr are summarily dispatched by five *mantra*-sprinkled arrows. So the

90. Kṛṣṇahari Dās, 47–50.

91. Kṛṣṇahari Dās, 52–53. The creation of a new city and the relocating of inhabitants from another is central to the story of Kālketu in the *Caṇḍīmaṅgal* of Kavikaṅkan; see Kavikaṅkan Mukundarām Cakravartī, *Caṇḍīmaṅgal*, 66–83, secs. 109–36 (the *pālā* performed on the night of the third day). For an analysis of this settlement process, see Ronald B. Inden, "The Hindu Chiefdom in Middle Bengali Literature," *Bengal, Literature and History* (East Lansing, MI: Asian Studies Center, 1967), 21–46.

king himself sets off, swearing to teach that *phakir* something about real *phakirī*. It is like Raghunāth himself assaulting Laṅkā. When his massive forces reach the Begavatī River banks, they pause. Satya Pīr, now in *sannyāsī*'s garb, approaches in the form of Satya Nārāyaṇ. He greets the *mahārāj* to ascertain his intentions. The king declares he is there to fight and, after winning, plans to turn Sandhyāvatī into his personal slave by way of retribution.[92] Because of his dream, he knows that this is the *sannyāsī* whom he spurned and who has been behind it all.

> "The head of that *sannyāsī* will be cut off right before my eyes!" At the command of the *mahārāj*, two soldiers leapt to attack the *sannyāsī*. Anticipating them, Satya Nārāyaṇ reflexively acted. He silently repeated (*jap*) the personal names of Nirāñjan, the Stainless, and his body mysteriously metamorphosed into adamantine rock. The blast of shot from the soldiers' muskets streaked like so many shooting stars, but the pellets splintered apart upon impact with his body, split open, the sound reverberating like the crack of a bird's egg. Witnesses all were dumbfounded. Clearly his death had not been inscribed, for he was still very much alive. Flooded with an unimaginable fear, everyone scattered. Satya Pīr gave chase, raising his staff, intent on slaying them; once again he resorted to his magical control of the created world (*māyā*). He waded into the field of battle and assumed the terrifying image of pestilence and death. Everyone panicked, lost their nerve, what little strength they had left draining away as they fled. By the power of *mantras*, he froze everyone in their tracks. Reciting the personal names of Nirāñjan, his body suddenly expanded upward to a height of fourteen hands. His skin turned black as pitch, his face monstrously terrifying, and in his hand, his staff transformed into a magical cudgel. Everyone who bore witness to this spectacle could only shake with fear.[93]

Two brave souls challenge him with sharply pointed missiles, but he simply snatches them from the air and sends them back, splitting open their unfortunate heads. The engagement seems to be over, but the king himself shows signs of continued resistance, so Satya Nārāyaṇ

> assumed his four-armed form, holding the conch, disc, club, and lotus. He towered directly over the *rājā*. When Basanta Rājā beheld that magnificent four-armed image, he quickly pulled a cloth around his neck and began to sing hymns of praise. "You are not a mere mortal, but the manifest Nārāyaṇ. Please forgive any offense I may have committed for I am lowly and despicable."
>
> Satya Pīr then explained the nature of this magical subterfuge. "I am not just Nārāyaṇ; I am a *phakir* of Āllā. You may recall that previous incident when a beggar came to you asking for a goose, but you refused to make that gift; that was your mistake, your great offense. That failure led directly to the destruction of Jhāḍakhaṇḍa.

92. Kṛṣṇahari Dās, *Baḍa satya pīr o sandhyāvatī kanyār punthi*, 56–57.

93. The image from the scroll painting held in the British Museum that graces the cover of this volume illustrates this scene.

I am a god (*devatā*) to *hindus*; I am a *pīr* to *musalmāns*. I have come to receive the worship and service (*sevā*) of both communities (*kūl*). I am Satya Nārāyaṇ, I am Satya Pīr."[94]

The army retreats and Basanta Rājā then smartly institutes the regular worship of Satya Bhagavān.

Satya Pīr returns to his mother in another emotion-laden reunion. Then the angel Jibril descends to remind Satya Pīr that he must go to Mālañcā to deal with the *pīr*-torturing king, Maidānav. As he starts to take leave of his mother, Sandhyāvatī weeps, rehearsing her various misfortunes—according to form, the author breaks into a formal lament (*bāramās*) of Sandhyāvatī's tribulations enumerated through the twelve months of the year.[95] As her son prepares to depart, she changes her tack and insists that she too should go, just as Gupicānd's four wives tried to accompany him as *joginīs*; but Satya Pīr summarily dismisses the suggestion.[96] Feeling remorse, he does tarry longer than is prudent, and that delay comes to the attention of Āllā, who makes it clear that his command is not to be ignored! The *paygambar* ensures he gets the message. Chastised, Satya Pīr waits until his mother is asleep, takes some of her bangles, and then dons his ascetic's garb.

Rudrākṣa beads around his neck, he wound his hair into a coil, which draped down, matted. He donned an ochre robe and picked up his mendicant's staff. His limbs glistened the golden color of the sun, his whole body was radiant, resplendent; the deerskin that hung loosely over his body broadcast a compelling image of majesty. From his left ear swung a gold earring. Everything about him glistened the color of gold. This erstwhile *sannyāsī* picked up in his right hand the flute of the *avatār* Kānāi, with the other he picked up the bows and arrows of Rām and Lakṣmaṇ. The ascetic's staff of the *avatār* Nitāi [Nityānanda] magically appeared, as did the plow of the *avatār* Balarām, and all the implements of the ten *avatārs* as well. Satya Nārāyaṇ then slipped the jeweled bracelets from Sandhyāvatī's arms and hung them casually in his hair. The measure of Satya Pīr's majesty could scarcely be calculated.[97]

94. Kṛṣṇahari Dās, *Baḍa satya pīr o sandhyāvatī kanyār punthi*, 57.

95. The *bāramās* (twelve-month lamentation) has a long history in Bengali letters wherein the poet describes the cycle of emotional trauma—usually of separation from the object of love or devotion—through the metaphor of the cycle of the seasons. For contemporary social use of lament, including the *bāramās*, see James M. Wilce, *Eloquence in Trouble: The Poetics of Complaint in Rural Bangladesh*, Oxford Studies in Anthropological Linguistics (New York: Oxford University Press, 2003).

96. Kṛṣṇahari Dās, *Baḍa satya pīr o sandhyāvatī kanyār punthi*, 61–62. Gupicānd, or Gopīcāndra, is the subject of several famous *nāth* tales. For the four wives' attempt to accompany Gopīcānd, see Bhābanidās, "Gopīcāndrer pāñcālī," in *Gopīcāndrer gān*, ed. Aśutoṣ Bhaṭṭācāryya, 3rd ed. (Kalikātā: Kalikātā Viśvavidyālay, 1965), 283–85, ll. 355–428.

97. Kṛṣṇahari Dās, *Baḍa satya pīr o sandhyāvatī kanyār punthi*, 63–64. A similar formulaic description of his sartorial style is repeated a few pages later, 70–71.

When Sandhyāvatī awakes, he is gone. She goes mad with grief, but eventually gathers her wits sufficiently to summon a magical talking *śuyā* bird to track him; it reports that Satya Pīr is wending his way toward Mālañcā country.[98]

After the village of Nandipur, Satya Pīr reaches the banks of the Gomani. The current is fast, the waves high, and there is no boat. A lounging crocodile offers to ferry him across for the price of a goat, but if he produces no goat, he promises to eat half of the *pīr*'s body in payment. With no goat handy, Satya Pīr meditates on God and does enter the mouth of the crocodile. When he reaches the belly, he summons his powers and tears it apart. The crocodile magically transforms into a nymph, *vidyādharī*. Cursed by Indra for a misstep in her dance, she has waited twelve years for release by the touch of Satya Pīr, for she knows him to be the *avatār* of the Kali Age. She pays her profound respects, and then a chariot arrives from heaven to escort her back to her rightful place.[99]

Satya Pīr heads on to Mālañcā, picking his way through obscure paths till he reaches the settlement of Kesarā Nagar. The village headman, Bhimā, is a thief who, after slyly estimating the value of the gold bracelets hanging in Satya Pīr's hair, feigns hospitality, only to steal them later. Satya Pīr confronts Bhimā, who affects ignorance. Satya Pīr erupts in anger, and in a matter of seconds all four of Bhimā's sons are struck down, blood spurting from their mouths as they writhe in agony and die. Bhimā, too, he curses to lose his head in the town of Akullapur. Bhimā and his wife are dumbstruck as the *pīr* makes sure they understand whom they have offended: he is Satya Nārāyaṇ for *hindus* and Satya Pīr for *musalmāns*. Bhimā repents, returns the bracelets, then offers nine rupees' worth of *sinni*. Mollified, Satya Pīr restores life to his sons. But he does not lift the malediction; some years later, as a result of his shenanigans, Bhimā meets his fate in the village of Akullapur.[100]

The *pīr* proceeds through a host of settlements, some well-known, others not; at long last he reaches the land of Mālañcā, the capital of which perches on the Damudar River. The magnificence of the king's residence rivals the palaces of Laṅkā. He calculates that for best effect, he should replace his *phakir*'s garments with the more opulent dress of a *sannyāsī*. Once again his clothes and accoutrements magically transform. He is greeted with affection and respect by everyone he meets—no one suspects he is really a *pīr*. And so he enters the court of Maidānav Rājā and is seated in honor beside the king.[101] He claims to be on pilgrimage, but that he has heard that the king is a great devotee and so has detoured. The king

98. The four wives of Gopīcānd similarly dispatch their parrot to trace his whereabouts, which was across the Gomati River in the town of Suripu; see Bhābanidās, "Gopīcandrer pāñcālī," 319–20, ll. 1420–55.

99. Kṛṣṇahari Dās, *Baḍa satya pīr o sandhyāvatī kanyār punthi*, 67–68.

100. Kṛṣṇahari Dās, 68–70.

101. Kṛṣṇahari Dās, 70–71.

queries the provenance of the bracelets hanging in his hair. Satya Pīr reports that he received them from a young woman living in the forest named Sandhyāvatī; she had no husband, but bore a son named Satya Nārāyaṇ. Satya Pīr continues: the boy's grandfather is named Maidānav, a *vārindri brāhmaṇ*, an assertion challenged by the king.[102] Then Satya Pīr reveals his identity as a *phakir*. The queen secretly meets Satya Pīr and questions how her *brāhmaṇ* daughter could be connected to a *phakir*; she advises him to decamp before her husband has him killed. Her two sisters, Rūpavatī and Mālāvatī, would show him out, but he refuses. When Satya Pīr tells the saga of Sandhyāvatī, they know it to be true. Recognizing him, Rūpavatī asks to cook for him, but he declines, for he only eats uncooked food: a small handful of rice flour, mixed with sugar, milk, and plantain; anything else would be an indulgence. The women press him to leave, but Khodā himself has guaranteed his safety.[103] The next day he appears in his mendicant's dress,

> He had the prophet's mantle draped over his shoulders, sandal smeared on his face, a ruby diadem gracing his forehead. Around his neck hung a string of prayer beads, under his right arm was tucked the *Bhāgavat purāṇ*. In his hand he fingered a *tulsīmālā* as he performed *jap*, the recitation of the names of God. With wooden sandals on his feet, he stepped lightly like a wagtail bird. The body of Sandhyā's son radiated in brilliance. In his left hand he carried a Korān and in his right hand his mendicant's staff. He did not wear the head covering of either a *phakir* or *vairāgī*. One leg sported an anklet, while the other was bare. The aureate limbs of this saint's body shone like molten gold as he walked. People talked and gossiped, but no one could fathom it. And that is how he entered the city.[104]

The townsfolk are flabbergasted and crowd around, hearing him recite *bichmillā* and then the name of Rām in the same breath. Neither the scriptural *agamas* or the *nigamas* has prepared them for this: to hear the *Bhāgavat purāṇ* and Korān mixed together. They are unsettled, for he is praising the gods of the *hindu* folk and paying respects to the *phakirs* of the faithful *momins*.[105]

He makes his way to the palace and petitions to see the king, but the king flies into a rage. He orders the durwan to give the beggar a handful of rice and shoo him away, but Satya Pīr keeps insisting on seeing the king in person. They go back and forth till, exasperated, one of the king's personal eunuchs (*khojā*) attempts to intervene, suggesting that the mendicant must be smoking too much *gāñjā*.[106] Satya Pīr still refuses to budge. Aggravated, the king orders the *pīr* be jailed and

102. *Vārendra brāhmaṇs* are one of the two top clans of *kulīn brāhmaṇs*, the other being *rāḍhī*. The historical region of *vārendra* settlement was in the north, with *rāḍhī brāhmaṇs* to the south. See Ronald B. Inden, *Marriage and Rank in Bengali Culture*, esp. chap. 1.

103. Kṛṣṇahari Dās, *Baḍa satya pīr o sandhyāvatī kanyār punthi*, 72–75.

104. Kṛṣṇahari Dās, 75–76.

105. Kṛṣṇahari Dās, 76.

106. When the eunuch speaks, his language is a *pidgin hindustāni*, telling his non-Bengali origins.

executed without delay. It takes a small army of highly trained soldiers to bind him and throw him into jail. Coming to feel Satya Pīr's tribulations as he languishes in jail, Jibril delivers a flower from Āllā that, laced with secret syllables, magically sunders his irons and breaks open the jail as soon as he touches it to his forehead. Satya Pīr is freed.[107]

Satya Pīr visits the queen's sister Mālāvatī, revealing his true identity and his plan to escape to Mālāvatīpur in the shapeshifted guise of a seven-year-old boy. Pretending to be an orphan, he winds up at the home of a *brāhmaṇ* named Kuśal. He convinces the childless *brāhmaṇ* that he is quite positive he is a *vārendri brāhmaṇ*. When asked, he says his name is Satya, but he does not know his *gotra* classification. They take him in. The *brāhmaṇ's* wife, Anandi, rejoices at their fortune, but when she goes to cook for him, he tells her it is his habit only to take uncooked food, again reciting the ingredients for *sinni*.[108]

Back in Mālañcā, Maidānav decides to sacrifice the *phakir* to the goddess Kālī, but when his minions reach the jail, he is nowhere to be found. As Maidānav fulminates, Satya Pīr is already far far away, living as a young boy in the home of the *brāhmaṇ* Kuśal, the tutor of the king's two sons, Śyāmsundar and Dāmodar. Attempts to tutor Satya fail, moving Kuśal to raise his staff to strike Satya, but his wife intervenes. In dreams, Satya eventually reveals to them who he is—"I am Satya Nārāyaṇ, I am Satya Pīr." They accept, and from that point forward he is free to do as he pleases.[109] After bathing in the Nur River, Satya Pīr picks up a Korān, but Kuśal is adamant that he not read it. When asked why, he replies that for a *brāhmaṇ* to read the Korān or recite the name of God, *bichmillā*,[110] would mean loss of social standing, nor could he ever enter *vaikuṇṭha*, heaven.

> Chuckling, Satya Nārāyaṇ said, "Who ever said that those names [of God] could not be conjoined? There is but one supreme lord, *brahmā*, not two. God as creator (*kartā*) is singular, Nirāñjan Gosāi. One recites (*jap*) the names of Brahmā, Viṣṇu, Maheśvar. Untold numbers of Brahmā-eggs can be found in each pore of his skin; though he has no hands or feet, he holds and embraces this created world of existence. Though he has no mouth, he eats; with no ears he yet hears; with no eyes he sees.[111] No one

107. Kṛṣṇahari Dās, *Baḍa satya pīr o sandhyāvatī kanyār punthi*, 78–82.

108. Kṛṣṇahari Dās, 82–84.

109. Kṛṣṇahari Dās, 85–87.

110. It should be noted that here and in the passage that follows, this author uses *bichmillā* as a proper name of Āllā, not as the benediction that opens the Korān that says "In the name of God . . ." Very occasionally the reference seems to be the incipit verse of the Korān, but even that is not always clear.

111. This is a reference to the previously noted *śloka* in the *Svetāśvatara upaniṣad* 3:19, which translates as: "Without hands or feet he moves and he grasps, without eyes he sees, without ears he hears. He knows all, yet no one can know him. [People] call him the most excellent primeval man." The Sanskrit of the upaniṣadic verse reads: *apāṇipādo javano grahītā paśyatyacakṣuḥ sa śṛṇotyakarṇaḥ / sa vetti vedyaṃ na ca tasyāsti vettā tamāhuragryaṃ puruṣaṃ mahāntam //*; see chap. 1, n. 59.

can fully cognize that he is inherent within, innate to all things created. The very one who is called Nirāñjan, the Stainless, people call Bichmillā. There is no distinction whatsoever between Viṣṇu and Bichmillā. People may discern one stream going this way, another that, but they all come together and are mixed in the ocean. The thirty-four social ranks (*jāti*) actually make for a single group. Though people take different paths, they end up mixed together." When he heard this exposition, the [*brāhmaṇ*] *ṭhākur* was stunned.[112]

The *brāhmaṇ* realizes he needs to study the Korān. He does not know how to read the script, but with the help of Āllā he is soon able. From then on he keeps a Korān in the house.

It is the sixth of Jyaiṣṭha (May–June), the day for Ṣaṣṭhī *pūjā*, the celebration of the goddess who looks after children. When Bhāṇḍārī Ṭhākur calls for Kuśāl to perform the *pūjā* for the king's two sons, Satya Pīr causes his adopted father to fall ill, so he can replace him. Kuśāl gives instruction and off he goes. He is presented to the king's wife Priyāvatī, who wonders who he is, but her two sisters, Rūpāvatī and Mālāvatī, have already figured out his disguise. Satya Pīr begins the *pūjā* by ritually rinsing his mouth while remembering Śrī Viṣṇu; then the queen offers flowers. The saint places his finger in his ear and recites *bichmillā*. When the queen hears this, she angrily throws away her flowers and water offering, but the *pīr* pretends to be nonplussed. "How can the word *bichmillā* come out of the mouth of a *brāhmaṇ*?" she sharply retorts. So they start again and complete the ritual, the food offerings (*naibedya*) cleansed with Gaṅgā water. Satya Pīr meditates on Khodā, recites the *mohāmmadi kalamā*, and finishes the *pūjā*. The queen gives the expected *dakṣiṇā*, but Satya Pīr toys with her, making it disappear and reappear, refusing and accepting, while Rūpāvatī and Mālāvatī gleefully play along. Finally he accepts her tribute and goes home, much to the joy of Anandi and Kuśāl the *brāhmaṇ*.[113]

Kuśāl is getting on in years, so Satya Nārāyaṇ begins to serve as tutor. At one point Śyāmsundar mocks Satya Nārāyaṇ for his limited knowledge of the texts, and a violent scrap ensues. When the blows come, using his God-given powers, Satya Pīr turns his body hard as stone; when he retaliates, he strikes Śyāmsundar once, but his blow is so hard it kills him. The god Yam arrives to fetch him. The king orders Satya Pīr put to death, but it takes more than twenty men to subdue him. Eventually they manage to strap him over the mouth of a cannon. Satya Pīr meditates on Lokmān Hākim, who appears, and together they meditate on the names of Āllā and the Prophet. When the cannon roars, belching smoke and fire, Satya Pīr emerges unscathed.[114] Then soldiers tie a massive boulder to his legs and

112. Kṛṣṇahari Dās, *Baḍa satya pīr o sandhyāvatī kanyār punthi*, 87–88.

113. Kṛṣṇahari Dās, 88–91.

114. Lokmān Hākim (Luqmān) here is a somewhat elusive figure who seems to conflate the popular Arabic Jahaliyya figure and the Luqmān found in Qur'ān 31; he is known for his wisdom and insight

throw him into the river. Satya Pīr continues to pray to Karim Kartā, the Creator, and suddenly the rock floats and he rides it like a boat. No one can believe it.[115] Confusion reigns, and Maidānav has Kuśāl imprisoned, for which his wife Anandi blames Satya Pīr. He manifests his four-armed form to console her, but naturally she is frightened. He then gently explains that he is a *devatā* and *pīr* in a single human body and that he will appear as whatever deity she may invoke. "For my birth in this Kali Age I take the name Satya Pīr. I have taken birth in this Kali Age to make my presence known. I am the *devatā* of the *hindu* and the *pīr* of the *momin*. Whatever one desires, I can effect. I am known as the son of Sandhyāvatī." And then he explains the entire saga of his birth and Sandhyāvatī's years of suffering. Because she the old *brāhmaṇ's* wife has been good to him, he gives her the boon that she will have a son, and off he goes to the king's palace.[116]

Satya Pīr somehow slips into the palace jail unseen and changes places with his adopted father. When summoned, he reveals to the king that he is actually the son of Sandhyāvatī, but the king will hear nothing of it. As he did with Anandi, Satya Pīr patiently explains that he is a *devatā* for *hindus* and a *pīr* for *momins*, to teach both clans to promote his service (*sevā*). He promises to revive the king's son if he will offer *sinni*, but the king puts his fingers in his ears, muttering "Viṣṇu Viṣṇu," closing his ears and his heart to any such suggestion. He orders his *laskārs* to bind Satya Pīr to be sacrificed in the Kālī temple, but while his guards hesitate, Satya Pīr metamorphoses into a white fly and flies off.[117] The constable responsible for killing the prisoner is named Tularām, so when Satya Pīr flies off, the king vents his rage on his ineffectual executioner and cuts out his tongue with much gushing of blood. From afar Satya Pīr, still in the form of a fly, watches the spectacle with dismay, then flies off.[118]

Satya Pīr wings his way to heaven where he approaches Indra, the King of the Gods, sitting on sacred *kuśa* grass, resplendent in his four-armed form. Satya Pīr is seated beside him and they discuss the dire situation in Mālañcā and Maidānav's continued refusal to acknowledge the validity of the *pīrs*. Satya Pīr then requests Indra to send storm clouds to flood Mālañcā, and he readily agrees. When summoned, each of the twelve storm clouds comes forward, boasting of prowess in various types of inundations and promising to do the deed in anywhere from one hour to seven days. Together they ride down to earth on Indra's elephant and begin

into the mechanics of this world, so it is likely that the cannon would count among machines that could be successfully manipulated. In Kṛṣṇahari's text, you may recall, he is depicted in the opening chapters as the analogue of Viśvakarmma, architect of the gods.

115. Kṛṣṇahari Dās, *Baḍa satya pīr o sandhyāvatī kanyār punthi*, 92–94. The ordeals of both Mānik and Gāji as well as the legend of Badar Pīr come to mind.

116. Kṛṣṇahari Dās, 94–96.

117. Satya Pīr will use this same trick of changing into a white fly in the episode of Kāśīkānt in his later adventures noted below; we have also seen the same technique used by Bonbibī above in chap. 4.

118. Kṛṣṇahari Dās, *Baḍa satya pīr o sandhyāvatī kanyār punthi*, 97–99.

their work—light rains, followed by winds, lightning, thunder, then torrential pelting sheets of rain. The waters are rapidly rising in Mālañcā, and soon people, horses, and elephants are being swept away. Rūpāvatī and Mālāvatī meditate on Satya Pīr and are saved when they offered *sinni*. Meanwhile the king struggles to stay alive.

Satya Pīr promises these good women that if the king will but offer a little *sinni*, everyone will be saved and come to no grief in the floods. The items for *sinni*, of course, are not immediately available, so the women find their way to a nearby town, its market controlled by one shyster merchant named Bīrbalā, who tries to con them, but they call his bluff. Being called a cheat ignites Bīrbalā's anger.[119] Satya Pīr miraculously materializes to investigate the commotion and Bīrbalā turns to strike him, which naturally angers the *phakir*.[120] Satya Pīr enlists the help of a poisonous serpent, a *nāginī*, to slay Bīrbalā's seven-year-old son as retribution, which will also conveniently demonstrate his power. The snake performs as asked. Grieving, the boy's mother remembers that the sacred texts instruct them to take a snakebite victim to the banks of a river, where the poison may be drawn out and life restored.[121] So they haul him to the verge of the Nur River, where Satya Pīr approaches the dead child and whispers a *brahma mantra* in his ear. Though it has been three days, the child regains consciousness. Bīrbalā finally fully reckons the power of the *pīr* and, foreswearing all interest in the profits off the bangles, submits to Satya Pīr, who shows him grace. The couple are overjoyed, and the wife heads home with her now-revived son, while Bīrbalā seeks out the two sisters, expresses his abject misery at his wrongdoing, and returns their bangles and then some.[122]

Satya Pīr assures the lives of all those stranded in the flood. He conjures a boat with his heaven-sent powers and collects King Maidānav. The king refuses to change his attitude; he insists that he is a good upstanding *vārendra brāhmaṇ* and has done nothing wrong to warrant the destruction of his city. Satya Pīr confronts the king for his horrible treatment of *phakirs*, and then rehearses the saga of Sandhyāvatī and the unbearable pain Maidānav caused his own daughter out of fear of a bastard child. "I am that child and I have come here as a *phakir*." The king is adamant and still refuses to acknowledge him, the recitation only inciting his further ire. Round and round they go, repeating the same arguments with the king still refusing to offer *sinni* or to acknowledge Satya Pīr, for, he asks, "What *pīr* has ever heaped goodness on a *hindu*?" Satya Pīr explains that all will be well if

119. Kṛṣṇahari Dās, 99–104.

120. There is a lengthy give-and-take here where Satya Pīr details Bīrbalā's faults and failings, somewhat uncharacteristic of the rest of the text, but perhaps a not-so-subtle commentary on the character of gold, silver, and jewelry merchants as swindlers.

121. The popular wisdom is that if one takes a victim of snakebite to the river, an *ojhā* (master of snakes and poisons) might be able to revivify the corpse, a practice with at least hints of *tantrik* necromancy; see Stewart, "Process of Surface Narrative."

122. Kṛṣṇahari Dās, *Baḍa satya pīr o sandhyāvatī kanyār punthi*, 104–10.

the king will offer *śinni* to the tombs of *pīrs*, but the king counters that as a good *vārendra brāhmaṇ* he would lose all social rank and heaven as well. There is no possible way he would undertake such an act. Then he chides Satya Pīr for falsely claiming to be Satya Nārāyaṇ. Satya Pīr settles the issue by manifesting his four-armed celestial form. Agape, Maidānav is finally convinced and rejoices in the fact that it is his daughter who has given birth to Satya Nārāyaṇ, his own Lord. At long last he can relent; he eats and sleeps.[123]

As Maidānav sleeps, Satya Pīr flies back to Indra's heaven, where he greets that four-armed lord and again petitions his help. He wishes to enlist the help of Viśvakarmma to rebuild the city and environs that the rains destroyed. Indra agrees and Viśvakarmma is summoned; he declares that he will rebuild everything within ten hours, so that when Maidānav awakens, his city will be restored. He not only rebuilds it, but exceeds its previous magnificence, erecting palaces and pavilions, open spaces, and living quarters for all. Soon the inhabitants begin to return, and the streets and stables are filled with horses and elephants and the markets with people. Those who perished in the floods are restored, but strangely without any memory of it. The city is back to normal in no time. Queen Priyāvatī and her sons, Śyāmsundar and Damodar, enter the palace and rejoin the king. Satya Pīr arrives amidst a certain fanfare, but he notices that the king does not seem as happy as he had expected.[124]

The king is still suffering the horrible loss of his eldest son Harihar, who was devoured by a crocodile while bathing in the river. He was only twelve at the time. Satya Pīr, who had not realized there was a deceased first son, promises to locate him, so off he goes to the river to interrogate the crocodiles. The crocodiles are cooperative and gather to pay their respects to Satya Pīr. When he asks who is responsible, who ate the crown prince Harihar when he came to bathe, Tirimiṅgā, the elder among the crocodiles, replies in the negative and vouches for all his clan, for, he declares, they are only fish-eaters. The old crocodile summons Neñjā Muḍā, the constable of the crocodiles, to investigate deeper downstream and along the swampy byways. After a while, the constable finds one very ancient crocodile named Hāṅguḍā who protests that he has eaten elephants and horses by the thousands, but never a human. As he is testifying, another crocodile named Baṅgaḍā comes forward and identifies the culprit as Chedaḍā, who is quickly summoned. Chedaḍā, who is also quite old, feigns memory loss and indicates he is not sure, that he does not clearly recall ever eating a boy. Satya Pīr sees through it, quickly utters the names of Āllā in *jikir*, and the old croc splits right apart. Half of him is crocodile, the other half young Harihar.[125] Satya Pīr magnanimously grants

123. Kṛṣṇahari Dās, 111–17.

124. Kṛṣṇahari Dās, 117–19.

125. There is an unstated and very clever visual/verbal pun here: Harihar is of course the combined form of the deities Kṛṣṇa (Hari) and Śiv (Har). Throughout this passage the author has used *kumir* for

Chedaḍā what is left of his natural life, and he slips back under the waters, but Harihar, on shore, lies insensate. Satya Pīr realizes that he will have to journey to Yam's abode to recover the boy's life, and so he does. Yam's residence is a house in Sandhyamani Nagar in Pātāl, so Satya Pīr stretches his own body four times its normal size, into that of a giant, then smears himself head to toe with oil infused with the secret incantations (*śabda*) of *brahma*, and off he flies. As soon as he arrives, he transfigures back into his normal form of Satya Pīr.[126]

When he lands, one of Yam's messengers tries to capture him. Satya Pīr gets the upper hand in the tussle and eventually finds his way to an audience. Yam is puzzled as to how Satya Pīr can be standing there before him and not be dead. But recovering his wits, he politely inquires why he has come, and Satya Pīr explains his mission. When he entreats Yam to return Harihar's soul, Yam informs him that the boy is not to be found in his settlement. He has been spirited away and has taken the form of a *bhūt pret* roaming the earth as a hungry ghost. Yam opines that he will be born again, but it will take untold numbers of lives to release him from the abominable practices he has already undertaken as a *bhūt*. Satya Pīr presses him further, and Yam reveals that Harihar can be found in a particular tamarisk tree in the Gardens of Āduni along with countless others *bhūts* and *prets*.[127] When Satya Pīr arrives, he hears the *bhūt* sentinels chirping away in their incomprehensible language. As soon as the sentries spot Satya Pīr and report, the king of the *bhūts* orders his minions to attack. Satya Pīr senses the danger, settles himself, and begins to recite the names of God, and the bodies of the *bhūts* instantaneously burst into flames with the fire of *brahma*, and they bail out of the trees in a tumble and flee.[128] Realizing Satya Pīr's formidable powers, the king of the *bhūts* asks him why he has ventured into their lair. Satya Pīr calmly recites the saga of Harihar, whom he wishes to retrieve. With their help, Satya Pīr finally locates him, but the task of bringing him back is complicated, so once again he petitions God, and begins to recite the *kalemā*, initiating a cleansing process which will restore Harihar. As he is purified, Satya Pīr whispers in his ear the revivifying *mantras* of the *kalandars*. As the boy regains consciousness, he can remember nothing. Satya Pīr explains all

---

crocodile, rather than the more common *kumbhīr*. As soon as the prince is recovered he is called the prince or *kumār*. When Chedaḍā splits apart, at least some in the audience would realize that after he ate Harihar, Chedaḍā had become the analogue to Harihar, a combined figure, *kumirkumār* (crocodile and prince combined), though the compound is left unconstructed.

126. Kṛṣṇahari Dās, *Baḍa satya pīr o sandhyāvatī kanyār punthi*, 119–22.

127. The tamarisk (*Caryophyllales*, *Tamaricacae*, here likely *Tamarix gallica var. indica*) is a shrub or small tree with reddish brown bark containing high concentrations of salt. It proliferates along waterways and grows up to twenty feet (unlike its cousins in the Middle East and Africa which can tower sixty feet). The Indic version produces a dense but wispy canopy, which is perfect for protecting *bhūts* and *prets*. It is not to be confused with the tamarind.

128. This same strategy was used by Gāji when he dispersed the ghosts and goblins the goddess Caṇḍī had supplied to Dakṣiṇā Rāy; see chap. 5.

that has happened to the incredulous young man, who, when it finally sinks in that he has been dead for forty years and Satya Pīr has restored his life, falls down and begs Satya Pīr to become his master, *murśid*. Satya Pīr readily agrees, so he sits him down and carefully instructs him in the four *kalemās*,[129] before sending him back to his father. It is not hard to imagine how tearful that family reunion is. The king, having once again experienced firsthand the power of the *phakir*, gratefully orders his servants to prepare a hundred thousand *ṭākās*' worth of *śinni* as offering. He also has prepared additional items appropriate to a more elaborate *pūjā*, in keeping with his brāhmaṇical status.[130]

After the commotion settles, Satya Pīr initiates the king into the recitation of the *kalemā*, and the king's heart is moved; he is profoundly transformed. He prostrates himself at the feet of Satya Pīr when he receives his own secret name of initiation, and all parties assembled pay their respects. Satya Pīr reminds the king of his long-lost daughter Sandhyāvatī and how badly she has fared as a result of the king's shortsighted and bigoted actions. When Satya Pīr describes the circumstances of the pregnancy—how God sent down the flower to impregnate her—he goes on to declare, "I am not a human, I am the *jindā pīr* of the Kali age. . . . I reign everywhere covered by the skies. That one you as king call Lord Īśvar—he is my servant." Then *śinni* is distributed to everyone, but a recalcitrant *brāhmaṇ*, one Gokul Paṇḍit, refuses to touch it until Satya Pīr persuades him in an outburst of earth-shattering power.[131]

Brooding on Sandhyāvatī, his long-forgotten daughter, the king has no idea in which part of the forest she can be found. Satya Pīr assures him that he knows the way and will take Harihar with him to fetch her. The king assembles an appropriately royal entourage with all the requisite attendants, staff, aides, and so forth, all to be transported on elephants and horses. Satya Pīr demurs at the offer of a royal ride, for it is not meet for a *phakir*. They are on the Nur River, so he pushes off by boat while Harihar and company travel alongside on the riverbank. At the small outpost town of Bāināṭ, the local garrison officer mistakes the retinue for a raiding party and launches his soldiers to check the procession before it reaches the settlement. In his inexperience, Harihar is frightened and shies away. Using his powerful control over the created world of *māyā*, Satya Pīr assumes the form of a soldier himself and handily subdues the advance party. He then ceremonially makes his way to the local king and presents himself, explaining that the retinue are simply passing through so that King Daināv's son, Prince Harihar, can visit the home of a relative. Satya Pīr cannot help noticing that the king has in his household one princess by the name of Līlāvatī, so he proposes that, to keep peace, she be married to Harihar. The king, sensing the advantages of liaison with the powerful

129. Six is the usual number.

130. Kṛṣṇahari Dās, *Baḍa satya pīr o sandhyāvatī kanyār punthi*, 122–26.

131. Kṛṣṇahari Dās, 126–27.

King Maidānav—and having little choice since his men have just been defeated—instantly agrees. Knowing that Maidānav is a *brāhmaṇ*, the petty ruler is troubled that some of his own past actions, such as eating meat, may come back to haunt him and compromise his and his daughter's social standing. Satya Pir reassures him that those matters are for God to decide. The king gives the order to make the wedding arrangements, promises one lakh of *ṭākās*, and happily submits as vassal to the righteous but absent King Maidānav with the gift of his daughter Līlāvatī to the crown prince. Harihar is pleased, but a little puzzled at just why Satya Pīr is making his marriage arrangements when his relatives, especially his parents, are not present, but he does not dwell on the matter after Satya Pīr's instruction.[132] At the appropriate time, the *paṇḍits* perform the needful rituals, recite their Vedic *mantras*, and the coupled solemnize their vows. Everyone rejoices.[133]

As Līlāvatī prepares to depart with her groom of a few days, her mother laments the all-too-sudden leave-taking, and it is she, rather than Līlāvatī, who needs to be consoled. Harihar formally takes leave of his new in-laws, and the retinue continues forward on elephants, while Satya Pīr walks; together they head to Sandhyāvatī's forest abode. Before they arrive, Satya Pīr visits his mother in a dream and tells her they are traveling towards her. Sandhyāvatī worries at the prospect of some foul play, for she has been abandoned with her bastard child and cannot understand why now her brother may be on his way. When they arrive, Harihar confirms Satya Pīr's explanation, and she reluctantly believes it. She summons her trusted vassal Cānd Khā̃ to help her finalize arrangements for her permanent departure. She deputes him Rājā in her stead and vests him with the responsibility of looking after all of her subjects, to see to the welfare of her small kingdom and the weal of all its residents. All of her subjects are in shock and weep, but Cānd Khā̃ assures her of his honorable commitment to her and to her father. Sandhyāvatī takes personal charge of her talking *śuyā* bird, who has been her close companion since the time of Satya Pīr's departure, and her other personal effects are loaded onto carts. Her attendants follow. Just after Nandipāl village, they reach the banks of the Nur River. Switching to the water course, they make their way steadily but slowly toward the Mālañcā. Eventually they glimpse the ramparts of the city in the distance and ease up to the landing *ghāṭs*. News is sent ahead, including the intelligence that Harihar has married, an unexpected turn of events that ever-much delights his father.[134]

132. Harihar—whom the narrator identifies as Satya Pīr's uncle (*māmā*) as they make ready to leave—clearly has not realized that Satya Pīr is a relative, his nephew by virtue of Satya Pīr being given birth by Sandhyāvatī, Harihar's younger sister; but their seniority is reversed by virtue of Harihar taking Satya Pīr as his *murśid*.

133. Kṛṣṇahari Dās, *Baḍa satya pīr o sandhyāvatī kanyār punthi*, 127–30.

134. Kṛṣṇahari Dās, 130–33.

Finally comes the reunion. Sandhyāvatī meets her mother, who is contrite over the agonies her daughter has suffered on behalf of Satya Pīr. Meanwhile Rūpāvatī, sister of the queen, joins the reunion and organizes elegant foods for all to celebrate. Satya Pīr joins them and triumphantly proclaims that now his mother's worries should finally dissipate. No sooner have they reunited than—much to everyone's surprise—Satya Pīr informs his mother that Āllā's work is not finished and he must depart. She cries with the same biting sorrow as the unfortunate Kauśalyā felt when Rām entered the forest in exile. He tries to reassure her that he will return in due course—and with that he slips away. After saying goodbye to his mother, he takes his leave of everyone in the family, starting with his father King Maidānav, the queen Priyāvatī, then the three princes; then he meets with all the servants and retainers. He visits Mālāvatī and Rūpāvatī on his way out. He has righted the wrong done to his mother, reunited the family, and his responsibilities toward them are fully discharged, his family mission accomplished. But according to the command of Āllā, he has more work to do, and off he dances in his inscrutable play.

Thus ends the Mālañcā Chapter of Satya Pīr's story.[135]

6.5. THE NEVER-ENDING MISSION OF SATYA PĪR

If we look to the remaining nine stories that make up the second half of the *Baḍa satya pīr o sandhyāvatī kanyār punthi*, there is no story that tells of Satya Pīr returning to his mother as promised. The rest of the saga traces Satya Pīr's peregrinations around Bengal, and while the plots are often analogous to those of the main hagiographical narrative that constitutes the first half of the book, the order seems random and the tales only loosely connected to one another. Many of the motifs will by now be familiar. As the moral of each story is drawn, Satya Pīr's identity as a *devatā* or god for the *hindus* and a *phakir* for the *momins* is confirmed, often including instruction to recite in *jikir* or *jap* the names of Āllā, of the Prophet, and occasionally of Phātemā. The sequence starts with his visit to the city of Amar where he encounters King Śiśupāla. The king is about to sacrifice a boy to Ardhakālī, or Half Kālī,[136] to gain the boon of a son, for his five queens are barren. Satya Pīr averts the boy's death and lectures the king about the abominations

135. Kṛṣṇahari Dās, 133–34.

136. Today Arddhakālī is not normally found in a temple and is not normally associated with human sacrifice; she is conceived as a human female manifestation of Kālī, a Bengali housewife whose sari dropped as she had her hands full cooking. Before it could fall all the way down, she spontaneously sprouted two more arms to pull it back and maintain her modesty—and that is how people knew her to be an *avatār* of the goddess. See Sures Chandra Banerji's *A Brief History of Tantric Literature* (Calcutta: Naya Prokash, 1998), 472, and the story in more detail in Banerjee, *Tantra in Bengal: A Study in Its Origin, Development, and Influence*, 2nd rev. ed (1978; New Delhi: Manohar, 1992), 234–35 (personal communication from Rachel McDermott, May 2017).

of human sacrifice. He arranges to give five bananas to the queens to aid their conception, but when they go to the appointed place to collect them, he appears in disguise and begs for food. Only the youngest named Bindumatī has compassion and readily hands over her banana to the *pīr*, foregoing her own pregnancy. By her selfless act of honoring the *phakir*, she is soon rewarded with pregnancy, the only one of the sisters to be so. When she gives birth to a boy, jealousy and fear prompt the four co-wives to steal the baby, dump it in a box, and set it upon the waters of the Gaṅgā—the classic motif of heroes. The goddess herself soon intervenes to save the baby, which is nursed by the Mother Earth, Basumatī. In what appears to be an act of sympathy, Khoyājā Khijir mysteriously appears and discusses with Basumatī the degradation of the Kali age as they await the arrival of Satya Pīr to rescue the child. Satya Pīr does eventually collect the child and return it to its mother. In joy at having an heir, the king releases all prisoners, banishes the four evil co-wives, and arranges for the lavish worship of the *pīr*.[137]

Satya Pīr then encounters Hīr the cobbler, whom he severely tests in a classic trickster mode—demanding food he knows Hīr cannot provide, then in false anger having the tiger Nāgeśvarī eat Hīr's son Madhurām. Hīr and his wife eventually manage to scramble together a meal, but before they can serve the *śinni*, Hīr lectures the *pīr* about the inappropriateness of his anger, how it is disproportionate to the offense.[138] Satya Pīr is pleased with his devotee, accepts the *śinni*, restores the life of his son, and enlists Viśvakarmma to erect a palace for the cobbler and provide all the wealth it requires. That sudden change of fortune catches the attention of a jealous woman who reports to Mān Siṃha, who in turn confiscates Hīr's wealth and has him thrown in jail. The cobbler patiently recites an elaborate *cautiśā* poem in praise of Satya Pīr,[139] who is alerted to the cobbler's imminent demise and so visits Mān Siṃha in a dream threatening his death. Man Siṁha quickly releases the cobbler and restores his wealth. Satya Pīr blesses them all and heads toward Bagjoḍ town.[140]

On his way, Āllā himself tries to deceive Satya Pīr by placing in his path the accomplished and beautiful courtesan Śaśī. When she accosts him, the *pīr* transforms himself into a child, crawling on the ground. Naturally Śaśī goes to pick him up, so he magically turns himself into a parrot and flees; astonished, she concedes. Śaśī becomes his devotee and, at his command, distributes her considerable wealth to *brāhmaṇs* and bathes in the Saraju River to wash away her past sins. There, Satya

137. Kṛṣṇahari Dās, *Baḍa satya pīr o sandhyāvatī kanyār punthi*, 135–53.

138. Hīr's lecture to Satya Pīr about the comportment appropriate to a *phakir* (Kṛṣṇahari Dās, 159) seems to be a restatement of the *śīkṣāṣṭaka*, or the eight verses of instruction attributed to the *vaiṣṇav* god-man Kṛṣṇa Caitanya; see Stewart, *Final Word*, 170–72.

139. A *cautiśā*, or more properly, *cautriśa*, is a poetic form that starts each line with a different consonant and follows in alphabetical order.

140. Kṛṣṇahari Dās, *Baḍa satya pīr o sandhyāvatī kanyār punthi*, 154–77.

Pīr instructs her to locate a certain large stone to bring home. It is too heavy, so rather than fail, she decides the only honorable path is to commit suicide on that stone, but her efforts are thwarted by Satya Pīr. As she again falls at his feet, she faints, and while she is insensate, Satya Pīr meditates on his *guru*, Khoyājā, who miraculously appears for consultation, then disappears. When Śaśī revives, Satya Pīr instructs her to bathe again, while he moves the stone to a spot underneath a tree near the river. He leaves his personal imprint on that stone and instructs her to worship it day and night. She is then initiated as Jasi Phakirāṇī and she worships that stone, which has a special power for all who encounter it, as one unnamed female flower vendor soon discovers after refusing to proffer fresh flowers to Jasi for its worship.[141]

The remaining episodes diminish in length and follow what should by now be recognized as a finite set of formulaic plots, the storyteller no longer providing the rich descriptions and mind-bending digressions, rather opting for relatively straightforward and predictable narratives that assume the reader or listener will anticipate sufficiently to fill in the gaps. Two stories of Jasmanta the merchant and Śundi the trader follow much of the pattern of the merchant's tale that makes up the largest part of the *hinduyāni* trilogy noted above—a parallel that is confirmed by the fact that these are the only two tales in the entire text where Satya Pīr is not the primary focus of the narrative, but which also signals that the author was well aware of the merchant narratives, making those short tales an intertextual acknowledgement. In the first, Jasmanta promises to make a donation of great wealth to Satya Pīr if he is successful in his voyage, but upon return, he tries to shortchange him, which proves a disastrous decision. Everything is lost until his son recognizes the insult to Satya Pīr and corrects what his father has done. In the second of the merchant tales, Satya Pīr meets a somewhat hapless trader named Śundi, who is childless. After hearing their tale and in exchange for *śinni*, Satya Pīr provides him and his wife with two flowers. She is instructed to wash the flowers and then drink the water, and she will conceive—but they have to agree to one condition: the younger of the two sons must be handed over to Satya Pīr when asked. They faithfully perform as instructed and soon have two boys. Twelve years later Satya Pīr returns to collect on their promise. The merchant is heartbroken and pretends that his youngest is actually a girl. The *pīr* asks to see her, so the merchant presents the boy dressed in drag appropriate to his/her age. Satya Pīr exposes him (literally) and leaves with the boy in tow. Nothing is mentioned about what happens to the young man later.[142]

In my essay originally exploring the Satya Pīr materials, the interested reader can find synopses of the tale of King Kāśīkānt, whose wives are incited to dance lasciviously in the public space of the court as a result of the king's recalcitrance,

141. Kṛṣṇahari Dās, 177–86.
142. Kṛṣṇahari Dās, 186–206.

and the saga of Dhanañjay the milkman, whose stinginess and refusal to give a little food to the *pīr* causes him to lose everything before coming to his senses and having it all restored.[143] In the last two tales of *Baḍa satya pīr o sandhyāvatī kanyār puthi*, Satya Pīr shows mercy to his faithful devotee Maṅgalu the musician and then to the loathsome king Main Gidāl, who sacrifices every *musalmān* he can find to the goddess Kālī, but who has a change of heart when he meets Satya Pīr. Here the story simply ends.[144]

. . .

Each tale magnifies the strength and depth of Satya Pīr's miraculous powers and his ever-expanding circle of influence. The book is of special interest because it attempts to create a "life" (*bios*) for Satya Pīr on the order of hagiographies devoted to historical figures of the early modern period; only the earliest manuscript versions of the dual hagiography of Gāji and Kālu as told by Khodā Bakhś and by Kavi Hālumīr rival the length and number of episodes that make up Satya Pīr's adventures. The narrative code adopted by this *musalmāni* cycle clearly hinges first on a demand for recognition by the *pīr* in what is obviously a *hinduyāni*, *brāhmaṇ*-dominated world of anti-*phakir* kings. In *Baḍa satya pīr o sandhyāvatī kanyār puthi*, the land of Bengal is portrayed as generally hostile to *pīrs*; indeed, the opening gambit, which frames the tale, has Āllā and the Prophet deciding to intervene in worldly affairs to counter the acts of King Maidānav, to address his intolerance of *phakirs*, which provides the raison d'être of Satya Pīr's descent. In this frame, it is imperative that the worship of the *pīrs* be integrated into the practices considered normal for Bengal's inhabitants. King Maidānav, who serves as a metonym for the Bengali cultural environment, must be convinced: to persuade Maidānav of the *phakirs*' efficacy, and through that, Satya Pīr's legitimacy, is to convince Bengal of the same. But the approach is not always brutally head-on; instead, long-term, incremental, and seemingly roundabout strategies induce the desired end. In that strategy, Satya Pīr utilizes and manipulates those around the ultimate object of his obsession: officials in various capacities, wives, and sons. He just as often coaxes people to a new way of thinking and acting in this world. Once his power is acknowledged, he educates by demonstrating that the familiar hierarchical world of traditional Bengal still has value, but that there is a higher figure atop that hierarchy. Āllā is not the equivalent of Nārāyaṇ or Kṛṣṇa; he reigns supreme as the only God. Pragmatically, a new cosmology was articulated through these stories, one that subsumed wholly the preexisting order but displaced it downward, while the social hierarchy of traditional Indic society was finding itself being leveled into a new model of *musalmāni* brotherhood. It was the *pīr* who was equal to Nārāyaṇ.

143. Kṛṣṇahari Dās, 206–16; the synopses can be found in Stewart, "Alternate Structures of Authority," 41–46.

144. Kṛṣṇahari Dās, 206–20; for the words of closing, see chap. 3, this volume.

The three emplotments that make up the cycle of Satya Pīr stories do not represent a linear teleology, far from it. Much more accurately than most historical reconstructions can manage, they document the range of possibilities for understanding how this *sūphī phakir* could operate in a Bengali-conditioned world. These approaches do not record discrete moments to be understood serially or in some kind of succession, but rather highlight overlapping prospects that by the late nineteenth century were simultaneously circulating. The demand for recognition and the insinuation of the *pīr* into the traditional Bengali cosmology, the demonstration of efficacy of devotion to the *pīr*, confirmed through his displays of *karāmat*, and the elevation of Āllā effected by the explicit but subtle and sometimes not-so-subtle demotion of the *hinduyāni* hierarchy of celestial figures to establish equivalences between *devs* and *pīrs* and *devīs* and *bibīs*—each of these three had its sympathetic audience.

One of the common messages of these tales is that *brāhmaṇs* do not have to change the ways they function, they do not have to forego their obsession with ritual purity, though they are reminded that their hubris is not to the benefit of the rest of the Bengali world, that they need to acknowledge that there are other forms of power than those in which they traffic, that relationships based on the family are more significant than caste rankings, and that commensal restrictions are not so strict. Kings, much more than *brāhmaṇs*, tend to be the focus of Satya Pīr's attention, and those kings are made to understand that a properly dharmic rule is all-embracing, not selectively favorable to *hinduyāni* communities alone. In the end, the message seems to be that Āllā has made allowances for traditional Bengali understandings of the world to continue without interruption as long as the supremacy of the *pīr* and God's unity are acknowledged. That Satya Pīr had from the beginning of his narrative cycle adopted a *pūjā* offering of *śirṇi* as the best expression of devotion meant that people could make this accommodation without having to adjust what was commonly familiar. That would beg, then, the question of conversion, or perhaps more accurately, problematize the issue that undercuts the models of conversion that are naïvely predicated on Protestant constructs of intellectual assent as a prerequisite for reorientation, generating in its wake an exclusivity of belief and practice. Though these are fictional tales, whose characters operate in autotelic worlds of the authors' own making, and whose explicit religious positions are constitutive of a generic Islam, a simulacrum of historical perspectives, they connect to the world of everyday things by exploring alternatives to the received wisdom about the way things are, by insisting that a real-life offering of *śirṇi* to Satya Pīr will have positive real-life effects. These tales subtly, and by virtue of their myriad repetitions, incrementally persuaded their audiences to think of the world differently, a world where *jabans*, *turuskas*, *kābulis*, *saiyads*, and other *musalmāni* folk have become properly *hinduyāni* in the real sense of that word—Indic; and that Indic world could now understand how and why Āllā alone was supreme.

EPILOGUE

We began this inquiry with the simple question: what kind of cultural or religious work do the tales of the fictional *pīrs* do or try to do? Of the many things we can observe, perhaps most telling are the ways these seemingly simple tales explore how the same world can be configured and reconfigured, a feature that is intrinsic to fictions everywhere. The stakes, however, are very real, for these tales subjunctively reflect and refract issues of real life in the lives of their Bengali audiences and, I would argue, that relentless but usually indirect and gently suggestive critique ultimately confirms their pragmatic utility. The tales turn out to be anything but naïve, for their persuasive power is significant and continues to have a strong purchase on their audiences. For those of us who try to understand in religious terms how and why people believe the things they do, act the way they do, these tales suggest a very different process for our all-too-abrupt notions of conversion. Stories, we might argue, are powerful, even more compelling than scriptural authority, unless, of course, that scriptural authority itself relies on stories, parables, or myths to make its case. Narratives exert an exploratory power that stands in opposition to—and constantly assesses—the prescriptive world of doctrines and their derivative, sanctioned histories. It is not surprising that in the world of Islam, narratives that tell of the fabulous exploits of heroes and heroines, constantly reshaped for each generation, face the enmity of doctrine-driven reformists.

I have focused this inquiry on the early modern period that leads up to the contemporary world, at least in a few cases into the nineteenth century; by the early decades of the twentieth century, with the political strife that accompanied the instantiation of the categories of Muslim and Hindu into exclusive political identities, I thought the *kathā* traditions might have come to an end. Hidden away in the holdings of the India Office Library, where I was working in 1992, I ran across an unusual piece that initially puzzled me, for it was like no other. In the late 1920s, Sañjīv Kumār Bāgchi composed a drama titled *Satyanārāyaṇ nāṭya kāvya.*[1] The title page advertises the author as a singer, poet, accomplished wit, and connoisseur of humor, and the creator of instrumental "card music" (there is no explanation of what constituted "card music," but there are hints that playing cards were involved, or possibly a cotton carder). The photograph on the frontispiece is a self-advertised joke: handlebar moustache, military tunic over a dhoti, and the modest comment implying that he represents the new height of fashion—native costume below combined with the dress of the enforcers of the colonial masters above. The text, likely self-published by members of the author's family, covers ninety-six pages and is divided into twenty sections. The dialogue is all in song, the music of his own composition. The last four pages are given over to various lengthy encomia (all but one in English) from prominent appreciative fans, all servants of the Raj, such as Bhupendra Nath Mukherjee, Shaheb Bahadur Sub-Divisional Officer, Kushtia; Gokul Chandra Mozumdar, Sub-Divisional Magistrate, Kandi, Murshidabad; and Surendra Kumar Sen, Pleader Judge's Court, Secretary of Arya Pustakagar, Dinajpur; these and others cited comment on the extraordinary novelty of Bāgchi's "card music" and the biting comedy and social commentary that punctuates his more serious pious sentiments. While one need only begin the libretto to confirm the light-hearted manner of delivery of the Satya Nārāyaṇ and Satya Pīr narrative (taken from the *revā khaṇḍa* of the *Skanda purāṇa*), this text does what no other we have examined even hinted: in the preface titled "Why Do I Write?" the author proclaims that it is to lament the contemporary traffic in gods and goddesses and to mock the "religion of the bazaar." In prior centuries, the Satya Nārāyaṇ and Satya Pīr stories parodied different textual traditions, but this would appear to be the first self-declared parody of parodies.

Some years later as I puzzled over this unique piece, I would surmise that Mr. Bāgchi's *nāṭya kāvya* could well be counted as a marker of the end to the creative period of these narratives, perhaps of all of the *pīr kathās*, for as Northrop Frye observed in his *Anatomy of a Criticism*, the urge to parody begins to intensify when a particular genre and its conventions are exhausted.[2] As we have already noted, parody is always context-specific, a product of its distinctive historical moment in interaction with prevailing authoritative discourses.[3] If these observations hold, it would appear that I had stumbled onto an harbinger of Satya Pīr's demise after five centuries of vibrant presence in the lives of those in the Bangla-speaking region. My sense of foreboding, however, was premature, for it seems that Satya Nārāyaṇ

1. Sañjīvkumār Bāgchi, *Satyanārāyaṇ nāṭya kāvya*, 1st ed. (Dinājpur: Kālīpad Bāgchi and Raṇajir Kumār Bāgchi, 1334 BS [ca. 1927]).

2. Hutcheon, *Theory of Parody*, 36, quoting Northrop Frye's *Anatomy of a Criticism*, 103.

3. Dentith, *Parody*, 163–64; Hutcheon, *Theory of Parody*, xi, xiv.

as Satya Pīr, exercising that subjunctive quality, was simply shifting from the older print form to a new kind of performance suitable for a modern, clearly metropolitan, local colonial audience.

In June 1920, a scant few years before Bāgchi's production, M. L. Sāhā published a short piece titled *Satyanārāyaṇ*, which was composed as a script for a gramophone recording.[4] This experiment rendered in brief but dramatic dialogue the traditional trilogy of the poor *brāhmaṇ*, the woodcutters, and the merchant. After the title page, which included impressive personal information,[5] a cast of nine male and four female characters was listed, while the story itself covered only twenty pages of this foolscap printing (F 8vo, 6–1/2 × 4–1/2 inches), a short but standard size one expects from the popular and inexpensive *baṭ-tola* editions of texts, though this was a private printing by the author. Given the tenor of the text, we might speculate that it was a bit of a spoof, but there is no direct evidence of that. Because we do not have the actual gramophone recording, we cannot gauge the tone of the delivery, which might more clearly indicate how the drama was to be understood. But regardless of how the text is read, it is clearly an innovative attempt to deploy the new technology of the gramophone to convey the story of Satya Nārāyaṇ, who assumed the form of a *pīr* to make known the way to wealth and weal. Whether we choose to see the text as a parody or a religious production is of no consequence, for it is the entrance of Satya Pīr into the new world of technology that again underscores the ever-explorative nature of the tradition. Satya Pīr seems always to have found new avenues of expression, leading his promoters to explore these older ideas in a new form.

When she was a visiting scholar in North Carolina some years ago, my mourned colleague Papiya Ghosh gently suggested to me that the critique of syncretism that Carl Ernst and I had initiated several years earlier may have overemphasized the negative entailments of the concept,[6] for syncretism, she noted, was actively being used by intellectuals and activists in India to offer an alternative, an antidote to the Islamist and Hindutva drive for purity in their respective religious traditions. Satya Pīr and Satya Nārāyaṇ were routinely placed on the front lines of this attempt to argue for an inclusive perspective in the modern state. Similarly, she named Bonbibī as another example. At the time I quibbled at the suggestion because of the imprecision of the language (as I then saw it), but in a demonstration of the malleability of abstractions, the definitional edges of both syncretism and

4. M. L. Sāhā, *Satyanārāyaṇ: Grāmāphon rekarḍe samagra abhinay* (Kalikātā: by the author, 1920). Unfortunately, I was unable to locate any gramophone recording in the British Sound Archive, only this script from the British Library.

5. The title page included the address of the author at "5/1 Dharmmtolā Ṣṭrīṭ, Kalikātā," his "Poṣṭ Baks naṃ. 906," his four digit "Ṭeliphon naṃ. 2290," and his wire address as "Ṭeligrān Ṭhikānā 'Bāgjantra.'" We can only speculate regarding the reasons for such detailed personal information, though it does signal a complete embrace of new technologies.

6. Stewart and Ernst, "Syncretism."

secularism to which she alerted me have indeed become blurred for at least some of those who argue for and attempt to promote in public life some form of religious neutrality (syncretism is often paired with secularism, the latter signifying in the Indic context a promotion of pluralism). Many figures that hint of allegiances that cross the hard modern categories of Hindu and Muslim are marshalled in this effort to counter the communalism that has become so widespread.[7] In a sense, I realized, this was what the narratives of Satya Pīr and the other stories of *pīrs* and *bibīs* had always done, to bring together people of different ethnicities, of different social classes, and of course different religious orientations, in provocatively new configurations, disrupting the status quo, their activity redirected to new (reformulations of the old) regimes.

The *pīrs* and *bibīs* are not just being used to address intercommunal strife, but intracommunal conflict as well. Confirmation of this revitalized life of the stories of the *pīrs* and the audiences they target can perhaps best be seen in the public dramas performed in Bangladesh today. As my friend and colleague Syed Jamil Ahmed has so well documented in Bangladesh,[8] the figures of the fictional *pīrs* continue to challenge and critique the religious and political normativity of the Bangla-speaking world.

These public performances reminded me of the ways in which stories used to be told, using the scroll paintings as visual cues to the storyteller's performance. The traditions of scroll (*paṭ*) painting are still thriving, even as evidenced by my personal collection of scrolls purchased over the last four decades—illustrations of the *pīrs*, of the gods and goddesses of the *maṅgal kāvyas*, of Caitanya, and so forth. I was reminded of this when in 2010 I visited a small exhibition at Asia House in London titled "The Tiger in Asian Art." That exhibit included a partial scroll from the Victoria and Albert Museum (which I identified as the opening to the story of Bonbibī, though it bore no label) and a number of other scrolls and single-register depictions of Baḍa Khān Gāji, Dakṣiṇ Ray, and others by Maithili, Bengali, and Santali artists. Contemporary Bangladeshi artist Shambhu Acharya's paintings in the modified *caukapaṭ* style speak to a constantly rejuvenating world of the imaginary; working with a local singer of tales, he has helped to create a new cycle of

7. Once alerted, I discovered that there are a host of articles and even a couple of short monographs that argue this alliance; see for example Sutapa Chatterjee Sarkar, *The Sunderbans: Folk Deities, Monsters and Mortals* (New Delhi: Orient BlackSwan, Social Science Press, 2010), esp. the introduction and chap. 3; and Shams Shahriar Kabi, "Traditional Bengali Folklore *Gajir Gaan*: Non-Communal Artistic Contemplation," *Grassroots Voices* 7, no. 1 (July 2010): 16–30. The earliest article I have located that ever-so-briefly anticipates this move is Aparna Bhattacharya, "Worship of Satyapir, an Example of Hindu Muslim Rapprochement in Bengal," *Proceedings of the Indian History Congress* 32, no. 2 (1970): 204–7.

8. Syed Jamil Ahmed, "Performing and Supplicating Mānik Pīr: Infrapolitics in the Domain of Popular Islam," *TDR: The Drama Review*, vol. 53, no. 2 (Summer 2009): 51–76. See also of course his full-length studies of performance previously cited.

Baḍa Khān Gāji stories that are now little more than a decade old as he described to me in 2010.

As the tales of the fictional *pīrs* and *bibīs* seek new creative outlets, we find their stories moving into new discursive realms that connect with unexpected literatures. Novelist Indra Das has linked the tales of Bonbibī and Dakṣiṇ Ray to the worldwide confreres of shapeshifters. His story, titled *The Devourers*,[9] begins with a professor of history attending a Calcutta performance of *bāul* musicians—depicted as ganja-smoking antinomians who occupy the liminal space between ordinary society and its hallucinatory and seamy sensual underbelly. As the story unfolds, the action segues to a stranger past world. A mysterious figure entices the professor to listen to a very different history that will be like nothing any historian has ever recorded. Going back four centuries, we meet Fenrir, a therianthrope whose name invokes the ancient Norse shapeshifter Fenrisúlfr. As he traverses Persian lands en route to India, he lives on the edges of society with other shapeshifters of legend: werewolves, vampires, *jinns*, *rākśasas*, and the like. Driven by an uncharacteristic urge, he rapes Cyra, a mortal and a prostitute, producing an offspring that shares the humanity of the one and the soul-eating qualities of the other and, like other shapeshifters, the ability to absorb the experiences, linguistic skills, and other knowledge of those they consume. While it would be easy, perhaps far too easy, to read this tale allegorically, as the successive expansions of Middle Eastern, Persian, Mongol, and European power as they intruded into the South Asian subcontinent, in its final chapters it invokes explicitly the misty hybrid origins of Bonbibī, who migrates to and eventually controls the Sunderbans—a subtle reinterpretation of the *Bonbibī jahurā nāmā*'s narrative of Bonbibī ontogenesis, raised by tigers, who, as we have repeatedly seen, are often themselves shapeshifters. Suddenly the frequent bodily transformations by Satya Pīr, Baḍa Khān Gāji, and others we have encountered become indexical of and participate in a larger transcultural imagination, the stuff of mythologies over the world and, closer to our times, the comic book superheroes and their antagonists.

It is fitting, then, that in their production of the previously cited *Folktales from India: The Sunderbans*, Vivalok Comics deploys modern color print technology to fuse the visual form of the old hand-painted scroll or *pāṭ* with the text embodied in comic book form. That particular storybook illustrates the tales of Mānik Pīr, Bonbibī, Baḍa Khān Gāji, and others. The effort to utilize the comic book medium as a vehicle for exploration is self-conscious on the part of the creators, who remark, "In the Indian context, comics are but a logical continuation of the strong pictorial and narrative tradition that it already has. The '*pata chitras*' or scroll paintings of Bengal and the '*phad*' of Rajasthan exemplify this. Both these techniques combine the excitement of both the oral and the visual form of story

9. Indra Das, *The Devourers* (New York: Del Ray Books, 2017). I am indebted to Ahmed Tanvir, graduate student at Brown University, for alerting me to this work.

telling." Quoting Scott McCloud in the epigraph to the piece, "Comics are often thought of as the joining of two art forms: writing and drawing. But what happens between the panels isn't about either, it's the author's imagination." And I would add, the reader's. Consistent with the impulse behind the original creation of the stories of the *pīr kathā*, the Vivalok creators go on to observe their own experience of growing up with the superheroes and other characters of comic books: "We have all mentally mimicked the world of these characters, which though unreal, provided an insight into the real world. Comics are viewed as the *unfolding of alternative spaces*."[10] The stories—here the *pīr kathās*—explore places and events not possible otherwise, stimulating the imagination in ways that constantly challenge expected boundaries. What better confirmation of the timelessness of these tales than to hear the delightful screams of my godson Samar and his older brother Anhad, as they play out the stories of Bonbibī, Baḍa Khān Gāji, and Dakṣiṇ Rāy on the bed with their grandmother Nilu, tirelessly reenacting their adventures, each time a new triumph as they relive tales that never seem to get old.

. . .

10. Ghosh, comp., *Folktales from India: The Sunderbans*, 3; emphasis added.

WORKS CITED

PRIMARY TEXTS IN BANGLA AND SANSKRIT

These primary texts are alphabetized according to full name (starting with given name or title) as printed on the title page, and for manuscripts as it appears in the signature line or *bhaṇitā*, because many of the authors' names include titles that do not correspond to surnames, and those titles often function as part of, or in lieu of, surnames.

Ābbās Āli Nājir. *Kalir phakīrer khelā*. Lakpur: by the author, 1920.

Ābdur Rahim. *Gājikālucāmpāvatī*. Ḍhākā: Ābdul Latiph and Ābdul Hāmid at Hāmidīyā Lāibrerī, Cak Bājār, n.d. [ca. 1890s?].

———. *Gājikālu o cāmpāvatī kanyār puthi*. Ḍhākā: Hāmidiyā Lāibrerī, 1961.

———. *Gājikālu o cāmpāvatī kanyār puthi*. Maymansiṃha: Prīṇṭār Śrī Ābdur Rahim at Rahimni Jantra in Mahakumā Kiśor Gañj, 1282 BS [ca. 1875].

Ābul Kālām Mohāmmad Jākāriyā, ed. *Bāṅglā sāhitye gājī kālu o cāmpāvatī upākhyān*. Ḍhākā: Bāṃlā Ekāḍemī, 1396 BS [1989].

Āhmād Śariph, ed. *Baṅglār sūphī sāhitya*. Ḍhākā: Baṃlā Ekāḍemī, 1371 BS [ca. 1964].

Ālamgīr Jalīl and Sāmīyul Islām, eds. "Ā̃ṭkuḍe rājār pālāgān o kissā saṃkalan." *Lok sāhitya* 15, (Pauṣ 1385 BS [January 1979]): 1–197.

Āli Roja. "Āgama." In *Baṅglār sūphī sāhitya*, edited by Āhmad Śariph, 336–43. Ḍhākā: Baṃlā Ekāḍemī, 1371 BS [1964].

Anonymous. "Baḍo bhāsān." *Lok sāhitya* 51 (Phālguṇ 1397 BS [February 1991]): 1–184.

Anonymous, "Cāmpāvatī kanyār pālāgān—Part 1." *Lok sāhitya* 1 (Āṣāḍh 1370 BS [ca. 1963]): 55–104; "Cāmpāvatī kainyār pālāgān—Part 2." *Lok sāhitya* 2 (Āśviṇ 1370 BS [ca. 1963]): 127–75.

Anonymous. *Mānikpīrer jahurānāmā*. Pāñcānan Maṇḍal, comp. In *Punthi Paricay*, vol. 2. Śāntiniketan: Viśva Bhārati, 1364 BS [1958], 318–20. MS 937, 1 folio of 4 pages, incomplete, n.d.

Anonymous [Rasmay]. *Manohar phāsarār pālā: Satyanārāyaṇ pāñcālī*. 10th ed. Kāñthāi: Nihār Press, 1313 BS [ca. 1906].

Anonymous. *Satyadever pāñcālī*. Bengali MS no. 874H, Dhaka University. Complete, 10 folios, dtd. 1218 BS [ca. 1811].

Anonymous. *Satyadever pāñcālī*. Bengali MS no. 3688, Dhaka University. Complete, 18 folios, dtd. 1239 BS [ca. 1832].

Anonymous [attributed to Jaymuni]. *Satyadever pāñcālī*. Bengali MS no. 1316, Dhaka University. Complete, 12 folios, dtd. 1273 BS [ca. 1866].

Anonymous. *Satyanārāyaṇ pāñcālī: Nalanīler palā*, 6th ed. Kāñthāi: Jatīndranāth Jānā at Nīhār Press, 1340 BS [ca. 1933].

Anonymous. *Satyanārāyaṇ pustak*. Kṛṣṇakanta Rāy Collection, Bengali MS no. K-434, Dhaka University. Complete, 8 folios, dtd. 1157 BS [ca. 1750].

Anonymous. "Sonāi kanyā" in "Caṭṭagrām gītikā." *Lok sāhitya* 57 (Āṣāḍh 1399 BS [ca.1993]): 1–101.

Anonymous [Harinārāyaṇ?]. *Trilakṣya pīrer pāñcālī*. Bengali MS no. 74, Dhaka University. Complete, 3 folios, dtd. 1246 BS [1839].

Anonymous [Harinārāyaṇ?]. *Tinlakṣya pīrer pāñcālī*. Bengali MS no. 1313, Dhaka University. Complete, 3 folios, dtd. 1259 BS [ca. 1852].

Anonymous. "Yoga kalandar." In *Baṅglār sūphī sāhitya*, edited by Āhmad Śariph, 87–116. Ḍhākā: Baṃlā Ekāḍemī, 1371 BS [1964].

Āriph. *Lālmoner kecchā*. Kalakātā: Sudhānidhi Yantra, 1274 BS [ca. 1867].

———. *Lālmoner kecchā*. Kalakātā: Viśvambhar Lāhā, 1276 BS [ca. 1869].

Aśutoṣ Bhaṭṭācāryya, ed. *Gopīcāndrer gān*. 3rd ed. Kalikātā: Kalikātā Viśvavidyālay, 1965.

Baṇkim Bihāri Majumdār. *Satyanārāyaṇer kathā*. Kalikātā: Bhavanīpur Somaprakāś Pres, 1284 BS [ca. 1877].

Bhābanidās. "Gopīcāndrer pāñcālī." In *Gopīcāndrer gān*, edited by Āśutoṣ Bhāṭṭācāryya, 273–324. 3rd ed. Kalikātā: Kalikātā Viśvavidyālay, 1965.

Bhāratcandra. "Satyapīr kathā." In *Bhāratcandra granthāvalī*, edited by Kṣetra Gupta and Viṣṇu Basu, 1–3. Kalikātā: Basumati Sāhitya Maṇḍir, n.d.

———. "Satyapīr vratkathā." In *Bhāratcandra racanāsaṃgraha*, edited by Kṣetra Gupta and Viṣṇu Basu, 430–35. Kalikātā: Bhaumik eṇḍ Sans, 1974.

Bhāratcandra Rāy. "Satyanārāyaṇ vratkathā." In *Bhāratcandra granthāvalī*, edited by Vrajendranāth Bandyopādhyāy, 391–96. Kalikātā: Baṅgīya Sāhitya Pariṣat, 1357 BS [ca. 1950].

Bidubar Ghoṣ. *Satya nārāyaṇ pustak*. Bengali MS 747B, Dhaka University. Complete, 12 folios, dtd. 1265 BS [ca. 1858].

[Caitanya Prasād Poddār Mahāśay]. *Satyanārāyaṇer puthi*, 2nd ed. Noyākhālī: Yogendramohan Poddār, 1315 BS [10 August 1908].

Candrakānt Sarkār. *Satyanārāyaṇ nāmak granthaḥ arthāt vratprakāś o mahimā varṇan*. Edited by Rajanīkānt Sarkār. Kalikātā: Umeścandra Madak at Jñān Dvīpak Pres, 1281 BS [ca. 1874].

Chaiyad Hāmjā Sāheb. *Chahi baḍa lālmon*. Kalikātā: Hāji Āijaddīn Āhmad eṇḍ Sans at Gāouchiyā Lāibrerī, 1344 BS [ca. 1937].

———. *Chahi baḍa lālmon*. Kalikātā: Śrī Rāmlāl Śīl at Niu-Bhikṭoriyā Pres, n.d.

Dayāl. *Śaṅkara gadya pālā*. Bengali MS B-7484, Bāṅglā Bibhāg, Kalikātā Viśvāvidyālay.

Dhīrendra Nāth Mukhopādhyāy. *Śani satyanārāyaṇ o trilakṣadever pāñcālī*. Kalikātā: by the author, 1319 BS [ca. 1912].

Dīnhin Dās. *Śrīśrīsatyanārāyaṇer pāñcālī: Līlāvati o kalāvatī upākhān*. Edited by Sītānāth Basāk. 72nd printing. Kalikātā: Sītānāth Ādarśa Lāibrerī, 1979.

Dvāraknāth Pāl. *Satyanārāyaṇer pāñcālī: Kṛṣṇa yudhiṣṭhīr saṃvād o kalāvatār upākhyān*. Ḍhākā: Lachman Baśak at Ḍhākā Bāṅglā Press, n.d. [1285 BS (ca. 1878)].

Dvija Aśvinīkumār. *Śrīśrīsatyanārāyaṇer pāñcālī: Pūjāpaddhati, dhyān, pranām, phardamālā evaṃ daridra brāhmaṇer upākhyān sambalita*. Kalikātā: Subhāṣnāth Pustakālay, n.d.

Dvīja Kavibar. *Bāghāmbarer pālā: Satyanārāyaṇ pāñcālī*. 10th ed. Kāñthāi: Nihār Press, 1322 BS [ca. 1915].

Dvija Dīnarām. *Nārāyaṇer dever pāñcālī*. Edited by Abdul Karim. *Baṅgīya sāhitya pariṣat patrikā* 12, no. 4 (1312 BS [ca. 1905]): 189–92.

Dvija Ghanarām. *Satyanārāyaṇ itihās*. Edited by Mahendranāth Ghoṣ. Kalikātā: Bhabanīpur Orieṇṭāl Pres, 1292 BS [ca. 1885].

Dvija Raghunāth. "Satyanārāyaṇer punthi." Edited by Satiścandra Rāy. *Baṅgīya sāhitya pariṣat patrikā* 24, no. 1 (1324 BS [ca. 1917]): 21–38.

Dvija Rāmbhadra. "Satyadev saṃhitā." Edited by Vyomakeś Mustaphī. *Baṅgīya sāhitya pariṣat patrikā* 8, no. 2 (1308 BS [ca. 1901]): 131–36.

Dvija Rāmdhan. *Satya nārāyaṇer punthi*. Kalikātā: Rāju Pāblikeśans, n.d.

Dvija Rāmkṛṣṇa. *Satyanārāyaṇer pāñcālī*. Kalikātā: Aruṇoday Ghoṣ, 1281 BS [ca. 1874].

———. *Satyanārāyaṇer pustak*. Edited by Vīrcandra Cakravarttī. Ḍhākā: Ḍhākā Giriśyantra, 1283 BS [ca. 1876].

Dvija Viśveśvar. "Satyanārāyaṇ pāñcālī." Edited by Vrajsundar Sānyāl. *Baṅgīya sāhitya pariṣat patrikā* 8, no. 3 (1308 BS [ca. 1901]): 193–200.

Garīb. *Iblich nāmār puthi*. Kalikātā: Śrī Akṣaykumār Rāy eṇḍ Kompāni, 1287 BS [ca. 1880].

Garibullāh. *Śāh garībullāh o jaṅganāmā*. Edited by Muhammad Abdul Jalil. Ḍhākā: Bāṃlā Ekāḍemī, 1991.

Gaurīśaṅkar. *Satyanārāyaṇ pustak*. Bengali MS no. 1584B, Dhaka University. Complete, 19 folios, dtd. 1726 *śaka* [ca. 1804].

Gayārām. *Madanmañjari pālā: Satyanārāyañ pāñcālī*. Khāñtāi: Madhusudhan Jān at Nihār Press, 1334 BS [ca. 1927].

Ghanarām Cakravarttī. *Dharma maṅgal*. Edited by Piyūṣkānti Mahāpātrā. Kalikātā: Kalikātā Viśvavidyālay, 1962.

———. *Satyanārāyaṇ ras sindhu*. Edited by Praphullakumār Bhaṭṭācāryya and Kālīpad Siṁha. Barddhamān: Barddhamān Sāhitya Sabhā, 1353 BS [ca. 1946].

Golokcandra Sengupta. *Satyanārāyaṇ pāñcālī*. Midnapur: Nibaraṇcandra Dāsgupta at Hari Sabhā Pres, 1319 BS [ca. 1912]).

Hājī Muhammad. "Surat nāmā" [alt. Nur jamāl]. In *Baṅglār sūphī sāhitya*, edited by Āhmad Śariph, 171–91. Ḍhākā: Baṃlā Ekāḍemī, 1371 BS [1964].

Hālumīr. *Baḍo khā̃n gājīr kerāmati*. In *Bāṅglā sāhitye gājī kālu o cāmpāvatī upākhyān*, edited by Ābul Kālām Mohāmmad Zākāriyā, 309–510. Ḍhākā: Bāṃlā Ekāḍemī, 1396 BS [1989].

Haridev. *Haridever racanāvalī: Rāy maṅgal o śītalā maṅgal*. Edited by Pañcānan Maṇḍal. Sāhityaprakāśikā, vol. 4. Śāntiniketan: Viśvabhāratī 1466 BS [ca. 1959].

Haridev. *Rāy maṅgal*. In *Haridever racanāvalī: Rāy maṅgal o śītalā maṅgal*, edited by Pañcānan Maṇḍal, 1–172. Sāhityaprakāśikā, vol. 4. Śāntiniketan: Viśvabhāratī 1466 BS [ca. 1959].

Harimohan Śarmma. *Satyakathā*. Ḍhākā: Harimohan Basāk at Ḍhākā Giriś Pres, 1277 BS [ca. 1870].

Īśāncandra Rāy. *Satyanārāyaṇer pāñcālī*. 1st ed. Kalikātā: Akṣay Kumār Rāy eṇḍ Koṃ, n.d. [1876].

Īśvarcandra Kar. *Satya nārāyaṇer pāñcālī*. Bariśāl: Denovandoo Kar at Satya Prakāś Yantra, 1930 *saṃvat* [ca. 1872].

Jaidi or Jayaraddhi. "Mānikpīrer jahurānāmā." In *Punthi paricay*, edited by Pāñcānan Maṇḍal, 305–18. Śāntiniketan: Viśva Bhārati, 1958; MS no. 936, 12–1/2 folios, dtd. 1224 BS [ca. 1817], incomplete.

Jatīndranāth Bhaṭṭācārya, comp. *Bāṅgālār vaiṣṇavbhāvāpanna musalmān kavir padsaṃjuṣā*. Kalikātā: Kalikātā Viśvāvidyālay, 1984.

K. Sadānanda. *Pāñcālī satyanārāyaṇ kathā*. Kāśī: Raghunandan Prasād at Bhavanna Tulsī Pustakālay, 1929 [Bangla in nagari script].

Kālīpada Devśarmma. *Śrīśrīsatyanārāyaṇer pāñcālī*. Ḍhākā: by editor at Bāherak Hari Sabhā, 1327 BS [ca. 1920].

Kaliprasād Dattaja Mahāśay. *Satyanārāyaṇ granth*. Ḍhākā: Jagadānanda Basu at Ḍhākā Giriś Yantra, 1281 BS [ca. 1874].

Kāśīrām Dās. *Mahābhārat*. Edited by Maṭilāl Bandhyopādhyay. Re-edited by Dhīrenda Ṭhākur. Kalakātā: Tārācā̃nd Dās eṇḍ Sans, n.d. [1988?].

Kavi Āriph. *Lālmoner kāhinī*. Edited by Girīndranāth Dās. Gokūlapur, Cabbiś Pargaṇās: Śrīmati Karuṇāmayī Dās, 1984.

Kavicandra Ayodhyārām Rāy. "Satya nārāyaṇ kathā." Edited by Vyomakeś Mustaphī. *Baṅgīya sāhitya pariṣat patrikā* 8, no. 1 (1308 BS [ca. 1901]): 61–72.

Kavikaṅkan Mukundarām Cakravartī. *Caṇḍīmaṅgal*. Edited by Sukumār Sen, rev. ed. Naẏ Dillī: Sāhitya Akādemī, 2007.

Kavi Kaṇva [= Kavi Karṇa]. *Ākhoṭi pālā: Satyanārāyaṇ kathā*. MS no. 59B, Dhaka University. Complete, 14 folios dtd. 1273 BS [ca. 1866].

Kavi Karṇa. *Pālās of Śrī Kavi Karṇa*. Compiled, edited, and translated by Bishnupada Panda. 4 vols. Kalāmūlaśāstra Series, vols. 4–7. Kapila Vatsyayan, series editor. New Delhi: Indira Gandhi National Centre for the Arts and Delhi; Motilal Banarsidass Publishers, 1991.

Kavivallabh. *Satyanārāyaṇ punthi*. Edited by Munsī Abdul Karim. Sāhitya Pariṣad Granthāvalī no. 49. Kalikātā: Baṅgīya Sāhityer Pariṣat by Rāmkāmal Siṃha, 1322 BS [ca. 1915].

Ketakādās Kṣemānanda. *Manasāmaṅgal*. Edited by Bijanbihārī Bhaṭṭācārya. New Delhi: Sāhitya Academy, 1977.

———. *Manasā Maṅgal*. Edited by Jatīndramohan Bhaṭṭācāryya. Calcutta: Calcutta University, 1949.

Khondkār Riyājul Hak, ed. *Gājīr gān*. Bāṁlā ekāḍemī phoklor saṃkalan, no. 66. Ḍhākā: Śāmsujjāmān Khān, Parikālak, Gobeṣaṇā Saṃkalan o Phoklor Bibhāg, Bāṃlā Ekāḍemī, 1402 BS [1999].

Kiṅkar Dās. *Matilāler pālā: Satyanārāyaṇ pāñcālī*. Khāñtāi: Nihār Press, 1322 BS [ca. 1915].

———. *Rambhāvatī pālā: Satyanārāyaṇ pāñcālī*, 4th ed. Khāñtāi: Madhusadan Jān at Nihār Press, 1331 BS [ca. 1924].
———. *Śaśidhar pāla: Satyanārāyaṇ pāñcālī*. Khāñtāi: Madhusudan Jān at Nihār Press, 1322 BS [ca. 1915].
Kṛṣṇadās Kavirāj. *Caitanya caritāmṛta*. Edited by Rādhagovinda Nāth, with the commentary "Gaurkṛpataraṅgiṇī ṭīkā" by the editor, 3rd ed. 6 vols. Kalikātā: Sādhanā Prakāśanī, 1355–59 BS [ca. 1948–52].
Kṛṣṇahari Dās. *Baḍa satya pīr o sandhyāvatī kanyār puthi*. Kalikātā: Nuruddīn Āhmad at Gaosiyā Lāibrerī, n.d.
Kṛṣṇarām Dās. *Kavi kṛṣṇarām dāser granthāvalī*. Edited by Satyanārāyaṇ Bhaṭṭācāryya. Kalikātā: Kalikātā Viśvavidyālay, 1958.
———. *Rāy maṅgal*. In *Kavi kṛṣṇarām dāser granthāvalī*, edited by Satyanārāyaṇ Bhaṭṭācāryya, 165–248. Kalikātā: Kalikātā Viśvavidyālay, 1958.
Kṛttibās. *Rāmāyaṇ*. Edited by Harekṛṣṇa Mukhopādhyāy, with an introduction by Sunitikumār Caṭṭopādhyāy. Kalakātā: Sāhitya Saṃsad, 1386 BS [1979].
Lālā Jayakṛṣṇa Sen. *Harilīlā*. Edited by Dineścandra Sen and Basantarañjan Rāy. Kalikātā: Kalikātā Viśvavidyālay, 1928.
M. L. Sāhā. *Satyanārāyaṇ: Grāmāphon rekarḍe samagra abhinay*. Kalikātā: by the author, 1920.
Mahāmmad Āinaddin Sāheb. *Nachihate āhale kali*. Kalikātā: Phasih Uddin Ahāmmad, Mahāmmadī Lāibrerī, 1337 BS [ca. 1930].
Mahāmmad Kārim Bākhs. *Śāhā gāji kālu gītābhinay, pratham khaṇḍa*. Jāiyānpur, Rājśāhī: by the author, printed in Kalikātā by Śrī Bimalcaraṇ Cakrabartī at Nāgendra Ṣṭīm Priṇṭiṅg Oyārks, 1326 BS [ca. 1919].
Meghnāth Bhaṭṭācāryya. *Satya nārāyaṇ vratkathā*. Kalikātā: Saṃskṛta Pres Ḍipajiṭorī, 1306 BS [ca. 1899].
Muhammād Munśi. *Bonbibī jahurā nāmā kanyār punthi*. Kalakātā: Osmāniā Lāibrerī, 1390 BS [ca. 1983]. Reprint, 1393 BS [ca. 1986].
Munśī Ābdur Rahim Sāheb. *Gājikālu o cāmpāvatī kanyār puthi*. Kalikātā: Nuruddin Āhmmad at Gāosiyā Lāibrerī, 2001.
Munśi Bayanuddīn. *Bonbibī jahurānāmā*. Sisvādaha: by the author, 1284 BS [ca. 1877].
———. *Bonbibī jahurānāmā*. Kalikātā: Āfājuddin Āhāmmad, from 337-2 Upper Chitpur Road, 1327 BS [ca. 1920].
Munśi Mohāmmad Hāphej Ālī Deoyān. *Gupta māraphat bā nadhihate pherāun*. Kalikātā: Gaosiyā Lāibrerī, Nūruddīn Āhammad, n.d.
Munśī Mohāmmad Khater Sāheb. *Bonbibī jahurānāmā*. Kalikātā: Śrī Rāmlāl Śīl at Niu-Bhikṭoriyā Pres, 1325 BS [?] [ca. 1918?].
———. *Bonbibī jahurā nāmā: Nārāyaṇīr jaṅga o dhonā dukher pālā*. Kalikātā: Nuruddīn Āhmmad at Gaosiyā Lāibrerī, 1394 BS [ca. 1987].
———. *Bonbibī jahurā nāmā: Nārāyaṇīr jaṅga o dhonā dukher pālā*. Kalikātā: Nuruddīn Āhmmad at Gaosiyā Lāibrerī, 1401 BS [ca. 1994].
———. *Bonbibī jahurnāmā: Nārāyaṇīr jaṅga ār dhonā dukher pālā*. Kalakātā: Ji Ke Prakāśanī, 1409 [ca. 2002]. Reprint, 1416 [ca. 2009].
Munsī Mohāmmad Pijiruddīn. *Mānik pīr kecchā*. Kalikātā: Gāosiya Lāibrerī, n.d. [ca. 1872?].

Munsi Nachiraddin Chāheb and Adhin Mahāmmad Hādek Orephe. *Jālālātal phokarā.* Kalikātā: Āli Hāniphi, printed by Mūnsi Golām Māolā Chāheber Moratajabi Pres, n.d. [1878].

Nanā Gājī. *Iblisnāmā.* Edited by Khandkār Mujāmmil Hak. Ḍhākā: Khośroj Kitāb Mahal, 1390 BS [ca. 1987].

Niṣākar Ghoṣ, *Satyanārāyaṇ pāñcālī.* Bengali MS no.747A, Dhaka University. Complete, 12 folios, n.d.

Phajlar Rahmān. *Bhaṇḍa phakīr.* Kalikātā: by the author at Niu Sarasvatī Pres, 1321 BS [c. 1914].

Phakīr Rām. *Satyanārāyaṇ pā̃cālī.* N.p., 1270 BS [ca. 1863].

———. *Śrīśrīsatyanārāyaṇer phakīrāmī kathā: Pujāpaddhatti o śabdārtha sambalitā.* Edited by Raghunandan Śatapathī. 1382 BS [ca. 1975]. Reprint, Bānkuṛa: Vikrampur Jagadbandhu Catuṣpaṭhī, 1978.

Premnāth Bhaṭṭācāryya, comp. *Satyanārāyaṇ pāñcālī: Līlāvatī o kalāvatī upākhyān sambalitā,* 2nd ed. N.p.: by the editor at Bāndhav Press in Utrāil Kumuk Bhavan, n.d.

Prāṇkiśor Ghoṣ. *Śrīśrīsatyanārāyaṇer punthi.* Edited by Kumudkānta Devśarmmā. Kalikātā: Aśīm Kumār Ghoṣ at Jayaguru Prakāśālay, 1375 BS [ca. 1968].

Priyanāth Ghoṣāl, ed. *Śrīśrīsatyanārāyaṇ: Trividha kathā.* Kalikātā: by the editor at Ripon College, 1910.

Priyanāth Ghoṣāl Jñānvinod. *Satyanārāyaṇ vratvyavasthā, pūjāpaddhati o pañcavidha māhātmyakathā.* Kalikātā: Peṭrik Pres, 1310 BS [ca. 1903].

Rādhāmohan Tarkālaṃkār Bhaṭṭācāryya. *Satya nārāyaṇ vratakathā.* Kalikātā: Prakāścandra Bandhyopādhyāy [Bhaṭṭācāryya] at Nūran Sen Press, 1814 *śaka* [ca. 1892].

———. *Satya nārāyaṇ vratkathā.* Kalikātā: Prakāścandra Bandyopādhyāy at Nūtan Sen Pres, 1819 *śaka* [ca. 1897].

Rādhāmohan Ṭhākur, comp. *Śrīpadāmṛtasamudra.* Edited by Umā Rāy, with the Sanskrit commentary "Mahābhāvanusārinī ṭīkā" by the compiler. Calcutta: Calcutta University Press, 1391 BS [ca. 1984].

Rādhānath Mitra. *Satyanārāyaṇ,* 2nd ed. Kalikātā: Sāradāprasād Mukhopoādhyay, 1889.

Raghunāth Cakravartī. *Satyanārāyaṇ punthi.* Edited by Caitanyaprasād Poddār. Kalikātā: Eṇ. El. Śīl Pres, 1277 BS [ca. 1870].

———. *Satyanārāyaṇ punthi.* Edited by Caitanya Prasād Poddār Mahāśay, 2nd ed. Noyākhālī: Yogendramohan Poddār, 1315 BS [ca. 1908].

Rājcandra Rāy, trans. *Satyanārāyaṇ nāmak granthaḥ.* Kalikātā: Jñānoday Pres, 1268 BS [ca. 1861].

Rām Śāstrī, ed. *Śrīśrīsatyanārāyaṇ vratkathā bā satya nārāyaṇer pāñcālī.* Kalikātā: Kṛṣṇa Bhaṭṭācāryya at Vāṇī Pustakālay, 1327 BS [ca. 1920].

Rāmāi Paṇḍit. *Dharmapūjā bidhān.* Edited by Nanīgopāl Bandyopādhyāy. Compiled by Yogīndranāth Rāy Bāhādur. Sahitya Pariṣad Granthāvalī no. 56. Kalikātā: Rāmkāmal Siṃha from Baṅgīya Sāhitya Pariṣat Mandir, 1323 BS [ca. 1916].

———. *Śūnyapurāṇ.* Edited by Bhaktimādhav Caṭṭopādhyāy. Kalikātā: Phārmā Ke El Em Prāibheṭ, 1977.

———. *Śūnyapurāṇ.* Edited by Cārucandra Bandhyopādhyāy, with an introduction by Muhammād Śahidullāh and Basantakurmār Caṭṭopādhyāy. Kalikātā: Satiścandra Mukhopādhyāy from Basumatī Sāhitya Mandir, n.d. [1336 BS preface (ca. 1929)].

Rāmdayāl Bandyopādhyāy. *Satyanārāyaṇer pāñcālī*. 2nd ed. Ḍhākā: Brajdās Bābājī at Giriś Pres, 1279 BS [ca. 1872].

Rāmeśvar. "Ākhoṭi pālā." In *Rāmeśvar racanāvalī*, edited by Pañcānan Cakravartī, 536–49. Kolkata: Baṅgīya Sāhitya Pariṣat, 1371 BS [ca. 1964].

———. *Ākhoṭi pālā: Satyanārāyaṇ pañcālī*. 3rd ed. Khāñtāi: Madhusudan Jān at Nihār Press, 1924.

———. *Rāmeśvarī satyanārāyaṇ pāñcālī*. 5th ed. Khāñtāi: Madhusudān Jānā, 1330 BS [ca. 1923].

———. *Satyanārāyaṇ*. Edited by Trailoknāth Datta, 2nd ed. Kalikātā: by the editor, 1283 BS [ca. 1876].

———. "Satyanārāyaṇ vratkathā." In *Rāmeśvar racanāvalī*, edited by Pañcānan Cakravarttī, 509–28. Kalikātā: Baṅgīya Sāhitya Pariṣat, 1964.

———. *Śrīśrīsatyanārāyaṇ o subacanī vratkathā bā pāñcālī*. Edited by Śrīmantu Cakravartī. Kalikātā: Māyā Lāibrerī, n.d.

———. *Śrīśrīsatyanārāyaṇer pāñcālī: Līlāvatī, kalāvatī o daridra brāhmaṇ upākhyān (pūjādravya o pūjāpaddhati sambalita)*. Edited by Paśupati Caṭṭopādhyāy. Kalikātā: Jenārel Lāibrerī, n.d.

———. *Śrīśrīsatyanārāyaṇer pāñcālī: Pūjāpaddhati, dhyān, praṇām, pharddamālā, evaṃ darīdra brāhmaṇ upākhyān*. Edited by Tīrthanāth Bhaṭṭācāryya Kāvyatīrtha. Kalikātā: Oriyeṇṭ Lāibrerī, n.d.

Rāmeśvar Bandyopādhyāy. *Satyapīrer kathā*. Edited by Nagendranāth Gupta. Kalikātā: Kalikātā Viśvavidyālay, 1336 BS [ca. 1929].

Rāmeśvar Bhaṭṭācārya. *Satyanārāyaṇ*. Edited by Rādhāvallabh Śīl. Kalikātā: Hindu Press, 1276 BS [ca. 1869].

Rāmeśvar Śarmma. *Satyanārāyaṇ*. Kalikātā: Nṛtyalāl Śīl, 1281 BS [ca. 1874].

Rāmgopāl Rāy. *Satyamaṅgal bā satyanārāyaṇ dever vratkathā o pūjāpaddhati*. Kalikātā: Jayakṛṣṇa Caudhurī, 1835 *śaka* [ca. 1913].

Rāmkānth Nyāyapañcānan Bhaṭṭācāryya. *Bāṅgālā pāñcālī kathā: Reva khaṇḍokta satyadev vrat kathāmūlak*. Edited by Rasrañjan Sen Gupta. Kahliśākoṭ, Bariśāl: n.p., 1322 BS [ca. 1915].

Rasmay. *Galakāṭā phāsyarār pālā*. Bengali MS no. 214, Dhaka University. Complete, 17 folios, dtd. 1264 BS [ca. 1857].

Rāsvihāri Sāṃkhyatīrtha. *Satyanārāyaṇ vrat kathā*. Edited with Bangla translation by Rāmdev Miśra. Murshidabad: Rāmdev Miśra for Haribhaktipradāyinī Sabhā of Baharampur at Rādhāramaṇ Press, 1315 BS [ca. 1908].

Ratneśvara Tantrajyotiṣaśāstrī, ed. *Śrīśrīsatyanārāyaṇ o śubhacunī pūjāpaddhati*. Kalikātā: Puṣpa eṇḍ Koṃ., n.d.

Reyājuddin Āhmād. *Bāul dhvaṅsa fatwa*. Calcutta: Mohammadi Press, 1925.

Rudradev. "Rāy maṅgal: Rāy gāji yuddha, ratā bāuliyā puṣpadatta baṇik pālā." In *Dvādaś maṅgal*, edited by Pañcānan Maṇḍal, 121–48. Sāhityaprakāśikā, vol. 5. Śāntiniketan: Viśvabhāratī, 1373 BS [1966].

Rūpa Gosvāmin. *Bhaktirasāmṛtasindhu*. Edited with Bengali translation by Haridās Dās. Includes the commentaries "Durgasaṃgamanī ṭīkā" of Jīva Gosvāmin, "Artharatnālpadīpikā" of Mukundadāsa Gosvāmin, and "Bhaktisārapradarśiṇī ṭīkā" of Viśvanātha Cakravartin. 3rd ed. Mathurā: Haribol Kuṭīr from Śrī Kṛṣṇajanmasthān, 495 GA [ca. 1981].

Śāh Muhammad Sagīr. *Iusuph jolekhā*. Edited by Muhammad Enāmul Hak. Ḍhākā: Māolā Brādārs, 1408 BS [2001].

Sāiyad Śāh Mohāmmad Āli, *Mithya-pīr*. Kochagrām, Dinajpur: by the author; printed in Kalikātā by Mohāmmad Reyājuddin Āhmād at Reyāul-Islām Press, 1325 BS [ca. 1918].

Saiyad Sultān. *Nabīvaṃśa*. Edited by Āhmād Śariph. 2 vols. Ḍākā: Bāṃlā Ekāḍemī, 1978.

Samir Rāy. *Banbibī o nārāyaṇīr pālā*. Kāśīnagar, Cabbiś Pārgaṇas: n.p., 1990.

Sañjīv Kumār Bāgchi. *Satyanārāyaṇ: Nāṭya kāvya*. Dinājpur: Kālīpad Bāgchī and Raṇajit Kumār Bāgchī, 1334 BS [1927].

Śaṅkarācārya. *Satyanārāyaṇer pāñcālī*. Edited by Gaurāṅgasundar Bhaṭṭācāryya. Baṭ-tolā edition. Kalikātā: Rājendraī, n.d.

Śaṅkarācārya and Rāmeśvar. *Śrīśrīsatyanārāyaṇ o śubhacunī pūjāpaddhati*. Edited by Rateśvar Tantrajyotiṣaśāstrī. Kalikātā: Puṣpa eṇḍ Koṃ., n.d.

———. *Śrīśrīsatyanārāyaṇer pāñcālī: Līlāvati, kalāvatī o daridra brāhmaṇ upākhyān*. Kalikātā: Rāmnāth Dās at Tārācāñd Dās eṇḍ Sans, n.d.

———. *Śrīśrīsatyanārāyaṇer pāñcālī: Līlāvati, kalāvatī o daridra brāhmaṇ upākhyān*. Edited by Avināścandra Mukhopādhyāy and Sudrendranāth Bhaṭṭācāryya. Kalikātā: Śrī Kārttik Candra Basu at Kalikātā Ṭāun Lāibrerī, 1360 BS [ca. 1953].

———. *Śrīśrīsatyanārāyaṇer pāñcālī: Līlāvatī kalāvatī daridra brāhmaṇer upakhyān (pūjādravya, pūjāvidhi, dhyān o praṇām sambalita)*. Edited by Gaurāṅgasundar Bhaṭṭācāryya. Kalikātā: Rajendra Lāibrerī, n.d.

Śaṅkarācāryā and Rāmeśvar Bhattācāryya. *Śrīśrīsatyanārāyaṇer pāñcālī: Līlāvatī, kalāvatī o daridra brāhmaṇer upākhyān*. Edited by Paṇḍit Śrī Kālīprasanna Vidyāratna. Kalakātā: Akṣay Lāibrerī, n.d.

Satyānanda. *Satyar pāñcālī*. Kṛṣṇakanta Rāy Collection, MS no. K-67, Dhaka University. Complete, 17 folios, dtd. 1171 BS [ca. 1765].

Satyanārāyaṇ Bhaṭṭācāryya, ed. *Rāimaṅgal*. Bardhamān: Sahitya Sabhā 1363 BS [ca. 1956].

Sāyeb Munsī Ābdul Ohāb. *Gāji kālu o cāmpāvatī kanyār punthi*. Kalikātā: Munsī Ābdul Hāmād Khān. Reprint, Kalikātā: Śrīmahāmmad Rabiullā at Hāmidīyā Press, Es Rahmān aṇḍ Sans Printer, 1315 BS [ca. 1908].

Śekh Khodā Bakhś. "Gājī kālu o cāmpāvatī." In *Bāṅglā sāhitye gājī kālu o cāmpāvatī upākhyān*, edited by Ābul Kālām Mohāmmad Jākāriyā, 1–307. Ḍhākā: Bāṃlā Ekāḍemī, 1396 BS [1989]

Śivacandra Sen. *Satyanārāyaṇer pāñcālī*. Edited byNibāraṇcandra Basu. Ḍhākā: by the editor at Bhikṭoriā Pres, 1328 BS [ca. 1921].

Śrī Jān Ārāmullā. *Iblich nāmār puthi*. Kalikātā: Viśvambhara Lāhā, 1284 BS [ca. 1877].

Sujit Kumār Maṇḍal, ed. *Bonbibir pālā*. Kalakātā: Aṇimā Biśvās Gāñcil, 2010. Includes text of Munśī Mohammad Khāter Sāheb's *Bonbibī jahurā nāmā* and *Bonbibī pālā* adaptation for *yātrā* stage performance; and the texts of *Bonbibir 'Ekani' pālā*, *Bonbibir pālā*, and *Dukhe jātrā*.

Surnāth Bhaṭṭācāryya. *Śrīśrīsatyanārāyaṇ vratkathā*. Kalikātā: by the author at Bi. Pi. Emer Pres, 1321 BS [ca. 1914].

Śyāmākānt Tarkapañcānan, ed. *Satyanārāyaṇ vratkathā*. Vārāṇasī: Vāmārañjan Ṭhākur, 1330 BS [ca. 1923].

Śyāmcaraṇ Kaviratna, ed. *Satyanārāyaṇ o śubhacanīr kathā*. 2nd ed. Kalikātā: by the editor through Gurudās Caṭṭopādhyāy at Bengal Medical Library, 1315 BS [ca. 1909].

Vaiṣṇav Dās, comp. *Padakalpataru*. Edited by Satiśacandra Rāy, with an introduction by the editor. 5 vols. Sāhitya Pariṣat Granthāvalī, no. 50. Kalikātā: Rāmakāmal Siṃha for the Baṅgīya Sāhitya Pariṣat, 1322–38 BS [ca. 1915–31].

Vasantakumār Dāsī. *Meyeder vratkathā bā vrat māhātmya*. Edited by Rākhālcandra Dās. Kalikātā: Mahendranāth Kar at Mehendra Lāibrerī, n.d. [1340 BS (ca. 1933)].

Vṛndāvan Dās. *Caitanya bhāgavat*. Edited with Bengali commentary "Nitāikaruṇākallolinī ṭikā" by Rādhāgovinda Nāth. 6 vols. Kalikātā: Sādhanā Prakāśanī, 1373 BS [ca. 1966].

Vyāsadeva. *Satyanārāyaṇa nāmaka granthaḥ*. Sanskrit text edited by Rājacandra Rāya, Bengali translation by Dharmadās Mukhopādhyāy. Kalikātā: Kāśīnāth Śīl at Jñānoday Yantra, 1268 BS [ca. 1861].

PRIMARY TEXTS IN TRANSLATION

'Abdullāh Ḥusain Bilgrāmī. *The Romance Tradition in Urdu: Adventures from the Dastan of Amir Ḥamzah*. Translated by Frances W. Pritchett. New York: Columbia University Press, 1991.

Abolqasem Ferdowsi. *Shahnameh: The Persian Book of Kings*. Translated by Dick Davis. With a foreword by Azar Nafisi. New York: Penguin Books, 2016.

Aḥmad Ibn Muḥammed Al-Thalabī. *Lives of the Prophets* [Arā'is al-Majālis fī Qiṣaṣ al-Anbiyā']. Translated by William M. Brinner. Leiden: E. J. Brill, 2002.

Anonymous. "*Campavati Kainyar Palagan*: Anonymous Muslim Folk Poem of Bengal." Translated by Edward C. Dimock, Jr. Learning Resources in Bengali Studies. New York: Learning Resources in International Studies, 1974 [circulated in mimeograph].

Anonymous. "The Erstwhile Bride and Her Winged Horse: Anonymous *Manohara Phāsara Pālā*." In *Fabulous Females and Peerless Pīrs: Tales of Mad Adventure in Old Bengal*, translated by Tony K. Stewart, 149–71. New York: Oxford University Press, 2004.

Anonymous. *Iskandernamah*. Translated by Minoo S. Southgate. New York: Columbia Universitry Press, 1978.

Burton, Richard F. *A Plain and Literal Translation of the Arabian Nights Entertainments, Now Entitled the Book of the Thousand Nights and a Night*. 4 vols. London: Kama Shastra Society, 1885–86.

Digby, Simon, trans. *Wonder-Tales of South Asia*. Edited by Leonard Harrow. Jersey, Channel Islands: Orient Monographs, 2000. Reprint, Delhi: Oxford University Press, 2006.

Doniger, Wendy, trans. *The Laws of Manu*. With an introduction and notes by Wendy Doniger with Brian K. Smith. London: Penguin Books, 1991.

Dvīja Kavibara. "The Disconsolate Yogī Who Turned the Merchant's Wife into a Dog: Dvīja Kavibara's *Bāghāmbara Pālā*." In *Fabulous Females and Peerless Pīrs: Tales of Mad Adventure in Old Bengal*, translated by Tony K. Stewart, 95–119. New York: Oxford University Press, 2004.

Eaton, Richard M., trans. "Forest Clearing and Growth of Islam in Bengal." In *Islam in South Asia in Practice*, edited by Barbara D. Metcalf, 375–89. Princeton: Princeton University Press, 2009.

Gayārāma Dāsa. "The Princess Who Nursed Her Own Husband: Gayārāma Dāsa's *Madanamañjarī Pālā*." In *Fabulous Females and Peerless Pīrs: Tales of Mad Adventure in*

Old Bengal, translated by Tony K. Stewart, 195–233. New York: Oxford University Press, 2004.

Ghosh, Saswat, comp. *Folk Tales from India: The Sunderbans*. Vol. 1. With illustrations by Dipankar Bhattacharya. New Delhi: Vivalok Comics, 2003. Contains the stories of Mānik Pīr, Gāji, and Bonbibī.

Husayn Ibn Mansûr Hallâj. *La Passion de Husayn Ibn Mansûr Hallâj*. Translated by Louis Massignon. 2 vols. New ed. Paris: Gallimard, 1975.

ibn Isḥāq. *The Life of Muhammad: A Translation of ibn Isḥāq's Sīrat Rasūl Allāh*. Translated by A[lfred] Guillaume. 1955. Reprint, Karachi: Oxford University Press, 1967.

Jones, Alan, trans. *The Qur'ān Translated into English by Alan Jones*. Cambridge: Gibb Memorial Trust, 2007.

Kavi Ārif. "The Wazir's Daughter Who Married a Sacrificial Goat: Kavi Ārif's *Lālmoner Kecchā*." In *Fabulous Females and Peerless Pīrs: Tales of Mad Adventure in Old Bengal*, translated by Tony K. Stewart, 29–50. New York: Oxford University Press, 2004.

Kavi Kaṇva. "The Fabled *Beṅgamā* Bird and the Stupid Prince: Kavi Kaṇva's *Akhoṭi Pālā*." In *Fabulous Females and Peerless Pīrs: Tales of Mad Adventure in Old Bengal*, translated by Tony K. Stewart, 67–94. New York: Oxford University Press, 2004.

Kavikankan. *Chandimangal*. Translated by Edward Yazijian. New Delhi: Penguin India, 2015.

Ketakā Dāsa. "The Manasā Maṅgal of Ketakā Dāsa: Behulā and Lakhindar." In *The Thief of Love: Bengali Tales from Court and Village*, translated by Edward C. Dimock, Jr., 195–294. Chicago: University of Chicago Press, 1963.

Kiṅkara Dāsa. "The Bloodthirsty Ogress Who Would Be Queen: Kiṅkara Dāsa's *Śaṣīdhara Pālā*." In *Fabulous Females and Peerless Pīrs: Tales of Mad Adventure in Old Bengal*, translated by Tony K. Stewart, 172–94. New York: Oxford University Press, 2004.

———. "The Mother's Son Who Spat Up Pearls: Kiṅkara Dāsa's *Matilāl Pālā*." In *Fabulous Females and Peerless Pīrs: Tales of Mad Adventure in Old Bengal*, translated by Tony K. Stewart, 120–48. New York: Oxford University Press, 2004.

———. "The Unwilting Garland of Faithfulness: Kiṅkar Dāsa's *Rambhāvatī Pālā*." In *Fabulous Females and Peerless Pīrs: Tales of Mad Adventure in Old Bengal*, translated by Tony K. Stewart, 51–66. New York: Oxford University Press, 2004.

Kṛṣṇadāsa Kavirāja. *Caitanya caritāmṛta of Kṛṣṇadāsa Kavirājā*. Translated by Edward C. Dimock, Jr. Edited by Tony K. Stewart. With an introduction by the translator and the editor. Harvard Oriental Series 56. Cambridge, MA: Department of Sanskrit and Indian Studies, Harvard University, 1999.

Kṛṣṇa Dvaipāyana Vyāsa. *The Bhagavad Gītā in the Mahābhārata*, translated by J. A. B. van Buitenen. Chicago: University of Chicago Press, 1981.

———. "Nala." In *The Mahābhārata*, translated by J. A. B. van Buitenen. Chicago: University of Chicago Press, 1975, vol. 3, bk. 3 (32a), 319–64.

Mīr Sayyid Manjhan Shattārī Rājgīrī. *Madhumālatī: An Indian Sufi Romance*. Translated by Aditya Behl and Simon Weightman, with Shyam Manohar Pandey. With introduction and notes by the translators. Oxford World's Classics. New York: Oxford University Press, 2000.

Muḥammad ibn 'Abd Allāh al-Kisā'i. *Tales of the Prophet (Qiṣaṣ al-anbiyā')*. Translated by Wheeler M. Thakston, Jr. Great Books of the Islamic World. Chicago: Kazi Publications, 1997.

Munśī Mohāmmad Khater Sāheb. "Bonbībī, Protectress of the Forest," translated by Sufia Mendez Uddin. In *Tales of God's Friends: Islamic Hagiography in Translation*, edited by John Renard, 301–11. Berkeley: University of California Press, 2009.

Pollock, Sheldon, trans. *A Rasa Reader: Classical Indian Aesthetics*. New York: Oxford University Press, 2016.

Quṭban Suhravardī. *Mirigāvatī: The Magic Doe*. Translated by Aditya Behl. New York: Oxford University Press, 2012.

Saiyad Sultān. "Curbing Moses' Hubris: Khoyāj Khijir's Instruction to Musā in the Bengali *Nabīvaṃśa* of Saiyad Sultān." Translated by Tony K. Stewart and Ayesha A. Irani. Typescript.

Somadeva Bhaṭṭa. *Tales from the Kathāsaritsāgara*. Translated and with an introduction by Arshia Sattar and a foreword by Wendy Doniger. London: Penguin Books, 1994.

Śrī Kavi Karṇa. *Pālās of Śrī Kavi Karṇa*. Translated and compiled by Bishnupada Panda. 4 vols. Kalāmūlaśāstra Series, vols. 4–7. New Delhi: Indira Gandhi National Centre for the Arts. Delhi: Motilal Banarsidass, 1991.

Stewart, Tony K., trans. "The Exemplary Devotion of the 'Servant of Hari.'" In *The Religions of India in Practice*, edited by Donald S. Lopez, Jr., 564–77. Princeton: Princeton University Press, 1995.

———, trans. *Fabulous Females and Peerless Pīrs: Tales of Mad Adventure in Old Bengal*. New York: Oxford University Press, 2004.

———, trans. "The Goddess Ṣaṣṭhī Protects Children." In *The Religions of India in Practice*, edited by Donald S. Lopez, Jr., 352–66. Princeton: Princeton University Press, 1995.

———, trans. "The Rescue of Two Drunkards." In *The Religions of India in Practice*, edited by Donald S. Lopez, Jr., 375–88. Princeton: Princeton University Press, 1995.

———, trans. "Satya Pīr: Muslim Holy Man and Hindu God." In *Religions of India in Practice*, edited by Donald S. Lopez, Jr., 578–97. Princeton: Princeton University Press, 1995.

———, trans. "The Tales of Mānik Pīr: Protector of Cows in Bengal." In *Tales of God's Friends: Islamic Hagiography in Translation*, edited by John Renard, 312–32. Berkeley: University of California Press, 2009.

Sunan An-Nasâ'i. *The Book of Kind Treatment of Women*. Translated by Nâsiruddin al-Khattâb. Compiled by Imâm Hâfiz Abû Abdur Rahmân and Ahmad bin Shu'aib bin 'Ali An-Nasâ'i. Edited and referenced by Hâfiz Abu Tâhir Zubair 'Alî Za'î. 6 vols. Riyadh: Darussalam, 2007.

Śvetāśvatāra Upaniṣad. Translated by Robert Ernest Hume. In *Thirteen Principal Upaniṣads: Original Sanskrit Text with English Translation*, translated by Robert Ernest Hume, edited by N. C. Panda. Rev. ed. Vol. 2. New Delhi: Bharatiya Kala Prakashan, 2012.

Vallabha. "Satyanārāyaṇer punthi." Translated by David Cashin. In Cashin, *The Ocean of Love: Middle Bengali Sufi Literature and the Fakirs of Bengal*. Skrifter utgivna av Föreningen för Orientaliska Studier no. 27: 251–82. Stockholm: Association of Oriental Studies, Stockholm University, 1995.

Vipradāsa. *La victoire de Manasā: Traduction française du Manasā Vijaya, poème bengali de Vipradāsa (XVᵉ)*. Translated by France Bhattacharya. Collection Indologies 105. Pondichéry: Institut Français de Pondichéry, École Française d'Extrême-Orient, 2007.

Wensinck, A. J. and J. P. Mensing, comps. *Concordance et Indices de la Tradition Musulmane. Les Six Livres*, al-Dārimī's *Le Musnad*, Mālik's *Le Muwatta'*, and Aḥmad ibn Ḥanbal's *Le Musnad*, vols. 1–8. 2nd ed. Leiden: E. J. Brill, 1992.

MONOGRAPHS, DISSERTATIONS, FIELD STUDIES, AND TWO NOVELS

Āhmad, Oyākil. *Bāṃlā romānṭik praṇayopākhyān*. 6th printing. Ḍhākā: Khān Brādārs eyāṇḍ Kompāni, 2004.

Ahmed, Rafiuddin. *The Bengal Muslims, 1871–1906: A Quest for Identity*. New York: Oxford University Press, 1981.

Ahmed, Shahab. *What Is Islam? The Importance of Being Islamic*. Princeton: Princeton University Press, 2016.

Ahmed, Syed Jamil. *Acinpakhi Infinity: Indigenous Theatre of Bangladesh*. Dhaka: The University Press Limited, 2000.

———. *In Praise of Nirañjan: Islam, Theatre and Bangladesh*. Dhaka: Pathak Samabesh, Losauk, 2001.

Amin, Shahid. *Conquest and Community: The Afterlife of Warrior Saint Ghazi Miyan*. Hyderabad: Orient Blackswan, 2015.

Assmann, Jan. *Religion and Cultural Memory: Ten Studies*. Translated by Rodney Livingstone. Stanford, CA: Stanford University Press, 2006.

Awn, Peter J. *Satan's Tragedy and Redemption: Iblīs in Sufi Psychology*. With a foreward by Annemarie Schimmel. Studies in the History of Religions. Leiden: E. J. Brill, 1983.

Bakhtin, M. M. *The Dialogic Imagination: Four Essays*. Edited by Michael Holquist. Translated by Caryl Emerson and Michael Holquist. Austin: University of Texas Press, 1981.

Bāndyopādhyāy, Asit Kumār. *Bāṅglā sāhityer itibṛtta*. 4 vols. 1365–80 BS [ca. 1958–63]. Reprint, Kalikātā: Modern Book Agency, 1373–90 BS [ca. 1966–83].

Banerjee, Sures Chandra. *Tantra in Bengal: A Study in Its Origin, Development, and Influence*. 2nd rev. ed. New Delhi: Manohar, 1992. Originally published in 1977.

Banerji, Sures Chandra. *A Brief History of Tantric Literature*. Calcutta: Naya Prokash, 1998.

Baudouin, Charles. *Le Triomphe du héros: Étude psychoanalytique sur le mythe du héros et les grandes épopées*. Paris: Librairie Plon, 1952.

Bāuliyā, Raṇajit Kumār. "Sundarban añcaler ādibāsī saṃskṛti o sāhitya." PhD diss., Calcutta University, 2010.

Behl, Aditya. *Love's Subtle Magic: An Indian Islamic Literary Tradition, 1479–1545*. Edited by Wendy Doniger. New York: Oxford University Press, 2012.

Benke, Theodore. "The *Śūdraśiromaṇi* of Kṛṣṇa Śeṣa: A 16th Century Manual of *Dharma* for *Śūdras*." PhD diss., University of Pennsylvania, 2010.

Bera, Gautam K. and Vijoy S. Sahay, eds. *In the Lagoons of the Gangetic Delta*. New Delhi: Mittal Publications, 2010.

Bhatia, Varuni. *Unforgetting Chaitanya: Vaishnavism and Cultures of Devotion in Colonial Bengal*. New York: Oxford University Press, 2017.

Bhaṭṭācāryya, Āśutoṣ. *Bāṅglā maṅgalkāvyer itihās*. 6th ed. Kalikātā: Mukhārji āyāṇḍ Koṃ Prāibheṭ Limiṭeḍ, 1381 BS [1975].

Bhattacharyya, Shatarupa. *The Magnificent World of the Littoral: The Northern Bay of Bengal on the Eve of Colonialism*. Saarbrücken: LAP Lambert Academic Publishing, 2012.

Bhaumik, Kalpanā. *Pāṇḍulipi paṭhan sahāyikā*. Ḍhākā: Bāṃlā Ekāḍemī, 1399 BS [1992].

Blurton, T. Richard. *Bengali Myths*. London: The British Museum Press, 2006.

Bodman, Whitney S. *The Poetics of Iblīs: Narrative Theology in the Qur'ān*. Harvard Theological Studies 62. Cambridge, MA: Harvard Divinity School, 2011.

Booth, Wayne. *A Rhetoric of Irony*. Chicago: University of Chicago Press, 1974.
Bose, Neilesh. *Recasting the Region: Language, Culture, and Islam in Colonial Bengal*. Delhi: Oxford University Press, 2014.
Bouillier, Véronique, and Claudine Le Blanc, comps. *L'usage des héros: Traditions narratives et affirmations identitaires dans le monde indien*. Bibliothéque de l'École Pratique des Hautes Études Sciences Historiques et Philologiques Tome 343. Paris: Librairie Honoré Champion, 2006.
Bühnemann, Gudrun. *Pūjā: A Study in Smarta Ritual*. De Nobili Research Library Publications, vol. 15. Vienna: Institute for Indology, University of Vienna, 1988.
Butler, Judith. *Gender Trouble: Feminism and the Subversion of Identity*. New York: Routledge, 1990.
Cakravartī, Amarkṛṣṇa. *Dakṣiṇeśvar Dakṣiṇrāy: Ek laukik debkalper anupam rupkathā*. Edited by Debabrata Bhaṭṭācārya. Kalakātā: by the editor at De Buk Sṭor, 1412 BS [2005].
Casey, Edward S. *Getting Back into Place: Toward a Renewed Understanding of the Place-World*. 2nd ed. Bloomington: Indiana University Press, 2009.
———. *Imagining: A Phenomenological Study*. 2nd ed. Bloomington: Indiana University Press, 2000.
Cashin, David. *The Ocean of Love: Middle Bengali Sufi Literature and the Fakirs of Bengal*. Skrifter utgivna av Föreningen för Orientaliska Studier no. 27. Stockholm: Association of Oriental Studies, Stockholm University, 1995.
Chandola, Anoop. *The Way to True Worship: A Popular Story of Hinduism*. Lanham, MD: University Press of America, 1991.
Chatterjee, Kumkum. *The Cultures of History in Early Modern India: Persianization and Mughal Culture in Bengal*. New Delhi: Oxford University Press, 2009.
Chatterjee Sarkar, Sutapa. *The Sunderbans: Folk Deities, Monsters and Mortals*. New Delhi: Orient BlackSwan, Social Science Press, 2010.
Chatterji, Suniti Kumar. *The Origin and Development of Bengali Language*. 2 pts. in 3 vols. 1926. Reprint, Calcutta: George Allen Unwin, 1975.
Curley, David L. *Poetry and History: Bengali* Maṅgal-kābya *and Social Change in Precolonial Bengal*. New Delhi: Chronicle Books, 2008.
Dās, Girīndranāth. *Bāṃlā pīr sāhityer kathā*. 1st ed. Kājipāḍā, Bārāsat, Cabbiś Pargaṇa: Śehid Lāibrerī, 1383 BS [ca. 1976].
———. *Bāṃlā pīr sāhityer kathā*. 2nd ed. Kalikātā: Suvarṇarekhā, 1998.
———. *Baṅger pīr o pirāni kathā*. Bijaynagar, West Bengal: by the author, 1409 BS [ca. 2002].
Das, Indra. *The Devourers*. New York: Del Ray Paperbacks, 2017.
Dās, Śaśāṅk Śekhar. *Bonbibi*. Kalakātā: Loksaṃskṛti o Ādibāsī Saṃskṛti Kendra, Paścimbaṅga Sarkār, 2004. Reprint, 2018.
———. "Bonbibi o grām bāṃlā." PhD diss., Calcutta University, 1989.
Das, Sudhir Ranjan. *Folk Religion in Bengal: A Study in Vrata Rites*. Calcutta: S. C. Kar, 1953.
Dasgupta, Shashibhusan. *Obscure Religious Cults*. 3rd ed. Calcutta: Firma KLM, 1969.
Davis, Dick. *Epic and Sedition: The Case of Ferdowsi's Shahnameh*. Washington, DC: Mage Publishers, 1992.
Delehaye, Père H[ippolyte], S. J. *The Legends of the Saints: An Introduction to Hagiography*. Translated by V. M. Crawford. Notre Dame, IN: University of Notre Dame Press, 1961.
Dentith, Simon. *Parody*. London: Routledge, 2000.

Deutscher, Guy. *Through the Language Glass: Why the World Looks Different in Other Languages.* New York: Picador, Henry Holt, 2010.

d'Hubert, Thibaut. *In the Shade of the Golden Palace: Ālāol and Middle Bengali Poetics in Arakan.* South Asia Research. New York: Oxford University Press, 2018.

Doniger, Wendy. *Śiva: The Erotic Ascetic.* New York: Oxford University Press, 1981.

———. *Splitting the Difference: Gender and Myth in Ancient Greece and India.* Chicago: University of Chicago Press, 1999.

Doniger (O'Flaherty), Wendy. *Asceticism and Eroticism in the Mythology of Śiva.* New York: Oxford University Press, 1973.

Dunham, Mary Frances. *Jarigan: Muslim Epic Songs of Bangladesh.* Dhaka: The University Press Limited, 1997.

Eaton, Richard M. *The Rise of Islam and the Bengal Frontier, 1204–1760.* Berkeley: University of California Press, 1993.

Eliade, Mircea. *Patterns in Comparative Religion.* 1958. Reprint, New York: New American Library, 1963.

Fauconnier, Gilles. *Mappings in Thought and Language.* Cambridge: Cambridge University Press, 1997.

Fauconnier, Gilles, and Mark Turner. *The Way We Think: Conceptual Blending and the Mind's Hidden Complexities.* New York: Basic Books, 2002.

Flora, Giuseppe. *On Fairy Tales, Intellectuals and Nationalism in Bengal (1880–1920).* Supplement no. 1, Alla Rivista Degli Studi Orientali, vol. 75. Pisa: Istituti Editoriali e Poligrafici Internazionali, 2002.

Franke, Patrick. *Begegnung mit Khiḍr: Queellenstudien zum Imaginaren im traditionellen Islam.* Beiruter Texte und Studien 15. Stuttgart: Franz Steiner Verlag, 2000.

Frye, Northrop. *Anatomy of a Criticism: Four Essays.* Princeton: Princeton University Press, 1957.

———. *The Secular Scripture: A Study of the Structure of Romance.* The Charles Eliot Norton Lectures 1974–75. Cambridge, MA: Harvard University Press, 1976.

Fuchs, Barbara. *Romance.* New York: Routledge, 2004.

Fuller, Jason D. "Religion, Class, and Power: Bhaktivinode Thakur and the Transformation of Religious Authority among the Gaudiya Vaisnavas in Nineteenth-Century Bengal." PhD diss., University of Pennsylvania, 2005.

Gaṅgopādhyay, Baren. *Bonbibīr upākhyān.* Kalakātā: Nāth Brādārs, 1978.

Genette, Gérard. *The Architext: An Introduction.* Translated by Jane E. Lewin. Foreward by Robert Scholes. Berkeley: University of California Press, 1992.

———. *Narrative Discourse: An Essay in Method.* Ithaca: Cornell University Press, 1980.

———. *Palimpsests: Literature in the Second Degree.* Translated by Channa Newman and Claude Doubinsky. Foreword by Gerald Prince. Lincoln: University of Nebraska Press, 1997.

———. *Paratexts: Thresholds of Interpretation.* Translated by Jane E. Lewin. Cambridge: Cambridge University Press, 1997.

Gentzler, Edwin. *Contemporary Translation Theories.* London: Routledge, 1993.

Ghosh, Amitav. *The Great Derangement: Climate Change and the Unthinkable.* Chicago: University of Chicago Press, 2016.

———. *The Hungry Tide.* London: HarperCollins, 2004.

Gruber, Christine and Frederick Colby, eds. *The Prophet's Ascension: Cross-Cultural Encounters with the Islamic* Miʿrāj *Tales*. Bloomington: Indiana University Press, 2010.
Gupta, Eva Maria. *Brata und Ālpanā in Bengalen*. Wiesbaden: Franz Steiner Verlag, 1985.
Halder, Epsita. "Of Blood and Tears: Tracing Self and Community in Karbala Narratives of Bengal (Late 19th to Early 20th Century)." PhD diss., Jadavpur University, 2017.
Halevi, Leor. *Muhammad's Grave: Death Rites and the Making of Islamic Society*. New York: Columbia University Press, 2007.
Halman, Hugh Talat. *Where the Two Seas Meet: The Qur'ānic Story of al-Khiḍr and Moses in Sufi Commentaries as a Model of Spiritual Guidance*. Louisville: Fons Vitae, 2013.
Haq, Muhammad Enamul. *A History of Sufi-ism in Bengal*. Dacca: Asiatic Society of Bangladesh, 1975.
———. *Muhammad enāmul hak racanāvalī*. Edited by Mansur Musā. 5 vols. Ḍhākā: Bāṃlā Ekāḍemī, 1398–1404 BS [ca. 1991–97].
Hazra, R. C. *Studies in the Upapurāṇas*. 2 vols. Calcutta: Sanskrit College, 1958.
Hewson, Lance, and Jacky Martin. *Redefining Translation: The Variational Approach*. London: Routledge, 1991.
Hosen, Jāhāṅgīr. *Dakṣiṇbaṅger aitihyabāhī loknāṭya*. Ḍhākā: Mohammad Śāh Ālam Sarkār at Samācār, 2014.
Hutcheon, Linda. *A Theory of Parody: The Teachings of Twentieth-Century Art Forms*. 1985. Reprint, Urbana: University of Illinois Press, 2000.
———. *Irony's Edge: The Theory and Politics of Irony*. London: Routledge, 1994.
Inden, Ronald B. *Marriage and Rank in Bengali Culture*. Berkeley: University of California Press, 1976.
Irani, Ayesha A. *The Muhmamad* Avatāra: *Salvation History, Translation, and the Making of Bengali Islam*. New York: Oxford University Press, forthcoming.
———. "Sacred Biography, Translation, and Conversion: The *Nabīvaṃśa* of Saiyid Sultān and the Making of Bengali Islam, 1600–Present." PhD diss., University of Pennsylvania, 2011.
Iser, Wolfgang. *The Fictive and the Imaginary: Charting Literary Anthropology*. Baltimore: Johns Hopkins University Press, 1993.
Jalais, Annu. *Forest of Tigers: People, Politics, and Environment in the Sunderbans*. London: Routledge, 2010.
James, William. *Pragmatism: A New Name for Some Old Ways of Thinking*. New York: Longmans, Green, 1907.
Kane, David M. *Puthi-Poṛa: "Melodic Reading" and Its Use in the Islamisation of Bengal*. London: Sylheti Translation and Research, 2017.
Karamustafa, Ahmet T. *God's Unruly Friends: Dervish Groups in the Islamic Middle Period, 1220–1550*. 1994. Reprint, London: Oneworld Publications, 2004.
Karim, Abdul. *A Social History of the Muslims of Bengal, down to A.D. 1538*. Dacca: Asiatic Society of Pakistan, 1959.
Kermode, Frank. *The Classic: Literary Images of Permanence and Change*. The T. S. Eliot Memorial Lectures 1973. Cambridge, MA: Harvard University Press, 1975.
Khānam, Māhmudā. *Madhyajugīya bāṃlā sāhitya hindī suphī kāvyer prabhāv*. Ḍhākā: Bāṃlā Ekāḍemī, 1410 BS [2003].
Korom, Frank J. *Village of Painters: Narrative Scrolls from West Bengal*. With photographs by Paul Smutko. Sante Fe: Museum of New Mexico Press, 2006.

Kuhn, Thomas. *The Structure of Scientific Revolutions*. Chicago: University of Chicago Press, 1962.
Lacan, Jacques. *The Four Fundamental Concepts of Psycho-Analysis*. Edited by Jacques-Alain Miller. Translated by Alan Sheridan. London: Hogarth Press, 1977.
Lakoff, George, and Mark Johnson. *Metaphors We Live By*. Chicago: University of Chicago Press, 1980).
Lefevre, André. *Translating Poetry: Seven Strategies and a Blueprint*. Assen: Van Gorcum, 1975.
Leoni, Francesca et al. *Power and Protection: Islamic Art and the Supernatural*. Oxford: Ashmolean Museum, 2016.
Luckmann, Thomas. *The Invisible Religion: The Problem of Religion in Modern Society*. New York: Macmillan, 1967.
Macherey, Pierre. *A Theory of Literary Production*. Translated by Geoffrey Wall. London: Routledge, 1978.
Maṇḍal, Śaśaṅk. *Britiś rājatve sundarban*. Kalakātā: Punaśca, 1995.
Mannan, Qazi Abdul. *The Emergence and Development of Dobhasi Literature in Bengal (up to 1855 AD)*. 2nd ed. Dacca: Bangla Academy, 1974.
Marvin, Brian D. "The Life and Thought of Kedarnath Dutta Bhaktivinode: A Hindu Encounter with Modernity." PhD diss., University of Toronto, 1996.
McCutchion, David. *Brick Temples of Bengal: From the Archives of David McCutchion*. Edited by George Michell. Princeton: Princeton University Press, 1983.
McCutchion, David, and Suhṛdkumāra Bhaumik. *Patuas and Patua Art in Bengal*. Calcutta: Firma KLM, 1999.
McDaniel, June. *Making Virtuous Daughters and Wives: An Introduction to Women's Brata Rituals in Bengali Folk Religion*. Albany: SUNY Press, 2003.
Mir, Farina. *The Social Space of Language: Vernacular Culture in British Colonial Punjab*. South Asia across the Disciplines. Berkeley: University of California Press, 2010.
Mitra, Sanatkumar, ed. *Tigerlore of Bengal*. Kolkata: Research Institute of Folk-Culture, 2008.
Mitra, Satiścandra. *Yaśohar-khulnār itihās*. 3rd ed., vol. 1. Calcutta: Dasgupta, 1963.
Miyā, Muhammad Śāhjāhān. *Bāṃlā pāṇḍulipi pāṭhsamīkṣā*. Ḍhākā: Bāṃlā Ekāḍemī, 1390 BS (1984).
Murrin, Michael. *Trade and Romance*. Chicago and London: University of Chicago Press, 2013.
Naskar, Debabrata. *Cabbiś parganār laukik devdevī: Pālāgān o loksaṃskṛti jijñāsā*. Kalakātā: De'j Pābiliśiṃ, 1406 BS [1999].
Nida, Eugene A. *Towards a Science of Translating*. Leiden: E. J. Brill, 1964.
Nida, Eugene A., and Charles R. Taber. *The Theory and Practice of Translation*. Leiden: E. J. Brill, 1969.
Niyogi, Tushar K. *Tiger Cult of the Sundarvans*. Calcutta: Anthropological Survey of India, 1996.
Pollock, Sheldon. *The Language of the Gods in the World of Men: Sanskrit, Culture, and Power in Premodern India*. Chicago: University of Chicago Press, 2006.
———, ed. *Literary Cultures in History: Reconstructions from South Asia*. Chicago: University of Chicago Press, 2003.

Pritchett, Frances W. *Marvelous Encounters: Folk Romance in Urdu and Hindi.* New York: Riverdale Publishing, 1985.
Rank, Otto. *The Myth of the Birth of the Hero: A Psychological Interpretation of Mythology.* Translated by F. Robbins and Smith Ely Jelliffe. New York: Robert Brunner, 1952.
Renard, John. *Friends of God: Islamic Images of Piety, Commitment, and Servanthood.* Berkeley: University of California Press, 2008.
———. *Islam and the Heroic Image: Themes in Literature and the Visual Arts.* Columbia: University of South Carolina Press, 1993.
———, ed. *Tales of God's Friends: Islamic Hagiography in Translation.* Berkeley: University of California Press, 2009.
Reynolds, Frank E., and Donald Capps, eds. *The Biographical Process: Essays in the History and Psychology of Religion.* The Hague: Mouton, 1976.
Rocher, Ludo. *The Purāṇas.* In *A History of Indian Literature,* edited by Jan Gonda, vol. 2: *Epics and Sanskrit Religious Literature,* fascicle 3. Wiesbaden: Otto Harrassowtiz, 1986.
Rose, Margaret A. *Parody//Meta-Fiction: An Analysis of Parody as a Critical Mirror to the Writing and Reception of Fiction.* London: Croom Helm, 1979.
Roy, Asim. *The Islamic Syncretistic Tradition in Bengal.* Princeton: Princeton University Press, 1983.
Śahīdullāh, Muhammad. *Bāṃlā sāhityer kathā.* In *Śahīdullāh racanābalī,* edited by Ānisujjāmān. 3 vols. Ḍhākā: Bāṃlā Ekāḍemī, 1994, 2:1–504.
———. *Śahīdullāh racanābalī.* Edited by Ānisujjāmān. 3 vols. Ḍhākā: Bāṃlā Ekāḍemī, 1994.
Sapir, Edward. *Culture, Language and Personality.* Edited by David G. Mandelbaum. Berkeley, CA: University of California Press, 1949.
Śarīph, Āhmad. *Bāṅgālī o bāṅglā sāhitya.* 2 vols. Ḍhākā: Bāṅglā Ekāḍemī, 1390 BS [1983].
Sartre, Jean-Paul. *The Imaginary: A Phenomenological Psychology of the Imagination.* Translated by Jonathan Webber. Revised by Arlette Elkaïm-Sartre. London: Routledge, 2004.
Schimmel, Annemarie. *Islam in the Indian Subcontinent.* Leiden-Köln: E. J. Brill, 1980.
Scholes, Robert E. *Fabulation and Metafiction.* Urbana: University of Illinois Press, 1979.
Sekh, Ābdul Khāyer. "'Musalmānī' pūthi sāhitya: Anusandhān o parjālocanā." PhD diss., Calcutta University, 2015.
Seligman, Adam B., Robert P. Weller, Michael J. Puett, and Bennett Simon. *Ritual and Its Consequences: An Essay on the Limits of Sincerity.* New York: Oxford University Press, 2008.
Sen, Dīneścandra. *Baṅgabhāṣā o sāhitya.* Edited by Asit Kumār Bandyopādhyāy. 2 vols. 1896. Reprint, Kolakātā: Paścimbaṅga Rājya Pustak Parṣad, 1986.
Sen, Dineshchandra. *The Folk-Literature of Bengal.* Calcutta: Calcutta University Press, 1920.
———. *History of Bengali Language and Literature.* Rev. ed. Calcutta: Calcutta University Press, 1954.
Sen, Sukumār. *Bāṅglā sāhityer itihās.* 7 bks. in 5 vols. 1347–65 BS. Reprint, Kalikātā: Eastern Publishers, 1383–88 BS [ca. 1976–81].
———. *Baṭ talār chāpā o chabi.* Compiled and edited by Subhadrakumār Sen. 1984. 2nd ed. 2008. Reprint, Kalakātā: Ānand Pābliśārs Prāibheṭ Limiṭeḍ, 2015.
———. *Islāmi bāṅglā sāhitya.* Kalakātā: Ānand Pābliśars Prāibheṭ Limiṭeḍ, 1400 BS [ca. 1993].

Sengupta, Amitabh. *Scroll Paintings in Bengal: Art in the Village*. Foreward by Kapila Vatsyayan. Bloomington, IN: AuthorHouse, 2012.

Sircar, Jawhar. *The Construction of the Hindu Identity in Medieval Western Bengal: The Role of Popular Cults*. Kolkata: Institute of Development Studies, 2005.

Stewart, Tony K. *The Final Word: The Caitanya Caritāmṛta and the Grammar of Religious Tradition*. New York: Oxford University Press, 2010.

Stille, Max. "Metrik und Poetik der Josephsgeschichte Muhammad Sagirs." Master's thesis, Ruprecht-Karls-Universität Heidelberg, 2011.

———. "Poetics of Popular Preaching: *Waz Mahfils* in Contemporary Bangladesh." PhD diss., Universität Heidelberg, 2016.

Suvorova, Anna. *Masnavi: A Study of Urdu Romance*. Translated from the Russian by M. Osama Faruqi. Karachi: Oxford University Press, 2000.

———. *Muslim Saints of South Asia: The Eleventh to Fifteenth Centuries*. London: Routledge Curzon, 1999.

Talgeri, Pramod and S. B. Verma, eds. *Literature in Translation: From Cultural Transference to Metonymic Displacement*. London: Sangam, 1988.

Tarafdar, M. R. *Husain Shahi Bengal 1494–1438 A.D.: A Socio-Political Study*. 2nd rev. ed. Dhaka: University of Dhaka, 1999.

Taraphdār, Mantajur Rahmān. *Bāṃlā romāṇṭik kāvyer āoyādhī-hindī paṭbhūmi*. Ḍhākā: Ḍhākā Viśvavidyālay, 1971.

Taylor, Charles. *Modern Social Imaginaires*. Durham, NC: Duke University Press, 2004.

Thomasson, Amie L. *Fiction and Metaphysics*. Cambridge: Cambridge University Press, 2008.

Todorov, Tzvetan. *The Fantastic: A Structural Approach to a Literary Genre*. Translated by Richard Howard. With a foreward by Robert Scholes. Ithaca: Cornell University Press, 1975.

———. *Genres in Discourse*. Translated by Catherine Porter. Cambridge: Cambridge University Press, 1990.

Toury, Gideon. *In Search of a Theory of Translation*. Tel Aviv: The Porter Institute for Poetics and Semiotics, 1980.

Uddin, Sufia M. *Constructing Bangladesh: Religion, Ethnicity, and Language in an Islamic Nation*. Chapel Hill: University of North Carolina Press, 2006.

White, David. *Sinister Yogis*. Chicago: University of Chicago Press, 2009.

White, Hayden. *Metahistory: The Historical Imagination in Nineteenth-Century Europe*. Baltimore: Johns Hopkins University Press, 1973.

———. *Tropics of Discourse: Essays in Cultural Criticism*. Baltimore: Johns Hopkins University Press, 1978.

Whorf, Benjamin Lee. *Language, Thought, and Reality*. Boston: MIT Press, 1956.

Wilce, James M. *Eloquence in Trouble: The Poetics of Complaint in Rural Bangladesh*. Oxford Studies in Anthropological Linguistics. New York: Oxford University Press, 2003.

Wittgenstein, Ludwig. *Philosophical Investigations*. German text with English translation by G. E. M. Anscombe, P. M. S. Hacker, and Joachim Schulte. Rev. 4th ed. Chichester: Wiley Blackwell, 2009.

Zakaria, Saymon. *Pronomohi Bongomata: Indigenous Cultural Forms of Bangladesh*. With a foreword by Tony K. Stewart. Dhaka: Nymphea Publications, 2011.

SECONDARY WORKS: ARTICLES AND ESSAYS

Afšār, Īraj. "Fāl-nāma," *Encyclopædia Iranica*, 9:172–76. New York: Bibliotheca Persica Press, 1999.

Ahmed, Syed Jamil. "Manik Pir as a Subaltern Trickster: Grandiloquent Tales of Extra-Scriptural Imagination." *Depart Magazine*, 9th issue, accessed December 2, 2018, www.departmag.com/index.php/en/detail/189/Grandiloquent-tales-of-extra-scriptural-Imagination.

———. "Performing and Supplicating Mānik Pīr: Infrapolitics in the Domain of Popular Islam." *TDR: The Drama Review*, vol. 53, no. 2 (Summer 2009): 51–76.

Aquil, Raziuddin. "Miracles, Authority, and Benevolence: Stories of *Karamat* in Sufi Literature of the Delhi Sultanate." In *Sufi Cults and Evolution of Medieval Indian Culture*, edited by Anup Taneja, 109–38. Indian Council of Historical Research Monograph Series 9. New Delhi: Indian Council of Historical Research in Association with the Northern Book Center, 2003.

Bhattacharya, Aparna. "Worship of Satyapir, an Example of Hindu Muslim Rapprochement in Bengal." *Proceedings of the Indian History Congress* 32, no. 2 (1970): 204–7.

Bhattacharyya, Shatarupa. "Localising Global Faiths: The Heterodox Pantheon of the Sundarbans." *Asian Review of World Histories* 5, no. 1 (January 2017): 141–57.

Chanda, Ipshita. "*Bonobibir Johurnama:* A Method for Reading Plural Cultures." *Delhi Journal of the Humanities and Social Sciences* 2 (2015): 51–62.

Costa, Benjamin. "Literature of the Tiger-Cult in Bengal (*Raymangal* et al.)." Unpublished Typescript.

Culler, Jonathan. "Presupposition and Intertextuality." *Modern Language Notes* 91 (1976): 1380–96.

Dās, Girīndranāth. "Loknāṭya bonbibi pālā evaṃ ekai viṣaye duṭi ādhunik nāṭak." *Lokśruti: Loksaṃskṛti viṣayak ṣānmāsik patrikā* 10 (1399 BS [1993]): 83–85.

Davis, Donald R., Jr. "The Evolution of the Legal Subject in Classical Hindu Law." Unpublished typescript.

Dimock, Edward C. "Muslim Vaiṣṇava Poets of Bengal." In *Languages and Areas: Studies Presented to George V. Bobrinskoy on the Occasion of His Academic Retirement*. Chicago: University of Chicago Press, 1967, 28–36.

Eaton, Richard M. "Sufi Folk Literature and the Expansions of Indian Islam." *History of Religions* 14, no. 2 (November 1974): 117–27.

Falasch, Ute. "The Islamic Mystic Tradition in India: The Madari Sufi Brotherhood." In *Lived Islam in South Asia: Adaptation, Accommodation, and Conflict*, edited by Imtiaz Ahmed and Helmut Reifeld, 256–72. New Delhi: Esha Béteille, Social Science Press, 2004.

Fauconnier, Gilles, and Mark Turner. "Metonymy and Conceptual Integration." In *Metonymy in Language and Thought*, edited by Klaus-Uwe Panther and Günter Radden, 77–90. Amsterdam: John Benjamins, 1999.

Ghoṣ, Ajoy Kumār. "Viṣṇupurer pir sthān." In *Bā̃kuḍār khoyālī: Jaṅgalmohal saṃkalan*, edited by Arabinda Caṭṭopādhyāy, 125–43. Pratāpabāgān, Bā̃kuḍā: E. Ṭi. Pres, 2014.

Green, Nile. "Ostrich Eggs and Peacock Feathers: Sacred Objects as Cultural Exchange between Christianity and Islam." *Al-Masāq* 18, no. 1 (2006): 27–78.

Hatley, Shaman, "Mapping the Esoteric Body in the Islamic Yoga of Bengal." *History of Religions* 46, no. 4 (May 2007): 351–68.

Hijiya, James A. "The Gita of J. Robert Oppenheimer." *Proceedings of the American Philosophical Society* 144, no. 2 (June 2000): 123–67.

Hiltebeitel, Alf. "Listening to *Nala* and Damayantī." In Hiltebeitel, *Rethinking the Mahābhārata: A Reader's Guide to the Education of the Dharma King*, 215–39. Chicago: University of Chicago Press, 2001.

Hora, Sunder Lal. "Worship of the Deities Olā, Jholā and Bōn Bībī in Lower Bengal." *Journal and Proceedings of the Asiatic Society of Bengal* 20, no. 8 (1933): 1–4.

Hossain, Nisir. "Folk Painting." In *Arts and Crafts*, edited by Lala Rukh Selim, 499–510. Cultural Survey of Bangladesh Series 8. Dhaka: Asiatic Society of Bangladesh, 2007.

Inden, Ronald B. "The Hindu Chiefdom in Middle Bengali Literature." In *Bengal, Literature and History*, edited by Edward C. Dimock, Jr., 21–46. East Lansing, MI: Asian Studies Center.

Irani, Ayesha A. "Love's New Pavilions: Śāhā Mohāmmad Chagīr's Retelling of *Yūsuf va Zulaykhā* in Premodern Bengal." In *Jāmī in Regional Context: The Reception of ʿAbd al-Raḥmān Jāmī's Works in the Islamicate World, ca. 9th/15th–14th/20th Century*, edited by Thibaut d'Hubert and Alexandre Papas. 692–751. Leiden: Brill, 2018.

———. "Mystical Love, Prophetic Compassion, and Ethics: An Ascension Narrative in the Medieval Bengali *Nabīvaṃśa* of Saiyad Sultān." In *The Prophet's Ascension: Cross-Cultural Encounters with the Islamic* Miʿrāj *Tales*, edited by Christine Gruber and Frederick Colby, 225–51. Bloomington: Indiana University Press, 2010.

Iser, Wolfgang. "The Reality of Fiction: A Functionalist Approach to Literature." *New Literary History* 7, no. 1 (Autumn 1975): 7–38.

Jakobson, Roman. "On Linguistic Aspects of Translation." In *On Translation*, edited by Reuben A. Brower, 232–39. Cambridge, MA: Harvard University Press, 1959.

Jameson, Frederic. "Magical Narratives: Romance as Genre." *New Literary History* 7, no. 1 (Autumn 1975): 136–63.

Kabi, Shams Shahriar. "Traditional Bengali Folklore *Gajir Gaan*: Non-Communal Artistic Contemplation." *Grassroots Voices* 7, no. 1 (July 2010): 16–30.

Knysh, Alexander. "Waḥdat al-Wujūd." In *The Oxford Encyclopedia of the Islamic World*, 5:510–11. New York: Oxford University Press, 2009.

Korom, Frank J. "'Editing' Dharmaraj: Academic Genealogies of a Bengali Folk Deity." *Western Folklore* 56, no. 1 (1997): 51–77.

Marzolph, Ulrich, and Richard van Leeuwen, with Hassan Wassouf. "Qamar al-Zamân and Budûr." In *The Arabian Nights Encyclopedia*. 2 vols. Santa Barbara: ABC Clio, 2004; 1:341–45.

Miller, J. Hillis. "Narrative." In *Critical Terms for Literary Study*, edited by Frank Lentricchia and Thomas McLaughlin, 66–79. 2nd ed. Chicago: University of Chicago Press, 1995.

Mills, Samuel Landell. "The Hardware of Sanctity: Anthropomorphic Objects in Bangladeshi Sufism." In *Embodying Charisma: Modernity, Locality and the Performance of Emotion in Sufi Cults*, edited by Pnina Werbner and Helene Basu, 31–54. London: Routledge, 1998.

Mitra, Sarat Chandra. "On a Musalmani Legend about the Sylvan Saint Bana-bibī and the Tiger-Deity Dakshiṇa Rāy." *Journal of the Department of Letters* 10 (1923): 154–72.

Norton, John D. "Ignorance and Indifference." *Philosophy of Science* 75 (January 2008): 45–68.
Oakley, Todd. "Conceptual Blending, Narrative Discourse, and Rhetoric." *Cognitive Linguistics* 9 (1998): 321–60.
Orsini, Francesa. "The Social History of a Genre: *Kathas* across Languages in Early Modern North India." *Medieval History Journal* 20, no. 1 (2017): 1–37.
———."Texts and Tellings: *Kathas* in the Fifteenth and Sixteenth Centuries." In *Tellings and Texts: Music, Literature, and Peformance in North India*, edited by Francesca Orsini and Katherine Butler Schofield, 327–58. Cambridge, UK: OpenBook Publishers, 2015.
Rāy, Kānāi Lāl. "Satyapīr." *Bāṃlā Ekāḍemī Patrikā*, edited by Mohāmmad Hārun-ur-Raśid (Śrāvaṇ-Āśvin 1399 BS [ca. 1992]): 71–82.
Rescher, Nicholas. "Coping with Cognitive Limitations." In *Studies in Epistemology: Nicholas Rescher Collected Papers,* vol. 14: 147–55. Frankfurt: Ontos Verlag, 2006.
———. "On Ignorance and the Limits of Knowledge." In *Studies in Epistemology: Nicholas Rescher Collected Papers,* vol. 14: 157–79. Frankfurt: Ontos Verlag, 2006.
———. "On Learned Ignorance." In *Studies in Epistemology: Nicholas Rescher Collected Papers,* vol. 14: 131–45. Frankfurt: Ontos Verlag, 2006.
———. "On the Ways and Vagaries of Fiction." In *Studies in Epistemology: Nicholas Rescher Collected Papers,* vol. 14: 70–105. Frankfurt: Ontos Verlag, 2006.
Roy, N. B. "Studies in Islamic History." *Visva Bharati Annals* 4 (1951): 70–84.
Roy, Sonali. "Hindu-Islamic Folk Goddess in Bengal: Bonbibi." *The Appollonian* 4, nos. 1–2 (March–June 2017): 66–74.
Roy, Tapti. "Disciplining the Printed Text: Colonial and National Surveillance of Bengali Literature." In *Texts of Power: Emerging Disciplines in Colonial Bengal*, edited by Partha Chatterjee, 30–62. Calcutta: Samya, 1995.
Schinkel, Anders. "Imagination as a Category of History: An Essay Concerning Koselleck's Concepts of *Erfahrungsraum* and *Erwartungshorizont*." *History and Theory* 44, no. 1 (February 2005): 42–54.
Sonn, Tamara. "Tawḥīd." In *The Oxford Encyclopedia of the Islamic World*, 5:332–41. New York: Oxford University Press, 2009.
Stewart, Tony K. "Alternate Structures of Authority: Satya Pīr on the Frontiers of Bengal." In *Beyond Turk and Hindu: Rethinking Religious Identities in Islamicate South Asia*, edited by David Gilmartin and Bruce B. Lawrence, 21–54. Gainesville: University of Florida Press, 2000.
———. "In Search of Equivalence: Conceiving Muslim-Hindu Encounter through Translation Theory." *History of Religions* 40, no. 3 (Winter 2001): 261–88. Anthologized in *India's Islamic Traditions: 711–1750*, edited by Richard M. Eaton, 363–92. Delhi: Oxford University Press, 2003. Anthologized in *Figuring Religions: Comparing Ideas, Images, and Activities*, edited by Subha Pathak, 229–62. Albany: SUNY Press, 2013.
———. "Popular Sufi Narratives and the Parameters of the Bengali *Imaginaire*." In *Religion and Aesthetic Experience: Drama—Sermons—Literature*, edited by Sabine Dorpmüller, Jan Scholz, Max Stille, and Ines Weinrich, 173–95. Transcultural Research–Heidelberg Studies on Asia and Europe in a Global Context. Heidelberg: Heidelberg University Press, 2018. Also accessible at DOI: 10.17885/heiup.416.

———. "The Power of the Secret: The Tantalizing Discourse of Sahajiyā Scholarship." In *The Legacy of Bengal Vaiṣṇavism in Colonial Bengal*, edited by Ferdinando Sardelli and Lucien Wong. London: Routledge, 2019.

———. "The Process of Surface Narrative: Corpse Worship." In *Sarpa-saṃskṛti o manasā*, edited by Añjan Sen and Śekh Makbul Islām, 181–94. Kalakātā: Baṅgīya Sāhitya Saṃsad, 2012.

———. "Religion in the Subjunctive: Vaiṣṇava Narrative, Sufi Counter-Narrative in Early Modern Bengal." *Journal of Hindu Studies* 6, no.1 (2013): 52–72.

———. "The Subject and the Ostensible Subject: Mapping the Genre of Hagiography among South Asian Chishtīs." In *Rethinking Islamic Studies: From Orientalism to Cosmopolitanism*, edited by Carl W. Ernst and Richard Martin, 227–44. Columbia: University of South Carolina Press, 2010.

Stewart, Tony K. and Carl W. Ernst. "Syncretism." In *South Asian Folklore: An Encyclopedia*, edited by Margaret A. Mills and Peter J. Claus, 586–88. London: Routledge, 2003.

Sur, Sujit. "Folk Deities of Sunderbans—Some Observations." In *In the Lagoons of the Gangetic Delta*, edited by Gautam K. Bera and Vijoy S. Sahay, 141–68. New Delhi: Mittal Publications, 2010.

Talgeri, Pramod. "The Perspectives of Literary Translation: From Cultural Transference to Metonymic Displacement." In *Literature in Translation: From Cultural Transference to Metonymic Displacement*, edited by Pramod Talgeri and S. B. Verma, 1–11. London: Sangam, 1988.

Thomasson, Amie L. "Fictional Characters and Literary Practices." *British Journal of Aesthetics* 43, no. 2 (April 2003): 138–57.

Tuana, Nancy. "Coming to Understand: Orgasm and the Epistemology of Ignorance." In *Agnotology: The Making and Unmaking of Ignorance*, edited by Robert N. Proctor and Londa Schiebinger, 108–45. Stanford: Stanford University Press, 2008.

Uddin, Sufia. "Beyond National Borders and Religious Boundaries: Muslim and Hindu Veneration of Bonbibi." In *Engaging South Asian Religions: Boundaries, Appropriations, and Resistances*, edited by Mathew N. Schmalz and Peter Gottschalk, 61–84. Albany: SUNY Press, 2011.

LANGUAGE AND REFERENCE SOURCES

Bāṃlādeśer āñcalik bhāṣār abhidhān. Compiled by Muhammad Śahīdullāh. 2 vols. Ḍhākā: Bāṃlā Ekāḍemī, 1380 BS [1973].

Bāṅgālā bhāṣār abhidhān. Compiled and edited by Jñānendramohan Dās. 2 vols. 2nd ed. 1344 BS [1937]. Reprint; Kalakātā: Sāhitya Saṃsad, 1986.

Baṅgīya śabdakoś. Edited by Haricaraṇ Bandyopāyāy. 2 vols. Niu Dillī: Sāhitya Akādemī, 1978.

Bāṁlā ekāḍemī bāṃlā bānān abhidhān. Compiled and edited by Jāmil Caudhurī. Revised and enlarged. Ḍhākā: Bāṃlā Ekāḍemī, 2008.

Bāṃlā ekāḍemī bāṃlādeśer āñcalik bhāṣār abhidhān. Edited by Muhammad Śahidullāh. 3 vols. 1372 BS (1965). Reprint, compiled into a single volume by Sayad Ālī Āhsān et al. Ḍhākā: Bāṃlā Ekāḍemī, 2000.

Bāṃlā ekāḍemī vyavahārik bāṃlā abhidhān. Edited by Muhammad Enāmul Hak. Emended and edited by Śivprasanna Lāhiḍī and Svarociś Sarkār. Ḍhākā: Bāṃlā Ekāḍemī, 2009.

Bangla Academy Bengali-English Dictionary. Edited by Mohammad Ali, Mohammad Moniruzzaman, and Jahangir Tareque. Dhaka: Bangla Academy, 1994.

Banglapaedia: National Encyclopedia of Bangladesh. Edited by Sirajul Islam and Ahmed A. Jamal. 2nd. rev. ed. 10 vols. Dhaka: Asiatic Society, 2012. The encyclopaedia is also issued in Bangla as *Bāṃlāpiḍiyā: Bāṃlādeśer jātīya jñānkoṣ*. Both versions of the encyclopedia are available online and in print.

Bengali and English Dictionary (bāṅgālā o iṃrājī abhidhān). Compiled and edited by Gopee Kissen Mitter (Gopī Kṛṣṇa Mitra kartṛk saṃśodhita). Revised and improved. Calcutta: Calcutta School Book Society, 1868.

Catalogue of the Bengali Printed Books in the Library of the British Museum. Compiled by James Fuller Blumhardt. London: Trustees of the British Museum, 1886.

Catalogue of the Library of the India Office, Vol. II, Part IV—Bengali, Oriya, and Assamese Books. Compiled by James Fuller Blumhardt. London: Eyre and Spottiswoode, 1905.

Catalogus Catalogorum of Bengali Manuscripts [Bāṃlā puthir tālikā samanvay: Saṅkalak o samapādak yatīndramohan bhaṭṭācāryya]. Compiled and edited by Jatindra Mohan Bhattacharjee. Calcutta: Asiatic Society, 1978.

Century Dictionary: Bengali to English. Compiled by Subalacandra Mitra. Rev. ed. Calcutta: New Bengal Press, 1961.

Companion to Johnson's Dictionary, Bengali and English. Compiled by John Mendies. 3rd rev. ed. Calcutta: Printed by C. B. Lewis at the Baptist Mission Press, 1876.

A Descriptive Catalogue of Bengali Manuscripts in Munshi Abdul Karim's Collection. Compiled by Abdul Karim and Ahmad Sharif. English edition with an introduction by Syed Sajjad Husain. Dacca: Asiatic Society of Pakistan, 1960.

A Dictionary of the Bengali Language (Bengali-English)—Bāṃlā iṃrejī abhidhān—in which the Words are Traced to their Origin and their Various Meanings Given. Compiled by William Carey. 2 vols. 1818. Reprint, New Delhi: Asian Educational Services, 1993.

Dictionary of Foreign Words in Bengali. Compiled by Gobinlal Bonnerjee. Revised and enlarged by Jitendriya Bonnerjee. Calcutta: University of Calcutta, 1968.

An Etymological Dictionary of Bengali: c. 1000–1800 A.D. Compiled by Sukumar Sen. Calcutta: Eastern Publishers, 1971.

Hobson-Jobson: A Glossary of Colloquial Anglo-Indian Words and Phrases, and of Kindred Terms, Etymological, Historical, Geographical, and Discursive. Compiled by Henry Yule and Arthur C. Burnell. New edition edited by William Crooke. 1886. Reprint, Calcutta: Rupa and Co., 1986.

The Modern Bengali Dictionary for Non-Bengali Readers. Compiled and edited by Kumar Bandyopadhyay. 4 vols. (in progress). Calcutta: Asiatic Society, 1999-.

Mudrita bāṃlā granther pañji 1853–1867. Compiled by Jatīndramohan Bhaṭṭācārya. Kalikātā: Paścimbaṅgā Bāṃlā Ākādemi, 1993.

A Mussalmani Bengali-English Dictionary. Compiled by William Goldsack. Calcutta: By the compiler at D. N. Banerjee at the Banerjee Press, 1923.

Persian-English Dictionary: Including the Arabic Words and Phrases to Be Met With in Persian Literature. Compiled, revised, and enlarged by F. Steingass, from Johnson and

Richardson's *Persian, Arabic, and English Dictionary*. 1892. Reprint, London: Iran University Press, Routledge and Kegan Paul, 1984.

Perso-Arabic Elements in Bengali [*Bāṅglāy phārsī-ārabī upādān*]. Compiled by Shaikh Ghulam Maqsud Hilali. Edited by Muhammad Enamul Haq. Dhaka: Bangla Academy, 1967.

Prācīn o madhyayuger bāṅglā bhāṣār abhidhān. Compiled and edited by Mohāmmad Ābdul Kāium and Rājiyā Sultān. 2 vols. Ḍhākā: Bāṅglā Ekādemī, 2008–9.

Present Day Colloquial Bengali for Foreign Students. Compiled by M. L. Das. Dhaka: M. L. Das, n.d. [1985?].

Samarthakosha: Bengali and English Dictionary [*Samarthakoṣ: Bāṅgālā o iṃrijī abhidhān evaṃ garhasthya darpaṇ vā dravyaguṇābhidhān o pauraṇik caritābhidhān*]. Compiled and published by Anupakṛṣṇa Mitra. 5 vols. Kalikātā: Sarmarthakoṣ kāryyālāy, 1301 BS [ca. 1894].

Samsad Bengali-English Dictionary. Compiled by Sailendra Biswas. Revised by Subodhchandra Sengupta. 1969. Reprint, Calcutta: Mohendra Nath Dutt, Shishu Sahitya Samsad Private, Ltd. 1972.

A Sanskrit Dictionary: Etymologically and Philologically Arranged with Special Reference to Cognate Indo-European Languages. Compiled by Sir Monier Monier-Williams. New enlarged ed. 1899. Reprint, Oxford: Clarendon Press of Oxford University, 1974.

Second Supplementary Catalogue of Bengali Books in the Library of the British Museum Acquired during the Years 1911–1934. Compiled by J. V. S. Wilkinson and James Fuller Blumhardt. London: British Museum, 1939.

The Student's Dictionary of Bengali Words and Phrases. Compiled by Benimadhav Ganguli. 9th ed. Calcutta: Keshavlal Auddy and Nilmony Auddy, 1918.

Students Favorite Dictionary (Bengali to English). Compiled by Ashutosh Dev. Calcutta: N. C. Mazumdar at B. P. M.'s press, 1968.

A Supplementary Catalogue of the Bengali Books in the Library of the British Museum Acquired during the Years 1886–1910. Compiled by James Fuller Blumhardt. London: Longmans, 1910.

. . .

MANUSCRIPTS CONSULTED: SATYA PĪR

The literature dedicated to Satya Pīr far and away exceeds any others in the *pīr kathās*, so too their print editions. I chose to cite the print edition when available because of its easier access, but only when the print edition and the manuscripts were consistent one with the other. The few variations, if relevant, are marked in the body and footnotes of the text itself. I have included the names of every author I could locate. I have marked with asterisks the manuscripts I consulted in my survey, limiting myself exclusively to complete manuscripts. It should be noted that because of funding constraints, the bulk of the manuscripts I consulted were housed in repositories in Bangladesh. Large numbers of the authors listed below have only incomplete manuscripts, which I did not consult due to the limitations of time. I refer the interested reader to Jatindra Mohan Bhattacharjee's *Catalogus Catalogorum of Bengali Manuscripts*, which proved invaluable in this search. It should be noted that there are a handful of printed texts by authors that are not listed in Jatindra Mohan's catalogue because the original manuscripts are in private collections or the text went straight into print. The interested reader can compare this list with the primary texts in works cited. The texts are alphabetized in Bangla word order according to the rules in the *Catalogus Catalogorum.*

* Complete manuscripts only consulted (46 different authors, 115 manuscripts)
† Largest numbers of complete manuscripts

Anonymous * [13 different texts]
Amarsiṃha Dvija
Asitcaraṇ
Ātmārām Dvija
Oyālij Dās
Kaviratna Dvija
Kaṇva Kavi * [multiple stories]
Karṇa Kavi * [same as Kaṇva Kavi]
Kālī Caraṇ Dvija
Kāśīnāth
Kiṇkar
Kiṇkar Dās *
Kumudānanda Datta
Kṛṣṇadās Dvija
Kṛṣṇadhan Dvija
Kṛṣṇa Bihāri
Kṛṣṇahari Dās
Kṛṣṇamohan
Kṛṣṇarām Dvija
Kṛṣṇaśaṇkar *
Kautukarām Caṭṭopadhyāy
Khokanrām Dās
Gaṅgādās
Gaṅgārām Kavi *
Gaṅgeś *
Gadādhara Cakravartī
Guṇanidhi Paṇḍit
Gurudās Dvij
Guruprasād
Gokulācārya
Govindacaraṇ Dvij
Goloki Candra Majumdār
Gohara Phakīr
Gaurīśaṅkar *
Ghanarām
Jagadānanda
Jagannāth
Janardan Bhaṭṭācārya *
Jayānanda Dās
Jaimini *
Jaymuni *
Tāher Māmud
Dayāl *
Dāmodar Dās
Diṇarām Dvij *
Dinahīn Dās *
Durgāprasād *
Daivākinandan
Dvijabar Dukhi *
Dhanañjay
Nandakumār Dvij
Nandarām *
Narahari
Nidhirām
Niṣakar Ghoṣ *
Paṇḍit Dvij *
Phakirām Kavibhuṣaṇ *†
Phāijullā
Vallabha Kavi [Dās] *†
Vikal Caṭṭopadhyāy

Vijay Ṭhākur
Vidubar Ghoṣ *
Vidyāpati
Viśvanāth Dvij
Viśveśvar Dvij *†
Becarām
Brajdās
Bhāgirathī Dās
Bhāratcandra *
Bholanāth Devsarmma
Mathureśa
Manohar Sen *
Mahādev
Mukunda Dvij
Mukul Dvij
Yogirām Siṃha
Raghunāth *
Raghurām Dvij
Rasmay *
Rāghav Dvij
Rāmkanta Dev
Rāmkṛṣṇa Dvij *†
Rāmcandra Dvij *
Rāmcandra Mukhti
Rāmjivan
Rām Dvij *
Rāmdhan Dvij
Rāmnārāyaṇ Dvij
Rāmprasād Dvij
Rāmbhadra *†
Rām Mānikya
Rāmlocan Dvij
Rāmsundar Sīl
Rāmānanda Dvij
Rāmeśvar Dvij *†
Rasmay *†
Lālmohan
Leḥta Phakīr
Śaṅkar Kavi
Śaṇkarācārya *†
Śivcandra
Śivnārāyaṇ
Śivrām Dvij
Sukdev Dvij
Śyāmānanda Datta
Śyāmānanda Dvij
Satyananda *
Svarūprām Dās
Harāi Dās
Haricaraṇ Bandyopādhyāy
Haridās Dvij

INDEX

Ācārya, Mādhav, 139
Acharya, Shambhu, 258–59
ādibāsī (original inhabitants), xviii, xix, 134n58
agamas, 241
āgam śabda (yogic scriptural utterances), 8
agnotology, xiv–xv
Ahmed, Shahab, xvi
Ahmed, Syed Jamil, 257
aiśvarya (omnipotent lordship), 226
aitihāsik (historical), 33, 34, 39
Ājupā, 77, 78, 158, 165, 174, 187
Ākhoṭi pālā ["The Fabled Beṅgamā Bird and the Stupid Prince"] (Kaṇva), 222
alaṃkār [*alaṃkāra*] (poetic aesthetics), 79
Ālāol, 23n46
Alexander of Macedon, traditions associated with, 235
Āli, 40, 51
Alī, Oyājed, 16
Āllā [Allāḥ] (God), 19, 38, 49–51, 66, 73, 186, 193; aerial vehicle (*bimān*) of, 49, 50, 60, 61, 63; in *Baḍa satya pīr o sandhyāvatī kanyār puthi*, 1, 3, 4, 7–8, 10, 120, 191, 251, 253; as Bhagavān Satya Narāyāṇ, 13, 14; in *Bonbibī jahurā nāmā*, 127, 134, 152–54, 179; in *Gāji kālu o cāmpāvatī kanyār puthi*, 76, 80; *ḥadīth* and, 13, 36, 104–5; Indic gods/goddesses and, 107; intertextuality and encounters with, 119–20; in *Mānikpīrer jahurānāmā*, 45, 46–50, 57, 58n62, 60–63, 69, 70, 82, 83, 90, 96, 97, 98, 99, 112, 122; in *Mānik pīr kecchā*, 74; Nārāyaṇ equated with, 186, 225; as Nirañjan (Stainless One), 3, 4, 7, 13; *phakīrs* of, 236, 238; recitation of names of, 246, 250; repetition of qualities of, 89; revisions to history of Gāji and, 178–79; Satya Pīr and, 27, 28, 32, 199; as supreme and only God, xii, 253, 254. *See also* Khodā; Nirañjan [Nirāñjan]
aṃśa (part, portion), 39
Anatomy of a Criticism (Frye), 256
angels, 12, 91
animals, 14, 28, 84n27, 223–24; Bonbibī raised by, 126, 136; hero's society with, 44, 66; talking, 25; taming of wild animals, 84. *See also* crocodiles; elephants; tigers
antiquarian scholars, 20, 23
Āorajbibi, 18
aparādh (offense against *dharma*), 28, 30
appropriation, 183, 199, 212, 219; in *Bonbibī jahurā nāmā*, 176–77; conceptual blending and, 187; of *hinduyāni* world into *musulmāni* cosmology, 107, 187; *vrat* cycle and, 210, 212, 214
apsaras (celestial water nymphs), 90, 99
Arabian Nights, 175
Arabic language, 2n2, 12, 46, 234; tales of the prophets in, 121; technical jargon in, 27, 118, 182
'*Arā'is al-Majālis fi Qiṣaṣ al-Anbiyā*' ["Lives of the Prophets"] (Al-Thalabī), 121

Ardhakālī (Half Kālī), 250
Āriph, Kavi, 121, 222
Arjuna, 96
Arya Samaj, 20
Āsānbibi, 18
asatya (untruth), 191
Assam, Indian state of, 12
Assamese language, 195
Assman, Jan, xv
āstānā [*āsthān, āsthānā*] (ritual dais, abode), 208, 229
āsuras (power-hungry spirits), 193
Āśuri, 77
Āśvins (divine Twins, associated with Dawn), 232
Āṭhārobhāṭi (Land of the Eighteen Tides), 136, 140, 141–43, 152, 176, 177, 179; Kēdokhāli region, 128, 130, 180; *shari'ā* conduct of humans and animals in, 182. *See also* Sunderban forest
'Aṭṭār, 23n46
auliyās (saints), 40n16, 235
Avadhī language, 12, 22, 139, 175
avatār (descent of divinity), 4, 7, 107, 108, 134, 191, 193; Badar's descent, 194; Balarām, 239; for Kali Age, 1, 26, 27, 30, 46, 87; Kānāi, 55, 239; Nitāi, 239; soteriological function of, 87. See also *vaiṣṇav avatār* concept
avatīrṇa [*yavatirnya*] (to descend), 64, 70, 87–88, 108

Baḍa Khā̃ Gājī, 18, 40
Baḍa Khān Gājī, 17, 78, 79, 111, 185–86; in *Bonbibī jahurā nāmā*, 127, 130–32, 137, 151, 153; comic book version of stories about, 259; conceptual blending and, 187; control of tigers and, xviii; emplotment and, 200; in *Gāji kālu o cāmpāvatī kanyār puthi*, 155; in the *Rāy maṅgal*, 137–47, 152, 154, 203; revisions to history of, 174–82; in scroll paintings, 258. *See also* Gāji Pīr
Baḍa Pīr Sāheb, 18
Badar Pīr, xi, 40, 46–53, 65, 72, 186; birth (descent from heaven) of, 69, 82; descent into sensual realm, 66, 67; emplotment and, 200; Gaṅgā and, 48–51, 60, 66, 82–83, 96–97; as Kṛṣṇa, 98, 107; mainstream Islamic traditions and, 91; in *Mānik pīr kecchā*, 74; marriage to Princess Dudbibī, 67, 122; as Nārāyaṇ, 88; parody and, 94; as Rām, 56, 57, 67–68, 88, 98, 99, 107; in the *Rāy maṅgal*, 138; religious ideal and, 83–84; return to forgotten mission, 70; as the Summoner, 47–56, 65; tigers commanded by, 52–54, 66–67; as Viṣṇu, 98, 107, 218. See also *Mānikpīrer jahurānāmā*
Baḍa satya pīr o sandhyāvatī kanyār puthi [*The Great Story of Satya Pīr and the Virgin Girl Sandhyāvatī*] (Dās), 1–14, 72, 83–84, 253; emplotment in, 191; framed in nominally religious terms, 13; intertextuality and, 120; Satya Pīr's never-ending mission in, 250–53; significance of Satya Pīr in *musalmāni* terms in, 233–50; tales of *sūphī* saints and, 12–25; uncertainty and ambiguity in, 25–32
Badi 'al-Dīn Madār, 47n29
Baḍo khā̃n gājīr kerāmati (Hālumīr), 79, 155–56
bādsā [*bādsvā*] (ruler, king), 51–52, 54, 55–57, 60, 65, 66, 68, 89, 111
Bāgchi, Sañjīv Kumār, 256
Bāghāmbarer pālā ["The Disconsolate Yogī Who Turned the Merchant's Wife into a Dog"] (Kavibar), 222
Bakhś, Khodā, 79–81, 155–56, 157, 253
Bākhs, Mahāmmad Karim, 81, 156
Bakhtin, Mikhail, 91, 92n39, 116
Balarām, 239
Bali Rājā, 167
Balkans-to-Bengal complex, xvi
Bāndhyopādhyāy, Asit Kumār, 22
Baṅgabhāṣā o sāhitya (Sen), 22
Bāṅgāl, 229, 230
Bāṅgālī o bāṅglā sāhitya (Śariph), 24
Bangladesh, xvii, 12, 19, 24, 258
Bangla language, 2n2, 12, 18, 79, 102, 195, 256; audiences beyond law and theology, 118; Bangla literature, xvii, 22, 23; Bangla-speaking regions, xvii; as medium for Islamic discourse, 19; mixed with Oḍiyā, 225; *musulmāni bāṅglā*, 24, 25, 45, 90, 182; non-*musulmāni* texts translated into, 121; Persian and Arabic technical vocabulary used with, 118; Persianized, 134; *sādhu bhāṣā* (high literary mode), 16, 24, 206, 207; Sanskrit and, xi, 24; stability of diction in, 139
Bāṅglā pīr sāhityer kathā, 92
Bāṅglā sāhityer itihās (Sen), 25n54
barakat (additional power), 110, 128, 130, 135, 156, 179
bāramās (formal lament), 239
Basanta Rājā, 236, 237, 238, 239
Basanta Rāy, 18
Basumatī (Goddess Earth), 173, 251
baṭ talā (inexpensive printed books), 25, 157, 196

bāuls (wandering religious minstrels), 138, 141n73, 218, 259
Bayanuddīn, 123
Behl, Aditya, 23n46
Behulā, 122, 223–24
Benākī, 18
Bengal, 10, 12, 14, 72, 200; colonial, xvi; hereditary artisans in, 15; hierarchical society in, 95; influx of foreigners throughout history of, 26; Islamization of, 182; maritime trade networks and, xix–xx; riparian landscape of, xvii–xviii; vernacularization in, 92
Bengal Renaissance, 22n44, 93
beṅgamā [*beṅgama*] (fabled talking bird), 51, 52n46, 222
Berāhim, 125–26, 178
bhadralok (educated elites of Bengal), 22, 24, 93
Bhagavad gītā, 103n65, 148, 197, 205
Bhagavān (Supreme God), 9, 154, 178, 193
Bhāgavata purāṇa, 12, 119, 147, 153, 162, 178, 203, 241
Bhaktirasāmṛtasindhu (Rūpa Gosvāmī), 101
bhaktirasaśāstra, 101
Bhāratcandra, 16
Bhaṭṭācāryya, Rādhāmohan Tarkālaṃkār, 39, 41
Bhaṭṭācāryya, Surnāth, 207
Bhattacharjee, Jatindra Mohan, 203n17
bhāv [*bhāva*] (emotional state), 24, 80, 101, 135, 167, 178, 198–99; *anubhāva* (indicator of emotion), 101; *cintā* (anxiety), 101; *prema* (supreme love), 102; *sāttvika* (involuntary responses), 101; *vibhāva* (prompter/enhancer of emotion), 101; *viraha* (pain of separation), 100, 101–2; *viṣāda* (grief), 101; *vrīḍā* (shame), 101; *vyābhicāri* (transitory emotions), 101
Bhaviṣya purāṇa, 200, 211, 214
bhest [*beheśet, behest*] (heaven), 27, 30, 32, 172; Āllā in, 13, 31, 57, 87, 234; interchanged with *golok*, 196; Phātemā in, 125, 181; physical access to, 178; Prophet Mohāmmad in, 13, 31, 234
Bhimā, 240
bhūts (hungry ghosts), 127, 135, 152, 167, 178, 193, 198, 237, 247
Bibi Barakat, 33
Bībīnur ("Lady of Light"), 186
bibipālā (stories of the matrons), 18, 41–42
bibīs (matrons, ladies), 4, 6, 19, 25, 118, 178, 193; Bengali *imaginaire* and, 111; challenging adventures of, 44–45; *devīs* equated with, 186, 254; 186; mass-printed stories about, 16; miracles credited to, xii; myth vs. history paradigm and, 34, 35, 37, 38; *premākhyān* and stories of, 23; worldly needs and worship of, 151
Bidhātā (God of Fate), 4, 10, 13, 29, 30, 64, 89, 160
Bindumatī, 251
biographical image, 38, 44
biography, religious, 37, 38, 109
bios (life of the individual), 38, 41, 108
Birbalā, 245
Biśālākṣī, 18
Biṣam Rāy, 129
bismillā [*bichmillā*] ("In the name of God"), 163, 168, 236, 241, 242–43
Bonbibī, 18, 22, 93, 135, 152, 220; Baḍa Khān Gājī and, 137; battle with Nārāyaṇī, 127–28, 131, 151; comic book version of stories about, 259; conceptual blending and, 185; emplotment and, 200; as "fabricated" figure, 33; as late-arriving figure, 27; as mediator, 179; as Mistress of the Sunderban Forest, xii, xix, 126, 176, 259; in scroll paintings, 258; shape-shifting of, 132, 259
Bonbibī jahurā nāmā (Khater), 110, 123–24, 150–54, 186, 259; conceptual blending in, 185, 187–88; intertextual references in, 176; lack of humor in, 181; late composition of, 157; *Rāy maṅgal* (Kṛṣṇarām Dās) as precursor to, 137–50; revisions to history of Gāji and, 176–77; three episodes of, 125–33
Booth, Wayne, 107, 181n61
Brahmā (creator god), 138, 186, 242
brahma mantra, 245
brāhmaṇs (Indic priestly caste), xii, 2, 11, 12, 39, 97, 151, 192, 219, 251; Gāji Pīr and, 218; held in "high esteem," 31; in the Kali Age, 148; kings, 199, 227, 230–31, 234, 249; legitimation process and, 212; pregnancy and paternity attested before, 141, 150; Sandhyāvatī and, 28, 29; tale of poor *brāhmaṇ* and woodcutters, 205, 206, 214–15; *vārindri* [*varendra*] (high-ranking *brāhmaṇ*), 241, 242; wedding astrologers, 98
Buddhism, 43
al-Bukhāri, 235
Butler, Judith, 221

Caitanya (Rādhā), 3n4, 95n53, 182, 259
Caitanya, Kṛṣṇa, 3n3, 102n61, 192, 215n49, 219n53, 220; *śikṣāṣṭika* of, 251n138
Cakravartī, Ghanarām, 78–79, 189, 195, 203, 205

Cāmpāvatī (Cāmpā), 75, 79, 111n1, 153, 159–63, 169–74, 187, 199
Cāmuṇḍa (fearsome goddess), 237
Cāndbibī, 3, 4–6, 13, 27, 28, 31, 32, 88. *See also* Sandhyāvatī
Caṇḍī ("fierce" goddess), xviii, 18, 133, 162, 167; Gāji as nephew of, 167, 175, 186, 187; revisions to history of Gāji and, 175, 178, 179
Caṇḍī maṅgal, 140n71, 181n61, 217n51
Cānd Khā̃, 236–37, 249
Cāṇḍo, 152
Candraketu, 229
Capps, Donald, 38
Casey, Edward S., 42n19, 114
Cāṣīmahādev, 18
caste, 97, 192, 204
Catalogus Catalogorum of Bengali Mansuscripts (Bhattacharjee), 203n17
Caṭṭopādhāy, Suniti Kumār, 23–24
caudhurī (wealthy land-owner, headman), 132, 135–36
caukapaṭ (style of painting), 258
cautriśa (verse form), 79
Chāheb, Munsi Nachiraddin, 21
Christianity, 135, 175, 198, 207
cillākhāna (space for mediation and *jikir*), 158
citrakār (painter), 15
comedy, 41, 140, 256
"Coming to Understand: Orgasm and the Epistemology of Ignorance" (Tuana), xv
conceptual blending, xiii, 182–88, 194
Conference of the Birds ('Aṭṭār), 23n46
coral tree (*mādāra*), 145
cosmology, 26, 107–8, 153, 154, 253, 254; conceptual blending and, 186–87; *hinduyāni*, 107, 187, 188n, 232; incremental realignment and, 233; Kali Age and, 30; mainstream Islamic traditions and, 91; *musulmāni*, xix, 107, 187, 188n, 232; *purāṇik* (traditional), 194; religious ideal and, 42; shared presuppositions and, 181; *vaiṣṇav*-inspired, 87
Costa, Benjamin, 111n1
crocodiles, xix, 131, 138, 158, 165–66, 240, 246–47
Culler, Jonathan, 116–17, 118

Daināv, King, 248
ḍākinī (witches), 127, 135, 152, 167, 178
dakṣiṇa (donation to *brāhmaṇ* for services), 188, 243
Dakṣiṇ Rāy (Dakṣiṇā Rāy), 17, 18, 78, 79, 125n34, 128, 136, 151, 259; as benefactor of woodcutters, 218; as *brāhmaṇ*, 153; conceptual blending and, 187; conflict with Baḍa Khān Gājī, 131, 137, 138, 142–47, 163–69, 185–86; demonic hordes of, 130, 135; Dhonāi and, 129–30; emplotment and, 200; *jabans* eaten by, 160; *maṅgal* (auspicious appearance) of, 133; *maṅgal kāvyas* devoted to, 197; in the *Rāy maṅgal*, 137–50, 179–80, 203; revisions to history of Gāji's conflict with, 176–77, 181; in scroll paintings, 258; as shapeshifter, 179–80, 259; tigers commanded by, 138, 141, 143–44, 146–47, 149; wealth of Sunderbans controlled by, 127
Damayantī, 68, 150, 230n69
Dāmodar, 242, 246
dānavas (powerful celestial figures), 77
dāoān (summoner to join *ummā*), 47, 49
Daphagā Gāji, 51
Dapharkhā̃, 138
darbār (court), 87
Darbārbibi, 18
dargā (tomb), 46, 51n41, 73, 152, 178, 200
dārveś (Sufi mendicant), xviii, 19, 218
Dās, Girīndranāth, 33, 34, 39, 74n9, 92
Das, Indra, 259
Dās, Kāśīrām, 92
Dās, Kṛṣṇahari, 1, 4, 8, 9, 13, 72, 73, 85, 233; on *avatār* for the Kali Age, 27; on human action with respect to heaven and hell, 28; *maṅgal kāvyas* composed by, 78; salutations to Satya Pīr, 31
Dās, Kṛṣṇarām, 16, 97n56, 137, 138, 139, 141, 153, 197
Dāyānā Gāji, 138
Dentith, Simon, 95
Deoyān Gājī, 18
devatās (*hindu* deities), 159, 175, 228, 229, 239, 250
Dev Bhagavān, 178
Devdatta, 139, 140, 141, 151
devīpālā (song performances of goddesses), 18
devīs (goddesses), 14, 50, 178, 193, 254
Devourers, The (Das), 259
devpāla (tales of the gods), 18
devs (gods), 14, 178, 193, 254
Dhanañjay the milkman, 253
Dhanapati, 143
Dhanbibī, Queen, 56, 57
Dhanvantari, 202
Dharma (Indic god), xviii, 18, 91, 133, 186, 205
dharma (traditional Indic moral order), 3, 87, 205–6, 217
Dharmaketu, 140, 143
Dharma maṅgal (Cakravartī), 79, 205
Dharma Ṭhākur, *see* Dharma

Dhonāi, 128–33, 135, 151, 188
dialogics, 86, 116
disease, xviii, 12, 18, 220
dobhāṣī (two-language speech), 24
Doniger, Wendy, 68, 70n90
Dudbibī, 54–57, 58–62, 65, 97, 218; birth of Mānik Pīr and, 62–63, 68–69; fidelity to Badar Pīr, 68, 69, 70; insemination of, 62, 69, 104, 105; marriage to Badar Pīr, 67, 122; meaning of name, 88; as Sītā, 56, 57, 67–68, 88
Dukhe, 129, 131–32, 133, 151, 177, 188
Dunham, Mary Frances, 14n20
Durgā (warrior goddess), 18, 96, 133, 158
Dvāpara Age, 68

East India Company, 39
Eaton, Richard M., xvii*n*10, xviii*n*11, 19n30, 195n9, 201
elephants, 56, 80, 170, 216n50, 231; Gāji's escape from execution and, 76; Indra's white elephant, 80, 244
Eliade, Mircea, 29n56
emplotment, xiii, 41, 225; of gendered creativity, 198; from literary emplotment to social discourse, 189–201; *musulmāni*, 198–99; *vaiṣṇav*, 197–98
epics, 42, 92, 98, 174, 185, 206
epistemology, xiv
Ernst, Carl, 257
euhemerism, 111

fables, 42
Fabulous Females and Peerless Pīrs (trans. Stewart), xi, 222
færies (*hurparī*), 3, 13, 91, 159, 164, 172
Fa'l-i Qur'ān (Divination by Qur'ān), 98
fanā (ecstatic loss of self in God's presence), 106
fantastic genre, 35–36
Faraizis, 17
Fauconier, Gilles, 185, 187
Fenrisúlfr (Norse shapeshifter), 259
Firdausī, 174
folk literature, xii, xx, 25, 36
Folktales from India: The Sunderbans (Vivalok Comics), 259–60
Frye, Northrop, 41, 42, 43–44, 67, 69, 256; on ascent of hero, 70; on narratives as romances, 66; on realism, 82
Fuchs, Barbara, 73, 138, 191

Gadādhar, 3n3
Gāji (Jābbār Sāheb), 157
Gāji boi (Jābbār Sāheb), 157
Gāji kālu o cāmpāvatī (Khodā Bakhś), 79, 80, 155–56, 157
Gāji kālu o cāmpāvatī kanyār puthi (Ohāb), 71, 126n39, 154, 155; narrative strategies in fictional hagiography and, 72–81
Gāji kālu o cāmpāvatī kanyār puthi (Rahim), 137n63, 155–57, 176, 179, 180–81; conceptual blending in, 186–87; Dakṣiṇā Rāy's conflict with Gāji, 163–69; Gāji's love for Cāmpāvatī, 158–63; Gāji's marriage to Cāmpāvatī and ascetic trek, 169–74
Gāji Pīr, 71, 126, 218, 235; conflict with Dakṣiṇā Rāy, 163–69; escape from execution, 75–78, 81; fictional world of, 39; love for Cāmpāvatī (Cāmpā), 159–63; marriage to Cāmpāvatī and ascetic trek, 169–74; parody and, 94; in the *Rāy maṅgal*, 143; scroll paintings of, 15n20. *See also* Bada Khān Gāji; Jendā Pīr
gājīs (warrior saints), xii, 2, 19, 33, 131, 144, 152, 179
gandharva (celestial musicians), 10, 55, 67, 98
Gaṇeś (Śiva's elephant-headed minion), 39, 186
Gaṅgā (goddess as Ganges River), 39, 48–50, 66, 82, 83, 96–97, 173; Gāji as nephew of, 158–59, 166, 175, 186, 187; intertextuality and encounters with, 119–20; in Rahim's *Gāji kālu o cāmpāvatī kanyār puthi*, 158, 159, 165–67; revisions to history of Gāji and, 175, 178
gāñjā [*ganja*] (cannabis), 241, 259
gāoyārs (witnesses), 3, 7
Garīb, 21, 90n37
Garuḍa (Viṣṇu's avian mount), 149
Gauḍīya Maṭh, 20
gauḍīya vaiṣṇav movement, 92–93, 102n61, 108, 192, 209
Gaurī (goddess, consort of Śiva), 174, 178
Gayarām, 222
gender: gender confusions, 44, 67; gendered witness to powers of Satya Pīr, 221–32
Genette, Gérard, 92n39, 117n17
ghāṭs (river landing steps), 10, 48, 60, 162, 163, 249
ghazals (love poetry), 156
Ghoṣ, Bidubar, 208, 210–11
Ghoṣ, Niṣākar, 211
Ghosh, Amitav, xvi*n*5, 124
Ghosh, Papiya, 257
gitābhinay (drama built around songs), 156–57
Gokul Paṇḍit, 248
Golālbibī, 126, 136
gopī (cowherdess), see *gupini*

Gopīcānd, 18, 58n62, 239n96
Gosānī, Lord, 145
Gosvāmī, Rūpa, 80n21, 101, 102n61
Great Story of Satya Pīr and the Virgin Girl Sandhyāvatī, The. See *Baḍa Satya Pīr o Sandhyāvatī Kanyār Puthi*
Guñjar, Phakir, 59, 100, 101, 103, 104; on adventures of Mānik Pīr, 105; on impregnation of Dudbibī, 106
Gupicānd, 239
gupinis [*gopīs*] (cowherdesses), 55, 68, 88, 99, 100, 101, 103–4
gurus (*hinduyāni* or *musulmāni* teachers), 69, 127, 134, 233, 252

ḥadīths [*hadīs*] (stories of Muhammad or followers), 13, 36, 43, 104–5, 235
Ḥāfiẓ, 235
hagiography, xii, 37, 39, 81, 95; martyrdom in, 44; narrative strategies in, 72–81; as parody, 108; as subgenre of romance, 82
Hajrat Jāber, 18
Hak, Enāmul, 24
hākim (local judge), 132, 135
Halman, Hugh Talat, 85n28, 234n80, 235n84
Hālumīr, Kavi (Mīrā Chaiyad Hālumīr), 79, 155–56, 253
Hānumān, 142, 153
Hara (Śiva's elephant-headed minion), 174, 178
Haridev, 138, 177
Harihar, 246, 247, 248, 249
Harilīlā (Sen), 213
Hāsān, 40
hell (*dojakh, narak*), 5–6, 210
Hindavī language, 12, 22, 23n46, 139, 175
Hindi language, 214
Hindu category/identity, 18, 21, 191, 196, 201, 207, 214n47; Bangla language identified with, 214; communalism and, 257; Hindu nationalism, 20; identity politics and, 27, 187; incipient and not fully formed, 200–201; as monolithic label, 200; political strife and, 255; Sanskrit language and, 118; sectarian, xv
Hinduism, 23
hindus, 7, 240, 241, 244, 245
Hindustani language, 12, 79, 139
Hindutva, 257
hinduyāni cultures/populations, 14, 89, 95, 205; common perspective with *musulmāni*, 25; contact with indigenous populations, xviii; cosmology of, 107, 188n, 232; gods of, 96; hierarchical of celestial figures, 254; kinship and, 177; mythological narratives, 17
Hīr the cobbler, 251
history, xiii, xvi, 14, 35, 112
History of Bengali Literature and Language (Sen), 22
Hungry Tide, The (Ghosh), 124
Husāin (son of ʿAlī), 40
Husāin (Lālmon's husband), 223-25
Husāin Śāh [Shāh], 92, 111n1, 121, 122, 197n11
Hutcheon, Linda, xvii, 92n39, 93, 109, 176, 180

Iblichnāmā [*Iblīsnāmā*], 21, 90n37
Ibn ʿArabī, 235
identity, 25, 99; identity politics, xvi, 27, 187, 190, 197, 200; loss of, 44, 67; of modern Bengal, 25; nationalist, 24; political, xvi; primary marker of, 31, 177; religious, xvi, 214. *See also* Hindu category/identity; Muslim category/identity
Ilyas Shāhi dynasty, 111, 137
imaginaire, xiii, 20, 37, 123, 185, 193; conditions of possibility and, 109; defined, 114–15; reality of, 110–23; semiotic context of, 133–37
imaginal space, 114
India, xvii, 16, 19, 43, 99, 257, 259
Indra (Vedic deity), 10, 80, 240, 244
intentionality, authorial, 116
intertextualities, 23n46, 41, 116–17, 122–23, 174, 190; explicit or overt (E/OI), 119–20, 133, 134, 136, 137; *imaginaire* and, 185; implied or covert (I/CI), 120–22, 133–37; literary pedigree and, 176
irony, xvi–xvii, 41, 94–96
Īsā (prophet Jesus), 74n9, 175
Iser, Wolfgang, 115n10, 180n60
Iskandarnāma (traditions associated with Alexander), 235
Islam, xv, 2n2, 23, 45, 254; Bengali cultural legacy and, 108; generic form of, xii; "local" traditions and, 19; mainstream theological literature of, 87; mainstream traditions of, 91; martyrdom and, 44; mythologies of, xiii; waterways in expansion of, xx
Islāmi bāṅglā sāhitya (Sen), 23
Islamist reformers, 17, 257
Islamization, 35, 182, 220
Īśvar (Supreme Lord), 6, 76, 138, 142, 152; *avatār* of, 185; as combined *musulmāni* and *vaiṣṇav*, 147, 154, 178; as peace broker, 181; as servant of Satya Pīr, 248
itihās (historical story/explanation), 40

prolegomena to, 46–57, 107; religious ideal and, 82–83; romance of Mānik Pīr's birth, 66–70
Mānikpīr jahurānāmā (anonymous, 1958), 33
Mānik pīr kecchā (Pijiruddīn), 74, 119
Manohar phāsarār pālā ["The Erstwhile Bride and Her Winged Horse"] (Rasmay), 222
Mān Siṃha, 251
mantras (magical utterances), 179, 237, 238, 247
Marddhagājī, 40
mārphati (mystical) path, 21
martyrdom, 44, 146n87
marvelous genre, 35, 36
Marxism, 24
Maryam, 175
masjids (mosques), 10, 50, 73, 83, 97, 159, 173, 183, 197
masnavī (Persian story literature), 22, 23n46, 175
Matilāler pālā ["The Mother's Son Who Spat Up Pearls"] (Kiṅkar Dās), 222
māyā (magic of creation), 7, 147n90, 148, 172, 248
Mayadānav (Demon King), *see* Maidānav
McCloud, Scott, 260
merit (*puṇya*), 5
metaphor, 41, 183
metonymy, 41, 185, 200
Miller, J. Hillis, 86n33
mimesis, 114, 122–23, 133
mi'rāj (Mohāmmad's night journey), 13, 178
Mirigāvatī, 175
Miṣra, Rāmdev, 209
Mitra, Rādhānāth, 206
Mitra, Satiścandra, 111n1
Mobārak Gājī, 18
Mohāmmad [Muhammad], Prophet, 40, 88, 92, 134, 178; Brahmā equated with, 186; as *guru* of all *phakirs*, 127, 134; Hāji Kāji Muhammad, 57; intertextuality and encounters with, 119–20; *jikir* of, 236; lineage of, 121; *mi'rāj* (night journey) of, 8, 13, 178; Satya Pīr and, 1, 4, 5, 13, 26; tomb in Madinā, 125, 126
mokāms [*maqāms*] (stages of Sufi practice), 175
mokṣa (liberation, entry to heaven), 194
mollās [*marllās*] (mullas), 57, 95, 98, 100, 133, 193
momins [*mamins*] (faithful followers), 3, 47, 48, 64, 241, 244, 250
Monāi, 128
monologics, 86, 91
Mozumdar, Gokul Chandra, 256
mudras (hand gestures), 210
Mughal empire, xx, 26, 87, 98, 136, 174
Mukherjee, Bhupendra Nath, 256
Mukhopādhyāy, Dhīrendra Nāth, 207
Mukil, 60, 61
mukti (enlightenment), 106
Mukuṭ Rājā, 111n1, 162, 165, 166, 168, 169–71, 186
munis (sages), 48, 49, 54, 152, 186
Munśī, Mohāmmad, 123–24
murids (students), 126, 135, 235
murśids [*murseds, mursids*] (Sufi teachers), 19, 21, 48, 57, 126, 135, 179, 235, 248
Musā (Moses), 120, 235
Muslim category/identity, 191, 196, 201, 207, 214n47; communalism and, 257; Hindi (Urdu) language identified with, 214; identity politics and, 27, 187; incipient and not fully formed, 200–201; as monolithic label, 200; Muslim reformers, 19–20; Persian and Arabic languages associated with, 118; political strife and, 255; sectarian, xv
musulmāni cultures/populations, xii, xviii, 7, 13, 14, 89, 220; common perspective with *hinduyāni*, 25; cosmology of, xix, 107, 186, 187, 188n; emplotment and, 198–99; Islamic reform and, 19; kinship and, 177
mu'tazilah traditions, 118
myth-history conundrum, 33–39
mythology, xiii, 33–39
myths, xii, 42

nabī (prophets), 3, 13, 107, 178, 193, 235
Nabīvaṃśa (Sultān), 92, 121
nāginīs (female serpents), 245
nāgs [*nāgas*] (serpents), xviii, 110
naivedya [*naibedya*] (food offered to deity), 209, 243
Nala, 150
Nalanīler pālā (*The Tale of Nal and Nīl*), 227–32
narabali (human sacrifice), 129, 135
Nārāda (celestial gadfly sage), 138, 206, 207
narak (hell), 210
Nārāyaṇ, *see* Nirañjan [Nirāñjan]
Nārāyaṇ (supreme god of *vaiṣṇav*), 11, 13, 33, 48n33, 149, 153, 253; Āllā equated with, 186, 225; Badar Pīr as, 67; divine characteristics of, 226; intertextuality and encounters with, 119–20
Nārāyaṇī, 18, 125n34, 127–28, 131, 135, 151, 152, 187
narratives: *bhaṇitā* (signature line), 45, 70, 101, 196, 209n30; doctrine-driven reformists against, 255; intertextuality and, 120; miraculous events in, 34; monologic and dialogic, 86; narrative codes, xiii, 199–200,

205, 221, 232, 253; possible world theory and, 113; primary, 41–42; reality defined by narrative content, 112; romances, 66; royal threat to birth of hero, 69; structure and process of, 43–44; truth test and, 42–43, 85. *See also* romances
narratives, autotelic, 39–46, 85, 109, 114; *bios* as, 39–46, 109; critique of existing society and, 190; intertextuality and, 117, 122
nasihat nāmā (didactic literature), 16
Naskar, Debabrata, 18
nāth jogīs (ascetics), 18, 58n62, 91, 96
nāths (ascetics, followers of Gorākhnāth), 106, 111, 193
nationalism, 24
nattā ritual, 65
Naybibi, 18
Neñjā Muḍā (constable of crocodiles), 246
Nida, Eugene, 183
nigamas, 241
Nīlāvatī, 149, 153
Nirañjan [Nirāñjan] ("Stainless One"), 71, 76, 122, 158, 178, 193, 236; Gosāi, 242; recitation of names of, 238, 242. *See also* Āllā [Allāḥ]; Nārāyaṇ
Nityānanda [Nitāi] (Caitanya's ascetic companion), 3n3, 239

Oḍiyā language, 139, 195, 225, 232
Ohāb, Sāyeb Munsī Ābdul, 71, 75, 78, 80, 155, 158
Olābibī (*musulmāni* Matron of Cholera), xix, 18, 33, 40n15, 220
oli (*musulmāni* saint), 2n2, 131, 137, 178, 236; Baḍa Khān Gājī as, 152; Satya Pīr as, 3
Orephe, Adhin Mahāmmad Hādek, 21
Orientalist scholars, xv, 20, 23, 35
Orissa, Indian state of, 12

Pā̃ctolā, 158, 173–74
padma lotus, 112
Padmāvatī (Indic goddess), 23n46, 186
padres [*padris, pādris*] (Christian preachers), 49n36, 91, 111, 193
Pāglāi Pīr, 20
Pakistan, 19
Pāl, Dvāraknāth, 207
pālagān (narrative set to music), 12, 15
pañcadevatā (five deities), 210
pāñcālī (narrative poem), 15, 118
Pañcānanda, 18
pañcaratna (five-spired temple), 10n12
Panda, Bishnupada, 225
paṇḍits (*brāhmaṇ* priests, teachers), 229, 248, 249
parables, 42
paratextuality, 45, 117n17, 123, 156, 208
parody, xiii, xvi–xvii, xviii, 91–94, 95, 122; in *Bonbibī jahurā nāmā,* 133; in *Mānikpīrer jahurānāmā,* 96–109; of parodies, 256
paṭacitra [*pata chitras, paṭ*] (scroll paintings of Bengal), 15–16, 258, 259–60
Pātālanagar, underworld city of, 77, 110, 158, 179
paṭidār (painter), 15
paṭuā (painter), 15, 16
payār (couplet), 80
paygambars [*pekambars*] (messengers, apostles), 146–47, 152, 186, 235, 239
peacock feathers, royalty and, 52
peris [*paris*] (færies), 107, 178, 193
Persian language, 2n2, 12, 23, 46, 139; *masnavī* literature, 175; technical jargon in, 27, 118, 182
phad (scroll paintings of Rajasthan), 259–60
phakīrs [*phakirs, fakīrs, faqīrs*] (Sufi mendicants), xii, 5, 19, 42, 46, 96, 107, 163, 193, 250; of Āllā, 236, 238; anti-*phakir* kings, 3, 253; Baḍa Khān Gājī's band of, 138; Badar Pīr as, 49, 52, 55, 65; Bengali *imaginaire* and, 111; Gāji Pīr, 76, 78, 80; Guñjar, 59; *munis* (sages) as, 186; Muslim reformers' opposition to, 20; parody and, 95; punished by kings, 97; revelation of new *dharma* and, 211–12; as solitary figures, xviii; *vaiṣṇav* images of divinity and, 233
Phātemā (daughter of Muhammad), 119, 125, 126, 128, 134, 178; as Bībīnur ("Lady of Light"), 186; recitation of names of, 250
Phayajullā, 205
pherestās (angels), 4, 107, 162, 178, 193
Phulbibī, 125, 126, 136
Pijiruddīn, Munsī Mohāmmad, 74, 119
pīrānīs (female Sufi saints), 19, 42, 82, 192, 193
Pīr Gorācā̃d, 18
pīr kathās (stories of *sūphī saints*), xi, 13n18, 17, 23n46, 75, 81, 185, 218; artful diction in, 79; *avatār* for, 26; *Bildungsroman* genre compared with, 84; comic book version of, 260; emergence in times of transition, 26; interpretation and analysis of, xii–xiii; irony and parody in, 91–96; literary emplotment and, 189, 190–91; martyrdom in, 44; parody and, 256; as primary narratives, 41–42; stealth critiques embedded in, 109; subjunctive fictional world of, xvi, 85–90; trading voyages in, xix
Pīr Mobārak Baḍakhā̃ Gājī, 34

pīrs (Sufi saints), 14, 19, 107, 118, 193; as agents for Islamization, 220; Bengali *imaginaire* and, 111; *devs* equated with, 186, 254; as equivalent figures to hinduyāni deities, 39; as "friends of God," 37, 73, 96, 120, 221; *jindā pīrs* (especially accomplished *pīrs*), 74, 75, 157n7, 158, 248; mass-printed stories about, 16; miracles credited to, xii; *mithya pīrs* ("fake" *pīrs*), 20; Muslim reformers' opposition to, 20; myth vs. history paradigm and, 34, 35, 37, 38, 39; *pāñc pīrs* (five *pīrs*), 40n16; as part of everyday *musalmāni* world, 232; piety of ordinary householders and, 218; *premākhyān* and stories of, 23; revelation of new *dharma* and, 211–12; worldly needs and worship of, 151

piśācīs (ghouls), 193

polysystem theory, 184

Prabhākar, King, 143, 152

Prabhu Kartā (Master Creator), 76

pragmatics, xiii, 190, 194

prasād (leftovers of food offered to god), 209

prem [*prema*] (pure love), 172, 173

premākhyān [*prem kahānī*] (allegorical love narratives), 22–23, 23n46, 43, 174–75

presupposition, 116–17; logical (LP), 118, 133–37; pragmatic (PP), 118–19, 133, 134

"Presupposition and Intertexuality" (Culler), 116–17

prets (shape-shifting ghouls), 127, 135, 167, 178, 193, 198, 247

Pritchett, Frances W., 23n46

Priyāvatī, Queen, 3, 4, 6, 8, 246, 250

Pṛthivī (Mother Earth), 3, 29

pūjā (worship), 3, 14, 65, 97, 129, 133, 148, 165, 243; of Bonbibī, 176; respects paid to mounds of earth, 142, 143; of Satya Pīr, 203, 208, 248; in *vrat kathās*, 209

pūjāpaddhati (ritual instruction), 209, 210

pūjārīs (worshipers), 193

purāṇas (traditional Sanskrit literature), 185, 211, 219, 230

purāṇik (traditional) texts, 14, 98, 134, 153, 174, 191; *avatār* theory and, 206; parody of, 194; Satya Pīr and, 206; stories in Bangla and, 211

pūrṇa brahmā (godhead), 236

purohits (*brāhmaṇ* priests conducting rituals), 193, 211

Puṣpadatta, 141–42, 148, 149–50, 218

pūthi literature, 24

puthi poṛā, 15n20

Qiṣaṣ al-Anbiyā' ["Stories of the Prophets"] (al-Kisā'i), 121

Qur'ān, Arabic, 13, 14, 47n32, 119, 234–35. *See also* Korān

rachul [*racchul, rasul*] (apostle), 3, 4, 13, 125

Rādhā (Kṛṣṇa's consort), 61n66, 68, 91, 99

Raghunāth, 238

Rahim, Ābdur, 156, 157, 175, 187

rājās (kings), 65

rākṣas (cannibalistic demon), 130, 131, 135, 153, 178, 179, 259

Raktān Gājī, 18

Rām (*avatār* of Viṣṇu), 8, 13, 149, 227, 250; Badar Pīr as, 56, 57, 67–68, 88, 98, 99, 107; in exile, 150; Rām Nārāyaṇ, 55

Rām, Phakīr, 195

Rāmāi Paṇḍit, 186, 205

Ramakrishna Mission, 20

Rāmāyaṇ (Kṛttibās), 92

Rāmāyaṇa epic, 43, 121, 136, 217

Rāmbhadra, 207

Rāmbhāvatī pālā ["The Unwilting Garland of Faithfulness"] (Kiṅkar Dās), 222

Rāmdhan, Dvija, 207

Rāmeśvar, 16, 195, 213, 214

Rank, Otto, 69

ras [*rasa*] (refined aesthetic experience), 79–80, 104

Rasmay, 222

Ratā, 138, 141n73

rati śāstras (love manuals), 172, 174

Ratnāvatī, 149, 150

Rāvaṇ, 149, 153, 159, 227

Rāy maṅgal (Haridev), 78n14, 111n1, 137–38, 177

Rāy maṅgal (Kṛṣṇarām Dās), 78, 97n56, 127n41, 137–50, 151, 152–54, 203; conceptual blending in, 185–86, 188; revisions to history of Gāji and Dakṣiṇ Rāy, 174, 176, 178, 179–80; translational exchange economy in, 185

Rāy maṅgal (Rudradev), 138, 141n73, 149n98, 177, 180

realignment, incremental, 233

reclamation, 219

recognition, 211, 214

refraction theory, 182–83

religious ideal, 38, 42, 44, 82–85, 109

Rescher, Nicholas, xiv*n*2, 113

revā khaṇḍa, 200, 206, 211, 256

Reynolds, Frank, 38

Ṛg veda, 232

Rhetoric of Irony, A (Booth), 107

rhinos, 198, 224
risi (sages), 49
Rogeśvarī (goddess of diseases), 237
romances, xiii, 16–17, 41; allegorical, 22, 23n46; gender roles in, 198; as hagiography, 81, 82; hero birth motifs, 70; heroic, 12; loss of memory in, 67; mental landscape of, 66; Quest in hero stories, 75, 99; as segmented narratives, 138; semantic mode, 73; structural markers of, 43; syntactical structure, 73; "and then" structure of, 72. *See also* narratives
Rose, Margaret, 93
Rostam (legendary Persian warrior), 174
ṛta (cosmic and moral order), 232
Rudradev, 138, 141n73, 149n98
Rūmi, 235
Rūpavatī, 241, 245, 250

śabda (sound, word, incantation), 247
sādh dinner, 64
sādhu bhāṣā (high literary mode), 16, 24, 206, 207
sādhus (holy men), 99, 188, 194, 217–18
Śāhā gāji kālu gitābhinay (M. K. Bākhs), 81, 156–57
Śāhā Jalil, 126
sahajiyās (*tantrik* practice/practitioners), 106
Śahīdullāh, Muhammad, 24
Śāh Jālāl, 40
śaivas (worshipers of Śiva), 91, 111
saiyads (descendants of Muhammad), 254
Śājaṅgali, 126, 127, 128, 130, 134, 137, 151, 153; conceptual blending and, 185; revisions to history of Gāji and, 178
śāktas (worshipers of Goddess or Śakti), 91, 108, 111
Salafists, 17
Śalemānā, 138
Sāṃkhyatīrtha, Rāsvihāri, 209
saṃsār (experience of this-worldly life), 7
Sanātan, 127
Sandhyāvatī, 1, 6–11, 27, 32, 238, 244; as both *jabanā* and *brāhmaṇ*, 28, 29, 30, 31; forest abode of, 236, 237; impregnated with flower sent by Āllā, 6, 8, 10, 13–14, 30, 248; lament over tribulations of, 239; talking bird of, 249. *See also* Cāndbibī
Śani, 18
Śaṅkarācārya, 213, 214
sannyāsīs (ascetic renouncers), 3, 18, 91, 193, 233, 237; Bengali *imaginaire* and, 111; Satya Pīr in garb of, 238
Sanskritization, 206, 207, 209, 210, 211, 214
Sanskrit language, 2n2, 46, 118, 211; Bangla derived from, 24; literary tradition, 12; ritual instruction in, 210
Santoṣī Mā, 18
śāriat [*śarīyat*] (mainstream Islamic practices), 21, 176, 182
Śariph, Āhmad, 24, 34n4
Śarmma, Harimohan, 206
Sartre, Jean-Paul, 114
Śaśī, 251–52
Śaśidhar pālā ["The Bloodthirsty Ogress Who Would Be Queen"] (Kiṅkar Dās), 222
Ṣaṣṭhī (goddess protecting children), 18, 65, 78, 89, 220, 243
Sātbibi, 18
satya (truth), 4, 7, 191
Satya Dev, 196
Satya Nārāyan, 1, 8, 14, 29, 73, 178, 196, 244; Cakravartī's poems dedicated to, 78–79; conjoined with Satya Pīr, 185, 202, 204, 212, 239; four-armed form, 215, 238, 244; *hinduyāni* constituency of, 26; in *Nalanīler pālā*, 229, 232; shift from print to performance and, 256–57; *vaiṣṇav avatār* theory and, 205–7; Viṣṇu associated with, 27; worshipped in North India, 210
Satyanārāyaṇ (Mitra), 206
Satyanārāyaṇer pāñcālī (Pāl), 207
Satyanārāyaṇer puthi (Mahāśy), 79
Satyanārāyaṇ ithās [*Satyanārāyaṇ ras sindhu*] (Cakravartī), 78–79
Satyanārāyaṇ nāṭya kāvya (Bāgchi), 256
Satyanārāyaṇ punthi (Kavivallabh), 213
Satyanārāyaṇ ras sindhu (Cakravartī), 189, 203
Satyanārāyaṇ vrat, 207
Satya nārāyaṇ vratakathā (Bhaṭṭācāryya), 39
Satya Pīr, xi, 14, 18, 40, 61, 72, 185, 204n19, 248; as amalgamation of Nārāyaṇ and Khodā, 121–22; bastard births of, 30–31; birth of, 120; in *Brāhmaṇ*'s Tale, 215; charmed life of, 12; conjoined with Satya Nārāyan, 185, 202, 204, 212, 239; Dharma equated with, 79, 186; dual form of, 26, 31, 244, 250; emplotment and, xiii, 189–201; escape from execution, 243–44; as "fabricated" figure, 33; as "fake" *pīr*, 20; gendered witness to powers of, 221–32; historical emergence of stories about, 189, 192, 195, 202–3; Lālmon's Adventure and, 223–25; in the Merchant's Tale, 217; *musulmāni* constituency of, 26; never-ending mission of, 250–53; number of titles and

manuscripts concerned with, xiv; parody and, 94; pragmatic survival concerns and, 202; *premākhyān* and stories of, 23; printing of classic tales about, 17; religious ideal and, 83–85; Śani (Evil Eye) and, 207; scroll paintings of, 15n20; shape-shifting of, 259; shift from print to performance and, 256–57; significance in *musalmāni* terms, 232–50; in tale of Nal and Nīl, 227–32; *vaiṣṇav avatār* theory and, 205, 218–19; *vaiṣṇav* literature of, 199; in the Woodcutter's Tale, 215–16. *See also* Satya Nārāyan
Satya pīr pāñcālī (Phayajullā), 205
Satyar pāñcālī (Satyānanda), 210
Saytān [Śaytān] (Satan), 21, 61–62, 90, 99
Schinkel, Anders, 115n12
science, xiv, 26, 115
secularism, 124, 257
Secular Scripture, The (Frye), 43–44
Sekander, Śāhā, 75–77, 111, 131, 137, 158, 165, 174
Sek Pharid, 58
Śekh Khodā Bakhś, *see* Bakhś, Khodā
semantics, xiii, 190
Sen, Dīneścandra, 22
Sen, Gaura Candra, 211
Sen, Lālā Jaykṛṣṇa, 213
Sen, Sukumār, 22–23, 25n54, 34, 217n51
Sen, Surendra Kumar, 256
seṭerā ritual, 65
sevā (service to God), 14, 244
sexuality, 55n52, 62, 69, 139; licit and illicit, 99; miraculous impregnation and, 90; passion drowned by ascetic practices, 106; plaintain forest image and, 58n62, 67
Shāh, Sultān Husāin, 92
shahāda (testimony that Mohāmmed is Prophet), 107
Shāh nāmeh (Firdausī), 43, 174, 185
shapeshifters, 259
shari'ā (Islamic law), 95, 182. See also *śāriat*
shaykhs [*shāikhs, śekh, sekh*] (Sufi teachers), xviii, 193, 220, 237
Shi'i martyrs, 15n20
silsilās (lineages), xviii, 38n13, 39
Siṃhabāhu, 231
sin (*pāp*), 5–6
sinni [*śinni, śirṇi, śirṇī*] (food offering to *pīrs*), 73, 145, 204, 206, 208, 209; instructions for preparation and offering of, 210; Mānik Pīr and, 218; Satya Pīr and, 215, 216, 227, 229, 240, 245–46, 248, 252, 254
sirā (biography), 13, 40
Sītā [Sitya] (wife of Rām), 8, 136, 149, 227; Dudbibī as, 56, 57, 67–68, 88, 99; with Rām in exile, 150
Śitalā (goddess of smallpox), xix, 18, 40n15, 78, 119, 133
Śiva (one of three supreme deities), 39, 138, 146, 152, 158, 228, 246n125
Śivrām, 207
Skanda purāṇa, 200, 204n19, 206, 211, 256
Somadeva, 98
subjunctive mode, xvi, 87, 104, 112, 188n, 192, 194, 201, 257; dialogical activity and, 86, 107; emplotment and, 201; humor and, 181
Sultān, Saiyid, 92
Sultanate of Bengal, xx, 26, 87, 98, 121
Ṣultān Rājā, 65
Sunderban forest, 71, 110, 124, 132, 148, 158; animals of, xix, 136; Bonbibī as Matron of, xii, xix, 126, 176, 259; mangrove swamps of, 138, 142, 176; new world order of, 150–54. *See also* Āṭhārobhāṭi (Land of the Eighteen Tides)
Śundi the trader, 252
Śūnya purāṇ (Rāmāi Paṇḍit), 186, 205
sūphīs (Sufis), xii, 2, 136, 181, 198; brotherhood of, 177; Christianity and, 175; similarity to *vaiṣṇav* spiritual guides, 219, 220; as solitary figures, xviii; unity of God perspective, 27; *waḥdat al-wujūd* (Unity of Being) concept of, 187, 199
Śura, 77
śuyās (magical talking birds), 163
svarūp (essential nature), 236
svayaṃvar (bride choice), 231
Śyāmsundar, 242, 243, 246
syncretism, 23, 91, 182, 257, 258
synecdoche, 41
syntactics, xiii, 190

Tale of the Glory of Mānik Pīr, The. See *Mānikpīrer jahurānāmā*
Talgeri, Pramod, 185
Tantrajyotiṣaśāstrī, Ratneśvar, 210
tantrik [*tāntrik*] (practice of arcane rituals using the body), 89, 96, 99, 106
tapisvyā [*tapasyā, tapisyā, tapisvi*] (ascetic practice), 46, 48, 49, 59, 60; of Badar Pīr, 65, 73, 106; of Mānik Pīr, 65
Taraphdār, Mantajur Rahmān, 23n46, 43n20
Taylor, Charles, 114, 115
Thakur, Bhaktivinode, 20
Ṭhākur, Bhāṇḍārī, 243

Al-Thalabī, Aḥmad Ibn Muḥammed, 121
theology, xvi, 14, 38, 42, 91, 112, 115
theophany, 70
Thomasson, Amie L., 111–12
tigers, xviii–xix, 40, 158, 251; in *Baḍa satya pīr o sandhyāvatī kanyār puthi*, 9, 251; in *Bonbibī jahurā nāmā*, 130, 131, 136, 176–77, 179–80, 259; in *Gāji kālu o cāmpāvatī kanyār puthi*, 71, 158, 163–65, 166, 169–71; in *Mānikpīrer jahurānāmā*, 52–54, 66–67, 97; in *Nalanīler pālā*, 228; in the *Rāy maṅgal*, 138, 139, 141, 143–47, 149; tiger skin used for meditation, 49, 58n62
tīrtha (pilgrimage), 179
Todorov, Tzvetan, 35–36, 42, 43n21, 82n26, 110
tomb worship, 21
Toury, Gideon, 184
tragedy, 41
Trailokya Pīr [Trilakṣya Pīr, Tinlakṣya Pīr], 33, 207
transmigration, 88, 91, 98
Tretā Age, 55, 68, 228
Trilakṣya Pīr, 207
tripadi (triplets), 80, 100
tropes, literary, 41
Tuana, Nancy, xv
Tuṅgadhvaj, King, 204
Turner, Mark, 185, 187
turtles, 11–12, 28, 30, 31
turuks [*turuskas*] (Turks), 111, 165, 192, 254
"twilight language" (*sandhya bhāṣā*), 106

ucchiṣta (leftover food offerings), 209
ummā (community of Muslim believers), 47n29
uncanny genre, 35, 36
Urdu language, 12, 182, 214
Uṣās [Ūṣū] (Goddess Dawn), 230, 231, 232

vaikuṇṭha (*vaiṣṇav* heaven), 11, 13, 29, 32, 210, 227, 242
vairāgīs (ascetic *vaiṣṇavs*), 18, 20, 91, 193, 218; Bengali *imaginaire* and, 111; Satya Pīr and, 233
vaiṣṇav avatār concept, 87, 202–14, 218–20; *Brāhmaṇ*'s Tale, 214–15; Merchant's Tale, 216–18; Woodcutter's Tale, 215–16
vaiṣṇavs (worshipers of Kṛṣṇa), 3, 13, 18, 183; aesthetics of, 101, 103–4; Bengali *imaginaire* and, 111; *musulmāni* authors and themes of, 102; *pīr*'s image appropriated by, 220; sexo-yogic practices and, 106; tales of *pīrs* as seen by, 20–21; theophany, 70; united with *jābans*, 211–12; *vaiṣṇav* emplotment, 197–98; *yugavatār* construct and, 26. See also *hinduyāni*
Vaṃśadhvaj, King, 204
varṇas (castes, social ranks), 148, 150, 177
Veda, 230
vernacularization, 92
vidyādharis (celestial figures skilled in arts), 10, 11, 178, 193, 240
Vīrbhadra, King, 227, 231
virgin motherhood, 4, 29, 30, 68, 69
Viṣṇu (one of three supreme deities), 13, 27, 39, 67, 138, 199, 242; *avatārs* of, 96; Badar Pīr in form of, 98, 107; many forms of, 91; as *pekāmbar* (messenger), 186; Viṣṇu Nārāyaṇ, 205, 206, 215. *See also* Rām
Visvakarmmā [Viśvakarma, Visāi] (celestial architect), 50–51, 62, 69, 83, 97, 251; Maidānav's city restored by, 246; in the *Rāy maṅgal*, 142, 150, 153
vrats (ritual vows), 208–9, 210, 214, 220, 230, 232, 233
Vyāsa (legendary sage), 39

waḥdat al-wujūd (Unity of Being), 27, 187, 199
Way We Think, The (Turner and Fauccioner), 185
West Bengal, Indian state of, xvii, 12
What Is Islam? (Ahmed), xvi
White, Hayden, 41

yakṣas (nature-spirits), 39
Yam [Yama] (god of death), xii, 8, 9, 39, 44, 80, 135, 235–36, 247
Yaśodā, 96
yavatirnya, see *avatīrṇa* [*yavatirnya*]
yogic meditation, 19
Yudhiṣṭhīr (dharmic king of *Mahābhārata*), 207
yug (cosmic age or era), 205
yugavatār (descent for the age), 26, 88, 205
Yūsuf and Zulaykhā, romance of, 159n20, 175

Founded in 1893,
UNIVERSITY OF CALIFORNIA PRESS
publishes bold, progressive books and journals on topics in the arts, humanities, social sciences, and natural sciences—with a focus on social justice issues—that inspire thought and action among readers worldwide.

The UC PRESS FOUNDATION
raises funds to uphold the press's vital role as an independent, nonprofit publisher, and receives philanthropic support from a wide range of individuals and institutions—and from committed readers like you. To learn more, visit ucpress.edu/supportus.

www.ingramcontent.com/pod-product-compliance
Lightning Source LLC
Chambersburg PA
CBHW051558230426
43668CB00013B/1902
9780520306332